MINHAJ ET TALIBIN

MINHAJ ET TALIBIN

A MANUAL OF
MUHAMMADAN LAW
ACCORDING TO THE SCHOOL OF
SHAFII

BY

MAHIUDIN ABU ZAKARIA YAHYA IBN SHARIF EN
NAWAWI

TRANSLATED INTO ENGLISH FROM THE FRENCH EDITION
OF
L. W. C. VAN DEN BERG
BY
E. C. HOWARD
LATE DISTRICT JUDGE, SINGAPORE

Kitab Bhavan
New Delhi-110002

KITAB BHAVAN
Publishers, Distributors, Exporters & Importers
1784, Kalan Mahal, Darya Ganj
New Delhi-110002 (India)

Phone Nos. : (91-11) 23277392/93, 23274686
Websites : www.kitabbhavan.com
E-mail : kitabbhavan.kitabbhavan.com
nusrat@bol.net.in
nasri@vsnl.com

Ist Edition : 2008

ISBN 81-7151-381-6

Published in India by :
Nusrat Ali Nasri for Kitab Bhavan
1784, Kalan Mahal, Daryaganj
New Delhi-110002

Printed in India at :
Lahooti Fine Art Press
Daryaganj, New Delhi

PREFATORY NOTE

In the preface to his edition of the *Fath el Karib* in 1894, Mr. L. W. C. Van den Berg remarked that "from year to year European control over Moslem peoples is extending, so that it is unnecessary to insist upon the importance of rendering the two works that form the basis of the legal literature of the School of Shafii accessible, not only to a small number of Arabic scholars, but also to magistrates and political agents" to whom that language is for the most part unfamiliar. This being as true now as it was twenty years ago it is thought advisable to publish an English translation of the other and larger work referred to, the *Minhaj et Talibin*, which "occupies the first rank for deciding legal cases." In the preface to his edition of this treatise, published in 1882 at Batavia by the Government of the Netherlands Indies, Mr. Van den Berg explained that the French version, of which this book is a rendering into English, was not a mere literal translation of the concise Arabic text, which would have been unintelligible, but a paraphrase, based partly upon the *Moharrer* and the Commentary of Mehalli, and partly upon the two principal sixteenth-century commentaries on the *Minhaj et Talibin*—that is to say, the *Tohfat-el-Mohtaj* and the *Nihayat el Mohtaj*. It is not always possible to decide a question by reference to the *Minhaj* alone; and in such a case a Muhammadan jurist—alim, fakih, mufti or kadi, as it may be—has recourse principally to the *Tohfa* and the *Nihaya*, which Dr. Th. Juynboll, in his *Handbuch des islamischen Gesetzes*, 1910, calls "the two standard works in the whole modern Fikh-literature of the School of Shafii." It is hoped, therefore, that the present publication may be of some practical utility in the direction above indicated, and at the same time not without interest to the student of comparative jurisprudence.

CONTENTS

INTRODUCTION

In the Name of God, the Merciful, the Compassionate

Glory to God, the good, the generous, whose blessings are too manifold to be numbered; who poureth forth abundantly His grace and His justice, Who leadeth us in the right way; Who maketh to profit in the study of the divine law those His servants towards whom He showeth kindness, and whom He hath chosen.

To Him I offer praise the most high, the most perfect, the most pure, the most complete. I bear witness that there is none other god but He alone, whose power none shareth; that He is the One that loveth to pardon. And I bear witness that Muhammad is His servant and His preferred and chosen Apostle. God grant him His grace and His blessing, and crown him in heaven with favour and honour.

Now, the best way to manifest obedience towards God and make right use of precious time is assuredly to devote oneself to the study of the law. And many of our learned men of blessed memory have already published with this object concise but exhaustive works, of which in my opinion the best is the Moharrar of the imam Abu Kasim er Rafii, an authority whose accuracy is beyond question. It is a book of the very greatest usefulness, upon whose authority may rely not only the jurist anxious to ascertain the veritable doctrine of our school, but also any other person who seeks to instruct himself by obtaining information from it. Rafii intended to include in his work nothing which had not already been established by the majority of authorities, and he may be said to have remained faithful to this programme, in spite of the great difficulty of carrying it out.

Its prolixity, however, is an obstacle to this work being learnt by heart, except perhaps by some persons who devote themselves exclusively to the study of law, and consequently it appeared to me to be useful to compose an abridgment of it, in length not more than about half of the original volume, but introducing—if God will—some improvements.

In the number of these improvements should principally be mentioned the four following: In the first place, I have everywhere indicated the reservations, that are sometimes not indicated in the Moharrar. Secondly, it will be easy for me to quote from the Moharrar several passages in manifest opposition to the doctrine preferred in our school, as the reader will see, if it please God. In the third place, I shall replace by others clearer and more correct all the little used expressions employed by Rafii, as well as those that might suggest erroneous ideas, either because he wished to be too explicit, or because he was not sufficiently so. Finally, in cases where there is divergence of opinion among authorities I shall give an impartial exposition of the two opposing theories, the two sides from which one may consider the question in dispute, and the two methods of reasoning adopted in order to solve it; and then I will also, where there is occasion for it, quote separately the decisions of our imam Shafii, and note the relative value of the different appreciations.

In order to avoid any subsequent misunderstanding I hereby notify the reader that in the course of the work I shall employ the words *el adhhar* and *el mashur* to designate the doctrine which appears to me preferable, with this difference that I shall use *el adhhar* wherever the doctrine I reject is widely accepted, but otherwise *el mashur*. Similarly the words *el asahh* and *es sahih* will indicate what, in my opinion, is the better way of regarding and resolving a question; with this difference that where there are to be found authorities of repute who incline to the contrary opinion, I shall use the word *el asahh*, but otherwise *es sahih*. The word *el mazhab* will indicate the system which merits the preference in our school; while *en nass* will denote the personal opinion of our imam Shafii, even where his reasoning may appear to me to be weak, or in the case of an isolated decision. The word *el-jedid* means that in his first period, *i.e.* during his stay in Irak, Shafii was of the contrary opinion; and the words *el-kadim* and *fi kawl kadim* indicate that the theory quoted was abandoned by that imam in his second period, *i.e.* during his stay in Egypt. The expression *kil kaza* denotes that this way of regarding and resolving a question is not to be recommended, and that most authorities come to another conclusion, whether the method I disapprove is or is not defended by authorities of repute; and I employ the words *fi kawl* to mean that nearly all authorities have expressed the contrary opinion. And lastly, I must warn the reader that I begin all insertions of my own by the word *kultu*, and terminate them by the phrase *wallahu aalam*.

In case of words or orthographic signs that have been added or intercalated, the reader may rely upon it that the matter was incontestable and the insertion absolutely necessary. Similarly, wherever he may meet with a form of glorifying God differing from that in the

Moharrar or other books upon jurisprudence, he may rest assured that I have verified it from the most authoritative collections of traditions.

And, finally, to some questions I have assigned another place in their section, without keeping to the order in the Moharrar, either because I thought them better placed so, or because I wished to be more concise. I have even taken the liberty to invert the order of whole sections, in order to improve the general arrangement.

In consequence of what I have said I hope that this abstract will be at the same time a veritable commentary upon the Moharrar; for, on the one hand, I have omitted absolutely none of the rules and controversies discussed in that work, however small their importance, and, on the other hand, I believe that I have considerably improved it.

Moreover, I have already begun a work which will contain a discussion of all the debatable points in this abstract, a work in which I explain why I have sometimes had to depart from the text of the Moharrar, and sometimes added a reservation or a conditional modification, etc. But in almost all cases these changes were absolutely necessary and indisputable.

God, the generous, is my sole helper; in Him I put my trust; upon Him I lean. To Him I address my prayer, that He may cause to grow from my labour some benefit to myself and to all other believers; that He may be satisfied with me, my friends, and all the faithful.

NOTE

(SEE INTRODUCTION, PAGE xii)

The following four signs indicate doctrines considered by Nawawi to be preferable to the contrary opinion.

* = *adhhar* (clearer), where the doctrine rejected is widely accepted.

** = *mashhur* (well known), where this is not the case.

† = *asahh* (surer), where the contrary is maintained by authorities of repute.

†† = *sahih* (authentic), where this is not so.

(The signs immediately precede the passages to which they relate.)

The personal opinions of Nawawi are inclosed in square brackets [ ].

MINHAJ ET TALIBIN:

A MANUAL OF MUHAMMADAN LAW

BOOK 1.—LEGAL PURITY

CHAPTER I.—GENERAL PROVISIONS

God has said in the Koran—" We make clear water for cleansing come down from heaven." Thus to remove any impurity, whether slight or serious, it is necessary to make use of " water " in the proper sense of the word, a liquid that can be described as " water " without modification. Water whose nature has been altered by the addition of some foreign substance, such as saffron, loses its purifying quality, for the alteration prevents its being any longer described simply as " water." On the other hand a modification that does not prevent a liquid being still called " water " does not affect its purifying quality ; and consequently mere stagnancy, or mud, or moss, or some accidental object in a basin or a pipe, are of no consequence. And in the same way the introduction of substances that do not dissolve, such as aloes or grease or sand, cannot be regarded as modifying the nature of water.

It is blamable to proceed to purification with water heated by the sun, or with water that has already been used for an obligatory purification. According to some authors Shafii, in his Egyptian period, sustained that even water used for a purification not legally prescribed must on that account be considered improper for any ritual use, if the quantity does not amount to two *kollah.* So considerable a quantity cannot itself become impure by contact with impure substances, unless its nature is thereby modified.

The impurity of water ceases with the adulteration that causes it, whether it regains its original quality of itself, or by an increase in the quantity of liquid ; but if the impurity has merely been rendered imperceptible by the addition of musk, saffron, sand, or plaster, the water continues to be unsuitable for purification, as the impurity itself has not been removed.

A quantity of less than two *kollah* becomes impure by contact, but as soon as the amount is increased to this minimum the water becomes suitable for purification, if the impurity was unaccompanied by any adulteration of the quality. On the other hand, impure water, to which water suitable for purification has been added, remains impure until the minimum has been reached; but according to some jurists the mixture should be considered pure, though unsuitable for purification, if the quantity of impure is less than that of pure water.

**As an exception to the foregoing rules the body of a bloodless insect does not render a liquid impure. And one jurist is of opinion that nothing we have just said applies to impurity so slight as to be inappreciable.

[*In this latter opinion I concur.]

Running water is subject to the same rules as stagnant water, at least this is so according to the opinion expressed by Shafii in his second period, though that Imam at first admitted that running water can never become impure, unless by adulteration, however small the quantity of liquid.

†Two *kollah* are equal to about five hundred *ratal* of Baghdad.

The adulteration of water due to a change from a state of purity to one of impurity is shown by taste, colour, and smell; and when it is at first impossible to distinguish the pure from the impure, one must decide as best one can which of the two one ought to use, and then purify oneself with that one believed to be pure. This course, however, according to some jurists, is not lawful if other water can be procured whose purity is not subject to doubt. *A blind man is subject to these rules relating to the examination of the liquid. If of two liquids that resemble one another one is water and the other urine††, it is of no use attempting an examination, and recourse must be had to purification by sand, after mixing the contents of the two vessels. And finally if it is a question of water and rose-water, both pure, one washes first with one and then with the other; though some authors maintain that even in such a case one should first carefully ascertain the nature of the liquid to be used.

When one of two similar liquids has been chosen and used, the other must be thrown away, in order that no other believer, coming in his turn to perform his ablutions, may be assailed by the same doubts. Should this not have been done, and should a mistaken choice be believed to have been made, still the purification should not be repeated with the other liquid—such at least is Shafii's personal opinion. †But in such a case purification by sand also should be performed. A warning that a liquid is impure should be accepted, if grounds are given for it and it comes from a person worthy of confidence, and even without grounds if coming from a jurist of the school of which one is a follower.

Any sort of vessel may be used for the purpose of ablution so long as it is clean, except vessels of gold and silver, †of which the very acquisition is forbidden. †This prohibition does not include vessels merely gilt or silvered *or of valuable material or adorned with jewels, but does include such as are mounted or inlaid with gold or silver, if the precious metal is in great quantity and solely for ornament. †Thus it does not apply to the three following cases :—(1) if the gold or silver forms only a small part of the vessel and is of some use ; (2) †if the quantity is very small, even when solely for ornament ; (3) †if the quantity is considerable, provided it is of some use. †The position of the gold or silver is immaterial.

[The use of vessels mounted or inlaid with gold is totally forbidden by our school.]

CHAPTER II.—CAUSES OF SLIGHT CORPORAL IMPURITY

Section 1

There are four of these causes.

1. The issue from the body, by the urinary or stercorary passage, of any substance except sperm. As to matter from a wound, a fistula, an incision or any other opening in the proximity of the stomach, the following distinctions have been established :—(*a*) when either pas sage is obstructed and the opening is below the stomach, any issue—*even if accidental, *e.g.* a tænia—impairs the purity of the body ; (*b*) when either passage is obstructed and the opening is above the stomach, or (*c*) when neither is obstructed and the opening is below, *the purity of the body is unaffected.

2. Loss of consciousness, except by sleep in a sitting posture.

3. Contact between a man and a woman, *except when marriage between them would be prohibited on account of relationship, etc. *The impurity affects the person touching as much as the person touched. †Contact with a girl under age, and in general a very slight touch, as of hair, teeth, or nails, cause no impurity.

4. Touching with the palm of the hand the private parts of any human being, including oneself, or even, according to the opinion of Shafii in his second period, the anus ; but not including the parts of an animal. Touching the private parts of a corpse, of a child under age, or of a eunuch or mutilated person, cause impurity ; †as does also a touch with a mutilated hand. †But touching with the finger tips, and taking the parts between the fingers, do not cause impurity.

All persons in a state of impurity are forbidden—

1. To pray.
2. To walk round the holy temple at Mecca.
3. To carry the Koran, or touch its leaves, ††or binding. Such persons may not even touch a bag or box containing the sacred volume, †or a slate upon which any text has been written as an exercise. †They may carry the Koran among and at the same time with other objects, or carry a commentary, or gold pieces engraved with texts; but they may not turn over the leaves of a Koran, even with a piece of wood. †These provisions do not apply to a child under age.

[†It is permissible to turn over the pages of a Koran with a piece of wood; at least it has been so decided by jurists of Irak.]

A person who was at first assured of his state of purity, but who afterwards suspects that he is affected by a slight impurity, should conform to what he considers to be certain, and not concern himself with ulterior doubts. This rule holds good also in the inverse case, *i.e.* when a person is at first assured of being affected by a slight impurity, but is afterwards attacked by doubts as to the result of his examination. Finally, where he perceives he has been alternately pure and impure, without remembering which state had the priority, he should first try to recollect the state he was in before the question arose, and then consider himself as being in the contrary condition.

Section 2

Latrines must be entered left foot first, and quitted right foot first. No object upon which the name of God is inscribed should be taken there. One should squat down leaning rather on the left foot, and if possible avoid turning either face or back in the direction of Mecca, either position being rigorously forbidden on a desert plain where it is possible to choose any direction. To relieve a want of nature one should retire and conceal oneself from the public view. It is forbidden to pass urine into stagnant water, or into a hole, or so that the liquid is dispersed by the wind, or at a meeting place, or on the public road, or under a fruit tree, or while speaking to any one. After evacuation one should not wash oneself at the same place. When passing water care should be taken that all the urine is passed out of the body.

The following words are used on entering latrines: "In the name of God. O God, I seek refuge with Thee against male and female demons"; and on leaving, "I beseech Thy forgiveness. Praise to God that has kept evil afar from me and preserved me." Cleansing, after evacuation, can be effected either with water or with stones, but better with both. By "stone" is here understood any hard, clean object that can be used to remove filth and thrown away; *even a tanned piece of leather may lawfully be employed for this purpose. The use of stones alone suffices only when the excrement is not dry; but may be considered sufficient although extraordinary matters such as blood are excreted, or in spite of the excretion of an extraordinary quantity of matter, provided that the impurity does not extend beyond the sides of the orifice.

The rubbing with stones is three times repeated, either with three different stones, or with three sides of the same stone. A dirty stone must be cleansed before use. The Sonna insists upon each of the three cleansings being done separately. Each stone should be used in cleansing the whole of the part of the body requiring to be cleansed; though some jurists recommend apportioning the three stones, or three ends of the same stone, between the two sides and the middle. The Sonna requires the cleansing to be done with the left hand. *In the case of the excretion of a tænia, or of hard matters, a cleansing is not strictly necessary.

CHAPTER III.—ABLUTION

The following things are necessary to constitute a valid ablution:—

1. The intention to remove an impurity; or the intention to enable oneself to accomplish an act, for the validity of which bodily purity is a requisite; or the intention to perform ablution as a duty prescribed by law.†* If a person is in a state of chronic impurity, *e.g.* a woman whose menses are prolonged beyond the legal term, there can of course be no intention to remove an impurity whose removal is an impossibility; but the intention to render licit the act one desires to accomplish suffices in all cases.†† An intention to cool oneself by washing may be combined with the religious purpose here treated of;† but it is illicit to combine the intention to accomplish an obligatory purification with a purpose to perform an ablution which is merely recommended, *e.g.* for the recitation of the Koran. The intention is formulated at the moment of proceeding to the ablution of the face; though some learned authors maintain that, following the example of the Prophet, it may be formulated before this.† It is not necessary that the intention should refer to the entire ablution, it may be formed at the washing of each separate member of the body.

2. The washing of the face, *i.e.* the part of the head comprised from top to bottom between the place where the hair usually begins and the extremity of the lower jaw-bones, and from right to left between the ears. This includes also the part of the forehead upon which the hair

falls down, and the part of the head where the hair has been cut; but does not include the temples, *i.e.* the two white spots to right and left of the forelocks.

[A part of the head where the hair has been cut is rightly considered by nearly all learned men as belonging to the top of the head and not to the face.]

It is necessary to wash eyelashes, eyebrows, whiskers, moustache and imperial, both the hair and the skin covered by it. Some jurists, however, contend that it is not obligatory to wash the skin covered by the imperial when the latter is thick; and all agree that the beard need be washed like the eyelids, etc., only when it is thin, but, otherwise, merely on the surface. One learned author has even advanced the opinion that a special ablution of the beard, and in general of all the hair on the face, is not obligatory.

3. The washing of the hands and arms up to the elbows.** If one has lost part of a hand, one should wash what remains. The stump should be washed, if an arm has been amputated below the elbow; but if above, an ablution is not necessary, though always to be recommended.

4. The passing of the moistened hand over the skin of the top of the head, or if that be impossible over the hair covering it.† A proper washing, is of course, also quite licit; and the head may also be moistened while keeping the hand closed, if necessary.

5. The washing of the feet, including the ankles.

6. The observing of the prescribed order.† If any one, instead of practising a mere ablution, prefers to take a bath, for the purpose of removing an impurity, this is permitted; provided that the prescribed order is observed in plunging into the water, and one remains there some time, but not otherwise. [†Even a hurried bath is in all cases sufficient.]

The following practices have been introduced by the Sonna :—

1. The use of teeth-cleaners, or other hard substance capable of taking their place,† except fingers. This is particularly to be recommended before prayer and when the taste in the mouth is changed; but it can be practised at any time, except when fasting in the afternoon.

2. Beginning ablution by pronouncing the formula, "In the name of God." If neglected at the beginning the omission may be rectified by pronouncing the formula in the middle.

3. Washing the hands before commencing the ritual ablution. It is even considered blamable to dip the hands in a basin containing water for the ablution of several persons, without first washing them three times, unless one is sure they are quite clean.

4. Rinsing the mouth and cleansing the nostrils with water. *It is well to do these separately ; †first taking water three times in the hollow of the hand for rinsing, and then three times for the other purpose. Except in the case of persons fasting, these two practices are as a rule observed by every one. [*It is preferable to cŏmbine them, taking water in the palm of the hand three times for the two together.]

5. Repeating all ablutions and moistenings three times.

6. Resolving any doubt as to the validity or number of ablutions, by coming to a definite conclusion one way or the other.

7. The moistening of the whole head and ears ; though it is enough to moisten the turban if it is difficult to take off.

8. Separation of the hairs of the beard if it is very thick ; and even the fingers and toes.

9. The washing of the right side before the left.

10. Extending the ablution of the face upon the skin covered by hair ; as well as that of the arms and feet above the elbows and ankles.

11. Completion of the ablution without interruption, a precept which Shafii in his first period even called obligatory.

12. Performance of the ablution without the assistance of other persons.

13. Abstention from shaking the water off the body, †or removing it with a sponge or other similar object.

14. Terminating the ablution by pronouncing the following formula :—" I witness that there is no other god than God alone, whose power is shared by none. I witness that Muhammad is His servant and apostle. O God, receive me amongst them that repent, that keep themselves from sin, Thy holy servants. Glory to Thee, O God ! I praise Thee, and witness yet again that there is no other God but Thee. I implore Thy forgiveness. I turn again unto Thee."

[I intentionally omit the formulas given in the *Muharrar* for repetition by the believer during the ablution of the different parts of the body, as their authority has not been established.]

CHAPTER IV.—MOISTENING OF FOOT-GEAR

THE ablution of the feet may be replaced by that of the foot-gear, if not worn for more than a day and a night during a stay at a fixed abode, or more than three days and three nights when on a journey. This indulgence applies only to a case where the impurity has been incurred after the feet have been covered. When setting out on a journey after moistening the foot-gear at home, or *vice versâ*, the shorter interval of one day and one night must be observed. It is also necessary that the feet should be thoroughly cleansed before being covered ; that every part of the feet requiring ablution should be covered ; that the foot-gear should be quite clean when put on ; and that the same foot-gear should be able to last to the end of the way. It is also necessary that the march or journey should have some object ; and some jurists insist further that there must be a legal right to use the foot-gear worn.

†Permeable foot-gear, *e.g.* the slippers called *jermuk*, cannot be moistened ; †but a torn sole is no objection, if properly fastened.

The Sonna insists on the foot-gear being moistened from top to bottom with the fingers, as if one were tracing lines on it ; but it is strictly sufficient to moisten the part of the foot-gear corresponding to that portion of the foot of which ablution is prescribed, except only the sole of the foot and heel which it is not the practice to moisten, at least according to the teaching of our school. [This rule applies to the edges, as well as to the sole.]

Moistening of the foot-gear is not permissible if there is any doubt as to the time not being yet passed ; nor in the case of grave impurity, where the clothes must be changed and a bath taken before the indulgence of moistening the foot-gear can again be had recourse to. And when foot-gear that has been moistened is changed, the feet must be washed ; and also the head and arms, according to one author.

CHAPTER V.—BATHING

Bathing, or general ablution of the body, is necessary on all occasions when a person is affected with grave impurity. These occasions are :—

1. Death.
2. Menstruation.
3. Lochia ; †and confinement in general, even when unaccompanied by evacuation.
4. Sexual penetration.
5. Any effusion of semen ; recognisable by emission, sensation, odour, or appearance. In the absence of these signs no bath is necessary.

In all that concerns grave impurity a woman is subject to the same rules as a man. In a state of grave impurity it is illicit to accomplish the three religious acts prohibited to persons affected by any impurity ; and in addition it is forbidden to remain in a mosque, though one may walk through ; and forbidden to recite the Koran, though one may pronounce a few words from the sacred volume, if solely to glorify God.

For the validity of the bath there must be :—

1. An intention to remove a grave impurity, or to enable oneself

to accomplish an act requiring a previous bathing, or to take the bath as a duty prescribed by law. This intention must be formulated at the moment of entering the bath.

2. A washing of all parts of the body, both the skin and the hair covering it; but rinsing of the mouth and cleansing of the nostrils, acts required as we have seen by the Sonna in ordinary ablution, are unnecessary.

It may be added, however, that the best way of taking a bath is as follows :—

1. Begin by removing all filth from the body.

2. Then perform ablution; except that according to one author washing of the feet should be deferred until the end.

3. Wash carefully in all the folds of the skin, especially in places more liable to perspiration.

4. Pour water on the head.

5. Separate the hair of the head and beard, by passing the wet fingers through them.

6. Give priority to the right side.

7. Rub the whole body.

8. Repeat the whole three times.

A woman subject to menstruation should also rub with musk any parts of the body that bear traces of blood, or if she has no musk with any other perfume.

The Sonna does not insist on a fresh bath for each act requiring bodily purity, but does insist upon an ordinary ablution before performing such act, even when no impurity has knowingly been incurred since the last ablution. It has also ruled that the quantity of water for an ordinary ablution should not be less than one *modd*, and for a bath not less than one *saa*; in neither case is any maximum prescribed. A person affected with grave material impurity should first remove the filth from the part concerned, and then take a ritual bath as a mere bath does not suffice. Whether the impurity incurred is grave or slight, ritual ablution must be practised as well as a bath. [†The bath alone is always sufficient.]

A person wishing to take a bath for a grave impurity at the same time as the prescribed Friday's bath may lawfully perform these two duties simultaneously, provided that his intention applies to both.

[According to our school a bath alone is sufficient, even in the case of a person who has incurred both grave and slight impurity, irrespective of which has been first incurred.]

CHAPTER VI.—THINGS IMPURE IN THEMSELVES

THINGS not accidentally but essentially impure are :—

1. Every intoxicating liquid.

2. Dogs and pigs ; and any animal born of the copulation of a dog or a pig with any other—even a pure—animal.

3. Animals dead from natural causes, or killed otherwise than in accordance with the law relating to that matter. Only human corpses, and the bodies of fishes and locusts, remain pure, however death has been caused.

4. Blood, pus, vomit and droppings.

5. Urine and any other liquid issuing from the genitals of a living being ; †including sperm, except human sperm. [†The sperm of all living things is pure, except that of animals mentioned in 2.]

6. The milk of animals not eaten by man ; but not a woman's milk.

Everything that comes or has been cut from a living thing is consisidered, so far as regards its purity or impurity, as the body itself, after such thing has ceased to live ; except the hair of animals that may be eaten ; for these are considered pure, however the animal came by its death. †In the same way a clot of blood, a bit of chewed meat, or the natural moisture of a woman's private parts, are not impure.

Essential impurity cannot disappear in any way ; but it is otherwise with accidental impurity. An exception, however, is admitted in the case of wine that has changed into vinegar of itself, *i.e.* without the use of chemicals. †This is accepted as pure, even if the change is due to transference from a sunny to a shady place, or *vice versâ*. But if, on the contrary, wine changes to vinegar on the introduction of some substance producing that effect, it remains impure.

An animal's skin, rendered impure by its death, may be purified by tanning either outside **or inside. By " tanning " is understood the removal of everything superfluous by corrosives, but not by sun-heat or sand. †The use of water is not necessary to insure the legal effect of tanning. Moreover leather soiled after tanning is in the same condition as a piece of cloth or other object become accidentally impure, that is to say that this impurity can be removed by a thorough cleaning ; it is only the impurity caused by contact with a dog, or with something that has come from a similar animal, that necessitates purification of a special kind. Now in this latter case the object must be washed seven times, and one of these seven ablutions must be performed with sand, *a substance specially prescribed for this purification. †Sand that is impure or has been mixed with liquid cannot be used for this purpose. *In reference to this matter contact with a pig is regarded in the same way as that with a dog. The impurity caused by the urine of a little boy not yet weaned can be removed by a mere washing of the soiled object; but in cases of impurity other than the two we have just specified, if it has left no perceptible trace water must be passed over it, and if it has then purification must be continued until at least there remains no noticeable odour. Traces of colour or smell need not prevent use of the object, if it is impossible or difficult to remove them. One authority, however, insists that the odour should be entirely got rid off. [††When traces of impurity are left, both in colour and smell, the object cannot lawfully be used.]

†For an efficient washing it is enough to pour water on the object; it is not always necessary to soak the object in water, or press it with the fingers or wring it out; *while water flowing off an object washed without pressing, etc., remains pure after the impurity of the object has disappeared, provided there has been no modification of quality.

Purification of liquid matter is impossible, though some authors assert that grease is an exception to this rule, at least when of a nature to admit of washing.

CHAPTER VII.—ABLUTION WITH SAND

Section 1

Recourse may be had to ablution with sand, whether for slight or grave impurity, in the following cases:—

1. If there is no water. The traveller who is sure of this can at once have recourse to ablution with sand; he need not first search the neighbourhood; but if it is a mere supposition, he should first search his luggage, or make inquiries from his companions. If in a plain he should look around him; and if the ground be hilly search the vicinity as far as the horizon. Only if all his efforts are without success, is he permitted—when uncertain of the absence of water—to practise ablution with sand. †When not on a journey, the absence of water at a place, once ascertained, does not dispense with the necessity of another search on a second ablution becoming requisite; because water may in the interval have risen at a spot where previously there was none. If there is known to be water at so short a distance that a traveller in case of necessity would be willing to leave his route in order to reach it, then he must do so, unless he fear thereby to endanger his person or property, for in this latter case also ablution with sand is permitted If the certainty of being able to obtain water is acquired only at the last

moment before the time prescribed for prayer, it is better to defer the accomplishment of this religious duty and go and get the water, rather than to rest content with an ablution with sand. *On the other hand, if it is not a certainty but a mere supposition that is formed at the last moment, it is better to pay no heed to it and proceed at once to perform the ablution with sand. When there is some water, but in insufficient quantity for an ablution, still one should make use of it, rather than have recourse to ablution with sand; and water should even be purchased if this can be done at a reasonable price, unless the money is needed to pay a debt that is due, or for travelling expenses, or for the keep of persons or animals in one's charge. †An offer of water, or of a bucket to draw it with, must be accepted; but an offer of money with which to buy it need not. If one has forgotten to bring water with one, or left the skin containing it amongst one's luggage and cannot find it after a careful search, ablution with sand is lawful; *but in that case the prayer or other act of devotion must be repeated when the liquid is found. This repetition is not necessary if it is the luggage itself that cannot be found amongst that of other travellers.

2. If the water one has is required for drinking by the persons and animals in one's charge, either immediately or in the near future.

3. In the case of an ill or wounded person, if it is feared the patient may die in consequence of an ablution with water, or may lose the use of a limb. *This rule even extends to the case where an ablution, by aggravating a malady or an injury, might retard the cure, or disfigure some part of the body ordinarily exposed like the face. For the purpose of ablution extreme cold is regarded in the same way as a malady. In all cases where the use of water is dispensed with, ablution with sand must be practised upon any diseased or injured limb not covered with a bandage; and it still remains necessary, according to our school, to proceed to the ablution with water of all those parts of the body that are healthy or sound. In these circumstances a person who has incurred grave impurity has the option of beginning with sand or water as he pleases; for these are a substitute for bathing, a religious duty that does not require the observance of any definite order in the purification of the parts of the body. †On the other hand, a person who has incurred a slight impurity must perform the ablution with sand, only at the proper moment at which the prescribed order requires the washing of the diseased or injured limb; and so, should there be two injured limbs, they must be separately purified, carefully observing the prescribed order. If a part of the skin is covered over, as by splints that cannot be removed, the exposed part of the body must be washed, and the rest cleansed in the way we have explained. The splints, too, must

be completely moistened and wiped ; though, according to some opinions, a part is enough. When it is necessary to proceed to a second ablution in order to prepare for the accomplishment of another religious obligation, where no impurity has intervened since the first ablution ; the sick person, if on the earlier occasion he had incurred grave impurity, and consequently performed ablution in place of a bath, need not wash the sound limbs when practising the second. But if, on the contrary, the sick person had on the first occasion incurred only slight impurity, he must, on the second, again wash those limbs which, in the prescribed order, have their turn after the diseased or injured limbs. Some authors support the view that in both cases the ablution of all sound limbs should be repeated ; others contend that the indulgence accorded to a sick person previously affected with grave impurity should be applied equally when the impurity is merely slight. [†I prefer the latter doctrine.]

SECTION 2

Any kind of sand can be used for ablution, even medical powder, or sand mixed with dust ; but not mineral powder, nor pounded pottery, nor sand mixed with flour, etc. Some, however, are of opinion that the use of sand mixed with other substances is licit, if they are present only in very small quantity. ††The use of sand that has already served for a previous ablution is illicit, whether it still adheres to the body †or not. It is necessary that the sand should be specially obtained for the purpose of ablution. Thus sand swept up by the wind and blown upon a person about to practise ablution cannot legally be utilised, even if it be shaken upon the member to be rubbed with the special intention of accomplishing that duty. It is, however, permissible to be assisted in the ablution by another person ; though some authorities admit this only if one is prevented from performing it oneself.

The essentials to a proper performance of ablution with sand are :—

1. An actual removal of the sand to the limbs ; †*i.e.* it must be carried from the face to the hand, or *vice versâ*.

2. An intention to prepare oneself for prayer. A mere intention to remove an impurity incurred, †or to practise ablution as a religious duty, is of no value. It is formulated at the moment of carrying the sand to the limbs, ††and should continue until some part of the face is rubbed. When the intention is directed both to an obligatory and also to an additional prayer, then both of these become licit by the fact of a single ablution. An ablution, practised with the intention of making an obligatory prayer, will serve either for this or for an additional (*i.e.* optional) prayer ; but if the intention refers only to an optional

prayer, or even merely to a prayer in general, it can in that case be succeeded only by an optional and not by an obligatory prayer—at least according to our school.

3. A rubbing, first of the face and then of the hands and forearms with the elbows. The law does not insist on the sand reaching the roots of the small hairs that cover these parts of the body.

†When carrying the sand to the limbs it is not necessary to observe any order of succession among the different parts of the body; and this principle even goes so far that it is quite permissible to plunge both hands at the same time in the sand, and to rub the face with the right hand, and then the right hand with the left hand.

In ablution by sand the following acts are considered recommendable:

1. Beginning by uttering the words "In the name of God."

2. Rubbing both face and hands twice. [†It was the personal opinion of Shafii that this repetition is obligatory, even when a rag or something similar is used to rub with.]

3. Always giving priority to the right side of the body over the left.

4. Rubbing the face from above downwards.

5. Using no more than the necessary amount of sand, and throwing away the rest.

6. Completing the ablution without interruption, as is the case for a ritual ablution. [This rule applies also to the bath, where it is considered recommendable to begin by separating the fingers. When rubbing the hands for the second time a ring must be laid aside.]

When a person finds water, after having had recourse to ablution by sand because he thought there was none, the two following cases must be distinguished.

1. If the water is found before beginning the prayer, the ablution by sand is annulled, and one proceeds to the ritual ablution, if there be no obstacle to such use of the water found, *e.g.* if it be not required for drinking.

2. If the water is not perceived until after the prayer is begun. Here it is necessary again to distinguish two possibilities :—(*a*) if the time legally allowed for the prayer in question permits of completing the ablution and after it another prayer, **then these should be undertaken, and the ablution by sand is annulled ; and (*b*) if it is impossible to do this within the prescribed time, in which case the ablution by sand is valid, and the prayer may be continued.

According to some opinions an optional prayer is always annulled by the fact of finding water afterwards. †And if possible it is always better to interrupt an obligatory prayer in which one is engaged, and continue it after ablution, even if time does not permit of concluding an entirely new prayer, and where in consequence the finding of the water does not absolutely nullify the ablution with sand. †Those, however, who admit that an optional prayer, preceded only by ablution with sand, is not in all cases annulled by the fact of finding water, contend that in these circumstances the prayer must not exceed two *raka*, unless the previous intention has been formulated of accomplishing a greater number.

A single ablution with sand can never serve for more than one obligatory prayer; though it suffices for as many optional prayers as may be desired. *But a supererogatory prayer which is the consequence of a vow comes under the same rule as an obligatory prayer. An ablution for the prayer for the dead may be combined with that for an obligatory prayer.

†If one has neglected to accomplish one of the five obligatory prayers, and one cannot remember precisely which, the oversight may be repaired by performing one ablution followed by the five prayers. If an uncertain two of the five have been omitted, all five must be repeated, each with its separate ablution; or one may perform two ablutions each followed by four prayers, omitting from the second four the one that began the first. And if the same obligatory prayer has been twice omitted, there must be two ablutions, each followed by all five prayers.

Ablution by sand is not permitted before the hour prescribed for each prayer; and this prohibition applies not only to obligatory prayers, †but also to those additional ones that are made at fixed times.

Notwithstanding that neither water nor sand can be procured for ablution, one should still, according to the view supported by Shafii in his second period, perform the obligatory prayers at their legal time, repeating them when one or other has been found. Moreover a person living at a fixed place who has recourse to ablution with sand in consequence of a want of water, must again acquit himself of his religious duty after finding it; but no such obligation lies on a traveller, †unless his journey has been undertaken for an illicit end. *Similarly, if one has had recourse to ablution with sand on account of the cold, the prayer must be subsequently repeated and preceded by a regular ablution; but this repetition is not strictly necessary if the use of sand was caused by a sickness which prevented the use of water in general or its application to a part of the body not covered by a splint, except only in the case of a wound that bleeds profusely. But if it is a question of a part of the body covered by a splint, a distinction must be made. **If the part of the body to which the splint has been attached has incurred only a slight impurity a repetition is necessary—if the splint was not removed before the ablution with sand; * but this is not so in the case of a grave impurity.

CHAPTER VIII.—MENSTRUATION

Section 1

The age at which a woman can begin to have menses is nine years. The shortest period of continuance of one menstruation is one day and one night; and the longest fifteen days and fifteen nights. The shortest interval of purity between two menstruations is fifteen days; there is no legal limit for the longest period.

The legal consequence of menses is that the woman undergoing them is regarded as a person who has incurred a grave impurity. Besides this the law forbids her—

1. To pass through a mosque, if she fears she may soil the building;
2. To fast,—though she must perform an obligatory fast on recovering her normal condition. On the other hand, prayers omitted on account of menstruation need not be accomplished;
3. To be touched by a man on the part of the body between the navel and the knees, though according to some authorities this prohibition refers only to the act of coition.

When the discharge stops, acts that are illicit during menstruation remain so until the woman has taken a bath; with the exception of fasting and repudiation, which become licit at the moment of stoppage.

A hæmorrhage that continues after the legal term of the menstruation is a perpetual cause of slight impurity, as is also an unhealthy discharge of urine or semen; though they do not prevent fasting or prayer. Before, however, proceeding to these latter acts of devotion, the person subject to the infirmities mentioned, should wash the affected part and apply a bandage. After this, as soon as the hour of prayer has sounded, ritual ablution should be practised, and the prayer accomplished as soon as possible. ††What the law forbids here is any capricious delay. A delay rendered necessary for the regularity of the prayer is permitted. Thus, after ablution, the prayer may be deferred until one is suitably dressed; or until the congregation has assembled, if it is a public act of devotion. A person subject to irregular discharges such as we have just spoken of, must repeat a ritual ablution for each obligatory prayer, even when no fresh impurity has elapsed, †and renew the bandage each time. And, finally, a person whose discharges cease after ritual ablution must repeat it immediately, even if she is not usually subject to a return of her infirmity after it has ceased, or if while subject to returns she usually has an interval of purity sufficiently long to admit of an ablution and prayer.

Section 2

When a woman has reached the age of puberty all matter coming out of the womb constitutes menstruation, at least during the legal period. †Even yellow or colourless fluids are regarded as menstruous. As to irregular discharges that occur after the legal period of menstruation, it is necessary to distinguish the two following varieties :—

1. Discharges occurring for the first time. This category is subdivided into two kinds : (*a*) if the discharges are of distinct nature, *e.g.* plentiful and slight, the latter are considered as hæmorrhages and the former as true menses if continuing for not less than the minimum and not more than the maximum legal period, provided that the slight discharges continue at least for the minimum legal state of purity ; and (*b*) if the discharges cannot be regarded as distinct, either because they are similar or because their precise periods cannot be determined ; they are then looked upon as menses for one day and one night, and as a hæmorrhage for the rest of the month, *i.e.* for the 29 following days.

2. Discharges constituting a chronic infirmity, in such a way that the person in question is habitually subject to intermittent intervals of purity. This category also admits of two subdivisions : (*a*) if the person understands the ordinary course of her infirmity, and can rely upon her experience of the length of the periods observed, even once ; †any new indications being duly conformed to ; and (*b*) if the person has doubts upon the subject ; **she should then scrupulously observe the phases of her infirmity and act accordingly ; at least this is the opinion of all jurists except one, who considers such person to come under rule 1.

It is forbidden to persons subject to irregular discharges coming under case 2 (*b*) to indulge in coition. They may not touch a Koran, nor may they recite passages from this sacred scripture, except in prayer,—for their infirmity does not prevent their performing the obligatory prayers. †They may only accomplish a supererogatory prayer after taking a bath. Similarly, a woman subject to irregular discharges must observe the fast of the month of Ramadan, *i.e.* she must fast for the whole of this month, and then for the whole of another month. Thus she will be regarded as having fasted for fourteen days in each of these two months. Finally she must fast six days out of eighteen in a third month, *i.e.* first three days, then, after an interval of twelve, three more days, to make up the two missing days of the fast. She may also substitute for any fasting day another fasting day, provided that in that case she fasts on the third and seventeenth days following.

A person subject to the chronic infirmity we are discussing, who has but a confused recollection of what happened previously, should be of strict observance where she is certain; and, where doubtful, she should regard herself as impure concerning coition, but pure concerning the accomplishment of her religious duties. If there be uncertainty as to cessation of discharge, a bath should be taken before each obligatory prayer. †The hæmorrhage of a pregnant woman is regarded as a true menstruation; as is also an interval of purity in any woman, during the legal period of her menses.

The shortest period of lochia is one instant and the longest sixty days; the ordinary time is forty days. Their effect is to render illicit all acts forbidden in the period of menstruation. Lochia that continue for more than sixty days are subject to the same rules as menses that have exceeded the legal term.

BOOK 2.—PRAYER

CHAPTER I.—GENERAL PROVISIONS

Section 1

Five daily prayers are prescribed in the Book of God—

1. The midday prayer (*dhohr*). The legal time for this prayer commences at the moment when the sun begins to decline, and lasts until the shadows of objects equal their real height, plus the length of shadow cast at noon.

2. At this moment begins the legal time for the afternoon prayer (*asr*); it lasts until sunset. It is preferable, however, to accomplish this prayer before a shadow has become twice as long as the object causing it, plus the length cast at noon.

3. The evening prayer (*maghrib*) should be performed at the moment of sunset. In his first period Shafii admitted that the legal time for this duty extends until the red colour of the sky has disappeared; but in his second period he contended that it lasts no longer than is necessary for practising ablution, dressing suitably, listening to the first and second call, and accomplishing the five *rakas* that form the act of devotion. ††These acts, however, may if necessary be prolonged until the red colour of the sky has disappeared, provided they began at the right moment. [*Shafii's first opinion is preferable.]

4. The prayer of the night (*isha*) can be said as soon as the red colour of the sky has disappeared; and the legal time lasts till dawn. It is, however, preferable not to defer this prayer beyond the first third of the night; or, according to one author, beyond midnight.

5. The morning prayer (*sobh*); for which the legal time begins with the appearance of dawn, *i.e.* when the light of day first appears on the horizon, and lasts until sunrise. It is preferable not to defer this prayer beyond the rising of the sun.

[The following practices are considered worthy of blame :—

1. To call the evening prayer *isha* instead of *maghrib;* and to call the prayer of the night *atama* instead of *isha;* as did the Beduin in the time of the Prophet.

2. To go to rest before accomplishing the prayer of the night.

3. To engage in conversation after having said the prayer of the night; unless it is an edifying conversation.]

The following two practices have been introduced by the Sonna.

1. To finish a prayer as soon as the legal time permits; although, according to one authority, it is to be recommended to defer the prayer of the night until one goes to rest.

2. For the midday prayer, to wait until the heat of the day begins to diminish, at least when it is very hot; †a rule specially adapted to hot climates, and to public prayer if the mosque is situated at a great distance.

†A prayer not finished within the legal term is nevertheless regarded as performed with regularity and at the prescribed hour, if at least one *raka* is finished within the time; otherwise it counts only as an act of devotion made too late. If one is uncertain as to the exact time of day, one should try to determine it approximately, for instance, by observing cattle that go down to drink at fixed hours. *If, however, one afterwards becomes aware of having thus said one's prayer too soon, one should repeat it by way of reparation; but this is not necessary in the case where a prayer is discovered to have been made too late. A person who perceives that he has allowed the prescribed hour to pass should accomplish the omitted prayer as soon as possible, but the Sonna insists in this case that the proper order of daily prayers should be observed, and that the prayer of which the proper time is passed should be accomplished before the one next due after the time the error was discovered, provided that too long a delay would not thereby be caused.

It is blamable to pray—

1. At the moment the sun is on the meridian, except on Friday.

2. From the end of the time prescribed for the morning prayer, until the elevation of the sun has attained the height of a lance.

3. From the end of the time prescribed for the afternoon prayer, until the sun has set.

These rules, however, do not apply to—

1. Prayers made for a special reason: *e.g.* (*a*) a prayer said by way of reparation, when the legal time has been allowed to pass; (*b*) public prayer on occasion of an eclipse; (*c*) the salutation of a mosque; (*d*) prostrations of thanksgiving; (*e*) prostrations at the reading of the Koran.

2. Prayers performed in the holy land of Mecca.

Section 2

Prayer is obligatory only for an adult Moslem, sane and free from impurity. Thus an infidel who has been converted to Islam need not thereupon perform all the prayers which he would have said in his past life; but this obligation does lie upon the apostate who repents of his errors. Similarly the adult need not perform prayers omitted during his minority. But minors should be exhorted to prayer from tneir seventh year, and from their tenth forced to it, even with blows. Prayer is not obligatory for a woman during her menses, nor for a lunatic, nor for a person in a faint; but it is for a drunkard, *i.e.* such person must perform it after becoming sober.

When one of these causes of exemption from prayer ceases before the legal time has passed, the prayer must be performed, even if there be but time to pronounce the introductory formula "God is Great"; or, according to the opinion of one jurist, if there be time to finish the first *raka*. *As to the midday and evening prayers, they must, under these circumstances, be performed as long as their respective terms admit of the enunciation of the formula mentioned. If a minor attains puberty while praying, the prayer should be continued and concluded ††and then counts as performed during majority. ††Neither of course is repetition necessary when the signs of puberty occur immediately after the termination of a prayer, even though the legal time permit it; but a woman in whom menstruation manifests itself, or a person who goes mad, after the hour prescribed for a prayer has sounded, must afterwards perform it, if the time passed before the cause of exemption would have sufficed for concluding the act of devotion, had the latter been begun at the proper moment.

Section 3

The *adzan*, or first call to prayer, and the *ikama*, or second, are only prescribed by the Sonna, though some consider them to be rigorously obligatory, and that the Moslem community is collectively responsible for their observance. These calls take place only for the five obligatory prayers, or as some think also on occasion of all public prayers, as for the great festivals, etc. In his second period Shafii admitted as a recommendable practice that every one about to pray on his own account should begin by reciting aloud the words of the first call, except in a mosque where the congregation was assembled. During the same period the imam also recommended the reciting of the words of the second call, in the case of an obligatory prayer for which the legal time was already past, and which one was about to accomplish by way of reparation. [*I prefer Shafii's earlier doctrine, namely that it is commendable to recite in all cases the words of the first call.]

If several prayers have been omitted at the proper legal time, it is sufficient to recite once the words of the call, when these prayers are repeated one after the other by way of reparation.

**When persons praying together are all women, they omit the first call, repeating the words of the second only.

At the first call all the phrases are pronounced twice; those of the second only once. The words, "the hour of prayer is come," do not form part of the calls; they are recited twice in each case.

The Sonna has introduced the following practices in the calls to prayer:—

1. Raising the voice by degrees while repeating the second call.

2. Pronouncing distinctly the words of the first call.

3. Pronouncing the confession of faith in the first call at first in a low tone and then aloud.

4. Adding to the first call to morning prayer the phrase "prayer is better than sleep."

5. Standing up when reciting the first call and turning to the *kibla*, *i.e.* the direction of the holy temple of Mecca.

But the two following requirements are alone necessary for the validity of the calls:—

1. Observance of the due order of succession of the phrases.

2. Enunciation of the calls without interruption; though, according to one of our jurists, their validity is not compromised either by a few superfluous words or by a fairly long interval of silence.

The muezzin or person entrusted with the duty of crying the first call must be a male Moslem and have attained years of discretion. It is blamable to entrust this duty to any one who has incurred a slight—and still more a grave—impurity; and it is yet more blamable that any such person should cry the second call. In conformity with the Sonna a person chosen to perform the function of muezzin is usually of irreproachable character, with a fine, sonorous voice.

In the prayer the function of the imam is more important than that of the muezzin. [On the contrary, the function of the muezzin must be considered as the more important.]

Another essential condition for the validity of the first call is that the prescribed time for the prayer should have come; except in the case of the first call to morning prayer which may be chanted any time after midnight.

The following additional practices have been introduced by the Sonna:—

1. The chanting of the first call to morning prayer by two of the muezzins attached to the mosque, one before and one after the appearance of the dawn.

2. The repetition of the words of the muezzin by every person hearing the first call to any prayer; except the two phrases beginning with the word "come," *i.e.* "come to prayer," and "come to salvation," which should be replaced by the formula, "there is no force nor power but in God." [The phrase, "prayer is better than sleep," is also not to be repeated. It is preferable to substitute for it, "Thou art the truth and the right."]

3. A prayer for the Prophet, uttered after the call is finished both by muezzin and hearers; and then after that the following formula:—"O God, to whom are addressed this call and also the prayer which I am about to offer, grant to Muhammad thy benediction and grace, and make him to enter the abode of the blessed, as Thou didst promise. O Thou that art the most Merciful!"

Section 4

One of the conditions essential to the validity of prayer is to turn if possible towards the *kibla*, that is in the direction of the holy temple of Mecca. To this rule there are only two exceptions—(1) prayer made at a moment of danger; and (2) a supererogatory prayer made by a traveller.

As to this second cause of exemption, it is necessary to observe further that a traveller is permitted to accomplish his supererogatory prayers while still remaining on his mount, and even while continuing his journey, **be it long or short. If, however, one is travelling in a litter, one should take the required direction and accomplish thus the inclinations and prostrations wherever possible; †but no such obligation exists for the rider, unless he can comply with it easily. †It is specially to be recommended that one should place one's body in the right direction at the moment of pronouncing the introductory formula "God is great"; and also, according to some authorities, at the moment of proceeding to the final salutation. The traveller who has a valid reason for not turning towards the *kibla*, must not turn in any other direction, but remain in the position he happens to be in at the time; while a traveller, riding, may accomplish the inclinations and prostrations by merely bending the head—lower on the breast for the latter than for the former.

***The traveller on foot must accomplish the inclinations and prostrations like everybody else, and he must turn towards Mecca when bending down or prostrating himself, just as when pronouncing the introductory formula "God is great." But he is allowed to continue his journey during the *kiam*, and when uttering the confession of faith.**

The traveller whose mount or litter permits of his accomplishing the inclinations and prostrations in the usual manner, and of taking the direction of the *kibla*, all without alighting, may do this provided he stops. But he is forbidden to continue the journey while doing it.

When praying in the sanctuary of Mecca one may either turn to the wall or the door; but if the door happens to be open, the threshold must be at least two-thirds of an ell high. When praying on the roof of the sanctuary one may turn to a wall or to the door at choice.

A person who is himself able to ascertain the proper direction of Mecca should regulate his attitude by that and not by what he sees others doing. If unable to ascertain the true position, he should find out from some reliable person who is sure of it; only in the absence of such person may one have recourse to indirect methods, and even then it is forbidden to follow blindly the example of another. When unable to discover the position of the *kibla*, it is better—rather than to follow blindly the example of another—to pray in the position one may happen to be in, at the risk of having to repeat the prayer upon learning afterwards that it was the wrong direction. ††One should make fresh efforts to ascertain the direction of the temple of Mecca before performing each prayer. It is only in two cases, *i.e.* where personal information is impossible, and where one cannot oneself distinguish the indications of direction—as, for instance, if one is blind—that it is allowable to follow without examination the example of a reliable and sufficiently educated person; †but such a course is rigorously forbidden except where one is totally unable to find out oneself or to distinguish the indications.

*He who ascertains to the best of his ability the direction of the sanctuary of Mecca, and afterwards finds it to be mistaken, should repeat his prayer. If at the discovery the prayer is not yet finished, it should be begun again at once. If one's opinion alters with regard to the direction when at prayer, one should conform to that opinion, without repeating the prayer—even if it should happen three times, and four *rakas* be addressed in four different directions.

CHAPTER II.—MANNER OF PRAYER

The essentials that constitute prayer are thirteen—

1. *Niya*, or intention. With regard to the obligatory prayers this consists in the intention of accomplishing the prayer specially in view. †It should also refer to the obligation to accomplish that prayer, but there is no need to add that it is an obligation towards God, as this is understood. †The intention to pray late to replace an omitted or irregular prayer suffices also for the prayer made at the legal time.

and similarly an intention to accomplish a prayer at the legal time suffices for a prayer said late by way of reparation. So far as regards intention, a supererogatory prayer accomplished at a fixed time, or for a particular reason, follows the same rule as an obligatory prayer; but whether it is necessary that the intention should also refer to the idea of a voluntary work is a matter of controversy. [††No special intention with regard to this idea is necessary.] The simple intention to pray is sufficient in the case of supererogatory prayers that have no fixed time nor particular reason; and it should also be observed that intention is a matter of the heart and not of words, though this does not prevent it being commendable to formulate the intention at the moment of saying "God is great."

2. The *takbirat al ihram*, or introductory formula "God is great," obligatory for every one capable of pronouncing it. Though this formula is all-important, a few superfluous words may be added. Thus one may say, "God is the great,"†or "God the most high is great." But the addition must not be derogatory to the name "God." ††One may not say, "The greatest is God." The believer who cannot pronounce this formula in Arabic may provisionally make use of a translation, but he must as soon as possible learn to pronounce it in the ritual language. According to the Sonna the hands must be lifted to the height of the shoulders †at the moment of pronouncing the first syllable of the formula, and in any case the intention must not be separated from it. It is enough, according to some jurists, if the intention accompanies the first word of the formula.

3. The *kiyam*, or standing up. In an obligatory prayer this act is required of every one capable of it. It consists in straightening the backbone. If the body remains bent or inclined in such a manner as cannot ordinarily be described as "upright," the act is invalid; ††but if holding oneself erect is physically impossible, one may perform the *kiyam* as best one can, even in an inclining position. In this latter case one should if possible bend more when accomplishing the *rokua*. Similarly a person who can stand up but cannot bend or prostrate himself, may accomplish the *rokua* and the *sojud* as best he can. And finally a person who cannot stand at all may sit instead; but in this case it is better to sit in the manner called *iftirash*, rather than in that called *tarabba*, *i.e.* cross-legged. The manner of sitting called *ikaa*, *i.e.* on the buttock with the knees in the air is regarded as blamable. After the *kiyam* one bends forward for the *rokua*, until the forehead is before the knees, or, better still, on the spot where one is about to prostrate oneself. If unable to sit one can rest on the right side, or even on the back, for the whole prayer. *Kiyam* is not an essential part of supererogatory

prayers which can be performed sitting †or lying, even when one is able to get up.

4. The *kiraa*, or recitation of the Koran. After the introductory *takbir* the Sonna prescribes the pronunciation, first, of some invocation, and then of the formula, "I seek refuge with God from Satan the stoned"; both in a low tone. Our school insists upon the *tawoz*, as this formula is called, being repeated at the beginning of each *raka*, especially the first. The part of the Koran specially appointed for recitation in prayer is the first chapter called the *Fatiha*. It is recited at each *raka*; except when one is late at public prayer, when one may leave it out, in order to catch up the others. The whole of the chapter must be recited, including the words "in the name of God," correctly, and paying attention even to the double consonants. †If even a letter *d* is replaced by a *dh*, the recitation is invalid. The order in which the verses occur must be observed, and the recitation continued without interruption. The uttering of any word not in the text destroys this continuity. †On the other hand, the "amen" or any word left out by the imam may be added by the congregation. A long interval of silence, †or even a short intentional interval, invalidates the recitation. A person who cannot recite the first chapter of the Koran, should recite seven other verses of the holy book, consecutive if possible. [†In Shafii's personal opinion one may recite seven separate verses, even though one may happen to know by heart seven consecutive ones.] A person who does not know seven verses of the Koran may simply glorify God; †but in this case what is said must contain as many letters as the first chapter of the Koran. A believer who can recite absolutely nothing must remain standing in silence during the whole of the recitation.

The following are practices of the Sonna:—(*a*) At the end of the first chapter "amen" is said without doubling the "m," but with emphasis on the "a"—it may be pronounced short and at the same time as the "amen" said by the imam in the public prayers, but always aloud; and (*b*) at the end of the first chapter another is recited, except at the third and fourth *raka*, when only the *Fatiha* is repeated. [According to a decision of Shafii this does not apply to a person who may happen to be in advance of the congregation; he should repeat the additional chapter so that the congregation may catch him up.] In general the congregation need only recite the first chapter, even in the two first *raka*, merely listening to the imam while he reads the second. †Only if the imam cannot be heard, either on account of the distance or because he speaks too low, should one recite aloud the second chapter; (*c*) this supplementary chapter is usually chosen from among chapters

49–114 of the Koran, a longish one at the morning and midday prayers, a shorter one for the afternoon and night, and a very short one at evening prayer. On Friday chapter 32 is preferred at the first *raka,* and chapter 76 at the second, to be recited after the *Fatiha.*

5. The *rokua,* or bending. This act should consist in bending so as to touch the knees with the hands, keeping the rest of the body still. The action of standing up again should be distinctly separated from that of bending. The bending must be for the express purpose of prayer; not, *e.g.* for reading the Koran. In the best manner of doing it care should be taken to keep back and neck in a straight line, to place the legs perpendicularly and to take the knees in the hands, the fingers being separate and turned towards the *kibla.* At the moment of bending one pronounces the formula "God is great," holding the hands in the same position as formerly in the prayer; and one repeats three times, when in a bending position, the formula, "Praise to my illustrious Lord." At public prayer this is all the imam says. At private prayer one adds, "O God, I incline myself before Thee; in Thee I put my trust; to Thee I make my petition. Before thee I humble my ears, my eyes, my marrow, my bones, my sinews, and all that is supported on my feet."

6. The *aatidal,* or equilibrium of the body. This is standing still with the sole object of praying. Thus, to get up through fear is regarded as an infraction. The Sonna insists on the following practices besides:— (*a*) The raising of the hands when about to raise the head, and saying, "God hearkens unto him that praiseth Him." Then one gets up, pronouncing the formula, "O our Lord! To Thee be homage of all that is in the heavens or in the earth, and of all that exists." At public prayer this is all the imam says. At private prayer one adds, "O Thou to whom alone belong glory and praise. I declare true what Thy servant has just said; for we are all Thy servants; none can refuse when Thou givest, nor give when Thou refusest; nor can fortune render us happy, if it come not from Thee." (*b*) Pronouncing, during the *aatidal* of the second *raka* of the morning prayer, the following formula called *Kanut,* "O God, lead me, as Thou hast led those before me," etc., which, of course, the imam recites in the plural at public prayers. (*c*) ††Praying for the Prophet after finishing the *kanut,* holding the hands before the face, but not wiping it, as some do. (*d*) ††Intoning aloud of the *kanut* by the imam. At the end of each invocation the congregation say "amen," while they repeat the Lord's praises in a low tone. Those who cannot hear the imam say the *kanut* on their own account. The *kanut* is obligatory, not only at morning prayer, as we have just said, but also at all the other prescribed prayers when made

at a time of endeavouring to avert an imminent calamity. **At other times the formula is not recited at the other prayers.

7. *Sejud*, or prostration. It consists in touching with a part of the forehead the place intended to be touched while praying. The validity of the prayer is not affected by touching a place at the side, provided the deviation be not caused by a previous and unlawful movement. *In prostration one is not strictly obliged to rest one's hands, knees, or feet on the ground. [*On the contrary, this act must be rigorously observed.] The following practices are considered necessary for the validity of prostration :—(*a*) keeping still the different parts of the body, while resting the whole weight of the head on the ground ; (*b*) prostrating oneself with the exclusive object of accomplishing prayer ; (*c*) recovering the position called *aatidal*, if unfortunately one falls on one's face ; (*d*) †causing the upper parts of the body to be lower than the inferior. And besides these necessary elements of the *sejud*, it is commendable, in order to accomplish one's prayer after the most approved manner : (*a*) to say, " God is great," while prostrating oneself, but without lifting the hands ; (*b*) to place the knees first on the ground, then the hands, then the forehead, and last the nose ; (*c*) to exclaim three times, while remaining prostrate, " Glory to the Lord most high." At public prayer this is all the imam says. At private prayer each believer adds, " O God, before Thee I prostrate myself ; in Thee I put my trust, to Thee I make my petition. I humble my face before Him who hath created it, who hath fashioned it, who hath opened my ears and my eyes. Blessed be God, best Creator " ; (*d*) to place the hands on the ground close to the shoulders with the fingers together and turned towards the *kibla ;* (*e*) to take care that the knees are not touching each other, that the stomach does not rest on the thighs, and that the elbows do not touch the sides. This rule is obligatory not only in the *sejud* but also in the *rokua ;* only women and hermaphrodites pray with the limbs together.

8. *Jelus, i.e.* sitting still between the two prostrations required in each *raka.* After sitting one cannot lawfully get up for any purpose but prayer. Neither must one sit too long. The *aatidal* also should last only a short time. The best way of accomplishing the *jelus* is to observe the following practices :—(*a*) to exclaim on sitting, " God is great " ; (*b*) to sit in the manner called *iftirash ;* (*c*) to place the hands on the thighs, a little above the knees, extending the fingers ; (*d*) to say while sitting, " O Lord, pardon me, show me Thy mercy, help me in misery, succour me, nourish me, lead me and preserve me." After the *jelüs* one prostrates oneself a second time in the same way as the first ; **except that the Sonna has introduced the practice of sitting

a little after the second prostration, in order to rest, in every *raka* followed by another.

9. The *tashahud*, or confession of faith.

10. The *kaud* or sitting down when about to repeat the confession of faith.

11. The prayer for the Prophet.

Nos. 9 and 10 are considered essential elements only when followed by the final salutation, *i.e.* in the last *raka* of the prayer. In the other *rakas* they are only commendable acts. As to the *kaud* it is strictly allowable to accomplish it in any manner ; though, at the first, *tashahud*, the Sonna insists that the sitting should be in the manner called *iftirash*, *i.e.* on the heel of the left foot half bent on its side on the ground, the right foot being under the body with the toes turned towards the *kibla*. To recite the second *tashahud* one should sit, according to the Sonna, in the manner called *tawarok*, similar to the *iftirash* but with the left foot under the right side, and the hinder parts on the ground. †At public prayer, however, any one who is behind the others or has been guilty of some omission, should sit only in the manner called *iftirash*, both at the first and second *tashahud*. In both *iftirash* and *tashahud* the left hand is placed on the thigh close to the knees with extended fingers. [†The fingers should, on the contrary, be pressed together.] As to the right hand, one shuts the little, ring, and *middle fingers ; and raises the index finger when pronouncing the words of the *tashahud*—" that God," etc. ; but one should not alternately raise and lower it. *And finally one should hold the thumb pressed to the hand, like a person wishing to indicate by the position of his fingers the number 53. After the second *tashahud* one should pray for the Prophet ; *and it is even recommended by the Sonna after the first ; the Sonna insists upon a prayer for the family of the holy man after the second, ††but not after the first. Some authors consider it obligatory. The best manner of saying the *tashahud* is known to every one, so I confine myself here to pointing out that the minimum consists of the following words :—" Glory to God and salvation to thee, O Prophet. May the mercy and blessing of God come upon thee. May peace be bestowed upon us and upon all pious servants of God. I bear witness there is no divinity but God, and that Muhammad is the apostle of God." According to some authors one may still further compress the formula by omitting the words " and blessing " and " pious " and by replacing the words " Muhammad is the apostle of God " by the words " Muhammad is His apostle." [†The former phrase is preferable, as one reads in the Sahih or collection of traditions of Muslim.] The prayer for the Prophet should consist of the following words :—" O God, grant thy grace to

Muhammad and to his family"; but after the second *tashahud* the Sonna insists upon adding the rest of the formula up to the words, "worthy of praise and glorious." It also requires the addition of an invocation, by preference one of those directly transmitted to us from Muhammad, *e.g.* "O God pardon all my sins," etc.; but this invocation should not be longer than the confession of faith and the prayer for the Prophet together. A person who cannot say the confession of faith and the prayer for the Prophet in Arabic, should make use of a translation; and this is allowable also for invocations and glorifications that are not obligatory but merely commendable. †But this permission to use one's mother tongue is strictly limited to cases of absolute impossibility.

12. The *salam*, or final salutation. It consists of at least the words, *es-salam aleykum*, †though one may also say *salam aleykum*. [†According to Shafii these latter words alone are insufficient.] †The *salam* need not be pronounced with the intention of finishing the prayer. The best way of doing it is to use the words, "Peace be with you, and may God be merciful to you," saying them twice, looking first to the right and then to the left and thus giving salutation to angels, men, and spirits. This, however, does not apply to public prayer, for there the imam should in intention salute the congregation, and they return his salutation.

13. *Tertib*, or observance of the order of succession of the essential elements of prayer, *i.e.* the order in which we have just mentioned them. If this order is intentionally neglected, *e.g.* by prostration before bending, the entire prayer is annulled; if done by inadvertence, then the subsequent portion only is regarded as unaccomplished. If one perceives that one has omitted or failed to accomplish lawfully one of the essential elements of a certain *raka*, before coming to the same part of the next *raka*, one can repair the omission by beginning the prayer again at the part omitted; otherwise the defective *raka* is completed by the *raka* one is actually saying, and one begins the prayer again from the *raka* so completed. If at the end of a prayer one perceives one has omitted a prostration in the last *raka*, it is enough to prostrate oneself forthwith, repeating the confession of faith; but if the omission was in a previous *raka*, or one cannot remember for certain which *raka* it was in, then the whole *raka* must be repeated. Should one, after completing the *kiyam* of the second *raka*, perceive that a prostration has been omitted from the first *raka*, it is sufficient to prostrate oneself forthwith, at any rate if one has already sat down after the first prostration. Such procedure, however, is not sufficient, according to some jurists, if one sat down merely with the intention of resting; and if that be not the case, still

according to their doctrine, one must sit still and then accomplish the omitted prostration. Finally, some authorities support the view that a subsequent prostration will of itself always suffice, without prejudice to an expiatory prostration. A believer who, at the end of a fourfold prayer, perceives that he has forgotten two or three prostrations, and cannot remember exactly to which *raka* they belonged, should accomplish two further *rakas* by way of reparation. If four prostrations have been omitted, the remedy is one prostration and two *rakas* ; if five or six, three extra *rakas* suffice ; if seven, a prostration and three extra *rakas* are necessary.

[The following further practices are recommended by the Sonna :—

1. Keeping the eyes fixed on the place where one is about to prostrate oneself. According to some it is even blamable to close the eyes ; but this, in my personal opinion is going too far, unless one is afraid thus to endanger the efficacy of the prayer.

2. To pray only in a humble and submissive attitude.

3. To meditate upon the words of the Koran recited and the glorifying of God enounced in the prayer.

4. To intone the prayer with fervour and without preoccupation.

5. When standing up, to hold the hands under the breast, the left in the right.

6. To pronounce an invocation when prostrating oneself.

7. To lean on the hands when rising from the prostration and the *kaud*.

8. †To recite the Koran for a longer time in the first *raka* than in the second.

9. To glorify God at the end of the prayer.

10. To change one's place, at the end of an obligatory prayer, if one wishes to accomplish a supererogatory prayer ; it is even better to go home to accomplish such optional act of devotion.

11. For the women at a mosque to take their places behind the men, who should remain until the women have gone out.

12. That each person should leave the mosque on the side most convenient for his business ; but the right is preferred, if there be no special reason to go out by the left.

13. That at public prayer the congregation should cease to follow the example of the imam immediately after the final salutation, during which they should recite an invocation or something of the sort, and then reply to the imam's salutation. Should the latter salute only once, the congregation must still salute him twice.]

CHAPTER III.—CONDITIONS FOR THE VALIDITY OF PRAYER

SECTION 1

There are five essential conditions for the validity of prayer—

1. The certainty that the legally prescribed time has come.

2. The direction of the body towards the *kibla*.

3. Keeping the shameful parts of the body covered. The parts of the human body between the navel and the knees are called "shameful," and this rule applies to men †and to female slaves. In the case of a free woman, the whole body is regarded as shameful, with the exception of the face and the hands. By "cover" is meant obscuring the colour of the skin, even by dirty water or mud. †If one has no clothes mud is obligatory. All that is necessary is that the clothing should be arranged so as to veil the shameful parts from being seen from above or from the side, but not from below. This rule is infringed if the parts in question are exposed by the garment opening in front when the body is bent. One's coat should be fastened, and drawn tight across the waist; and if necessary, as much as possible of the shameful parts should be covered with the hand. When one is able to cover the shameful parts both before and behind, this should be done; but if one's garment does not suffice for this, it is better to conceal those in front; though some authors give preference to the hinder parts, and others contend that it is a matter of choice.

4. To be free from all impurity, even slight. A slight impurity incurred during the prayer nullifies it just as much as one that one has neglected to remove before beginning; although, according to the opinion entertained by Shafii in his first period, one can, in the first case, proceed at once to a ritual ablution, and subsequently continue the interrupted prayer. The controversy extends to all other causes of illegality in prayer not due to negligence on one's own part and which cannot be immediately removed. If, on the other hand, one can remove at once the cause of illegality, *e.g.* if the wind has accidentally exposed the shameful parts, and one readjusts one's garment at once, the illegality is without consequence. But if it is a case of responsible illegality, *e.g.* if one has allowed the time for moistening the footgear to elapse, then the prayer is annulled.

5. That not only the clothing and the body but also the place of prayer must be free from impurity. In case of difficulty one should endeavour to ascertain whether a thing is pure or impure. If a part of the clothing or of the body has become impure, and one does not know precisely which part, one should wash the whole of the body or clothes. ††Even if one supposes the impurity to have tainted only one corner,

a partial cleaning will not suffice. †This cleaning, however, can be done in two stages, *i.e.* by washing first one half and then the other; provided that an overlapping border be washed twice, otherwise an intervening space is considered to be still impure.

If the clothing is or has been in contact with any impure object, even though only a part of the clothes which have not been displaced incurred this impurity, the prayer is invalid. Similarly if anything of which the other end is in contact with an impure object is held in the hand, whether it is †or is not in motion. However, if it be merely the foot which rests upon something of which the other end is touching an impure object, the prayer is valid, unless there are other causes of nullity. ††The impurity of the ground below the breast at bending and prostration does not entail the illegality of the prayer.

If in a surgical operation it is necessary to join to the patient's bone the bone of an animal, one can, if the matter is urgent and no other can be found, utilise an impure bone. On recovery the patient is none the less able to accomplish a valid prayer. If, however, the operation was not necessary, the impure bone must be cut out, if this can be done without manifest danger, or even in any case according to some authors. ††Only in case of death is there never need to cut out the impure bone from the corpse.

One may lawfully pray after cleaning the shameful parts with pebbles, even if there are still traces of impurity; †but if while praying one has been in contact with a person so cleansed, the prayer is invalid. The dirt of the high-road, even when manifestly impure, is an excusable impurity, if not in immoderate amount, as it is very difficult to take precautions against it. Distinctions, however, are to be made in this respect as to the time of day, and the part of the clothing or body that is affected. Similarly, a small quantity of blood from the bite of a flea, or of dirt deposited by a fly, does not affect the validity of a prayer; †but a large amount of either, or even a small quantity spread over the skin by the flow of perspiration, does. [†According to the most competent authorities these impurities are always excusable.]

Blood from blisters is considered in the same way as that from flea-bites; except, according to some authors, if the blisters are pressed. Blood from a pimple, an ulcer, a blood-letting or a cupping glass, is assimilated by some authors to that from blisters; †but the majority consider it to have the same effect as hæmorrhage after menses, provided the flow is ordinarily of some duration. Otherwise this blood is equivalent to that of another person; *i.e.* it is never excusable. Some jurists, however, admit an exception to this rule, when the blood has flowed only in a small quantity. [†Pimples, ulcers, etc., come under the same rule as blisters; *and one may even accomplish prayer while tainted with the blood of another person, if in very small quantity.]

Pus and clear fluid substance coming from a wound are regarded by the law for this purpose in the same way as blood; and the same is the case with matter coming from ulcers or tumours, whether it has *or has not a fetid odour. [According to our school this matter is always pure.]

If any one prays in a state of impurity without knowing it he should, according to the opinion held by Shafii in his second period, repeat it on discovery by way of reparation; and the same obligation rests, according to our school, on any person who may have forgotten his state of impurity after having become aware of it.

SECTION 2

A prayer is nullified by any superfluous word, even if it consist of but one letter; or by too long a pause in its enunciation. †Coughing, laughing, weeping, groaning, or breathing, if of such a nature as to render perceptible to the ear at least two letters, nullify prayer; but not otherwise.

The following are considered excusable :—

1. Words uttered (*a*) because one cannot control the tongue; or (*b*) through momentary forgetfulness that one was engaged in prayer; or (*c*) through ignorance of the prohibition, if recently converted to Islam. †But this only applies to a small number of words, many are never excusable.

2. Coughing, etc., where avoidable.

3. Omission to recite the Koran through incapacity; †but to cry aloud is inexcusable.

*If superfluous words are the consequence of violence the prayer is nullified all the same. If one utters some passage from the Koran, even if it is to say something to some one else, *e.g.* Koran xix. 13, "O Yahya, take the holy scripture," the prayer is nullified, unless the passage comes in relevantly in the recitation.

The prayer is not nullified in the two following cases :—

1. If it is interrupted for glorifying God or for an invocation; provided this be not in addressing some one else, as *e.g.* in saying to some one who has sneezed, "God be merciful to you."

2. †If it is stopped unintentionally, even for a considerable time.

The Sonna recommends that any believer who may be obliged to interrupt his prayer by unforeseen circumstances, *e.g.* in order to tell the imam to let some one pass who has just come in, or to warn a blind man, should say, "Praise to God"; while a woman in similar circumstances should strike the back of the left hand with the right.

When the superfluous thing consists, not of a word, but of an act, the prayer is nullified if the act consists of something of a nature essential to the prayer itself, *e.g.* an inclination of the body; though such contravention is not condemnable if committed in ignorance. But if the superfluous act is not of this category, it does not nullify the prayer, unless it is a thing of great importance. Custom indicates what must be considered a thing of great importance; thus two paces or two knocks are not so considered as a rule, but three consecutive paces or knocks are. Similarly prayer is nullified by an indecent jump, but not by a slight though continuous movement, as *e.g.* counting the beads of a rosary, †or scratching oneself. †In all these cases faults due to inadvertence have the same effect as intentional faults.

Prayer is also nullified by eating, however little. [Two exceptions are admitted, when the act is done (1) through forgetfulness, without thinking what one is doing, and (2) without knowing that it is illicit.] †So rigorous is this prohibition that even a morsel of sugar in the mouth is enough to nullify the prayer, if any liquid from it be swallowed.

A practice has been introduced by the Sonna that any one about to pray should place himself near a wall, a column or a post stuck in the ground; or place before him a special carpet, or draw a line to stop passers-by, ††who are obliged to respect it.

[The following things are considered blamable if done during prayer:—

1. Turning round unnecessarily.
2. Lifting up the eyes to heaven.
3. Taking hold of one's hair or one's clothes.
4. Unnecessarily putting the hand into the mouth.
5. Standing on one foot when accomplishing the *kiyam*.
6. Retaining urine or stercoral matter.
7. Performing devotion in the presence of a repast one wishes to eat.
8. Spitting in front of one, or to the right side.
9. Placing the hand on the hip.
10. Bending the head excessively when bowing.
11. Praying at the public baths, or on the road, or at a place where ordure is deposited, or in a temple of unbelievers, or at a place for camels to lie down, or in a cemetery even if free from impurity.]

CHAPTER IV.—EXPIATORY PROSTRATION

THE Sonna has introduced the practice of accomplishing an expiatory prostration, whenever (1) Any prescribed duty has been neglected; and (2) any prohibited act has been done.

With regard to the first point, if it is a matter of negligent omission of one of the necessary elements of prayer, one should first correct oneself, and prostrate oneself immediately afterwards, observing for the supplementary prostration the rule mentioned when speaking of the *tertib*. But when the omission extends only to a part of a necessary element, *e.g.* the *kanut*, the *kiyam* accompanying it, the first *tashahad*, the *kaud* accompanying it, or the prayer for the prophet that is said after the first *tashahad*, then one may repair the error by prostrating oneself at once. Some authorities maintain, however, that this procedure is insufficient, if the omission was premeditated. [The same rule should be observed in case of omission of the prayer for the family of the Prophet, at any rate if this is considered as a duty introduced by the Sonna.] Negligent omission of the other practices of the Sonna has no need of such expiation.

In the second case, the doing of a prohibited act, even intentionally, does not necessarily involve the nullity of the prayer; if, *e.g.*, one has turned round, or taken a pace or two. One need not prostrate oneself to repair the error, if one has committed any such fault by inadvertence. But where an act would, if committed intentionally, nullify the prayer, one must prostrate oneself in reparation, if one commits it inadvertently. If, however, a fault is so grave as to nullify the prayer, even when committed inadvertently, an expiatory prostration is of no avail. This is the case if the prayer is interrupted by a long discourse. On the other hand, prolonging excessively one of the essential elements of prayer which should be accomplished rapidly, nullifies the prayer only if premeditated; if it is mere negligence it can be expiated by prostration. Among practices that should be rapidly accomplished are cited the *aatidal*, †and the *jelus* between two prostrations.

If one of the essential verbal elements has been misplaced, *e.g.* if one has recited the first chapter of the Koran during the *rokua* or the *tashahad*; †the prayer is not annulled, even if the act be intentional. †If, however, such fault has been committed negligently, an expiatory prostration is required. This forms an exception to the rule already mentioned, viz. that where an intentional act does not affect the validity of a prayer, it is not necessary to expiate by a prostration its inadvertent committal.

As to forgetting the first *tashahad*, the two following cases must be distinguished :—

1. If one remembers the error after finishing the prayer, one should not resume the formula, for the whole prayer would be nullified, at least if the resumption is done knowingly. Otherwise, *i.e.* if one has not thought of the prohibition, the law requires an expiatory prostration.

†The same rule applies if the resumption is due to ignorance instead of forgetfulness. Only a member of the community may resume the first *tashahad*, in these circumstances, when the imam gives him the example. [†This is even rigorously necessary.]

2. If one perceives one's error before finishing the prayer, one should, if not still standing, resume the first *tashahad.* One should also prostrate oneself. But if one has intentionally risen before finishing the prayer, without having enounced the first *tashahad,* the resumption of the omitted formula nullifies the whole prayer, even if one is not yet quite standing.

The *kanut,* if forgotten, is not resumed, if one remembers it only during the *sejud ;* but it is so if remembered before this, and one also accomplishes a prostration to repair the error, as soon as one is in a bending position.

If one does not know exactly what part of the essential element one has neglected, one should still prostrate oneself ; but if one merely suspects one has done some prohibited thing, an expiatory prostration is never required. Should one commit an irregularity by inadvertence, and be unable to remember whether it has already been expiated by a prostration; one should prostrate oneself ; and should one be uncertain if one has accomplished three or four *rakas,* one must perform another, followed by a prostration. †This prostration is even obligatory if the doubt has disappeared before the final salutation. The same rule applies to all cases where one has accomplished some practice without knowing if it was obligatory or not, for it is possible one may have performed a superfluous act. On the other hand, no expiatory prostration is required for an act which appears to have been necessary, even if one doubted it for a moment ; for example, if in the third *raka* of a prayer that consists of four *rakas* one is uncertain if it is the third or the fourth ; but if one remembers the truth before finishing the *raka* in question, one need not prostrate oneself to expiate one's fault. If, however, the doubt disappears only during the fourth *raka,* an expiatory prostration is required. **If it is only after the final salutation that one suspects having omitted a necessary practice, one need pay no attention to it.

At public prayer, an omission by a member of the congregation who has followed the lead of the imam, is the latter's business. This principle is carried so far that if one has repeated the final salutation in the mistaken belief that the imam had reached that stage, it can be pronounced a second time without an expiatory prostration. Even if one remembers, during the imam's *tashahad,* that one has omitted one of the essential elements of a *raka,* always excepting the intention and the introductory *takbir* without which the prayer is null, one need only repeat the missing *raka* without prostration, after the imam has pronounced the final salutation. Any omission by a member of the congregation after the final salutation is his own mistake, for which the imam is not responsible. Thus, if one has lagged behind the imam in the prayer, one should nevertheless pronounce with him the final salutation, and then continue one's act of devotion from the place interrupted, and finally accomplish an expiatory prostration for negligence. On the other hand, faults committed by the imam through inadvertence are imputable to the congregation; and for this reason the expiatory prostrations of the imam are accomplished by the whole community; and even if the imam does not prostrate himself to expiate his errors the congregation should do so, this at least was Shafii's personal opinion. When, though the congregation is ahead, one prays under the direction of the imam, and he is guilty of an omission, either †before or after one has begun to follow him, ††one should in both cases accomplish with him the expiatory prostration, and then at the end of the prayer prostrate oneself again to expiate one's having lagged behind. If the imam omits his prostration in these circumstances, the congregation is none the less obliged to accomplish it at the end of the prayer. This was so decided by Shafii himself.

The expiatory prostration is never accomplished more than twice, whatever the number of faults committed through inadvertence. It is performed like an ordinary prostration, and, according to the opinion of Shafii in his second period, between the *tashahad* and the final salutation. †It follows that no reason for its performance can arise, once the final salutation has been knowingly accomplished; or even inadvertently, if a long interval has ensued. Otherwise, according to Shafii's personal opinion, the fact of having inadvertently accomplished the final salutation, does not prevent performance of an expiatory prostration. †After the prostration has been accomplished one continues the interrupted prayer. However, if the imam has been guilty of some omission in the public Friday prayer, and the time prescribed for that ceremony has expired during the expiatory prostration, one proceeds immediately to the celebration of midday prayer; and after this the congregation again prostrates itself in order to expiate the fault of having exceeded the time allowed for the weekly prayer. †It should be added that if after prostration for a fault believed to have been committed, it appears that the fault never really existed, one should prostrate oneself again in order to expiate the error of having accomplished a superfluous prostration.

CHAPTER V.—PROSTRATIONS FOR READING THE KORAN, AND FOR THANKSGIVING

Prostrations for reading the holy scripture, introduced by the Sonna, are fourteen in number, according, at least, to Shafii in his second period, including two prostrations for the reading of Chapter XXII., but not including the prostration for the reading of Chapter XXXVIII., as the latter is a prostration of thanksgiving, commendable when the chapter is read out of prayer time, †but prohibited at prayer. The prostrations of which we are speaking are prescribed by the Sonna as well for the reader as for the hearers, the only distinction being that those accomplished by the hearers are but the necessary complement of those performed by the reader. [They are prescribed also for every person who happens to hear the reading of the holy scripture.]

When the reading of the Koran takes place during prayer, the imam and congregation, when praying on their own account, prostrate themselves as may be necessary in the case of each; but when the congregation prays under the direction of the imam, its prostrations must follow the lead given by him. Should any one omit a prostration performed by the imam, or *vice versâ*, the prayer of that person is nullified. A person about to accomplish a prostration for reading the Koran out of prayer time, should express his intention and then accomplish an introductory *takbir* raising his hands, adding another *takbir* when bending to the ground without raising his hands. He thus accomplishes the prostration as he would in prayer, and then, on rising, says the final *takbir* and the salutation. ††The introductory *takbir* is an essential condition for the validity of prostrations of this nature, *and so is the salutation. The believer must also comply with all the conditions requisite for the validity of prayer; the only exception being that during prostration at prayer the *takbir* is said without raising the hands both in bending down and in rising up. [As another exception it may be mentioned that one does not sit down to rest after prostration for the reading of the Koran.]

While prostrate, one should say: "My face is bowed before Him that hath created it, that hath formed it and opened mine ears and mine eyes by His energy and power." A person who reads a verse of the Koran at two different sittings, should prostrate himself each time: †and so should any one who reads at one and the same sitting a verse he has already read. For this purpose one *raka* is considered as one sitting, and two *rakas* as two sittings; but if one has read a portion of the Koran without prostrating oneself, and becomes aware of the omission only after a long interval, no prostration is necessary.

The prostration of thanksgiving is never accomplished during prayer ; it is prescribed by the Sonna on the occasion of any unforeseen happiness, or averted calamity, or on meeting a person stricken with some physical or moral infirmity. Such prostration is performed in public only when one perceives a moral infirmity, not in presence of a physical infirmity. It is accomplished in the same way as a prostration for the reading of the Koran.

A traveller may accomplish without alighting any prostrations for the reading of the Koran, whether during prayer †or out of prayer time, or any prostration of thanksgiving.

CHAPTER VI.—SUPEREROGATORY PRAYER

SUPEREROGATORY prayers are of two categories—

1. Those which are not prescribed by the Sonna to be performed at public prayer.

(*a*) Special acts of devotion combined with obligatory prayers, *i.e.* two *rakas* before morning prayer, two before midday prayer, evening prayer, and the prayer of the night. Some jurists, however, maintain that these *rakas* should not be combined with the prayer of the night; others insist on the accomplishing of four *rakas* before the midday prayer, or four after it; others on four before the afternoon prayer. All these *rakas* are no more than practices introduced by the Sonna; they are not of rigorous observance. It is only those founded upon some imperative text of the Sonna as to whose rigorous observance there is some dispute amongst authorities. Some authors add the two *rakas* to be accomplished in haste before evening prayer. [††These two last *rakas* are also meritorious acts, for a direction to perform them is found in al-Bokhari's collection of traditions called *as-Sahih*. There should also be considered as imperative precepts of the Sonna the accomplishing of four *rakas* after the Friday public prayer, and before it as many *rakas* as before the midday prayer.

(*b*) The prayer called *witr*, or *uneven*, consisting of a single *raka* at least, and at the most eleven, or according to others, thirteen, *rakas*. A person who wished to perform more than one, may either combine them, or, better, accomplish each separately. The combination is done by means of a *tashahad*, and, for the last two, two *tashahads*. The time prescribed for the *witr* is between the prayer of the night and the appearance of the dawn. According to some authors the *witr* may not consist of only one *raka* except where preceded by another supererogatory prayer performed after the prayer of the night; and the Sonna insists on the *witr* being the last prayer accomplished during the night. To-this rule there is but one exception, viz. that the prayer called *witr* may be followed by the prayer called *tahajud* (reveille) without requiring to be repeated ; a few jurists only maintaining that it is even then necessary to begin by praying a *raka* and then repeat the *witr*. It is commendable to add the *kanut* to the *witr* during the latter half of the month of Ramadan, and some consider this act to be commendable throughout the year. This *kanut* is the same as the *kanut* for morning prayer, except only that before beginning one pronounces the formula "O God, with sure trust in Thee we implore Thy succour and pardon," etc. [†On the contrary, this formula should be enounced after finishing the *kanut* ; it is also commendable to perform the *witr* at public prayer after finishing the prayer called the *pauses*, specially prescribed for the nights of the month of Ramadan.]

(*c*) The prayer called *doha*, *i.e.* late in the morning, consisting of not less than two, and not more than three *rakas*.

(*d*) †The salutation of a mosque. This act of devotion consists of two *rakas*, which may, however, be implicitly performed when one says any obligatory or supererogatory prayer, ††though it is not permissible to omit one of the *rakas* composing it, when accomplishing the act of devotion separately. [The salutation is not implicitly performed by saying a prayer for the dead, or by accomplishing a prostration for the reading of the Koran, or of thanksgiving. †It is repeated each time of approaching the sacred edifice.]

The legal time for such supererogatory acts of devotion as are accomplished before beginning some obligatory prayer is the time for that prayer ; and the legal time for such as are performed after finishing a prayer is the moment of accomplishing such prayer. In each case the legal time finishes at the same moment as the time for the prayer. *Where a supererogatory prayer, to be accomplished at a fixed time, has not been so performed, it is always commendable to practise it afterwards by way of reparation.

2. Supererogatory prayers prescribed by the Sonna to be performed at public prayer, on the occasion of the two yearly festivals, at an eclipse, or in time of drought. Acts of devotion of this category are in general of more importance than those which need not be performed at public prayer. †In spite of this, however, prayers of sub-category 1 (*a*) have priority over the prayer called *tarawih*, †though the Sonna prescribes that the latter must be accomplished at public prayer, and no such precept exists for supererogatory prayers in general. The believer who has performed the introductory *takbir* for more than one *raka*, may at choice accomplish the *tashahad* either for two *rakas* at once, or for each *raka* separately. [††It is forbidden in these circumstances to perform

the *tashahad* for each *raka* separately.] The intention to say a certain number of *rakas* does not prevent the performing of a greater or smaller number, provided one expressly changes one's intention as to the number before deviating from the original idea, otherwise the prayer will be nullified. If, however, it is only by inadvertence that one has begun a third *raka* while the intention was to perform two, one may lawfully finish the third, although the intention has not previously been changed, †if only one sits down immediately upon becoming aware of one's error. Only after having thus sat down may one lawfully recommence and terminate the *raka* in question.

[Of supererogatory prayers those performed at night are of most value, especially those said at midnight, and after them those said at the end of the night. It is commendable to pronounce the final salutation each time one finishes two *rakas*. The Sonna has also introduced the nocturnal prayer called *tahajud*; but it blames the practice of passing the whole night without going to bed, especially the night of Friday. It also blames the omitting of the *tahajud*, if one is in the habit of accomplishing it.

BOOK 3.—PUBLIC PRAYER

CHAPTER I.—GENERAL PROVISIONS

Section 1

The Sonna imperatively prescribes the coming together of the faithful to perform in congregation the obligatory prayers. The performing of the Friday public prayer in congregation is a matter of rigorous observance; and some jurists maintain it to be the same with the daily prayers, and that all male believers are collectively responsible. This obligation, however, exists only in countries where Islam is an officially recognised religion. Inhabitants of such a country refusing to observe it should be executed. †The precept of the Sonna concerns the men only, and does not mention the women, whose presence at public prayer is not even a meritorious act. [†According to Shafii's personal opinion public prayer is an obligation for which the community is collectively responsible. Some authors maintain the obligation to be individual.]

It is preferable to pray publicly in a mosque, but neither is this rule applicable to women; and the more numerous the congregation the more valuable the prayer, provided the crowd be not attracted by any heretical innovations of the imam, and the neighbouring mosques be not deserted in consequence. It is recommended to reach the mosque so as to be present at the introductory *takbir*, the believer being considered to take part in the prayer if he begins this formula before the imam has finished it. Some authors, however, maintain one may arrive at any time before the *kiyam*, or even at the first inclination; ††and, strictly speaking, there is yet time so long as the final salutation has not been pronounced. The imam should perform his duty without either wasting time or neglecting any essential part or practice of the prayer. He need not haste, however, if all the congregation ask that the prayer should be accomplished slowly; but it is blamable to do this in order to give time to those that are late to join. *The imam may wait a moment if he sees a person come in at the inclination or the last *tashahad*, provided no distinction be made between the members of the community. [According to our school it is even commendable to wait under the circumstances.] But with the exception of the moment at the inclination and the *tashahad* of which we have just spoken, one never waits at public prayer. And according to the Sonna any one who has made his prayer either alone †or in company with others should repeat it with the congregation when he enters the mosque at the moment the same act of devotion is being accomplished. According to the opinion of Shafii in his second period, it is the first prayer which is then considered as the obligatory prayer; †though one should formulate an intention for the second, as if it also were obligatory.

Whoever neglects attendance at public prayer is deserving of the most severe blame, even according to authors who see in that act only a precept of the Sonna. But it is not necessary to go to the mosque if one has a valid general or personal excuse. Amongst excuses of a general character may be ranked rain, or a storm in the night, ††or too much mud on the road. Among personal excuses are reckoned illness, excessive heat or cold, impossibility of satisfying hunger or thirst, the necessity of preserving oneself from some impurity, the fear of incurring some injury to person or property, the pursuit of an importunate creditor, the avoiding of some chastisement by a few days' concealment, want of decent clothing, preparations for a voyage in company of a caravan about to start, the fact of having partaken of some food of disagreeable odour, wish not to leave a relative at the point of death, and finally the illness of any person to whom assistance is indispensable or to whom one is bound by ties of friendship.

Section 2

At public prayer it is forbidden to pray, not only under the direction of a person whose prayer is known to be nullified, but even under that of a person the nullity of whose prayer one has reason to presume. Thus where two persons cannot agree upon the true direction of the *kibla*, even after doing their best to ascertain it; or if they differ as to which of two vessels for ablution is pure; one may not lawfully pray under the direction of either. The same if a choice has to be made from several vessels, even if the most of them are known to be pure. †But the vessel used by the imam should be used by the congregation until proof of its impurity, and one may even lawfully use without personal examination a vessel used by another, if one has no good reason for doubting its purity. Impurity of vessels for ablution gives rise to the following particular case:—when five similar vessels belong to five different individuals praying together in public, and amongst them one is impure but it is not known which, each of the five believing his own to be pure; then each should use his own vessel for ablution; but in order to be sure to avoid praying under the direction of an imam using an impure vessel, each should assume the function of imam at one of the five obligatory prayers, beginning with the morning prayer. †Then the prayer for the night should be repeated on their own account by four of them, *i.e.* all except the one who has already presided as imam, who should repeat on his own account the evening prayer. †A follower of Shafii praying under the direction of a follower of Abu Hanifa who has touched the private parts or has been bled without removing the impurity, lawtully performs his religious duty in the latter but not in the former case; the ground of the distinction being the probable intention of the follower of Shafii, whose school does not admit impurity from bleeding. It is not permitted to follow as imam, either a person who prays under the direction of another, or a person obliged to repeat his act of devotion, *e.g.* one who, though living at a fixed place of abode, has recourse to ablution by sand.

According to the opinion of Shafii in his second period it is not lawful for one who can read and write to pray under the direction of an illiterate person. This latter phrase comprises—

1. He who suppresses a letter or a *tashdid* in the recitation of the first chapter of the Koran.

2. A stammerer who pronounces two letters as one, where the grammar does not require it.

3. A person who by defect of pronunciation substitutes one letter for another.

One illiterate may, however, pray under the direction of another illiterate, though it is blamable to be imam when one has a difficulty in pronouncing the letter "t" or the letter "f" or does not know the exact use of the vowels. And if this last defect is so grave as to alter the sense of the words, *e.g.* if instead of saying "an'amta" one says "an'amto" or "an'amti," the prayer is nullified, at least if the person in question ought to have known better. But if such person is merely perplexed and has time enough still to learn, he should be considered illiterate only if the mistakes are made in the reading of the first chapter of the Koran; mistakes in the other parts of the prayers do not affect their validity, or disqualify the imam making them.

Neither a man nor a hermaphrodite may lawfully pray under the direction of a woman or of a hermaphrodite. A person who has performed ablution with sand or moistened the footgear may as imam lead another who has accomplished ritual ablution. A man standing may follow the lead of one sitting or lying on the side; and a free adult may pray under the direction of a minor or a slave. Shafii himself says that the blind is in this respect as he that can see. †And an individual with no bodily infirmity may pray under the direction of one subject to an unhealthy issue of urine or sperm; or a woman in a state of purity follow the lead of one subject to hæmorrhage after menses, provided the latter is in no uncertainty upon the subject. If it subsequently appears that an imam under whose direction one has prayed is a woman or a notorious unbeliever, or even according to some a secret unbeliever, the prayer should be repeated. But this is not necessary if it merely appears afterwards that the imam had incurred some, or even a grave impurity, or was secretly in contact with some impure object. [†The personal opinion of Shafii, which is generally accepted, is to the effect that the unbeliever who has concealed his infidelity should be considered in this matter as if he had openly proclaimed it.] †The rule applying to the case of a woman under whose direction one has erroneously prayed applies also to that of an illiterate person; *while inversely a repetition is necessary if one has taken for a hermaphrodite an imam who appears afterwards to be a man.

A man of irreproachable character has more right to be an imam than a person of notorious misconduct; †and a savant more than one who can merely read and write, or who has the merely negative quality of having done nothing wrong. A savant, or even a merely lettered man, has more right than an older man or one of undoubted descent; but according to the opinion of Shafii in his second period age has precedence over birth. Where two persons are equal in all these respects preference will depend on cleanliness of clothing or body, sonority of voice, profession, trade, and so on. An owner of landed property, even if not otherwise the most worthy of the congregation, has a better right to be imam than he who possesses nothing; and if incapable of assuming the functions himself, he has a right to nominate the imam. The master has a right of precedence over the slave living on his land; but the law accords him no such precedence if the slave is under contract of enfranchisement. †The tenant has precedence over the lessor, the lender over the borrower; and in his province the Governor has precedence over the learned man or the landowner.

SECTION 3

No one may place himself in front of the imam, and an infraction of this rule nullifies the prayer, according at least to the opinion supported by Shafii in his second period. There is, however, no objection to being on the same line with him, though it is always commendable to keep a little distance. Whether one is before or behind depends on the position of the heels. At public prayer in the Masjid-al-Haram at Mecca a circle is formed round the sanctuary; †and in that case a person on the other side to the imam may approach nearer than he. One can also approach nearer the wall if imam and congregation make their prayer inside the sanctuary and turn in two different directions. If in these circumstances the congregation consists of one man, he may place himself on the imam's right, and any one coming afterwards should place himself on the left. Then the imam moves forward a little, or, better, the others move back. If the congregation in the sanctuary consists originally of two men, or of a man and a minor of the same sex, they should place themselves behind the imam. The same rule applies to a congregation composed of one or more women.

In general, men should place themselves in front behind the imam, then male minors; and last of all the women, the person who directs their prayer being in the front rank among them. When praying under any one's direction, one should not occupy a place apart, but place oneself if possible in one of the rows. Otherwise, immediately after the introductory *takbir*, one should draw some one towards oneself, and the person so drawn must comply with this demand. The congregation should be kept informed of the movements of the imam, either by looking at him or at other members close by, or by the *muballigh* or person specially charged with communicating to the congregation in the large mosques the acts and words of the imam.

If the imam and a member of the congregation are in a mosque, the distance between them is immaterial, whatever may be the shape of the edifice; but if they are praying in a plain it must never exceed three hundred cubits more or less; according to some jurists this is the absolute maximum. If the question relate to two persons or two rows, the distance is measured between these persons or rows, and not between the last person of the last row and the imam. It is of little importance if the plain is private property, real property or part property; ††or if the distance is cut by a public road or an unfordable stream. If the imam and the person praying under his direction are in different buildings, *e.g.* one in the interior and the other in the vestibule of a mosque or in a chamber apart, the following distinctions are to be observed:—

1. The place of the follower is to right or left of the imam. In this case they must be in the same storey, †interrupted or not, of the buildings.

2. The place of the follower is behind the imam. ††In this case there must not be between the two buildings a greater distance than three cubits.

3. According to another system three hundred cubits is the maximum

distance permitted between the two buildings as in the case of the plain; but in any case, for the validity of the prayer it is necessary that there should be no separation between the two places, or that at least they should communicate by an open door. If there intervene an obstacle to passage but not to sight, opinions differ. All authors, however, agree that if a wall intervenes the prayer is invalid. [†I prefer the second system.]

If a person can lawfully follow, as imam, another person in another building, he can in his turn lead the other's prayer, in spite of a separation.

If one is in a higher or lower position than the imam, it is necessary that at least some part of the body should be at the same height. If one be outside the mosque and the imam inside, with nothing intervening, the distance should be measured from the edifice, or, according to some authors, from the last rows of the congregation. Under these circumstances a wall or a locked door prevent participation in public prayer, †as do also a door closed but not locked, and a railing. [It is blamable for a believer to be in a higher or lower position than the imam; unless it is the only position possible, in which case it is even praiseworthy One should not begin a prayer before the muezzin has finished the second call, nor begin a supererogatory prayer at the moment when the muezzin has already begun the second call; but such prayer if already begun should be concluded unless one fears that the time for public prayer will thus be taken up.]

Section 4

One can only pray under the direction of another if one has formulated the intention of following his lead or of performing public prayer, an intention which should accompany the introductory *takbir*. ††There is no difference in this respect between a Friday and any other public prayer; but if the intention be lacking the prayer is void, even though otherwise completely accomplished. The law does not insist that the intention of the congregation shall refer to any special imam; but the prayer is void if such intention be formed, and there is an error as to the person. On the other hand, it is not necessary that the imam should formulate the intention to perform his functions, though it is a commendable practice. An error committed by an imam in designating some particular person about to pray under his direction does not prejudice the validity of the prayer.

A person who prays in order to perform his religious duty at the time prescribed by law may take as his imam a person who prays in order to accomplish his duty by way of reparation. One may also perform an obligatory prayer under the direction of an imam who is accomplishing a supererogatory prayer; and perform midday prayer under the direction of an imam who is accomplishing afternooon prayer, and *vice versâ.* The midday prayer may even be performed under the direction of an imam who is accomplishing the morning or evening prayer; but in that case the believer should act as if he were behind the congregation, and accomplish afterwards the *rakas* that are in his own prayer but not in that of the imam. When the imam proceeds to the *kanut* at morning prayer, or to the last *jelus* of the evening prayer, one may then either follow him or leave the congregation. *And so, on the other hand, one may perform morning prayer, taking as imam one who is accomplishing that for midday, though the latter is longer than the former; and then one may either pronounce the final salutation and leave the congregation as soon as the imam begins the third *raka,* or remain quietly in one's place to the end of the ceremony without taking part in it, and pronounce the final salutation along with the imam. [This latter course is the better.] When the believer has an opportunity of performing the *kanut* of the second *raka,* while the imam is not speaking, he should do so; but if this be impossible he may either omit that formula or cease to pray under the direction of the imam and recite it by himself ††It must always, however, be quite understood that one cannot perform under the direction of an imam a prayer which differs in its essential practices from that which the imam himself is accomplishing. Thus one may not perform one of the five obligatory prayers under the direction of an imam who is accomplishing prayer on the occasion of an eclipse, or a funeral prayer.

Section 5

One should follow the imam in the different acts constituting prayer, commencing each shortly after the imam, without waiting for him to finish it. Strictly speaking, however, one can begin each act at the same time as the imam, with the exception of the introductory *takbir.* †If one is still occupied with another essential element of the prayer, *i.e.* when the imam has already finished such element, while one is still occupied with the preceding, the prayer is not therefore nullified. This only occurs when the interval between the imam and the member of the congregation amounts to two essential elements of the prayer, without valid excuse. If such excuse exists, *e.g.* if the imam has hurried over the recitation of the Koran, and bent in prayer before the member of the congregation has finished his recitation, that member should, according to some authors, follow the imam, omitting the remainder of his recitation. ††Others think the recitation should first be concluded, and the imam followed afterwards. But the interval between imam and member must never exceed three essential elements of importance, *i.e.* which cannot be hurriedly accomplished. If this should occur, the member must stop praying under the direction of the imam, according to some opinions; †or else he should follow the imam in what he is actually doing, and accomplish what has been omitted after the imam has pronounced the final salutation. In case the member of the congregation is unable to conclude the recitation with the imam, because occupied with the introductory invocation, he is considered excusable.

This only applies to a member of the congregation who has been present at the ceremony from the beginning. One who is behindhand because he arrived late, and has in consequence not yet finished his recitation when the imam bends in prayer, †should stop his recitation, bend, and join the imam in the *raka,* provided the imam be not at the moment occupied with the introductory invocation or the *tawuz,* for in this case the recitation should be continued as much as possible. When behindhand like this, after pronouncing the introductory *takbir,* one should pay no attention to the practices introduced by the Sonna, but limit oneself to the recitation of the first chapter of the Koran, unless one is quite sure of being able to catch up the others. A member of the congregation who during the *rokua* perceives he has omitted the recitation, or is uncertain about it, should not go back, but should pray one *raka* after the imam has pronounced the final salutation. If this recollection or doubt occurs after the imam has bent in prayer, but before the member has done so, he should first proceed to the recitation and then has an excuse for remaining behindhand. Others, however, think he should bend in prayer with the imam, and accomplish the omitted portion after the final salutation. If the member of the congregation has preceded the imam in saying the introductory *takbir* his prayer is null; but if he has only preceded him in the recitation and the *tashahad,* his prayer is valid and he has legally acquitted himself of his duty before God. Some authors, however, prescribe that in these circumstances the prayer should be recommenced with the imam. Finally, if one has preceded the imam in some material act, *e.g.* inclination or prostration, the prayer is nullified, if the error affects two essential elements; otherwise not. A few authorities contend that the prayer is nullified even if only one essential element is affected.

Section 6

When the imam stops praying the congregation ceases legally to pray under his direction. Each member indeed can stop praying under the direction of the imam whenever he pleases; though according to one authority such a course is only lawful if there be some valid excuse for withdrawing from public prayer. With respect to this, there should be added to the excuses already mentioned the case where an imam unnecessarily prolongs a prayer, or omits some important precept of the Sonna, such as the first *tashahad*.

*One may begin a prayer on one's own account and resolve afterwards to continue it under the direction of the imam, even if the latter has already begun. Even if the imam be already occupied with a different *raka*, one can still take him as model, and get up and sit down when he does. When, under these circumstances, the prayer of the imam terminates first, one should act like any other person who was not present at the beginning. But if one is finished before the imam, one can either leave the congregation, pronouncing the final salutation on one's own account, or wait and finish the prayer along with the imam. The part of the prayer which the imam is accomplishing at the entry of a late arrival, is considered, so far as the latter is concerned, as the first part of the prayer. Consequently, in the part of the prayer he has still to make on his own account, he must repeat the *kanut* pronounced by the imam, if this formula is of strict observance. Similarly a member who joins the congregation at one of the *rakas* of evening prayer should say the *tashahad* in his own second *raka*; but it should be remembered that an arrival at the moment the imam bends in prayer is considered to have been present at the entire *raka*. [Provided one keeps still before the imam gets up after the *rokua*; even when the latter is accomplished in the most simple manner.] *If one is doubtful of having participated in a *raka* at the right moment, that *raka* cannot count.

On joining the congregation one should accomplish the *takbir* twice, once as introduction to the prayer, and once for the inclination. One *takbir* will not suffice for the two acts; except, according to some authors, in a supererogatory prayer. ††One *takbir* is of no use if performed without thinking of the double function of this formula. When a person joins the congregation at the moment the imam is performing the *aatidal*, the later portions of the prayer are valid for him on accomplishing one *takbir*; †and such person should say with the imam the *tashahad*, and the formulas beginning with the word *sobhana*. †A person who does not arrive before the prostration, an act of no profit to him, need not say a *takbir* on joining the congregation. But after the imam's final salutation the person behindhand in this way should get up and pronounce the formula in question, provided he has sat under the direction of the imam at the place he performed the *jelus* in a former *raka* accomplished on his own account; †otherwise he should omit the *takbir* altogether.

CHAPTER II.—PRAYER ACCOMPLISHED ON A JOURNEY

SECTION 1

OF prayers that fall to be performed in the course of a long journey, undertaken with a lawful object, only the fourfold prayers may be abridged. This indulgence of the law does not extend to a prayer whose proper legal time has been allowed to pass by when not travelling. *If this oversight has occurred when travelling, the prayer can be performed afterwards abridged, if the journey is not yet over, but not after one's return home.

A traveller leaving a town is considered to have begun his journey when he has passed not only the ramparts †but also the habitations of the neighbourhood. [†These are of no account.] If the town has no ramparts the journey begins after passing the last buildings, without considering what ruins or gardens may be in the neighbourhood; and the same principle applies also to a village. The journey of a nomad living in a tent begins from the limit of the camp. The journey may be considered at an end when one has repassed these same boundaries. If the traveller stops anywhere intentionally for four days, the journey is suspended for that period, by the mere fact of arrival at this temporary halting place. ††But in the four days is included neither the day of arrival nor the day of departure. On arriving at a town with the intention of stopping only as long as the finishing of one's business requires, prayer may be abridged for eighteen days; or according to some opinions four days, while according to others there is no restriction of time. There are authorities too who consider an abridgment warranted if the delay is caused by fear of being attacked, but not during a stay for some commercial object. However this may be, our rite does not allow abridgment if a long stay is anticipated.

SECTION 2

Prayer may be abridged if a journey extends to at least forty-eight miles of Hashim. [This distance is the equivalent of two days' journey with loaded camels. Distances on land and sea being the same, prayer may be abridged even where a ship might under full sail cover the distance in an hour.]

The traveller must from the start have a fixed destination. Therefore he cannot abridge prayer if either—

1. He wanders aimlessly here and there, whatever the distance may be.

2. He is looking for a debtor or a slave whose whereabouts he does not know, and after finding whom he means to return home.

If of two roads leading to the same destination one chooses the longer for some reason or other, *e.g.* because of the level or the security, prayer may still be abridged. *But this is not so if the choice be made from mere caprice. A slave, a wife, or a soldier travelling under the authority of other persons, and ignorant of their destination, may not abridge prayer; even when such persons have an idea the journey will be long, only the soldier may abridge prayer, not the slave or the wife. If a person starts with the intention of making a long journey, and returns voluntarily before completing it, it is finished none the less, and if he starts again it is considered a new journey.

No one has the benefit of abridging prayer who leaves their abode for an illicit purpose, *e.g.* as a fugitive slave, or a wife deserting her husband. †It is the same if a journey begun lawfully is continued unlawfully; while, on the other hand, prayer may be abridged on a journey continued with a lawful object though unlawfully begun.

A traveller who has prayed even for a moment under the direction of an imam who is accomplishing the entire prayer without abridgment, should also finish it without abridgment. This principle is carried so far that a traveller cannot invoke the right of abridgment, if he has begun his prayer under the direction of another traveller, who in the middle of it incurred some unforeseen impurity, *e.g.* a nasal hæmorrhage, and was replaced by another imam who did not abridge. If under these circumstances the first imam rejoins the congregation and resumes his functions after the disappearance of his impurity, the traveller must yet continue his prayer without abridgment. A prayer accomplished by a traveller without abridgment because following an imam must be repeated entire in regular fashion, if it has to be repeated because of some fault of the traveller or the imam, or because the latter is afterwards discovered to be impure. The same rule is observed if one has to repeat a prayer accomplished under the direction of an imam one supposed to be a traveller but afterwards discovered to be living at a fixed abode, or of an imam with regard to whom one did not know whether he was a traveller or not. On the other hand, one may lawfully abridge prayer after having formulated one's intention; when, at the moment of formulating that intention, one knew that the imam was not living at a fixed abode, though uncertain if he intended to abridge prayer or not. †One may even, in this state of uncertainty, formulate the intention conditionally, *i.e.* "if the imam abridges the prayer I will do so with him, but otherwise perform it in the ordinary manner."

To abridge prayer lawfully one must intend to do so from the beginning, and avoid anything incompatible with that intention, throughout the whole act of devotion. Thus a believer cannot claim a right to abridge prayer if :—(1) he has begun the prayer intending to shorten it, but has afterwards hesitated to keep to this intention ; or (2) he is not sure of having had the intention of shortening the prayer ; or (3) if the imam gets up to perform a third *raka,* and one is not certain if it is in order to accomplish the entire prayer without abridgment, or by inadvertence.

The prayer is nullified, if one begins intending to shorten it, and then in spite of that knowingly begins the third *raka,* without special cause for deviating from one's original idea. But if this is a mere inadvertence one may either :—(1) resume one's position, and after a prostration by way of reparation pronounce final salutation ; or (2) change one's intention and accomplish the whole prayer without shortening it ; but in that case one should first resume one's position, and then get up again at once to perform the later *rakas.*

Another essential condition for the lawful shortening of prayer is that one must be able to consider oneself as a traveller throughout the entire duration of the act of devotion. If one expects to arrive at one's destination during prayer, or if one's vessel arrives in port, the prayer must be normally accomplished.

**On a journey of at least three days it is better to abridge prayer than to perform it in the ordinary way. But the traveller is recommended to observe the fast of the month of *Ramadan,* rather than exercise his right to break it, at least when this can be done without danger.

Section 3

During a journey that admits of abridgment of prayer, one may combine the midday and afternoon prayers, and the evening prayer with that of the night ; performing the combined prayers at the usual time of the earlier or of the later of the two. According to one jurist this may be done even when the length of the journey does not admit of the shortening of prayer. If one is actually travelling at the legal time for the midday or evening prayer, it is better to postpone it until the time of afternoon prayer or of the prayer of the night, as the case may be, and accomplish the two prayers together.

One may anticipate a later prayer only on three conditions :—

(1) One must first perform the prayer for which the legal time has

come. Its illegality involves that of the second, anticipated, prayer—but not *vice versâ*.

(2) One must intend to combine the two prayers, when one begins the first, or at least before its completion.

(3) The two prayers must not have any considerable interval between them; otherwise the second prayer must be postponed to its proper time. Whether an interval is considerable or not is a matter of custom.

††The believer who has had recourse to lustration with sand may lawfully combine prayers, as well as one who has performed ritual ablution or bathed. Asking for something in a hurry between the two prayers is not considered a breach of continuity. If, after combining two prayers one remembers that one has omitted from the former some essential element, both are nullified and must be repeated together, but if it is one of the essential elements of the second that has been omitted, the error may be rectified by recommencing the act of devotion at the place of omission, if no long interval has elapsed. If a considerable interval has been allowed to ensue, the second prayer only, not the first, is nullified; and the combination of the two prayers becomes unlawful. If uncertain whether the omitted portions belonged to the first or second prayer, both prayers should be separately repeated at their respective legal hours.

††If the second prayer has not been anticipated, but the first postponed to the legal time for the second, they can be combined without observing the order, without causing one to follow immediately on the other, and even without formulating an intention to combine them. But this intention should have existed already when one resolved at its prescribed hour to postpone the first, otherwise one is guilty of an irregularity, and the first prayer counts merely as an act of devotion performed too late.

If, when one wishes to combine two prayers by anticipating one of them, one arrives at a fixed place of abode before beginning the second, their combination becomes unlawful; but this is not so if one has already begun, and still less if one has finished, the second prayer. And if, in a case where the first prayer has been postponed, one reaches a fixed abode after having accomplished both, both remain valid; but if they are not finished before arrival, the first counts only as an act of devotion accomplished too late. Rain is a good reason for combining two prayers by anticipating the second; while, on the other hand, Shafii in his second period decided that it is no excuse for a postponement. Anticipation is, however, permitted only where rain is actually falling at the beginning of each prayer, †and at the moment of final salutation in the first. Snow and hail, when sufficient to wet the clothes, are regarded as rain. *This faculty of combination refers especially to the believer performing public prayer in a distant mosque, who is afraid of getting wet before reaching home if he starts at once.

CHAPTER III.—PUBLIC PRAYER ON FRIDAYS

Section 1

Public prayer on Fridays is obligatory only for adult male Moslems, sane, free, domiciled in the place, and not obliged to remain at home by sickness, etc. It is not obligatory for any one with a valid excuse for not attending daily public prayer, for one under contract of enfranchisement, ††for one partially enfranchised. Those for whom public prayer on Fridays is not obligatory have nevertheless a right to be present, provided they can legally perform midday prayer; though the law allows them the option of leaving the congregation after the midday prayer, before proceeding to that for the week. This rule does not apply to believers who, having a mere accidental excuse for absence, such as sickness, etc., happen to be in the mosque at the time of weekly prayer; these are forbidden to leave, unless their sickness is increased by remaining. Weekly public prayer is obligatory even for decrepit and sickly persons, if they have means of transport and can endure it without pain. The blind should attend, if he can find some one to lead him. The inhabitants of a village should perform weekly prayer, if they are in sufficient number for it, otherwise they should go for this purpose to a neighbouring town or village, if a call can be heard from the one to the other, in the silence of the night. If the distance is too great for this, then there is no obligation to go.

The law forbids any one who should attend the Friday prayer beginning a journey upon that day immediately after the sun has begun to decline, unless he happens to have to take the road that leads to the place of meeting, or he is afraid of incurring some detriment from leaving later and consequently being obliged to remain in the rear of the caravan. According to the opinion of Shafii in his second period this rule applies also to the case of a person wishing to leave a little before the sun begins to decline, at least if the journey is merely allowable; but if the departure is commendable or obligatory, one may chose what hour one pleases. [†A journey, whether it be merely allowable, or commendable, or obligatory, is in all cases subject to the prohibition to start on Friday at the time mentioned.]

†Persons who are not obliged to take part in the Friday prayer,

should still, according to the Sonna, be present at the public midday prayer on that day. It is better, however, that they should not take part in it, but remain concealed, unless the cause of their absence from the Friday prayer is a matter of public notoriety. It is also recommended to believers who consider themselves temporarily excused from attending the Friday prayer, to postpone the midday prayer on that day as long as possible, until sure of being unable to go to the weekly function: but those, on the other hand, who have a permanent excuse, such as women and sickly persons, should perform the midday prayer as soon as the hour has sounded.

Besides the conditions already mentioned, the law has established for the validity of weekly public prayer, the following:—

1. It must take place at the time prescribed for midday prayer. If this is past, the Friday prayer cannot be performed, as it may not be accomplished too late by way of reparation. If one is afraid that the legal time does not suffice for its completion, one should say the midday prayer and no more; and if the legal time expires during the ceremony, it should be concluded as an ordinary midday prayer. Only one author maintains that this prayer should be accomplished from beginning to end. A person who arrives late and lags behind should finish his act of devotion as a midday prayer; though according to some authors he should finish the weekly prayer as if nothing were the matter.

2. Public weekly prayer must be performed in a place surrounded by edifices inhabited by members of the community; *so that people living in tents in the desert cannot accomplish it.

3. In the same town, public prayer on Friday cannot be performed in different places, either simultaneously or successively, unless the town be so extensive that its inhabitants cannot easily assemble in one spot. Some jurists do not admit this exception; others think that any town divided by a large river should be considered in this respect as two separate towns; others again are of opinion that in the case of several villages with contiguous buildings, the ceremony may be held in as many places as there are distinct communes. When Friday public prayer has been accomplished in one place, and others proceed to perform it in too near a neighbourhood, the former alone is lawful, unless the Sultan attends the latter, in which case it alone is lawful, in spite of not having priority. To determine which of two public prayers has priority it is necessary to observe the time of the introductory *takbir*; or, according to some authors, the moment when the congregation disperses. while a third doctrine maintains that the important point is the beginning of the first sermon. If two public prayers begin at the same time, or if is not certain if one began first, the ceremony should be begun over

again. When, on the contrary, it is known that one began before the other, but it is not certain which, or it has been forgotten, then midday prayer only must be accomplished. One jurist maintains that even then one should perform the Friday prayer.

4. Weekly public prayer can be accomplished only in congregation, and is in that respect subject to the rules detailed in Chapter I. of this Book. The congregation must consist of at least forty Moslems, adult, sane, free men, domiciled in the place, *i.e.* who leave it neither in winter nor summer, except by necessity. The ††Friday prayer is regularly performed even if the congregation consist only of forty sick persons. The imam can be included in the legal forty. If the congregation wholly or partly disperses during the sermon, leaving less than forty behind, the continuation of the service is invalid; but if they return after a short interval it can be resumed from the place of interruption. *If the interval is long the whole ceremony must be begun over again; and if the congregation disperses during the prayer, the latter is nullified. Only one author thinks this is not so if at least two persons remain in the mosque. *The weekly service may be performed under the direction of a minor, a slave, or a traveller, provided there are forty persons present besides them. *If the imam has contracted an impurity, whether grave or slight, the service is still lawful if forty persons besides him are present, but not otherwise. ††But if one begins the prayer at the *rokua* under an impure imam the whole *raka* is invalid.

5. Before beginning the prayer the imam must deliver two sermons, consisting of five parts:—(*a*) the praise of God; (*b*) the prayer for the Prophet, consisting like (*a*) of certain special words; (*c*) an exhortation to virtue, ††of which the wording is not prescribed. These three parts must occur in each of the three sermons. (*d*) A recitation of a verse of the Koran in one of the two sermons. Some authorities maintain that this recitation should take place in the first sermon; others that it should occur in both; yet others that it is not obligatory at all. (*e*) An invocation, as the word is ordinarily understood, for the good of Moslems, in the second sermon. A few authors consider it not obligatory. The sermons must be delivered in Arabic, observing the proper order of succession of (*a*), (*b*) and (*c*); and the proper time must have arrived, that is the sun must have begun to decline. The imam remains standing, if possible, when delivering each sermon, but sits down during the interval between them. The sermons should be pronounced so that at least the minimum legal congregation could hear them. Shafii, in his second period expressed the opinion that it is not absolutely prohibited for the members of the congregation to speak a few words when listening to the sermons. The Sonna insists on th

congregation being silent when listening to the imam. [†The order of succession of the parts of the sermons is not a matter of rigorous observation.] *The following are essential conditions for the validity of the sermons :—(*a*) uninterrupted delivery; (*b*) absence of any grave or slight impurity in the imam, who (*c*) must be decently dressed. The Sonna has introduced the following additional practices :—(*a*) delivery from a pulpit or other elevated place; (*b*) a preliminary salutation by the imam of those close to the pulpit, his turning towards the congregation when mounting the steps, and salutation of the whole congregation when taking his seat; it is only then that the first call is intoned; (*c*) eloquence, intelligibility and conciseness; (*d*) turning neither to the right nor to the left; (*e*) leaning during delivery upon a sword, stick or something similar; (*f*) remaining seated between the sermons as long as is required to recite chapter 112 of the Koran.

After the second sermon the muezzin intones the second call to prayer, while the imam hastens to descend from the pulpit so as to be facing the *mihrab* before the second call is finished. He then says a prayer consisting of two *rakas*; in the first he recites aloud chapter 62 of the Koran, and in the second chapter 63, both after reciting chapter 1.

Section 2

The Sonna recommends every believer to take a bath before attending Friday public prayer. Some authorities extend the recommendation to those who do not attend the service. The bath can strictly be taken at any time after dawn, but it is preferable to take it as soon as possible before going to the mosque. †Those unable to take a bath should have recourse to ablution with sand. The Sonna also prescribes—

1. The taking of a bath on the occasion of each of the great festivals; at an eclipse, or in time of drought; when about to wash a corpse; on recovery from an attack of insanity or a fainting fit. It is prescribed to an infidel upon his conversion, and for pilgrims to Mecca. The bathing of a person about to wash a corpse is more imperative than the Friday bath; though Shafii in his first period maintained the contrary opinion. [*This former opinion is the better; being accepted by the majority of authorities and based on several authentic traditions, while only one authentic tradition supports the opinion adopted by Shafii in Egypt.]

2. Going to the mosque early, on foot, in a state of composed meditation.

3. On the way, and in the mosque before the service begins, reciting a portion of the Koran, or glorifying God.

4. Refraining from outstripping other members of the congregation on their way to the mosque.

5. Wearing one's best clothes, using scent, paring the nails, and removing any disagreeable bodily odour.

[The Sonna also recommends the recitation of chapter 18 of the Koran, both on the day and night of Friday, and to pronounce on that day several invocations and prayers for the prophet. Once the first call has been entoned, those present at the service are rigorously prohibited from occupying themselves with commercial or other affairs, in the preacher's presence. A bargain, however, struck in contravention of this rule, cannot be legally invalidated on that ground. It is considered blamable to conclude a bargain even before the first call if the sun has already begun to decline.]

Section 3

A person who takes part in the Friday public prayer from the inclination in the second *raka* is considered to have been present at the whole ceremony; and all he needs to do is to perform one single *raka* more, after the imam has pronounced the final salutation. But if he enters after that inclination, he is considered to have been absent at the whole prayer; and should perform midday prayer in four *rakas*, after the imam's final salutation.

†Each member of the congregation should have an intention to accomplish the Friday public prayer under the direction of the imam. If the imam is obliged to discontinue Friday public prayer, or any other prayer, by reason of a slight impurity, etc., *another may continue the function. Only, in the case of Friday public prayer, the imam may be replaced solely by a member of the congregation who has prayed under his direction until the moment when the impurity was ascertained, †but who need not have been present at the sermons or even at the first *raka*. It is clear, however, that if the substitute has been present from the beginning of the first *raka*, the ceremony continued under his direction will be valid both for him and for the congregation; †otherwise it will be valid for the congregation only and not for him. The substitute should continue the function just as the imam himself would have done, whether he has been present since the beginning of the prayer, or whether he came late and so is behind the congregation. Consequently if he has still to perform two *rakas* and the congregation only one, he should proceed at once to the *tashahud* after finishing his first *raka*. Then he should inform the congregation that they may cease praying under his direction, or wait until he has

finished his second *raka* and finish the service together. †The congregation need not renew their intention when continuing the service under the direction of a substitute.

If the crowded condition of a mosque obliges the believer, when making his prostration, to rest his body, not on the ground but on the body of one of his neighbours, the prostration is still valid. ††If prostration is quite impossible he must wait till the others get up ; he must not substitute for the prostration a mere nodding of the head. Under these circumstances the following distinctions are to be drawn :—

1. If the believer has still time to prostrate himself before the imam bends in prayer in the second *raka* he should do so, and after rising he should :—(*a*) take part in the recitation if the imam is still standing; (*b*) †bend his body with the imam if the latter has already begun the inclination of the following *raka*, acting like a person who has arrived late ; (*c*) take part in that portion of the prayer with which the imam is occupied, if the latter has already finished the inclination of the next *raka*, but not pronounced the final salutation, and then after the service perform a supplementary *raka ;* (*d*) but he has missed the service altogether if the imam has already pronounced the final salutation.

2. If the believer has no time to prostrate himself before the imam bends in prayer in the second *raka*. One author is of opinion that he should prostrate himself as soon as possible and finish the prayer on his own account, *but other authorities think he should bend his body with the imam. †This inclination, though the imam's second, is considered to be the believer's first, and so his *raka* consists of the inclination of the imam's first *raka* and the prostration of the second. †This, however, does not prevent one accomplishing in this way the entire Friday prayer. The authors referred to go so far as to consider the whole prayer nullified if the believer prostrates himself on his own account, while knowing that he ought to incline with the imam.. But if he has so prostrated himself through oversight or ignorance it is only that first prostration which does not count ; and if he has occasion to prostrate himself a second time, the latter prostration is valid. †One has thus accomplished all the essential elements of a *raka*, and is considered to have performed the Friday prayer, provided the two prostrations are finished before the imam pronounces the final salutation. When, owing to forgetfulness, the member of the congregation has lagged so far behind that the imam is already bending in the second *raka* when he is still prostrated in the first, he should, according to our school, bend in prayer with the imam.

CHAPTER IV.—PRAYER IN CASE OF DANGER

Section 1

There are three categories of this prayer :—

1. When the enemy comes from the direction of the *kibla*, the imam should draw up his army in two or more lines, and pray with all his soldiers up to the prostration, when one of the lines should prostrate itself with him for the two prescribed prostrations of the first *raka*, while the other soldiers remain on guard. Then before beginning the second *raka* those who at first remained on guard perform two prostrations on their own account, and after that the whole army begins the second *raka* with the imam. In this *raka* the soldiers who remained on guard during the prostrations of the first *raka* prostrate themselves with the imam, while the others remain in their turn on guard until the imam sits down, when they prostrate themselves on their own account. The *tashahad* and the final salutation should be accomplished by all together. This manner of prayer was introduced by the Prophet of God at the battle of *Osfan*. It is also permissible for the two divisions of a single line to remain on guard by turn in the two *rakas ;* †or even a single division may remain on guard in the two *rakas* while the imam prostrates himself, provided, as we have just seen, that these omitted prostrations are accomplished at the end of each *raka*.

2. When the enemy does not come from the direction of the *kibla*, and consequently it is impossible to face the prescribed point without exposing the rear or the flank, the imam should perform the prayer twice, each time with a separate portion of the army while the other portion is held ready to repel an attack. This was done by the Prophet of God at the battle of *Batn-Nakhl*.

3. When one only of two divisions of an army is in face of the enemy, the imam first prays one *raka* with the other division, and when he is about to begin the second *raka* this division stops praying under his direction, pronounces the final salutation, and relieves the division on guard, which then joins the imam and accomplishes the second *raka* under his direction. After the imam has sat down for the *tashahad*, the whole army performs another *raka* on its own account—the second so far as the soldiers are concerned—and this *raka* finished, the army begins to pray again under the direction of the imam and pronounces with him the final salutation. This course was adopted by the Prophet of God at the battle of *Zat ar Rika*, †and is better than that followed t *Batn-Nakhl*. After the departure of the first division the imam

should recite some passage of the Koran until the arrival of the second. On finishing this recitation he says the *tashahad ;* though this, according to one jurist, should be deferred until the second division has joined him. In the case of evening prayer the imam should pray two *rakas* with the first division and one with the second. *This is better than the other way about, though the latter is also permissible. The imam should so arrange that the second division may arrive either during the first *tashahad* of the second *raka*, or, †better, during the *kiyam* of the third. In the case of a fourfold prayer he should pray two successive *rakas* with each of the two divisions, *though he may also divide his army into four and pray a single *raka* with each. The entire army is responsible for the negligences that each division may commit in the *raka* it prays under the direction of the imam, *i.e.* its first *raka ;* †and the same responsibility exists for faults of this nature committed by the second division in the second *raka*, but not for those of the first division in its own second raka. A negligence of the imam in the first *raka* is imputed to the whole army, but if it occurs in his second *raka*, *i.e.* the first of the second division, it is imputed to that division only.

The Sonna prescribes that in these three categories of prayer weapons should not be laid aside ; and one jurist considers this to be of rigorous observance.

4. In the midst of a battle or other imminent danger, one must pray as one can, whether riding or afoot. One need not turn in the direction of the *kibla*, †and may even, if necessary, omit most of the practices of which prayer consists. Prayer, however, can never be performed shouting ; and one must always, if possible, lay aside weapons if ever so little blood-stained ; but if circumstances do not permit the laying aside of one's weapons, one may, if it is absolutely necessary, pray while holding blood-stained weapons in the hand, *without being obliged to repeat this act of devotion later. If it is impossible to perform the bending and the prostration, one makes only a sign of the head, lower in the latter case than in the former. One can pray like this both in combat and flight where combat or flight is permissible ; and also when escaping from a fire, a flood, a fierce beast, or even a pressing creditor who threatens his debtor with bodily restraint ; †but such a course is not permissible for a pilgrim to Mecca who is afraid of invalidating his pilgrimage by arriving too late for the ceremony at Mount Arafa. *If one has prayed in this manner in presence of a troop of persons supposed erroneously to be the enemy, one's prayer must be performed over again on discovering the mistake.

Section 2

The law forbids a man to clothe himself in silk or to use it as carpet or covering. A woman may wear clothes of silk; †but neither may she use this material for carpet or covering. †A guardian may clothe in silk a minor of whom he has charge. [†A woman may use silk also as carpet or covering; at least it has been so decided by jurists of *Irak*, and others.]

Silk clothes may, however, be legally worn by men:—

1. When urgently necessary; *e.g.* in case of extreme heat or cold, or if some unforeseen attack obliges him to snatch up the first thing he can find, and he can find no other.

2. For the sake of health; *e.g.* if infected with itch or other cutaneous malady, or to protect himself from vermin.

3. In time of war; brocade having qualities that render it particularly useful to the soldier.

It is forbidden to use a material composed of silk and threads of some other stuff, if the weight of the silk exceeds the weight of the other threads, †but if otherwise it is permissible. Silk lace or embroidery is not forbidden, if the coat is not ornamented in an extravagant manner.

And finally one may lawfully wear an impure coat when not praying or performing some other act of devotion; but except in case of urgent necessity such as an unforeseen attack, one may not cover oneself with dogskin or pigskin, †nor with the skin of any animal that has died a natural death.

**It is not forbidden to burn in a lamp oil that has become impure.

CHAPTER V.—PUBLIC PRAYER AT THE TWO GREAT FESTIVALS OF THE YEAR

Section 1

This prayer is prescribed by the Sonna only, though some authors maintain it is a rigorous obligation for which the community is collectively responsible. The prayer may be accomplished either in public or on one's own account. Slaves, women, and travellers should take part in it as well as other believers. The legal time for this prayer is between sunrise and the moment when the sun begins to decline, but it is preferable not to begin the ceremony before the elevation of the sun has reached the height of a lance.

The prayer consists first of two introductory *rakas;* then is pronounced the introductory invocation; and after that are said seven *takbirs*, with a pause between each two *takbirs* of a length sufficient for the recitation of a verse of the Koran of medium length. On the termination of the *takbirs* the confession of faith is pronounced, followed by another *takbir* and a glorification of God, preferably in the following terms :—" Praise to God," " Glory to God," " There is no god but God," or " God is great." Finally the *tawaz* is accomplished and the first chapter of the Koran recited. In the second *raka* five *takbirs* precede the ordinary recitation of the Koran, and the hands must be raised at each *takbir*. Neither the seven nor the five *takbirs* mentioned are obligatory, nor any of them ; and they have no object once the recitation has been begun, though Shafii in his first period admitted that they could if necessary be performed so long as the inclination had not begun. The chapters of the Koran which should be recited after the first chapter are, in the first *raka* chapter 50, and in the second chapter 54, both aloud and without any omission.

After the two *rakas* are finished the Sonna requires two sermons of the same component parts as the two Friday sermons. At the end of the fast the sermons contain an exhortation with regard to the special contribution prescribed on that occasion ; while at the feast of victims the congregation should be exhorted to accomplish the sacrifice. The first sermon is preceded by nine *takbirs* and the second by seven, accomplished in either case one after the other without interruption.

At these two festivals it is commendable—

1. To take a bath at midnight, and according to one jurist at dawn.
2. To use scent, and dress in one's best clothes, as on Friday.

The ceremony should take place preferably in a mosque, or according to others, in a plain, provided there be no obstacle to either of those courses. In any case the imam should instruct his substitute to preside at the prayer in the mosque for those whose strength does not permit them to follow the rest of the community to the plain. The others make their way to the plain by one road and return by another. The congregation should assemble early, but the imam arrives only at the time the prayer begins. At the feast of victims the ceremony should be performed in haste.

[At the end of the fast some nourishment should be taken before the ceremony, but not at the feast of victims. In either case one should go to the ceremony on foot, in a state of composed meditation. Before going every one except the imam may say a supererogatory prayer.]

Section 2

It is commendable to entone the *takbir*, on the eve of the two festivals, at sunset, in the inns, on the roads, in the mosques, and in the bazaars,

**takbirs* which are continued until the imam begins the ceremony. On the eve of the feast of victims the Mecca pilgrims replace the *takbirs* by the cry of *labaika*. †The Sonna makes no mention of *takbirs* to be entoned immediately after evening prayer on the eve of the breaking of the fast. The Mecca pilgrims begin the *takbirs* from the midday prayer of the *Yum-an-nahr* or day of the feast of victims, and continue them until morning prayer on the last of the next three days called *ayam-at-tashrik*. *Those who are not on pilgrimage are subject to the same obligation as the pilgrims. One authority maintains that the *takbirs* of these believers should begin at evening prayer on the eve of the feast of victims, another thinks they should commence from morning prayer on the day of Mount *Arafa*. According to this view, which has prevailed in practice, the *takbirs* continue until the afternoon prayer of the last of the days called *ayam-at-tashrik*. *If when performing one of the special acts of devotion or some supererogatory prayer one is guilty of omitting some obligatory prayer one should say *takbirs* also on the days called *ayam-at-tashrik*. The most usual form of the *takbir* is the following :—" God is great, God is great, God is great. There is no god but God. God is great, God is great. Praise be to God." It is commendable to add : " God is great in his greatness. I offer Him numberless praises. Glory be to God morning and evening." If on the thirtieth day of the month of *Ramadan*, before the sun has begun to decline, it is legally ascertained that the new moon has been seen on the previous night, the fast should be at once broken, and the festival prayer accomplished. But if the proof be only attained after sunset the day just ended counts as a fast day ; while if this takes place after noon but before sunset one breaks the fast without celebrating the festival prayer, as the hour is past. *Under these latter circumstances the prayer can be accomplished at any moment according to some ; but one jurist has expressed an opinion that the next day must be considered the legal one, and that the prayer performed then at the prescribed hour, is not too late.

CHAPTER VI.—PRAYER ON THE OCCASION OF ECLIPSES

This prayer is prescribed by the Sonna. One begins by formulating a special intention to perform it, and then recites the first chapter of the Koran. One bends one's body, gets up, again recites the first chapter, stands still and at the end prostrates oneself. This constitutes one *raka*, after which another is performed in the same manner ; but never a third, even if the eclipse be not yet over when the second is finished

†Should the eclipse terminate sooner than the prayer, one of the two inclinations may not for that reason be omitted. To accomplish it in the best and most approved manner possible one recites the two first chapters of the Koran at the first *kiyam ;* and at the second, besides the first chapter about 200 verses of the second ; at the third about 150, and at the fourth about 100. At the first inclination one repeats the formula " Glory to God " as long as would be necessary for the repetition of 100 verses of the second chapter of the Koran ; at the second inclination this formula is repeated for as long as it would take to repeat 80 verses ; similarly for the third a time of 70 verses ; and for the fourth 50. †The prostrations should not last too long. [††On the contrary they should be prolonged as much as possible according to what is stated in the two collections of traditions called *Sahih* by al-Bokhari and Muslim, while al-Bawaiti quotes a decision of Shafii tending to show that the prostrations should last as long as the preceding inclinations.]

According to a precept of the Sonna prayer on the occasion of eclipse should only be accomplished in congregation. The imam repeats aloud in the case of a lunar, but not in that of a solar eclipse. Then he delivers two sermons as on Friday, and finally exhorts the congregation to repent and do good. A person joining the congregation at the imam's first inclination is considered to have been present at the whole *raka,** but not one arriving at the second inclination or the second *kiyam.*

The legal time for prayer on the occasion of an eclipse of the sun is considered to have elapsed when it reappears in its full splendour, or sets still obscured. The legal time for prayer on the occasion of an eclipse of the moon is considered to be over at the end of the eclipse or at sunrise ; but according to the opinion adopted by Shafii in his second period, neither the appearance of the dawn, nor the setting of the moon while still obscured, have any effect upon the legal time.

If the time of a prayer on occasion of eclipse coincides with that of a public weekly prayer, or with any obligatory prayer, that obligatory prayer has the priority, at any rate if it is feared there may not be time for it unless begun at once. If there is time one should first perform the prayer on occasion of eclipse, then pronounce the Friday sermons with references in them to the eclipse, and lastly accomplish the weekly or daily obligatory prayer. If a festival or eclipse coincides with a burial prayer, the latter should be first accomplished.

CHAPTER VII.—PRAYER IN TIME OF DROUGHT

THIS prayer also has been introduced by the Sonna, and is said when there is great need of rain. It is repeated two or three times if the drought continues. When preparations have been made for it but the rain falls before the congregation assembles, they should still meet to render thanks to God and invoke Him, ††and then proceed to the prayer as if nothing had happened.

The imam should first command the faithful to fast for three days, to repent of their sins, and to seek the favour of God by being charitable and refraining from injustice. On the fourth day one goes to the plain, fasting, in ordinary clothes, with head bent in sign of humility. Children, old people †and domestic animals should accompany the community; and even the presence of infidels cannot be forbidden at this ceremony provided that they are the subjects of a Musulman prince and do not mix with the believers.

The prayer consists of two *rakas* like that on the occasion of the two festivals, except that according to some authorities the 71st chapter of the Koran is recited in the second *raka*, †and that the ceremony need not take place at the time prescribed for the festivals. The sermons are the same as at the festivals, except that for the formula "God is great" are substituted the words "I ask pardon of God." In the first sermon is pronounced also the following invocation :—"O God grant us an abundant rain, to moisten the soil, for our benefit and profit and the fertilisation of the earth, a rain that may spread everywhere upon all lands for a length of time. O God, grant us an abundant rain, and reduce us not to despair. O God, grant us Thy pardon, for Thou lovest to pardon. Cause the heavens to pour down an abundant rain." The imam turns in the direction of the *kibla* after beginning the second sermon, and on its termination turns again to the congregation and utters the most pressing invocations, both in a low tone and aloud. When turning towards the *kibla* he turns back his cloak so that the right side is to the left and the left to the right; and Shafii in his second period decided that it must be turned back again so as to place the upper part below and *vice versâ*, while the congregation imitates his movements. [The cloak is worn turned about in this way until one has got home and taken off one's things. If the imam will not perform the prayer, the congregation has the right to do so on its own account; but there is no objection to the imam delivering the sermons after the prayer, instead of before as usual. The Sonna has also introduced the following usages :—

1. Exposing oneself to the first rain of the year, with no clothes on but what is required to cover the shameful parts, so that the rain may wet the body all over.

2. Taking a bath on that occasion, or performing ritual ablution in water of some torrent.

3. Saying "glory to God" on hearing the thunder or seeing the lightning, but without continuing to look at it.

4. Exclaiming during the rain, "O God, may this rain be beneficial to us." Then one utters some invocation, and at the end of it says, "A favourable rain has been sent us by the goodness and mercy of God." It is blamable to substitute for this formula the words, "We have had rain through the influence of such and such star," or to conjure the wind in a similar way.

5. Asking God to abate too abundant rains, if they are causing damage. This supplication is made in the following words :—"O God, be Thou our help ; but be not against us," without accomplishing a regular prayer.]

CHAPTER VIII.—INTENTIONAL OMISSION OF PRESCRIBED PRAYERS

A SANE adult Moslem who refuses to pray and denies the obligation is an apostate and punishable as such ; even if he has merely neglected prayer through laziness, without denying its obligation, he is none the less punishable with death. ††Capital punishment is liable to be incurred by the omission of even one single prescribed prayer, the moment its time is passed, if done designedly and without offering any excuse. One should begin by exhorting the culprit to repentance, and if this be unavailing strike him upon the neck. Some authorities prefer that he should be pricked with a sharp instrument until he either prays or dies. After his death, however, his body is washed and wrapped in a winding sheet. Prayers are said for the repose of his soul, and he is buried among the faithful. Nor does the law insist upon removing all trace of the grave in which he is laid.

BOOK 4.—FUNERAL CEREMONIES

Section 1

One should think often upon death, and prepare oneself for it by repentance, and by refraining from injustice, especially if one is ill.

††A person about to die is laid upon the right side, with the body turned towards the *kibla*. If the bed is not large enough the dying person is laid on the back, the face and the soles of the feet turned towards the *kibla*. The confession of faith is said so that the sick person may hear it, but without inconveniencing him; the 36th chapter of the Koran is recited, and everything done to fix his attention upon his Lord. After death the eyelids are closed, and a bandage placed under the cheeks; the joints are rendered as supple as possible; the whole body is covered with a piece of light cloth; and some heavy object is placed on the stomach. Lastly the corpse is placed on a bier or something of the sort, and after the clothes have been taken off is turned towards the *kibla* as before death. This duty is incumbent upon the most suitable relative.

As soon as death is ascertained one hastens to wash the body. This ablution, the wrapping of the body in a shroud, the prayer for the repose of the soul of the deceased, and the burial, are obligations for which the survivors are collectively responsible. The washing of a corpse must always extend to all parts of the body. The person accomplishing it removes the impurity, †but he need not formulate the intention. The corpse of a person drowned, if the body has been completely wetted, need not be washed again. An infidel can, if necessary, perform the ablution. [According to Shafii's personal opinion the body of a drowned person should be washed.]

The best way of performing the ablution is as follows. The corpse is taken to some place isolated and concealed, where it is placed on a table. Ablution is then practised with cold water, while the corpse remains covered with a shirt upon the table, inclined backwards. The spine of the corpse is supported on the right hand, the thumb being in the hollow of the neck, and the back of the deceased resting on the right knee. The left hand is then pressed down hard upon the abdomen of the corpse, in order to expel the excreta. The body is laid upon the back; and the shameful parts washed with the left hand, covered with a rag. The left hand is then covered with another rag, and the fingers introduced into the mouth of the deceased. The teeth are rubbed and the nostrils cleansed. After this one proceeds to ritual ablution as in the case of a living man; and when it is terminated the head and beard are washed with a decoction of lotus leaves or some analogous plant, and the hair and beard are softly combed with a comb of which the teeth are not too close together. Any hairs that may come out should be put back again. Then one proceeds to the ablution of the front of the body, first the right side then the left. Then the corpse is laid upon the left side in order to wash the right side and the back, from the neck to the heels; and on the right side in order to wash the left side and the back in the same way. Such is the first ablution of the body. It is commendable :—

1. To repeat the ablution once or twice, and to employ for the first ablution a decoction of lotus or marsh-mallow.

2. To pour clear water on the body, from above to below, after the liquid containing the lotus or marsh-mallow has flowed away.

3. To put a little camphor in the water used at each of the three ablutions.

If after the ablution some impurity still comes from the body, one should simply remove it; though some authors consider that one should proceed to a fourth ablution, if the impurity comes from the shameful parts; while others think a new ritual ablution to be obligatory in such a case.

A man's corpse is washed by a man, and a woman's by a woman; though the master can wash the body of a woman who was his slave, and the husband that of his wife. Similarly the wife may wash the body of her husband; but in all cases where the ablution is performed by a person of the other sex, the hands should be wrapped in rags so as not to touch the body. †When at the place of decease persons of the same sex as the deceased cannot be found, nor persons of the other sex allied by kinship or marriage, the ablution cannot take place, and recourse must be had to lustration with sand. The ablution of the corpse of a deceased person is obligatory for those who have to pray for the soul; but in the case of a woman this duty is incumbent on the relatives, and firstly those within the prohibited degrees. †They even have priority over the husband. In default of relatives a woman not of the family may be called upon for this duty, and it is only in the last resource that recourse is had to the male relatives, in the order in which they are called to pray for the deceased. [With the exception of a cousin on the father's side and the other relatives with whom marriage is not forbidden, for they are considered for this purpose as not being of the family.] †A husband has priority over all other male relatives.

It is forbidden to perfume the corpse of a person deceased during *Ihram*, and to cut off a hair or a nail as a memento; †but it is permissible to perfume the body of a woman deceased during a period of legal retirement, though the use of scent was legally forbidden her when alive. According to the opinions maintained by Shafii in Egypt, in the case of a person not deceased during *Ihram* one may lawfully cut the nails and the hair, even of the armpit, the pubis and the moustache. [*Such a proceeding is always blamable.]

Section 2

After the ablutions are finished the corpse should be wrapped in a shroud, which is subject to the same rules as the clothes which the dead person might wear during life, in such a manner as to cover at least the shameful parts. Any testamentary disposition tending to nullify this precept is without legal effect. It is preferable to wrap a man's corpse in three shrouds, though four or five may be used; but as to women five shrouds are recommended by law. If using three shrouds, the corpse is simply enveloped three times; but if five are employed, one begins by dressing the body in a shirt and turban and then wraps it round three times, in the case of a man; while a woman is first dressed in a cloak, a veil and a shirt, and then enveloped twice. According to one jurist, however, the body of a woman should first be dressed in a mantle and veil, and then wrapped round thrice. The Sonna has prescribed that the shroud should be of white material; and that the expense is a first charge upon the succession; while, if the deceased person has left nothing the expense must be borne by those liable for the maintenance of the deceased, *i.e.* the relatives, the master †or the husband. One spreads first the finest and largest shroud, the second above it, and the simplest last, not forgetting to scatter aromatic spices upon each. One lays the body on the back upon these three shrouds, and places with it camphor and spices. The thighs are pressed close together, and each opening of the body stopped with cotton. The shrouds are then wrapped round and pressed tightly together. The bands on the thighs and other parts of the body are not detached until the corpse is just about to be lowered into the grave.

The body of a person deceased during *Ihram* is not wrapped in sewn shrouds; neither is the head covered. In the case of a woman deceased during *Ihram*, the face only should remain uncovered.

†It is better to have the bier supported between the two poles than to have it carried by four persons. In the former case a man places the two front poles on his shoulders with his head in the middle, while two men bear the poles behind, one on the right and one on the left. If four persons are employed two bearers are placed in front of the bier and two behind. It is commendable that those who form part of the funeral procession should walk immediately in front of the bier, which should be carried rapidly to the cemetery, unless it is feared some lesion may thereby be caused to the body.

SECTION 3 (1)

Prayer for the repose of the dead consists of seven essential elements :

1. The intention, which is formulated like that in other prayers. It is enough to have the intention of performing one's duty to God ; though some authorities consider necessary an intention of accomplishing an obligation for which Moslems are collectively responsible. The intention need not refer to a particular deceased person ; but if one does so and afterwards discovers one has made a mistake, the prayer is void. If one is present at two or more simultaneous funerals, one may formulate an intention for all at once.

2. Four *takbirs ;* †though the prayer is not void if five are said. However, if the imam begins a fifth, †it is better that those present should cease to pray under his direction, and either pronounce at once the final salutation or wait quietly till they can do so with him.

3. The ordinary final salutation.

4. The recitation of the first chapter of the Koran, after the first *takbir.* [This chapter can be recited just as well after one of the three other *takbirs.*]

5. The prayer for the Prophet, which is performed after the second *takbir.* ††The prayer for the family of the Prophet is not obligatory.

6. A special invocation for the repose of the soul of the deceased, after the third *takbir.*

7. The *Kiyam,* at least according to our school, if it is possible.

The Sonna requires also that the hands should be raised when performing the *takbir,* and that the first chapter should be said in a low tone, though some consider that it should be recited aloud if the ceremony takes place at night. †It is commendable to pronounce the *tawuz,* without the introductory invocation.

At the third *takbir* one pronounces the formula :—" O God, this is Thy servant, and the child of parents who are Thy servants," etc. These vords are preceded by the following :—" O God, pardon our living and our dead, absent and present, old and young, women and men. O God, cause him amongst us to whom Thou accordest life to live in the observance of religion, and to die in the faith him whom Thou willest to die." To this last formula is added in the case of a little child :—" O God, may this child be the forerunner of his parents in Paradise, may his loss be reckoned to them as a sacrifice to Thee, may it be to them a warning and an example, and may this child be their intercessor with Thee. May the weight of this loss be placed in the heavenly balance to their profit at the day of judgment, and patience be poured upon their hearts." And lastly at the fourth *takbir* one says these words :—" O God, deny us not the recompense due to him; lead us not into temptation after his death; and pardon both us and him.

The prayer is void if, without valid excuse, one has lagged so much behind the imam as to be still engaged upon one *takbir* when the imam has already got to the next. A person who arrives after the ceremony has begun should pronounce a *takbir*, and then say the first chapter of the Koran, even though the imam may have finished it; but if the imam has already got to the next *takbir* before such person has begun the recitation he should omit it, and join the imam in saying the *takbir*. †If the imam is finishing the next *takbir* while one is still reciting the first chapter, one should stop doing so and follow the imam for the remainder of the prayer. If the imam has reached the final salutation when one arrives, one should accomplish all the *takbirs* and glorifications of God, though according to one jurist the latter are not rigorously necessary under the circumstances.

The conditions essential for the validity of a prayer for the repose of the dead are the same as in the case of ordinary prayer, except that it need not be accomplished in public, the prayer of one man being sufficient. According to some authors, however, there must be at least two persons to accomplish this prayer; others say three, others four. †A funeral prayer may validly be performed by women, if there are no men in the place. Funeral prayer is said for one who dies far from his own people. It should take place before burial, but it can be repeated afterwards, †especially if at the moment of death one is among those responsible for its due execution.

Funeral prayers should never be performed on the tomb of the Prophet.

SECTION 3 (2)

Shafii, in his second period, adopted the doctrine that the *wali* of the deceased is more competent to be imam in the prayer for the repose of his soul than the chief of the state or of the town. In this connection is understood by *wali* any male relative of the deceased, whether entitled to succession or not, *i.e.* (1) father, (2) grandfather or other agnate ancestor, (3) son, (4) grandson, (5) brother—*whole brother having priority over half-brother on the father's side ; (*b*) son of whole brother, (7) son of half-brother on father's side, (8) other agnates in order of succession, (9) cognates. If two persons are equally related to the deceased, priority should, according to the personal opinion of Shafii, be accorded to the elder, if of irreproachable character. But a free man always has priority over a slave, even though the latter may be more nearly related to the deceased.

The person presiding as imam at a burial service should place himself near the head of the corpse if a man, but in the case of a woman he should place himself behind the body. A single service will suffice for several deceased persons at once. It is forbidden to pray for the rest of the soul of an infidel ; it is not necessary even to wash his corpse, though the body of an infidel subject of a Moslem prince should be wrapped in a shroud and buried. In the case of a Musulman known to be dead, prayer for the repose of his soul is obligatory, even if only a part of the body has been found. An abortion that has uttered a cry or wept at birth is buried like an ordinary person. *If, uttering no cry, it has given some sign of life, as palpitation of the heart or movement of a limb, prayer is obligatory ; but if there are no such signs it is unnecessary, even if four months be passed.

It is unnecessary to wash the body of a martyr, or to pray for the repose of his soul. By martyr is understood any one who dies in war against the infidels. *Thus a soldier who dies after the end of the war, or fighting against rebels, or, according to our school, in consequence of an accident, is not considered as a martyr. †A martyr dying in a state of grave impurity need not be washed. The impurity should be removed, but not the blood from his wounds. His blood-stained garments are the shroud of the martyr. If these are an insufficient covering, they should be supplemented with a shroud of some kind.

Section 4

The grave should always be deep enough to retain the odour of the body and protect it from wild beasts. It is commendable that it should be so deep and wide that the deceased could stand up in it and lie down in it with his whole length. It is better, if the earth is hard enough, that the grave should be hollowed out laterally rather than a simple trench. The corpse is introduced head first, drawn softly by that part of the body, preferably by men, *i.e.* in the first instance by those who have the precedence in the burial service. [In the case of a married woman, the husband has the better right to carry out the deposition, though not to lead in the prayer.] The people who place the corpse in the grave should be of uneven number. The corpse should be laid on the right side, facing the *kibla* and leaning against the wall, with the back supported by a brick or something similar. The entrance of the grave should also be walled with bricks. Those present then throw in three handfuls of sand, and the grave is filled up by means of the shovel. The earth forming the tomb may rise above the level of the ground to the height of a span; ††and it is better that the surface should be plane rather than convex. Two persons are not buried in the same grave except in case of necessity, when the one having most merit must be placed on the side of the *kibla*. Sitting or walking on a tomb is forbidden, and any one wishing to visit it should approach in the same manner as to the living person.

The Sonna has introduced the practice of making visits of condolence before the burial and three days after. A Musulman performs this duty to a fellow-believer by saying:—"God grant you large compensation for the loss you have suffered; may He pour resignation upon your heart; may He pardon the sins of the dead." If it be an infidel whom the Musulman is consoling, he says:—"God grant you large compensation for the loss you have suffered; may He give you the necessary patience"; while an infidel says to a Musulman:—"God pardon the sins of the dead, and pour resignation upon your heart." It is permissible to deplore the loss of any one before and after death; but it is forbidden to compose for this purpose an elegy or a funeral oration containing nothing but an enumeration of the good qualities of the deceased. It is also forbidden to utter lamentable cries, or to manifest extravagant signs of sorrow, as *e.g.* by striking the breast.

[Some special rules are here added:—

1. One should make haste to pay the deceased's debts and execute his testamentary depositions.

2. It is blamable to wish for death in order to avoid some misfortune, but not to avoid something incompatible with religion.

3. The Sonna recommends a sick person to take care of himself and to take medicine; but it is blamable to force any one to do so.

4. Parents and friends of the deceased may kiss his face.

5. There is no objection to making an announcement of the death, in order to call people to the burial service, etc., provided this be not done in the manner practised in the time of paganism.

6. The person performing the funeral ablution should see no more of the body than is strictly necessary for the proper performing of his

duty, and should never look at the shameful parts. Ablution with sand is enough, if circumstances prevent washing the body with water.

7. A person who has incurred a grave impurity, and even a woman during menstruation, can attend to the washing of a corpse; and such persons themselves require after death no greater ablution than any one else.

8. The person entrusted with the ablution of a dead body should be a reliable person. Should he perceive that the deceased had some good quality of body he may mention the fact; but he must not mention any bodily defects, unless for some useful purpose.

9. If two brothers, or two wives, both claim precedence at a funeral, the matter must be decided by lot.

10. An infidel is more competent than a Musulman to preside at the funeral of an infidel relative.

11. It is blamable to use a shroud dyed with red carthamine, or one of an exorbitant price. A piece of material that has been washed is better for this purpose than one which is quite new. A minor is subject to the same rules as an adult, so far as regards the shrouds and cloths to be used at the interment.

12. It is meritorious to use spices for the embalming of the dead; some authorities even regard it as obligatory.

13. A bier should be borne by men only; even if the body be that of a woman.

14. It is forbidden to carry the bier carelessly; or so as to cause apprehension lest the body fall to the ground.

15. It is recommended to carry the body of a woman so as to be concealed from the public gaze, *e.g.* in a coffin.

16. One may not ride, except when returning from the burial.

17. There is no objection to a Musulman attending the funeral of an infidel relative.

18. It is blamable to make a noise, or to light fires, during a funeral.

19. If the dead bodies of Moslems are so mixed with those of infidels that it is impossible to distinguish them all must be washed and prayed for. In this case one may either: (*a*) perform a burial for all at once declaring one's intention of applying it only to the repose of the souls of those who were Moslems; this is considered the better course and was recommended by Shafii himself; or (*b*) pray for each body separately, on the understanding that the prayer is valid only in the case of a Musulman; in this case the formula used is "O God, pardon him, if he was a Musulman."

20. It is requisite for the efficacy of a funeral prayer that the corpse

should first be washed; and it is even blamable to pray before the corpse has been wrapped in a shroud. Consequently no prayer is said for the repose of the soul of a person crushed to death by the fall of a house, whose body cannot be recovered from under the *débris*.

21. When performing a burial service it is not lawful to stand in front of the bier or of the grave. Those two precepts are admitted by our school. The prayer may, however, be said in a mosque. The Sonna insists upon those present being placed in at least three lines.

22. Every person attending a burial service, who has not already prayed for the repose of the soul of the deceased should join the others in doing so; but he need not repeat it if he has already done it.

23. A burial service may not be deferred in order to allow more people to attend.

24. The body of the suicide is washed, and prayer said for the repose of his soul, just as in other cases.

25. When the imam has the intention of accomplishing a prayer for the repose of the soul of a deceased person who is absent, and a person praying under his direction has the intention of praying for the repose of the soul of another whose body is present, or *vice versâ*, the prayer of the latter is valid all the same.

26. It is recommended that corpses be interred in some recognised cemetery. It is blamable to pass the night there.

27. It is also commendable to cover the grave with a piece of cloth of some sort during an interment, even in the case of a man, and to say during the deposition :—"In the name of God, and in accordance with the precepts of the religion of His apostle. God grant him His grace and His blessing."

28. A dead body may not be laid on a carpet; nor may the head be placed on a pillow.

29. It is blamable to place a corpse in a coffin, unless the earth be damp or soft.

30. It is permissible to proceed to a burial at night, and even at an hour in the daytime when it is blamable to pray, provided it be not intentionally chosen, for any other time is better.

31. It is considered blamable to plaster a tomb, to adorn it with a monument, or place inscriptions upon it. Monuments erected in a public cemetery should be demolished.

32. It is recommended :—(*a*) to water the grave, (*b*) to place pebbles as a pavement, (*c*) to mark the position of the head with a stone or a piece of wood, (*d*) to have the graves of relatives together in one spot (*e*) to visit graves. Visiting graves, however, is commendable in men only; in women it is blamable, some authorities even forbidding it

altogether in their case. Others allow women this visit as a right but not as a merit.

33. A person visiting a tomb should pronounce a salutation, recite some portion of the Koran, and invoke the grace of God upon the deceased.

34. It is forbidden to carry a corpse to another town—though some authorities consider it merely blamable—unless the death occurred in the neighbourhood of Mecca or Medina—or, according to a decision of Shafii, Jerusalem—for then it may always be carried into one of these holy cities. All, however, agree that it is forbidden to disinter a body, whether in order to carry it elsewhere or for any other reason, except in case of necessity, *e.g.* if the body has been buried without being washed, or if buried in a misappropriated shroud or piece of ground, or if a valuable object has accidentally fallen into the grave, or if the face of the deceased was not turned towards the *kibla*, etc. †On the other hand, a corpse may not be legally disinterred under the pretext of wrapping it again in a shroud.

35. The Sonna prescribes to those taking part in funerals not to hasten away from the grave as soon as the body is buried, but to wish the deceased person a happy abode.

36. The neighbours should prepare food for the family of the deceased for the first day and night after the interment; one should even persuade the survivors to take something. But it is forbidden to prepare a meal for the hired mourners.

BOOK 5.—ALMS CONTRIBUTION, OR CHARITY TAX

CHAPTER I.—ASSESSMENT ON CATTLE

SECTION 1

ALMS is not obligatory except on cattle properly so called, *i.e.* camels, horned cattle and small cattle; it is not exacted upon horses, slaves or the offspring of small cattle and gazelles. It is not leviable upon camels unless there are at least five. On this number one *shah* is due, on ten camels two *shahs;* on fifteen three *shahs;* on twenty four *shahs;* on twenty-five one she-camel called *bent-makhad;* on thirty-six one she-camel called *bent-labun;* on forty-six one she-camel called *hikka;* on sixty-one one she-camel called *jaza;* on seventy-six two *bent-labuns;* on ninety-one two *hikkas;* on one hundred and twenty-one three *bent-labuns;* and after this on each forty head one *bent-labun,* and on each fifty one *hikka.*

By *bent-makhad* is understood a yearling she-camel; by *bent-labun* a two-year-old she camel; by *hikka* a three-year-old she-camel; and by *jaza* a four-year-old she-camel. By *shah* is understood a young animal; either a yearling lamb (others say six months), or a two-year-old kid (others say one year). †Where a *shah* is due the taxpayer may give a lamb or a kid at his choice, whether the small cattle of the country consists principally of sheep or goats. †Either a male or a female *shah* may be given, and when paying assessment on less than twenty-five camels one may give a camel instead of a *shah.* Instead of a *bent-makhad* one may give a *bent-labun* as the latter is the more valuable. If the only camels one possesses have redhibitory defects, it is as if one had none. And on the other hand the taxpayer is never obliged to give a very valuable animal. †An *ibn-labun, i.e.* a male two-year-old camel may not be given instead of a *bent-labun* or of any she-camel; but a *hikk* or three-year-old male camel may be substituted for a *bent-makhad* or yearling she-camel, †though not for a *bent-labun.*

If the number of camels in a drove be a multiple of both forty and fifty, *e.g.* two hundred, the taxpayer is not, according to our school, obliged to give always four *hikkas;* he may give either four *hikkas* or five *bent-labuns.* Thus the owner of a drove containing only *hikkas* or only *bent-labuns* may give four of the former or five of the latter; while the owner of a drove containing neither may buy, as he prefers, four *hikkas* or five *bent-labuns*. According to some jurists, however, such owner should give those that would be most advantageous for the poor; ††and in any case an owner possessing both is not considered to have paid the assessment if he has given an inferior lot, either by deceiving the inspector, or because the latter has failed in his duty. Otherwise, if the owner has acted honestly and the inspector done his duty, there is no ground for complaint, once the animals have been accepted; †but the difference between the value of the animals given and what was due must be made up, either in money or, according to some authorities only, in kind. The taxpayer who is liable for a *bent-makhad*, but has none, though he has a *bent-labun*, may give this latter and take back two *shahs* or twenty *drahms;* if he is liable for a *bent-labun*, and does not possess one, he may either give a *bent-makhad* and also two *shahs* or twenty *drahms*, or give a *hikka* and take back two *shahs* or twenty *drahms*. The right of choosing between *shahs* and *drahms* belongs to the payer. The taxpayer may always in these circumstances decide whether to give a *hikka* and take back its excess value over the *bent-labun* he was owing, or to give a *bent-makhad* plus the difference between its value and that of a *bent-labun*. Only he must not give an animal having redhibitory defects. The taxpayer has even the right :—

1. To give she-camels two degrees more valuable than what is required, *e.g.* a *hikka* instead of a *bent-makhad*, and to take back the double excess, *i.e.* four *shahs* or forty *drahms;* or

2. To give she-camels two degrees less valuable than what is required, *e.g.* a *bent-makhad* instead of a *hikka*, plus the double deficit, *i.e.* four *shahs* or forty *drahms;* †both on condition that *bent-labuns* cannot be procured.

According to the best opinion there is no excess if a *thaniya* or five-year-old she-camel is given instead of a *jazaa* or four-year-old she-camel. [†On the contrary, nearly all authorities admit that there is an excess in such a case.]

One cannot supply the deficit nor take back the excess of one degree of value, by giving or taking one *shah* and ten *drahms* instead of two *shahs* or twenty *drahms;* but if it is a difference of two degrees one may give or take either four *shahs* or forty *drahms* or two *shahs* and twenty *drahms*.

As to horned cattle the levy is void on less than thirty head. Of thirty one *tabia* or yearling calf is taken. If there be more than thirty head in the herd a *tabia* is taken for each thirty, and a *mosinna* or two-year-old calf for each forty. Nothing is taken from small cattle in less number than forty. On forty, one *shah* is levied ; on one hundred and twenty-one, two *shahs ;* on two hundred and one, three *shahs ;* on four hundred, four *shahs ;* and on each additional hundred, one *shah.*

SECTION 2

Where a flock or herd consists of animals of the same kind the ordinary levy is made with this modification that, taking due count of their respective values, a kid may be exchanged for a lamb, and *vice versâ,* as they are both included in the word *shah.* But if the animals are of different kinds, *e.g.* sheep and goats, the assessment is made, according to one jurist, on the more numerous kind ; or, if the two kinds are in equal number, on that which is the more advantageous for the poor. *According, however, to the majority of authorities, the taxpayer may in these circumstances give whichever kind he prefers, taking due count of their respective value and number. If, for instance, there are thirty goats and ten sheep, the assessment, according to this theory, is one goat or one sheep, provided the value of the animal given is equal to three-quarters of the average value of a goat, plus quarter of the average value of a sheep. A sick animal, or one with redhibitory defects is not sufficient, unless there are none but animals of this sort. Neither is a male animal accepted except in the two following cases :—

1. If, as we have already mentioned in the preceding section, the law insists upon its acceptance.
2. †If there are none but males.

If there are none but little ones, one must be contented with such, according to the opinion maintained by Shafii in his second period. One may not take for the assessment a ewe that has just lambed, nor an animal that is being fatted, nor one in calf, nor one of exceptional value, without the owner's consent.

Cattle belonging to two joint owners is taxed as if it belonged to a single individual. This is also the case where two neighbours have mingled their flocks or herds ; provided there is no separation between the animals of the two owners, either at the watering-place, the meadow. the stable, or the place where they are milked ; †and provided there is only one herdsman, and one male animal for breeding purposes. †It does not matter whether the flocks or herds were mingled intentionally or accidentally. *In the case of fruit, grain, precious metals and merchandise, it is taken as indicating that the owners have mixed their respective quantities, if they have jointly the same overseer, threshing-floor, shop, caretaker, store, etc.

There are two other essential conditions for the tax on cattle being due—

1. That the property has been in one's possession for a whole year. This rule admits of one exception. In the case of a flock or herd of which the original number already reached the *nisab* or taxable minimum, the new-born animals become taxable in the year of their birth; but animals added by purchase, etc., become so only in the year following. The declaration of births made by the owner at the end of the year is presumed to be correct, and it is only in case of grave suspicion that he may be required to confirm his declaration on oath. If during the year one loses possession of some head of cattle and replaces them later in the year, or if an exchange of cattle of the same kind takes place between two owners, the yearly period for the purpose of taxation begins only from the date of acquisition.

2. That the cattle have been turned out to graze; for there is no ground for the tax if the animals have passed most of the year in the stable. †Even cattle fed in the stable for half the year or less are taxable only if the owner turned them out to graze also during this period, and if the fodder given in the stable was comparatively in such small quantity that the animals could have gone without it and been hardly the worse.

In default of these two conditions the tax cannot be levied. †Cattle is also not considered taxable if: (*a*) it is turned out to graze separately; or (*b*) it is, though grazing, fed with hay, etc.; or (*c*) it is used to plough or irrigate the land.

If the animals are accustomed to go down together to the watering-place, the assessment takes place while they are all there; otherwise in the stables or enclosures of the respective owners. An owner whose moral character inspires confidence is believed on his word when he declares the number of his taxable animals; otherwise this presumption does not exist, and the animals must be counted, after having them driven into some narrow space.

CHAPTER II.—ASSESSMENT ON PRODUCE

This tax is limited to plants fit for food, such as, among fruit, dates, and grapes, and among grains and vegetables, wheat, barley, rice, lentils and other such commonly eaten products. According to Shafii's earlier opinion it is levied also on olives, saffron, *wars*, carthamine, and honey.

The *nisab* or taxable minimum of produce is five *wask*, which is equal to sixteen hundred *ratal* of Baghdad, or, according to the measure of Damascus, to three hundred and forty-six *ratal* and two-thirds. [†This last amount is three hundred and forty-two *ratal* and six-sevenths, †as the *ratal* of Baghdad is one hundred and twenty-eight *drahms* and four-sevenths. Some authorities reject the four-sevenths, and according to others one hundred and thirty *drahms* is the proper estimate.]

When dates or raisins are intended to be dried, the weight is not estimated until after they have been so dried ; otherwise the weight of dates or grapes is ascertained immediately after the plucking. Grain and vegetables are weighed without chaff, etc., while the minimum taxable of those that remain enveloped, such as rice and *alas*, is ten *wask* instead of five. In determining the quantity of produce taxable those of different nature may not be combined, but those of different species may. The taxpayer is in this case assessed on the total, taking count of the respective quantities of each kind. If this is impossible one takes the mean. Thus the *alas* may be combined with ordinary wheat, of which it is a species, and the assessment made on the total; but the *solt* is a distinct plant, though some jurists maintain it to be a species of barley and others a species of wheat. The fruit and other taxable produce of a particular year may not be combined with that of the year following, but those of the same year must always be totalled, even if the harvest be in different seasons. However, according to some jurists the totalling of the fruit of a whole year is not necessary where some only begin to grow after the gathering of others ; but even these authorities agree that the rest of the produce of a single year must in all cases be combined. *By fruits of the same year is understood all produce gathered in that year, irrespective of the time it was sown or began to grow.

In the case of land irrigated only by rain—or in no need of artificial irrigation, the roots of trees and plants obtaining moisture by the proximity of water—the assessment on produce is one-tenth of the crop ; but fields irrigated by means of tanks or water-wheels, or with water that has been paid for, are assessed at only half this rate. ††Water brought in conduits is regarded legally as rain-water. Where the irrigation is half natural and half artificial the assessment is three-fourths of the tenth. Where one kind predominates, it should be regarded, according to one jurist, as being the sole kind ; *others, however, think an inquiry should be made as to which has contributed the more to the growth of the trees and plants ; while others are of opinion that the number of times irrigation of each kind has taken place should be considered.

The tax is due on the appearance of signs of maturity in the case of fruit, and in the case of other produce at the moment the grain begins to harden. It is then that the Sonna has introduced the practice of making a valuation of the fruits and determining the amount due by the owner. **This valuation should include all the trees and can be made by a single expert, who should be a †free man of irreproachable conduct.

*After the valuation, the portion of the poor is separated from that of the owner, who should hand over the former as soon as the drying is finished. According to our school this obligation should be explicitly notified to the proprietor, who should declare his assent to it; though some authors consider that the separation of the two parts is legally accomplished by the mere fact of valuation. In any case the owner is responsible only for the amount of his assessment and not for the delivery of particular fruit, and so may still sell the total yield of his garden. An owner who alleges that fruit has been lost to him after valuation, either in some obscure way as by theft, or in some visible accidental manner of public notoriety is presumed to be correct if he takes an oath to that effect. If, on the other hand, he alleges as the cause of the loss something which, though visible in its nature, is not of public notoriety, ††he must first of all establish its existence in general, and only when this has been done can his oath be accepted to the effect that the calamity in question has injured his garden in particular. Should the owner complain of injustice on the part of the expert, or that the latter has combined produce of dissimilar kinds, his assertion cannot be accepted, †except in the case of some kinds of produce which, though different, can easily be confused.

CHAPTER III.—ASSESSMENT ON GOLD AND SILVER

The *nisab* or taxable minimum of silver is two hundred *drahms*, and that of gold twenty *mithkal*, of the standard weight in use in Mecca. One-fortieth is levied on each of these precious metals; but debased gold and silver are not taxable, unless the quantity of pure metal amounts to the *nisab*. Where a vessel or other object is composed of gold and silver in two unequal parts, the proportion of the two parts themselves being known, but it not being known which is gold and which is silver, the vessel is assessed as if it were composed of a quantity of gold equal to the larger part and also of a quantity of silver equal to that larger part, unless the owner prefers to have the metals separated.

The tax is levied on illicit ornaments and other objects of gold and silver, *but not on such as may legally be used. Among illicit objects are reckoned gold and silver vessels, and also chains and bracelets if belonging to a man who has obtained them in order to wear them.

†But if a man buys a bracelet or other ornament, without intending to wear it, or in order to lend it to a woman who can lawfully wear it, he is not liable to pay tax on it. The same is the case with a man who has bought a broken ornament to mend and sell. A man may not lawfully wear gold, except at the nose or the end of a finger, if these have been mutilated. Gold may also be applied to the teeth to prevent their becoming loose. But if a man has lost a finger he may not replace it by one in gold; neither may he wear a ring in which the jewel is attached by means of small gold hooks. As to silver the law permits a man to wear it in the form of a ring, and to adorn with it his weapons and accoutrements, such as a sword, lance, or belt; †but he may not ornament with silver what he does not himself carry, his saddle or bridle. This of course does not apply to women, who may lawfully wear all sorts of ornaments both in gold and silver, †as well as stuffs embroidered with threads of the precious metals. †Only they should abstain from adorning themselves with gold or silver in an excessive and prodigal manner, wearing for instance a chain of the weight of two hundred *dinar*, a restriction which is applicable also to the ornamentation of weapons and accoutrements. †A man may possess a Koran adorned with silver, a woman one ornamented with gold.

Lastly, it is an essential condition for the tax on the precious metals becoming due that the owner should have had possession of them for a whole year.

Pearls and precious stones are not taxable.

CHAPTER IV.—ASSESSMENT ON MINES, TREASURE AND MERCHANDISE

Section 1

On gold or silver extracted from a mine one-fortieth is due. One jurist says a fifth; another a fortieth if there is difficulty in the extraction, otherwise a fifth. Our school admits only the imposition of the *nisab* or minimum mentioned in the last chapter for each of the two precious metals, without possession for a whole year being necessary.

The quantities extracted are added together in order to determine the total amount to be assessed, if the exploitation has been uninterrupted; but it is not necessary that it should have been continually remunerative, this at least is the opinion adopted by Shafii in his second period. A forcible interruption is considered as no interruption, and so the quantities extracted may still be combined; but this is not permissible in the case of a voluntary interruption. In other words one cannot add what the mine has already produced to what is extract subsequently, except to determine if the latter has reached the taxable minimum. This principle applies to all taxable precious metals, whether they come from a mine or not.

**On discovered treasure a fifth should be paid by way of assessment, according to our school, provided the amount is not less than the taxable minimum, and that it consists of coin. A whole year's possession is not necessary. By treasure is understood a hoard buried in the time of Paganism. A discovered hoard, dating from a period when Islam had already been introduced into the locality, belongs to the owner who buried it. If the owner is unknown, it becomes simply lost property, and the finder must then conform to the rules which will be given when treating of that subject. The hoard is considered to be lost property when it is not known if it was buried before or after the conversion of the country to Islam. One becomes owner of the treasure and owes assessment on it only if it was discovered on an uncultivated portion of the public domain, or when clearing an uncultivated portion of one's own property. A hoard discovered in a mosque or on the public road is regarded simply as lost property, whatever may be its date, at least according to our school. Treasure discovered on the property of another belongs to the actual proprietor if he claims it, otherwise to the previous holder and so on and ultimately to the original owner. In case of dispute between seller and purchaser, landlord and tenant, or borrower and lender, the presumption is in favour of the actual occupier provided he confirms the truth of his assertion on oath.

Section 2

Assessment on merchandise depends on two conditions—possession for a whole year, and attainment of the *nisab* or minimum taxable value. This latter is the same as for the precious metals, and should be the value obtaining *at the end of the year, or according to the opinion of one jurist both at the beginning and end of the year—or as another thinks, throughout the whole year. †If goods are sold in the course of the year for an amount less than the *nisab*, and other goods bought with the money, possession dates from the purchase. †If at the end of the year the value of goods is under the *nisab*, one owes nothing for that year, and begins to reckon another. Objects acquired in order to profit by their exchange are regarded as merchandise, whether obtained by purchase †or as dower or as compensation for divorce, but not when obtained by gift, nor when consisting only of firewood gathered in the forest, nor when taken back after sale in consequence of redhibitory defects.

When goods are bought for a sum of money which is itself taxable, the year's possession is reckoned from the date of obtaining the money; but if the amount is under the *nisab*, or if goods are acquired by exchange for other goods already in one's possession, the year begins only from the date of purchase. Some authorities, however, admit an exception to this rule when taxable cattle are given in exchange for goods, in which case duration of ownership of the cattle is added to duration of ownership of the goods. Profit obtained in the course of the year by sale or exchange is added to capital if this profit consists of goods and not coin; *otherwise it is not included in the total taxable. †All increase of merchandise, whether by animals in which one trades giving birth to young, or by trees bearing fruit, is regarded as taxable merchandise, the possession of which dates from that of the original merchandise.

The assessment on merchandise is one-fortieth of the value. When goods are bought for money the price constitutes the real value, whether less than the *nisab* †or not; but where goods are exchanged they must be valued in the money of the place. In this last case, if there are two kinds of money of equal currency, the following distinctions must be drawn:—

1. If the value reaches the *nisab* only when expressed in one of the two kinds, it should be expressed in that kind.

2. If the value reaches the *nisab* when reckoned in either kind, then it should be reckoned in that which is most advantageous for the poor. According to some authorities the taxpayer has the choice.

The value of goods sold is estimated according to the price stipulated; that of exchanged goods is valued in the money current in the place.

Slaves owned for purpose of trade in them are liable both to the tax at the end of the fasting month and also to the ordinary tax on merchandise. In the cattle trade the owner of a herd which reaches the *nisab* either under Chapter I. or as merchandise, owes the assessment under that heading; if the *nisab* is reached in both, then only the tax on cattle is paid. Shafii so decided during his Egyptian period. If at the beginning of a certain year one has become possessed of goods exchanged six months afterwards for a herd of cattle, it is the assessment on merchandise which is payable at the end of the year in question, after which the tax on cattle is payable in due course. This opinion also was adopted by Shafii in his second period.

In a joint stock company a sleeping partner is personally responsible for the tax both on the joint capital and on the profits; at least where it is agreed that the acting partner does not become legally entitled to his share in the profits by the mere fact of drawing up the balance sheet, but only on distribution. †This, however, does not prevent the entire assessment being always based on the total profit, and not on the capital. If, on the other hand, it is agreed that the managing partner becomes legally entitled to his share of the profits by the mere fact of having drawn up the balance sheet, a sleeping partner is responsible only for the assessment on the joint capital and on his part of the profit ; while it is the managing partner who, according to our school, is responsible for his own share.

CHAPTER V.—PAYMENT AT THE END OF THE FASTING MONTH

This tax is due from the night preceding the festival at the end of the fasting month. Those who die after sunset are still liable for it, but not those who are born after that moment. The Sonna does not allow payment to be deferred until after prayer on the festival, and the law absolutely forbids its postponement until the next day after the feast.

An infidel is not subject to this tax at the end of the fasting month, †unless on account of his slave or Moslem relative. A slave is not liable on his own account, but authorities are not agreed upon the case of one undergoing gradual enfranchisement. The partially enfranchised slave owes the tax in proportion to his liberty. The payment is not obligatory for insolvent persons, those *i.e.* who have no more food than is necessary for their subsistence and that of people dependent on them for the day and night of the feast. And, besides, the believer should only pay this contribution after he has supplied the necessary needs of his household.

Any one who owes this payment for the breaking of the fast for himself, owes it also for those dependent on him, though a Moslem owes nothing for an infidel slave, relative, or wife. A slave owes nothing for his wife, nor a son for his father's wife ; though as regards the son this rule is the subject of controversy. *If a husband is insolvent, or a slave, his wife is liable for this payment on her own account, unless she is herself a slave ; †and the master of a female slave owes it for her, if she is married to some one who is free, but poor. [†A free woman married to a slave does not owe this payment on her own account ; such is Shafii's personal opinion.]

When a slave is absent, and his whereabouts is unknown the master still owes the tax for him, according to our school. Some authorities consider it as due only on the return of the slave ; one maintains that under these circumstances the master owes nothing.

†If a person possesses no more than a *saa* of food, he should give what he has in payment for himself. If he has more than a *saa*, he should pay first for himself and then in order for his wife, infant child, father

mother, grown-up child. Now the assessment on food stuffs is one *saa* for each taxable individual, *i.e.* six hundred and ninety-three *drahms* and a third. [†According to the method of calculation adopted in the chapter relating to the assessment on produce, the *saa* is equal to six hundred and eighty-five drahms and five-sevenths.]

The food that is given in alms at the breaking of the fast should be such as is liable to ordinary assessment, *though cheese may also be given. It must be food commonly consumed in the place. Only a few authors maintain it to be enough to give what one has and consumes oneself; and a few others think one may give what one likes. It is permissible to give better food than one has oneself, but not an inferior kind. According to one doctrine quality is determined by price; †but according to the generally received opinion the more substantial food should be looked upon as of superior quality. Thus corn is better than dates or rice, †while dates are inferior to barley but better than raisins. One may give on one's own account a *saa* of some kind of food and for one's relative a *saa* of some superior kind, but the tax is not properly paid by giving for each person a *saa* of different kinds of food. When the people of the place eat various kinds of food so that it is impossible to say which is the most common, the taxpayer may give whatever he thinks best, though the very best kind is to be preferred. †As to the payment due for an absent slave, this must be made in the food of the place where the slave is.

[Grain and vegetables given as payment of the tax at the breaking of the fast must be free from redhibitory defects. A father may legally pay this tax for his infant child from the latter's estate, and similarly for his grown-up son with the latter's consent. One may do it for any one with his consent. When a slave belongs in common to two persons of whom one is solvent and the other insolvent, the solvent owner owes half a *saa*; †if both are solvent but their contributions are of different kinds, each gives half a *saa* of food, without regard to the particular kind given by the other.]

CHAPTER VI.—PERSONS AND OBJECTS LIABLE TO ASSESSMENT

Section 1

The tax is due only from a free Moslem proprietor. It is, however, due from an apostate, if he does not legally forfeit his property by the mere fact of apostacy. But it is not due from a slave undergoing gradual enfranchisement. It is levied from—

1. The property of a minor, a lunatic, †and a slave partially

enfranchised; provided in the latter case that what belongs to him as a free man is not below the *nisab* or taxable minimum.

2. Property usurped by another, strayed camels, and goods deposited with a person who denies the deposit—all these only on recovery.

3. Property purchased, even before possession has been taken; though according to others the tax on such property is the subject of controversy, as also in the case of the second category.

4. Property in another town. The assessment on this is due immediately, if there is full power to dispose of it; otherwise it is treated as in 2.

5. Debts due to one. A debt relating to a certain quantity of cattle, and a debt which cannot be exacted, such as that due to a master from a slave undergoing gradual enfranchisement, are not subject to assessment. In his first period Shafii extended this principle to all debts due to a person, whether relating to goods or money; but during his Egyptian period he drew a distinction in this respect between a debt which can be immediately exacted and one which is due only at a fixed date. The tax on the former is due at once, except when the debt cannot be recovered owing to the insolvency of the debtor, etc.; otherwise it is regarded as coming under the second category; though some authors think the assessment is due even before the debtor has satisfied his obligation. *The fact of being a debtor does not prevent one's being due for the tax on one's property; though according to one opinion assessment cannot be insisted on in the case of so-called "hidden" property owed to others, *i.e.* precious metals and merchandise. *An exception, however, must be made in the case where a person's debts are so considerable that the judge has been obliged to declare him bankrupt, and that he has remained in a state of legal incapacity for a whole year, in which case his property is regarded as coming under the second category, as he has not had the free disposition of it. As to claims on the estate of a deceased person, the tax has preference over a debt to a private individual; though according to one authority the debt has preference, and according to another they are claims of equal importance.

6. Booty obtained in war against the infidel, even before distribution, provided it consist of one and the same kind of taxable property, that those having a claim to it prefer that it should remain in common, and that a whole year has elapsed since this decision. The entire booty is then subject to assessment, whether the share of each of the owners amounts to the *nisab*, or whether the total alone does so; and the tax is paid in the place where the booty was constituted common property.

But if those having a claim to the booty have expressed no wish to keep it in common, it is assessable only after distribution.

7. Marriage dower, *i.e.* when a woman has stipulated, as dower, a definite quantity of a specified taxable kind of cattle, she owes the assessment on it at the end of a year.

*A person who has leased a house to another for four years, at a rate of eighty *dinars* paid in advance, owes assessment only during the tenant's occupation, *i.e.* at the end of the first year he must pay assessment on twenty *dinars*, at the end of the second on twenty for one year and on twenty for two years, at the end of the third on forty for one year and on twenty for three years, at the end of the fourth on sixty for one year and on twenty for four years. According to another opinion assessment on eighty *dinars*, and nothing more, is due at the end of the first year.

Section 2

The tax may be exacted as soon as it is due, *i.e.* as soon as the existence of the taxable property and the categories of persons having claim to it have been ascertained. Such as consists of so-called "hidden" property, *i.e.* precious metals and merchandise may be given personally to those entitled to it; and, according to the opinion maintained by Shafii in his second period, this may even be done in the case of the so-called "visible" property, *i.e.* cattle and produce. This distribution may be effected through an agent, or by the Sovereign, his officials and delegates; *and this latter method is even considered the better, unless the ruler is a tyrant.

An intention of performing one's duty towards God must be expressed by saying: "Here is the portion of my substance which I owe as assessment," or "as legal alms." It is not enough to say, "This is the portion of my substance which I owe," †or "This is legal alms." It is unnecessary to specify the property on which one is paying assessment; but if one does so, the gift counts as assessment on that particular property only. Expression of intention is obligatory on the guardian of a minor or the curator of a lunatic, when paying the tax for those entrusted to their care. †When payment is made by an agent, it is sufficient to express the intention when the amount is handed to him; it is not necessary for the agent to repeat it when paying in at the receiving office. It is, however, preferable that the agent also should himself express an intention, if he personally distributes it to the ultimate recipients. If the distribution is effected through government, the only expression of intention required by law is from the tax-payer, but if this is omitted the act has no value, even if an intention is expressed by the distributing official. †It is only when the assessment is recovered from a refractory taxpayer that expression of an intention is unnecessary on his part and is replaced by that of the ruler or his officer.

Section 3

It is not lawful to pay the assessment before one possesses the taxable minimum, but one may do so before the period of one year has expired, †so long as one is not two years in advance. As to the alms at the breaking of the fast, one may pay it in advance from the beginning of the month of Ramadan, †but not earlier. ††Assessment on fruit may not be paid until signs of maturity have appeared, nor in the case of grain and vegetables until the seeds have begun to harden; but it may then be done immediately. In order that this anticipated payment should be valid the law insists that the owner should remain liable until the end of the year, as it is not till then that the tax is due; it is also necessary that the person who accepts an anticipated share in the proceeds should not lose whatever claim he has at the end of the year. If after such anticipated acceptance a person loses his right to a share in the distribution of alms—even though he should regain it in the course of the year—the anticipation is, according to some authors, nullified. This right, however, is not considered to be lost merely because the person receiving an anticipated share has thereby ceased to be poor.

A taxpayer may only recover what he has bestowed in advance upon a person who appears afterwards to be no longer entitled to alms, if he has reserved to himself this right in all eventualities, †a reservation implied in the words, "This is the alms I owe you, which I give you in advance." †On the other hand, it cannot be recovered if the taxpayer did not state that the payment was in advance, and the person having a claim to it declares that he was not aware of it. †In legal proceedings the presumption is in favour of the recipient, on oath. If a claim for recovery is found good, the person who has received the advance is responsible for the accidental loss of the property delivered, †up to its full value on the day of delivery. †Nothing is due for a diminution in the value. †The separate fruit need not be given back.

A taxpayer who is in arrears is responsible for property due by him for alms, even in case of accidental loss; but not if such loss occurred before the tax was due. *In the case of accidental and partial loss before the due date, the owner owes assessment only on what is left. If the loss was caused through his fault, after a year's possession but before the tax was due, the owner owes the full assessment in spite of the loss, for the assessment adheres to the property as if the recipients were co-proprietors; or, according to one jurist, as if it were secured to them. One author maintains, however, that there is here a stipulated responsibility, not a real right. *The sale of taxable property before paying the assessment is invalid so far as relates to the amount of the tax, but valid for the remainder.

BOOK 6.—FASTING

CHAPTER I.—GENERAL PROVISIONS

SECTION 1

THE fast of the month of Ramadan becomes obligatory, *i.e.* commences, either upon the termination of the thirty days of the preceding month of Shaban, or from the first appearance of the new moon. The testimony of a single irreproachable witness—or of two, according to one authority—is sufficient to establish the fact of this appearance. †If there be only one, he must unite all the requisites of an ocular and unexceptionable witness; so that the testimony of a slave or a woman cannot be accepted. If the fast has been begun on the testimony of a single irreproachable individual, but the moon is not seen for the next thirty days, †the fast must still be terminated after that period, even though the sky may have been cloudless. †A sight of the moon in any place renders obligatory the commencement of the fast in that neighbourhood, but not in places situated at a great distance. By great distance is understood a distance which permits of the abridgment of prayer, or, according to others, a distance that causes an appreciable difference in the rising of the heavenly bodies. [†The latter opinion is the better.]

When, by reason of the above rules, the fast is not yet obligatory in a certain place, †a traveller, arriving from a place where the moon has already been seen, should conform to the local observance. And he should act in the same way on arrival at a place where the moon has already been seen, coming from one where it has not yet been observed. But if in this way on arrival at a place he celebrates with the inhabitants the feast at the end of the fasting month, he must make up afterwards for the day's fasting he has thus omitted. †A passenger on a ship leaving on the morning of the feast and arriving the same day at a distant place where the inhabitants have not yet terminated the fast, should conform to the local observance during the rest of the day.

SECTION 2

The intention is an essential condition for the validity of fasting. For the obligatory fast it should be formulated before the end of each night; ††without, however, it being necessary to do this in the latter half of the night, or to abstain after having done so from eating and coition. ††If one goes to sleep after formulating it, it is not obligatory to renew it on awaking. As to a supererogatory fast it is enough to formulate the intention on the day selected for the fast, provided the sun has not yet begun to decline; though according to one authority it can be done even later. ††Another doctrine, however, requires that the intention and the other conditions essential for the validity of fasting must in all cases exist from the beginning of the day. In the case of an obligatory fast the intention must have special reference to this fast. The most complete way of expressing an intention for the fast in the month of Ramadan is to use the following words :—"I intend to fast for the coming day, in order to perform my duty towards God, in the month of Ramadan of the present year." With regard to the words "perform," "duty," and "towards God," there is here the same diversity of opinion amongst scholars, as with regard to the formulating of an intention for prayer. ††One can, if need be, omit any special indication of the year, when expressing an intention as to fasting.

When, on the thirtieth night of the month of Shaban, one formulates the intention of beginning next day the fast of Ramadan, provided it is then the first of that month, the fast accomplished that day counts for that of the first of Ramadan only if one had reason to think that it would be the first day of that month, if *e.g.* the moon's appearance had been asserted by a slave, a woman or minors of sufficiently developed intelligence. For these persons, though incapable of furnishing legal proof of the moon's appearance, can render it probable, if they are otherwise worthy of confidence. In default of such reason for believing that the moon has appeared, a fast accomplished by virtue of the conditional intention above-mentioned is of no value, even if it afterwards appeared that it was really the first day of Ramadan on which one fasted. But if, on the other hand, it is on the thirtieth night of Ramadan that one expresses an intention to fast on the following day, provided it is not the first day of Shawal, this fast is always valid, if the day in question is really in the month of Ramadan.

A believer who is himself unable to ascertain the beginning of the month of Ramadan—if, *e.g.* he is in prison—should do his best to find out indirectly, and then fast for an entire month. If by doing this his fast happens partly to correspond with the ensuing month of Shawal, he is none the less considered to have accomplished his duty, †even if a little late. And if, under these circumstances, he has fasted for an incomplete number of days, while the month of Ramadan that year was a full month of thirty days, he can make up afterwards the single day that is wanting. On the other hand, a believer who in such circumstances begins fasting by mistake before the first day of Ramadan, must all the same continue fasting for the whole of that month, if this is still possible when he perceives his error. Otherwise, according to the opinion adopted by Shafii in his second period, he should repeat the fast afterwards, by way of reparation, as soon as he has perceived his error.

A woman, even when undergoing menstruation, may lawfully formulate during the night an intention to fast next day, and subsequently accomplish that act of devotion, provided that bleeding ceases before dawn, and provided also that in that same night the legal time for the menstruation is more than half over, †for the ordinary term of the menses of the woman in question.

Section 3

When fasting, the following abstinences are rigorously prescribed :—

1. Abstinence from coition.

2. Abstinence from vomiting. ††Vomiting nullifies the fast, even if one be sure that nothing coming out of the body has gone back again. Involuntary vomiting does not count, †nor a clearing of the throat followed by a spitting of white froth. As to fluids descending from the head into the mouth they must be rejected, †for if kept in the mouth or swallowed the fast is broken.

3. Abstinence from allowing anything whatever to enter what is understood by the interior of the body. Some authorities consider that the fast is not broken unless the body has strength to digest what is thus introduced as nourishment or medicine. All authorities agree that introduction into the head, stomach, intestines or bladder breaks the fast; and that it is of no importance whether the introduction takes place by sniffing or chewing or by a clyster, or through some wound penetrating into the stomach or touching the membrane of the brain. †The fast is also broken if one lets any liquid fall, drop by drop, into the ear. There are two other conditions established by the law as being required before the fast can be considered broken. (*a*) Introduction of substances must take place by an opening, and penetrate into the interior of the body. Thus the fast is not broken if oil happens to filter through the pores of the skin into the body, nor if collyrium applied to the eyes leaves a certain taste in the throat. (*b*) This introduction must be intentional. Thus the fast is not broken if a fly or a mosquito or the dust of the road or a little flour siftings enter the body, nor if the saliva is inadvertently swallowed, before it has left its original place of ormation. On the other hand, the fast is broken: (*a*) by tasting saliva

which has re-entered the mouth after leaving it ; (*b*) by putting into the mouth a thread moistened and still wet with saliva ; (*c*) by swallowing saliva mixed with any other substance, or saliva which has become impure. †One may, without breaking the fast, swallow all at once the saliva which has accumulated in the mouth ; but according to our school fluid remaining in the mouth or nostrils after clearing the throat or sniffing and then introduced into the body does break the fast, at least, if it be in considerable quantity, not otherwise. Similarly particles of food between the teeth, carried away by the saliva and swallowed, are of no consequence for the fast, when they cannot be distinguished and removed. Forced deglutition does not break the fast ; but it is broken if one swallows anything which one has been forced merely to take into the mouth. [*This last circumstance does not break the fast any more than the former.] Nor is the fast broken by inadvertently eating something ; †but it is broken if this negligence is often repeated. [†Even in this case the fast is not broken.] And similarly, according to our school, with respect to coition.

4. Abstinence from onanism ; otherwise the fast is broken. It is the same in the case of emission of semen due to touching or kissing a woman, or sharing a bed with her ; but not if it is due to lewd thoughts or looks. It is for this reason that it is blamable to embrace a person during the fast, if one is of a passionate temperament, and in any case it is better not to do so. [†This rule is of rigorous observance.]

The fast is not broken by cupping, or by the application of leeches.

Care should be taken in the evening not to eat until first assured that the sun has set ; †though strictly one may rely upon indirect information as to that fact. In the morning one can eat as long as one has reason to believe that the night is not yet over. [And even if one is doubtful upon the matter.] When one has done one's best to ascertain the proper time for taking one's meal either before the beginning or after the end of the day, but it appears after all that a mistake has been made, that day's fast is nullified. If one has taken some nourishment without thinking of the exact time, and it does not afterwards appear that any contravention has occurred, the fast is nullified in the case of an evening meal, but not in that of a morning one. If one has some food in the mouth on the appearance of the dawn, but immediately rejects it, the fast is not nullified ; and similarly with regard to coition.

Section 4

Essential conditions for the validity of fasting in general are faith, mental lucidity, and absence of menstrues or lochia for the whole day.

††There is no objection to one's sleeping the whole day; *nor is the fast invalid by reason of a state of unconsciousness, provided there be in the day at least one instant's recovery.

Fasting is not permitted on either of the two great annual festivals, nor during the three days called *ayyam-at-tashrik*, at least according to the ideas of Shafii in his second period. †Nor may one accomplish a supererogatory fast on an "uncertain" day, for it is then generally speaking illegal, except to make up for a day of fast which has been neglected, or to accomplish a vow, or when it happens to coincide with a fixed date at which one is in the habit of fasting. The thirtieth day of the month of Shaban is called an "uncertain" day if the appearance of the new moon has been established only by public rumour, or by the testimony of minors, slaves, or persons of notorious misconduct. A day when the moon is invisible by reason of clouds is not an "uncertain" day.

During the month of Ramadan the Sonna recommends—

1. Breaking the fast as soon as possible, by eating some dates, if one has any, or, if not, by drinking a little water.
2. Putting off the meal taken before the fast to the last moment one is sure the prescribed time has not yet come.
3. Abstinence from lying and evil-speaking.
4. Not allowing oneself to be carried away by passion.
5. Bathing before dawn in order to remove all impurity.
6. Not applying cupping glasses.
7. Embracing no one.
8. Not exciting the appetite.
9. Refraining from chewing.
10. Saying, when breaking the fast, "O God, I have fasted to Thy glory; and I now break the fast with food that cometh from Thee."
11. Frequently bestowing alms.
12. Frequently reading the Koran.
13. Withdrawing often into a mosque, especially during the last ten days of the month.

Section 5

The fast of the month of Ramadan is obligatory for every believer provided he be of sound mind, an adult and able to support it. A minor should be exhorted to it from his seventh year, if he is strong enough. A sick person may omit to observe it, if he fears that it may seriously affect his health; and so may a person undertaking a long journey with a lawful object; with this distinction, however, that the exemption of the latter begins only from the second day, that of the former from the moment he falls ill. If in spite of this exemption the traveller or the sick person begins the day with fasting, he may break the fast when he pleases, ††except on arriving at his destination, or on recovery, as the case may be.

Such traveller or sick person must, after breaking the fast, make up afterwards for the days omitted. A similar duty lies upon the following persons :—

1. A woman who has her menses during the fast.
2. Any person who breaks the fast without lawful excuse.
3. Any person who forgets to formulate an intention before fasting.
4. Any person who is unconscious for at least one whole day.
5. An apostate. But the born infidel who is converted need not make up for the days on which he would have fasted, had he been a Moslem.

There is no obligation to make up for a neglect due to minority or madness. †A minor who attains puberty on a day begun fasting should finish that day fasting, and that is all that is necessary. If he has begun the day not fasting, it is not necessary to make up for it. †It is the same with a lunatic who has come to his senses, or a converted infidel, these also being exempt from any obligation to fast on the day of the change, unless it was already begun fasting. On the other hand, the omission must be made up for afterwards by any one who improperly breaks a fast, or forgets to formulate an intention, but not by a traveller or sick person whose cause of exemption has ceased after the breaking. Our school goes so far as to extend this rule to the case where the cause of exemption has ceased before a breaking of the fast by a traveller or a sick person, unless on the preceding night a special intention was formulated to fast next day. It is necessary to make up for the lost day, if one has taken anything on an "uncertain day" which turns out afterwards to be a day of the month of Ramadan.

Abstinence from anything that breaks the fast, during the rest of a day on which the fast has already been broken, is a feature peculiar to the month of Ramadan ; it is not required when fasting in consequence of a vow, or to make up for a lost day.

Section 6

A person dying before he has been able to make up for days of fast of the month of Ramadan omitted by reason of a valid excuse, owes nothing by way of reparation, as no contravention can be imputed to him. But if, on the other hand, he had been in a position to make up for the days lost, there must be deducted from his estate, by way of expiatory fine, a *modd* of foodstuff for each day. Shafii, in his second period, abandoned the doctrine that the *wali*, or representative of the deceased, should accomplish the fast in his place. This rule applies also to a fast in consequence of a vow or by way of expiation. [*The original doctrine of Shafii is preferable, understanding by *wali* in this connection any relative, agnate or cognate, without distinction of sex or degree. Even a person who is not of the deceased's family can accomplish this fast, †not of his own accord but with the authorisation of the *wali*. It is not necessary after a death to accomplish a prayer or a spiritual retreat left undone by the deceased, nor to replace these acts of devotion by any expiatory fine paid out of the estate. One jurist, however, pronounces in favour of the obligation to accomplish a spiritual retreat neglected by the deceased.]

*An expiatory fine of a *modd* of foodstuff per day is due also from a person who abstains from fasting on account of advanced age. If a pregnant woman, or one who is suckling an infant, omits fasting for the sake of her own health, she should make up for it afterwards; but she owes nothing in the way of fine. *If, however, she omits it for fear of hurting the health of the child, she must not only make up for it afterwards, but pay an expiatory fine in addition. †These principles with regard to a suckling woman apply also to any other person who breaks the fast in order to avoid imminent danger; but not to the believer who breaks the fast of the month of Ramadan without a definite lawful excuse. We shall speak in the following section of the breaking of the fast by coition.

The believer who has to make up for a fast neglected in the month of Ramadan but who unnecessarily defers this act of devotion until the next Ramadan, owes also an expiatory fine of a *modd* of foodstuff for each day, multiplied by the number of years the accomplishment of this duty has been put off. And if, under these circumstances, the believer dies, without having made reparation for his fault, though able to have done so, there must be levied from his estate an expiatory fine of two *modd* for each day of fast neglected, *i.e.* one for the contravention and another for having deferred the reparation.

The expiatory fine is given to the poor and the indigent. Several *modd* may be given to the same individual. The foodstuffs given are the same as those given for the tax at the end of the fast.

Section 7

Expiation properly so called, and not merely an expiatory fine, is obligatory if one has violated the fast on a day of the month of Ramadan by intentionally indulging in coition, which is considered under the circumstances not only as a contravention but as an immoral act. Expiation is therefore not obligatory in the following cases :—

1. When one has indulged in coition forgetting that it was a fast day.

2. When one has violated in this manner a fast other than that of the month of Ramadan.

3. When one has broken the fast of the month of Ramadan by some act other than coition.

4. When one has indulged in coition during a voyage, intending to use one's right to break the fast, †or otherwise.

5. When one has indulged in coition under the erroneous impression that it was still night.

6. When one has indulged in coition, after having eaten through forgetfulness, and thinking the fast had so been broken, even though this idea was erroneous, and the fast was really broken by the coition.

7. When, forgetful of the fast, one has committed the crime of fornication ; or in the case of a traveller who has broken the fast in this way, wishing to use his right to sleep with a woman, without first ascertaining whether she was prohibited for him or not.

Expiation for coition is due by the man who has indulged in it ; or, according to one jurist, by the man and the woman together ; though, according to another, each is separately liable for the entire expiation. Expiation is also obligatory for the unbeliever who, after seeing the new moon, indulges in coition on one of the following days, even if he be the only person who has seen it and the other people of the place have not yet begun their fast. The expiation must be repeated as many times as there are broken fast days, and it remains none the less obligatory though a voyage is begun immediately afterwards. Our school extends this principle to the case of illness, though in other respects both traveller and sick person may break the fast when they please. ††Expiation has no effect upon the obligation to make up for the broken fast days.

Expiation consists in the freeing of a slave. If one has no slave, one must fast for two consecutive months ; and if one is not capable of this, one must feed sixty indigent persons. *If all three methods are impossible, the transgressor remains personally liable for the expiation of his fault, which he must accomplish as soon as he has the means of doing so. †One may always discontinue a fast undertaken by way of expiation, and substitute for it the feeding of indigent persons, when assailed by violent sexual desire. †A poor man may not lawfully give to his family what he owes by way of expiation.

CHAPTER II.—SUPEREROGATORY FASTING

THIS fast is recommended by the Sonna on : (1) Monday ; (2) Thursday ; (3) the day of Mount Arafa ; (4) the *aashura*, or 10th day of the month of Muharram ; (5) the *tasua*, or 9th day of the same month ; (6) the days called " white days," *i.e.* the 13th, 14th, and 15th of each month, because the moon is then full ; and (7) six days of the month of Shawal, at one's choice, but preferably six consecutive days.

It is blamable : (1) to choose a Friday or Saturday for a supererogatory fast, except when fasting for several consecutive days ; (2) to undertake a perpetual fast, if one fears to incur thereby some injury to person or property ; otherwise it is commendable. But a perpetual fast may not include the two great annual festivals, nor the three days called *ayyam-at-tashrik*."

A person who undertakes voluntarily a supererogatory fast or prayer may stop when he pleases without making any reparation ; but when one has begun an additional fast to make up for some neglect, this act of devotion must be completed. This must be done both in the case where immediate reparation is necessary, *i.e.* where an obligatory fast has been broken without lawful excuse ; †or where the neglect need not be immediately made up for, as when the fast is broken in any other manner.

BOOK 7.—RELIGIOUS RETIREMENT

Section 1

This retirement is always commendable, but particularly upon the ten last days and nights of Ramadan, in order to include if possible the "night of power," believed to be the twenty-seventh. Shafii, however, inclined to think that this night is that of the twenty-first or twenty-third.

The retreat can only be accomplished in a mosque, preferably a *jama masjid.* In his second period Shafii maintained that a woman cannot perform this act of devotion in her private chapel, *i.e.* the room of her house specially set apart for family prayer. If one has vowed to undertake a retreat in *masjid-al-haram* at Mecca, it is there that it should take place; and similarly if a vow is made to accomplish a retreat in the great mosque at Medina or in the *masjid-el-aksa* at Jerusalem. The mosque at Mecca may be substituted for that at Medina or Jerusalem, but not *vice versâ.* In the same way the mosque at Medina may be substituted for that at Jerusalem, but not *vice versâ.*

† It is necessary to remain in the mosque long enough to be able to say one has sojourned there; though according to some jurists it is enough to have passed through the edifice without stopping, while others insist on a stay of at least one day.

Coition nullifies a retreat. So does any voluptuous contact, *e.g.* touching or kissing a woman, if any lascivious feeling is thereby provoked, but not otherwise. Coition in forgetfulness of the retirement is subject to the same rules as in regard to the fast. On the other hand, there is no objection to using scent and ornament, and taking nourishment during a retreat. One may also enter into retirement during the night only. A vow "to undertake a retreat on a fast day" is obligatory as is also a vow "to undertake a retreat fasting," or "to fast in retirement." †In all these cases the two acts of devotion must be combined.

Religious retirement requires a previous intention which, where the retreat is the consequence of a vow, is formulated in the same way as an intention for a necessary act of devotion. If the retirement has no previously fixed term, the intention to undertake a retreat is enough, however long may be the stay in the mosque. If the devout person leaves the mosque intending to return to it, the intention must be formulated anew, even if at the beginning the intention was for a definite time. But if one left the mosque in order to satisfy a want of nature a renewal of intention is not rigorously necessary. Some authors, however, insist on the intention being renewed in all cases where the mosque is left for a long time, without reference to the motives of this absence; while others consider no such obligation exists at all. If one has vowed an uninterrupted retirement for a definite time, but afterwards quits the edifice for a valid reason, the retreat cannot be regarded as interrupted, and there is no need to renew the intention. Other jurists, however, insist on the intention being renewed, even in these circumstances, after each absence not necessitated either by a want of nature or by bathing to remove some grave impurity.

Religious retirement can be lawfully accomplished only by a sane Moslem free from grave impurity—including, in the case of a woman, menstruation. A retreat is nullified by apostasy, or drunkenness, both of which, according to our school, are retro-active. But madness and loss of consciousness supervening during retirement have no such effect upon what has already been accomplished, unless the person has been carried out of the mosque. The time passed by the believer in the mosque in a state of unconsciousness is considered as part of the retreat, but this is not so in the case of madness, or menstruation obliging the person to quit the edifice. A state of grave impurity also necessitates the believer quitting the mosque, if he cannot take a bath on the premises; if he can, it is not necessary for him to leave for this purpose though it is permissible. The time during which menstruation or any grave impurity continues must be deducted from the period of retreat.

Section 2

A vow to enter a state of retirement for a fixed time without interruption should be accomplished; ††but continuity is not obligatory, unless expressly declared. ††But a vow of a retreat "for a day" may not be divided up into twenty-four hours on different days. The believer who vows a retreat for a definite period only, *e.g.* a week, and who accomplishes it partially, but uninterruptedly, should observe continuity if obliged to make up afterwards for his omission; but, on the other hand, the person who has not begun continuously is not obliged to continue so later, when making up for any lost days. *It is lawful to undertake an uninterrupted retreat, reserving a right to leave the mosque in case of any unforeseen occurrence; and it is not necessary then to make up for lost time. This last rule, however, presupposes that the retreat is to expire at a fixed date, *e.g.* "at the end of the month," otherwise lost time would have to be made up for.

Continuity is interrupted by any exit without valid excuse; though it is understood that there is no objection to one limb of the body being outside the edifice, or to leaving it in order to answer a call of nature. For the latter purpose one may go to one's own house, even if at a considerable distance, †if not too far. The believer who leaves in order to answer a call of nature, and falls ill on his return to the mosque, does not diminish the virtual effect of his act of devotion, if the interruption was short, and he followed the same road. Neither is continuity interrupted if one leaves the mosque for the following reasons:—

1. In consequence of some malady obliging one to leave.
2. In consequence of menstruation; at any rate in the case of a long period of retirement. *On the other hand, there is interruption from this cause, if the period of retirement was so short that a woman is ordinarily free during this interval.
3. Through forgetfulness, at least, according to our school.
4. †In order to go to a minaret, isolated from the principal edifice, and perform one's duties as muezzin.

After these exits and absences from the mosque it is necessary to make up later for the time lost; except when the mosque is quitted in order to answer a call of nature, for then it is never necessary to compensate for the interruption.

BOOK 8.—THE PILGRIMAGE

CHAPTER I.—GENERAL PROVISIONS

THE *hajj*, or pilgrimage, *and the *omra*, or visit to Mecca, are obligations towards God which can be accomplished only by Moslims. The guardian puts himself into a state of *ihram* for his pupil, and the curator for the lunatic entrusted to his care, for one cannot do this for oneself if unable to understand the nature of this act of devotion. As to the obligatory pilgrimage and visit, a journey to Mecca can never count for one or the other, unless one has put oneself into a state of *ihram* on one's own account, *i.e.* unless one is a free, sane, adult Moslem. So the poor man is capable of it, but not the minor or the slave.

The obligation to accomplish the pilgrimage or the visit exists only for such believers as are not only capable of legally performing it but also in condition of doing so personally or by intermediary. As to the power of accomplishing this act of devotion in person, it depends on four conditions—

1. Possession of a sufficient quantity of provisions, sacks and money for the voyage there and back. Some authors do not insist on possession of funds for the return journey, if family or near relatives are not left behind at the place from which one starts. A man who gains only enough to live from day to day is not obliged to go to Mecca if the distance be great; but if the distance be short and enough is gained on one day to support him for several the journey is obligatory.

2. Possession of a mount, if the distance from Mecca is two days' journey. If one cannot ride without a great deal of difficulty, one need not go unless in a pannier, if one can find a companion to occupy the other half. Any person who lives at a less distance from Mecca than two days' march, and who can walk, must make the pilgrimage, even if afoot; but if he is too feeble for such an undertaking, he is considered in the same way as a person living at too great a distance. Before such a journey can be looked upon as obligatory, the law insists also that provisions for the nourishment of self and mount must be the property of the pilgrim, and that he has not acquired them to the prejudice of his creditors, or of persons he has to support during his absence. †In the same way the expenses of the pilgrimage may not be deducted from

those of the pilgrim's household nor from what he has to give to a slave whom he needs as a servant. †But he is obliged, if necessary, to sell his merchandise to defray the expense of the pilgrimage, if by so doing he is enabled to take his journey to the holy city.

3. The security of the road. The pilgrimage is not obligatory if danger is feared for person or goods, from wild beasts, enemies or brigands, unless one can take a safer road. *One should go by sea, if that way seems the safer; and if necessary pay for an escort. Nor need one go at all unless one can get water and necessary provisions at reasonable prices at the places where travellers usually obtain their supplies. A reasonable price is one considered moderate in that country and at that time. It is also necessary that one should be able to procure forage for one's mount at each stage of the journey. A woman need not go unless accompanied by her husband or by some relative within the prohibited degrees, or by at least three trustworthy females. †The law does not require each woman in a caravan to be accompanied by her husband or a relative. †A woman on pilgrimage should remunerate the individual who accompanies her and who has undertaken the journey solely on her account.

4. Ability to make use of one's mount with no great difficulty. A blind man is exempt from the duty of pilgrimage if he has no guide. The rules just mentioned with regard to a woman's companion, apply also to a blind man's guide. A person who is incapable by reason of imbecility is subject to the same law as any other person, so far as regards the duty of going on pilgrimage to Mecca, except that he is not entrusted with money for the journey, and his curator should accompany him or employ some one else to do so.

Permission to be represented by a substitute at the pilgrimage is granted in the following cases :—

1. When a person dies without fulfilling his obligation of going to Mecca, the pilgrimage should be accomplished by another person for the deceased, defraying the expense out of the estate.

2. When one cannot go to Mecca by reason of paralysis, etc., one's duty is to send a substitute, at least if one is rich enough to pay for such a substitute and can find one at a reasonable price. This remuneration is of course subject to the pecuniary obligations already mentioned as incumbent upon any one who undertakes the pilgrimage in person. But the law does not insist in these circumstances that the maintenance of the family should be assured in advance for the whole period of going to Mecca and returning from it.

†When a son wishes to employ some one to accomplish the pilgrimage for the sake of his father, the person addressed upon the subject is not

obliged to consent—and still less is he bound to comply when approached by some one who is not even a member of the deceased's family. But if a son offers to make the pilgrimage for his father, the latter is bound to accept his offer, or indeed that of any other person.

CHAPTER II.—STATIONS

One should put oneself into a state of *ihram, i.e.* begin the pilgrimage, in the month of Shawal or Zulkada, or on one of the ten first nights of Zul Hijja. As to the permissibility of not putting oneself into a state of *ihram* until the night preceding the feast of sacrifice, authorities are not in agreement. ††If he puts himself into a state of *ihram* on any other month, the believer can only accomplish a visit, an act which can be performed at any time of the year. The pilgrimage takes place only at one fixed time.

The stations at which one must stop in order to put oneself into a state of *ihram* are as follows :—

1. For the inhabitants of Mecca, the holy city itself. According to some authorities all inhabitants of the sacred territory may place themselves in a state of *ihram* at their own domicile.
2. For pilgrims from Medina, Zul Holaifa.
3. For those from Syria, Egypt and the north of Africa, Johfa.
4. For those from Tahama and Yemen, Yalamlam.
5. For those from south or north Nejed, Karn.
6. For those from the east, Zat Irk.

It is preferable to put oneself in a state of *ihram* at the entrance of these stations, although strictly speaking this may even be done when leaving them for Mecca. If the pilgrim does not pass through one of these places, he should place himself in a state of *ihram*, as soon as he arrives in the vicinity of the nearest to his route ; or, if he passes near two of them, †when close to that which is the farther from Mecca. If he passes near none of them, he should place himself in a state of *ihram* when at a distance of two days' march from the holy city. A pilgrim domiciled between the holy city and one of the stations should enter a state of *ihram* at the place where he resides. If a believer passes through one of the stations, not intending to accomplish a pilgrimage, but resolves afterwards to perform this religious duty, he should begin the state of *ihram* at the place where he adopted this decision. But no one arriving as a pilgrim may pass a station without putting himself in a state of *ihram* ; and if he neglects to do so he must go back to the station indicated by law, unless the time for the ceremonies is at hand, or the road is not safe. In these two last cases an expiatory sacrifice must be performed; †but not if the pilgrim duly returns to the station. Unless a pilgrim does so return, an expiatory sacrifice is always due for a neglect to put oneself in a state of *ihram* at the proper station. One can always place oneself in a state of *ihram* on leaving one's domicile, before arriving at one of the stations, and this is indeed the course to be preferred. Only one author maintains it to be better not to put oneself into a state of *ihram* until one's arrival at a station indicated by law. [*This latter doctrine is preferable, and in accordance with authentic traditions.]

The stations for the visit are the same as those for the pilgrimage, on arrival at least from outside the sacred territory. Otherwise, *i.e.* if one is already at Mecca for the pilgrimage, one should first of all proceed to the nearest part of the boundary of the sacred territory, without reference to one's country of origin, then cross this boundary if only by a single pace, and place oneself in a state of *ihram* at this same station. *The believer, however, who has taken part in the ceremonies of the visit, without first recrossing the boundary of the sacred territory in order to renew his *ihram*, may make reparation for his fault by an expiatory sacrifice. According to our school an expiatory sacrifice is not obligatory for those who cross the boundary of the sacred territory after having renewed their *ihram* for the visit. The places most to be recommended for crossing the sacred territory and renewing *ihram* for the visit are: Jarana, then Tanaim, and lastly Hodaibiya.

CHAPTER III.—*IHRAM*, OR STATE OF CONSECRATION

SECTION 1

THE believer who goes to Mecca may put himself into a state of *ihram*—

1. Precisely; by formulating an intention to accomplish the pilgrimage, the visit, or both.

2. Generally; by merely formulating the idea of *ihram*, without special reference to the act to which it is to relate. The precise manner is to be preferred, though one jurist maintains the contrary opinion. The general intention may, during the months of pilgrimage, serve at the believer's choice, either for the pilgrimage, the visit, or both; but one cannot lawfully take part in any ceremony without first making up one's mind upon the subject. †On the other hand, a general intention at any other time of the year applies only to the visit; and never to the pilgrimage, even if one wait until the time prescribed for that duty.

3. By saying—"My *ihram* will be the same as such an one's." If the person indicated did not put himself into a state of *ihram* at all, these words are held to imply a general intention. According, however,

to the opinion of some authorities, such a proceeding has no legal consequence, if the person in question is known not to have put himself into a state of *ihram*. Where the former intention was precise, the later accomplishment must of course be in the same precise manner. If the death of the person indicated prevents the nature of his *ihram* being known, both pilgrimage and visit must be accomplished together in the manner called *kiran*, and part taken in the ceremonies of both.

Section 2

When placing oneself in a state of *ihram*, one should formulate one's intention and pronounce the sacramental words *labaika*, etc. The words without the intention are of no effect; ††but the intention is good, even without the words. The Sonna has introduced the following usages :—

1. Taking a bath when putting oneself in a state of *ihram*; or, if there be no water, having recourse to ablution with sand. The bath is repeated on making one's entry into the holy city; on the occasion of the halt at Mount Arafa; at Mozdalifa on the morning of the feast of sacrifice; and lastly on the three following days, called *ayyam-al-tashrik*, when one repeats the ritual lapidation.

2. To use scent, when putting oneself into a state of *ihram*, both for the body †and for the clothes. There is no objection to one's continuing to wear these perfumed garments after having placed oneself in a state of *ihram*, nor to having about one's person some object that gives an agreeable odour; †but one must not put them on again after having once taken them off, under penalty of an expiatory fine.

3. That women should stain the hands red when putting themselves into a state of *ihram*; and that men should put off clothes that are sewn, and put on special garments called *izar* and *rida*, both of white stuff. On his feet a man may only wear sandals.

4. Performing two *rakas*, when putting oneself into a state of *ihram*. But it is preferable to do this latter only when about to continue the journey to Mecca, whether on foot or not; only one author considers that the state of *ihram* should follow immediately upon the two *rakas*.

It is recommended to a person who has put himself in a state of *ihram* to repeat frequently and aloud the words "labaika," etc., especially when changing his position, *e.g.* mounting a horse or dismounting, ascending or descending some elevation, or when rejoining a caravan; but not during the circuit of the Kaba. However, according to the earlier idea of Shafii, the formula is commendable also when making this circuit, provided it is not said aloud. It is composed the following words :—" Behold me, O God, behold me, behold me. No one shareth Thy power. To Thee the glory, the riches, the empire of the world. No one shareth Thy power." On seeing anything astonishing one says : " Behold me, of a truth the true life is that of the other world." After pronouncing this formula the believer adds a prayer for the Prophet, and lastly beseeches God to permit him to enter Paradise to show Himself satisfied with him, and grant him escape from everlasting fire.

CHAPTER IV.—ENTRY INTO MECCA

Section 1

It is preferable—

1. To make one's entry into the holy city before the halt at Mount Arafa.
2. To take a bath at *Zu Tuwa,* if arriving by the Medina road.
3. To make one's entry near the place called *Thaniya Kada.*

On first catching sight of the Kaba or sanctuary one exclaims, " O God, may this temple grow in glory and grandeur, esteem and veneration. May the number of those that extol its greatness and grandeur exceed the number of those that come hither, as pilgrims and visitors, to praise its worth and distinction, its glory and magnificence. O God, salvation cometh from Thee ; make us live in faith." The mosque built round the *Kaba* is then entered by the gate called the Banu Shaiba, and one begins at once to make the circuits called " of arrival." These circuits are specially prescribed for the pilgrim who has made his entry into the holy city before attending the ceremony at Mount Arafa. When one enters the city without any idea of accomplishing a pilgrimage or visit, it is none the less commendable to put oneself into a state of *ihram* for one or other of these acts of devotion. According to one jurist this is even a matter of rigorous observation ; unless one is continually going in and out of Mecca, *e.g.* as a woodcutter or hunter.

Section 2

The circuits, of whatever category they may be, consist of obligatory practices, and of practices introduced by the Sonna.

The obligatory practices are as follows :—

1. To cover the shameful parts.
2. To be exempt from all filth and impurity. Any impurity incurred by the believer during the circuits necessitates ritual ablution or a bath, after which the circuit may be continued from where it was left off.

According to the opinion of one jurist, it must be begun all over again from the beginning.

3. To keep the sanctuary on one's left hand.

4. To begin the circuit from the place in the Kaba inclosing the Black Stone; and to face this stone with all the front of the body each time it is passed. A circuit begun at any other place does not count, and if the believer has in such way arrived at the Black Stone, he should begin a new circuit from there. Neither does a circuit count if one has walked upon the *Shazarwan* or basement of the sanctuary, nor if one has touched the wall of the sanctuary with the hand by stretching out the arm above the *Shazarwan*, nor if one has passed, on one's way, through the two entries of the *Hijr*. However, authorities are not all agreed as to the touching of the wall.

5. To make the circuit of the Kaba seven times, without leaving the mosque that surrounds it.

The practices introduced by the Sonna are as follows:—

1. Making the circuit on foot.

2. Beginning each circuit by touching the Black Stone with the hand, the lips and the forehead. If the crowd of devout people prevents one touching the stone with lips and forehead, it is enough to touch it with the hand and then kiss the hand. If necessary it can suffice to point the finger at the Black Stone.

3. Not touching the corner stones on the Syrian side of the Kaba, *i.e.* those placed at the north and west corners. As to the corner stone on the Yemen side, *i.e.* the south corner, one places one's hand upon it, and then simply kisses the hand.

4. Beginning a circuit by uttering the following formula:—"In the name of God; God is great; O God, I believe in Thee; I declare the truth to be in Thy Book; I trust in that which Thou hast promised; and I conform to the practices of Thy Prophet Muhammad, to whom grant Thy grace and blessing."

5. When opposite the door of the sanctuary pronouncing this formula: "O God, this temple is Thy dwelling; this sacred territory belongs to Thee; the security found here comes from Thee; and this is the place to seek refuge with Thee from fire everlasting." To this formula an invocation may be added if so desired. An invocation believed to have been used by the Prophet is to be preferred to a recitation from the Koran, but not one not so derived.

6. Making the first three circuits in the way called *ramal, i.e.* with short quick steps, and the others at an ordinary pace. This rule is specially to be observed when one is going, immediately after the seven circuits, to perform the ritual walk between the hills Safa and Marwa;

and, according to one authority, when performing the circuits called "of arrival."

7. Saying, during the *ramal*, "O God, may this pilgrimage be looked upon with favour by Thee; may my sins be pardoned; and may the walk that I am about to perform be agreeable to Thee."

8. Wrapping oneself with one's *rida* in the manner called *idtiba*, during the *ramal*; ††as also when executing the ritual walk. The *idtiba* consists in passing the middle of the *rida* under the right armpit, and putting the two ends over the left shoulder, so that the right shoulder is left bare. The *ramal* and the *idtiba* are not prescribed for women.

9. Keeping in the circuits as close to the sanctuary as possible, unless the crowd of devout people prevents the *ramal* being possible, in which case it is better to perform the circuits at a little distance. But if it is feared to come thus into immediate contact with women, it is preferable not to execute the *ramal*, and to perform all the circuits at an ordinary pace, keeping near the Kaba.

10. Performing the successive circuits uninterruptedly.

11. After finishing the circuits, performing two *rakas*, placing oneself behind the *Makam Ibrahim*. The recitation in each consists respectively of Chapters 109 and 112 of the Koran.

When accomplishing the circuits at night, the above-mentioned formulas, etc., are uttered aloud. According to one jurist the last two practices, Nos. 11 and 12, are obligatory, and not merely precepts of the Sonna. When a person in a state of *ihram* is carried round the sanctuary by another not in that condition, the circuit counts for the person carried. The same if the bearer also is in a state of *ihram*, and has already performed the circuits on his own account. †If, however, a person who has not yet accomplished the circuits, though in a state of *ihram*, carries round the sanctuary another in like state, the circuit counts for the person carried if such is the intention of the bearer; but if the latter's intention is to perform the circuit either for himself alone, or for himself and the person carried, the circuit counts only for himself.

SECTION 3

After finishing the circuits and the prayer, one touches the Black Stone with the right hand, and then kisses that hand. Then one leaves the mosque by the gate called the gate of Safa in order to perform the ritual walk, a ceremony which consists in traversing seven times the distance between the hills of Safa and Marwa, beginning at the former. This walk may be taken either just after the final circuits, or after those "of arrival." But it must not be separated from the latter by the halt at Mount Arafa. In any case the walk is only done once; and if accomplished immediately after the circuits "of arrival" it is not repeated again after the final circuits. It is commendable—

1. To mount the hill of Safa and that of Marwa to the height of six feet, saying: "God is great, God is great, God is great; glory to God; God is great for having led us hither, and He is worthy to be praised for His goodness towards us; there is no God but He that is the One, whose power none shareth. To Him be the empire of the world; to Him the glory. It is He, the Beneficent, that giveth life and death from His hand; He is the Almighty." Then one offers up a prayer, either for some spiritual, or for some worldly, benefit. [These glorifyings and prayers are repeated twice or even thrice.]

2. To walk at an ordinary pace at the beginning and end of the road, but to run in the middle. The places where the speed should be altered are indicated.

Section 4

It is recommended that the imam or his substitute should preach a sermon at Mecca on the seventh day of the month of *Zul-Hijja,* after midday prayer. It consists of a single discourse exhorting the congregation to proceed next morning to Mina and obtain information as to the ceremonies about to be performed. Next morning the preacher sets out for Mina, followed by the pilgrims. There they pass the night, and as soon as the sun is risen proceed to Mount Arafa. [The pilgrims do not go straight there, but stop on the way at Namira near Mount Arafa, until the sun begins to decline.]

On Mount Arafa, as soon as the sun begins to decline, the imam preaches two sermons, and then accomplishes with the congregation the midday and afternoon prayers combined. The audience remains there until sunset glorifying God and offering prayer, and uttering many times the confession of faith. After sunset one goes to Mozdalifa and performs evening prayer and the prayer of the night combined, the former being said late.

For the validity of the halt at Arafa, the law insists absolutely that one must actually have been on some part of the mountain bearing that name; even if only for some other reason, as to seek a fugitive slave. It is necessary that one should be capable of taking part in religious ceremonies in general, and not in a fainting condition; while, on the other hand, there is no objection to sleeping upon the sacred mountain. The legal time for the halt at Arafa begins on the day bearing that name, from the moment the sun begins to decline; ††and it lasts until dawn on the next day, called *yum-en-nahr*, or day of the immolation of victims. A person quitting the assemblage on Mount Arafa, and not returning before sunset, owes for this contravention an expiatory sacrifice; but the observance of this precept is merely commendable; only a single author maintains it to be obligatory. If one returns to Mount Arafa before sunset one cannot be blamed, †nor even if it be only during the night. The believers who by mistake have only been on Mount Arafa the tenth day of the sacred month have none the less fulfilled their duty, unless their number was inferior to the number of devout persons ordinarily there at that time, in which case their halt counts only as an act performed late. Those who halt at Arafa on the eighth of the month, and perceive their error before the time prescribed for the ceremony has gone by, should repeat their act of devotion at the legal time. †If they perceive it too late they must still satisfy the requirements of the law by way of reparation.

Section 5

The night is passed at Mozdalifa. A pilgrim who quits this villag before or after midnight has not failed in his duty, provided he return before the dawn. Only the pilgrim who is not there in the second half of the night, owes an expiatory sacrifice; though the necessity of this sacrifice has been considered doubtful as in the case of that already mentioned with regard to Arafa.

The Sonna prescribes that women and weak men should start early for Mina, but not before midnight. The other pilgrims remain at Mozdalifa, and as soon as possible after morning prayer they set out for Mina, taking with them from Mozdalifa pebbles for the lapidation. On arrival at the place called Al Mashar al haram, they halt until dawn, uttering invocations. Then they proceed to Mina, where they arrive a little after sunrise. There each pilgrim must throw seven pebbles on a heap of stones called *jamrat-al-akaba*. During this ceremony the cries of *labaika* are momentarily interrupted, and replaced at each cast by "God is great." Any person who has brought a victim should immolate if after the lapidation.

Next one has one's head shaved or one's hair cut, the former being preferable, though women may content themselves with the second. **This shaving or hair-cutting is an essential part of the ceremonies, whether of a pilgrimage or of a visit. Three hairs at least must fall under the razor or the scissors, or be pulled out or burnt. The cutting may be effected either at the end of the hairs or at the roots. It is even recommended to a perfectly bald person to have the razor passed at least once over his head. After the hair has been cut or shaved, one returns to

Mecca to accomplish the final circuits, and the walk if not yet taken. Then one returns to Mina for the third time.

The Sonna insists upon observing the proper order of the ceremonies —lapidation, immolation, head-shaving or hair-cutting, circuits—as they have been described. One may lawfully proceed to accomplish any of them from midnight preceding the day called *yum-en-nahr, i.e.* of the sacrifice of victims. For the immolation there is no prescribed time. The time allowed for the lapidation lasts until the end of the *yum-en-nahr*. [††The immolation should take place on the *yum-en-nahr*, as Rafii himself points out at the end of the next chapter.] For head-shaving or hair-cutting, for the circuits, and for the walk, no time is prescribed by the law.

When we said above that the act of shaving the head or cutting the hair is an offering to God, we should have added that after accomplishing the lapidation and this offering, the pilgrim has recovered the first degree of his *tahallol* or normal condition ; he can dress as usual, shave, pare his nails, *and even go hunting or execute a marriage contract. [*A marriage contract is still forbidden him. When the pilgrim has accomplished the final circuits, he has then entirely recovered his normal condition. He can do, after that, everything that was prohibited him on account of his state of *ihram*.]

Section 6

On his return to Mina the pilgrim passes there the next two nights, those *i.e.* separating the three days called *ayyam-at-tashrik*, and repeats each day the lapidation at the *jamrat-al-akaba*, and at the two other heaps of stones in the vicinity, each lapidation consisting of seven distinct casts. It is permissible to leave Mina on the second of the *ayyam-at-tashrik* before sunset, after the lapidation, without waiting to pass the night of the third day. Only, if the departure does not take place until after sunset, then the night must be passed at Mina and next day's lapidation duly performed. The lapidation on the *ayyam-at-tashrik* may be commenced as soon as the sun has begun to decline ; and must be finished before sunset, or, according to others, before the appearance of dawn on the morrow.

The following are conditions for the validity of the lapidation :—

1. That it is accomplished in seven successive casts, one by one.
2. Observing the proper order of the different heaps of stone.
3. That the stones thrown are pebbles.
4. That they are really thrown. It is not enough to deposit them at the place mentioned.

The Sonna has introduced the practice of employing pebbles of ordinary size. The law does not require: (1) that the stones should remain where they are thrown; or (2) that the person performing the lapidation should immediately leave the stone-heap.

A person who has not enough strength to accomplish himself the ceremony of lapidation should ask another to do it for him. *Any one who has omitted the lapidation on the first or second day can still make it good on the morrow, without an expiatory sacrifice. This sacrifice is, however, formally prescribed for any one who omits the lapidations altogether. According to our school an expiatory sacrifice is due if three out of the seven casts have been omitted.

The lapidations over, one may leave Mecca, after once more performing the circuits of the sanctuary as a farewell; a further stay in the holy city not being permitted. These farewell circuits are obligatory; their omission requiring an expiatory sacrifice. Only a single author maintains they are merely prescribed by the Sonna, and that consequently their omission has no need to be expiated. Even, however, in the case of those who admit that these farewell circuits are obligatory, the pilgrim is allowed to be exempt from the necessity of any expiatory sacrifice, if, after leaving Mecca without performing them, he returns before having covered a distance permitting him to abridge prayer, ††but not otherwise. A woman in whom menstruation manifests itself during her stay in Mecca, need not wait until it is over in order to perform her farewell circuits; she may leave without accomplishing them.

The Sonna has introduced a custom that the pilgrim, after taking part in the ceremonies we have just described, should drink the water of the sacred fountain Zamzam and visit the tomb of the Prophet at Medina.

SECTION 7

The essential elements of the pilgrimage are five: the *ihram*, the halt on Mount Arafa, the circuits, the walk, and the act of head-shaving or hair-cutting—at least, according to the authorities who consider this last as a necessary ceremony. If one of these elements is omitted the pilgrimage is wholly void, and this error cannot be made up for by any expiatory sacrifice. The five ceremonies mentioned, with the exception of the halt on Mount Arafa, are also essential elements of the visit.

The pilgrimage and the visit may be accomplished together in three different ways—

1. In the way called *ifrad, i.e.* first performing the pilgrimage, and then putting oneself into a state of *ihram* in order to accomplish the visit, as if one lived at Mecca.

2. In the way called *Kiran, i.e.* by putting oneself into a state of *ihram,* for both acts of devotion, before arriving at the prescribed station. One is then considered, when accomplishing the ceremonies of the pilgrimage, to have performed at the same time those of the visit. The putting oneself into a state of *ihram* in order to accomplish the visit in the pilgrimage months is enough to enable one to combine the two acts, provided that before performing the circuits one places oneself in a state of *ihram* for the pilgrimage also ; but the inverse proceeding is not permitted by the law, according to the opinion maintained by Shafii in his second period.

3. In the way called *tamatto, i.e.* by putting oneself into a state of *ihram* for the visit, at the station indicated by the law, and while accomplishing this act of devotion ; and then after this remaining at Mecca until the time of the pilgrimage and placing oneself in a state of *ihram* for this last duty, as if one lived in the holy city.

The first method is the best, then the third, and lastly the second, though one authority has maintained that the third method is the best. Any one who follows it, however, owes an expiatory sacrifice in the three following cases :—

1. If he does not live in the neighbourhood of the Masjid-al-haram, or sacred mosque built round the Kaba ; *i.e.* when his domicile is at a greater distance than two days' march. [†This distance is not to be computed from Mecca, but from the boundary of the sacred territory.

2. If the visit takes place in one of the pilgrimage months, and in the same year in which he performs the pilgrimage.

3. If he has not returned to the prescribed station, in order to place himself in a state of *ihram* for the pilgrimage.

This expiatory sacrifice is due from the moment of entering upon a state of *ihram* for the pilgrimage ; but it is better to perform it on the day of the immolation of victims. The believer who is unable to perform the expiatory sacrifice during his stay in the sacred territory should fast for ten days ; *i.e.* three days during the pilgrimage, preferably before the day of Mount Arafa, *and the other seven on his return home. It is also commendable that the three and the seven should be consecutive days ; *and if the three first have not been observed during the pilgrimage, a short interval should elapse between their observance and that of the seven. A person choosing the second of the three methods must make the expiatory sacrifice, in the same way as if he had chosen the third. [Unless he lives in the neighbourhood of the sacred territory.]

CHAPTER V.—ACTIONS FORBIDDEN DURING *IHRAM*

DURING *ihram* abstinence from the following things is obligatory :—

1. Covering the head, even partly, with anything whatever, except in case of necessity. Nor is it permitted to wear any article of clothing that is sewn or woven or tied round the body, unless one has no other. These precepts, however, apply only to men. A woman's face is subject to the same rule as a man's head ; but a woman may wear sewn clothing, *except gloves.

2. The use of scent, whether on the clothes or on the body ; and the use of cosmetics for the hair or beard ; though it is not even blamable to wash the body and head with mallow water.

3. Cutting the hair or the nails. The expiatory fine of three *modd* of foodstuffs is only incurred in full when at least three hairs or three nails have been cut ; one *modd* only being due for a single hair or a single nail, and two *modd* for two hairs or two nails. A person who is unable to observe this abstinence, should have his whole beard shaved and pay the expiatory fine.

4. Coition. This act nullifies the visit always, and even the pilgrimage if one has been guilty of it before attaining the first degree of *tahallol.* It must be expiated by the sacrifice called *badana, i.e.* the immolation of a camel, and subsidiarily a cow, or seven head of small cattle. One must continue to take part in the subsequent ceremonies, and must afterwards repeat all the ceremonies, even in the case of a supererogatory pilgrimage, or of a visit. †This repetition should take place as soon as possible, and in any case after no long interval.

5. Hunting any animal fit for food, other than a domestic animal. [This rule extends to any animal born of such animal and of one that may be killed.] Hunting is forbidden on all the sacred territory even when one is not in a state of *ihram.* Any one who has killed an ostrich must make reparation by a *badana ;* an antelope or a wild ass is expiated by the sacrifice of a cow ; a gazelle by a full-sized goat ; a hare by an *anak* or goat of less than one year ; and a jerboa by a *jafra* or weanling kid. Wild animals that have not been thus appraised are expiated by the most suitable domestic animals, according to the opinion of two irreproachable experts. If the law cannot be satisfied by the sacrifice of an animal, one should pay the value of the animal killed.

6. Cutting or plucking, upon the sacred territory, even if not in a state of *ihram,* any vegetable whatever that has not been sown or planted by man. *For cutting or plucking plants or trees one is liable for an expiatory sacrifice. In the case of a large tree one owes a cow ; in the case of a small tree or a plant, a sheep. [Our school does not distinguish

between what is planted by man and what is not. One is merely permitted to cut the galingale, and thorny plants, such as the *ausaj*, etc., such at least is the opinion of most authorities. †One may also lawfully take such plants as are necessary as fodder for one's beasts, and medicinal plants one may require.]

Hunting is also forbidden in the immediate neighbourhood of Medina; but a breach of this rule involves no responsibility, according to the opinion maintained by Shafii in his second period.

A hunter having to expiate the killing of an animal may, at his choice, either—

1. Kill the animal he owes and give the meat to the poor of the sacred territory; or—

2. Have the value of the animal he owes estimated, buy foodstuffs to this amount, and distribute to the poor as in 1; or—

3. Fast a whole day for each *modd* of foodstuffs owed in virtue of alternative No. 2.

If the animal killed is one which cannot be compensated for, No. 2 or No. 3 must be chosen. As to the expiatory fine for shaving the head or cutting the hair, one may choose between the sacrifice of a *sha*, or a present of three *saa* of foodstuffs, in each case to the profit of six poor persons; or one may fast for three days. †But the expiatory sacrifice incurred for omitting some obligatory duty, such as putting oneself into a state of *ihram* at one of the stations, always consists in the sacrifice of a *sha*; and this immolation cannot be replaced by any other act of devotion, unless it is impossible to find a *sha*. In this latter case one may buy foodstuffs to the value of the animal for poor persons, or, subsidiarily, fast a day for each *modd*. The expiatory sacrifice due for not choosing the prescribed time for the halt on Mount Arafa, also consists of a *sha*, but may be replaced in the same way as for the person who has unlawfully followed the third way of combining the pilgrimage and the visit. †It must take place during the pilgrimage, which must be accomplished afterwards by way of reparation. On the other hand, the expiatory sacrifice for committing some illicit act, or for omitting some obligatory duty, is not confined to any legal term; *but it must be performed in the sacred territory, and the meat belongs of right to the poor who are domiciled there.

As to persons accomplishing the visit, the best place for them to perform their expiatory sacrifices is Murwa. The best place for pilgrims to do so is Mina. This rule applies also to the immolation of victims which the pilgrim or the person accomplishing the visit have brought to the holy city in fulfilment of a vow. ††This immolation, like the others, should take place preferably on the day of the feast of victims.

CHAPTER VI.—CAUSES THAT PREVENT THE ACCOMPLISHMENT OF THE PILGRIMAGE

The believer who is prevented from continuing the ceremonies is considered to be thereby released from his state of *ihram*, and fully restored to his *tahallol* or normal condition. Some authors, however, insist that, to have this result, the cause of prevention must be individual, or that it must apply to all the pilgrims without exception. Illness is not a valid cause of prevention; **unless a right to interrupt the ceremonies was expressly reserved at the time the *ihram* was undertaken; but a person who leaves his state of *ihram* in this way must in any case sacrifice a *sha*, at the place where the cause of prevention arose.

[A return to a state of *tahallol* only occurs when the intention to do so is combined with a sacrifice and with the cutting of the hair, etc.; at least according to the authorities who consider this last act as an essential ceremony. *In default of a *sha*, the immolation may be replaced by the purchase of foodstuffs to the value of the animal, and subsidiarily by a fast of a day for each *modd*. *This is the only way in which one can be immediately released from a state of *ihram*.]

When a slave has put himself into a state of *ihram* without his master's consent, the latter may oblige him to return to his normal condition. In the same way a husband may break the *ihram* of his wife, if she undertakes a supererogatory pilgrimage without his permission; *and the same is the case if the pilgrimage be obligatory. A person who has been prevented from continuing a supererogatory pilgrimage is not required to repeat it later; but this is so in the case of a recognised obligatory pilgrimage. As to a pilgrimage which, though obligatory, has not been expressly recognised as such, it must be repeated only if one has the power to accomplish it.

A pilgrim who has allowed the prescribed time for the halt on Mount Arafa to pass by, cannot be released from his state of *ihram* until he has performed the circuits, the walk, the cutting, etc., of the hair; though the obligation to accomplish these two last ceremonies has been called in question by one authority. In any case the believer under such circumstances owes an expiatory sacrifice, and must afterwards perform his act of devotion.

BOOK 9.—SALE OR BARTER

CHAPTER I.—GENERAL PROVISIONS

For the validity of a contract of sale or exchange the law requires mutual consent, *i.e.* that the vendor should make an offer of the goods, *e.g.* by saying, " I sell you," or " I make you owner " of such and such a thing, and that the purchaser should declare his consent, *e.g.* by saying, " I buy the object," " I accept the ownership," or " I accept it." There is no objection to the purchaser first declaring his wishes, *as by saying, " Sell me such and such a thing," and the vendor replying, " I sell it you," which constitutes a valid agreement. †A sale may also equally well be implied in words such as, " I give you the thing for such and such a sum." But the law forbids that any long interval should elapse between the declaration of the vendor and that of the purchaser ; and it requires the acceptance to be similar to the offer, for if one party says, " I sell you the thing for one thousand debased pieces of money," and the other replies, " I buy it for a thousand good pieces," there is no legal sale. In the case of a mute person a sign is as good as consent expressed in words. Each contracting party must be capable of managing his affairs.

[Another condition essential to the validity of a sale is that no violence must be used against either party, except such as is authorised by law. An infidel is forbidden : (1) *to buy a copy of the Koran, or a Moslem slave (unless his ancestor or descendant)—the latter is freed by the mere fact of such purchase ; or (2) to buy weapons of war, unless he is the subject of a Moslem ruler.]

There are five conditions necessary for the legal sale of any thing—

1. It must be a pure substance. Thus, a dog cannot be sold, nor wine. Nor can anything that has become impure be sold ; if it is impossible to remove the impurity, as in the case of impure vinegar, milk, or fat.

2. It must be of some use and consequently of some value. Thus, vermin cannot be sold, nor useless wild animals, nor *e.g.* two grains of corn, etc., nor an object of mere amusement like a musical instrument or an article only used in playing a game. As to this last category, however, some authors consider sale permissible if the materials have

an intrinsic value. †The sale of water is allowed, even by the banks of a river, and sand may be sold even in the desert.

3. The vendor must be able to deliver it to the purchaser. Thus, a domestic animal or a slave that has escaped or property that has been misappropriated by another person cannot be sold, ††unless to a person able in fact to bring back the animal or slave or recover the property. One may not sell the half of a vase or of a sabre, for these things cannot be materially divided without great loss of value ; †but this is permissible in the case of a piece of cloth, each portion of which retains its proportional value. One may not sell any pledged article without the creditor's consent ; nor a slave who has committed a crime and who can consequently be seized by the injured party as damages. There is no objection, however, to the sale of a slave who is himself in debt, *or who is liable to corporal punishment under the *lex talionis*, or otherwise.

4. The vendor must be the real owner. The sale of another's goods is null. In his first period Shafii was of a different opinion, and considered the sale of another's goods, without the knowledge of the owner, as a conditional sale, *i.e.* a sale having full legal effect if the owner subsequently approves of it, but not otherwise. But the sale of the property of a person to whose succession one will be called, and whom one supposes to be living, but who it subsequently transpires was dead at the time of the contract, is considered to be valid.

5. The thing must be distinctly known to the two contracting parties. Thus " one of two coats " cannot be sold without determining which ; but one *saa* may be sold from a heap of grain, whether the number of *saas* in the heap is known †or not. A sale cannot be effected, in block and without indicating the respective quantities, of " as much corn as can be stored in such and such a room," nor for " as much gold as the weight of such and such a stone," nor for " as much as so and so has sold his horse for," nor for " a thousand pieces of money consisting partly of *drahms* and partly of *dinars*." Where a certain quantity of " pieces of money " has been stipulated for, the price is considered sufficiently determined if one coinage only is current in the locality ; but where two coinages are current, the one intended must be specified. A particular heap of grain may legally be sold at the rate of one *drahm* the *saa*, though the number of *saas* is not known ; but if the sale is for " one hundred *drahms* at one *drahm* the *saa*," ††the contract is void unless there are really just one hundred *saas* of grain. A thing sold is deemed to be sufficiently known to the two parties if it is in their sight and they have inspected it ; *but a thing not there cannot be sold unless both parties have previously seen it. Another doctrine admits the validity of such a sale, but allows the purchaser the faculty of refusing

the goods after inspection. If the thing sold is not there, the fact of previous inspection suffices in the case of things ordinarily durable for that interval. If the whole of a thing may be estimated by partial inspection, it is enough to have seen a part, *e.g.* the outside of a heap of grain, or a sample. This is so also in the case of a natural envelope, such as the rind of a pomegranate, an eggshell, or the lower covering of nuts and almonds. Inspection of a thing means the inspection of those parts of it from which its quality may be judged. †A mere description of the thing as in the contract of *salam* is not enough for an ordinary sale. Consequently the *salam*, but not a sale, may be effected by a blind man. It is only, according to some jurists, when such person has become blind before reaching the age of discernment, that the contract of *salam* is forbidden him.

CHAPTER II.—ILLICIT GAIN

FOODSTUFFS cannot be legally exchanged for others of the same nature, unless: (1) it is a cash transaction; (2) the two quantities are equal; and (3) each party takes possession of what is due to him then and there.

If the foodstuffs exchanged are not of the same kind, *e.g.* corn and barley, the first and third conditions are still obligatory, but not the second. By foodstuff is understood anything that serves for the internal nurture of the body, whether as principal nourishment, seasoning, fruit, or medicine. Flours produced from different products of the soil are deemed to be of different kinds, as also liquors such as oil and vinegar. *The same rule applies to meat and milk from different animals.

Quantities are ascertained to be equal either by measure or weight, according to their nature—the custom of the inhabitants of the Hejaz at the time of the Prophet being observed with regard to this matter, or if it be not known the custom of the local market. Some jurists maintain one must always go by the measure others by the weight; others allow choice. Money is subject to the same rules as foodstuffs. Goods from which illicit gain can be derived may not be bartered for in a lump without specifying the exact quantity, even if after the transaction the quantities are ascertained to be equal. Equality must be ascertained when the products are mature and dry. Thus unripe dates cannot be bartered for other dates, ripe or unripe; nor grapes for grapes or raisins. Products not intended to be dried, like cucumbers and some kinds of grapes, may not be exchanged at all with others of the same nature. Only one authority maintains that in this case an equality ascertained after plucking suffices to render the exchange valid. Equality cannot be ascertained after the substances have been converted into flour, ptisan or bread ; but only when the grains are still intact. However, in the case of oleaginous plants like sesame, equality can be ascertained either when the grains are still intact or after preparing the oil ; or in the case of raisins either while dry or after the preparation of vinegar or must. As to milk one has the choice between its ordinary state, butter or skimmed milk ; but not in any other condition, such as cheese or *akit.* Equality cannot be ascertained after products have been cooked, fried, or roasted ; but there is no objection to their being heated in order to separate them from other substances, as in the case of honey or butter from which wax or milk has thus been extracted.

A sale is void if the prohibition of illicit gain has been violated by both parties, or by one only. No distinction is made between the exchange of products of a different nature and of a different species. Thus one cannot barter a *modd* of preserved dates and a *drahm* for a *modd* of the same substance and a *drahm,* nor a *modd* of this substance and a *drahm* for two *modds* or two *drahms,* nor a certain quantity of good and debased coin for the same quantity of good or debased coin. It is forbidden to barter meat for an animal, whether of the same kind as the meat, *or not, and whether eatable or not.

CHAPTER III.—OTHER ILLICIT SALES

Section 1

The Prophet has forbidden the following sales :—

1. The sale of the services of a male animal required to cover a female. According to some authors this prohibition relates to the sale of male sperm, while according to others it refers to payment for the use of the male. Sperm may not be sold at all, whether the transaction is called a sale †or a hire.

2. The sale of younglings to be brought forth later from the fœtus of an animal. No object may be sold by stipulating that the price shall not become due until such and such a fœtus bears young.

3. The sale of an embryo, *i.e.* of what a female animal bears in the womb.

4. The sale of the product of a future project, *i.e.* of a being still within the loins of the male.

5. A "touch" sale, expression which means : (*a*) the sale, *i.e.* of a piece of cloth already folded, that is bought by merely touching it, and renouncing in advance the right of option accorded by law after seeing it ; or (*b*) a sale concluded by saying, "When you have touched this coat I have sold it you."

6. A "throw" sale, *i.e.* if two persons mutually exchange their goods, and the sale is effected by this alone, without any preliminary examination on either side.

7. A "stone" sale; effected by saying, "Of these pieces of cloth I sell you the one upon which falls this stone thrown in the air"; or a sale that becomes irrevocable by throwing a stone; or by stipulating, "I sell you such and such an object, and you will have a right of option until I have thrown this stone."

8. A "double-face sale"; *i.e.* one effected by the words, "I sell you such and such an object, either for one thousand pieces of money in cash, or for two thousand at the end of a year"; or, "I sell you this slave for one thousand, if you will sell me your house for the same amount."

9. Any "qualified" sale; *i.e.* a sale on condition that the purchaser will sell or lend some other object to the vendor; or the purchase of a cultivated field on condition that the vendor will reap the harvest; or the purchase of a piece of cloth on condition that the vendor will make a coat out of it. †All these kinds of conditional sales are null.

The law does not forbid at a sale the stipulation of conditions that merely modify it, and do not affect the contract itself; such as—a reservation of a right of option; a stipulation that the vendor shall not be held to guarantee the absence of redhibitory defects; a reservation of the right of plucking fruit; the stipulation of a term for payment, of a security or of a personal guarantee for the payment of the price agreed upon, if it is not a cash transaction—provided always that there is no uncertainty as to the term, the security or the guarantee. It may also be stipulated that payment be made in the presence of witnesses, †without its being necessary at that time to designate the witnesses by name. If, under these circumstances, the purchaser does not deposit the necessary security, or the person designated does not bring it, the vendor has the right to relinquish the contract. **The sale of a slave on condition that he will be freed, is quite valid; †and the vendor has the right to proceed against the purchaser to enforce the enfranchisement agreed upon. †On the other hand, the sale would not be valid if the vendor reserved a right of ownership after the enfranchisement, or stipulated that the enfranchisement should be by will, or contract, or at some future time, *e.g.* a month.

The following stipulations are considered admissible:—

1. Any condition resulting from the very nature of the sale, such as taking possession, or redhibition; or even a condition without any reasonable object (itself without effect), as, *e.g.* to take only a certain kind of food.

2. A stipulation that goods should have some special, useful quality,

as, *e.g.* that a slave should know how to write, or that a beast should be with young, or have milk in the udder. Such stipulation confers on the party insisting on it the right to withdraw from the contract if the thing sold has not the stipulated quality. According to a single jurist a stipulation that a beast should be with young nullifies a contract.

†On the other hand, the law regards as null the sale "of a beast or a slave with the embryo." It prohibits the sale either of the embryo alone, or of the beast or the slave "without its embryo." It is illicit to sell in any way a slave pregnant with a free child. When a female is sold, the embryo is *ipso facto* comprised in the transaction.

Section 2

Some kinds of sales, though forbidden by the Prophet, are not necessarily null when concluded; the prohibition referring only to accessory circumstances, not to the essence of the contract. Amongst these are cited the following:—

1. A sale concluded between a townsman and an inhabitant of the desert or of the country, in the following circumstances:—(*a*) when the townsman sees a stranger arrive with objects of prime and general necessity for sale at the current rate of the day, and is able to persuade him to transfer the whole to himself, with the avowed object of retailing them at a higher price; and (*b*) when the townsman goes out to meet people bringing their goods to town, and buys these products before they are aware of the current rate. On learning the fraud of which they have been victims these people have even the right to cancel the contract.

2. Outbidding; *i.e.* it is forbidden to outbid, as soon as the vendor has accepted the offer of another person, even though this may not yet be irrevocable.

3. A sale or purchase effected with the object of supplanting a competitor. It is blamable to persuade a purchaser to cancel a revocable sale, in order to sell him a similar object; or to persuade a vendor to cancel a contract, in order to be able to buy the thing oneself.

4. Trickery, consisting in offering a higher price for something, not in order to obtain it but with the object of deceiving another person as to its value. †Under these circumstances, however, the person cheated has no right to cancel the sale.

5. A sale of dates or grapes to make wine of.

The law does not permit the sale of a female slave that involves her separation from her child before the latter has attained the age of discernment, or—according to one authority—the age of puberty. *Any sale or donation involving such separation is null.

A sale is also considered illegal where one buys goods giving at the same time a sum of money as earnest, which sum becomes part of the price if the purchaser is satisfied with the things, but is otherwise considered as a gift to the vendor.

Section 3

In the case of a sale of two objects at the same time, the sale of one of which is illegal, *e.g.* a sale of vinegar and wine, or of a slave and a freeman, or of one's own slave and that of another person, or of a slave without the consent of another co-proprietor, *the contract is valid with regard to what has been legally sold, without prejudice to the purchaser's right, if ignorant of the circumstances, to cancel the sale. Even if he knew of it, or would prefer the contract to remain valid, he has a right to claim a proportional diminution of the total price agreed upon. A single authority maintains that the purchaser cannot insist upon any such diminution if he prefers to keep the object which has been legally sold him. A vendor can never cancel a contract of this sort. The sale of two slaves is not *ipso facto* cancelled by the accidental death of one, before the purchaser has taken possession, at least according to our rite; but the purchaser may decline to fulfil the contract, or, if he prefer, claim a proportional reduction of the price.

*Contracts of different kinds may be combined, as *e.g.* a contract of hiring with a sale or with a *salam* contract. In such a case the price agreed upon is divided proportionally between the obligations undertaken. Even in the case of a sale combined with a marriage contract, not only is the validity of the marriage admitted, *but also that of the sale, and of the stipulation of dower. Whether in any case there is a combination or a plurality of contracts depends upon whether one price only has been stipulated, or a separate and distinct price for each contract. If it is said, "I sell you this for so much and that for so much," two bargains have been concluded. Subject to this rule plurality may also be determined by the number of persons taking part in the transaction as vendors or purchasers; and if two persons appoint one person to act for them, or one person appoint two agents, †it is the number of these agents that must be considered.

CHAPTER IV.—RIGHT OF OPTION OR CANCELLATION

Section 1

The right of option, called *majlis, i.e.* "of the sitting," is the inalienable right to cancel a contract concluded by both parties, so long as they have not yet separated. This right of option obtains for all agreements of the nature of a sale, *e.g.* exchange of gold or silver or of foodstuffs, the contract of *salam*, mere transfer of a thing purchased, sharing, compromise for an equivalent, etc. It even exists if one purchases a slave of whom one is the ancestor or the descendant, and whose enfranchisement consequently take place *ipso facto* on that purchase. When, in these circumstances, it is admitted that the ownership of the slave remains with the vendor as long as the right of option lasts, or even that it remains in suspense during that interval, the doctrine must also be admitted that either of the contracting parties can cancel the agreement upon the spot. But if, on the contrary, it is held that the ownership of the slave is at once transferred to the purchaser by his taking possession, then it follows that the vendor alone enjoys a right of option. No such option exists in the delivery of a debt, nor in a marriage contract, nor in a gift, †whether accompanied or not by a remuneration, †nor in the exercise of a right of pre-emption, †nor in a contract of hiring, nor in a farm lease, nor in stipulating dower.

Neither does a right of option exist in the following two cases :—

1. If the parties declare their approval of the contract. If only one does so, he loses his right of option, but that of the other party remains, until he makes a similar declaration.

2. If the parties separate without any express reservation. A right of option remains, however, as long as the separation has not taken place ; even though the parties remain together for a long time, or get up and walk about together. Custom indicates what is to be understood by the word " separation."

†In the case of sudden death of one of the parties, his right of option is transferred to his heir ; similarly, in a case of sudden madness the right passes to the curator. If proceedings are taken and one party asserts and the other denies the fact of separation or cancellation, the presumption is in favour of the one that denies.

SECTION 2

The contracting parties may by special stipulation reserve a right of conventional option, *i.e.* the faculty of cancelling the contract within a certain time. Such stipulation may be made either by one of the contracting parties or by both. It is admissible in all agreements of the nature of a contract of sale, except only those in which possession must be taken upon the spot, as in the exchange of goods subject to the prohibition of illicit gain, and in the contract of *salam*. The faculty can only be reserved for a specified time, not exceeding three days, from the conclusion of the bargain, or—according to others—from the separation of the parties.

*The ownership of the thing sold remains with the vendor, if a right of option has been stipulated by him; or with the purchaser if the stipulation was his; and it remains in suspense if both made the stipulation. However, if the contract is not subsequently cancelled by an exercise of the right of option, the ownership of the goods is considered to have been the purchaser's from the time the bargain was concluded; while if, on the contrary, the contract is cancelled, the vendor's ownership is considered to have been uninterrupted.

Cancellation or approval of a sale concluded under reservation of a right of option should be announced in explicit terms, such as, "I wish the bargain to be cancelled," or "suppressed," or that "the goods be returned"; or "I approve the contract," or "I wish it to be carried out." Cancellation may also be manifested by facts indicating that one considers oneself owner of the goods, *e.g.* by cohabitation between the vendor and the slave he has sold, or by her enfranchisement; as also by a second sale of the goods, or by hiring them to another person, or by giving in marriage a female slave. †Similar acts on the part of the purchaser are considered as showing that he approves the bargain concluded; but exposing the goods for sale does not constitute an act of ownership, either on the part of the vendor or the purchaser, and consequently does not suffice to establish approval or cancellation.

Section 3 (1)

A purchaser has a right of option on account of defects in the thing bought, of which he has become aware only after taking possession, but which existed previously. The following, for instance, are redhibitory defects in a slave:—castration; tendency to debauchery, theft or desertion; incapacity to retain urine when lying down; a bad breath; a fetid odour from the armpits. An animal such as a horse or mule, etc., is considered to have redhibitory defects, if it is stubborn or bites. In a word any defect is called redhibitory that affects the substance or the value of the thing sold in such a way as to render it unfit for the use to which it is lawfully destined, at any rate if the object is usually exempt from such defect. No distinction is made between defects already existing at the time of the contract and those that may occur later; but defects originating after taking possession cannot give rise to redhibitory option; unless they are the consequence of some previous fact, *e.g.* if some bodily member of a slave has to be amputated under the law of talion for a crime committed before taking possession. †In this latter case the slave may be returned to the vendor ; but not if he dies of an already contracted malady. †On the other hand, redhibition is admissible if the slave has to be put to death for previously abjuring Islam.

*A sale under an express condition that the vendor shall not be responsible for redhibitory defects is permitted only in the case of animals and slaves, and only in regard to hidden defects existing at the time of the contract unknown to the vendor, who is otherwise fully responsible. Thus this stipulation does not affect the vendor's responsibility for defects supervening between the conclusion of the contract and taking possession ; †for this responsibility cannot be excluded from the agreement under any pretext, as during that interval the goods are at his risk and peril.

Should the purchaser not become aware of certain redhibitory defects until after the accidental loss of an object of which he has taken possession, or until after enfranchising a slave, he can still none the less sue the vendor for damages, *i.e.* he can claim a proportional reduction in the price. †Under these circumstances the value of the object is reckoned at the lowest rate obtaining between the contract and taking possession. And the right of redhibition remains also in the case of accidental loss of what has been given by way of price, in which case the purchaser can still none the less return any defective articles he may have received, and claim either objects analogous to those he gave by way of price or the value of those objects. But where a purchaser perceives the existence of defects only after transferring the property to a third person, †he is not entitled to any damage ; though the right of redhibition is renewed if the property returns to the ownership of the first purchaser. However, according to some, this last rule applies only to the case where an article is returned to the first purchaser by reason of redhibition.

Redhibition should be effected without delay, as quickly as custom requires. It is understood that if one becomes aware of some such defect while praying or at a meal, redhibition may be deferred until one has finished ; or until daybreak, if it occurs during the night. If the vendor or his agent is in the place the article should be returned either by the purchaser or some one acting on his behalf. But it is better not to concern oneself about the vendor but take the matter at once before the court. If the vendor is absent and has no representative in the place, there is all the more reason to adopt this latter course. †If possible, witnesses should be called to prove the fact of redhibition, and they should look after the object until it has been restored to the vendor or to the Court. †If it is impossible to call witnesses, cancellation need not be pronounced before meeting the vendor or his agent or coming into court

After discovering redhibitory defects, use of the thing bought is absolutely forbidden. Thus the right of redhibition is lost if one continues to make use of the services of a purchased slave, or even if one leaves the saddle or shabrack on the back of a mount. But it is permissible to ride an animal back to the vendor if it is so mischievous one can neither lead nor drive it. In every case where the purchaser loses his right of redhibition in consequence of his own fault or negligence, he loses also all claim to damage.

The right of simply returning the defective article ceases when the latter is allowed to deteriorate still further in possession of the purchaser; unless the vendor consents to take it back as if no deterioration had occurred, in which case the purchaser may either return it or keep it without compensation on the part of the vendor. But if, on the contrary, in consequence of the deterioration, the vendor declines to take back the object sold, the purchaser can only force him to do so if he offers to pay compensation for the further deterioration while in his possession; or he can, if he prefer, keep the thing himself and claim damages for the original redhibitory defects for which the vendor was responsible. If the parties are in agreement as to the best way of arranging their difficulties in the matter, no one has any right to force them to adopt any other; †but otherwise the court should authorise the arrangement proposed by the actual possessor who wishes to keep the thing in dispute. The purchaser should also inform the vendor without delay of any accident that may befall the article sold, so that the latter may be able to declare his wishes; for if the purchaser puts off doing this, without valid excuse, he loses both his right of redhibition and his right to claim damage. If damage to the thing sold is necessary before redhibitory defects can be discovered, as for instance in the case of an egg, a coconut, or a melon, and one is not aware of the noisome or rotten condition of the thing until it is opened, right of redhibition remains intact, *and one is not liable for damage. But if it is possible to ascertain the existence of redhibitory defects in some way that does less damage to the goods, then the general rule relating to defects supervening after taking possession must be observed.

Section 3 (2)

Where two slaves with redhibitory defects have been bought together, both should be returned to the vendor. *Even if only one of the two is affected, both must be returned; and the vendor may refuse to accept the one without the other. If a slave with some redhibitory defect has been bought from two co-proprietors, each may be proceeded against in proportion to his share; *and, similarly, if two persons have purchased a slave from another, each may sue on his own account.

Where defects are asserted by the purchaser and denied by the vendor, the presumption is in favour of the latter, provided he confirms his statement on oath.

Any increase which continues to form part of the object bought, *e.g.* the fattening of an animal, must be returned with it in case of redhibition; but things that exist separately from it, such as the young of an animal, or the rent of a house, are unaffected. These latter belong to the purchaser, whether the redhibition takes place after he has taken possession †or before. But children or young animals born of a mother already pregnant at the time of the contract must be returned.

Employing a slave as a domestic servant, or cohabiting with one not virgin does not prevent redhibition, provided of course the purchaser was at the time unaware of the defects. On the other hand, the deflowering of a girl after taking possession is considered a damage that renders simple redhibition impossible; if done before taking possession this even constitutes a crime against the property of another.

Section 4

It is rigorously forbidden to sell an animal put aside for a few days in order to increase the amount of its milk at the moment of sale. Such fraud gives the purchaser a right of cancellation, provided he makes use of it without delay. According to some authorities the right can still be exercised three days after discovery. If the purchaser has already consumed the milk from the animal, he should return the beast to the vendor together with a *saa* of dry dates, or—according to some—a *saa* of any kind of foodstuff forming the main ordinary nourishment in that locality. †A *saa* is the amount due, however much milk has been consumed. And this right of cancellation is not limited to cattle, but admitted for all animals serving for nourishment, and also for a female slave and a she-ass. Only, in these cases, it is not necessary to pay the vendor any compensation for loss of milk,—though this has been contested as to the female slave.

The following acts are considered to be of the nature of fraud and to give rise to a right of cancellation of sale:—

1. Damming irrigation water or mill water in order to let it flow at the moment of sale.

2. Painting the face of a female slave red, or dyeing her hair black, or curling it.

†But dirtying a slave's clothes with ink, to make a purchaser believe he knows how to write, is no ground of cancellation.

CHAPTER V.—PROPERTY SOLD, BEFORE THE PURCHASER HAS TAKEN POSSESSION

Section 1

The vendor is responsible for the thing sold, until the purchaser has taken possession; so that if it is accidentally lost, the contract is *ipso facto* cancelled, and the price need not be paid. *The purchaser cannot relieve the vendor of this obligation, as it is a rule of public interest. However, if the loss has been caused voluntarily and knowingly by the purchaser, this circumstance is considered to amount to a taking possession by him, and the responsibility consequently devolves upon him. But in the contrary case, *i.e.* if the purchaser has caused the loss involuntarily, there is the same divergence amongst authorities as with regard to a person who involuntarily eats food unlawfully taken from him by his host. The same rule that obtains in case of casual loss is applied by our rite to loss caused by the vendor; *but loss caused by a third person does not necessarily imply a dissolution of the contract, but confers on the purchaser the right of either demanding the execution of the engagement or of withdrawing from it. In the first case the purchaser, in the second the vendor, can proceed against the third person.

If it is not a case of total loss, but only of a deterioration in the value of the object sold, the law establishes the following distinctions:—

When the deterioration accidentally supervenes before taking possession, and the purchaser declares he does not wish to make it a ground of cancellation, he cannot claim to have a part of the price remitted; and still less of course where the deterioration is caused by himself. On the other hand, deterioration caused by a third person confers on a purchaser a right of cancellation; or, if he does not wish to withdraw from the agreement, a right of proceeding against that third person. If deterioration has been caused by the vendor, our rite prescribes that the purchaser may choose between a cancellation and an execution of the contract, both without any claim to damage.

A purchaser is forbidden to resell anything bought before he has taken possession of it; whether the second sale be to the original vendor or to some one else. Hiring, pledging or giving is prohibited as much as selling, so long as possession has not been taken; but the enfranchisement of a slave may take place first. What is given in exchange for goods, by way of price, is subject to the same law as the goods themelves, at least if it is a certain definite object; that is to say that the vendor cannot transfer its ownership to any one else before taking possession.

On the other hand, one may lawfully alienate, even before really taking possession, the following :—

1. What one has temporarily entrusted to the care of another by way of deposit.
2. Funds contributed to a society or company.
3. Funds contributed to a joint stock company.
4. A thing pledged, if one has paid the debt.
5. Property inherited.
6. The balance due from a guardian upon the majority of a minor.
7. An article one has lent for use.
8. Property bought at an auction sale.

For one is already owner of these things before actually taking possession.

Before taking possession it is unlawful to sell foodstuffs upon which one has advanced money, or to substitute other foodstuffs for those stipulated in the contract of *salam* or advance ; but it is permissible to replace the money advance by something else, at least according to the opinion maintained by Shafii in his second period. If, however, the money advanced, and the effects with which it is agreed to replace it, are capable of giving rise to some illicit gain, the mutual taking possession must be proceeded with at once. As an example may be cited the substitution of *drahms, i.e.* silver coin, for *dinars* or gold coin. †When, on the other hand, the things substituted and those for which they are substituted are not both of them capable of giving rise to illicit gain, *e.g. drahms* replaced by cloth, the law does not insist upon certain definite articles at the time of stipulation, and it is not necessary to take possession at once.

Section 2

One may also lawfully agree to replace, not only what one has borrowed, but also anything one has caused the loss of, and is consequently responsible for. In doing so the following distinctions should be observed, with regard to taking possession on the spot.

Except in accordance with the provisions of Chapter IV. of Book 12, *the sale of a credit to any one but the debtor is void. Thus one cannot purchase the slave of Zaid with a hundred pieces owed one by Amr. Neither may Zaid and Amr exchange debts owed them by a third person ; any agreement to that effect is void.

The taking possession of immovable property is not effected by a mere surrender of it to the purchaser ; the law insists that he must be put in the state of being able to dispose of it, after the vendor has removed his belongings. †If the two contracting parties are not present at the place where the purchased property is, whether movable or immovable, possession should be taken within a reasonable time. The taking possession of movable property is effected by simple delivery, or by conveyance to the place where the purchaser is. That is to say, if the sale has not been concluded at the vendor's it is enough to convey the goods to the place where the purchaser is; but if the sale has been concluded at the vendor's, then this is not enough, and the things must be taken to the domicile of the purchaser. And further, where the sale takes place in the vendor's house, the purchaser cannot waive his right to receive the goods at his own house, seeing that the vendor has no benefit in keeping in his house what he has sold. If the vendor consents to the things remaining, he is considered to have lent the purchaser his house or his store for that purpose.

Section 3

The purchaser has no right to take possession of the goods before paying the price, unless the vendor has allowed him time for payment.

When something is bought by measure or weight, such as a piece of cloth or a strip of land so long, or a certain amount of cheese, the measuring or weighing must take place at the same time as the delivery. As example of a sale by capacity may be cited one concluded thus: "I sell you this piece of cheese at one *drahm* the *saa*," or "I sell you these ten *saas* of cheese for such a sum." If it is a question of the sale of a certain quantity of foodstuffs, etc., that the vendor can claim from Zaid and sells again to Amr in equal quantity, the measuring must take place twice, first to transfer the ownership of the goods from Zaid to the vendor, and then to transfer it again from him to Amr. The taking possession would be illegal if in these circumstances one simply said to Amr, "Take what Zaid owes me," and Amr proceeded to comply with this invitation.

Section 4

When the vendor refuses to deliver the goods to the purchaser until the latter has paid the price of them, and the purchaser on his part declares he will not pay before taking possession, it is the vendor who should take the first steps. One jurist, however, has maintained the opinion that it is the purchaser who should begin by paying; another considers that there is no obligation upon either to begin, but whoever fulfils the agreement thereby obliges the other to do so also; a third thinks that both parties should be forced to carry out the agreement simultaneously.

[If the price consists of a certain definite object, the first two of these opinions are inadmissible; *and both parties should simultaneously deliver the articles agreed upon.]

After delivery by the vendor the purchaser should pay the price agreed upon, if he has it with him. If he has not, the following circumstances should be distinguished:—

1. If the purchaser is insolvent. In this case the vendor can declare him bankrupt; the sale is *ipso facto* cancelled, and the vendor can reclaim the thing sold and delivered.

2. If the purchaser is solvent, and his property (*a*) is in the town or its neighbourhood. In this case the court may prohibit him from engaging in any further trade, until he has paid the debt, but the sale is not cancelled. But if his property (*b*) is at a distance that permits the abridgment of prayer, the vendor need not wait †but may either cancel the contract or if he prefer it await the arrival of the money, after having had the purchaser forbidden to engage in any further trade, as indicated under (*a*).

It must be understood, however, that this does not prevent the vendor always having a right to detain the object he is selling until payment, if otherwise he runs a risk of losing both the price and it. And the purchaser has the same right with regard to the price. So that the difference of opinion among jurists has regard only to disagreement between vendor and purchaser as to which of the two should begin the execution of a contract of sale, without prejudice to the adverse party.

CHAPTER VI.—SIMPLE TRANSFER; PART TRANSFER; TRANSFER AT A PROFIT, OR AT A LOSS

SIMPLE transfer consists in buying a thing and then saying to a third person who is aware of the price agreed on, "I wish to transfer to you my rights and obligations under this contract. If he accepts a price must be paid equal to that agreed upon. An agreement of this sort is subject to the same rules and has the same legal consequences as an ordinary sale; but it is unnecessary to mention any price as the grantee knows this already. Any subsequent reduction in the price made by the vendor in favour of the original purchaser goes to the entire profit of the grantee.

Part transfer is identical to simple transfer, with the sole difference that only a part of the thing purchased is transferred, not the whole. Part transfer is valid, not only where the part transferred is indicated.

but also where a third person is made to participate in the sale, without expressly mentioning any particular portion of the thing sold. In the latter case each participant takes half; though according to some authorities such a proceeding is illicit.

It is lawful to make a transfer at a profit, *i.e.* to buy, *e.g.*, something for one hundred *drahms,* and then to offer to transfer it to a third person at a profit of "one drahm in ten," or "eleven for ten"; while transfer at a loss consists in saying, "I sell you what I have just bought at a loss of ten for eleven," and in that case the difference between the price of the purchase and that of the transfer is one in eleven, or, according to others, one in ten.

If the transfer has been made "for the price of the purchase," the transferee owes only the price and nothing more; but if the words used by the purchaser were "for what it has cost me," he owes, besides the price of the purchase, what the original purchaser has paid by way of remuneration to the measurer, the broker, the watchman, the cleaner, the repairer and the dyer he may have employed, and also the price of the dye and other substances he may have used to increase the value of the thing purchased. These expenses, however, are not taken into account if the original purchaser has himself cleaned, measured, or transported the article, nor if another person has done so gratuitously.

It is obligatory, in every transfer, that both contracting parties should be aware of the price of purchase, or what takes the place of it. ††Otherwise the agreement is void. The law admits a presumption in favour of a declaration by the transferrer with regard to price and term of payment, whether the price has been paid in coin, or other articles given instead, and with regard to redhibitory defects supervening while the goods were in his possession.

*If a transferrer declares he has bought the goods for one hundred pieces of money, while in reality he had them for ninety, he loses the ten pieces and any other profit he would otherwise have made; but this does not give the transferee a right to cancel the agreement. †If, after an agreement has been concluded, the transferrer declares that the article transferred at a profit for one hundred really cost him one hundred and ten, and that thus the transferrer is really at a loss, the agreement is void, unless the transferee consents to accept the truth of this subsequent declaration of the transferrer. [†This circumstance does not render the transfer invalid.]

But if, on the contrary, in such circumstances the transferee does not accept the subsequent declaration of the transferrer with reference to the price, and the latter can allege no adequate excuse for his former erroneous statement, his later declaration is inadmissible, even if he could prove the truth of it. †His only remedy then is to call upon the transferrer to take an oath that he was ignorant of the real price of purchase. Where, however, the transferrer can allege an adequate excuse for his former erroneous declaration with regard to the price, he may at his choice either challenge the transferee to take an oath, or prove the truth of his later declaration.

CHAPTER VII.—SALE OF TREES, FRUIT, AND STANDING CROPS

Section 1 (1)

If one says, "I sell you this land," or "this courtyard," or "this plot of ground," the buildings and trees upon it are *ipso facto* comprised in the bargain. This rule, however, according to our school, does not apply to the case of a pledge or security. Plants whose roots remain in the soil for more than one year, such as the *katt* and chicory are considered to be trees and consequently included in a sale of land; but this is not the case with plants whose roots give only a single crop, like wheat, barley and other grain. Although in consequence the vendor remains owner of these plants, our school does not forbid the sale of a field that has growing grain on it; but the purchaser can make this a cause of cancellation, if he was not aware of it. †Previous sowing does not in itself form an obstacle to the delivery of a piece of ground, and the loss or accidental deterioration of the crops renders the purchaser liable as depository, from the moment of surrender by the vendor. Planting shoots is the same thing as sowing. †If the purchaser does not renounce the purchase upon perceiving that the land has been sown, he loses the right to damage he would otherwise have on the ground that he had had no use of the land until the harvest.

The combined sale of a field and the crops on it is void, both as regards the land and as regards the crops; though some jurists maintain that this rule is of doubtful application, so far as the land is concerned.

A sale of land includes the stones that may happen naturally to be upon it, but not those brought there by the hand of man. A purchaser has, however, no right to cancel the contract, if at the time of concluding the bargain he knew such stones were there; but he may oblige the vendor to remove them. If the purchaser was unaware of the condition of the ground, the same principle should be observed, if the stones can be removed without injury to the soil. If this is impossible, the purchaser may, at his choice, either cancel the contract on the ground of redhibitory defects, or oblige the vendor to remove the stones and level the soil. As to the obligation of the vendor to indemnify the purchaser, under these circumstances, authorities are not in agreement. I prefer the view which admits that a reasonable indemnity may be claimed; of course only in a case where the stones are removed after possession has been taken, for before this a purchaser has no right to any compensation.

In a sale the following things are understood to be included:—

1. In the sale of a "garden" are included the ground, trees, walls, and—according to our school—the buildings, that may be in it.

2. In the sale of a "village" are included all buildings and empty ground within the circuit of the walls; ††but not the fields outside.

3. In the sale of a "house" are included the ground, and all buildings, including baths; but not movable furniture, such as pails, pulleys, and beds. Included are also fixed doors, with their hinges, washing-house vats, fixed shutters, fixed stairs, ††upper and lower mill stones, †and the keys of fixed locks.

4. In the sale of an "animal" is included any shoeing of iron or other material applied to the soles of the feet.

5. In the sale of a "slave" are included the clothes he is wearing. [†The sale of a slave does not include the clothes he is wearing.]

Section 1 (2)

The sale of a tree includes that of the roots and leaves; but as to the leaves of a mulberry tree authorities are not agreed. Such sale includes also the branches, except those already withered. A tree can be sold either on condition that it be torn up or cut down or on condition that it shall remain where it is. The latter is assumed, if no condition be mentioned. The sale of a tree does not extend to the soil in which it is planted, but the purchaser has a right to use the ground as long as the tree remains; and if the tree dies, he must remove it.

The fruit of a palm that has been sold belongs to the vendor or to the purchaser according to agreement. If no stipulation has been made, the fruit belongs to the purchaser if it has not been fertilised by the vendor, but otherwise to the latter. As to trees that bear fruit but no flowers, such as the fig and vine, the fruit belongs to the vendor if it has already appeared at the time of sale, otherwise to the purchaser. But in the case of fruit that grows out from flowers that then fall off, as with apples and apricots, it belongs to the purchaser if not yet formed, †and also even if formed, if the flower has not yet fallen. If the bargain is concluded later than this, the fruit belongs to the vendor.

When one sells "the palm trees of a garden that have already produced spathes of which some are fertilised," all the fruit is the vendor's, unless the purchaser has made a special stipulation reserving for himself the spathes not fertilised. †If, on the contrary, it is a question of the palm-trees, not of a single garden, but of two distinct gardens, of which only one has fertilised palms, then each must be separately considered. If the fruit remains the vendor's, he is obliged to gather it at once, if such is the agreement; but otherwise he may leave it on the trees until the proper season for plucking it. Both contracting parties have a right to water the ground when necessary if it is profitable for the tree or the fruit, and neither may place any hindrance in the way of this being done; but if the watering is harmful to the tree or the fruit, it can only be done by mutual consent. If watering is harmful to the tree only, but not to the fruit, or *vice versâ*, the contract should be cancelled if the two parties cannot agree about it, unless the injured party is willing to enter into an arrangement. Some jurists maintain, however, there is always a right of watering under any circumstances. The purchaser can compel the vendor to gather the fruit, or water the tree, if the tree only has been sold and the fruit absorb the sap.

Section 2

The fruit of a tree may be sold as soon as it has begun to ripen, either without expressing any condition, or on condition that it be gathered, or on condition that it remain some time longer on the tree. On the other hand, it cannot be sold apart from the tree until it has begun to ripen, unless it is stipulated that it must be gathered immediately, and the fruit so gathered prematurely is of some use. For example this is not the case with pears. Some authorities, however, maintain the validity of a sale of ripening fruit, unreservedly, if the purchaser is already the owner of the tree. [If, in such a case, the vendor has stipulated that the fruit must be plucked immediately, the purchaser is not obliged to carry out the obligation.]

A combined sale of fruit and tree is lawful, without the addition of any special agreement; but a stipulation that the fruit must be plucked at once is in this case inadmissible. The law forbids a sale of green standing grain, unless it is stipulated that it be at once plucked out or reaped; but the sale of grain, whether with the ground, or after ripening, is permitted unreservedly.

For the validity of a sale of ripening grain or fruit the law requires that the true subject of the bargain can be seen, *i.e.* that one can see the fig, the grape, or the barley. Products of the soil having hidden grains, such as corn in the ear or lentil seeds in their pods, cannot be sold without these envelopes. Shafii even advocated, in his second period, the prohibition of a sale with the envelopes. This prohibition, however, does not relate to products of the soil whose envelope is only removed at the moment of eating; nor to those with two envelopes, such as nuts, almonds, and beans, which may lawfully be sold in their inner, but not in their outer, envelope. A single authority maintains, however, that a sale in the outer envelope is legal, if the products be not yet dry.

The first sign of maturity in fruit that does not change colour is the fact of its being seen from the outside to attain its full development, and of having acquired its agreeable taste; and an appearance of red and black in fruit that changes. It is enough that a part of the fruit, however small, arrives at maturity, to render lawful the unconditional sale of that fruit. If the fruit of one or more gardens is sold, in some of which only maturity has begun, the rule given in the second part of the preceding section with regard to fertilisation must be observed.

A person who sells fruit beginning to ripen should, although remaining owner of the tree, continue to water it, as well before as after the transfer of the fruit to the purchaser, until the gathering. However, after the transfer of the fruit to the purchaser, the latter has the right to dispose of them; and it is he upon whom the loss falls, in case of frost or other similar occurrence. This at least is the opinion entertained by Shafii during his Egyptian period. If the fruit deteriorates because the vendor neglects to water the tree, the purchaser has even the right to cancel the contract; but in the case of fruit sold before the appearance of signs of maturity, under the express condition that the purchaser shall gather it immediately, any loss from deterioration caused by insufficient watering by the vendor falls, according to the best doctrine, upon the purchaser, if the latter delays the gathering agreed upon.

In general, the law does not permit a sale of fruit, even mature, in the case of a tree or plant that does not ordinarily yield its fruit all at one time, but at different intervals, so that new fruit appears on the same tree or plant along with that already grown, as *e.g.* in the case of figs, or of cucumbers. The validity of such a sale is admitted only—

1. On condition that the purchaser must immediately gather the fruit sold him.

2. In a case where the peculiarity exists only for a few scattered fruits. *But the purchaser always has a right of cancellation, †unless the vendor allows him to take the new fruit as well.

It is forbidden to barter—

1. Corn in the ear for husked corn; an exchange called *mohakala.*
2. Dates on the tree for dry dates; an exchange called *mozabana.*

On the other hand, as an indulgence, the law allows the contra-

called *araya, i.e.* the barter of dates on the tree for dry dates placed at the foot of it; or the exchange of grapes on the vine for raisins; provided in both cases that the amount is less than five *wask.* If the quantity be greater than this, the law admits the validity of such an exchange only if it takes place by two or more different transactions. The contract of *araya* necessitates an immediate taking possession by each party, *i.e.* the measuring and delivery of the dry dates on the one hand, and on the other the transfer of those on the tree. *An exchange of this kind cannot be effected with regard to any other fruit, except dates and grapes. Some authors maintain that only persons with insufficient money to buy green dates can have recourse to this form of contract; but this is not so.

CHAPTER VIII.—DISPUTES BETWEEN VENDOR AND PURCHASER

Where the two contracting parties are agreed upon the validity of a sale; but not upon its details, as *e.g.* the amount or nature of the price, stipulation of a time within which payment should be made, or the quantity of the goods sold; and if neither party is able to prove his case, they should both take an oath as to the falsehood of what is alleged by the adverse party, and the truth of their own statements. The vendor is the first to be sworn; though, according to one jurist, it is the purchaser; and another thinks that they have an equal right to the priority. According to this last authority the court should decide according to circumstances who should have the priority. And some authorities maintain that the priority should be decided by casting lots. *A single oath, combining a denial and an affirmation, is sufficient on the part of each, but the denial must always be pronounced first. Thus one should say, "I did not sell for this sum, but I sold for that."

††When the oath has been taken by both parties, the contract is not considered as being immediately dissolved. The court should first endeavour to persuade the parties to a reconciliation. If this is unsuccessful, then each of the parties has a right to cancel the contract, or, if necessary, the court decrees its dissolution. Some maintain that cancellation must always be decreed by the court. Upon cancellation, however effected, the purchaser must return the thing bought; or its value, if he has already disposed of it either by conversion into immovable property or by enfranchisement or by sale, just as if it had been accidentally destroyed. *The value of an article is that it had on the day it was lost. In case of accidental deterioration, but not total loss,

the purchaser must all the same return the article to the vendor, and indemnify him for the loss in its value.

Disputes between the heirs of the contracting parties are regulated by the same principles as disputes between the parties themselves.

If a dispute has arisen, not about the details, but about the very nature of a contract; as, for example, when one of the parties asserts, "I sold you the article for so much," and the other replies, "No, you gave it me;" no affirmative oath is then necessary, and each party need only swear that he denies his opponent's assertion. After this, the one who has received the donation must return the article received, together with any increase or profit he may have derived from it. †If one of the parties maintains and the other denies the legality of a sale, the presumption is in favour of the former, if he confirms his statement on oath. If, after a cancellation of a contract in the manner referred to, the purchaser brings to the vendor a slave with redhibitory defects as the one he purchased and the vendor asserts that it was another that he sold and delivered, the law admits a presumption in favour of this latter statement. †Similarly, in the contract of *salam*, it is the creditor who enjoys this advantage.

CHAPTER IX.—SLAVES

†A SLAVE who has not been designated by his master to carry on commercial transactions, can buy nothing without first obtaining his master's authorisation. Consequently a person who has sold anything to such a slave without the necessary authorisation, can claim back the goods, not only if they are in the slave's possession but also if the master has them. If the goods are accidentally lost while in possession of the slave, the latter is personally responsible for the payment of the price, even after his enfranchisement; but if they are so lost while in the master's possession, the vendor can claim payment either from the latter, or from the slave after his enfranchisement. A debt contracted by a slave is subject to the same rules as a purchase made by him.

A slave authorised to transact business in general can enter into any engagement up to the value of the things entrusted to him; but if the authorisation extends only to specified acts, he may not pass the limits prescribed. Even a slave authorised unconditionally may not of his own initiative conclude a marriage, nor engage his own services, nor authorise a slave of his own, nor give away for nothing the things entrusted to him, nor enter into commercial relations with his master. Desertion does not necessarily cancel an authorisation: for this the master's withdrawal is required. On the other hand a slave is not regarded as having been authorised, merely because his master has not objected to his transactions. The law insists upon a formal declaration on the part of the master. An affirmation of an authorised slave, with regard to his commercial undertakings, is admissible in a court of law.

A person who knows that a certain individual is a slave should not enter into commercial relations with him, until he has ascertained if he has been duly authorised. This can be done either by asking the master, or by requiring the slave to furnish proof of the position he claims, or by learning the matter from public notoriety. This public notoriety, however, is a controverted point. In any case an oral affirmation by the slave to the effect that he has been authorised is insufficient.

When an authorised slave has received the price of an article he has sold and it is accidentally lost while in his possession, the purchaser can, in case of a legal seizure of the article, cite as guarantor either the slave or his master. Some authorities, however, maintain the contrary opinion so far as regards the master; others consider that the citation of the master is inadmissible unless the slave's goods have been seized. The same divergence of opinion exists upon the subject of the master's responsibility for the payment of the price, in case of seizure of an object bought by an authorised slave. In general the slave himself cannot be seized for a debt of a commercial nature; nor can payment be exacted from the master; but things supplied by the latter alone constitute the joint security of the creditors, †as well as profits realised by the slave in other ways, as by hunting, etc. Everything that a slave, even if authorised, acquires, belongs *ipso facto* to his master; he can acquire nothing for himself, even if his master wished personally to transfer to him a right of ownership.

BOOK 10.—SALE BY ADVANCE

Section 1

The *salam* or advance is a sale of goods that have not been seen, but are specified in the contract. Besides the conditions necessary for an ordinary sale, there are required for the legality of a *salam* the following additional conditions :—

1. The payment of the value advanced must take place on the spot. It is permissible to promise an advance at first in vague terms, provided it is afterwards specified with precision, and paid upon the spot ; but it is not permissible to transfer, as an advance, a debt due from a third person, even if the latter pays immediately. There is no objection to the person who receives the advance touching it and depositing it with the person who made it. It need not consist of coin ; and may even consist of the use of some object, but possession must still be taken on the spot. In the case of dissolution of contract of *salam*, what has been advanced may be reclaimed, where it is some particular object still existing, though a few jurists maintain that the advance may then be replaced by other things of value. This faculty, however, is limited in their opinion, to cases where the objects advanced were not specified in the contract, but afterwards, though upon the same occasion. *Inspection of what is given by way of advance suffices to ascertain the quantity.

2. The goods upon which the advance has been given must be regarded as a debt due by the person receiving their value in advance. Consequently, if one says, *e.g.* " I advance you this piece of cloth for this slave here," there is neither a *salam* nor an ordinary sale. But if one says, " I buy from you a piece of cloth of such and such a description, for these pieces of money," to which the other party replies, " I sell you the piece of cloth," it is an ordinary sale, or according to others, a contract of *salam*, that has been concluded.

3. According to our school the place of delivery must be indicated ; at any rate if the *salam* is effected in a place which is either unsuitable for it, or would necessitate much expense in transport. Otherwise no stipulation as to place of delivery is required. Delivery of the goods

can be effected either at once or within a given time ; but if no time is agreed upon, it should be done at once. Others maintain that an omission to stipulate a time of delivery nullifies the *salam*. In all cases, if the delivery is not effected at once, a time must be determined on, either according to the months of the Arabs, or according to those of the Persians or Greeks. A mere enumeration of a certain number of months, not mentioning any particular calendar, is held to refer to the lunar year. In case of an agreement concluded in the middle of a month, its remaining days are taken into account ; so that, for example, a term " of one month " expires thirty days later. †The time may also be indicated by saying " at the festival " or " at the month of Jumada."

SECTION 2 (1)

The conditions permitting one legally to receive an advance on goods are four—

1. The goods should be of a nature to admit of their delivery at the term stipulated. Consequently an advance may be received for goods coming from another place only when they are regularly brought for sale to the place of delivery ; otherwise such a course would be inadmissible. When an advance has been given on produce to be found everywhere, but which happens to be unprocurable at the moment stipulated for delivery, *the contract is not necessarily cancelled, but the creditor can at his choice either claim its cancellation, or have patience and wait until the things arrive. †A creditor never has any right to cancel the contract before the expiry of the term fixed, even though he may know for certain that the goods cannot be delivered him within the time agreed.

2. There must be a precise specification of the amount, either by measure of capacity, or by weight, or by number, or by measure of length, except as follows :—Produce ordinarily sold by capacity, may be specified by weight, or *vice versâ* ; but the quantity may not be specified in two ways. Thus one may not stipulate for one hundred *saas* of corn to weigh so many pounds. Melons, tomatoes, cucumbers, quinces, and pomegranates are estimated only by weight ; while nuts and almonds are calculated either by weight, †or, when the sizes vary very little, by measure. Bricks are sold by number, or weight, but not by measure. In the latter case the contract is invalid, unless it is the local custom, †when it becomes a regular sale. An advance cannot be given upon a certain quantity of fruit from some village specially mentioned ; †but this may be done in the case of a large village which is sure to have a sufficient supply at the due date.

3. The quality must be known, or at least those essential qualities on which depends the object of the purchase. They must be mentioned in the contract, without, however, making an enumeration so meticulous as to cause great difficulty in finding goods to correspond to the description. Consequently a *salam* is forbidden with respect to articles with which this is impossible. Such is the case, for example, with a combination of qualities, each with a particular object, as in the eatable known as *harisa,* the medicine *majun,* the perfume called *ghaliya,* shoes, or a compound antidote. †On the other hand a *salam* is lawful in the case of goods which, though composite have a single particular object. Instances of these are the materials known as *attaba* and *khazz,* cheese, *akit,* honey, date vinegar and grapes ; †but not bread, at least according to most jurists.

4. The things should not be difficult to obtain, by their very nature—like game, in places where it is rare—nor of a quality rarely met with, though of an article itself not at all rare, such as pearls of an enormous size, precious stones of a certain shade of colour, a slave with her sister or child, etc.

SECTION 2 (2)

Domestic animals, and slaves, can be dealt with in a contract of *salam.* In the case of slaves their nationality should be specified, as, *e.g.* "a Turkish slave" ; or their colour, stipulating, for example, "a white slave," and mentioning whether he should have a tawny or a ruddy complexion. Besides this, when dealing in slaves, sex, age, and approximate height should be indicated ; but it is not necessary to specify whether a slave has brown eyelashes, or is fat, etc. In the case of camels, horses, mules and donkeys, sex, age, colour and species are mentioned ; in the case of birds, species and size of the body ; in the case of meat it must be stated if it is beef, mutton or goat, and if it is a castrated animal, or one with milk, or one for fatting. It should also be mentioned if the meat comes from the leg, shoulder, or rib. Bones must be accepted in customary proportion with meat.

As to cloth, its nature, length and breadth must be mentioned, and the quality of the stuff determined, whether it is coarse or fine, hard or soft, rough or delicate. Unless otherwise agreed upon the material is assumed to be unbleached. An advance may be given on washed cloth, and on material of which the threads have been dyed before weaving, as is the case with striped cloth. By analogy the validity of an advance on cloth dyed after weaving may also be admitted. [†Most authorities deny the legality of an advance upon this material.]

In the case of dates, the colour, species, origin, and the size of the fruit should be mentioned, and whether they are old or fresh. Wheat, barley, and other cereals, and beans, are subject to the same rule as dates. The things necessary to be known when stipulating about honey are—whether it is from the mountains or the town, summer or autumn honey, white or yellow ; but it matters little whether it is old or fresh. It is forbidden to give an advance upon what has been cooked or roasted, but there is no objection to doing so upon goods heated by the sun. *An advance is also illegal upon the heads of slaughtered animals, and upon things having individuality, such as worked pots, skins of animals, earthen jars, saucers, bottles, lanterns, kettles ; but it is lawful when given, *e.g.* upon the small square vessels called *satal*, or on pots or saucers, etc., of metal cast in a mould—upon things, in a word, that are made in the mass and resemble one another. †It is not necessary to mention whether the things are good or bad, for even if nothing is said about it one is assumed to have promised that they are in good condition. Both the contracting parties must be aware of the quality of the goods ; and a third person should also be aware of it, in order that they may appeal to his decision in case of disagreement.

Section 3

The substitution, for the thing stipulated, of another different in nature or kind, is totally prohibited. Some jurists, however, maintain the legality of a substitution, provided the difference is only in kind ; but they admit that the other party is not obliged to accept anything but what was agreed on. It is even permissible to offer, but never obligatory to accept, an inferior quality to that stipulated. †The person who has given the advance cannot refuse to accept produce of the same kind as, but of a superior quality to, that promised him.

If the debtor brings the goods before the time agreed upon, the creditor may refuse to accept, if he has a valid reason for so doing, *e.g.* if it is an animal he will have to feed, or if a hostile incursion is apprehended at the moment ; but otherwise he cannot refuse, especially if the debtor has good ground for anticipating delivery, *e.g.* if he wishes to redeem a pledge, *or even if he merely wants to discharge his obligation.

If, after expiry of the term agreed upon, a creditor meets his debtor elsewhere than at the place stipulated, he cannot prevent the latter fulfilling his engagement upon the spot, if the transport of the goods would involve some expense ; ††nor can he in such a case recover the value of the goods for breach of contract. But the creditor may refuse to accept the things, if the place of meeting is not a safe one. †In all other cases the creditor is bound to accept the goods, even though the place be not that agreed upon.

Section 4

A loan is a meritorious act on the part of the creditor, and is effected by the following words :—"I lend you this," "I advance you this," "Take this and give me something similar in exchange," or, "I make you owner of it, till you pay me an equal sum." The law requires for the validity of this agreement †that the offer should be accepted, and that the lender should be capable of disposing of his property freely. Anything that can be made subject to a contract of *salam* can be lent, *with the single exception of a female slave, with whom the lender can lawfully have intercourse. †On the other hand what cannot be made the subject of a contract of *salam*, cannot be lent. If the things lent are measurable, an equal quantity of similar things must be returned ; but if the things lent are not measurable, then things resembling them must be returned ; or, according to some jurists, the value of these. If the lender meets the borrower at a place other than that where the contract was made and asks the return of the loan, his demand is admissible ; but if the transport of the object borrowed would cause expense, he can claim only its value at the place of agreement.

The lender may not stipulate for a return of produce of a better quality than that lent ; nor for interest of any sort or kind ; and if the borrower adds anything extra, when returning what was borrowed, it is pure generosity on his part. A stipulation that produce of an inferior quality to that lent shall be returned, and a stipulation that the borrower shall in his turn lend something to the lender, are void ; †but the contract remains otherwise valid. It is the same with the stipulation of a term of payment, if entirely in favour of the debtor ; †but if it is in the creditor's favour, for example, if the loan is made at a moment when a town is about to be sacked, and payment is to be made when quiet has returned, then the stipulation is equivalent to a return of produce of better quality, and consequently the contract itself is void. A creditor may legally stipulate for a pledge or personal security for the return of the loan.

Ownership of things lent is transferred only by taking possession ; or, according to one authority by a disposal on the part of the borrower, †though this does not prevent the lender being able to claim their return, as long as they are still undisposed of in the borrower's possession.

BOOK 11.—PLEDGE OR SECURITY

SECTION 1

SECURITY cannot be legally given except by mutual consent of the parties interested, *i.e.* by offer and acceptance. There may be added a stipulation, of the very essence of the contract, to the effect that the creditor shall have a right of preference on the sale of the thing pledged; or a stipulation tending to strengthen the contract, as, *e.g.* that it should be concluded in the presence of witness; or even a stipulation without any reasonable object. But a stipulation that would prevent the creditor exercising his right would nullify the contract. A stipulation profiting the creditor to the detriment of the debtor, *e.g.* allowing the former exclusive and unlimited use of the article, is null, *and consequently nullifies the contract. *A stipulation that all increase in the thing shall remain pledged with him is unlawful, and causes the illegality, but not the nullity of the contract. The contracting parties must have the free disposition of their property; consequently the goods of a minor or a lunatic cannot be given in security by the guardian or curator, except in case of absolute necessity or obvious advantage. It is only on the same condition that a guardian or curator may stipulate a pledging of property in order to secure the payment of debts due to the persons in their charge, for under ordinary circumstances these debts should be recovered as soon as possible.

†The thing given as security should be something definite and precise. An undivided share in something owned in common by several persons may be given in security; or even a slave without her child, or, *vice versâ*, the child without its mother, although in these cases a sale would be unlawful, and consequently in case of an execution sale mother and child must be put up to auction together. In this latter case the proceeds are divided between creditor and debtor in proportion to the value of the mother and of the child. First the mother alone is put up to auction, and then both together; the difference gives the value of the child. The pledging of a slave guilty of a crime, or of an apostate slave, is subject to the same rules as their sale. The pledging of a slave to be enfranchised under the provisions of a will, and that of a slave-

whose enfranchisement may become obligatory before the satisfaction of the debt, are void, according to our school.

In the case of pledging of things liable to rapid deterioration that may be preserved in a dry state, like dates, drying must be resorted to. If this is impossible, giving such produce in security is only lawful in the case of a debt due immediately, or due before deterioration is likely to commence. Otherwise the contract may be effected only on the express condition that the thing shall be sold and the proceeds of the sale remain pledged ; and even then the sale may only take place at the moment it is feared deterioration will begin. The proceeds thus remain pledged, instead of the thing itself. A stipulation tending to exclude the right to sell under these circumstances nullifies the security, in the same way as an omission to stipulate with regard to the sale and the price, at least when it is known that deterioration will occur before the due date. *If this fact is not known, the absence of such a clause does not invalidate the contract. If something has been pledged which, though not naturally liable to rapid deterioration, is accidentally exposed to such an occurrence, as for instance wheat that has become damp, the security remains valid, in spite of the accident.

It is lawful to borrow a thing in order to pledge it, a proceeding which one authority regards as coming under the same rules as a gratuitous loan, *but most consider as a real security. In any case one must mention the nature, amount, and details of the bond and of the other sureties ; and if the thing lent is accidentally lost when in the creditor's possession he is not liable for it. The owner of an article borrowed in this way cannot claim to have it back once it is in the creditor's possession. On the expiry of the term allowed for payment, or, if the contract admits of it, at once, the owner must, on the creditor's demand, sell the article lent, if the debtor has not yet paid. The owner of the article can then, of course, seize the debtor's goods and recover the amount of the sale.

Section 2

Security may be given only for a definite, obligatory debt. Consequently it is not permitted to a person who desires in that way to secure the execution of some real obligation, such as the restitution of some object unlawfully usurped or borrowed ; or to secure some future debt, such as the repayment of a sum of money he intends to lend some one. Security is given in the following words :—" I lend you these pieces of money, provided you pledge me your slave." To this offer the answer is, " I accept the loan, and grant you the security asked for." Or the offer may be made thus, " I sell you this article for so much provided the coat is pledged to me," and the answer, "I buy the article, and grant you the security asked for." One may not secure by a pledge the periodical payments resulting from an enfranchisement by contract, nor the price stipulated for contract work before it is finished, or, according to others before it is begun, because these are not as yet definite and obligatory debts. On the other hand, security may lawfully be given for the payment of the price of a thing sold during the period of the right of option. The payment of a debt may be secured by two pledges even when successive; but according to the doctrine adopted by Shafii in Egypt, one may not pledge with a creditor an article already pledged him for another debt.

The security becomes irrevocable only when the creditor has taken possession of the object pledged. Possession may, however, be taken by the creditor's agent. The creditor may not appoint the debtor or his slave as his agent for this purpose. Authorities are not agreed as to whether he may so appoint the debtor's generally authorised slave; but he may certainly appoint the slave undergoing gradual enfranchisement. The pledging of an article already in possession of the creditor, either as deposit or because illegally usurped, becomes irrevocable only from the moment when he could have taken possession of it, if he had not had it already. *And in such a case the law requires that the debtor should declare that the change in the nature of the possession has taken place with his full consent. Subsequent pledging can never relieve a creditor from the consequences of any usurpation of which he may have been guilty; but he is freed from them *ipso facto* if the owner entrusts the article to his care as a deposit. The security is *ipso facto* revoked if the debtor disposes of the thing pledged, before the creditor has taken possession, in a way which causes him to lose the ownership of it, *e.g.* if he gives it away, or pledges it to some one else, provided it is effectively taken possession of. The same consequence is recognised by law if, before possession has been taken, the debtor begins the contractual enfranchisement of his slave, *or provides for his freedom in his will, or if a female slave is rendered pregnant by him; but not if he merely cohabits with her, or gives her in marriage to some one else. †Neither is security nullified by death, nor by lunacy, of one of the contracting parties, before possession has been taken; nor by a liquid that has been pledged becoming fermented; nor by the flight of a pledged slave.

After the creditor has taken possession, the debtor can no longer dispose of the pledged object, so as to lose the ownership of it. As to the validity of an enfranchisement authorities are not agreed. *As a rule it is considered valid in the case of a solvent debtor, who should in that case pledge the value of the slave at the moment of enfranchisement. But if the debtor is insolvent, and consequently unable to execute the intended enfranchisement †the slave is not thereby freed, even though afterwards redeemed. The pledging of a slave who is to be enfranchised at a certain date, or who has been conditionally enfranchised is lawful; and the expiry of the term, or the fulfilling of the condition, before the due date of the security, has the same effect as a simple and voluntary enfranchisement. If the term does not expire, or the condition is not fulfilled, until after that date, ††the enfranchisement takes place *ipso facto*, whether the master is solvent or not.

After the creditor has taken possession, the debtor can no longer—

1. Pledge the thing to another person.

2. Give a pledged female slave in marriage.

3. Lend the thing pledged; at least where the debt is due at once, or at a term expiring before the loan.

4. Cohabit with a pledged female slave. A contravention of this precept involves the consequence that a child born of this cohabitation is considered free.* Upon the question whether the mother becomes free by this maternity there is the same difference of opinion as with regard to the simple, voluntary enfranchisement of a pledged slave. †But it is agreed that in these circumstances a female slave is *ipso facto* enfranchised by reason of her maternity, upon the expiry of the due date of the security, even if the debtor is insolvent; and that the latter is bound to pledge the value of the slave, if she dies in childbirth.

A debtor remains owner of a pledged article, and can make what use of it he likes, provided he does not diminish its value. He may ride a pledged beast, or live in a house he has given in security. On the other hand, he may not build on or cultivate pledged land; but if he has already done these unlawful acts, he is not obliged to root up what has been planted, or take down the buildings either before or after the debt has become due, unless in the latter case the value of the ground with the plantations or constructions on it is insufficient to pay the debt, and the value of the land will be increased by their removal. When it is possible for the debtor to use the thing pledged, without its being actually in his charge, it should remain in the creditor's possession; but if this is impossible it should be intrusted into the charge of the debtor, if he demands it, to be held on sufferance. The creditor has the right to have this restitution effected before witnesses, if he has reason to doubt the debtor's honesty.

A creditor may always allow a debtor to dispose of a pledged article, even in a manner not otherwise permitted by law; but this authorisation may be revoked at any time before the debtor has made use of it. If under these circumstances a debtor has disposed of a pledged article, not knowing that the authorisation has been revoked, he is in the same position as an agent who has acted in ignorance of the revocation of his appointment. But a creditor cannot give a debtor permission to sell a pledged article before the debt is due, whether this is done in order so to obtain an earlier payment, or on the understanding that the proceeds will be pledged instead of the article itself.

Section 3

When the security has become irrevocable by possession having been taken, the creditor has a right to keep the article pledged, without prejudice to what has been said in the preceding section, as to the use which the debtor can make of it. The parties may if they like agree to intrust the article to the care of a third person of irreproachable character; or to two such persons, at the same time stipulating for a joint or separate performance of their duties by the depositaries. †If nothing has been stipulated with regard to this, neither can do anything in the matter alone. If a depositary is dead, or has ceased, by notorious misconduct, to be worthy of confidence, the contracting parties can deposit the article where they please; or if they cannot agree about it, the court may order its sequestration.

A creditor may insist on the sale of a pledged article if the debt has not been paid by the due date; and he is entitled to payment out of the proceeds, in preference to any other person. The sale is effected by the debtor or his agent, but never without the creditor's previous authorisation. If the creditor refuses the required authorisation the court will notify him that in default of his authorisation the debtor will be released from his obligation. When, on the other hand, it is the creditor who claims either the payment of the debt or the sale of the article, and the debtor refuses, the court will order the latter to fulfil his obligation or sell the article, and if he persists in his refusal after this order, the court may itself proceed with the sale without the debtor's concurrence. †But the creditor can never effect the sale in the absence of the debtor even with his consent. When it has been agreed that the sale shall be effected by a depositary, the latter may if necessary proceed with it without the debtor's concurrence, keeping the proceeds as depositary, *i.e.* at the debtor's risk, until the creditor has taken possession. In case of a legal seizure of the article pledged and sold in this way by a depositary the purchaser may cite as guarantee either the depositary or the debtor, who is in any case ultimately liable towards the depositary. This citation as guarantee is admissible even if the proceeds of the sale are accidentally lost when in charge of the depositary. A depositary may sell a pledged article only at a reasonable price, and for cash, in locally current coin. If after the sale, but before the expiry of the time of option, another person bids more, the first bargain should be cancelled and the thing sold to the highest bidder.

A debtor must provide for the up-keep of a thing pledged, and a creditor has a right to have this enforced by the court. On the other hand, a creditor may not prevent a debtor from improving or repairing the article ; for example a debtor may have his pledged slave bled ; for the property is his, and he has only intrusted it to the creditor as a deposit.

The loss of a pledged object does not affect the debt ; and as to the responsibility of the creditor, it does not matter whether the security is valid or not, for in any case it is a deposit intrusted to his care.

It is illegal to stipulate that the thing pledged shall be considered as sold to the creditor upon the expiry of the term allowed for payment of the debt. Such stipulation renders illegal both security and sale.

A thing pledged remains on deposit until the due date ; consequently there is a presumption in favour of the creditor's statement on oath in any proceeding against him for loss of the article ; but not, according to most authorities, if it is a question of the restitution of a pledge.

A creditor who intentionally cohabits with a female slave pledged to him, is guilty of the crime of fornication ; and the excuse cannot be admitted by the court that he was ignorant of the prohibition of intercourse with such person, unless he has recently become a Muhammadan, or was brought up in the country far from the society of men acquainted with the law. †He may allege as an excuse that the debtor gave him permission ; and in this special case, though not guilty of fornication, he is liable to the slave for dower, if he forced her to cohabitation, and the child is his, and free from its birth. And, finally, he owes the debtor the value of the child as damage.

When a pledged article is lost by the fault of a third person, and the creditor receives from that person another article in its place, it is regarded as the thing pledged. Any proceeding against the individual in question to oblige him to replace the original pledge, must be taken by the debtor. †If he declines to make good his right in the matter, the creditor can do nothing as against the third person. Similarly, if a pledged slave is assassinated by a third person, the debtor alone can claim an application of the *lex talionis ;* but the contract of security is cancelled *ipso facto.* But if, on the other hand, there is only occasion for inflicting a pecuniary penalty, either because the debtor has pardoned his slave's assassin, or because the homicide was not intentional, neither debtor nor creditor can of their own initiative remit the penalty.

The security given does not extend to increase from the thing pledged, if this increase consists of what has individual existence, like the fruit of trees, the young of animals, or the children of slaves. However, if an animal with young or a pregnant slave has been given in security, and the pregnancy continues until the debt falls due, *beast and slave must be sold as they are, with their offspring, if already born. *Where the pregnancy does not occur until after the security has been given, though it may exist at the moment of sale, the mother alone is pledged, and the creditor has no claim to the offspring.

Section 4

When a pledged slave commits a crime involving a penalty under the law of talion, the rights of the injured party have the first preference, and the security is cancelled by the capital penalty, or by a legal sale of the slave to recover the price of blood. The capital penalty has the effect of cancelling the security, both if imposed at the instance of the debtor as owner of the slave, or at that of a third party; ††but where the debtor, not a third party, claims, from whatever motive, only a pecuniary penalty, then the security is unaffected, and the slave remains pledged as if nothing had happened. When a slave pledged by his master kills another pledged to the same master, both securities are cancelled by the execution of the criminal; but when there is ground only for a pecuniary penalty, the master of the delinquent can claim this amount in place of the dead slave pledged to him. The culpable slave must then be sold, in spite of the security, and the proceeds remain pledged, by law, with the master in place of the dead slave. According to others, however, a sale is unnecessary, and the slave who has committed the crime, replaces *ipso facto* the dead slave. If murderer and victim were both of them slaves pledged to the same creditor for a single debt, he must resign himself to this diminution in his security. If the two individuals were pledged for two distinct debts, he may transfer to the remaining slave the debt for which the security has been lost to him, if he has good reason to do so.

A security is cancelled by the accidental loss of the thing pledged. The article itself is released by a renunciation on the part of the creditor, or by the remission of the debt. As a security is indivisible, the article remains pledged as long as the debt is not either remitted or paid in full. On the other hand, when half the share in a slave is pledged for one debt, and the other half for a second debt, a remission of one of them releases the half share. A slave owned jointly by two masters and pledged by them, is proportionately released by a remission granted to one only.

Section 5

In all disputes between debtor and creditor about anything pledged, or about the quantity of it, the presumption is in favour of the former's assertion, if substantiated on oath; provided that it is not a security which the debtor was obliged to effect. For if, *e.g.* in a sale, one of the parties has stipulated that the other shall pledge him something in order to insure the due execution of the contract, both parties must take an oath. If in any proceeding brought against two persons who together pledged a slave of whom they were joint owners, for a debt of a hundred pieces of money, one admits the fact and the other denies it, the slave is considered to have been pledged only on the part of the owner who admits, *i.e.* for fifty pieces; while the other owner has the advantage of a presumption in his favour, provided he substantiates his denial on oath. This presumption, however, like any other, can be legally disproved, and the owner who admits may even be called as a witness to this effect, in order to show the falsity of his partner's assertions.

In any proceeding with regard to the taking possession of the thing pledged, the following distinctions must be observed :—

1. The article is in the debtor's possession; or it is in the creditor's, but the debtor says he usurped it. In both these cases the law admits a presumption in favour of the debtor, on oath; †and it is the same if he states that he delivered it to the creditor, but not as a pledge.

2. The debtor, having admitted that the creditor took possession of the article as a pledge, withdraws this admission as being untrue. In this case the debtor may only insist that an oath be administered to the creditor; though other jurists maintain that he cannot even do this, and that the claim of the creditor should be at once allowed, unless the debtor can give some adequate explanation of his previous admission. Proof on his part that this admission had been based on false documents, would be regarded as a satisfactory explanation.

If one of the two contracting parties alleges that a pledged slave is guilty of a crime, and the other denies it, the presumption is in favour of the latter, on oath. Even if the debtor declares that the crime was committed before possession was taken, *the law still admits a presumption in favour of the creditor's denial on oath. †But in these circumstances the oath of the creditor does not in any way affect the debtor's obligation towards the injured party. This obligation consists, at the debtor's choice, either in the value of the slave or in the indemnity due for the crime, whichever is most advantageous for him. If in such a case the creditor should refuse to be sworn, the court should administer the oath to the injured party, not to the debtor himself; and after the oath has been taken the slave should be sold for the damage, but not to reimburse the creditor to whom he was pledged. And lastly, if the creditor has consented to the sale of a pledged slave who is guilty of a crime but afterwards asserts that he withdrew his consent before the sale took place, while the debtor alleges he did not do this until after the sale, †the presumption is in favour of the creditor.

When a debtor owes two debts, each of a thousand pieces of money, one only being secured by a pledge, he may declare, when paying one thousand pieces, that he is thereby clearing off the most onerous debt, and the law will presume that this is the truth. If he has omitted to make this declaration at the time of payment, he may do so afterwards; though some authorities maintain that in this case the security is proportionally distributed.

Section 6

At the death of a debtor his debts must be paid, so far as the amount of his assets allow, the latter being regarded as the joint security of the creditors. Only one author maintains that the estate can be seized for debt in the same way as the person of a slave for the pecuniary consequences of a crime committed by him. *The estate is distributed amongst the creditors in proportion to their claims, unless there is some legitimate cause for preference, which is in any case independent of the amount due. †Where the heir has disposed of the estate, without there appearing to be any debt, and a properly authenticated debt is subsequently established, as *e.g.* by the redhibition of some article sold; the dispositions made by the inheritor are not *ipso facto* nullified, but they must be revoked, if there is no other way of paying the debt. It is undisputed that the inheritor can keep the estate and pay the debts from his own means. The obligation to pay the debts so far as the estate will allow, does not in any way affect the rights of the inheritor; and the profits of the estate, of a separate character, such as those realised from the labour of slaves or from births subsequent to the opening of the succession, belong to the inheritor, and cannot be included when determining the amount seizable for the payment of the debts.

BOOK 12.—BANKRUPTCY, ETC.

CHAPTER I.—BANKRUPTCY

Section 1

A person whose debts exceed the value of his property should be declared bankrupt, upon the demand of his creditors, but bankruptcy should never be declared on account of debts not yet due. *A declaration of bankruptcy for debts due does not render other debts not yet due claimable before the due date. If a person's debts are counterbalanced by his property, and he can also gain a livelihood by his labour, there is no ground for a declaration of bankruptcy. †This is so also if he cannot work, and consequently his support is a charge upon his assets. A bankruptcy is not declared on the initiative of the court, but as has been said on the demand of the creditors. If all the creditors do not support the application, the total of the debts due to the petitioning creditors, taken together, should amount to a sum sufficient to authorise the declaration. †Proceedings in bankruptcy may also be begun upon the demand of the debtor.

An immediate consequence of bankruptcy is that the debtor becomes *ipso facto* dispossessed of the administration of his property; while the court should in the presence of witnesses explain to him the measures taken with regard to the matter, so that he may abstain from any further disposition of his property. Only one jurist maintains that a sale, donation, or enfranchisement made by a bankrupt should remain suspended until it becomes clear whether these dispositions can be maintained without prejudicing the payment of the debts. If this is the case they should be regarded as valid, according to this jurist, but not otherwise. *On the other hand, most authorities maintain the nullity of these arrangements, for the same reason as for all others. †A declared bankrupt cannot transfer his property to his creditors, in order to free himself from his obligations, without the permission of the court; ††though there is no objection to his taking an advance on goods he promises to deliver by a certain date, nor to his making a purchase and stipulating for a delay in payment. These future obligations are on his own personal responsibility, and have nothing in common with his property that has been seized. Bankruptcy also leaves intact purely personal rights, such as legal capacity to marry, repudiate or divorce a wife, claim an application of the law of talion, or grant a pardon in accordance with it. An admission made by a bankrupt, concerning a right or obligation that has become effective before the bankruptcy, *binds the creditors; but they are not obliged to take into consideration an admission regarding obligations that become effective only at a later or indeterminate date, †unless it has reference to a crime. A bankrupt can of his own accord return goods he has just bought, on account of redhibitory defects, if such redhibition profits the estate. †But he is prohibited from dealing with anything he may obtain afterwards; either by hunting, or by a testamentary disposition, or by purchase—at least when it is admitted that this last contract is not absolutely null when effected by a bankrupt. †The bankruptcy of a purchaser does not give a vendor the right to cancel a bargain, if he has knowingly entered into it; he cannot even claim the goods back; otherwise, both cancellation and reclamation are permitted him. †If the law forbids this reclamation on the part of the vendor, neither can he prove as creditor for the amount of the price.

Section 2

After the declaration of bankruptcy the court should hasten to sell the bankrupt's property and distribute the proceeds amongst the creditors. First of all are sold things liable to deteriorate, then slaves and domestic animals, then other movable property, and lastly immovable property. The sale takes place in presence of the bankrupt and the creditors, each object being sold at the market where such things are usually sold; and nothing can be sold except at a reasonable price, payable immediately, in locally current coin. A creditor who has stipulated for some particular article is not obliged to take coin, and if such article is not among the assets it must be purchased to satisfy him. If, on the contrary, the creditor does not insist on the very thing stipulated for, the debt can be paid in coin; except in the case of a contract of *salam*, for this contract does not admit of any similar conversion, even by consent of the parties interested. The court, when proceeding to the sale of the bankrupt's property, should never deliver it before receiving the price; and money coming from the sales and recoveries should be immediately divided amongst the creditors, unless the sums are so small as to make this impossible. In the latter case distribution may be deferred until the amount in hand has been increased by the sale of other objects, or the recovery of other debts due to the estate.

In order to proceed to this distribution, the law does not require that the creditors present must prove that there are no others ; but a creditor who only presents himself after a distribution retains all his rights to his share in what remains of the assets. According to some authorities the previous distribution should in such a case be annulled.

If the bankrupt sold an article before the declaration, and this article is subject to legal seizure by a third party, while the price paid has been already spent, the purchaser can only prove like an ordinary creditor ; but if the article has been sold by the court after the declaration of bankruptcy, a seizure gives the purchaser the right to claim back the price as a privileged creditor. Only one authority maintains that a purchaser can never enjoy this privilege.

The support of persons dependent upon the bankrupt is a charge upon the assets until the distribution is finished, unless the bankrupt is himself capable of supporting them by his labour. †But all the property of the bankrupt must be realised. It is even necessary to sell his house and any slave who may be working as his servant, without any regard to the state of his health or to the rank he occupies in society. All that should be left him is a bundle of clothes sufficient for decency, *i.e.* a shirt, a pair of trousers, a turban and a pair of slippers ; to which in winter should be added a cloak. There is also exempted from sale the food necessary for the nourishment of the bankrupt and his family until the distribution is over.

After the final distribution the bankrupt need not work or hire out his services as domestic servant or workman, in order to pay what remains of his debts ; †but his creditors may oblige him to put out to service his female slave enfranchised by reason of maternity, and to lease out property realised in her favour. A bankrupt who says he is in a state of absolute insolvency, or who after the distribution of his property declares he has no more at all, must, if this is denied on the part of the creditors, prove the truth of his assertion ; at least this is so in the case of commercial debts, like those arising from a purchase or a loan. †In all other cases the law allows a presumption in his favour, provided he substantiates his declaration on oath. Proof of absolute insolvency can be furnished at any time ; but the witnesses called to establish it must have an accurate knowledge of the private life of the bankrupt. They must declare positively and expressly that the bankrupt is "absolutely insolvent." A merely negative deposition, *e.g.* that the bankrupt "possesses nothing," is not enough. When the bankrupt's insolvency is established in this way the creditors have no right to demand bodily restraint, nor that the bankrupt be adjudged personally as a pledge ; they must wait until he has collected sufficient money to pay his debts. In the case of a stranger whose financial position is accurately known to nobody, and who consequently cannot prove his "absolute insolvency," the court should appoint some one to examine the state of his affairs, and this expert should then appear as a witness if he thinks the evidence of absolute insolvency to be conclusive.

Section 3

A vendor can, in case of bankruptcy, break the contract and claim back goods the price of which has not yet been paid him. †This right must be exercised without delay, for the reclamation is not admissible as soon as the bankrupt has disposed of the thing bought, either by cohabitation in the case of a female slave, or by enfranchisement, or by sale. This right of reclamation is not confined to a sale properly so called, but extends to all contracts involving the transfer of property for an equivalent. It is, however, admitted only under the three following conditions :—

1. That the time for payment has fallen due.

2. That payment cannot be obtained on account of the bankruptcy ; †for there is no ground of reclamation where the bankrupt's property is sufficient to meet all his engagements, but he nevertheless refuses to pay ; or where payment cannot be obtained because the debtor, though solvent, has absconded. On the other hand, the vendor may not be deprived of his right to cancellation and reclamation if the creditors wish to keep the goods at the price agreed upon between him and the bankrupt.

3. That the bankrupt purchaser is still the owner of the property ; for there is no right of reclamation if he is no longer its owner, or if he has entered into a contract of enfranchisement with a purchased slave. On the other hand, the right of reclamation is not affected by the fact that a bankrupt has given in marriage a purchased slave.

If the goods have been accidentally damaged, the vendor has the choice of either taking it back as it is, or claiming, for the payment of the price, his share of the assets, like any other creditor. If the deterioration in value is due to him or to a third person, he may choose between the property as it is, or a claim as ordinary creditor for the amount agreed upon, minus the deterioration. †Deterioration due to the bankrupt purchaser is regarded as accidental, so far as reclamation is concerned.

In the case of a sale of two slaves, one of whom dies after the purchaser has taken possession, and the purchaser then goes bankrupt, the slave still living may be claimed back, and for the dead slave the vendor may claim his share in the assets as an ordinary creditor. According to the opinion of Shafii in his second period, the right of reclamation in this case is not invalidated by the fact that a part of the price has already been paid to the vendor. So that if the two slaves were of the same value, and the vendor has already received half the total price agreed, he may still claim back the living slave for the amount still due. Only one jurist maintains that he must in such a case keep the part payment already received, and claim his share of the assets, for the other half, as an ordinary creditor.

When the property has undergone an increase inseparable from it, as in the case of an animal that has become fat, or a slave that has learnt a trade, the vendor profits by its reclamation ; but when the increase has an individual existence, like the fruit of trees or the young of animals, the purchaser keeps it, and the vendor can reclaim only the original thing and nothing more. In the case of a slave's child, an increase separable by nature but not by law, the vendor may claim it along with the mother, on paying its price ; or if this is not convenient, both must be sold, and the price fetched by the mother paid to the vendor. According to others, however, reclamation is altogether inadmissible in such a case. If a slave is pregnant at the time of reclamation, but not at the time of sale, or *vice versâ,* †the vendor's right extends both to mother and child. The fruit of the date palm hidden in its envelope, or that already formed by means of fecundation is subject to nearly the same rule as the embryo hidden in its mother's womb and the child just born, *i.e.* it is better to include it in the reclamation. In the matter of the reclamation of a piece of ground which has been sown or built upon by the bankrupt, he, the vendor and the creditors may by common agreement proceed to pluck up the shoots or remove the buildings if they think fit. The ground is then returned to the vendor in its primitive condition. But if the creditors or the bankrupt object to this uprooting or removal, the vendor has no right to enforce it, but must receive back the land with the crops or buildings on it. Thus he only has a choice between two courses : either to appropriate crops and buildings on paying their value, or to uproot or remove them at his own risk, and deliver them to the bankrupt, plus damage, if any. *In no case can the vendor claim back the land, even if he abandons to the bankrupt crops and buildings.

If the property consists, for example, of corn that the bankrupt has mixed with other corn of the same or an inferior quality, the vendor can claim back the same quantity of the mixture ; *but if on the contrary the bankrupt has added corn of a better quality, reclamation is inadmissible. Corn ground by the bankrupt, or a coat cleaned by him, without in either case any increase in value, are subject to reclamation, and the vendor need pay nothing extra for the work done. *But if the value is increased, the corn or the coat should be sold, and a part of the price proportionate to the increase in value should be returned to the bankrupt.

Where the bankrupt has stained the cloth purchased in some dye belonging to him the three following cases are to be distinguished :—

1. The value of the cloth is increased by exactly the value of the dye. In this case the bankrupt becomes part owner of the cloth, for the amount of the value of the dye.

2. The increase in value is less than the price of the dye. In this case the bankrupt cannot profit by more than the increase in value of the cloth.

3. The increase in value is greater than the price of the dye sold by itself. †In this case the bankrupt takes the whole of the increase.

Where the bankrupt has purchased from one and the same person both cloth and dye, the vendor reclaims simply both, unless the value of the cloth, after manipulation, exceeds the value it had previously. In this latter case reclamation is impossible, and the vendor can claim his share in the distribution of the bankrupt's effects, like any other creditor.

Where cloth and dye have been purchased from two different persons, the law admits three distinctions—

1. The value of the dyed cloth does not exceed the previous value when undyed. In this case the vendor of the dye loses his right of reclamation.

2. The value of the dyed cloth exactly equals the sum of the values of cloth and dye. In this case the two vendors should jointly reclaim the cloth, and become co-proprietors of it.

3. The value of the dyed cloth is greater than the sum of the values of cloth and dye. †In this case the bankrupt takes the whole of the increase in value.

CHAPTER II.—INCAPACITY OF LUNATICS, MINORS, AND SPENDTHRIFTS

SECTION 1

THE incapacity of a bankrupt in relation to his creditors; that of a debtor with regard to an article pledged by him; that of a sick person who may not deprive his legitimate heirs, by testamentary disposition, of more than a third of his property; that of a slave whose property belongs to his master; and that of an apostate, whose goods are confiscated for the benefit of Moslems; all these will be found treated of in those parts of my work dealing with these special classes of individuals. Here it remains for me to speak of the incapacity of lunatics, minors, and spendthrifts.

A person in a state of lunacy is incapable of administering his property, and not responsible for what he says. His incapacity ceases with its cause. The incapacity of a minor ceases at puberty only if his intelligence is then sufficiently developed to allow of his being intrusted with the administration of his property. The age of puberty is fixed by law for both sexes at fifteen years completed, unless in the case of a boy nocturnal pollutions have already manifested themselves. But whatever may be the physical development of the body, a child is never considered to have reached puberty before the age of nine. When the hairs of the pubis begin to grow it is a sign of puberty in the case of an infidel child †but not in that of a Moslem. As to girls, menstrues and pregnancy are also signs of puberty.

The intelligence of a minor is considered to be sufficiently developed for him to manage his property, under the following circumstances:—

1. When he is able to perform his religious duties properly.
2. When he behaves himself reasonably in his affairs.
3. When he abstains from everything incompatible with an irreproachable character.
4. When he is not a spendthrift; *i.e.* he does not waste his substance by allowing himself to be deceived in commerce by obvious frauds, by throwing his money into the sea, or by ruining himself in illicit pleasures. †On the other hand, prodigality does not include expenditure on charity or good works, nor even exorbitant expense on the table or the toilet.

The degree of intelligence of a minor should be estimated in different ways, according to the different categories of persons. Thus the son of a merchant should be examined with regard to purchase and sale or his aptitude at a bargain; the son of a farmer should undergo inquiry as to his knowledge of cultivation and the proper employment of labour for that purpose; and the son of an artisan should give proof that he understands his trade; while a girl should show herself apt in all that has to do with spinning and cotton and the best way of protecting food from the cat, etc. This examination should be undergone at least twice; according to some before the minor has reached the age of puberty, and according to others after. †Some insist upon a previous examination, maintaining that engagements entered into by a minor before puberty are invalid. †But according to these authors, the pupil should be given, before his majority, an opportunity to prove the development of his intelligence, for example, by making a bargain; though the guardian and not the pupil is the person who must actually conclude it.

The minor who, having attained the age of puberty, has an intelligence insufficiently developed to be entrusted with the management of his property, remains in a state of incapacity; otherwise his incapacity ceases *ipso facto* on his attaining his majority. His property is then intrusted to him; though others maintain that the court should in all cases decree the cessation of the guardianship. A person who, immediately upon attaining his majority, begins to waste his substance, should be formally declared incapable; only a few jurists maintain that incapacity recommences *ipso facto* under guardianship as before.

†A person who has attained majority cannot be pronounced incapable owing to notorious misconduct.

An adult afflicted with idiocy should be placed under the care of the court, or according to others under that of the person who would be his guardian if he were a minor. This difference of opinion is also manifested with regard to an adult who is mad. A person in a state of incapacity through idiocy can neither sell, buy, nor enfranchise slaves, nor make a donation, nor marry without the consent of his curator. If he buys or borrows anything, and if after delivery it is lost when in his possession, he is not responsible either during or after his incapacity, whether his condition was or was not known to the injured party. He may marry with the consent of his curator, †but under no circumstances may he meddle with the management of his property or admit the existence of debts contracted before or since his incapacity. Neither is his admission of any value *as to any damage caused by him; but it is taken into consideration if it relates to an offence punishable by a definite penalty or under the law of talion. He can, moreover, repudiate or divorce his wife, pronounce an injurious assimilation with regard to her, or disavow a child by means of anathema. As to religious practices an idiot is subject to the same law as other believers; but he cannot personally take part in the distribution of what he owes in charity; and if he wishes to perform an obligatory pilgrimage, the curator should intrust to some reliable person what is required for his maintenance on the journey. Moreover, the curator may forbid his undertaking a voluntary pilgrimage, if the expense would exceed his ordinary maintenance, even if he has already begun it; and as our school considers the idiot as a person prevented from continuing his act of devotion, his *ihram* ceases *ipso facto*.

[If it is admitted that the expiatory sacrifice due in these circumstances may lawfully be replaced, the idiot should fast instead of sacrificing a *shah* or giving food to the poor, as he is incapable of disposing of his property. However, if he is able to gain on the way what is enough to cover the extra expense of a voluntary pilgrimage, his curator is not legally entitled to prohibit this act of devotion.]

Section 2

A father is the guardian of his children during their minority. In default of the father the guardianship reverts to the father's father, and then to a testamentary executor appointed for that purpose by the father or father's father, and as a last resort to the court, which, however, may depute some reliable person as administrator. †A mother can never be guardian in her own right, but the father or father's father may so appoint her by will.

A guardian should manage the affairs of a minor like a good father. Thus he should in building use clay and bricks baked in a furnace, not bricks dried in the sun or plaster. He will not sell immovable property, unless it is absolutely necessary or the advantage is obvious; but he may alienate movable property, even by exchange or on credit, if his ward's interest requires it. In the case of a sale on credit, however, he should always have the transaction certified by witnesses, and stipulate for security. As to a right of pre-emption, he should exercise it or not as his ward's interest requires. He may pay what is due by the minor as legal alms; and should furnish him with what is necessary to enable him to live decently.

When a ward, after attaining majority, makes a claim against his father or father's father, alleging that the latter has not acted as a good father of a family with respect to the sale of his property, the guardian has a presumption in his favour if he takes an oath; but if the claim is against a testamentary executor or an administrator appointed by the court, the presumption is in favour of the ward.

CHAPTER III.—COMPROMISE, AND RIGHT OF WAY

Section 1

Compromises are of two kinds; the first, those come to between two litigants, is itself divided into two kinds—

1. A compromise about an obligation admitted by the other party, or legally established in some other way. When in these circumstances there is a consent to accept an object not claimed in the place of one claimed, this consent is regarded as similar to a sale, though the word

"compromise" may have been used; and consequently there must be observed all the rules of a sale, such as the right of pre-emption, redhibition for defects, prohibition from disposing of the article before taking possession, and the necessity of mutually taking possession, if both are capable of giving rise to illicit gain. When one consents to accept, instead of the thing claimed, the use of something else, this consent has the effect of a contract of hiring, of which all the particulars must be exactly observed. And lastly, if one consents to accept only a part of what one might claim, this consent is regarded as a true donation, subject to the law ordinarily governing such kinds of contract. But in all these cases †the word "compromise" and not the word "sale" must be employed. Moreover, if one says to some one, "Give me such and such a thing by way of compromise instead of your house," †this proposal has no legal effect unless there has already been some dispute about the house. There is, however, no objection to replace a debt in this way by some definite object. If, in these circumstances, it is on both sides a question of things giving rise to illicit gain, a mutual taking possession must take place at once; †otherwise this is not necessary, at least if what is given in exchange for the article originally due is something definite. If, on the other hand, one debt is substituted for another, the latter must be immediately converted into some definite object; though we have seen that authorities are not agreed as to taking possession in such a case. When compromising in such a way that one accepts the part payment of a debt, one really grants a remission as to what is left; and in this case one may make use of the word "remission" or "diminution," just as well as of the word "compromise." A permission granted to the debtor to pay in a certain time what is due immediately, or *vice versa,* is quite invalid; but this does not prevent the debtor being able, with the exceptions mentioned, to anticipate payment of a debt due at a certain time. On the other hand, one may accept, by way of compromise, five pieces of money paid at once, instead of ten paid by a certain date; for in this case it is not the same sum that the debtor has to pay, these five pieces paid at once dispensing him from paying the rest. But the inverse compromise to this is not permissible, that is, one may not stipulate for ten pieces at a certain date instead of five immediately.

2. A compromise about an obligation not established by an admission or in any other way. Such a compromise is invalid when the denial of the opposite party relates to the obligation itself, †even partially. †A phrase such as "I propose to compromise upon the subject of the house you are claiming," cannot be regarded as an admission.

The second kind of compromises consists of those concluded between the plaintiff and a third party. Now it is a perfectly lawful compromise when some third party declares to the plaintiff, "The defendant admits his obligation and has authorised me to come to a compromise with you." An agent has also power to compromise, in these circumstances, on his own account, for then it is as if there had been on his part a preliminary purchase of the thing in dispute. When the defendant's agent declares that the latter totally denies the claim, the compromise between the plaintiff and the agent upon the subject of litigation has the same effect as the purchase of something unlawfully usurped; that is to say the agent has concluded of his own accord a compromise whose validity depends upon whether the plaintiff can have the thing delivered him. A compromise is in any case invalid if the defendant denies the obligation, and his agent has not communicated this circumstance to the plaintiff.

SECTION 2

It is forbidden to make use of a public way, serving as communication between two places, in such a manner as to obstruct the passage. Thus it is forbidden to construct at one's house a balcony opening upon the road, or to make a covered passage between two houses; though both are lawful if at such a height as to allow of a man standing upright to pass underneath If it be a road along which riders and caravans habitually pass, the balcony or the roof of the covered passage must be of sufficient height to allow of the free passage underneath of a camel carrying a litter, including the baldachin and its supports. It is forbidden—

(1) To compromise upon the subject of these rights, relating to any public way; or

(2) to construct a bench upon the public road, or plant a tree on it. According to other authorities, however, this precept does not include benches or trees that do not in any way obstruct the free passage of the road.

If it be a question, not of a public road, but of a blind alley, access to it is forbidden to persons not living there; †and even these should obtain the previous permission of their neighbours. By a person living there is understood the occupant of a house with a door in the blind alley, but not a person whose house merely adjoins it with a bare wall. †Each inhabitant of the blind alley has a right to that part of it only comprised between the corner of the public road and his house door. The inhabitants alone have the right to make doors leading into the blind alley, for entrance and exit; †persons who have only a bare wall on it may not pierce this wall, unless they carefully nail up any door they may make there. An inhabitant whose house already has one door opening on the blind alley, may not make another further from the corner of the road, without his neighbour's consent. Even if it is nearer the corner the new door may not lawfully be made without the knowledge of the neighbours, unless at the same time the old one is shut up; in this latter case no one has any right to object. †Nor have the neighbours any right to object if the owner of two houses proposes to make a door of communication between the two, whether the doors of these houses open on to two different blind alleys, or whether one opens into a blind alley and the other into the street. In all cases where neighbours wish to oppose the opening of another door, they may compromise for a sum of money. Every householder has a right to make new windows opening on to a blind alley, in order to get more light.

A wall between two properties is either a party-wall or not. If it is not a party-wall, the neighbour may not place beams against it without the knowledge of the owner, at least, according to what was admitted by Shafii in his second period; nor can he force the owner to allow him to do so. If the owner permits him to do so without payment, it is as if he had lent him the use of the wall; and he may at any time withdraw this permission, without being liable for damage, †even though the neighbour may have already begun his intended construction. If the owner withdraws his permission, he may at his choice either permit the building for a consideration, or he may insist upon its demolition, and claim damages for any injury done to the wall. Some authorities, however, maintain that the owner may only claim compensation under these circumstances, and cannot insist upon demolition. If, on the other hand, it is for a consideration that the owner has granted permission to rest upon the wall beams supporting some construction, *e.g.* if he has rented out for this purpose the use of the top of the wall, he must keep to the articles of the contract of letting. †If the following expressions have been used:—"I sell you the top of my wall to support your building," or "I sell you the right to build upon it," it is a sale combined with a contract of letting; and the owner, once the construction has begun, has no longer under any circumstances the right to demolish the wall. Even if the wall falls down and the owner rebuilds it, a neighbour who has bought a right of construction upon the original wall can exercise his right upon the wall newly erected. It is necessary that the portion of the wall concerned should be specified by mentioning both length and width, whether the permission has been granted for a consideration or not. There should also be indicated the nature and the height of the walls of the building it is intended to build upon the wall in question, and the nature of the roof with which it is to be covered. When permission is asked to build on another's land, it is sufficient to indicate the area of the proposed building.

As to a party-wall, according to the theory adopted by Shafii in his second period, neither of the part-owners has a right to rest beams on it without the other's consent ; nor to fix a bolt in it, nor open a window, except on the same condition. Each part-owner may, however, support things against it, or open a shop for goods, so long as the wall is not damaged. Such acts are lawful also in the case of a wall which is not a party-wall. A part-owner may not oblige his neighbour to contribute to the repairing of a party-wall, at least according to the opinion adopted by Shafii in his second period ; but if the wall falls into ruin, he may rebuild it at his own cost and his own profit. In this case he obtains exclusive possession of it, and may dispose of it as he pleases, either by making it serve as a foundation for other buildings, or by demolishing it ; and if the neighbour should then object to its demolition, and offer to pay his share in the expense of rebuilding and up-keep, he cannot be forced to agree to this proposal. Where, however, one of two part-owners of a party-wall fallen into ruin wishes to rebuild it with the *débris* to which both have equal right, the other may object to this ; but if they help each other and build it together their joint rights in the party-wall become as before. It is permissible for one of the part-owners to grant to the other who alone undertakes to rebuild it, a larger share in the party-wall than he had before ; for in that case these increased rights are considered as being the reward of his labour.

One may grant to one's neighbour, for a consideration, the right to deflect a course of water, or to throw snow, upon property of which one is the owner.

When two proprietors dispute about the ownership of a wall between their properties, and the buildings belonging to one of them are so closely fixed in to the wall, that both must have been constructed at the same time, he is regarded as the owner of the wall ; otherwise they must be looked upon as joint owners. Consequently the wall must be adjudged in this case to that party who is able to prove his ownership ; and if neither can do this, the court should administer an oath to both of them. If both, or neither, substantiate their statements on oath, the wall should be declared a party-wall ; but if one only does so, the wall should be adjudged to him. The circumstance that one of two neighbours has rested beams on a disputed wall, cannot of itself add weight to his claim. The flooring between two storeys of a house belonging to different persons is subject to the same law as a wall between two properties. It is necessary to consider if the floor can have been made after the construction of the upper storey. If this is the case, it is presumed that the floor is, so to speak, a party-floor; but if it is not so established, the floor is presumed to belong to the proprietor of the lower story.

CHAPTER IV.—TRANSFERENCE OF DEBTS

For the validity of a transference the law requires the consent of the transferrer and of the transferee, †but not that of the debtor. A person who owes nothing, however, cannot be made the subject of such a transference; though some authorities maintain that this is possible, with the consent of the person in question. A debt transferred must be obligatory. It can refer to things sold by weight or measure †or otherwise. It is lawful to transfer the price of a sale during the period of option, either by the purchaser designating to the vendor a third person who will pay him the price agreed upon, †or by the vendor designating a third person to whom the purchaser should pay the money. A slave undergoing enfranchisement by contract may designate to his master another person who will make him the periodic payments; though the master may not transfer to any other person his claim upon the slave for these same payments. The amount and nature of a transferred debt should be known, as in the case of the original debt. Only one jurist admits the legality of a transference of camels due as the price of blood, both on the part of the claimant and of the debtor. A debt extinguished by transference must be of the same nature and amount as the transfer; †the due date of both must be the same; †and they must both refer to the same coin or goods.

A debtor who pays his creditor by transferring him a claim, is thereby free of the debt; and the person whose liability is transferred is at the same time freed as regards his first creditor, while becoming responsible towards the transferee. Consequently, the transferee cannot proceed against the transferrer, even if he meets with difficulty on account of the bankruptcy of the other party, or by reason of his denial confirmed on oath. Even if the latter is already a bankrupt at the moment of the transference, without the knowledge of the transferee, the latter has still no claim against the transferrer; though other authorities allow him this remedy if the transfer was on the express condition of the debtor's solvency.

A transfer by a purchaser, as to the price agreed upon, *is annulled by a restitution on account of redhibitory defects; but, according to our school, a similar transfer by the vendor stands good, even though the goods are subsequently returned him on account of such defects. A transfer with regard to the price of a slave sold is also null, if the interested parties, *i.e.* the vendor, purchaser, and transferee, are agreed that it is really a free man they have disposed of by mistake, or if one of the parties proves this in court. When, in such circumstances, the transferee alone denies to the slave the liberty admitted by the vendor and purchaser, the latter have the right to insist upon the transferee confirming upon oath his ignorance of the liberty of the person in question ; and it is only after taking this oath that the transferee can claim from the purchaser payment of the price transferred.

In case of a dispute between two persons, one of whom contends that he appointed the other his agent to take possession of something due by a third party, while the other maintains that the debt was transferred to him and he acted not as agent but as transferee, or if the case turns upon the question whether the word "cede" used by the parties implies a mandate or a transfer, the one who asserts the fact of an appointment as agent has a presumption in his favour, if his statement is confirmed on oath. All authorities, however, are not agreed in admitting this presumption in the latter case, *i.e.* where the dispute is about the meaning of the word "cede." If one of the parties in litigation maintains that he transferred his claim to the other, while the latter asserts that he was merely authorised to receive the sum due, the law presumes that this latter statement is the truth, if confirmed on oath.

CHAPTER V.—GUARANTY

SECTION 1

A PERSON who is incapable of managing his affairs cannot be a surety. A guarantee on the part of a bankrupt has the same effect as a purchase by him; †and that on the part of a slave without his master's authorisation is considered void. If a master has authorised his slave to go surety, indicating as guarantee what the slave gains by his labour, or some other thing, it is the property indicated which is liable to seizure ; †otherwise the following rule must be observed. In the case of a generally authorised slave, everything he actually possesses and everything he has gained after his authorisation may be seized ; but in the case of a slave not authorised to trade, the profits of his labour are alone liable. †It is necessary that the surety should know the creditor, but the latter need not accept or even subsequently approve him. It is generally agreed that one may go surety for a person without his consent ; †one need not even know him.

A guaranty can only be given for a debt, which must be—

1. Certain ; though in his first period Shafii accepted the validity of a guarantee on a future obligation. Our school also admits a guarantee as to the indirect consequences of a sale, even after payment of the

price ; *i.e.* one can go surety to the purchaser for the return of the price paid by him, in case of a legal seizure, redhibition or deterioration.

2. Obligatory. One may not go surety for the periodic payments arising out of an enfranchisement by contract ; †but one may do so for payment due by reason of a contract of sale, even during the continuance of a right of option. A guaranty relating to the payment of a contractor is regulated by the same principles as a security with reference to a similar obligation.

3. Known. This, at any rate, is what Shafii decided in his Egyptian period, when he also gave it as his opinion that the remission of an unknown debt is null, unless it is a case of camels due as price of blood, †in which latter case he also admits the validity of a guaranty. †An agreement in the following terms :—" I go surety for so-and-so's debt up to an amount of from one to ten *drahms* is not regarded as a guarantee for an unknown debt, and one is then liable for the maximum. [†In such a case one is responsible for a maximum of nine *drahms.*]

Section 2

Our school admits the validity of personal security. One can go surety for the person of a debtor without knowing the amount of the debt. In every other case personal security can only be given where an ordinary guarantee can also be given. Our school admits personal security even for a person liable to a penalty depending upon the will of the injured party as under the law of talion, or liable to punishment for defamation ; but a third party can never go bail for the person of a criminal liable to a definite punishment, *i.e.* one that cannot be remitted. One may go bail for the person of a minor, a lunatic, a man in prison, an absent person and even a dead man.

In this last case it is necessary to produce the corpse, for its identity to be established by witnesses ; but in other cases a personal bail has for its effect that one has undertaken to bring the debtor alive to the place where he has to pay his debt, at least if such place has been previously indicated, or if not to the place where the guarantee was given. The guarantee has been fulfilled once the debtor is brought to the place, so that the creditor is able to seize his person. It has been fulfilled also if the debtor presents himself of his own accord and places himself at the disposition of his creditor, in order to fulfil his engagement ; but a mere appearance of the debtor is not enough, unless he declares he comes to answer to his bail. When one has become bail for a debtor, who subsequently absconds, and nobody knows where he is, there is no longer need to produce him ; and the guarantor, even if he has already made inquiry as to the debtor's whereabouts, may still insist on a delay necessary to enable him to go and look for the debtor and procure his return. When this is over, the guarantor may be imprisoned, unless he brings the debtor. Some jurists maintain, however, that in these circumstances the guarantor can never be obliged to bring the debtor, if the latter has gone away as far as will permit of an abridgment of prayer. †If a debtor is already dead and buried at the moment when a guaranty was given for his person, the guarantor is not responsible for the payment of the debt; and personal security is in such a case null and void, even if a clause has been added to the effect that the guarantor shall be liable for the payment of the debt, where the burial of the debtor prevents his being brought. †And, finally, personal security is not valid without the debtor's consent.

Section 3

For the validity of a guaranty, ordinary or personal, such words must be used as clearly indicate the obligation undertaken, as "I go bail for what so-and-so owes you," or "I take his debt on myself," or "I undertake it," or "I answer for his person," or "I become bail, security, guarantor, responsible for bringing you the debtor; and if I do not bring him, I will pay for him." But if, on the other hand, one says, "I will pay the money or bring the debtor," it is a mere promise and not a personal guaranty. †Guaranty, whether ordinary or personal, cannot be made conditional; nor may the exact moment of the debtor's appearance be lawfully specified. But it may be stipulated that the debtor shall be brought immediately, or that he shall not be brought before the end of the month. One may also guarantee payment by a certain time of a debt due immediately, as well as the immediate payment of a debt due on a certain date. †The guarantor need never pay off a debt before the date agreed upon between him and the creditor.

A creditor may at his choice seize either the guarantor or the original debtor. †He cannot accept the security on condition that the principal debtor shall be free from seizure. The guaranty ceases with the principal debt, and consequently the guarantor is released by a remission of the original debtor. On the other hand, a release of the guarantor does not affect the obligation of the original debtor. Upon the death of the principal debtor, or of the guarantor, the death is recoverable from the goods of the deceased; but the position of the survivor is unaffected. A guarantor, on proceedings being taken against him, may cite the original debtor, and force him to discharge his debt to the creditor, unless he has gone security without the debtor's knowledge; but† the

N

guarantor cannot proceed against the original debtor, before the creditor claims payment. A guarantor who pays, without reference to the debtor, may still sue the latter if guaranty and payment were effected with his consent. * But if the debtor disapproved these, the guarantor has no remedy against him. †The debtor's consent to the guaranty renders him liable to the guarantor ; but not his mere consent to payment by the latter. †If a guarantor has persuaded a creditor to accept debased money instead of the good pieces due by the debtor, or a coat worth fifty pieces instead of one hundred pieces, he can claim from the debtor no more than he has actually paid.

If one discharges another's obligation without his knowledge and without any guaranty, one is not substituted for the creditor so as to be able to proceed against the debtor ; but the debtor's consent to payment by a third party not a guarantor involves this substitution, whether or not such a right has been expressly reserved. †This right of substitution remains intact, even where the creditor and the third party convert the debt into another of a different nature.

The law requires that before proceedings are taken, either under a guaranty or by right of substitution, that payment took place in presence of two male witnesses, or of one male and two female witnesses ; or even of a single male witness—but in this last case the guarantor or substitute should take an oath. If there are no witnesses, the payment made by the guarantor or the substitute, in the absence of the debtor, gives him no right to proceed, whether there is †or is not a rejoinder on his part. Our school, however, admits such right to proceed, even without witnesses, where payment is substantiated by a declaration of the creditor, or where it has taken place in presence of the original debtor.

BOOK 13.—PARTNERSHIP

FOUR kinds of partnerships are to be distinguished—

1. Personal (sherkat-al-abdan), a contract by virtue of which some persons unite for the exercise of their trade or profession, as a partnership of two or more porters or workmen so that their profit is held in common and divided amongst them. Such a partnership does not require equal contribution, nor that the partners should all have the same trade.

2. Universal (sherkat-al-mofawada), in which the profit gained by each partner is held in common by all, and all are jointly responsible for the debts of each.

3. Commercial, in participation (sherka-al-wujuh), in which two persons, well known as merchants, each buy goods as if for himself, under particular conditions as to time of payment; the goods being then sold in common and the profits divided between the two.

All these three kinds of partnership are null and void.

4. Particular (sherka-al-inan), which alone is permitted, provided that the share of each partner is expressly indicated. †Thus a partnership of this kind cannot exist where there is merely an agreement to combine and nothing more. No particular partnership can take place except between persons capable of appointing or being appointed an agent.

The share capital must consist of things sold by measure or weight, and not otherwise. Some jurists even maintain that these contributions must consist in gold or silver coin. All agree that the shares must be mixed together so as to be indistinguishable. This cannot take place unless the contributions are of the same nature and quality. Thus one partner cannot bring good coin and another debased. These rules, however, apply only to the common stock collected to form a conventional partnership; for if two persons obtain anything as undivided property in some other way, as by inheritance, sale, etc., and allow each other unrestricted right to trade with it, this is a perfectly legitimate partnership, without, however, there being any combination of funds subscribed, and without there being any question of things sold by measure or weight. It follows therefore that the rule that the funds of a partnership must consist of things sold by measure or weight can be eluded by a mutual and partial exchange of the things contributed, combined with an authorisation to dispose of them at pleasure. The law does not insist that the share contributed by each partner shall be equal; †nor even that the exact amount must be known at the time of the contract of partnership.

No partner may dispose of the common funds, except in a reasonable manner. Thus he cannot of his own accord sell either on credit or for any coin not legally current in the place; and he is personally responsible if he allows himself to be deceived by any obvious fraud. Neither can he take with him on a journey partnership funds; nor send them to a commission agent, without the permission of the other partners.

Each partner has a right to terminate the contract of partnership at any moment; but can then no longer dispose of the common funds. This rule, however, must be understood in the sense that if one partner says to another, "I release you from our contract," or "You can no longer dispose of my share in the common funds," he is not himself released from his obligations towards the partnership. A partnership terminates upon the death, lunacy, or disappearance of one of the partners.

Profit and loss must be shared in proportion to the contribution of each partner, without regard to the value of the labour of each. Any stipulation to the contrary would involve the illegality of the contract. But in these circumstances the partners retain a right of action against each other for any salary that may be due for their respective services, and what dispositions they may have made with regard to the common funds remain intact. And any profit made or loss incurred, before the legality of the contract was called in question, must be shared in proportion to the capital contributed.

Each partner is considered as the depositary of the common funds intrusted to him; which implies that his word is presumed to be true as to restitution, deterioration or accidental loss of such property. If he alleges some visible cause of the loss, he need only prove that the accident took place, his word being enough to show the accident did also cause the loss of the object in dispute. If one partner possesses something he says is his, while another says it belongs to the partnership or *vice versâ*, the presumption is in favour of the person in possession; but if he asserts that the thing belongs to him in consequence of a division amongst the partners, the presumption is in favour of the party that denies this fact. And finally there is a presumption in favour of a partner who asserts that a thing was purchased, either for the partnership or on his own account, against any other partner who maintains the contrary.

BOOK 14.—PRINCIPAL AND AGENT

Section 1

For the validity of an appointment as agent, it is necessary that the principal should have the right to do in person what he authorises his agent to do, whether it concerns his own property, or something else of which he has a right to dispose. Thus a minor, a lunatic, a woman—as to marriage—or a person in a state of *ihram*, cannot appoint an agent; but a guardian may do so on behalf of his pupil. A blind person, though incapable of himself buying or selling anything because he cannot see it, may nominate an agent for this purpose.

An agent must himself be capable of doing on his own account what he is appointed to do for another. Consequently, neither a minor, nor a lunatic, nor—as to marriage—a woman, nor a person in a state of *ihram*, can be appointed an agent.

There are, however, certain circumstances in which one may rely upon the word of a minor, *e.g.* when in the name of his parents he allows some one to enter the house, or when he brings a small present from them. †A slave may be appointed an agent to receive a woman in marriage, but not to give her away.

The object of an appointment as agent must be—

1. The property of, or a right acquired by, the principal. †Thus, for example, the appointment of an agent to sell a slave one is about to purchase, or to repudiate a woman one is about to marry, is considered null and void.

2. An act which may be performed by another person. Consequently, to appoint an agent to perform one's religious duties is unlawful, with the exception of the pilgrimage, visit, distribution of charity and sacrifice. An agent may not be appointed to depose as a witness, take an oath of continence, pronounce an anathema or other oaths †or an injurious comparison. On the other hand, sale and purchase, donation, contract of *salam*, security, marriage, repudiation, and in general all civil conventions may be effected or revoked through an agent. Similarly, an agent may accept what a third party owes his principal; he can fulfil the latter's obligations, appear in court for him either as plaintiff or defendant, *and by occupation in his name acquire possession

of an object not belonging to any one, as *e.g.* by clearing waste land, by hunting, or by picking up dry wood. A judicial confession should be made personally by the interested party, †and cannot be made through an agent; but it is permissible to apply by agent for the application of a penalty that may be remitted, as under the law of talion, or of a penalty for defamation. Only a small number of authorities refuse to allow this unless the principal is present.

3. Known; at least in part, for complete precision is unnecessary. Thus, an appointment as agent in the following terms is invalid:—" I give you general authority as my agent in business, important or otherwise," or "for all my affairs," or "I intrust my property to you." On the other hand, there is no objection to an appointment as follows:—" I appoint you my agent for the sale of all my property, and the enfranchisement of all my slaves." It follows also from this principle that when giving any one power of attorney to purchase a slave, the kind must be specified; or, in the case of a house, its situation; but in † neither case is it necessary to mention the price.

The principal must make use of words that leave no doubt as to his consent. Thus, for example, he should say, "I appoint you my agent for such and such a business," or "I intrust it to you," or "You will be my agent;" and consent is also sufficiently expressed by saying, "Sell this for me," or "Enfranchise such and such a slave." For the validity of an appointment as agent the law does not require an express acceptance on the part of the agent; though some authorities maintain the contrary opinion, in a case where the principal has merely indicated the nature of the contract, as, for instance, by saying, "I appoint you my agent." Where, however, the principal has disclosed the nature not of the contract but of the act, by saying, *e.g.* "sell" or "enfranchise," even these authors do not insist upon an express acceptance.

†An appointment as agent cannot be made to depend upon a condition; but there is no objection to the business confided to the agent being made so to depend. †The words, "I appoint you my agent and you will be so again after I have revoked the appointment," constitute a valid power of attorney for the present, but it lapses upon revocation, for there is then a new appointment depending upon a condition. †The same principle applies to the cancelling condition; whether, *i.e.* the revocation of the appointment may or may not be conditional.

Section 2

An agent appointed to effect a general sale may accept in payment of the price only such coin as is legally current in the locality. He may not

sell on credit; nor may he allow himself to be deceived by any obvious fraud—such a fraud, that is, as is seldom capable of deceiving an average person. In any case the agent is personally responsible to the principal for damage, when there has been delivery of the goods. If the power of attorney specifies that a sale shall be at a fixed time, the same rule must be applied; †but it is quite legal to leave the time to the discretion of the agent, who should then guide himself by what is usually stipulated as to the time. An agent appointed to sell a thing cannot buy it for himself, nor for a minor of whom he is the legal guardian; †but there is no objection to his selling it to his father or to his adult child. A power to sell implies a power to receive the price and deliver the goods. A delivery of the goods before the receipt of the price is at the agent's risk. An agent appointed to buy must not purchase a thing with redhibitory defects, except on his own responsibility. If the object is worth the price stipulated, in spite of redhibitory defects, the purchase is chargeable to the principal, if the agent was unaware of the defects, †but not otherwise. If the thing is not worth the price paid, the purchase does not bind the principal, if the agent knew of the defects. If he was not aware of them, the agreement rests intact, except for the right of option, which in these circumstances the law allows both to principal and agent.

An agent, if able to carry out his instructions, may not delegate a third party to do so, without his principal's consent; but if he is unable to conclude the affair through incapacity or on account of his social position, such delegation is quite lawful. It is so also where there are many agencies that one person cannot execute alone; but in this case our school admits delegation only for that part of his duty that exceeds the agent's power. A power of delegation accorded by the principal in explicit terms, such as, "Choose a substitute for yourself," does not affect the position of the substitute, who remains always the agent's agent. †Consequently his authority terminates either by a revocation of his appointment by the agent, or by a revocation of the latter's own appointment. Where, on the other hand, the principal says to the agent, "Choose me another person to replace you if you should require a substitute," and the agent chooses such a substitute, the latter becomes the direct agent of the principal. †And it is the same where the principal has accorded a faculty of substitution, without indicating whether the substitute is to act for him or for his agent.

[1. In all cases where the substitute acts directly for the principal, an agent cannot revoke his appointment; nor is his appointment *ipso facto* revoked by the revocation of the agent's appointment. On the other hand, the agent is equally independent of the substitute.

2. Even where an agent has a right of delegation, he can appoint as substitute only a person worthy of confidence; unless the principal has indicated some particular person.

3. †Where an agent has made use of his power to appoint as substitute a person worthy of confidence, who is afterwards guilty of notorious misconduct, he cannot of his own accord revoke his appointment.]

Section 3

If in an agent's power of attorney there is a formal injunction to sell, either to a person specially mentioned, or at a certain date, or at a particular place, the agent must act in conformity with this clause. Authorities, however, are not in complete agreement as to the place, especially if the agent is unaware that such place has been indicated with a particular object. A power of attorney to sell for "one hundred pieces of money" does not imply any authority to sell for less; but the sale may be effected at a higher price, unless expressly forbidden by the principal.

Where an agent had been appointed to purchase a *shah* of a certain quality for a *dinar* received for that purpose, and he buys for that price two *shahs* of the required quality, but neither of them is worth the price, the principal is not obliged to confirm the purchase. *He would be bound to confirm it, if each of the two *shahs* had the value mentioned, and in that case the ownership of the property would be transferred to the principal by the fact of his agent's taking possession. Where a principal instructs an agent to give some definite object in exchange for the goods, and the latter buys on credit, †or *vice versâ,* the purchase has no effect as against the principal. An agent who does not conform to his principal's instructions, with regard to the sale of his property or an exchange for some definite object, disposes of the goods of another in such a way as to cause the nullity of the contract. A purchase effected by an agent without naming his principal, and on his own responsibility, does not affect the latter; †and it is the same where the vendor says, "I sell you this thing," and the agent answers, "No, I buy it for so-and-so." Finally, according to our school, an agreement expressed as follows:—"I sell this to your principal Zaid," to which the agent answers, "I buy it for him," is null and void.

An agent is considered as the depositary of everything intrusted to him in virtue of his appointment as agent; and, even where he does not act gratuitously, he is responsible for loss or accidental deterioration only if he has exceeded his powers. †However, an error of this sort upon his part does not of itself involve the revocation of his appointment. In all cases the immediate consequences of a contract concern only the agent who has effected it, and not the principal. Thus the inspection of the goods, the irrevocableness of the contract upon the separation of the parties, and mutual taking possession upon the spot, are the affair of the agent, not of the principal.

The price agreed upon may be recovered by the vendor in the following ways :—

1. If the price has been left by the principal to the agent, the vendor may cite both of them.

2. If this is not so, and the price consists of some definite object, the vendor can cite only the principal.

3. If neither of these suppositions is the case, the vendor can cite only the agent ; at any rate if the principal entirely denies the agency, or declares he knows nothing about it. †Where, on the other hand, the appointment is admitted by all the interested parties, the vendor may cite both principal and agent, even though the price is not a definite object. In such a case the agent is regarded as the principal debtor, and the principal as his security.

In case of a legal seizure the purchaser has a remedy against the agent if the latter has received the price, even though this price may have been accidentally lost when in his possession, †and even though he may have informed the purchaser he was not acting on his own account. The agent may in his turn proceed against the principal. [†The purchaser has also the right to proceed directly against the principal in case of a legal seizure.]

Section 4

An appointment as agent may at any moment be revoked by the principal ; and the agent on his part may also at any moment give it up. A revocation pronounced in presence of the agent, as, for example, in the following words :—" I cancel the power of attorney," or " I annul it," or " I release you from it," operates as an immediate dismissal of the agent. A revocation in the agent's absence has the same effect, though one authority maintains that in such a case the revocation has no effect until communicated to the agent. An agent may give up his appointment, as, for example, by saying, " I resign," or " I return you your power of attorney." The appointment terminates of itself where either party loses a right to dispose of his own property, as by death or loss of reason, †or by temporary loss of consciousness following upon a fit. It ceases also of itself when the article which the principal has instructed his agent to dispose of no longer belongs to him. A mere disavowal of an agent by his principal who has forgotten his engagement, or who wants to conceal his intentions, does not involve a dismissal; but this is certainly involved in a premeditated disavowal, with no other object in view.

In the case of a dispute as to the essential nature of an appointment as agent, *e.g.* where the agent maintains that the principal instructed him to sell something on credit, or to buy it for twenty pieces of money; while the latter contends that it was to be sold for cash, or bought for ten pieces; the presumption is in favour of the principal, if he takes an oath.

The law considers as null and void a purchase effected by an agent—

1. Of a female slave for the price of twenty pieces of money; if the agent tells the vendor he has been instructed to buy at that price, and the principal afterwards states on oath that he said only ten pieces.

2. For a price consisting of a definite object belonging to the principal; if the agent declared either before or after the purchase that it was not on his own account, but for another, and the principal afterwards disavows this on oath. However, the nullity in this case occurs only where the vendor admits he was informed of the fact that he was dealing with an agent; for if this is denied by the vendor on oath, the purchase remains and the agent is personally responsible for payment. If the sale is not effected for some definite object, but on credit, the principle to be followed is still the same; that is to say, the purchase is void if the agent has disclosed his true character to the vendor and this is admitted by the latter; but the agent is himself liable if he has not done so, †or the vendor states on oath he did not know it. Finally, in all cases where the purchase remains chargeable to the agent, the law recommends the court to persuade the principal to give an explanation of his disavowal to the agent, *e.g.* by saying, "If I had instructed you to purchase this slave for twenty pieces of money I would have resold her to you with pleasure for that amount which seems to me exorbitant;" to which the agent may reply, "I buy her," with the object of thus acquiring a female slave with whom cohabitation is permitted him.

Where an agent maintains he has not exceeded his powers, and his principal asserts that he has, there is a presumption in favour of the latter; or, according to one authority, in favour of the former. There is general agreement that an agent's declaration must be accepted when he affirms upon oath that a certain article in his possession has been accidentally destroyed, or that he has restored to his principal what the latter intrusted to his keeping. Where an agent does not act gratuitously, some authorities are of a different opinion, so far as concerns restitution. If the agent maintains that he effected the restitution by means of a messenger of the principal, the messenger's word presumed to be true, and not that of the agent; ††and in that case the principal is not required to pronounce upon his attorney's declaration. Where an agent contends that he received the price of a sale and that it was accidentally lost, and the principal denies these facts, there is a presumption in favour of the latter, so long as the delivery of the goods has not yet taken place; after this our school admits a presumption in favour of the agent. Where some one has been instructed to pay a debt, and says he has done so, but the creditor denies receiving the money, the latter has a presumption in his favour, provided he takes an oath. An appointment as agent is never presumed; consequently an agent must always prove his assertions, if contradicted by his principal, with the exception of the special cases mentioned in which his word is believed. ††On the same principle the administrator of an orphan's property is obliged, if the fact is contested, to prove that he has handed over all that remains in his hands to his ward upon his attaining his majority.

†Neither an agent nor a depositary can refuse to hand over to the owner what they hold of his, under the pretext that such restitution must take place in the presence of witnesses, for their word suffices to establish this. But a person holding by usurpation, or any one enjoying no legal presumption in his favour as an agent does, may refuse restitution except in the presence of witnesses.

If a person asserts that he has been instructed by some one having a right to do so to take possession of property in possession of a third party, whether as payment of a debt or as restitution of a definite object, the debtor may pay the debt or restore the object to the agent, if he sees fit to acknowledge the character he claims. However, according to our school, he cannot be obliged to pay the debt or restore the object to the agent, unless the latter proves his right to act as agent. †On the other hand, in such a case, if the claimant states he is acting as transferee, the restitution or payment is obligatory, unless the debtor denies. [Our school acknowledges a similar obligation where the claimant derives his right from his being an heir, and the debtor admits this.]

BOOK 15.—ADMISSION

Section 1

An admission is valid only when made by a person who can dispose freely of his property. Thus an admission by a minor or a lunatic is null and void. But where an individual, regarded as a minor, admits having attained puberty in consequence of nocturnal pollutions, he must be believed, without being sworn, if he has attained an age at which emission is legally presumed to be possible. Where, on the other hand, a minor says he has reached his majority, on no other ground than his having attained the required age of fifteen, he must prove this circumstance. The consequences of an admission made by an idiot or a bankrupt have already been dealt with. An admission by a slave, asserting upon his part an obligation to undergo a purely corporal punishment, is accepted in a court of justice; but his admission relating to an offence for which a pecuniary penalty may be imposed, involves only his own personal obligation, if it is contested by his master. The slave is bound to discharge this obligation upon his enfranchisement, but the admission does not render him liable to seizure. Moreover, a slave's admission in a civil matter is not accepted at all, if it relates to his master's rights or property, unless in the case of a slave generally authorised to trade. In this latter case it is accepted, and the slave must discharge the resulting obligation, either out of the profits he has realised, or out of the funds intrusted to him by his master. A sick person's admission upon his deathbed is valid, according to our school, whether made in favour of some third party or in favour of one of his heirs. An admission made before a last illness enjoys no right of priority over one made on a deathbed, if it is a matter of two admissions about the same thing in favour of two different persons. †Nor is there any right of priority where a person, in health or on his deathbed, makes an admission in favour of some one; and after his death his heir makes an admission about the same thing in favour of some one else.

An admission is of no value if obtained by violence. The person in whose favour an admission is made should be capable of possessing and exercising rights over the thing it refers to. Thus an admission made in favour of an animal is invalid; but an obligation would be created by the following words :—"I admit owing such and such a thing to its master on account of that animal," or "I admit owing to the child of which Hind is pregnant such and such a thing which the child will be able to claim as inheritance or legacy." This admission is equally invalid if some cause is assigned that cannot legally exist; but it is valid if the cause has not been expressed. †A denial on the part of the person in whose favour an admission is made, results in the ownership of the property not being transferred. A revocation of an admission followed by such denial must be accepted, if the admission was an error, and the denial is immediately followed by the revocation.

Section 2

An admission is usually made in the following words :—"Such and such a thing belongs to Zaid;" and if it is about a debt, "I am his debtor," or "I owe it him." An admission with regard to real property or some definite object should be made as follows :—"The thing belonging to so and so is with me," or "I hold it." If one merely says to some one, "You owe me a thousand pieces of money," and the other merely answers, "Weigh it," "Take it then," "Weigh the money," "Take it," "Put your seal on it," or "Put it in your purse," this cannot be considered as an admission; but it does amount to an admission if he answers, "Certainly," "Yes," "You are right," "You have given me a receipt for it," "I have paid you," or "I admit it." The words, "I admit," without adding "what," or "I will admit my debt," *i.e.* in the aorist tense instead of the past, do not constitute an admission; but the words, "Certainly," or "Yes," in answer to a question such as, "Don't you owe me this sum?" do so. However, authorities are not agreed as to the answer, "Yes." †There is an admission also where one says to some one, "Pay me the thousand pieces you owe me," and he answers, "Yes," or "I will pay you them to-morrow," or "Let me have a day's time," or "Let me have time to sit down," or "To open my purse," or "To look for my key."

Section 3

An admission must refer to something not belonging to the person making it. Thus, an admission as to "my house," or "my coat," or in the words, "My claim upon Zaid I admit belongs to Amr," is null and void. In the phrase, "I admit such and such a thing now belongs to so-and-so, but until I made this admission it belonged to me," the first part implies an admission, and the second is considered as null. And secondly the thing with reference to which the admission is made must be in the possession of the person making the admission, since the consequence of the admission is that he is obliged to deliver the object. However, the admission will be valid even where the thing, at the moment of the admission, is not yet in the possession of the person making the admission; provided he obtains possession of it before the time fixed for the delivery.

An admission that the slave of a third party is free, renders the person making it liable under it, if afterwards he obtains possession of the slave by purchase. If the admission is to the effect that the slave is already free, the purchase must simply be considered as a ransom. But if otherwise, that is if the admission is merely of an intention to enfranchise the slave of a third party, the purchase is considered a ransom only on the part of the person making the admission, but an ordinary purchase on the part of the owner, at least according to our school. Consequently to the vendor alone belongs the right of option, both that called "of the sitting," and that which is the effect of a special agreement.

An admission need not refer to a known object. Thus, if one admits owing somebody "a thing," the creditor must be contented with whatever the debtor says he meant, provided only that it is "a thing" in the legal acceptation of the word, *i.e.* a thing of some value and capable of being owned. †He would even have in these circumstances to content himself with some valueless thing, if of the same kind as *e.g.* a grain of corn; or with an object which, though not capable of legal ownership, may be acquired and possessed, such as a trained dog, manure, etc. Only those things of which the acquisition and possession are forbidden, *e.g.* a pig or an untrained dog, may be refused as having no legal utility. A debtor cannot discharge an obligation resulting from any such admission by performing an act of mere politeness, *e.g.* by visiting his sick creditor, or returning his salute. An admission of owing some one something "of value," "of high value," "of great value," or "of much value," involves an obligation merely to give something not entirely valueless;—†for instance, even a female slave enfranchised on account of maternity;—but a dog, or the skin of a dead animal, would not suffice. The expression "I admit owing him so much," is equivalent to "I admit owing him something"; while the simple repetition of "so much," or "thing," in an admission, have no consequence at all. If, on the contrary, one says, "a thing and a thing," or "so much and so much," uniting the words by the conjunction, one owes two distinct things.

If one says, "I owe you such a *drahm*," or "I owe it you," one owes only a single *drahm*; but one owes two, according to our school, if one says, "such and such a *drahm*," putting the word "*drahm*" in the accusative singular. And according again to our school, one owes only a single "*drahm*," when the word is in the nominative or the genitive, or where the conjunction "and" has been omitted. An admission expressed as follows, "a thousand plus a *drahm*," may be explained as though the word "thousand" did not refer to *drahms*, but to something else. ††But "twenty-five *drahms*," can refer to nothing but *drahms*. ††A modification to the effect that "the *drahms* I admit are *drahms* of an inferior weight," must be accepted; but if the *drahms* current in the locality are not debased coin, the modification must immediately follow upon the admission. Such a modification may be made later only where the *drahms* current in the locality are not of the usual weight. At least Shafii so decided. An admission in the words, "I owe him from one to ten *drahms*," †involves an obligation to pay nine; but an admission of "one in ten" means eleven if the preposition is used in a conjunctive sense, and ten if in an arithmetical one; though otherwise, *i.e.* if used in the ordinary sense, it means only one.

SECTION 4

An admission of owing "a sword in a sheath," or "a coat in a box," does not imply the sheath or the box; and similarly an admission of owing "a sheath containing a sword," or "a box containing a coat," does not involve the contents. And so too, if one admits owing "a slave with a turban on his head," ††one is not supposed to have included the turban; but, on the other hand, one owes everything spoken of when the admission is of "an animal with its saddle," or "a coat adorned with embroideries."

The expression "a thousand pieces of money in my father's inheritance," implies an admission that the estate is burdened with a debt of this amount; but the expression "a thousand pieces of money in the inheritance my father will leave me" is considered as a mere promise of a future donation. Moreover, if one admits owing any one "a *drahm*," and repeats this last word without saying anything else, one owes a single *drahm*; but if one repeats the word "*drahm*," and adds the conjunction "and," then one owes two. By saying "a *drahm* and a *drahm* and a *drahm*," one owes two for the two first times the word is pronounced. The third has no effect if used only to confirm the obligation resulting from the other two. On the other hand, a third *drahm* must be paid in the following cases :—

1. If the third *drahm* was pronounced with the intention of creating a new obligation.

2. †If the third was pronounced with the intention only of confirming the admission in the first.

3. †If the third was pronounced with no special intention.

An admission made in vague terms, *e.g.* "something and a coat," obliges the debtor to specify more precisely the object of his admission when required to do so by the creditor; ††and should he refuse to do so the latter may force him to do so by having him committed to prison. When the debtor specifies the object of the admission in a more precise manner, but the creditor contends that this declaration is made in bad faith, the latter must prove his allegation, for he is the plaintiff, and the presumption is always in favour of the defendant. An admission of "a thousand" pieces of money, followed by a second admission of "a thousand" pieces, involves the payment of only one thousand pieces; and where these two admissions do not refer to the same sum, the smaller is *ipso facto* included in the greater. On the other hand, the two admissions give rise to two distinct obligations where the particulars are not the same; or if one first says, "I received ten pieces of money on Saturday," and then afterwards, "I received ten of them on Sunday."

*An admission constitutes a novation, or substitution of one obligation for another; consequently the words, "I owe him a thousand pieces of money for the wine or the dog he sold me," or "I owe him a thousand pieces of money I have already paid him," result in the person using them having to pay the sum admitted.

If one says, "I owe him such and such a sum as the price of a slave purchased by me, of whom I have not yet taken possession, and I will pay him as soon as he has delivered me this slave," our school considers the sum mentioned as the price offered for the slave, though the payment is not obligatory before delivery takes place. According to our school nothing is due upon the admission of a debt of a thousand pieces of money under the restriction "If God wills"; but an admission of a debt creates an obligation, even if it is added that nothing is owing. On bringing one thousand pieces of money, after admitting owing this sum, and saying, "Here they are, as a deposit," *one has the presumption on one's side, provided one takes an oath, where the opposite party contends having yet another credit of the same amount; while on the contrary our school admits a similar presumption in favour of the creditor, where the debtor, on remitting him the amount, does not use words implying a deposit, but speaks to him of "my obligation," or "my debt."

[†Where it is allowed that one can validly declare afterwards that the sum one admits owing was remitted to the creditor only as a deposit, it follows that from the time of the original admission the debtor has a claim against the creditor for loss, and that he can demand restitution of what has been, as it were, intrusted to the latter's good faith. If one has used the expression "six thousand pieces of money are with me," or "I have them upon me," one still has the presumption in one's favour if one afterwards maintains that it was only a deposit, or if one alleges that the sum mentioned has been restored or accidentally lost.]

An admission of a sale or a gift followed by a taking possession of the object does not admit of a subsequent retractation upon the ground that the contract was illegal or the admission the result of an error. All that the debtor can do is to have an oath administered to the creditor in whose favour the admission was made; and it is only if the latter refuses to be sworn that the court may tender the oath to the debtor, who can then free himself from the debt by taking it. When one admits "that a certain house belongs to Zaid," and afterwards corrects oneself and admits "that it belongs to Amr"; or when one admits that one has illegally usurped "the house of Zaid," and subsequently declares "that it was the house of Amr"; the house should be delivered to Zaid, *but Amr can claim the value of it.

An admission may be accompanied by all sorts of exceptions, provided that the clauses containing them are pronounced at the same time as the admission and do not render it illusory. Thus if one says, "I owe him ten, less nine less eight pieces of money," one owes nine. Such a clause of exception may even refer to a thing of a different kind from that admitted, for instance, "I owe a thousand pieces of money minus a coat," in which case the value of the coat must always be considered less than the sum mentioned. A clause of exception is also admissible with reference to definite objects, *i.e.* one may admit, *e.g.* "This house is his, except this room," or "These *drahms* are his, except this *drahm*." However, with regard to this last class of objects, jurists are not all in agreement, though the great majority adopt the admissibility.

[In saying, "These slaves belong to so-and-so, except one," one makes a valid admission, but one should immediately declare which one is intended. ††If, in such a case, all the slaves die except one, and the person who made the admission declares that this was the slave he intended to except, the presumption is in his favour, if he confirms on oath the truth of his words.]

SECTION 5

An admission of paternity is admissible only on condition that it is in conformity with law and common-sense; thus, one cannot recognise a child that is notoriously another's. The interested person must consent to the admission if legally capable of doing so; thus an admission does not establish paternity with regard to an adult who opposes it, unless it is legally proved in some other way. †A minor legally recognised as a child cannot annul this by his mere denial upon majority. It is permissible to recognise one's child after death, or during minority, †or after attaining majority; and this recognition is sufficient to give one a claim upon the estate. Where an adult is recognised as their child by two different persons, the paternity is established of the one he accepts as his father. The consequence of a similar recognition in the case of a minor will be explained in the book about foundlings. A declaration on the part of a master "that the child of one of his slaves is his" is sufficient by itself to establish filiation, *but not to enfranchise the slave on account of maternity. The same rule applies to a declaration as follows:—"Such and such a slave belonging to me is the mother of my child." On the other hand, the words, "She conceived while belonging to me," implies enfranchisement on account of paternity. The child of a slave who has frequently shared her master's bed, has no need of special recognition in order to establish filiation. The child of a married slave is the child of the husband; and in such a case a recognition of paternity by the master would be null and void.

A recognition of relationship, such as, "so and so is my brother," or "my paternal uncle," establishes that relationship, if made under the conditions just mentioned, and provided the person whose paternity is involved is dead. Such recognition is permissible †even though the deceased denied the imputed paternity; but in every case it is necessary that the person making the declaration should be the deceased's universal heir. †A declaration, however, that one considers a certain individual as one's brother, gives him no claim to any share in the estate, not even to a share in the portion of the person making the declaration. †An adult heir can never of his own accord establish filiation between a third party and the deceased, if there are other heirs, minors. If filiation is admitted by one of the heirs and denied by another, it remains established if the one denying it dies, leaving no other heir except the one who admits it. †And it is established also where, after the father's decease, his son, universal heir, admits that persons of unknown descent are his brothers, while these persons recognise their own filiation, but deny that of the person who makes the admission. †Lastly, where the known heir is excluded from the succession by a person whose relationship he admits, *i.e.* if *e.g.* he admits "that his deceased brother left a son," the admission has reference to family rights, but gives no claim to the succession.

BOOK 16.—LOAN

Section 1

It is necessary that a lender should be legally capable of disposing gratuitously of his property, and that he should have a right to convey the use of the object lent. Thus a lessee or a tenant may lend what they hold as such, ††but not a borrower. There is, however, no objection to the latter allowing a third party the use of a thing borrowed, instead of using it himself. Things that are not consumed by use can alone be the subject of this contract; whence it follows that a female slave may be lent as a servant, or to a woman, or to a man within the prohibited degrees, but not to a man who can legally cohabit with her. It is blamable to lend a Moslem slave to an infidel.

†The law insists that the lending should be expressly mentioned, *e.g.* by the words, "I lend you," used by the lender, or "lend me," said by the borrower. It is sufficient if only one of the two parties has thus expressed himself, provided that the other has shown his consent by his conduct. By saying, "I lend you my horse on condition that you feed it," or "on condition that you lend me yours," one does not effect a loan, but an irregular contract of hiring, for which a reasonable payment should be made.

The cost of restitution of the thing lent must be borne by the borrower, who is liable for damage if it is even partly destroyed, except by mere usage, even though no negligence can be imputed to him. But where, on the contrary, the thing lent is lost or damaged merely by usage, †the borrower is not responsible; though even in this case some authorities consider that he is. †A person who borrows something from a lessee or a tenant is not responsible as a borrower, but just as if he were himself the tenant or lessee. Nor would there be any responsibility where a principal lends his agent an animal which dies in the latter's possession in consequence of work ordered by the principal; nor where an animal dies in the possession of a trainer, to whom the owner intrusted it for the purpose of being trained.

A borrower can use the thing borrowed only in accordance with the agreement. Thus, if a piece of land has been lent to be sown with corn.

it may be sown also with similar cereals, unless this has been expressly forbidden ; but if it has been lent to be sown with barley, it cannot be sown with a grain like wheat, which is more prejudicial to the soil. A permission to sow in general is lawful, and gives a borrower the right to sow what he likes. Permission to build or plant implies a right to sow ; but not *vice versâ*. ††Permission to build neither implies nor is implied by permission to plant. ††Lastly, it is forbidden to lend a piece of land without stipulating the use to which the borrower may put it.

Section 2

The lender has the right to demand back, and the borrower to return, the article lent, whenever they please, even where one of them had stipulated for a definite period. To this rule there is one exception ; where a piece of land has been lent for the interment of a corpse, it cannot be taken back until the remains have been duly buried.

Where the owner takes back a piece of land lent for building purposes or for sowing, with no time of restitution mentioned, the borrower is obliged to demolish the buildings or uproot the crop only if this has been specially stipulated. In default of such stipulation the borrower cannot be obliged to do so ; and if he does so of his own free will, †he need not level the ground. [*Levelling is obligatory under these circumstances.]

Where the borrower refuses to demolish buildings or uproot crops without compensation, the owner cannot force him to do so, but may choose one of two courses. He can either leave them on the land, charging the borrower a rent ; or himself carry out the demolition or uprooting, compensating the borrower for the loss of his buildings or his crop. Some authorities maintain that the owner of the land can also appropriate the buildings and crops, paying their value to the borrower. If the owner has not declared, on taking back his land, whether he prefers to retain the buildings or crops, paying compensation to the borrower, or whether he prefers to have them removed, he cannot have them removed later without paying compensation. This rule applies just as well where the borrower pays the compensation of which we have spoken, as a rent, †as where he does not pay it. And some authors maintain that if the owner refuses to decide, the court should sell the land with everything built or sown on it, and pay the owner and borrower their proper share out of the proceeds ; †but the majority are of opinion that the court should not interfere until both parties have declared their wishes with regard to the buildings and the crops. During this period, however, the owner may visit and utilise his land, while the borrower may not visit it without the owner's permission, merely for the sake of amusement, †though he cannot be prevented from going there at any time to water the crop or repair the buildings. Both lender and borrower retain their right to sell what belongs to them; though, according to some jurists, the borrower can only sell his crop or buildings to the owner of the land. A loan, in which a definite time of restitution is specified, is subject to the same rules as regards demolition and uprooting as the loan for an indefinite period with which we have just dealt. Only one authority maintains the contrary opinion, *i.e.* that in these circumstances the borrower is not liable for any indemnity if, upon the restitution of the land, he wishes to demolish or uproot what he has built or sown. ††An owner who has lent his land with the avowed object of having it cultivated by the borrower, without stipulating for any particular time of restitution, should always, when taking back the crops, leave them standing until the next harvest. ††In this case, however, he can charge a rent for the whole period that may elapse between the restitution and the harvest. Where, on the other hand, the owner has stipulated for a specified time of restitution, and the harvest does not occur before this, the borrower should uproot his crop on the expiry of the term, at any rate if the delay is caused by his own fault, if *e.g.* he did not sow the field at the usual time. Where a torrent has carried away the crop on to another's seed field, the crop belongs to the original owner, †but he must remove it upon the first notification.

Where a person mounts a horse and says to the owner, " You have lent it me," and the owner replies, " No, I have hired it to you," as well as in a similar dispute between the owner of a field and the sower, our school admits a presumption in the owner's favour. A similar presumption is admitted by our school in the owner's favour where the possessor of something says, " You lent it me," and the owner answers, " No, you usurped it." Whatever may be the result of the proceedings whenever in these circumstances the thing in dispute is destroyed before restitution, the holder is always responsible, either as borrower or as usurper; †with this difference, that a loan involves responsibility only for the value of the thing when lost, and not for the maximum value it may have reached during the period of possession, nor for its value on the day upon which possession was taken of it. Where an owner claims, on account of usurpation, a higher value than the thing had on the day it was lost, he must take an oath as to the surplus value.

BOOK 17.—USURPATION

SECTION 1

USURPATION includes all acts of encroachment, in bad faith, upon the rights of another. Thus the following categories of persons must be considered usurpers :—

1. One who mounts another's beast, or sits upon another's carpet, even without moving it.

2. One who enters a house and drives out the owner ; or without entering himself prevents the owner from entering. This last precept has been contested, though not strongly.

3. A tenant who prevents the owner of a house from entering his room, though leaving him in the peaceable possession of the rest. This act, however, constitutes a usurpation of the room only, not of the whole house.

4. One who enters a house intending to take possession of it, even though the owner may not be there at the moment. If the owner is there, and is not driven out, the fact of entering in this way amounts to a usurpation of half the house. Where, however, the person entering is physically weaker than the owner, the act does not imply a usurpation.

A usurper should immediately restore an object he has taken possession of. He is responsible for any injury, even if accidental, that may happen to it while detained by him, in the same way as if he had caused the loss of an object in some one's lawful possession. Thus a person who opens a sack lying on the ground, so that the contents escape ; or opens one placed upright, so that it falls down and the contents escape in this way ; is in either case liable for damage. If, however, in the latter case, the sack does not fall down in consequence of being opened, but the loss is caused by the wind or some other fortuitous cause, such as an earthquake, he is not liable. A person who opens a bird cage and then shakes it to make the animal fly out, is responsible ; but if he merely opens the cage *he is responsible only when the bird flies away at once, and not when it remains some time inside the open cage.

A person who derives possession from a usurper is responsible for the accidental loss of what he thus holds, even if unaware of the usurpation; with this distinction, however, that if he knew of it he must be considered as having usurped the thing from the original usurper, and to be just as responsible as he is; while if he was ignorant of the illegal manner in which it was come by, his responsibility is of the same degree only where the cause of his possession implies such responsibility. Therefore responsibility for accidental loss is admitted, where the third party has obtained the object from the usurper by way of loan, but not where it has been obtained as a deposit. But when a person who has received something from a usurper causes its loss exclusively through his own fault, the responsibility rests upon him in all cases, even though the usurper may have pressed him to take possession of it. Thus the responsibility is admitted of *an individual who is hungry and eats of a plate passed him by a usurper; and, carrying this principle further, the usurper's responsibility ceases if he passes the plate to the owner and the latter eats it.

SECTION 2

The responsibility of a usurper, in the matter of the life of a slave, can never exceed the value of the individual at the moment of death, without distinguishing between death caused by the usurper, and accidental death. Injuries, not involving payment of a legal indemnity in the case of a free man, are compensated for by payment of the diminution in the slave's value. No attention is paid to whether these injuries have been caused by circumstances not under human control, or whether they are intentional, at least according to Shafii's original opinion. On the other hand, according to the opinion adopted by Shafii during his stay in Egypt, compensation for the intentional injuring of a slave, in such a way as to be liable to the payment of a legal indemnity, is subject to the laws that regulate the "price of blood" for a free man, though this compensation should be estimated according to the value of the individual. Thus, for example, for the loss of one hand, half the slave's value should be paid, just as in the case of a free man half the "price of blood;" without taking into consideration whether or not the value of the slave has undergone a similar diminution.

Compensation due for domestic animals consists, according to circumstances in payment of the value of the animal or a sum amounting to its diminution in value. As to other things liability differs according as they are or are not sold by measure or weight, and consequently can or cannot have an advance paid on them. †Such are water, sand, copper, precious metals in an unrefined state, musk, camphor, cotton, grapes, flour, but not the perfume called *ghaliya*, nor the medicine called *majun.* Compensation for the loss of articles such as these consists in restitution of similar things, whether the loss was intentional or fortuitous; only if they cannot be procured is payment of the value permissible. †This value is always fixed at the maximum from the moment of usurpation until the time when the impossibility of procuring an equivalent was perceived. If the measurable things usurped have been taken to another town, the owner may still demand restitution; he can even insist upon the value being paid immediately, until the usurped articles are brought back; but on their arrival the price provisionally paid must be returned. When the measurable articles have been destroyed at the place they were taken to, the owner can claim an equivalent in either place; and if there are no equivalents at the place where the demand is made, the usurper is liable for their value at the place where they are the dearer. ††However, an owner who meets a usurper at a place other than that of the loss, can only claim restitution of similar things there, if they do not involve expense for transport, as in the case of coin. If this is not the case he cannot claim at this place the restitution of similar things, but the usurper owes him simply their value at the place where they were lost. Finally, as to things not sold by weight or measure, the usurper always owes their maximum value in the period between the day of usurpation and that of loss; while in the case of intentional destruction of things not so sold and not usurped, the responsible person is liable only for the value ascertained on the day of the crime. To this rule only one exception is admitted; when a slave or a domestic animal is wounded, and death ensues without its being possible to attribute it directly to the wound, there is due the maximum value between the day of the crime and the day of death.

A loss of usurped wine involves no liability. It is unlawful to transfer usurped wine to an infidel subject of a Moslem prince, unless he has manifested an intention of drinking it immediately or selling it. However, as long as the usurped wine still exists, its restitution is obligatory, and this last rule even applies to juice of the grape not destined to fermentation, where this juice has been usurped to the owner's prejudice, if he is a Moslem. The same rule applies also to idols and to instruments of gaming or music, which one should break before returning, without incurring any liability. †However, if the owner asks the holder of these things for their return, they should not be all at once rudely shattered; but the different parts should be detached so as to return to their original condition, and it is only where the owner himself has rendered this impossible, that they may be destroyed in a more rapid manner.

In case of loss, either by his own fault or by accident, the usurper should not only compensate the proprietor up to the value of the thing, but owes him in addition an indemnity for the use he has made of it, at least in the case of something the owner could have leased out in the meantime, such as a horse, a slave, and so on. In the case of a female slave, the usurper owes this indemnity only if he has cohabited with her, and that she has died as a consequence of this. †It is the same with services rendered by a free man, during the period of usurpation. If it is not a question of the loss of the thing usurped, but of its deterioration, not caused by the usurper's usage, the latter, on restoring it is still liable for damage, plus an indemnity by way of rent for the use he has made or might have made of it. This principle must be applied also when the deterioration has been brought about by the usurper, *e.g.* where a usurped coat has been worn.

Section 3

††A usurper who declares that the thing in dispute has been lost, has a presumption in his favour ; provided he takes an oath to that effect, if the statement is contested by the owner. †In this case the owner must be contented to claim damage, according to the principles enunciated in the preceding section. The same presumption is established in the favour of a usurper, on oath, if contested by the owner, as to the value of the article, as to the clothes worn by a usurped slave, and as to the latter's natural defects ; but, on the other hand, the owner enjoys a presumption in his favour, if he maintains on oath the existence of accidental defects in the slave.

A usurper who restores something in dispute at a moment when its price has gone down, owes nothing by way of damage for this diminution in value. Thus when one has usurped, *e.g.* a coat of the original value of ten *drahms* that has gone down to one *drahm*, and has besides worn the coat until it is no longer worth more than half a *drahm*, one must pay back five *drahms* as damage, having regard to the rule that requires payment of the maximum value.

[†The usurper of a pair of shoes worth ten *drahms*, one of which is accidentally lost, so that he can restore only the other worth alone not more than two *drahms*, owes eight *drahms* as damage. This sum is due also where the loss is not accidental, but caused after usurpation, or while in the owner's possession.]

Deterioration of such sort as to lead to total loss, *e.g.* the use of cheese to make *harisa*, is legally regarded as the same. A single author maintains that even in that case the thing usurped should be restored as it is, together with an indemnity for the deterioration. Where a usurped slave commits a crime punishable by a fine for which his person may be seized, the usurper is liable up to the full value of the slave or of the sum due, whichever is the more advantageous for him, without prejudice to his liability towards the owner, in case of the slave's death. Under these circumstances the injured party has none the less the right to proceed by seizure against the usurper. Should he prefer to take similar action against the owner, and recoup himself out of what the latter has received from the usurper as damage, the owner can take fresh proceedings against the usurper to recover what he has had to pay the injured party. Similarly the owner has a claim against the usurper where, after the return of the slave, he has had to put him up for sale, in order to pay what was due for an offence committed during the period of usurpation.

The usurper of a field, who has removed earth from it, must restore it as it was at first. He must return the earth, or other earth of the same quality. The restitution of the earth that has been removed is obligatory, even without any demand from the owner, if it would be profitable to him. †Otherwise the usurper must wait for the owner's permission. The same principles must be followed if the usurper has dug a well, or filled up one that already existed. If the field has been re-established by the usurper in its original condition, and no permanent deterioration has been caused to it, damage cannot be claimed from the usurper, who is liable merely for reasonable compensation as rent, for the time employed in removing all traces of the usurpation. On the other hand, in the case of a permanent deterioration caused by removal of earth, the usurper owes damage in addition.

†A usurper of olive oil, etc., who has boiled the liquid so that part has evaporated without the total value being diminished, must, all the same, in case of restitution, compensate the owner for the amount lost. In the case where the value of the oil has diminished in consequence of the operation, without diminution in quantity, the usurper still owes damage. Diminution in quantity accompanied by a diminution in the value of the remainder renders it obligatory to compensate the owner for what has evaporated, and return him the rest with damages, if the diminution in value is ever so little greater than that caused by the diminution in quantity alone. †Stoutness acquired by a slave during usurpation cannot be held to compensate for a previous leanness during the same period; but if a slave who, during usurpation, has lost knowledge of his profession or trade, is in a condition to take to it again, the owner cannot claim damage for this. The fact that the slave has learnt a new trade or profession with the usurper does not in any way affect the latter's liability for knowledge lost.

†If usurped must ferments and then changes into vinegar, the vinegar must be returned to the owner with damages, when the value of the vinegar is less than that of the must. †When impure things, that consequently cannot be claimed back, such as wine that changes to vinegar, or the skin of an animal that has died a natural death and is afterwards tanned, have been usurped, the wine or tanned skin, although it has lost its impurity owing to the usurper, nevertheless belongs to the person from whom it was usurped.

SECTION 4

No increase in the value of a usurped article, consisting in simple amelioration, such as the cleaning of a coat, goes to the profit of the usurper; and the owner may even insist upon his restoring the thing to its original state, if this is possible, together with any damages that may be due. Where, on the contrary, the increase in the value of the thing has a separate existence, such as a building or a plantation, the usurper should in all cases restore the land to its original condition. †A person who dyes a piece of usurped cloth with his own dye, may be obliged to remove this dye if it is possible. If it is impossible, and the value of the cloth has not been increased by the addition, the usurper can claim nothing, but damages may be claimed from him if there is ground for this. Where, on the other hand, the dyeing has increased the value of the cloth, owner and usurper become its co-proprietors.

If a thing usurped has been mixed with something else belonging to the usurper, it should be separated from it if possible. If this separation is impossible our school considers the thing as destroyed, that is to say the owner can claim from the usurper either a return of the value or something of the same kind not so mixed. Thus a beam that has been usurped and used in building must be removed, even if it has been used in building a ship. The claim, however, cannot be immediately complied with, if made at a moment when the removal of the beam would cause danger to the persons or goods confided to the captain's care.

Cohabitation knowingly practised with a usurped female slave renders the usurper liable to the penalty for fornication; but not if unknowingly. In both cases, however, the usurper owes dower, unless the cohabitation was accomplished with the woman's full consent. In this latter case ††nothing is owing, and the woman is liable to be dealt with severely, if she has knowingly committed the crime. Cohabitation with a female slave purchased from a usurper, has the same consequences, so far as the purchaser is concerned, both as regards the penalty and the dower, as if the usurper himself had been guilty of it. The purchaser has no claim against the usurper for payment of the dower. When a usurper, or some one who has purchased from him a female slave, renders her pregnant, knowing that she was forbidden him, her child becomes the slave of the owner without regard to paternity; but if it was done unknowingly, the child is free, and considered to be the father's legitimate offspring. In this case, however, the father owes to the mother's owner the value of the child at the time of its birth.

Where, under these circumstances, the child's father buys the mother in good faith from the usurper, he has a claim against him; although, in general, the purchaser of anything usurped has no claim against the usurper, if the article is destroyed in his possession in a manner which renders him directly responsible towards the owner. *The same principle is followed in the case where the article has not been destroyed, but has only deteriorated. *Neither has the purchaser any claim against the usurper for payment of the indemnity due to the owner for his usage of the article; †but such claim is admitted for damages paid to the owner, whether for accidental loss or for injury caused, *e.g.* to a piece of land by demolition of buildings or uprooting of crops, if there was ground for such damages. A usurper who has paid damages for a purchaser can never claim them from him; even in a case where the latter could have claimed them from the former; but he may do so if the damage was incurred by the purchaser's own fault.

[Every person who derives his possession from that of the usurper, is subject to the same rules as have now been shown to apply to the first purchaser of a usurped object.]

BOOK 18.—PRE-EMPTION

Section 1

This right does not exist in reference to movable property, but only with regard to land and what is naturally included in it, like buildings and trees, †and fruit not artificially fertilised. There is no right of pre-emption in the case of a *hojra* supported on a roof, †even a roof held in common; †nor in the case of anything that cannot be divided without lowering the value, such as a bath or a mill.

Right of pre-emption exists only in favour of a co-proprietor of the immovable property sold. Thus, where there are two houses belonging to two different persons, both houses having a common outlet to the public road, neither of the two proprietors can, in case of sale, exercise a right of pre-emption with regard to the other's house, on the ground of common ownership of the outlet. ††He cannot even exercise a right of pre-emption with regard to the common outlet, unless the purchaser has another at his disposition, or can open a door upon the public way. There is a right to pre-emption only in the case of transfer of ownership for a consideration and irrevocably, and the transfer must be later than the acquisition of the pre-emptor's rights. Consequently pre-emption is admissible in the following cases: transfer by sale, dower, compensatory price, compromise in the matter of a crime, periodical payment, rent, advance. From these principles ensue the following conclusions:—

1. When, in a sale, a right of option has been stipulated, either by the two contracting parties, or by the vendor alone, a co-proprietor cannot exercise his right of pre-emption before the expiry of the optional time. Where, on the other hand, the purchaser alone has reserved a right of option, *the right of pre-emption can be immediately exercised, at least when it is admitted that in these circumstances the ownership is acquired by the purchaser at the moment of the contract.

2. *When the purchaser, on perceiving that the thing bought has redhibitory defects, wishes to return it to the vendor, while the pre-emptor wishes to accept the thing and waive the redhibition, the latter may exercise his right independently of the rupture of the original sal-

3. If two persons jointly buy a house, wholly or in part, neither can dispossess his co-proprietor by way of pre-emption.

4. *If a piece of land belongs to three co-proprietors, and the first sells his share to the second, the third cannot, by exercising his right of pre-emption, acquire the whole of the part sold, but only in proportion to his original share.

In pre-emption the transfer of ownership is effected without any adjudication on the part of the court; the price need not be brought; and the presence of the original purchaser is unnecessary. All that is required is the verbal declaration of the pre-emptor, such as, "I appropriate the whole of the land," or, "I take possession by right of pre-emption." In order that the pre-emption should have full effect, the law requires also that the price of the re-purchase should be delivered to the purchaser. On making this delivery of his own accord, or in consequence of an injunction, the pre-emptor becomes proprietor of the portion he wants. It is, however, also permissible that the purchaser may consent to allow credit to the pre-emptor for the amount of the re-purchase, and that it be pronounced by the court. In both cases delivery of the price of repurchase is unnecessary in order that the ownership of the property claimed should be transferred, although, in the latter case, that ownership can only pass to the pre-emptor on condition that he is present at the sitting, and shows that his claim is well founded. And finally, according to our school, ownership of a portion of an immovable property that the pre-emptor has not yet seen is never transferred.

Section 2

As to the compensation due to the purchaser by the pre-emptor, the law admits the following distinctions:—

1. When the purchase has been effected for a price consisting in things sold by measure or weight, the pre-emptor should indemnify the purchaser with similar things.

2. When the purchaser has given in exchange something not sold in this way, the pre-emptor should return him the value, *i.e.* the value the thing had on the day of sale, or according to others its value on the day the right of option expired, and on which consequently the sale became irrevocable.

3. *When the purchase has been effected on credit, the pre-emptor can at his choice either pay at once and take possession of the immovable property, or he can wait until the term has expired and do so then.

In the case of a combined sale of a portion of an immovable and of some other object, the pre-emptor can exercise his right all the same provided that he pays what may be considered the price of his portion, in proportion to the total value of the sale.

A portion of an immovable property transferred as dower is subject to a right of pre-emption on the part of a co-proprietor, for a price valued according to the proportional dower the woman in question could claim; and the same rule is observed with regard to a transfer as compensatory price in case of divorce. When the sale of an immovable property subject to pre-emption takes place for a contract price, and this latter is accidentally lost, the owner cannot exercise his right of pre-emption. Where, under these circumstances, the co-proprietor indicates the exact amount which has been paid in this way for the property, while the purchaser declares he knows nothing of it, the latter should confirm his ignorance on oath, and the claim is dismissed. †Neither can it be entertained, where the co-proprietor maintains before the court that the purchaser really knows how much he has paid, without any further indication on his part as to the exact amount.

A subsequent judicial seizure of what the original purchaser has given by way of price, nullifies both sale and pre-emption, at least where the price is some definite thing liable to seizure. Otherwise the things given as price may be replaced, and both the sale and the pre-emption hold good. A right of pre-emption remains unaffected by a seizure of what the pre-emptor has given the purchaser in compensation, whether this is a consequence of the pre-emptor's ignorance, †or whether he knew of the danger. A disposal of the purchased property by the purchaser, by way of sale, *wakaf*, lease, etc., is not *ipso facto* annulled by a subsequent pre-emption, but the pre-emptor can demand the cancellation of a disposal which, like *wakaf*, would render illusory a right of repurchase. In the case, however, of a disposal on the part of the purchaser, which, like a sale, admits of subsequent pre-emption, the person in whose favour this right originally existed may at his choice either exercise it with regard to the second sale, or demand the cancellation of that one, and exercise his right with regard to the former.

In case of dispute between purchaser and pre-emptor upon the subject of the price, the presumption is in favour of the purchaser's statement; and the same is the case where the latter denies the purchase or the status of co-proprietor upon which the plaintiff bases his right of repurchase. †This presumption, however, is destroyed, and the repurchase takes effect, if in these circumstances the co-proprietor who has sold maintains the purchase denied by the purchaser. And it is to this co-proprietor that the pre-emptor then owes the compensation originally due to the purchaser, unless the co-proprietor admits having already received the price. If he does admit it, in spite of the purchaser's denial; authorities are not agreed as to whether the compensation should be left in the hands of the co-proprietor pre-emptor, or whether the court should seize and keep it for whoever finally establishes his claim to it. This controversy is the same as that we have spoken of, about a confession that is denied by the person in whose favour it is made.

Where several co-proprietors have a joint right of pre-emption, they should exercise it in proportion to their respective shares; though, according to one jurist, they should do it by heads. When one co-proprietor sells the half of his share in a property, and then the second half to another person, it is understood that the right of pre-emption with regard to the first half belongs to the other of the original co-proprietors; but if the latter waives his right, the purchaser who has become owner of the first half, shares with him a right of pre-emption with regard to the second half. †A renunciation on the part of one of the two co-proprietors possessing a joint right of pre-emption, prevents him from making any later claim; the other co-proprietor should then decide, either to exercise his right upon the whole of the property put up for sale, or to renounce his part also. Thus he may not merely exercise his right in proportion to his own share; but the repurchase being indivisible, even a partial renunciation by one of the parties results in a devolution of the full and entire right of pre-emption to the other. When, of two persons having right to pre-emption, only one is present, he can at once exercise the right in its entirety, on condition of allowing the other to participate in it upon his return; †though he may instead postpone the repurchase until his co-proprietor's arrival. If two persons have bought in common a share in immovable property, the pre-emptor can exercise his right either against the two together or against one of them; †but where two of the co-proprietors have sold their respective shares to a single person, the pre-emptor should exercise his right separately with regard to what has been sold by each of his co-proprietors.

*A right of pre-emption should be exercised without delay, and the person having this right should speedily declare his wishes in the matter, in conformity with custom as soon as he has learnt of the sale. If that is impossible through sickness or absence or fear of enemies, he should appoint an agent to act for him, or, if he cannot find one, call witnesses and announce in their presence his intention of exercising his right of pre-emption. The right of pre-emption lapses †if no agent is appointed, or no intention expressed before witnesses, where this might have been done; but a person at prayer, at the bath, or at a meal can postpone his declaration until he has finished. A prolonged delay involves the loss of the right of pre-emption, even although the pre-emptor declares that he did not believe the person who brought the news of the sale, at any rate if it was brought him by two persons of irreproachable character, †or even by a single person worthy of confidence. He is permitted to disbelieve in the truth of the news of the sale only where it is brought him by persons whose deposition would not be accepted in a court of law. However, if the co-proprietor learns that the sale has taken place, *e.g.* for a thousand pieces of money, in consequence of which price he renounces his right of pre-emption; his right remains intact, in spite of his renunciation, if it subsequently transpires that the sale was concluded for five hundred only; though, on the contrary, it remains irrevocably lost if it afterwards appears to have been concluded for more than a thousand. Neither is there any loss of the right of pre-emption where the pre-emptor, meeting the purchaser after learning of the sale, salutes him, saying, "Peace be with you," or "God bless you in the acquisition you have made." However, all authorities are not in agreement as to the consequences of an exclamation which, like the latter, contains an invocation of the name of God.

†There is no right of pre-emption, if, after a sale by one of the co-proprietors, the other, who is thus entitled to appropriate the entire property, has himself sold his share also to a third party, even though this sale was effected in ignorance of the other.

BOOK 19.—JOINT-STOCK COMPANIES

Section 1

A joint-stock company is called *kirad,* or *Modāraba.* It exists between two persons, one of whom supplies funds to the other to trade with, on condition that the former has a share in the profit. The law requires that these funds :—

1. Consist in gold or silver coin ; consequently the company has no legal existence where the funds are given in the form of bullion, or gold or silver ornaments, adulterated coin, or goods.

2. Are of a known amount and consist in coins of known value ; though others maintain that it is sufficient to indicate the amount, *e.g.* "the contents of one of the two purses."

3. Are remitted to the managing partner ; for the money may not be left in the hands of the person who furnishes the funds.

It may not be stipulated that the sleeping partner should take part in the management, ††though his slave may be employed in the affairs of the company. The powers of the responsible partner are limited to trading and what depends on it, such as exposing for sale, and placing the stuffs in their covers or rolls. Thus when one forms a joint-stock company with some one in order that he may buy wheat and sell it after grinding and baking into bread, or when one instructs him to buy cotton thread and sell it after weaving, the company is *ipso facto* invalid. †Neither can one instruct the managing partner to buy certain specified goods, nor such as are of a rare kind, nor to trade with only one specified individual.

It is not necessary to stipulate any period of duration for the company; and if it is stipulated that after a certain time the responsible partner cannot dispose further of the funds, this stipulation will even involve the illegality of the contract. There is, however, no objection to instructing him to abstain from certain specified proceedings, *e.g.* to buy after a certain lapse of time.

Both partners, sleeping and managing, share in the profits to the exclusion of all others. Consequently the words, "I form a joint-stock company with you, and all that you gain will be yours," do not constitute a legal association ; though others maintain its validity. It is the same if the words used are "all the profit shall be mine;" though, according to others, this constitutes a commission agency. Besides this the share of each partner in the profits must be mentioned in their respective proportion. Thus one cannot associate with some one by stipulating, "You will have a part of the profits," or "a part in the profits," without indicating what part; †but one can do so by providing that "the gain shall be common to both of us," and then each partner can claim half. ††Although it is admitted to be a legal contract when the person who provides the funds says to the manager, "Half the gain will be yours," †if he says, "Half the gain shall be mine," and nothing more, the association is invalid. And this would also be the case if it were stipulated that one of the partners should have ten pieces of money from the profits, or should take all the profits of a certain nature.

Section 2

For the contract to be valid there should be an offer by one of the parties and acceptance by the other; though, according to some authorities, acceptance need not be formally announced, provided it exists in fact.

The relations between the managing partner and the sleeping partner are the same as those between agent and principal. †A managing partner cannot in his turn form a joint-stock company with a third person, participating both in the management and in the profits, even if the original provider of the funds authorises it. Without his authorisation such secondary association is considered wholly illegal, *i.e.* any dispositions the third person may make are considered to be those of a usurper; †and this principle is carried still further, for if the second managing partner buys on credit for the company, any profit that may result from this purchase goes entirely to the original manager, who owes nothing to the second except remuneration for his services, if there is occasion for this. It is, however, well known, that, according to the opinion of Shafii in his second period, a usurper who has effected a similar sale can keep the profit for himself. Only a few authorities maintain that in these circumstances the profit belongs also to the second managing partner who has obtained it. A purchase effected by the second managing partner, not on credit, but for cash, or for some specified thing belonging to the company, is absolutely null and void. There is, however, no objection to one person associating himself with two others by furnishing them with funds, either of the same or of different amounts; and similarly two persons supplying funds may associate themselves with a single managing partner. In the latter case the profits are shared between them in proportion to their capital, after deducting the share of the managing partner. In all cases where a joint-stock company is illegal, dispositions made in good faith by the managing partner remain intact; but the profit is for the person who supplied the funds, who owes the manager reasonable remuneration for his trouble. †It is only in a case where the contract is invalid owing to the sleeping partner reserving all the profit for himself, that the manager can claim nothing.

The managing partner should administer the society's affairs like the good father of a family; he is responsible if he allows himself to be caught by any obvious fraud. He is forbidden to sell on credit without the sleeping partner's authorisation, but he can alienate by exchange, and cancel a bargain on account of redhibitory defects, or keep a thing bought in spite of its redhibitory defects, as circumstances require. Redhibition is a right of the person who supplies the funds just as much as of the manager, and where the two are not agreed about the redhibition of a thing bought, that course should be adopted which offers the greater advantage. The managing partner can never in any case, on account of the company, enter into commercial relations with the person who provides the funds. He must not purchase goods to a larger amount than the capital of the company; nor must he buy a slave whose enfranchisement would be obligatory for the sleeping partner, except with his consent. †This rule applies also to the purchase of a slave married to the latter. In all cases where the managing partner effects a forbidden purchase, the person supplying the funds is not bound by it; but the managing partner is personally responsible if it was on credit. The managing partner cannot take the capital of the company with him on a journey without the authorisation of the sleeping partner, nor can he use it for his personal expenses whether at home *or on a journey. He must act in conformity with custom, *e.g.* he should place in covers or rolls the stuffs in his shop; he should at once personally ascertain the weight of precious or light articles, such as gold or musk, but this is not necessary with heavy or voluminous merchandise.

A managing partner may credit himself with the salary of employees, for any work he is not obliged to do himself as managing partner. *His share of the profits becomes his property only upon division, not upon his merely drawing up a balance sheet. Fruit, the young of animals, profit realised from slave labour, and the dower of a female slave given in marriage, belong to the person who supplies the funds; though others consider them as forming part of the profits of the company. Losses caused by a fall in price are deducted from the profits if possible, and should be compensated for in the same way. †This principle should be followed also in the case of a loss of part of the capital, whether by accident, usurpation or theft; †all on condition that the loss is incurred after the managing partner's administration has begun, for any previous loss constitute a diminution of the capital supplied.

SECTION 3

Each partner has a right to withdraw from the company, which is terminated *ipso facto* by the death or madness or even by the unconsciousness of one of the partners. After the dissolution of the company, on the wish of one of the parties, it is the managing partners' duty to proceed to the payment of the debts and the realisation of the capital, at least if it consists of merchandise. Only a small number of jurists maintain that realisation is not obligatory, at least if no profit is expected from it.

If the sleeping partner withdraws a part of the money before a profit and loss account has been drawn up, this fact constitutes a diminution of the total capital of the company; if after then it is a diminution both of the capital and of the profits. Where, for example, the capital is a hundred pieces of money, and the profit twenty, and the sleeping partner wishes to withdraw twenty more, a sixth of the sum claimed must be taken from the profits, all without prejudice to the share in the profits stipulated for by the managing partner. The remaining five-sixths are taken from the capital. If the sleeping partner wishes to withdraw a part of the capital of the company, and it appears that the company has incurred a loss, the loss must be shared both on the sum claimed and on the rest of the company's capital; but under these circumstances any profits which may subsequently be realised do not render it necessary to compensate the sleeping partner for the proportional diminution of the sum he wished to withdraw. Where, for example the capital of the company is one hundred pieces of money and the loss twenty and the sleeping partner expresses a desire to withdraw twenty more, this sum is diminished to a quarter, that is to five, and the capital of the company is thus reduced to seventy-five.

The declaration of the managing partner, confirmed on oath, is presumed to be true, when it relates to:—

1. The absence of any profit, or the total of the profit.
2. His purchase of a thing for the company, or on his own account.
3. The absence of any prohibition by the sleeping partner to effect a particular bargain.

4. The total amount of the funds supplied.
5. The loss of any article belonging to the company.
6. †The restitution of the sums or articles of value supplied.

In case of dispute as to the share in profits stipulated for by the managing partner, both parties should take an oath, and the court then awards the managing partner a reasonable remuneration for his trouble.

BOOK 20.—FARMING LEASES

SECTION 1

A FARMING lease (*mosaka*) is lawful only if concluded by a person enjoying a right to dispose of his property; consequently a minor or a lunatic is incapable of effecting it except through his guardian or curator. Plantations of palms or vines are alone subject to this contract; though Shafii in his first period admitted similar leases with regard to all kinds of fruit trees. Besides this a farming lease cannot be effected on condition that the cultivator shall plough the field and share the produce with the owner, whether the seed is provided by the one or the other. Such leases are called respectively *mokhabara* and *mozaraa.* But if between the palms there are bits of uncultivated land, a contract of *mosaka* may be combined with one of *mozaraa,* provided it is the same cultivator in each case, and that it would be difficult to proceed separately to the watering of the palms and to the ploughing of the intermediate portions of uncultivated land. †In the case of such a combination the law insists that the two contracts must be considered as forming one only, without the *mozaraa* predominating; but with that exception it matters little whether there is much uncultivated land between the trees or only a small portion. †Nor is it necessary that the fruit should be shared between cultivator and proprietor in the same proportion as in a division of the harvest. †A contract of *mokhabara,* one, *i.e.* by virtue of which the cultivator gives the seed, is never lawful, even as an accessory to a contract of *mosaka.*

Where, in defiance of the law, a contract of *mokhabara* is effected by itself, all the produce of the field belongs to the owner, who owes the cultivator nothing but a remuneration for his labour, and for the animals and implements used in ploughing. If necessary, however, both cultivator and proprietor may be made to share in the profits of the crop, without its being requisite for the latter to remunerate the former when recourse is had to one of the following ways of eluding the law :—

1. The cultivator has hired his services to the proprietor for half the seed, under condition of sowing the other half to the profit of the owner who on his part lends him half the field.

2. The cultivator lends his services to the proprietor for half of both the seed and the field, under condition of sowing the other half of the field with the rest of the seed.

SECTION 2

It is necessary that the fruit of the trees should become the exclusive and common property of the proprietor and the cultivator, and that the share of each should be proportionally determined as in a joint-stock company. Moreover, a contract of *mosaka* can be legally effected, *even after the appearance of the fruit, provided it is before the first signs of maturity, but the cultivator may not be given palm shoots for planting on condition that the trees become the common property of himself and of the owner. It is only after the shoots are already planted in the soil that the cultivator may be promised a share of the future fruit as a remuneration for his labour upon the trees, if at least a period of time has been stipulated equal to that in which the trees planted usually bear fruit. When on the contrary the time stipulated is shorter than this the whole transaction is illegal; though some authorities maintain its validity even then, provided the time is not so very short as to render it wholly impossible that the fruit can be gathered before the end of it. One of the joint owners of a plantation can undertake to look after the trees of the whole of it by himself, provided that he reserves to himself a certain quantity of the fruit, exceeding the portion that is his by right.

The law requires also :—

1. That the cultivator shall not take upon himself obligations of any kind not relating to the cultivation.

2. That the cultivator alone does the work, and occupies the garden or the orchard.

3. That the length of continuance of the labour is known. It may be stipulated, for example, that the contract shall expire after a year's time, or that it shall last longer. †But the length cannot be lawfully determined by the words : "until the fruit comes to maturity."

The words by which the contract may properly be expressed are : "I give you charge to water these palm-trees for so much," or "I cede you my plantation to be taken care of." The cultivator must then manifest his consent, without its being necessary to announce in detail in what the work is to consist.

In default of special agreement to the contrary, the contract relates to everything that is usually comprised in it; *i.e*, the cultivator must not only do all that is necessary to enable the fruit to ripen, but must also undertake all the work that has to be repeated each year, such as watering, cleaning the channels for the water, upkeep of the little reservoirs at the foot of the trees, fertilisation of the flowers, weeding, removal of dead branches hurtful to the development of the trees, construction of trellises for the vines, according to usage. †He must also protect and shelter the fruit, and also pluck and dry it. On the other hand, everything that is required in order to preserve the trees themselves, and all work that is not repeated each year, like the construction of walls and new water channels, is the duty of the owner. Neither party can withdraw from a contract of *mosaka;* consequently the cultivator who runs away before the expiry of the contract remains none the less liable for damage to the owner, even though the latter voluntarily undertakes to look after the garden. The court should engage another person at the cultivator's expense, to take care of the plantation, if the owner is not disposed to undertake it personally; and if the owner is unable to take the matter before the court, he can engage a workman of his own initiative. By doing so, however, he loses his right of proceeding against the absent cultivator, unless he has the cost of cultivation established by witnesses. If the cultivator dies the contract becomes part of the estate, and his heirs should continue it; but they have the choice either to cultivate the plantation in person, or to employ workmen to do so. If it is established that the cultivator has committed some fraudulent action, the owner may appoint an overseer; and if this is insufficient, may engage another person to complete the work at the cultivator's expense. Finally, in case of a judicial seizure of the fruit, the cultivator can always insist that the owner shall pay him a reasonable salary.

BOOK 21.—CONTRACT OF HIRING

SECTION 1

THE two contracting parties are subject to the same conditions as the vendor and purchaser. The contract is formulated by the words, "I give you this on hire," or "I make you lessee," or "I cede you the use of it for a year for so much;" to which the other party replies, "I accept," "I take," or "I wish to be the lessee of it." †The contract may also be expressed in the words, "I hire you the use of it," but not by saying, "I sell you the use of it."

The contract of hiring is of two kinds. It may either refer to a particular thing, such as the rent of immovable property, or the hiring of an animal or slave specially indicated; or it may refer to something not yet determined, such as the hiring of an animal of which only the species is described, or the hiring of some one's services for some work indicated in a general manner, for example to sew or to build. When one says to a workman, "I engage you to make such and such a thing," this hiring applies to a specified object; though according to the opinion of some authorities this is a contract of hiring of the second kind. Between the two kinds there is first of all this difference that the contract of hiring of the second kind cannot exist unless the rent or the workman's salary is paid at once; while this is not necessary in a contract of hiring of which the object is certain and specific. In the case of the latter the payment can be made either in cash at once or at a fixed date if such is the agreement. If nothing has been agreed upon as to this, the payment should always be made at once, and the ownership of the sum given as rent, etc., passes at once to the tenant or the workman. In all cases the law requires that the rent or the salary shall be known; consequently it cannot consist of a field or the upkeep of an animal. One cannot hire one's services to skin an animal stipulating for its skin as salary; nor stipulate for a right to a part of the flour, as reward for grinding corn; nor for the refuse that passes through the strainer in sifting grain. ††But it is permissible to engage a woman to give suck to a child slave, and to grant her at once a part ownership in it.

The use to which the thing hired is put, or the labour, should be of a nature of which the price can be legally fixed. Consequently one may take on hire :—

1. The services of a hawker, telling him he will not need to tire himself, provided there is a sale for the goods.

2. †Gold or silver coin, to be used as ornaments.

3. A dog for hunting.

It is necessary that the person letting on hire should be in a condition to deliver the gratification he engages to supply. From this it follows :—

1. That one cannot hire out a runaway slave ; nor goods that a third party has usurped.

2. That a blind man cannot hire himself out as a watchman.

3. That a field with no means of irrigation and as a rule insufficiently watered by rain cannot be taken for sowing. For the renting of a field for sowing is possible only if it has means of irrigation, or if there is usually sufficient rain to water it, or if there is †usually an accumulation of snow sufficient to be used for this purpose.

If a precept of the law renders the use of an object impossible, one should act as if it were a physical impossibility. Thus one may not lend one's services to take out a sound tooth ; a woman undergoing menstruation may not be engaged as servant in a mosque ; †and a married woman may not be engaged as nurse, etc., unless she obtains her husband's permission.

A term may be stipulated for the use of a thing or the engagement of personal services, if the object of the contract is not some specific article ; *e.g.* one may say, "I engage you to take such and such a thing to Mecca, on the first of such month ;" but it is not permissible to hire some particular thing, in order to make future use of it. †There is, however, no objection to one's letting one's house for a second year to the tenant of the first year, before its termination ; and hiring out by turns is also lawful. By this last is meant either that one hires one's mount to some-one to use for a part of the way only, or that one hires it to two persons to use alternatively on different days. In these cases the respective rights should be clearly announced in the contract before allotment.

Section 2

It is also necessary that the use should be known, and that its duration should be limited to a particular period, such as the rent of a house for a year ; or that the duration should be limited by the nature of what is stipulated, such as the hiring of a mount for the journey to Mecca, or hiring out one's services to make a coat of such and such a piece of cloth. †In such cases, however, the duration and nature of the agreement may not both be indicated; thus one cannot engage a tailor "for a whole day to make a coat of such and such piece of cloth." If one hires out one's services to teach the Koran, it is necessary to determine the length of the lessons or to specify the chapters that are to be taught; while in the case of a building the site, length, breadth, height, and materials must be indicated, if the agreement is to be determined by the nature of the work. A piece of land naturally adapted either for building on or for cultivation cannot be rented without specifying the particular use that is to be made of it; though it is sufficient to stipulate, *e.g.* that it is to be sown †without giving any fuller details as to the manner of cultivation. One may even say in general, "You can use it as you like," †or "You can sow it, or plant trees on it, as you like."

When an animal is hired as a mount, the rider must be indicated, either by presenting him to the owner; or by pointing him out so that there can remain no uncertainty as to his identity, but this latter method is disapproved by some authorities. It is the same as regards the manner in which the animal is to be ridden, *i.e.* it must be mentioned if a litter or any other burden is to be placed upon it. †Consequently a contract must be considered illegal which stipulates only that the animal shall carry "what is placed upon it" without specifying what. If nothing is agreed to upon the subject, nothing can be loaded upon the animal. If the contract refers to some particular animal, that animal must be specified. As to whether it must have been seen there is the same controversy as upon the subject of the validity of the sale of an object which is not there. Where, on the other hand, it is not a particular animal that is hired, but only one of a certain species, without regard to the individual, it is enough to mention the nature and species, and indicate whether it is male or female. In both cases, however, the daily journey should be stipulated; unless there are fixed stations on the road, when the animal must be rested at those stations, even if no stipulation has been made upon the matter. *When a beast of burden is hired, it is absolutely necessary in all cases that the two parties should know what it is to carry. Thus, if the goods are on the spot, they must be inspected, and raised with the hand if they are in packages; and if they are things to be found elsewhere, measure, weight, and quality should be mentioned. But it is not necessary to know the nature of a beast of burden, nor its qualities, when no particular animal is in view except in the case of transport of glass or other fragile articles that require extraordinary precautions.

Section 3

A Moslem cannot be hired to take part in the war against infidels, nor to perform his duties towards God, where an intention is necessary, except as far as regards the pilgrimage, and the distribution of the tax. On the other hand, a person may be engaged to perform funeral ceremonies, including burial, and to teach the Koran. Similarly a woman may be engaged to nurse a child and give it suck, either for both these obligations combined, or for one or the other, for they are two distinct obligations. To nurse a child means to look after it and wash both its head and body, to clean its clothes, put pomade on its hair, and ointment round its eyes, put it to bed and rock it to sleep. From these principles it follows that when a woman has been hired to nurse and give suck to a child, our school admits that the contract is *ipso facto* dissolved, so far as concerns the suckling, when the breasts are dry; but, in spite of this, it holds good for the nursing. †A copyist is not bound to bring ink at his own expense, nor a tailor thread, nor an eye-doctor collyrium.

[Rafii has shown in his commentary that in such a case everything depends on custom; if there is no custom, special stipulations should always be made with regard to the obligations just mentioned; otherwise the whole contract is null and void.]

Section 4

The landlord should give the tenant the keys of the house, and keep it in good repair; for if it is uninhabitable, and the landlord does not hasten to repair it, the tenant may cancel the agreement for the renting of it. It is also the landlord's duty to clear the snow from the roof; but the tenant has to clear away the snow fallen in the court yard, and have the house swept. In the case of an animal hired to ride, the owner must supply an *ikaf* or shabrack, a pack-saddle, a girth, a crupper, a nose-ring, except in the case of a camel, and a bridle; while litter, baldachin, mattress, blanket, and accessories must be supplied by the hirer. †Custom decides which of the two parties supplies the saddle. The packing of goods for transport is the duty of the owner of the animal, at least where a specified animal has not been hired; for in the latter case the expense of packing must be borne by the hirer, and the owner must accompany his animal to take care of it, and lend the rider assistance to mount and dismount, if it be at all necessary. In the case of a beast of burden the owner should accompany it in order to load and unload it, or to fasten and unfasten the litter. On the other hand, where some specified animal is hired, the owner need merely give the hirer opportunity to make use of it. The hiring of some specified animal is cancelled *ipso facto* by the death of the animal ; and in case of redhibitory defects, the hirer has a right to cancel the contract. If it is not a specified animal that has been hired, the death of the animal the owner had in view does not of itself give rise to the dissolution or cancellation of the contract, for he is obliged, if necessary, to supply another. *Provisions taken on a journey by the owner of the animal and by the hirer for their mutual nourishment, should be replaced with others by the party who has consumed them.

SECTION 5

A contract of hiring may be entered into for as long a period as the ordinary duration of the thing hired. According, however, to one jurist, the term can never exceed one year ; another fixes the maximum at thirty years.

The hirer may make use of the thing hired, either personally, or by an intermediary. The only thing insisted on is that a substitute empowered to ride an animal or inhabit a house should not be of an essentially different condition of life from that of the principal hirer or tenant. Thus, for example, one cannot sublet a house to a blacksmith or a scourer.

The owner cannot replace the thing whose use he has to permit, *e.g.* a house or a mount, by any other object, even of the same kind, at least if it is a case of something specified. *But a person who has engaged some one, *e.g.* to sew a coat or suckle a child, even if these are specified, may substitute another coat or another child.

During the term of the contract, †and even after its expiry, the hirer's possession is considered to be of the same nature as that of a depositary. Thus a person who hires an animal to carry a load or to ride, and does not use it, but merely ties it up somewhere, is only responsible if the stable collapses while the animal is tied up in it, and at a time when the animal could not have been injured if the person had made use of it. In case of the accidental loss of an article entrusted to the care of a workman, without any fault upon his part, for instance the loss of a coat he has been told to mend or dye, he is not responsible. This rule applies not only to the case where the workman has no exclusive possession of the article, for instance, where the owner sits by his side during the work, or makes him come to his house to do it, *but also to the contrary case. Some authors, however, maintain a different opinion, distinguishing between a workman on contract and an ordinary worl man, and contend that the former is responsible, but not the latter, who merely supplies his labour for a specified piece of work, or for a specified time.

A workman to whom a coat has been entrusted for scouring or mending, without mentioning any wages, cannot claim any wages after the termination of the work. Some authorities, it is true, maintain the contrary; while others contend that under these circumstances the workman should be remunerated, if that particular kind of work is his trade, though not otherwise. Obviously the latter are right.

In all cases where it can be shown to be the hirer's fault, he is responsible for the loss of the thing hired, as for instance if he gives more blows to an animal, or stops it more suddenly, than is usual; or if he allows it to be ridden by a heavier rider than himself; or if he allows a house which he has hired to be occupied by a blacksmith or a scourer. The same principle applies to the responsibility of a person who hires an animal for carrying a weight of one hundred *ratal* of wheat, and makes it carry a weight of one hundred *ratal* of barley, or *vice versâ;* or who hires it to carry a measure of ten *kafiz* of barley, and loads it with a measure of ten *kafiz* of wheat; for these changes really cause an aggravation of the beast's burden. But no responsibility is incurred by replacing ten *kafiz* of barley with ten *kafiz* of wheat. A person who hires an animal to carry one hundred pounds and loads it with one hundred and ten, owes to the owner a reasonable indemnity for the surplus; and he is responsible for the death of the animal if this is caused by the additional load, unless the owner accompanied him and consented to it. In these circumstances the hirer owes for the death of the animal an indemnity proportional to the extra service rendered, or, according to one jurist, half the value of the animal. Our school admits the responsibility of the hirer in a case where the one hundred and ten pounds are delivered to the owner of the animal, who undertakes the transport in ignorance of the excess; but if the owner undertakes the transport after ascertaining the weight and without raising any objection about the surplus, the law prescribes neither indemnity nor responsibility on the part of the hirer.

*When a piece of cloth is delivered to a tailor to make into clothing, and he makes a coat out of it and says that was the order given, and the owner says his order was for a shirt, the presumption is in favour of the owner, provided he takes an oath to that effect; and not only does he owe nothing to the tailor, but the latter is liable for damages.

SECTION 6

A contract of hiring remains intact, even where the hirer is prevented from making use of the thing hired, for example, if he has no combustibles for heating his bath, or cannot use it on account of a journey, or if he falls ill after hiring an animal for a journey. Nor can a contract of hiring be cancelled when the crop from a field hired for sowing perishes from some calamity. In none of these circumstances may even a partial remission of the amount of the hire be claimed. On the other hand, the contract is *ipso facto* dissolved by the death of the animal or of the workman ; at least if it is a specified animal or a particular workman ; but the consequences of this dissolution are not retrospective. Therefore the hire or the wages are due in proportion to the work done or the use made of the article. Except in the case of a hiring of the labour or services of a particular workman, the contract is not dissolved by the death of the contracting parties, even if the lessor be the trustee of a *wakaf*. †But where the hiring has been contracted by the trustee of a *wakaf* with a life interest, of the first generation, for a certain time, the contract is dissolved by his death before the expiration of that term. †On the other hand, if a guardian agrees that his ward shall go and work with some one as an apprentice for a salary, and for a term that expires before he can attain the age of puberty, the agreement holds good up to the expiration of that term, even though majority were attained before the legal age by the occurrence of nocturnal pollutions. The renting of a house is cancelled *ipso facto* by the fall of the building. But the renting of a field is not cancelled by a failure of its means of irrigation ; though the farmer may cancel the agreement. The usurpation of an animal or the escape of a slave also give a person who has hired them a right of cancellation.

When, after hiring out one's camels to some one, one leaves them at his domicile, he must apply to the court before proceeding to seize the camel-driver's goods for the cost of their up-keep. If the camel-driver has nothing that can be seized, the court should borrow money for him, and deliver it to the hirer if it can trust him ; if not, it should deposit the amount with some person worthy of confidence. In case of necessity the court can even proceed to sell some of the camels left in order to defray the cost of upkeep of the others. *Or, finally, the court can authorise the hirer to keep the camels at his own expense, in which case he can recover the cost from the owner.

The taking of possession of an animal by the hirer, or of a house by the tenant, and the fact of having kept the one or occupied the other until the expiry of the contract, suffice together to constitute an obligation to pay the price, even though no use has been made of the thing hired. It is the same where an animal is hired for a journey to some specified place, and kept until the time necessary for such a journey has expired. It is of no consequence whether it is or is not a particular specified animal, provided that in the latter case the owner really delivers to the hirer an animal that possesses the qualities stipulated. ††In the case of an illegal hiring, a reasonable remuneration is due, in proportion to the time during which the object is retained.

The contract is *ipso facto* dissolved where the owner does not deliver the object to the hirer within the time agreed upon; †but where no time has been fixed for the duration of the hiring, no such consequence follows even where an animal is hired for a journey to some particular place, and the owner delivers the animal to the hirer after the time for such a journey has expired. Nor is the agreement affected by the enfranchisement of a slave just hired; for in these circumstances, the freed slave can †neither break the engagement entered into by his master *nor recover from him the wages he might have gained for his services after his enfranchisement. The sale of an object hired out to a tenant is lawful, †and does not affect the hiring; *one may even admit the validity of the sale of an object hired out to a third party without the hiring being in any way affected.

BOOK 22.—OCCUPATION OF LAND

SECTION 1

EVERY believer may, by clearing it, appropriate any piece of land, situated in a Moslem country, that has never been cultivated or built upon. Infidel subjects of our Sovereign do not enjoy this right. Uncultivated land in an infidel country can be so occupied either by an infidel or a Moslem; provided it is not a piece of land from which a Moslem has been expelled, for this must return to its former owner by virtue of the *jus postliminii*. Land that has been cultivated or built upon belongs to its proprietor; and land that still bears traces of occupation previous to the conversion of the country to Islam, but of which the owner is unknown, is regarded as a thing lost, and consequently not susceptible of appropriation. *Where, on the other hand, the abandonment of the land dates from a period before the conversion ownership may be acquired by clearing it.

Land that, though uncultivated and unbuilt upon, serves as *harim* to other land already occupied, cannot be appropriated by clearing. By *harim* is understood land contiguous to other land, the use of which it renders possible. Thus, in a village the place of meeting of the inhabitants, the training ground, the place for the camels, the ditch for depositing filth, and so on, must be considered *harim*; while the *harim* of a well situated in uncultivated land consists of the place where one stands to draw water, the trough, the irrigation wheel, the reservoir, and the place necessary for the animal to turn the wheel. The *harim* of a house situated in uncultivated land includes the ditches for filth, for odure and for snow, and the space necessary to leave or enter by the door. One must also consider as the *harim* the reservoirs of a conduit of water, as far round as a well cannot be sunk without affecting the quantity of water or threatening the solidity of the reservoir. A house immediately surrounded by others has no *harim*.

One may dispose of one's property in conformity with custom, and one is responsible for the prejudice caused to one's neighbour only in the case of a disposition or act of an exceptional nature. †One may convert one's house, even if surrounded by other buildings, into a bath or a stable or establish a forge in one's shop situated perhaps in the bazar of the dealers in old clothes, provided that the shop is shut off on all sides from the neighbouring dwellings by walls.

†Clearing is permissible on the sacred territory of Mecca, with the exception of Mount Arafa. [Mozdalifa and Mina are subject to the same law as Mount Arafa.]

Clearing differs according to the object in view. Thus, if a habitation is to be built, it is necessary, before the habitation can be considered finished, that the land should be surrounded with a wall, that a part of it should be covered with a roof, and a door built, though the necessity of building a door has been called in question. In the case of an enclosure for animals, it is necessary to have a surrounding wall, but the land need not be covered with a roof. Authorities are not agreed as to the necessity of a door in such a case. If it is a matter of clearing a field, the sand must be removed from all parts of it, the land must be levelled and the necessary works constructed for its irrigation, unless the ordinary rains suffice; but the law does not require it to be sown. In the case of a garden, the sand must be removed, the land surrounded by a wall or a hedge, if such is the custom, and means of irrigation prepared; and, according to our school, trees must be planted.

When one has begun to clear land without finishing, or, what is more, when one has only marked a piece of land with stones or stakes, and not yet begun to clear it properly speaking, one is considered to be the first occupier, and one has a prior right to continue the work in preference to any other person. †However, it is forbidden to sell this purely personal right, and if in the meanwhile any one in good faith clears the land, he will be considered as the owner. Consequently, if the first occupier allows too long an interval to elapse before continuing the clearing the Sultan should notify him either to continue it or to abandon the land, allowing him a short respite if he asks for it. A person who has obtained a concession from the Sovereign has, so far as clearing is concerned, the same right of preference as a person who has begun to clear but not continued. Such concession is only to be given to a person able to complete his undertaking, and in proportion to the means at his disposal. This latter principle is applicable also to the preference that results from the simple occupation of which we have just spoken.

*The Sovereign may reserve a part of the uncultivated land, in order to pasture upon it—

1. Cattle given as capitation or assessment.
2. Cattle escaped from a stable or enclosure and seized by the police.
3. Cattle belonging to persons incapable of obtaining forage.

*He also has a right of dispensation with regard to the regulating of land so reserved, if it is necessary ; but he can never reserve uncultivated land for his own use.

Section 2

By enjoyment of the public road is understood the right of each person to go along it, to sit down and rest, to speak of one's business, etc., without in any way annoying the passers-by. One has no need of any special permission of the Sovereign in order to rest, etc., upon the public road ; and one may even shade the place where one sits with a mat, etc. If two persons want to occupy the same spot on the public road at the same time, chance should decide between them, or, according to others, the public authority. If any one who sits on the public road to sell his goods, leaves his place, either because he wishes to discontinue that means of livelihood, or because he wishes to occupy another place, he loses all his rights ; but if he goes intending to return, his rights remain intact, unless his absence is so prolonged that his customers go to some one else.

A learned man who habitually frequents a certain part of the mosque to pronounce his decisions and to teach, should be regarded in the same way as a person established upon the public way to carry on his business ; but if one is merely sitting in the mosque to accomplish a prayer, one has no right to occupy the same place again, in preference to another person, in order to say a later prayer. †A person who chooses a place in a mosque for prayer, and leaves it for some reason intending to return, does not lose his right to return to it, in preference to all other persons, if he wishes to finish the prayer he has begun. He need not even leave his cloak to show that the place is occupied. The traveller who takes up his quarters at a public inn, or the doctor-at-law who instals himself at a college, or the sufi at a monastery, should be left in peace, and their place should not be occupied by others, if they happen to leave it to buy necessaries, etc.

Section 3

"Visible" mines, those, that is, from which material can be extracted without preliminary labour, as in the case of deposits of naphtha, sulphur, pitch, or bitumen, or in the case of millstone quarries, do not become private property by exploitation, and no preferential right arises from first occupancy, nor even from a concession from the Sovereign. If the yield of the mine is not abundant, the first occupier can take from the mine what is enough for his needs ; †but if he wants to take more, it may be prohibited. †Drawing lots must decide the priority, where two or more persons want to begin the exploitation at the same time. "Hidden" mines, those, that is, from which nothing can be extracted without preliminary labour, as gold, silver, iron, and copper mines, *do not become private property by the mere fact of digging and exploitation, any more than "visible" ones ; but if a person clears uncultivated land, and discovers in it a "hidden" mine, he obtains the ownership of it, as an accessory to the soil.

Every one has an equal right to the water of rivers and springs in the mountains, if it is ascertained that no one has obtained exclusive possession of the water. If several persons wish to use it for the irrigation of their fields, and the quantity of water is not sufficient for an extensive employment, the owner of the highest land can water his fields first, then the next lower, and so on. None of them may retain more of the water than is required to inundate his fields to the height of the ankles ; and if it is the case of a field of varying level, each level should be separately considered in this respect. ††Water, even when common to all, becomes private property as soon as it is taken into any sort of vessel.

A person who sinks a well on uncultivated land, with the sole intention of procuring the water he requires, obtains in this way only a right of preference until he has left the place ; †but if he sinks the well in order to become the owner of it, he becomes proprietor of the water as well. In any case, whether or not the water becomes private property, the person who has sunk the well is never obliged to share the superfluous water with another person if the latter only requires it for agriculture ; ††but he must share the superfluous water with any person who wants to water his animals.

The water of common canals is distributed by means of wooden sluices in which holes are pierced, so that the distribution may take place either equally or in proportion to the respective rights of the co-proprietors. The partition may also be effected by turns, in virtue of special agreements between the owners having a right to the water.

BOOK 23.—WAKAF

SECTION 1

THE founder must be capable of declaring his wishes, and must be able to dispose of his property at his own will and pleasure, and the foundation must be of such a kind that perpetual use may be made of it. Thus it may not consist of foodstuffs or odoriferous plants, but with this exception, it may be either movable or immovable, or even such things as are capable only of individual possession, but not a slave or a coat unless a particular specified one, nor one's own person, †nor a slave enfranchised on account of maternity, †nor a trained dog, †nor one of two slaves without indicating which. †On the other hand the validity of a foundation is admitted that consists of buildings and plantations on another's land leased for that object.

A foundation, whether in favour of a certain particular person, or of several individuals all together, has no legal effect unless the beneficiaries could legally become proprietors of the goods given in endowment. Consequently a foundation cannot be made in favour of a fœtus, or of a slave by personal reference to him. A foundation in favour of a slave with no such express reference is understood as referring to his master. A foundation in favour of an animal is null and void, though, according to some, it is to the profit of the master in this case also. †It results from the principle already stated that one may endow in this way an infidel subject of a Moslem prince, but not an apostate, nor an infidel who is not the subject of a Moslem prince, nor one's self. A foundation for an illicit purpose, such as the construction of a Christian church or of a synagogue is null and void. But it is perfectly legal, whether it is made with a pious object, as in favour of the poor, of learned men, of a mosque or of a school; †or whether it is made with no manifestly pious intention, as when in favour of the rich.

The intention to endow a foundation should be expressed in explicit terms, as, for example, "I make such and such a thing a wakaf," or "My field shall be a foundation in favour of so and so." ††The phrases, "I consecrate," or "I devote to such and such pious use," are explicit; †as are also, "I make a sacred gift of such and such a thing," or "I make wakaf," or "it cannot be sold or given to another." On the other hand, the expression "give" without anything else cannot be considered explicit, even if it was the intention to found a wakaf; except when in favour not of one or many individuals, but of a category of persons or of the public, when it is so regarded. †The phrases, "I make such and such object a sacred thing," or "I wish it to remain for ever as it is," are not explicit; but the expression, "I destine this land to become a mosque," is enough to make of it a place devoted to religious worship.

†A foundation in favour of a particular person is not complete unless he accepts; an acceptance which can in no case follow upon a previous refusal. A foundation expressed in the words, "I make such and such a thing wakaf for a year," is null and void; but if the words used are, "I make it wakaf in favour of my children," or "in favour of so-and-so, and after him of his descendants," and nothing else, the foundation remains intact, even after the extinction of the family. *The usufruct then goes to the nearest relative of the founder, upon the day of the extinction of the beneficiaries designated by him. Our school regards as null and void a foundation made without designating an original beneficiary capable of enjoying it immediately, made *e.g.* "in favour of the child I shall have." On the other hand, it recognises the validity of a wakaf where one of the intermediary beneficiaries does not exist, *e.g.* where it is said, "I make a wakaf in favour of my children; and if I have none, then in favour of a person not designated, and after that in favour of the poor.

*The law considers null and void a foundation that has no object. Nor can it be made to depend upon a condition, as "I make wakaf, provided Zaid comes." ††It is also annulled by an option. †As to other conditions they should be faithfully executed, as that the property immobilised may not be leased, or that a mosque should be specially destined to a particular rite, such as that of Shafii. In this last case members of the school mentioned alone have a right of enjoyment, to the exclusion of all other believers; and this rule applies also to the foundation of a school or hostelry. †In the case of a wakaf in favour of two persons, and after them of the poor, the death of one causes his share in the usufruct to fall to the other, and not to the poor, who profit from it only after the death of both. This doctrine was defended by Shafii himself.

Section 2

A wakaf in favour "of my children and grandchildren," results in the usufruct being divided equally between all the children and grandchildren alive on the day of the foundation, even though one may have added "who are their descendants," or "generation after generation." Where, on the contrary, one has used the words, "in favour of my children, then of my grandchildren, then of my great-grandchildren who are their descendants," or "in favour of my children and my grandchildren, the one after the other," or "the former first," there is successive enjoyment by the different generations, and the first are merely fiduciary beneficiaries. †Besides, the grandchildren have on their own account no claim upon a wakaf made in favour of "children" only; but, on the other hand, grandchildren born of the founder's daughter are included in the expressions "posterity," "descent," "progeny"; or "grandchildren," unless one says "grandchildren bearing my name. "A wakaf in favour of "persons between whom and myself there are relations of patronage," should be divided into two equal parts, if the founder is both client and patron; but according to some jurists it is null and void.

An apposition preceding several words, joined to one another, refers to all of them; for example, in the phrase, "I make a wakaf in favour of those who are indigent, my children, my grandchildren and my brothers"—brothers and grandchildren are here proclaimed to be indigent equally with the children. It is the same with an apposition that follows, and with a reservation added to the principal words, provided these words are united by the conjunction "and"; thus, "I make a wakaf in favour of my children and grandchildren and brothers, who are indigent," or "except such as may be of notorious misconduct."

Section 3

*The ownership of the thing immobilised is transferred to God; which means that such object ceases, for men, to be subject to the right of private property, and that it henceforth belongs neither to the founder nor to the beneficiary. To the latter belongs the usufruct alone; and he may enjoy it, either personally, or by an intermediary, *e.g.* by lending him the object immobilised, or by hiring it out to him. The beneficiary of a wakaf is *ipso facto* the proprietor of what is obtained from a lease of the foundation, or of what it produces, as fruit, wool, and milk, †without forgetting slave-born children and the young of animals; though according to another theory these various offshoots become themselves wakaf, by virtue of the right of increase. After the death of a dedicated animal, the skin belongs to the beneficiary. Similarly, he becomes proprietor of the dower paid for a female slave with whom a third party has cohabited, either by error, or by right of marriage, †at least where it is admitted that a dedicated slave can legally be married. On the other hand, according to our school, the indemnity due by the murderer of a dedicated slave does not belong to the beneficiary, who should employ the money in purchasing another slave, who then becomes dedicated *ipso facto* in the place of the slave killed ; or, if this be impossible, he should at least employ the money in acquiring an undivided share in a slave.

The dedication of a tree is not, according to our school, terminated by the death of the tree ; for this does not prevent the continued use of the wood ; though according to some authorities, the tree should in this case be put up to auction, and the proceeds employed in the same way as the indemnity due for a slave killed. †The old mats and broken beams of a mosque may be sold, but only to be used as firewood. The ground of a mosque can in no case be sold, even though the building may have fallen into ruin, and though it be impossible to reconstruct it.

SECTION 4

Where the founder has reserved to himself the administration of the wakaf, or where he has conferred this duty upon another person, that disposition must be adhered to ; but if the founder has made no stipulation with regard to this, the administration must, according to our school, be intrusted to the court. The administrator of a wakaf must be a man of irreproachable character, fit for his duties physically and mentally. The functions of an administrator consist in keeping up and leasing the property immobilised, and in the collection and distribution of the revenues. If the administration has only been partly conferred upon him, he is forbidden to exceed the limits of his authority. In all cases the founder has the right to dismiss his administrator and appoint another, unless the administrator has been appointed in the deed of foundation itself. †A lease, effected by an administrator, remains good in spite of a rise in price, or the fact that another person offers more advantageous conditions.

BOOK 24.—GIFTS

A GIFT is a gratuitous transfer of property. When such transfer is made with the intention of obtaining a recompense in the other world, it is an alms; ††when the gift is brought to the donee to manifest one's respect for him, it is a present. It is an essential condition for the validity of a gift properly so-called that offer and acceptance be made in explicit terms; but in the case of a present neither offer nor acceptance are strictly necessary; it is enough that the object is brought by the donor and taken possession of by the donee. By saying to some one, "I want you to live in this house of mine, and that it shall pass to your heirs after your death," one makes a gift, as also by merely saying, "I want you to inhabit it," at least according to the doctrine adopted by Shafii in his second period, or by saying, "After your death it will return to me." Shafii in his first period expressed an opinion different from that adopted in his second as to the validity of a gift made in the following terms, "I grant you a life interest in this house," or "I make you a gift of it for life"; that is, if you predecease me it will return to me, but otherwise it will be yours irrevocably. Nowadays, however, in our school, both of the imam's opinions have equal currency.

Anything that may be sold may be given; anything that may not be sold, as an unknown or usurped thing, or an escaped animal, cannot be the subject of a gift. But in the case of things of very little value, such as two grains of corn, etc., a gift is permissible but not a sale. The gift of a debt due to one, implies the remission of the debt, if made to the debtor; †to any third person it is null and void.

As to the ownership of the thing given, this is transferred only upon the donee taking possession with the consent of the donor, or if one of the parties dies between the giving and the taking possession, by the agreement of the heirs. Some jurists, however, consider that under these circumstances the gift is *ipso facto* revoked.

A practice has been introduced by the Sonna, by which parents, at any rate when not of notorious misconduct, may by gift *inter vivos* distribute their property equally amongst their children, without distinction of sex; others, however, maintain that the provisions of the law of the distribution of property upon succession cannot be set aside in this way.

A father **or any ancestor may revoke a gift made in favour of a child or other descendant, provided that the donee has not irrevocably disposed of the thing received, *e.g.* by selling or dedicating it. Revocation is not prevented by a disposition leaving the right of ownership intact, such as pledging or gift, at any rate as long as neither have been followed by possession, conditional enfranchisement, giving in marriage a female slave, cultivation of a field, or even, according to our school, a contract of hiring. In a case where the donee first loses the ownership of the thing and afterwards recovers it, †the right of revocation does not revive ; and where, in the meanwhile, the thing given increases, the revocation applies only to that part of the increase which is incorporated with the thing itself, not that which has a separate existence. A revocation is made in the following words :—" I revoke my gift," or " I claim back the object," or " I wish the thing to become my property again," or " I wish to put an end to my donation " ; but it cannot be effected by mere implication, by ulterior dispositions affecting the thing given, such as sale, immobilisation, gift to another person, enfranchisement †or cohabitation.

In the case of a gift by which it has been expressly stipulated that there is to be no remuneration, a right of revocation belongs only to ancestors ; while a gift with regard to which no stipulation has been made about the matter is considered to have been made without any prospect of remuneration, if the donee is in any respect inferior in social position to the donor, and even if he is superior. Our school goes even further ; it accepts the same principle in the case of a gift between two persons of equal position. Where a remuneration is obligatory, but none has been specified, †it consists in the value of the thing given ; and the donor has in these circumstances the right to revoke the gift, if the donee forgets the remuneration. *A donation is admitted as valid when made with the reservation of a known remuneration ; ††a donation which must, however, be considered as a sale ; but, according to our school a gift made on the express condition of an unknown remuneration, is null and void.

In the case of a present made to some one, the receptacle is considered to be part of the present, and, if such is the custom, need not be restored, as one does not return the basket that has contained dates. Otherwise the receptacle remains with the donor, and the donee can only use it as, for example, a plate for the food given, provided always custom admits of this.

BOOK 25.—THINGS FOUND

SECTION 1

It is commendable to pick up what one finds, if one thinks one can keep it in safety. Some authorities even maintain this to be obligatory. If one has reason to doubt if one can keep a thing safely, the law neither recommends the above course, †nor does it forbid it, except for a person of notorious misconduct, in which case it is blamable. According to our school one is not obliged, on finding something, to call witnesses to see it; and, strictly speaking, a person of notorious misconduct, a minor, or an infidel subject of a Moslem prince, can pick a thing up in case of necessity. *But it should be removed from the possession of a person of notorious misconduct and deposited with one of irreproachable character; and one should never rely upon a person of notorious misconduct for announcing the discovery to the public, even if the object found be left in his possession, which is permissible if the person in question is watched by another. As to a minor it is his guardian who should take from him the thing found, make the public announcement, and appropriate it for his pupil, if he considers it proper for him to undertake the resulting obligations, *i.e.* in a case where it would be otherwise permissible for him to borrow money on his behalf. The guardian is responsible for a thing found which he has omitted to take from his pupil's possession, and which has been accidentally lost. *If a slave has picked anything up his action is null and an announcement made by him is void. On the other hand, his master who takes the thing from him is regarded as the person who has found it and picked it up.

[According to our school a slave who is undergoing enfranchisement by contract can pick up a thing found, with all the legal consequences, provided that the contract cannot be legally invalidated in any respect. In the case of a person who is partially free, the fact of having found something affects both him and his master; *and if he has only to serve his master once in two or three days, the object is considered as having been found by him or by the master in accordance with whether it was or was not a free day. This last principle is also applicable to all accidental benefices or expenses, with the single exception of an indemnity due for a crime which affects solely the person himself who is partially enfranchised.]

Section 2

Domestic animals that have nothing to fear from small carnivores, either in consequence of their strength, as in the case of the horse or the camel, or of their fleetness, as with the hare and the gazelle, or because they can fly, like the pigeon, can only be seized in a desert place with the intention of keeping them. This seizure can be effected as well by the court †as by any other person. Such animals when found in such a place cannot be seized in order to be appropriated; †but it is quite lawful to seize them with this intention when straying in a village. Domestic animals such as ordinarily become the prey of small carnivores —sheep, for example—can be seized and appropriated wherever found; and a person who seizes them in a desert place can at his choice—

1. Make a public announcement, and at once appropriate them.
2. Sell them, keep the price and appropriate it after making a public announcement.
3. Kill them and eat the meat; acts, however, by which one engages to pay the value to the owner upon his presenting himself.

Where, on the contrary, the animals in question are found in an inhabited place, the choice lies between the first two of these courses, †to the exclusion of the third. One may also seize a young slave who has not yet reached the age of discernment.

As to inanimate things found, if they are liable to rapid deterioration, like the paste called *harisa*, one may either sell them and appropriate the price after making the required public announcement, or take them at once and eat them. Others, however, maintain that sale is obligatory for a person who finds things of this sort forgotten in an inhabited place. Where, on the other hand, it is a question of things that can be preserved after manipulation, such as fresh dates that can be dried, one has the right either to sell them or to dry them, whichever course is rendered most advantageous by circumstances; if, at any rate, after finding them, one is willing to undertake their manipulation gratuitously. Otherwise the finder can sell a part to defray the cost of manipulation.

A thing picked up with the sole object of keeping it and returning it to the owner becomes a deposit, which one can get rid of at any moment by consigning it to the care of the court, which must accept it. According to the majority of jurists a public announcement is not obligatory in these circumstances.

Bad faith supervening after picking up a thing †involves no

responsibility, which arises only from bad faith at the moment of doing so. Such bad faith it is, according to our school, that prevents a public announcement in order to appropriate the thing subsequently.

Whoever picks a thing up intending to announce it, and appropriate it if the owner does not present himself, keeps the thing as a deposit, as long as the public announcement lasts, †and even until he declares his intention to appropriate it. One should first examine the nature, quality, quantity, wrappings and fastenings of the thing found, and then announce it in the markets, at the doors of the mosques, etc., for a whole day and according to custom. This notification should be repeated twice a day, *i.e.* morning and afternoon, then once a day, then once a week, and lastly once a month, †without interruption for the whole year that is prescribed for notifications. [†An interruption in the year prescribed for notifications does not render them absolutely illegal.] In the notification it is only necessary to give a superficial description of the thing found. The expense of the notification does not fall upon the finder, who picks a thing up merely in order to keep it and give it to the owner. The court should in such a case defray the expense, either from the public treasury, or by borrowing in the owner's name. The expense should, on the other hand, be borne by the finder if he picks a thing up in order to appropriate it; though, according to some authors, the owner should recoup him in all cases where the appropriation for some reason or other did not take place. †A thing of small value need not be announced for a whole year; it is enough if the notification lasts long enough to give reason to suppose that the loser has renounced his claim.

Section 3

A person who has notified the finding of a thing for a whole year, is not *ipso facto* its owner; he must also express his intention to appropriate it, in words such as, "I appropriate it." According to some, however, the intention alone is enough; while according to others appropriation takes place *ipso facto* upon the expiry of the required year. In any case appropriation is merely temporary; for if the original owner presents himself he can exercise his rights, under the following circumstances:—

1. The thing found should be returned him in kind, if the two interested parties are agreed about it; †or if the owner insists upon such restitution, even though the finder may prefer to replace the thing found by something similar.

2. When the thing found has been accidentally lost, the finder should

replace it by another similar object, or pay the value it had on the day he appropriated it.

3. Where the thing has deteriorated in the meantime, †the finder should restore it to the owner in the state in which he found it, and also pay damage.

If some one presents himself and claims a thing found, but can neither give a description of it, nor prove he is the owner, the person who has found it has no right to give it him. If some one comes and is able to give a description of the object but no other proof that he is the owner, the finder may give it him if he believes him to be speaking the truth; but, according to our school, restitution is never obligatory in such a case. Where restitution is made on the sole ground that the claimant gave a description of the thing, and the real owner comes later and proves his claim, the person to whom the thing was given may be called as surety. If in the meanwhile the thing has been destroyed in possession of the person who wrongly represented himself as the owner, the real owner may proceed either against the finder or against the person to whom he gave the object found; though the former may always recover from the latter what he has been obliged to pay the owner.

[††Objects found upon the sacred territory of Mecca, cannot be appropriated; but this does not affect the obligation to make a public announcement of their finding.]

BOOK 26.—FOUNDLINGS

Section 1

Children that have been abandoned must not be left to their fate; this is an obligation for which the Moslem community is collectively responsible. †The fact of finding a child should be established by witnesses. Authority over a child, in consequence of finding and taking care of it, can be exercised only by an adult, sane, free Moslem, of irreproachable character, and of sufficient intelligence to manage his own affairs. Consequently, a slave who takes charge of a foundling without his master's knowledge, has no right to keep it. Even if a slave, after finding a child, tells his master, and the latter lets it remain with him, or if a master authorises a slave to take charge of a child; it it is not the slave but the master who must be regarded as civilly responsible for it. A minor, a person of notorious misconduct, and one legally incapable, cannot legally take charge of a child they may find; and the same with an infidel in the case of a Moslem foundling. In all these cases the care of the child should be confided to another person.

If two individuals dispute possession of a foundling, the court should decide which of the two seems preferable, and, if necessary, confide the child to a third; but no one can dispute the claim of a person who has already taken a child to his home. †In a case where two persons, both of full legal capacity, jointly find a child, the court should prefer the richer to the poorer, and the one who is notoriously and positively irreproachable to the one about whom it can only be said that nothing is known to his disadvantage. In a case of complete equality in all respects chance should decide. A townsman who finds a child abandoned in a town, has no right to take it into the desert among the nomads; †but there is no objection to his taking it to another town; nor is there any objection to a stranger who finds a child in a town where he is temporarily staying, taking it to the town where he has his domicile. A stranger who happens to find a child in the desert may take it to a town. A nomad who finds a child in a town is subject to the same law as a townsman in similar circumstances; but a nomad who finds a child in the desert can keep it and bring it up at his home; unless, according to some jurists, the tribe has a habit of changing its place in search of new pastures.

The upkeep of a foundling is defrayed from property destined to such children in general, like wakafs made in their favour, or from the property of the foundling. This last phrase means the clothes, etc., in which he is wrapped, or upon which he is lain, the drahms there may be in his pocket, his cradle, and the dinars placed above or below his body. The law even considers as the child's property the deserted house in which he is found, but not the treasure buried underneath the place where he lay, †nor clothes or other objects placed in the neighbourhood. *A wholly destitute foundling should be brought up at the expense of the state; and, if necessary, every Moslem is obliged to assist him, as by way of loan; or, according to one author, as by way of upkeep. †A person who finds a child has the exclusive right to administer its property; but in all cases the expenses of its upkeep must be authorised by the court.

Section 2

A child that has been abandoned is regarded as a Moslem—

1. If it is found in a Moslem country, even though inhabited by infidel subjects of our Sovereign.

2. If it is found in a country conquered from the infidels, whose inhabitants have retained their property by virtue of a treaty, or hereditary possession by right of capitation; provided the country is not entirely destitute of believers.

3. †If it is found in a country not yet conquered from the infidels, but where there are some Moslems who have come either as prisoners of war or for a commercial object. If, on the other hand, the country is inhabited exclusively by infidels, the child also is regarded as an infidel.

The son of an infidel, declared to be a Moslem in consequence of the place where he is found, becomes none the less an infidel as soon as his origin has been proved; but a mere contestation of the presumption established by law in favour of the Moslem faith, is not sufficient, according to our school, to cause the child to be regarded as an infidel.

The Moslem faith of a minor, in general, is established in two other ways that have no reference to foundlings.

1. By the fact of being born of Moslem parents, even though only one of them may have been Moslem at the moment of the child's conception. If such a child, after attaining majority becomes an infidel, he must be regarded and punished as an apostate. Even a child

conceived at a moment both the father and the mother were infidel, becomes Moslem *ipso facto* upon the conversion of either parent during its minority; and must also be considered as an apostate if proof of infidelity is given upon majority. However, one of our jurists considers the child in these circumstances to be an infidel by origin.

2. By being made a prisoner of war by a Moslem; for in that case the child follows the religion of the person that has taken possession of it, unless the father and mother were made prisoners at the same time. †The fact of being made a prisoner of war by an infidel subject of a Moslem prince constitutes no reason for considering a child to be a Moslem. ††As a general rule, a minor, even though he may have attained the age of discernment cannot become a Moslem unless at least one of his parents is converted to the faith of the Prophet.

Section 3

If a foundling, upon his majority, does not himself admit that he is a slave, every one must consider him as free, until another person has proved the legal presumption in the matter to be false. If a foundling, upon his majority, admits he is the slave of a particular person, who does not deny it, the admission should be accepted by the court; unless the child previously admitted he was free. However, our school does not consider it an obstacle to an admission of being a slave that a foundling has already disposed of his property or person in a manner only compatible with freedom, *e.g.* by entering into a contract of sale or marriage. In spite of any dispositions of this nature the child's admission of being a slave must be admitted both as regards his origin and with reference to his subsequent actions; but his previous acts remain valid in all cases where such an admission would prejudice other persons who, believing him to be free, have in good faith entered into relations with him. The debts of a foundling who upon his majority admits being a slave are recoverable from anything he actually possesses. *Where the status of slavery of a foundling is maintained in legal proceedings by a person who has not the child with him in his house, the court can take no notice of his claim unless he proves the truth of his statement. In a case where the statute of slavery is not alleged by the foundling himself but by the person who finds him, the court can never give credit to the statement of the latter, unless the fact is established by sufficient evidence.

A minor, whether or not he has attained the age of discernment, kept by some one as a slave, without it being known if he is a foundling or not, should be regarded as really the slave of the person employing him; †and on his majority he cannot change his status by merely declaring himself to be free. Such a change is admissible only upon legal proof. And if any one proves that a certain foundling is a slave the latter should be treated as such; but before this can be admitted, not only must a general right of ownership be proved, but the cause must be shown, only one authority considering the former alone sufficient.

When a free Moslem declares a foundling to be his child, this declaration is enough to give him a right to bring up the child in preference to all other persons. A similar declaration by a slave also establishes filiation; though one of our jurists admits it only on condition of the master's approval. †On the other hand, a declaration of this kind made by a woman has not the same consequences. In a case where two persons dispute the paternity of a foundling the law admits no presumption in favour of a Moslem over an infidel subject of a Moslem prince, nor of a free man over a slave. In the absence of other proof recourse must be had to a physiognomist to discover the true father of the child. The person indicated by the physiognomist as the real father must be so considered; but, if there be no physiognomist, or if the physiognomist cannot venture to decide, or declares that the child is the child of neither competitor, or that he finds traces of filiation with respect to both of them, then the child on his majority must himself decide to which of the two persons he inclines by his character, etc. *Finally, in a case where each party succeeds in legally proving the truth of his affirmation of paternity, these proofs mutually annul each other.

BOOK 27.—JOB WORK

THIS form of agreement occurs when one says, for example, "Whoever brings me back my fugitive slave will be rewarded in such and such a manner," or when one makes use of any other phrase indicating the work that is to be done for some obligatory remuneration. In consequence one can claim nothing for doing a piece of work without the master's consent, or one that another person had been employed to do. A third party may promise a reward to any one who brings back the fugitive slave of another person; but in that case the person who undertakes the work can proceed only against the person who promised him the reward. If some one says, "Zaid promises a reward of so much to any one who brings back his slave," a person who brings back the slave has no case against the speaker if Zaid denies it. It is not necessary that the offer of a job should be formally accepted by the person undertaking it, even in the case of something that is to be delivered to a particular person.

The contract is valid if the work to be done is not known, †as well as where its extent is ascertained; provided in both cases that the amount of the remuneration is known. Thus, one may not say, "Whoever brings me back the slave shall have a coat," or "I shall reward him"; although, under these circumstances, the person undertaking the job can still claim, if he succeeds, reasonable remuneration for his trouble. In case of a promise to reward any one "bringing back a slave from such and such a place," the person who undertakes the job can claim only a proportional reward if he finds the fugitive in some nearer spot. If two persons together bring back a slave, they should jointly claim the promised reward; but if the reward has been promised to some particular person and another assists him in the work, the person with whom the master made the contract can alone claim the entire reward, at least, where the other shared the work in order to assist him. But if the second has taken part in it for the sake of the master, the original contractor can only claim a reward proportional to what he has done, and the other can claim nothing.

Each of the contracting parties may cancel the agreement before the job is completed under the following conditions:—

1. Nothing is due to the person undertaking the job if the cancellation takes place before the work is begun; or if the person so undertaking wishes to cancel the agreement later.

2. †If the master wishes to cancel the agreement after work has been begun he owes to the other party reasonable remuneration for what has been accomplished.

The master has the right to increase or diminish the remuneration so long as the work is not finished; without prejudice, however, to the contractor who has begun it, who in these circumstances always has a right to demand reasonable remuneration instead of accepting the change in that promised. The contractor cannot claim the promised reward, if, *e.g.* a slave he has undertaken to bring back dies on the way or escapes again; nor has he any right to retain the recovered property in order to secure payment of what is due to him.

The law admits a presumption in favour of the master when the latter denies that a condition, alleged by the contractor, has been added to the promise; or if he contends that the contractor has not been diligent in bringing back a fugitive. In case of a dispute upon the subject of the amount of the promised remuneration, both parties should take an oath to the truth of their assertions.

BOOK 28.—DISTRIBUTION OF ESTATES

SECTION 1

FUNERAL expenses are a first charge upon the total of the deceased's estate; next his debts must be paid; and then his testamentary dispositions may be executed, but only with regard to one-third of what is left of the estate, after deducting the debts. The remaining two-thirds of the net estate belong to the heirs.

[Special privileged claims, such as the charitable tax, the price of blood, security, and the return of things sold and not paid for in case of bankruptcy, are prior charges even to funeral expenses.]

The grounds of legitimate succession are four in number—relationship; marriage; patronage; in the sense that the patron is heir to the enfranchised slave, but not *vice versâ;* and, finally, religion, for in default of heirs of the first three kinds, the inheritance passes to the state, and this acquisition has all the effects of an ordinary succession. Legitimate male heirs are ten in number: (1) son; (2) son's son and other agnate descendants; (3) father; (4) father's father and other agnate ancestors; (5) brother; (6) brother's son, except in the case of a son of a uterine brother; (7) father's whole brother, and father's half-brother on father's side; (8) son of (7); (9) surviving husband, not divorced, who has not repudiated the deceased: (10) patron. Legitimate female heirs are seven in number: (1) daughter; (2) son's daughter, and other female descendants of a son, provided they are agnates; (3) mother; (4) grandmother, and the other ancestresses mentioned in section 5 of this book; (5) sister; (6) surviving wife, not divorced nor repudiated; (7) patroness.

In a case where all the male heirs just mentioned present themselves, father, sons, and wife share the succession to the exclusion of the others. If all the heiresses appear, then daughters, sons' daughters, mother, whole sisters, and wives alone share in the estate. Finally, should all possible male and female inheritors claim their portion, then the succession belongs exclusively to the father, mother, sons, daughters, and husband or wives.

The primitive doctrine of our school did not allow cognates a share in the succession, and the heirs indicated in the Koran could never obtain more than their determinate portions. Consequently, in default of persons legally entitled to it, the remainder of the inheritance escheated to the state. For this reason modern authorities have introduced the rule that, in all cases where the public money is not administered in accordance with the law, the heirs indicated in the Koran, with the exception of husband and wife, may, after receiving their respective portions and in default of other legitimate inheritors, demand that the remainder of the estate should be proportionately distributed amongst them. The state is even excluded by cognates, if the deceased has left no legitimate heir. By "cognates" are understood all relatives, except those already mentioned as legitimate heirs. They are of ten different kinds of relationship: (1) mother's father and, in general, any ancestor or ancestress who is not a legitimate heir or heiress; (2) daughters' children; (3) any brothers' daughters; (4) sisters' children; (5) uterine brothers' sons; (6) father's uterine brother; (7) father's brother's daughters; (8) father's sisters; (9) mother's brothers and sisters; (10) relatives of all these persons, male and female.

Section 2

The portions fixed by the Book of God are of six categories—

1. Half the estate is assigned to five individuals: (1) husband, if the deceased has left no children nor son's children; (2) only daughter; (3) son's only daughter; (4) only whole sister; (5) only half sister on father's side.

2. A quarter of the estate is assigned to: (1) husband, if the deceased has left children or son's children; (2) wife, if the deceased has not left children nor son's children.

3. An eighth of the estate is assigned to the wife, if the deceased has left children or son's children.

4. Two-thirds of the estate are assigned to: (1) two or more daughters; (2) two or more daughters of sons; (3) two or more whole sisters; (4) two or more half sisters on the father's side.

5. A third is assigned to: (1) mother, if the deceased has left no children nor son's children, nor two brothers, nor two sisters; (2) two or more brothers or uterine sisters; (3) father's father, when called to the succession along with the brothers.

6. A sixth is assigned to seven individuals: (1) father, if the deceased has left children or son's children; (2) father's father, under the same circumstances; (3) mother, if the deceased has left either children or

son's children, or brothers or sisters; (4) grandmother; (5) son's daughter, when she is called to the succession along with the deceased's daughter, *i.e.* her father's sister; (6) one or more half sisters on the father's side called to the succession along with the whole sister; (7) brother, or only uterine sister.

Section 3

Father, son, and husband are never excluded from the succession; son's son, or other agnate descendant, is excluded by son or other agnate descendant of a nearer degree, even though in another line; but an agnate ancestor can be excluded only by a nearer agnate ancestor of the same line. Whole brother is excluded by father; son's son and half brother on father's side are excluded also by whole brother; while uterine brother is excluded by father, father's father, child, and son's child. Whole brother's son is excluded by six persons: father, father's father, son, son's son, whole brother, and half brother on father's side; son of half brother on father's side is excluded also by whole brother's son. Father's whole brother is excluded by the same persons and by the son of deceased's half brother on the father's side; father's half brother on the father's side is excluded also by father's whole brother. Father's whole brother's son is excluded by all the persons last mentioned, and then by father's half brother on the father's side; while the son of father's half brother on the father's side is excluded also by father's whole brother's son. A patron is excluded by all agnates.

Daughter, mother, and wife are excluded by no one. Son's daughter is excluded by son and by two or more daughters of deceased; unless she inherits by way of agnation owing a special legal disposition. Mother's mother is excluded only by the mother herself; father's mother only by the father or mother. Now in the same line of succession more distant relatives are excluded by nearer ones, and more distant ancestors in the paternal line are even excluded by nearer ancestors in the maternal line, *but not *vice versâ*. Thus father's mother's mother is excluded by mother's mother. Whole sister is excluded by the same persons as whole brother; and half sister on the father's side is excluded also by two or more whole sisters. Patroness is subject to the same rule as patron.

If the estate is entirely disposed of amongst the portions of persons designated in the Koran as entitled to a share, agnates receive nothing by virtue of their right of agnation; but otherwise they can claim what remains of the estate, after deducting these portions.

Section 4

A son is universal inheritor when he alone is called to the succession; and this principle applies also where the deceased leaves several sons. On the other hand, an only daughter can never claim more than the half, nor two or more daughters more than two-thirds. In case of concurrent claims by sons and daughters, the whole estate belongs to them, in such proportion that a son's share is equal to that of two daughters; while son's children, in default of other heirs, are subject in this respect to the same rule as for deceased's children. In case of concurrent claims by a son and by children of another predeceased son, the latter are excluded from the succession; but in case of concurrent claims by an only daughter and by children of a predeceased son, she can only claim half, and the remainder falls to the share of the son's children, if they include a male. Otherwise, *i.e.* where the son left only daughters, they can only claim a joint sixteenth. Where, in these circumstances, the deceased leaves, not an only daughter, but several daughters, called to the succession along with children of a predeceased son, the law assigns to the daughters together two-thirds of the estate, and the remainder falls to the son's children, provided they included a male. Otherwise, *i.e.* where the son left only daughters, they have no right to the succession, unless they are called to it as agnates, because otherwise the remainder of the estate would fall to the share of agnates further removed. As to son's son's children, etc., in case of concurrent claims with deceased's children, they are subject to the same rule as son's children.

As a general rule, where agnate descendants are called to the succession, the result is that any female descendant of the same degree of relationship also inherits by right of agnation. The same applies to any female descendant of a nearer degree of relationship, if otherwise she would be excluded from the two-thirds' share assigned her by the Koran.

Section 5

A father can claim only the portion fixed by the Koran, if he is called to the succession along with a son or son's son; but in default of children and son's children he inherits by agnation; and if a daughter or son's daughter has a concurrent claim, the law assigns him—

1. A sixth, as heir designated in the Koran.
2. The remainder, after deducting daughter's and son daughters' portions, as agnate.

A mother can never claim more than a third or a sixth, as explained in the second section of the present book; while her portion is only a third of what remains of the estate after deducting the husband's or wives' portions, in case of concurrent claims by the father and the husband or wives of the deceased.

Father's father is subject to the same law as father, except that—

1. Brothers and sisters are always excluded by the latter; whereas whole brothers and sisters and half-brothers and half-sisters on the father's side, are called to the succession along with the former.

2. A father excludes his own mother, *i.e.* deceased's father's mother, who is not excluded by deceased's father's father, *i.e.* by her husband.

3. A father reduces a mother's share to a third of the remainder, in case of concurrent claims by her and the husband or wives; which is not so in the case of father's father.

A grandmother can claim a sixth; if both father's mother and mother's mother have survived deceased, the two grandmothers share this fraction between them. By grandmother is understood not only father's mother or mother's mother, but also all other paternal or maternal ancestors of the female sex not related to the deceased through males; **and this even includes father's father's mother, or her mother Thus the law calls to the succession every ancestor connected with the deceased, either exclusively through women, or exclusively through men, or connected with deceased's agnate ancestor exclusively through women, but not those female ancestors in whose line a male interposes between two women.

Section 6

If the deceased leaves only whole brothers and sisters, they share the estate as if they were deceased's children. Half brothers and half sisters on the father's side are subject to the same law as whole brothers and sisters, except in the case called *mosharaka, i.e.* where a woman leaves as her heirs a husband, a mother, two uterine brothers or sisters and a whole brother. In this particular case the whole brother participates, along with the two uterine brothers or sisters, in the third assigned them by the Koran; but if, in these circumstances, it is the case of a half brother on the father's side, and not of a whole brother, the half brother inherits nothing. In the case of concurrent claims by whole brothers or sisters along with half brothers or sisters on the father's side, the same rule is applied as obtains in the case of children called to the succession along with children of a predeceased son; except that the son's daughters inherit by right of agnation where there exists an agnate of the same or an inferior degree; while a whole sister or a half sister on the father's side inherits by right of agnation when she has a brother, *i.e.* where there exists an agnate of the same degree. A uterine brother or sister may claim a sixth ; two or more uterine brothers or sisters may claim a third, and in this case males have no advantage over females.

Whole sisters or half sisters on the father's side also inherit by right of agnation when they have concurrent claims along with deceased's daughters or sons' daughters ; they can then claim a portion as if they were brothers ; except that half sisters on the father's side are excluded by whole sisters only if there also exists a daughter of the deceased.

Sons of whole brothers or of half brothers on the father's side, are subject as a general rule to the same provisions as relate to their respective fathers, whether both categories are represented, or only one. They differ from their respective fathers only in the four following respects :—

1. They do not reduce the mother's share to a sixth.
2. They are excluded by the father's father.
3. They do not cause their sisters to inherit by right of agnation.
4. They are excluded from the succession in the case called *mosharaka,* of which we have spoken.

Father's whole brother or father's half brother on the father's side is subject to the same rule as deceased's whole brother or half brother on the father's side, whether the two categories of uncles are represented, or only one. This principle extends also to father's brother's sons, and other agnates properly so called, *i.e.* by reason of relationship.

By inheritors by right of agnation are understood the legitimate inheritors to whom the Koran does not assign a definite fraction of the estate, but who, in default of persons entitled to such fraction, share amongst them the entire succession, and who, if there are persons so entitled, can claim only the remainder, after deducting the portions prescribed in the Book of God.

Section 7

In default of agnates properly so called, *i.e.* by reason of relationship, the patron or patroness must be accepted as such and may claim the estate or what is left of it, after deducting the portions assigned by the Koran to the heirs we have just mentioned. In default of patron or patroness, their agnates are called to the succession of an enfranchised slave ; but in this case the law recognises as agnates only those properly so called, and not a daughter or sister inheriting as agnates by a special legal disposition. Agnates of patron or patroness share the succession as if they were agnates by reason of relationship ; but the *brother or brother's son of the patron or patroness have priority over the father's father. In a case where the patron or patroness are themselves enfranchised slaves without agnates, it is their patron and subsidiarily his agnates that the law calls to the succession, and so on. Thus a woman is never heiress by right of patronage, except to the estate of her own enfranchised slave, or of a person connected with the latter by relationship or enfranchisement.

Section 8

In case of concurrent claims by father's father along with brothers and sisters, whether whole brothers and sisters, or half brothers and half sisters on the father's side, and where there are no other inheritors who can claim a portion specified in the Koran, the law assigns to the first, either a third of the estate, or the option of sharing with the brothers and sisters as if he were himself a brother, whichever is more advantageous for him. If the father's father claims a third, brothers and sisters share the remainder. On the other hand, where, in the above circumstances, there are other inheritors who can claim a portion specified in the Koran, the law allows the father's father to choose whichever of three alternatives is the most advantageous for him: (1) a sixth of the estate; (2) a third of what remains after deducting the portions of those inheritors; (3) sharing with the brothers and sisters as if he were himself a brother. In these circumstances the following provisions also must be observed:—

1. Where the estate is exhausted by the portions specified in the Koran, *e.g.* where a woman leaves as her heirs two daughters, mother, husband, father's father, and whole brothers and sisters or half brothers and half sisters on the father's side, a sixth is still given to the grandfather; and recourse must be had to a proportionate reduction of the respective shares, as otherwise they would exceed the total estate. This excess and consequent reduction is called *awl*.

2. Where, after deducting the portions specified in the Koran, there remains less than a sixth of the estate, *e.g.* where a woman leaves as her heirs two daughters, her husband, and her father's father, the latter should still have his sixth, while observing the proportional reduction rendered necessary by the *awl*.

3. Where, after deducting the portions specified in the Koran, there remains precisely a sixth of the estate, *e.g.* where a woman leaves as her heirs two daughters, her mother and her father's father, the latter obtains this sixth and nothing more.

In the three cases mentioned brothers are entirely excluded from the succession.

In the case of concurrent claims by father's father, not with brothers and sisters or half brothers and half sisters on the father's side, but with both whole brothers and sisters and also with half brothers and half sisters on the father's side, the same rules must be observed; but in this particular case half brothers and half sisters on the father's side are not always excluded by whole brothers and sisters. It is only, under these circumstances, when the grandfather prefers to content himself with the portion assigned him by the Koran, rather than to claim a fraction of the remainder of the total estate, or participate with the brothers and sisters, that the existence of a whole brother amongst the persons entitled has the effect of excluding the half brother and half sisters by the father's side. Where there are no whole brothers, but one only whole sister, and also where, beside the father's father, there are two or more whole sisters, the estate is exhausted by the respective fixed portions of a third and two-thirds, and nothing is left for half brothers and half sisters by the father's side. Father's father, on being called to the succession concurrently with full sisters or half sisters on the father's side, is admitted to share as if he were a brother, *i.e.* the sisters cannot then be considered as heirs able to claim a specified portion according to the Koran, except in the particular case called *el akdariya*. This is where a woman leaves husband, mother, father's father, and a whole sister or half sister by the father's side. Then the husband can claim half, the mother a third, the grandfather a sixth, and the sister half. As the sum of these fractions exceeds the total of the estate, recourse must first be had to proportional reduction; then the portions of the grandfather and of the sister must be combined, and two-thirds of the total taken for the grandfather, and one-third for the sister.

Section 9

An infidel cannot succeed to the estate of a Moslem, nor *vice versâ*. An apostate cannot inherit nor be inherited from. Infidels inherit among themselves, whatever their respective religions may be; **but between infidel subjects of a Moslem prince and infidels not so subject there is no right of inheritance. Neither can a slave be an heir; but, according to the opinion adopted by Shafii in Egypt, the partially freed slave is capable of having heirs, though he cannot himself inherit. A person who has killed another cannot succeed to the estate of the person killed; though some authorities admit an exception to this rule in the case of a homicide for which the perpetrator was not in any respect to blame.

When two persons, called respectively to succeed to each other, perish together in a shipwreck, or the fall of a building; or if they die apart, either simultaneously, or in such circumstances that it is not known which predeceased the other, there is no inheritance as between them, and both estates go to other heirs.

The property of a prisoner of war, or of an absent person of whom there has been no news, should be sequestrated, until the death has been legally established, or until the lapse of such time as may justify its presumption. Then the court, after thorough examination, should declare that there is a presumption of death, and proceed to the distribution of the estate amongst those entitled at the moment when the presumption was declared. If the absent person is an inheritor, his portion should be sequestrated ; but the other inheritors obtain at once what is legally due to them.

If, when an estate falls to be distributed, there is a woman pregnant whose child will or may inherit, the rights of this child should be reserved intact until its birth, in the best way that may be possible, while respecting the rights of the other inheritors. If the child is born alive, and at a time indicating that conception took place before the inheritance fell due, it inherits as if it had been already born then ; otherwise it does not inherit. In any case the estate must be sequestrated until the delivery of the child, at least, if there are no other heirs, or if the other heirs are excluded by the posthumous infant. That is to say that when, in these circumstances, there are, besides the posthumous infant, other inheritors not excluded by the law, a distinction must be made between heirs that have a portion specified in the Koran, and those that have not. The former receive at once their respective portions, subject, if necessary, to a proportional reduction ; while the latter receive nothing. There is an example of the former case when the deceased leaves a pregnant wife who can claim an eighth, and his two parents can each claim a sixth, all subject to proportional reduction ; and one of the latter when the deceased leaves only children. According to some authorities there should be reserved out of the estate a sufficient provision in case the woman should give birth to four children at once ; though naturally there is eventually given to the posthumous child only what is really due to him.

When a hermaphrodite is called to a succession by reason of a title that makes no distinction between heirs and heiresses, as by uterine fraternity or patronage, the matter is simple ; but otherwise it should only be given at first what is due to it on the more disadvantageous hypothesis ; the remainder being sequestrated until it becomes evident which sex is preponderant. The fact of being an heir by reason of a disposition of the Book of God is no objection to claiming also as an inheritor by reason of agnation. Thus the master who has married enfranchised slave inherits from her both as husband and as patron; and the cousin on the father's side who has married his cousin inherits from her both as husband and as agnate.

[However, if it happens as the result of an incestuous marriage between mother and son that the same person is daughter and uterine sister of the deceased, she inherits only in the former character, though some jurists admit a succession under both denominations, even in these circumstances. Incestuous marriages such as these are customary among fire-worshippers, and might happen accidentally in Moslem families.]

If two persons have an equal right by reason of agnation, and one can also claim a portion specified in the Koran, by reason of some other relationship, this latter portion is assigned him without prejudice to his right to participate with his coinheritor. Thus, where there are two sons of a father's whole brother or father's half brother on the father's side, of whom one is also uterine brother of the deceased, the latter takes from the estate the sixth assigned him by the Koran, and the remainder is shared equally by the two cousins. Where, however, in these circumstances, the deceased has also left a daughter, the latter obtains the half specified in the Koran, and the remainder is shared equally by the two cousins; though, according to some jurists, the law assigns the entire half that remains to be disposed of to the cousin who is also uterine brother. A person who could strictly claim two portions specified in the Koran, by virtue of two distinct causes, is considered to be entitled only under the "predominant" cause. By this term is understood that cause which would exclude the other, if it were a case of two persons, or one which cannot be excluded, or that of which the exclusion is the more limited. As an example of the first kind of predominant causes may be quoted the case of a daughter who is also uterine sister, as may happen when a fire-worshipper has married his mother, or where a Moslem has accidentally concluded a like incestuous marriage, and the mother gives birth to a daughter. As an example of the second kind may be quoted the case of a mother who is at the same time a half sister on the father's side, such as may happen by the birth of a daughter of a marriage between a father and his daughter; and as an example of the third kind where a mother's mother is at the same time half sister on the father's side, as may happen where a father marries his daughter and she gives birth to a daughter who in her turn is also married by the father. In this case the daughter who is first married to her father becomes mother's mother and half sister on the father's side to the children born of the second incestuous marriage.

SECTION 10 (1)

Where all the inheritors claim by right of agnation or what is equivalent to it and they are all of the same sex, they should share the estate in equal portions; but in the case of concurrent claims by male and female agnates, each man counts for two women. In both cases, however, the number of heads is the "numerical basis of distribution," which means that the estate is divided into as many lots as there are persons entitled to a share. Where there are concurrent claims, by reason of agnation, by heirs entitled under the Koran to equal portions, the numerical basis of distribution is the denominator of the fraction of these inheritors. Thus, the numerical basis of the fraction $\frac{1}{2}$ is two, of the fraction $\frac{1}{3}$ three, of the fraction $\frac{1}{4}$ four, of the fraction $\frac{1}{6}$ six, and of the fraction $\frac{1}{8}$ eight. In the case of two fractions having different denominators of which one is a multiple of the other, as $\frac{1}{3}$ and $\frac{1}{6}$, the numerical basis of distribution is the greater denominator. When of two denominators one is not a multiple of the other, but they have a least common multiple, the numerical basis is found by multiplying the particular factor of each of the denominators by the other. Thus the numerical basis of $\frac{1}{6}$ and $\frac{1}{8}$ is twenty-four. Where the denominators have no least common multiple, they must be multiplied by one another, and the product constitutes the numerical basis of distribution. Thus the numerical basis of $\frac{1}{3}$ and $\frac{1}{4}$ is twelve.

Numerical bases are seven in number; two, three, four, six, eight, eleven, and twenty-four; and of these bases the following can give rise to *awl*, *i.e.* to proportional reduction of the shares, or—what comes to the same thing—to an enlarging of the basis.

1. A basis of six becomes: (*a*) seven, *e.g.* in case of concurrent claims by a husband and two whole sisters or half sisters on the father's side; (*b*) eight, if there is also a mother; (*c*) nine, if there is a uterine brother in addition to (*b*); (*d*) ten, if there are several uterine brothers, in addition to (*b*).

2. A basis of twelve becomes: (*a*) thirteen, *e.g.* in case of concurrent claims by a wife and two whole sisters or half sisters on the father's side; (*b*) fifteen, if there is also a uterine brother; (*c*) seventeen, if there are several uterine brothers in addition to (*a*).

3. A basis of twenty-four becomes twenty-seven, *e.g.* in case of concurrent claims by two daughters, father, mother, and wife.

In the case of two fractions having the same denominator the calculation is easy, *i.e.* it is only necessary to multiply these fractions by the common denominator to obtain whole numbers with exactly the same proportion; and the addition of these numbers gives the numerical basis ; but if the two fractions have different denominators then the following cases must be distinguished :—

1. One of the denominators is a multiple of the other ; they are thus mutually divisible, as 6 or 9 by 3 ; and the fractions are multiplied by the greatest.

2. They have a greatest common divisor, as 2 in the case of 4 and 6 ; then the fractions are multiplied by the least common multiple.

3. Their greatest common multiple is the number 1, as with 3 and 4 ; then the fractions are multiplied by the product of the two denominators.

Denominators of which one is a multiple of the other, have at the same time a greatest common divisor, but not *vice versâ*.

SECTION 10 (2)

When the numerical basis is known, and it allows of giving to all those persons entitled to share in the estate portions in whole numbers, the calculation is easy ; but in the case of portions composed of a whole number and a fraction the following cases must be distinguished :—

1. The fractions have the same denominator. Then the numerators must be rendered divisible by the number of heads. This is done, if there be no least common multiple, by multiplying the numerical basis by the number of heads ; or, otherwise, by multiplying, either the basis by the particular factor of the number of heads in question, or the number of heads by the particular factor of the basis, while observing in both cases the proportional reduction, if necessary.

2. The fractions have two different denominators. Then each numerator should be rendered divisible by its respective number of heads, after having reduced this number to its particular factor, if there exists a least common multiple. Then, in case of an equality in the number of heads that cause the two different fractions, it is necessary, in order to know the final basis, to multiply the number of heads by the numerical basis, while observing the proportionate reduction, if necessary. Where the two numbers of heads in question differ, the multiplication is made by the greater, if one is a multiple of the other ; and by the particular factors, if the two numbers have a least common multiple. Finally, if the numbers of heads are mutually indivisible, the numerical basis is multiplied by the product of these numbers. In this way is obtained a final numerical basis admitting of division without fractions ; and following the same principle the calculation can be made with fractions having three or even four different denominators, which is the greatest possible number.

If one wishes to know the number of shares that fall on the final basis to each category, one has only to multiply the number of the shares obtained on the original basis, by the multiplicator of that basis; and afterwards to divide the product by the number of heads. The quotient will be the separate portion of each inheritor.

Section 10 (3)

When the deceased leaves heirs of whom one dies before the distribution of the estate, leaving no other inheritors besides those of the original succession, who can claim the same portions in the second as in the first, the distribution takes place as if the deceased inheritor had never existed. This happens, for example, if a deceased person leaves only brothers and sisters, or sons and daughters; and one of these heirs dies before distribution, leaving no other heirs than his coinheritors in the original succession.

Where, on the other hand, the inheritor deceased before distribution leaves other heirs, or his coinheritors are called to his succession in different portions from their shares in the original estate, these different portions must first be separately determined. If the number of shares assigned to the deceased inheritor in the original estate permits also of assigning to his own inheritors portions consisting of shares in whole numbers, the calculation is easy. Otherwise the number of shares in question must be rendered divisible by the basis of the second succession; *i.e.* the basis and portions of the original succession must be multiplied by the particular factor of the basis of the second, at least if there exists a least common multiple of the number of shares fallen to the lot of the deceased inheritor, and the basis of his succession. If there is no least common multiple, the portions must be multiplied by that basis. Each inheritor in the original succession takes finally the portion due to him from that estate, multiplied by the multiplicator above mentioned; and a person called to the second succession obtains, from the first estate, the portion he would have from the second, multiplied by the portion of the deceased, or by the particular factor if there exists any least common multiple of the numbers in question.

BOOK 29.—WILLS

Section 1

Capacity to make a will is accorded by the law to every one, whether Moslem or not, without distinction of sex, who is adult, sane, free; and even according to our school to a person otherwise incapable by reason of imbecility. It is not possessed by a madman, by a person in a faint, nor a minor; though one jurist maintains that this incapacity does not extend to a minor who has attained the age of discernment. Neither can a slave make a will, unless—according to some jurists—he is enfranchised after doing so, and renews its dispositions before his death.

Testamentary dispositions for the public benefit must have some lawful object; thus a legacy cannot be made for the upkeep of a Christian church or a synagogue. Those in favour of one or more individuals are permitted only on condition that the person designated is capable of exercising a right of property. Thus a legacy in favour of a child conceived has effect only upon the double condition that such child is born alive, and that the conception has already taken place at the moment of the disposition, *i.e.* that the birth takes place before the expiry of six months. If the birth takes place after an expiry of six months the child is not considered as having been conceived before the testamentary disposition, at least if the husband or the master has not ceased to have commerce with the mother. *Otherwise conception is admissible up to a maximum of four years. A legacy in favour of a slave falls to the master, unless the slave is enfranchised before the testator's death. As to a subsequent enfranchisement followed by acceptance on the part of the slave, the effect depends upon the question whether ownership of the legacy has or has not been acquired since the testator's death. Testamentary dispositions in favour of an animal are absolutely null, whether an intention is manifested to make the animal a proprietor, or whether nothing is announced as to that; but when there is merely a declaration that the legacy is to be used so that the animal may never be in want of necessary nourishment, the traditional doctrine tends to admit its validity.

A legacy for the upkeep of a mosque is lawful, †and even one "for the profit of a mosque," specifying nothing further. However, in this case, the disposition is considered to have been made not only for the upkeep properly so called, but also for any amelioration of the edifice. A legacy may also be left to an infidel, †whether or not the subject of a Moslem prince, †to an apostate, *and to a person who afterwards murders the testator. *A legacy in favour of a legitimate heir is valid only if unanimously approved by the coinheritors, after the succession has been opened. This approbation is strictly necessary even if the coinheritors renounce their claims to the succession, and it cannot be given before the testator's death. For the disposition can be invalidated only by the fact that coinheritors exist at the time of death; and this cannot be known before that event. A testamentary disposition leaving each inheritor his legitimate portion is void; but there is no objection to leaving one of one's heirs a specified object of the same value as the portion he can legally claim. †But the disposition must be approved by the coinheritors.

The following things may be left by will:—

1. "The child with which a certain slave is pregnant," words which imply the condition that the child is born alive, and at a time indicating that conception had already taken place at the moment of the disposition.

2. The usufruct of things that are not consumed by use.

3. †The future fruit of a tree, the future young of an animal, and the future children of a slave.

4. One of two slaves at the choice of the legatee.

5. An impure thing, provided its use is not forbidden by the law, *e.g.* a trained dog, manure, grape juice not intended for fermentation.

A legacy of "one of my dogs" has effect if the heir gives any dog that belonged to the deceased. If the deceased had no dogs it is void. A person owning dogs among his property may leave them either all or part, even though the dogs form the larger half of the estate. When one possesses two tambours one of which is a musical instrument of diversion and the other an instrument that may lawfully be used, *e.g.* a war drum or one used by pilgrims, the legacy of "a tambour" and nothing more refers to the latter. A legacy of the tambour of diversion is void, unless it can also be used as a war or pilgrim drum.

Section 2

Testamentary dispositions may not exceed a third of the estate; and those made in contravention of this precept of the law, may be reduced to the portion which may be disposed of, upon the application of the legitimate heir. If the heir declares his approval of the disposition, it is effective, whatever its amount may be ; but according to one jurist it is then considered as a mere donation upon the part of the heir, and the legacy itself remains void for as much as exceeds the third.

The reduction is carried out by forming a lump total of all the property existing on the day of the decease, or, according to others, the day the disposition was made. In the portion that may be disposed of are included : enfranchisements of which the condition has been fulfilled by death, liberalities *inter vivos* made during the last illness, such as *wakaf*, gift, simple enfranchisement, and remission of debts. If all this exceeds the third which may be disposed of, the following rules must be observed in the reduction :—

1. Where the testamentary dispositions consist only in enfranchisement of slaves, a drawing of lots must decide which of them shall be deprived of their liberty in consequence of the reduction.

2. Where the testamentary dispositions consist in liberalities of other kinds, all are subject to a proportionate reduction.

3. Where the testamentary dispositions consist both in the enfranchisement of slaves and in other liberalities, it is necessary first to divide the portion of which one may dispose in proportion to the amount of the two categories of the legacy, and then to proceed under 1 and 2. One authority, however, maintains that the enfranchisements should always have their effect up to the full amount of the portion of which one may dispose, in preference to all other liberalities.

4. Where the third of which one may dispose has been exceeded, not by testamentary dispositions, but by liberalities *inter vivos*, bestowed during the last illness, no proportional reduction takes place ; but earlier liberalities are executed in preference to later, until the amount of which one may dispose is exhausted. If these liberalities are of the same date and the same nature, *e.g.* the enfranchisement of all one's slaves, or the remission of all one's debts ; the enfranchisement is carried out by drawing lots, up to the amount of which one may dispose, but the remissions are reducible by so much in the pound. Liberalities *inter vivos* of the same date, but of different nature ; and in general all engagements entered into, not by the deceased in person, but through agents are also carried out at so much in the pound ; except in the case of enfranchisements, for in that case the rule explained under 3 must be observed. According to one authority, however, enfranchisement has still the preference even in this case.

A single exception is admitted to the rules given as to casting lots, that is to say if, *e.g.*, the deceased has left only two slaves, Salim and Ghanim, and has declared before his death, " If I give his liberty to

Ghanim, Salim shall be free too," and has afterwards enfranchised Gahnim in his last illness. In this case Ghanim alone becomes free, if it transpires that the two enfranchisements together exceed the third of which one may dispose; and one cannot have recourse to drawing lots to decide between him and Salim.

If the deceased has bequeathed a specified object, at that locality, of which the value does not exceed the third of which one may dispose, while the rest of the estate is elsewhere, this object cannot be wholly delivered to the legatee immediately after the death; †and he cannot even be permitted the free disposition of a third, before the entire assets are got together, and become capable of being shared.

Section 3

A person who becomes so ill as to be in danger of death may no longer dispose of his property for nothing to a greater amount than one-third; but should he against all hope recover, these dispositions cannot be invalidated. A sick person, not in any danger, may freely dispose of his property; and even if he unexpectedly dies during this sickness, his dispositions have all the same their full legal effect. This is not the case where death is caused by the malady in question, even though the latter may not be regarded as of a dangerous nature, for then it is manifested to be really dangerous. In case of uncertainty as to the character of the malady, it should be ascertained by two doctors, free men of irreproachable character.

The following are considered by the law to be dangerous maladies—colic, pleurisy, constant flow of blood from the nose, chronic diarrhœa, phthisis, commencement of paralysis even where merely partial, vomiting out of food in an unchanged condition, and even vomiting in general if very violent and accompanied by pain or effusion of blood, and also continuous or intermittent fever, but not quartan fever. The following circumstances are by our school regarded as analogous to a dangerous malady—being made a prisoner of war by infidels who do not usually give quarter; being in a desperate battle between two armies of equal force; being condemned to death by the law of talion, or to be stoned to death; being in a ship in the middle of a tempest or a rough sea; a woman in grievous pangs of childbirth, before or after confinement, so long as the fœtus has not broken the membrane.

A testamentary disposition is expressed by the words—"I leave him such and such a thing," "give it him," "give it him after my death," "I make it his," "it shall be his after my death;" but the mere words "it is his" constitute an admission, and not a legacy. On the other hand, where one says, "It is his in my succession," this is a valid testamentary disposition. A testamentary disposition can also be expressed in a way which, though not explicit, still indicates the last wish of the deceased, *e.g.* by giving witnesses a writing that contains it.

A legacy in favour of a category of persons, as "the poor," does not require acceptance, but becomes irrevocable by decease; while, on the other hand, a legacy in favour of one or more particular persons should be formally accepted by them. The acceptance or renunciation of a legacy cannot take place during the testator's life-time; and it is not even rigorously necessary that the legatee should declare his decision immediately after the decease. Moreover, a legacy lapses if the legatee predeceases the testator. If he dies after the testator, but before accepting the legacy, the right of acceptance passes to his heirs. As the question at what period the legacy becomes the property of the legatee, some jurists consider that the legatee becomes owner from the death of the testator, under the condition that he accepts the legacy; others maintain the contrary, *i.e.* that he becomes owner only upon acceptance. *Others maintain that, before acceptance, the legacy remains in suspense, but that the legatee is regarded as having been the owner since the decease, if he accepts; and that otherwise the heirs have never lost the ownership. These three different doctrines as to the ownership of a legacy between the death of the testator and acceptance by the legatee, exist also with reference to fruit and the profit realised by a slave bequeathed by will, and with reference to other expenses, like the keep of the slave, and the tax to be paid for him on the breaking of the fast. According to the authorities who admit that the legacy remains in suspense until the legatee has accepted or repudiated it, the latter is nevertheless obliged to defray provisionally the cost of the keep of the slave or animal bequeathed.

Section 4

A legacy "of a *shah*," and nothing more, implies as well a large animal as a small one, a sound animal as one having redhibitory defects, an animal of the ovine as well as one of the caprine race, and even a male animal of one of these kinds, †but not a very young animal that can still be looked upon as *sakhla* or *anak*. A bequest of "a *shah* of my flock" is regarded as void, if the testator had no flock of *shahs*; but if it is a bequest of "a *shah* of my estate," one must be bought and given to the legatee, if the testator has left none. The expressions "camel" and "she-camel," in a testamentary disposition, include both the Bactrian and Arabian species; but the expression "camel" does not include "she-camel" or *vice versâ.* †The expression "animal of the camel race" includes both camel and she-camel. "Cow" excludes "bull," which in its turn includes only males; while, on the other hand, according to our school, the expression "mount" includes horse, mule, and donkey.

"Slave" includes a child, a woman, an individual with redhibitory defects and an infidel; though, according to some authorities, an injunction to an heir to enfranchise a slave means a slave who may be lawfully enfranchised by way of expiation. A bequest of "one of his two slaves" is *ipso facto* annulled by the death of both, accidental or otherwise, before the testator's decease; while the bequest becomes direct and simple by the death of one of the two slaves, accidental or otherwise. Where one instructs one's heirs to enfranchise "several slaves," they should give their liberty to three at least, and if the value of three exceeds the third of which one may dispose, it is necessary, according to our school, not to buy merely a share of a slave for the amount that remains of the third after the purchase of the two first, but to buy and enfranchise two slaves of a total value approaching as near as possible to the third of the estate; after which the excess goes to the profit, not of the legatee, but of the heirs. An injunction to enfranchise "two-thirds of a slave," involves merely an obligation to buy and enfranchise that share.

A legacy in favour of "the child such-and-such a woman is pregnant with," goes to the profit of both children, if she gives birth to twins; †and to the living, if one is born dead. Where, on the contrary, the testator added, "if it is a boy" or "if it is a girl," the giving of birth to a twin boy and girl nullifies the disposition. The legacy can only be claimed by the boy to the exclusion of the girl where the testator adds, "if she bears a boy in her womb." †This last form of legacy is still valid if the woman gives birth to twin boys; and the heir, in these circumstances, may give the object bequeathed to whichever child he chooses.

A legacy in favour of his "neighbours" extends to the inhabitants of forty houses in four different directions; one in favour of *savants* to all who occupy themselves with sciences relating to the law, *i.e.* Koranic exegesis, prophetic traditions, and jurisprudence; but it does not include mere reciters of the Koran, men of letters, interpreters of dreams, or doctors; nor does it include, according to most authorities, theologians properly so called.

A legacy in favour of the "poor" includes the "indigent," and *vice versâ.* Where both categories are jointly benefited, the legacy must be divided into two equal portions, and one given to each category, provided it comprises three persons at least. Of course the testator may also bequeath to one of the persons composing the category in question more than to the others so entitled; but according to our school a legacy "to so-and-so and to the poor" results in the person designated being unable to claim more than each separate poor person however small the portion may be, provided it is of some value. The person designated may not, however, be entirely excluded.

A bequest, moreover, may be made, not only in favour of a certain specified category of persons, without indicating their number, *e.g.* "to the Alids," but also to a specified number, *e.g.* "three persons" of a certain category, or to "the relatives of so-and-so." In this latter case, it should be observed that the phrase includes all the relatives, even those that are very distant, †but not those in a direct line, whether ancestors or descendants. †Relatives on the mother's side are not included in testamentary dispositions made by Arabs in favour of any one's "relatives," unless they are expressly named. Thus to know who the "relatives" are that are benefited by the testator, the nearest ancestor must be taken, and his descendants that have remained in the tribe must be regarded as the parents intended by the testator. If, on the other hand, the testator uses the expression "the nearest relatives," the legacy includes also the direct line, †it being always understood that son has priority over father, and brother over father's father; but with this exception the law grants no preference, in these circumstances, to either sex, nor by virtue of any right of succession. In consequence, father, mother, son, and daughter, are all considered as equal sharers in the legacy, and daughter's son has even priority over an agnate great grandson. †A legacy to one's own relatives does not include those that are legitimate inheritors.

Section 5

The usufruct of a slave or a house, or the rent of a shop, may be bequeathed. The legatee may then not only have the full enjoyment of the slave, but he is also owner of what the slave gains by his ordinary work; †and even of the dower, if it is a woman. †On the other hand, a child born of a slave during the usufruct follows the mother's condition, *i.e.* the legatee has the usufruct, but the ownership is the heir's. The latter also keeps the right of enfranchisement, and must provide for the slave's support, whether the usufruct is temporary or perpetual. The sale of an object of which the usufruct has been bequeathed to a third party for a specified time has the same consequences as the sale of a thing lent; †but in the case of a perpetual usufruct the thing can only be sold to the legatee. †If it is desired to ascertain whether a legacy exceeds the third of which one can dispose; the perpetual usufruct of a slave must be regarded as ownership; but if it is a case of temporary usufruct, the value of the slave's services must be calculated, having regard to the period during which the owner will be deprived of them.

*One may lawfully enjoin upon one's heir the accomplishment of a voluntary pilgrimage which one wished to accomplish oneself. The heir must then pay a visit to Mecca, †from the station fixed by the law, unless the testator has indicated some particular town for the pilgrimage to start from. As to an obligatory pilgrimage neglected by the deceased, this act of devotion has *ipso facto* to be defrayed by the estate, as we have seen. If, however, the testator has instructed the heir to pay it, either from the residue of the estate or from the third of which one may dispose, his last wishes must be observed. If the deceased has expressed no desire in the matter, the duty imposed on the heir to accomplish the obligatory pilgrimage that has been neglected must be defrayed from the residue of the estate, or according to others from the third of which one may dispose; but in any case this duty relates only to the journey as from the station fixed by law. †Moreover, any person, even though not belonging to the family, may accomplish the obligatory pilgrimage for the deceased, though not authorised to do so by him or by his heir.

The heir must also bear the pecuniary charges, resulting from fixed expiations which the deceased neglected to accomplish. As to alternative expiations, the inheritor may at his choice give foodstuffs or clothing to the poor, if there is occasion for it, †and even enfranchise a slave for this purpose. †In any case, and whatever may be the nature of the expiation, the heir may accomplish it at his own expense, if the estate is insufficient, and it counts none the less as an act of the deceased. †The result is the same when the expiation is accomplished by some one not belonging to the family, at least in the case of a gift of foodstuffs or clothing, but not where the expiation consists in the enfranchisement of a slave. And the soul of the deceased profits from alms and pious invocations made for its benefit, whether by the heirs or by any other person.

Section 6

A testamentary disposition may be wholly or partly revoked. It may take place either :—

1. Verbally, *e.g.* by uttering the words—"I cancel the will," "I annul it," "I revoke it," "I renounce," or "The thing I have bequeathed will be none the less my heir's;" or

2. By the fact of having disposed of the object bequeathed, by sale,

enfranchisement, dower, gift, or security; even where, in these two last instances, possession has not been taken by the donatee or creditor; or

3. By an injunction to the heir, contained in a later will, to dispose of the thing bequeathed in one of the ways mentioned under 2; or

4. †By an authorisation to sell the thing bequeathed; †by a putting up for sale though unsuccessful; or by mixing other wheat with the specified wheat bequeathed. Even if the legacy does not consist of specified wheat, but merely of "a *saa* of wheat" from a certain stack; the fact of mixing it constitutes a revocation, at least if the wheat added is of superior quality. But if it is of the same †or of inferior quality, the fact of mixing it with the original wheat does not imply a revocation of the legacy. And, finally, revocation results from the following facts—grinding the corn bequeathed; sowing one's field with it, kneading flour bequeathed, spinning cotton, weaving thread, making a shirt out of a piece of stuff bequeathed, building or planting on a piece of land bequeathed.

Section 7

The Sonna has introduced the practice of appointing testamentary executors to see to the payment of the testator's debts, the carrying out of his last wishes, and the guardianship of such of his children that are under age. An executor should be a Moslem, adult, sane, free, of irreproachable character, and a fit person to perform the duties intrusted to him. †However, an infidel subject of a Moslem prince may be appointed executor by a person of his own religion. Blindness is no cause of incapacity. An executor need not be a male; and the mother of children that are under age is considered the fittest person to bring them up.

An executor guilty of notorious misconduct should be relieved of his functions. This principle applies also †to a judge; but not to the chief of the state.

A right to appoint an executor to see to the payment of his debts and the carrying out of his last wishes belongs to every Moslem, adult, sane, and free; but the faculty of intrusting to an executor the guardianship of children under age belongs only to a testator who is himself their lawful guardian. An executor cannot by will appoint another person to replace him after his death, *unless this faculty has been formally accorded him by the original testator. There is no objection to an appointment of two executors in succession; as happens, for example, in the words, "I constitute you my executor until the majority of my son," or "until the arrival of Zaid, for then my son," or "Zaid will undertake this duty." On the other hand, one cannot appoint an executor to be guardian of one's children, during the lifetime of their father's father, who is their lawful guardian, if he is capable of performing this duty.

It is forbidden to give power to an executor to conclude a contract of marriage for the deceased's son during his minority, or to represent the deceased's daughter as her guardian, in a contract of marriage.

Forms of words by which an executor may be appointed are—"I name you my testamentary executor," "I intrust my affairs to you," etc.; but there is no objection to adding a term or a condition, provisional or absolute. It is necessary to define with precision the duty the executor is charged with; for if one merely says, "I name you my executor," the disposition is null and void. The nomination of a testamentary executor has no effect until the duty is accepted; †and this acceptance cannot take place during the testator's lifetime.

Where the testator has named two executors, neither can do anything without the other's concurrence, unless such faculty has been expressly accorded. A testator may revoke a nomination, and an executor, even after accepting, can give it up when he pleases. On a child's majority an executor guardian must render him an account of his guardianship, and in case of disagreement, the law admits a presumption in the executor's favour, as to the expense of his ward's support. On the other hand, the presumption is in favour of the ward, with regard to any sum the executor alleges having paid him after his majority.

BOOK 30.—DEPOSITS

The law forbids any one who is unable to keep it safely from accepting a deposit. Where a person accepts a deposit, being strictly speaking able to keep it, but not quite sure about it, the law regards him as merely blamable. On the other hand, the law considers it a meritorious act to accept a deposit, when one believes oneself to be in all respects capable of performing such a duty of trust. The depositor and the depositary should fulfil the same conditions as the principal and his agent. The contract is expressed on the part of the depositor by the words, " I constitute you depositary of this object," " I ask you to keep it," " I put you in my place to keep it ;" †but a verbal and formal acceptance is not required on the part of the depositary, provided he takes possession of the thing.

One should not accept a deposit on the part of a minor or a madman ; though one incurs all the obligations of a true depositary if one does so. On the other hand, a minor who has accepted a deposit is not responsible for it in case of loss, †unless that loss is caused by his own personal fault. A person legally incapable through imbecility is subject to the same rule as the minor. The contract ceases upon the death of one of the contracting parties, or upon the madness or unconsciousness of the depositary. The deposit may be claimed back by the depositor, or restored by the depositary at any time.

As regards responsibility, the following modifying circumstances are to be noted :—

1. A depositary who deposits the thing intrusted to him with a third person, without the original depositor's permission, or manifest urgency becomes responsible for any loss or deterioration, even accidental ; except, according to some authorities, in the case of a judicial deposit ; all without prejudice to the depositary's right to have the object transported by another person under his supervision to the place where he wishes to keep it, or to keep it in a shop of which he is only part proprietor. A depositary who is preparing to make a journey, should restore the deposit, either to the owner or his agent, or, if necessary, to the court. In default of the owner, his agent, and the court, the depositary may even, in these circumstances, deposit the thing with

another person worthy of confidence, without the latter incurring any ulterior responsibility. On the other hand, a depositary who buries the thing somewhere and then starts on a voyage is responsible for any loss or deterioration, even accidental, unless he has communicated the fact to some inhabitant worthy of confidence. If he takes the deposit with him on his journey, he is still responsible for accidental loss or deterioration, except in case of fire or hostile attack, unless he can find some one to whom he can lawfully transfer the deposit. Fire and hostile attack, and the fact that the place of deposit is liable to brigandage, have also, so far as regards the depositary's faculty of transferring the deposit, the same consequences as a voyage he is obliged to undertake. A depositary who falls dangerously ill should also return the deposit either to the owner or his agent, or to the court, or to a person worthy of confidence, or he should instruct his executor to do so, if he does not want to be still responsible for, though unable to exercise any control over it. It is only in case of absolute impossibility, *e.g.* in case of sudden death, that this ulterior responsibility is recognised.

2. A depositary who of his own accord transports a deposit from the original place or from his house to some other spot that is not so safe, becomes responsible for loss or accidental deterioration, but not if the new place is as safe as the original.

3. A depositary is responsible for the consequences of placing a deposit in contact with anything that may cause its loss or deterioration; and also for not giving sufficient fodder to an animal intrusted to his care, ††unless the owner himself so instructed him. He should give the animal the fodder with which the owner supplied him, and if the latter neglected to supply him with any, he should ask for it either from the owner himself, or from his agent, or from the court. †But it is obvious that if the owner sends him, with the animal, a person specially appointed to give it drink, the depositary is not responsible for the consequences that may result from that person's acts. Where a deposit consists of woollen garments, the depositary should expose them to the air so that they may not become worm eaten; and he should even wear them sometimes, if that is necessary to preserve them.

4. A depositary who has not scrupulously observed the directions given him by the owner as to the way the deposit shall be kept is responsible for all loss or deterioration that may result from his negligence. Thus where the owner has told him not to lie down on the top of a chest intrusted to him, and he does so, and the chest gives way beneath his weight, and its contents are crushed, the depositary is responsible; ††but no responsibility is recognised if, in these circumstances, the

deposit has not been crushed and destroyed by the fault of the depositary, but by accident or by another person's fault. The same rule should be observed where the owner has forbidden the locking of the chest with two padlocks, but the depositary has nevertheless done so. If some one is told, "Hold these drahms tight in your coat-sleeve," and he merely holds them in his hand, he is responsible for their loss, according to our school, if he lets them fall by inadvertence or when asleep, but not if the drahms are snatched away by a thief. If instead of holding them fast in his coat-sleeve, he puts them in his pocket, he is not responsible for any accidental loss. But if he holds them fast in his sleeve when he was told to put them in his pocket, he will then be responsible. If the owner, being at the market, gives the drahms to the depositary without indicating any particular manner of keeping them, the latter may, as he pleases, keep them fast in his coat-sleeve, hold them in his hand, or put them in his pocket, without being responsible for accidental loss; except that, if he keeps them in his hand, though no responsibility attaches to him if they are snatched away by a thief, he is responsible where loss is caused by his negligence or by his falling asleep. And where the owner directs the depositary to keep the money in a particular room, he should go there immediately and deposit what has been intrusted to him; for if he puts off doing this without good reason, he is responsible for the consequences.

5. The depositary is responsible for the loss or deterioration of the deposit caused in the following ways: (*a*) by putting it in a place where from its nature, it is not sufficiently secure; (*b*) by in some way imprudently calling a thief's attention to the deposit; (*c*) by indicating the deposit to some one who goes and claims it from the depositor. Even where a criminal forces the depositary to give him the deposit, the owner can none the less proceed in the first instance against the depositary; who, however, in his turn, can take action against the criminal.

6. The depositary is responsible where he makes use of a deposit in bad faith, *i.e.* wears the coat or rides the animal intrusted to his care. He is even responsible for taking a coat intending to wear it, or for taking drahms with the intention of using them; ††but a mere intention to commit such infidelity, followed by no attempt to execute it, is of no account. He is responsible if he mixes things intrusted to him with his own things, so that they are inextricably confused; †as also if he mixes the contents of two purses belonging to the same depositor. This responsibility of a depositary, once admitted from any cause whatever, does not cease by reason of his finally acquitting himself faithfully of his obligations; †but only where the depositor knowingly intrusts him again with the deposit.

A deposit should be returned to the depositor as soon as he calls for it; the law not permitting the depositary to retain it under any circumstances. He is responsible for accidental loss or deterioration wherever, except in case of violence, he is late in restoring the deposit.

In disputes between depositor and depositary, the law admits the following presumptions :—

1. The statement of the depositary on oath must be believed; if he does not allege a cause of accidental loss or deterioration; or if he alleges a cause by nature invisible, as theft; but his word alone, without an oath, is enough where he alleges a visible cause of public notoriety, such as a fire, at least if it is a general conflagration. But if the cause, though visible and of public notoriety, is not a general calamity, *e.g.* a partial conflagration, he must take an oath. A cause visible in its nature, but not of public notoriety, should first be legally proved, and after this the oath of the depositary is enough to show that the fire extended to the deposit in dispute.

2. The depositary's word confirmed on oath is also sufficient to establish a presumption that he has restored the deposit, either to the depositor or *e.g.* to the latter's heir; but there is no such presumption where the depositary's heir maintains that the deposit has been restored by the depositor to the person entitled to it, or that he has deposited it with a person worthy of trust, because he was going on a journey, and the latter asserts that he restored it to the owner himself. On the owner's demand, these facts must be proved.

A refusal to deliver a deposit of which the return is claimed by the depositor is of itself sufficient to cause the depositary to be responsible for any accidental loss or deterioration, even though in ordinary circumstances he would not be so responsible.

BOOK 31.—DISTRIBUTION OF THE PROFITS OF WAR AND OF BOOTY

Section 1

By "profits" are understood everything that the Sovereign collects from the infidels, except booty taken in the battle or in the pursuit by our cavalry. It includes a capitation tax, a tithe on commerce, property abandoned by flying infidels before being attacked, property of an apostate executed or deceased, and the estate of an infidel subject of a Moslem prince, deceased without heirs.

Profits of war should be divided into five equal portions, of which one is devoted to the five following objects :—

1. The public interest, *e.g.* the fortification of the frontiers, the amelioration of judicial institutions or the encouragement of the sciences, whichever at the moment is the most urgent.

2. The support of the Beni Hashim and the Beni Muttalib, *i.e.* the descendants of the Prophet's relatives, without distinction between rich and poor. The proportion between the pension thus allotted to the male members of the family and that of the females is the same as in the succession to a deceased person's estate.

3. The support of orphans, *i.e.* minors who have lost their father, **provided they are really poor.

4. Assistance granted to the indigent.

5. Assistance granted to strangers.

The distribution amongst the four last categories is effected while taking into consideration the number of persons entitled on the whole Moslem territory; though according to some jurists the yield of each country should be divided amongst those of its inhabitants who are entitled to it, without regard to the portions allotted elsewhere.

*As to the other four-fifths of the profits of war, these are applied to the support of the soldiers composing the permanent army, always held ready for the war against the infidels. Its administration is delegated to a special department organised by the Sovereign for that purpose, and to overseers appointed for each tribe and for each brigade. These overseers must make themselves acquainted with what concerns each soldier and his family; they should ascertain the sum necessary for his support and for that of his family, and see that this sum is correctly paid.

The first inscribed on the army registers are the Koraishites, and they are paid first before the others. They include all the descendants of Nadr ibn Kinana—*i.e.* (1) the Beni Hashim and the Beni Muttalib; (2) the descendants of Abd Shams; (3) the descendants of Nawfal; (4) the descendants of Abd-al-Ozza; (5) the descendants of the other relatives of the Prophet, according to the degrees of their respective generations.

After the Koraishites are inscribed upon the registers the descendants of the inhabitants of Medina who took the part of the Prophet against the inhabitants of Mecca, then the other Arabs, and lastly foreign nations converted to Islam. There should be struck out from the registers all those who have become blind, sickly, or for some other reason incapable of taking part in war; but a soldier who is ill or mad still receives his pay if recovery can be hoped for; *otherwise he is pensioned. After his death his pension is paid to his widow and children, *i.e.* to his widow until she remarries, and to his children until they are old enough to support themselves. Any excess of the four-fifths that may be left over should also be distributed amongst the soldiers of the permanent army, in proportion to their respective salaries; though the Sovereign may also apply it to the upkeep of the fortifications, or to the purchase of arms and cavalry horses. It must be noted that all that has been said in this section applies only to movable property; for as to immovable property forming part of the profits of war, it should constitute a *wakaf*, the revenue being then distributed as movable property.

Section 2

By "booty" is understood what is taken upon the infidels, either in the battle or in the pursuit; it being understood that the equipment of a dead enemy belongs *ipso facto* to the slayer.

By "equipment" is understood the clothes, boots, gaiters, cuirass, arms, mount, saddle, bridle, *bracelet, *belt, *ring, and *provisions a soldier has upon him; and also *a spare mount or beast of burden led at his side; but not the truss bound upon the crupper of his horse, at least according to our rite. This right to the equipment exists only when one has personally run some danger, attacking the enemy in front. Where one has merely killed an infidel by means of a projectile thrown from the ramparts of a fortress, or from a distance in the ranks, or where one has killed a sleeping infidel, a prisoner of war, or a person belonging to a routed army, no such recompense can be claimed. To establish one's right to his equipment, however, it is enough to have put the infidel *hors de combat*, even without killing him, *e.g.* by gouging out his eyes, or cutting off his hands or his feet; *or it is even sufficient to have made him a prisoner, or cut off his hands or his feet, without putting him entirely *hors de combat*. **Equipment is not included in the distribution of booty.

The booty that remains over after deducting equipments, cost of surveillance, transport, etc., is divided into five equal portions, one of which is divided in the same way and amongst the same persons as the first fifth of the "profits." †Rewards are paid out of the twenty-fifth part devoted to the public interest, at least if such is the order of the Sovereign; but the latter may also employ for this purpose money paid into the treasury at the end of previous expeditions. By "reward" is meant any extraordinary recompense promised by the Sovereign or the General in command to any one, whether a soldier or not, who accomplishes some feat to the detriment of the infidels, of whatever nature it may be. The amount of the reward depends upon the importance of the feat and the greatness of the danger incurred. The remaining four-fifths of the booty are given in entirety to those who have obtained it; making no distinction between movable and immovable property. All those are entitled to it who are upon the field of battle intending to fight, even though they may not personally have taken part in the combat. On the other hand, a person who does not arrive upon the field of battle until the issue is decided can claim nothing. Authorities are not agreed as to the right of persons arriving before booty has been gathered, though after the end of the fighting. The rights of combatants who die after the battle, and after the booty has been collected, pass to their heirs; †and it is the same with the soldier who dies after the battle, but before the collection of the booty. But the heirs of soldiers actually killed during the fighting can claim nothing, according to our rite. *Individuals engaged to conduct beasts of burden, or look after the baggage, and traders and artisans following the army, may all participate in the booty if they have actually fought.

A horseman's share is three times that of a foot soldier; no distinction being made between those that have one horse and those that have more, or between a man riding an arab horse and one that rides a horse of inferior breed. Soldiers mounted, not on horses, but on camels, etc., receive the same as foot soldiers; and the same is the case with horsemen mounted on animals that are thin and unfit for service, though one authority maintains that these share like other horsemen, unless the General in command has notified them to remain in the rear. A slave, a minor, a woman, and an infidel subject of a Moslem prince,

:ing part in a battle without being obliged to, receive a remuneration be determined by the Sovereign, but less than that received by those o participate in the booty. *These remunerations are payable out he four-fifths that remain disposable.

[††An infidel subject of a Moslem prince can claim no remuneration, ess he has served in the war without pay, and with the Sultan's cial authorisation.]

BOOK 32.—DISTRIBUTION OF THE PROCEEDS OF THE TAX

Section 1

Those entitled may be divided into eight categories :—

1. The poor, *i.e.* those who have nothing, and cannot gain their living. One may be legally called poor, though having a house, clothing, property at a distance of more than two days' journey, or debts due to one at a fixed date ; and even though able to gain a living by some work not suitable for one. Thus a learned man may be called poor though able, strictly speaking, to provide for his own needs by exercising some trade that would prevent him continuing his studies ; but this cannot be alleged as an excuse by a person who, wishing to perform some voluntary act of devotion, makes it a pretext for not working. To be admitted amongst the number of the poor, it is not necessary to be sickly, nor to abstain from asking for alms, at least according to what Shafii maintained in his second period. †On the other hand, a person is not poor if he has relatives—or if she has a husband—who should provide maintenance.

2. The indigent. In this category are classed those persons who, though possessed of property, or making a living that might, strictly speaking, be called sufficient, yet have not enough for their maintenance in the circumstances in which they happen to be.

3. Those engaged in the administration of the tax, *i.e.* the collectors, registrars, distributors, and the messengers to call together the tax-payers ; but not including the judge, or the prefect of the province.

4. Persons inclined to Islam who need some assistance in order to declare themselves openly to be converts ; or whose high social position gives hope of the conversion of other infidels. According to our rite these two categories of persons are admitted to be entitled.

5. Slaves undergoing enfranchisement by contract.

6. Insolvent debtors, provided their debt has a legitimate cause. [*Insolvent debtors should be assisted, even where their debts have no legitimate cause, if they manifest a firm intention henceforth to introduce better order into their business or their conduct.] *Persons of this category participate by the fact of being in difficulties, though the

debts may not yet be due for payment. [†On the contrary, before the debts become due, they are not entitled.] What we have said about this class of persons applies only to debtors who have contracted obligations in their own interest; for those who have done so with a laudable object should be compensated in all cases, even though they may be rich. Some authors, however, admit an exception in the case of an individual so rich in coin that he can easily meet his engagements.

7. Those "in the way of God," *i.e.* who take part in the war against the infidels, unless they share in the four-fifths of the profits of war. This category of persons are entitled without distinction of fortune.

8. Travellers without means to begin or to continue their journey; on the sole condition that the journey is not undertaken for an illicit purpose.

These persons we have now mentioned as being entitled must also be Moslems, not belonging to the families of the Beni Hashim or the Beni Mottalib, †nor under the patronage of any member of these two families.

Section 2

A person claiming a share in the proceeds of the tax should be admitted amongst the number of those entitled, if the Sovereign is certain that the claim is well founded, or dismissed at once, if the Sovereign is convinced of the contrary. In case of uncertainty a simple declaration of poverty or indigence is enough, without the claimant being obliged to produce proof; but if it is certain that the person in question was formerly in easy circumstances, he must then prove the loss of his property. †This rule applies also to those alleging, as the cause of their poverty, their being charged with the maintenance of a numerous family. A simple declaration is enough in order to share as a combatant for the faith or a traveller; but claimants under these two categories must restore what they have received, if it subsequently appears that they have remained at home. On the other hand, persons employed in the collection, slaves undergoing enfranchisement by contract, and debtors, must in all cases prove the ground of their claim. It is understood that in these cases sufficient proof includes not only the deposition of two witnesses of irreproachable conduct; but also public notoriety, †and a confirmation by creditor or master.

Poor and indigent persons never obtain more at one time than is necessary for the current year. [†According to Shafii's personal opinion, accepted by nearly all authorities, they should be given enough to support them for the rest of their life, according to average mortality, this sum being devoted to the purchase of some immovable property of which the revenue is applied to their maintenance.

A slave undergoing enfranchisement by contract, and the debtor, receive only what is necessary to pay what they owe. The traveller receives sufficient money to reach his destination or his domicile. The combatant for the faith should be provided with what is required for his maintenance and outfit, there and back, including the period during which he is on the frontier. A horse and arms are given him ; and these remain his property, even after the end of the war. The combatant and the traveller may even claim a mount all ready equipped, if they have to go a great distance, or if they are too weak to make the journey on foot ; and lastly they have a right to the necessary transport ; if their provisions or their baggage are so bulky that they cannot easily carry it themselves.

*A person who wishes to claim on two counts has to be content with what is due to him under one head only.

Section 3

The Sovereign or his subordinates employed for that purpose should divide the proceeds of the tax into eight portions ; or, where there are no special collectors, into seven. In default of one or more of the categories their portions go to the others by virtue of the law of increase. The portion of each category should be wholly divided up amongst the individuals composing it ; and similarly the taxpayer who prefers to effect the partition himself, should divide up the entire amount due by him, if all the categories of those entitled live in his place. In any case a category cannot legally be admitted to share in the distribution, unless it is composed of at least three individuals. The respective categories have each right to an equal portion ; but equality is not required between the shares of the individuals composing a category, unless the distribution is effected by the Sovereign, for in this case inequality of shares is forbidden if there is equality of need.

*The transfer of the tax collected in one district into another is illegal, except in the case of a district where none of the categories entitled exist. In this latter case the transfer is incontestably obligatory. According to those authorities who do not admit the prohibition of a general right of transfer, a transfer is obligatory if all eight categories do not exist in the district. Among the authorities who maintain the prohibition of a transfer, except in the case of a total lack of persons entitled, the majority allows the claim of the categories existing in the district to the share of those that are absent. There are some, however, who, though rejecting in these circumstances a transfer of the entire proceeds of the tax, admit none the less a transfer of the portions of the categories that do not exist.

A collector should be a free man of irreproachable conduct, and sufficiently instructed in the dispositions of the law relating to the tax. If, however, the amount due by the taxpayers, and the shares of those entitled are mentioned in his instructions, it is not necessary for him to have any profound knowledge of the subject. The month of collection should always be announced beforehand.

The Sonna has introduced the practice of marking animals due for the tax or as profits of war, with a red-hot iron on a part of the body where the hair is thin. It is blamable to mark animals upon the face. [†It is even expressly forbidden, according to a decision of Baghawi; while in the collection of Moslim, called Es-sahih, there is a tradition that the Prophet cursed whoever should commit a similar atrocity.]

Section 4

The Sonna prescribes also a supererogatory tax that may be given even to persons in easy circumstances and to infidels. It is given in secret, in the month of Ramadan, preferably to one's near relatives and neighbours. But it is recommended to those who owe a debt, or have to maintain a family, not to pay a tax on their property by way of charity until they have first discharged these obligations. [†It is even forbidden to spend in charity money required for the maintenance of those dependent on one, or for paying a debt that otherwise one can hope for no means of paying.] †It is commendable to be charitable out of one's superfluity, provided that too great a burden is not thereby incurred.

BOOK 33.—MARRIAGE

CHAPTER I.—GENERAL PROVISIONS

Section 1

Marriage is to be recommended for every man who feels the need of it, provided he is able to undertake the pecuniary obligations that result from it. Otherwise it is better to abstain and repress one's passions by fasting. Marriage is a blamable act for a man who does not feel the need of it, and is not able to support the expense; but not for one who, though not needing it, is yet able to undertake its obligations. It is preferable, however, that such a person should remain a celibate and devote himself entirely to religious practices.

[†Should such a man not possess a temperament suitable for an austere life, it is better for him to take a wife, though it is not strictly necessary. But it is blamable in him to marry if, though able to support the expense, he is physically incapable of fulfilling his marital duties, by reason of decrepitude, chronic malady, impotence, etc.]

One should preferably choose, as a wife, a virgin, of religious sentiments and well-established descent, not too nearly related to the husband.

The Sonna has introduced the practice of seeing a woman one proposes to marry, even without her knowing it, and even several times, before demanding her in marriage; but the suitor must not see any more of his future wife than the face and hands. The law forbids a male adult to look upon the shameful parts of a free adult woman, a "stranger" to him—*i.e.* not his near relative, wife or slave. This prohibition extends, in ordinary circumstances, to the face and hands, ††even though one may be sure of not feeling any lascivious sensations. Relatives within the prohibited degrees need conceal only that part of the body between the navel and the knees; or, according to some authorities, the parts of the body that are invisible when such women are engaged upon their household duties. †As to a female slave any one may see her body, except between navel and knees; and a girl under age need only conceal her *pudendum;* unless upon looking at either one experiences lascivious sensations, in which case they should cover the whole body. †A slave with regard to his mistress and a eunuch with regard to any woman, are considered as men within the prohibited degrees. A minor of either sex approaching majority should observe the law as if majority were already attained. Men may look at each other, provided they keep concealed the part of the body between navel and knees; but it is forbidden to look upon the body of a beardless youth, if it excites desire.

[†One should avoid altogether looking upon a beardless youth, for fear of exciting an infamous passion; this is Shafii's personal opinion. †The best authors consider a female slave as subject to the same rule as a free woman, so far as regards the prohibition of being seen.]

Women among themselves should observe the rule laid down for men; †though an infidel woman, subject of a Moslem prince, may not look upon a Moslem woman. †A woman may lawfully look upon the body of a foreigner, except between navel and knees, unless fleshly desires are thereby excited. [†It is forbidden for a woman to look upon a man, in the same way as for a man to look upon a woman.] A woman may look upon a relative within the prohibited degrees, as a man may. A prohibition of looking upon implies that of touching; though one may both look upon and touch any part of the body, for the purpose of bleeding, or applying a cupping glass, or dressing a sick or wounded member.

[It is permissible, if necessity requires it, to look upon any woman with whom one wishes to enter into commercial relations, or who is a witness in a court of law, or where it is necessary to give her some instruction, etc.]

A husband has a right to see all parts of his wife's body.

Section 2

One may ask for the hand of any woman who is unmarried, or whose legal period of retirement is finished; but a woman whose period is not yet completed may not be openly demanded in marriage. A woman repudiated in a revocable manner can never be demanded in marriage during her retirement, even indirectly. But one may, if one uses ambiguous terms, make a proposition of this nature to a widow, during her retirement, *or to a woman repudiated irrevocably. The law forbids asking for the hand of a woman who has already received and formally accepted a similar proposition from another, except with the consent of one's rival; *but until a woman has decided as to the first offer, there is no objection to making her a second. When a woman asks advice from a third party as to a man who has made her an offer of marriage, this third party is bound to give her sincere and truthful information.

It is commendable that a demand in marriage, as well as the contract, should be preceded by some edifying words ; ††though strictly speaking it is enough, for the validity of the marriage, that the bride's guardian should say these words, and that the husband should simply answer : " Glory to God, and grace to his apostle—God grant him his grace and blessing—I accept, etc." [††This fashion is not at all commendable.] The marriage is not legally binding, if the offer is separated from the acceptance by a long religious ceremony.

Section 3

A marriage is not constituted except by an offer, expressed in terms such as : " I give you in marriage," or " I give you for wife," followed by acceptance, expressed in terms such as : "I take her as wife," "I marry her," " I consent to marry her," or " I accept your offer." The validity of the marriage is unaffected by the husband or the guardian being the first to express his will ; but it is rigorously necessary that the guardian should make use of the words "give in marriage," or "give for wife." Arabic †or any other language may be used, provided that consent is expressed on both sides in explicit terms. Consequently, our school does not accept the validity of a marriage where the husband replies, " I accept," without specifying what, to the guardian who says to him, " I give you her in marriage ; " but there is no objection to the consent being expressed in the words : "Give her me in marriage," and "I give her you," or "marry her," and "I marry her."

The parties may not make their consent depend upon any condition ; and our school regards the contract as wholly null where a father, hearing his wife has given birth to a child, cries out, " If it is a daughter, I give her you in marriage ;" or where he says, " If my daughter is repudiated by her present husband, I will give her you in marriage, after her legal retirement. A contract of marriage may not be made for a certain term ; nor have a reciprocal character in such a way that the parties are mutually exempt from dower, *e.g.* by saying : "I give you my daughter in marriage on condition that you give me yours, and that the one's virginity becomes the other's dower," even though such proposal is accepted. †But a reciprocal marriage is perfectly regular, if the value of virginity is not taken into the calculation ; †it is nullified when such value enters however little into the amount of the dowers.

A marriage should be effected before two witnesses, free, male, of irreproachable character, sound in hearing and sight—though the necessity of being able to see is doubtful. †There is no objection to the witnesses being near relatives, *e.g.* sons of the bridegroom and bride, or their personal enemies. ††Nor does it matter if the reputation of the witnesses is doubtful; provided it is not notoriously bad; but the law insists positively upon their being free and Moslems. Though our school regards as null a marriage effected before witnesses whose incompetence from notorious misconduct was known at the time, this circumstance alleged after the celebration is only admissible if legally proved or admitted by the parties. It is not sufficiently established by a mere subsequent declaration of the witnesses themselves; and if only the husband admits the circumstances, while the wife denies it, the marriage is not null, but the law requires a separation; upon which the husband owes his wife half her dower, if he has not yet had connection with her, or otherwise the whole. It is commendable to choose as witnesses persons agreeable to the bride, at least where her consent is necessary to the marriage. However, it is not necessary to ask her advice as to the witnesses.

Section 4

A woman cannot give herself in marriage, even though her guardian should authorise her to do so. Nor can she give in marriage another woman, even as agent of the latter's guardian; nor effect a marriage as agent for the husband. However, if cohabitation ensues upon a marriage effected without a male guardian, proportional dower is due, and the couple are not guilty of the crime of fornication.

The guardian's admission is accepted as sufficient proof of a marriage where he has a right to dispose of the bride's hand as he pleases; but not where the bride's consent is also necessary. According to the opinion adopted by Shafii in his second period, the wife's admission must also be accepted, provided she is of age, and sane.

A father can dispose as he pleases of the hand of his daughter, without asking her consent, whatever her age may be, provided she is still a virgin. It is, however, always commendable to consult her as to her future husband; and her formal consent to the marriage is necessary if she has already lost her virginity. Where a father disposes of his daughter's hand during her minority, she cannot be delivered to her husband before she attains puberty. In default of the father, the father's father exercises all his powers. Loss of virginity puts an end to the right of disposing of a daughter's hand without her consent; and there is no difference in this respect between a loss caused by licit cohabitation and one that is the consequence of unlawful intercourse. On the other hand, the right remains intact where the loss has taken place without carnal connection, as for example in consequence of a fall upon the ground. Collateral agnates, such as whole brother, or half brother on the father's side or father's brother, cannot in any way engage the hand of a daughter under age; and a woman who has lost her virginity must manifest her consent in explicit terms, when collateral agnates give her in marriage. As to an adult virgin, it is enough that she does not oppose the choice of her collateral agnates.

The persons who have the right to assist a woman as guardian at her marriage are first of all the father, then father's father, then his father, then the whole brother or half brother on the father's side, then the latter's son or other agnate descendant, then father's whole brother or half brother on father's side; and lastly the other agnates in the order in which they are called to the succession, *it being understood that a whole brother always has priority over a half brother on the father's side. A son, though the nearest agnate, cannot give his own mother in marriage, since a right of guardianship does not pass into the descendant line; he can only do so if he is also son of the son of his mother's father's brother, or by right as patron or as judge representing the Sovereign. In default of agnates in the ascendant or collateral line, a woman should be given in marriage by her patron, †and after him by his agnates in the order in which they are called to the succession. In the case of an enfranchised slave who has no patron, but a patroness, she should be given in marriage by the individual who in these circumstances would be the guardian of the patroness, †without the latter's consent being necessary. After the death of the patroness, the right of assisting the enfranchised slave as guardian devolves upon the same person as does the patronage. Lastly, in default of patron, or agnates of patron or patroness, it is the Sultan who should assist the enfranchised slave who wishes to marry, as guardian of all the women in his empire who have no other, or whose guardian, whether agnate or patron, prevents the marriage by abusing his power. It is considered an abuse of power on the guardian's part, where an adult sane woman wishes to marry a suitable person and the guardian refuses to give her to him; †but not where she wishes to marry a particular individual, and her father wishes to give her to another who is also suitable.

SECTION 5

The following are incapable of assisting a woman at her marriage as guardian: a slave, a minor, a lunatic, a person whose intelligence is troubled by reason of senility, or by the work of a malicious spirit; and even, according to our school, a person legally incapable by reason

of imbecility. In case of incapacity of persons with a prior claim to guardianship, it falls to those who have second claim and so on. If the guardian is in a state of unconsciousness, and his attacks are usually temporary, it is necessary to wait until he comes to himself again, even though the state of unconsciousness should last several days. Under these circumstances, however, some jurists consider that the right of guardianship passes to the next of those entitled. †Blindness is no obstacle to guardianship; but notorious misconduct is, at least according to our rite. As to an infidel, he is only capable of assisting as guardian a woman who also is an infidel.

A state of *ihram*, whether of the guardian, or of the bride or bridegroom, is an obstacle to the validity of a marriage; †but the *ihram* of the guardian does not transfer the right of guardianship. The Sultan, or the judge for him, should then replace the guardian. [Even in the case where one of the two contracting parties, *i.e.* the guardian or the husband, appoints, previously to his state of *ihram*, a competent agent to conclude the marriage in his name, its validity is not to be accepted.

A legitimate guardian who is at a distance of at least two days' journey should be replaced by the Sultan, *i.e.* by the judge; †but if he be at a less distance, the court cannot proceed without his authorisation.

Guardians that have a right to dispose of the hand of a woman as they please, *i.e.* her father or father's father, can delegate an agent for this purpose, *even without indicating the husband they have in view. In this case the agent may give the woman to whatever man he pleases, provided it is a fitting match and not a mesalliance. As to a guardian who has no right to dispose as he pleases of the hand of the future bride, he should appoint an agent if she desires it, but abstain from doing so if she forbids it; †but where a woman asks her guardian to give her the requisite assistance for her marriage, without saying anything further the latter has a right to delegate an agent. ††But such guardian can never appoint an agent without first obtaining the woman's consent to the proposed marriage. A legitimate guardian's agent should say, "I give you in marriage the daughter of so-and-so." If it is the husband who is represented by an agent, the guardian says to him, "I give my daughter in marriage to so-and-so," and the agent answers, "I accept her as wife on behalf of my principal."

A father or father's father should, if possible, seek a husband for their adult daughter or grand-daughter in a state of lunacy; but as to an adult male lunatic his curator should not seek a wife for him, unless he is manifestly in need of one; and promises of marriage should never be made with regard to lunatics under age of either sex.

A guardian who has the right to dispose as he pleases of the hand of a woman cannot without good reason decline to perform his duty, if he is asked to effect a marriage desired by the woman in question; the same obligation rests upon the other guardians, where they are personally indicated by the law, *e.g.* where the bride has only one whole brother or half brother on the father's side. Where this is not the case, *e.g.* where she has several brothers, †any one of them should undertake the duty upon the woman's demand, though it is to be recommended that those individuals whose degree of relationship calls them equally to the guardianship should intrust this function to the wisest or the eldest, or decide the matter by lot if they cannot otherwise come to an agreement. †In these circumstances, however, if the bride does not object, she may, strictly speaking, be given in marriage by any one of those entitled, even though the lot may have fallen upon another.

If one of the persons entitled to the guardianship gives a woman in marriage to Zaid, and another gives her to Amr, she belongs to the husband who has the priority; and both marriages are void if effected at the same time or if it is not known which is the earlier. This is also the case, at least according to our school, when it is known that one of the marriages preceded the other, but it is not known which; but where one is at first believed to have the priority, and afterwards doubts arise upon the subject, the matter remains in suspense until the doubts are dissipated. When each of the two husbands asserts that the woman in question knows he has the priority, it is impossible, according to the opinion of Shafii in his second period, to admit any presumption in favour of the one or of the other; in default of legal proof the decision then depends upon the wife's admission. Consequently if she denies being married to any one the two husbands can only have an oath administered to her; and if she admits being married to one of them it is this last marriage that is to be accepted as valid, without prejudice to the other husband's right to question the marriage in a court of law, and if necessary have an oath administered to the wife. Such is the doctrine of authorities who allow an admission expressed in the form, "This object is Zaid's, not Amr's," as creating a pecuniary obligation towards the latter as well as a real obligation towards the former; while jurists who do not allow that in such a case Amr can claim any compensation do not allow either that the marriage can be attacked in the circumstances just mentioned.

†Father's father may lawfully effect a marriage by himself alone in his double character as guardian of the daughter of one of his sons, and as guardian or curator of the son of another of his sons. But a cousin on the father's side cannot in this way marry his cousin whose

guardian he is by right of agnation, for in these circumstances the guardianship devolves upon another agnate cousin of the same degree of relationship, and after him upon the judge as representing the Sovereign. A judge who wishes to marry a woman having no other guardian cannot marry her to himself, but must be replaced as guardian by his superior magistrate or by his substitute. With the exception of father's father no one can effect a marriage entirely by himself, neither as guardian of the two parties interested, nor as tutor of the one and agent of the other. †Nor can a marriage be effected by two agents, one of the guardian and the other of the bridegroom.

Section 6

A guardian can never give a woman in marriage to a man of inferior condition, except with her entire consent. Where there are several persons who, by their degree of agnation, are equally competent as guardian, the consent of all is necessary to a mesalliance, though it is only one of them that need preside at the celebration of the marriage. Agnates further removed can never oppose a mesalliance concluded by one more nearly related, acting as guardian, with the full consent of the woman in question; but a mesalliance concluded by one of the agnates intrusted with the guardianship, without the consent of the others equally competent is wholly illegal, even though the bride should have given her consent. A single authority maintains that in this case the validity of the marriage must be accepted, until the other agnates have demanded its dissolution by the court. A similar controversy exists where a father disposes of the hand of his virgin daughter, whether minor or adult, in favour of a man of inferior condition, without obtaining her consent. According to most authorities such a marriage is null and void, but according to the jurist just mentioned the contract is valid unless the wife applies for its cancellation. An adult wife should bring an action for this purpose at once, but a minor should wait until she has attained her majority. †Finally neither the Sultan as ultimate guardian, nor the judge for him, can legally give a woman in marriage to a man of inferior condition, even though she may desire it.

In order to determine whether the suitor is a good match, the following must be taken into consideration :—

1. Absence of redhibitory defects of body.

2. Liberty. A slave is not a suitable match for a free woman, nor an enfranchised slave for a woman born free.

3. Birth. An Arab woman makes a mesalliance by marrying

man belonging to another nation; a woman of the Koraish does so if her husband is not of the Koraish; a woman who is a descendant of Hashim or of Abd-al-Mottalib, *i.e.* who is of the same blood as the Prophet, can make a suitable match only in the same family. †In the case of marriages between persons belonging to foreign nations, like the Persians, genealogy must be taken into consideration as in the case of Arabs.

4. Character. A man of notorious misconduct is not a suitable match for an honest woman.

5. Profession. A man exercising a humble profession is not a suitable match for the daughter of a man in a more distinguished profession. Thus a sweeper, a barber, a watchman, a shepherd, or a servant at a bathhouse, is not a suitable match for the daughter of a tailor; while the tailor in his turn is no match for the daughter of a merchant or a second-hand dealer, who in their turn are no suitable match for the daughter of a learned man or a judge.

†Difference of fortune constitutes no cause of mesalliance; but inequality under one of the aspects above-mentioned is not compensated for by the husband being superior to his wife in other respects.

A father or father's father should never marry his son or his grandson to a slave; nor, according to our school, to a person with redhibitory defects; but with these two exceptions the law does not admit that a man can make a mesalliance by marrying a woman in any respect inferior to him.

Section 7

The curator of a lunatic minor cannot effect a marriage in his name; and the curator of an adult lunatic can do so only if the latter is manifestly in need of it, and then only with one woman at a time. As to a sane minor, his father or father's father can marry him to as many wives as the law permits. An insane woman, whatever her age, and whether she be virgin or not, should, if possible, be given in marriage by her father or father's father, not only if she needs it but also if it is in any way advantageous for her. But a husband ought not to be sought for a mad woman during her minority, unless she is under the guardianship of her father or father's father. †Upon her majority it is the Sultan who should find her a husband if she requires one, but not if it be merely for her advantage.

A person legally incapable by reason of imbecility cannot legally effect a marriage in his own name; his curator's authorisation is necessary for this purpose, unless the curator prefers to effect it himself in the name of the person legally incapable. Where the latter obtains the authorisation to marry a specified woman he cannot marry any other. He cannot even marry the woman specified unless he promises a proportional dower, or a definite dower, inferior to what the woman could claim as proportional dower. **The promise of even a definite and excessive dower does not, however, prejudice the validity of the marriage; for the promised dower is in that case *ipso facto* reduced to a reasonable amount. An authorisation granted to a person legally incapable to marry a woman not specified for a dower of at most one thousand pieces of money, gives him a right to take what woman he pleases provided her proportional dower does not exceed this sum. †If he is authorised generally without any restriction as to the woman or the dower, he can marry whom he likes provided her proportional dower does not exceed his means. †As to the curator, he can conclude no marriage in the name of the imbecile without his consent. Nor can he allow more than proportional dower, or a dower inferior to what the wife could claim as proportional dower; and if this limit is exceeded, though the marriage remains valid, the dower is *ipso facto* reduced to a reasonable amount. Only one authority is of opinion that in this case the marriage is null and void. Finally a marriage concluded by an imbecile without the authorisation of his curator is absolutely null; even though cohabitation should have resulted, he owes his wife nothing. Others, however, maintain that in this case he owes her proportional dower; and others consider he owes a small present, which should not be something quite without value.

A bankrupt is subject to no restriction as to his right to marry; but the expenses of the marriage must be defrayed out of what he gains personally, and not out of the estate.

The law regards as null and void a marriage effected by a slave without his master's consent, which may lawfully be given either by a general authorisation, or restricted to a specified woman or one of a certain tribe or place, in which case the slave must respect the will of his master. *However, a master cannot lawfully force his male slave to marry, nor, on the other hand, is he obliged to allow him to marry. A female slave cannot oblige her master to give her in marriage, unless according to some authors, cohabitation with her is prohibited to the master himself. †Moreover, when giving a female slave in marriage, a master acts by virtue of his right of ownership and not as guardian; this is why the faculty is granted not only to a Moslem with respect to his infidel slave, but also to a master of notorious misconduct, and to a slave who is undergoing enfranchisement by contract

CHAPTER II.—PROHIBITED MARRIAGES

Section 1

In the direct line it is forbidden to marry—

1. One's mother, *i.e.* not only the woman that bore one, but any that has borne one's ancestor or ancestress.

2. One's daughter, *i.e.* any woman of whom one is the ancestor. [The prohibition does not extend to children born of a criminal connection, though a woman can never marry her descendant, even a descendant by adultery or incest.]

In the collateral line one may not marry: one's sisters, nieces and aunts; understanding by "aunt" any whole sister, half sister on the father's side or uterine sister of one of his ancestors or ancestresses.

Relationship by fosterage is a cause of prohibition in the same way as relationship properly so called; and this prohibition extends to the same degrees. By foster mother is understood any person: (1) who has given one suck; (2) who has given the breast either to one's nurse, or to one's ancestor or ancestress; (3) who is the ancestress of one's nurse; (4) who is the ancestress of the man from whom is derived one's nurse's milk, and so on.

One may legally marry the nurse of one's brother or of one's grandchildren, the mother or the daughter of the nurse of one's own children, and the uterine sister or foster sister of one's half brother on the father's side or *vice versâ*.

By reason of affinity one may not marry—

1. The wife of one of his descendants or ancestors, there being no distinction between those properly so called and those by fosterage.

2. One's wife's ancestresses, understood in the same way.

3. One's wife's descendants by another husband, similarly regarded.

Affinity does not exist before marriage has been consummated by coition. A master who has cohabited with his slave should subsequently abstain from all commerce with her ancestresses or descendants; and all commerce with her is forbidden to her master's ancestors or descendants. It is the same in the case of illegal cohabitation by error, whether the error was on the man's side, or, according to some authors, on the woman's; but, on the other hand, coition that constitutes the crime of fornication has no legal consequence so far as affinity is concerned. *Affinity exists only in consequence of coition, and not by reason of other lascivious acts.

The fact of being aware that a woman with whom commerce is prohibited to oneself, but whom one does not know, is living in a large town does not prevent one marrying a woman of that town; but when one knows that such a woman is amongst a small number of women, but one does not know which she is, then one should abstain from marriage with any of them. If in case of marriage with one of the women of a large town, one perceives too late that one has accidentally married a woman with whom commerce is entirely prohibited one at any time, *e.g.* the wife of one's father or of one's son, cohabitation must be at once discontinued.

One may not have at one time two wives of whom one is the sister or the aunt of the other; without distinction between parentage properly so called and parentage by fosterage. Thus, if one marries at one and the same time a woman and her sister or her aunt, there is no marriage; and if one marries the two women the one after the other, the second marriage alone is void. A prohibition to have two women as wives at the same time implies a similar prohibition to have commerce with them by right of property, as in the case of two slaves; but such prohibition is no obstacle to the mere ownership in itself. Thus, a master who owns two female slaves of whom one is the sister or aunt of the other and who has cohabited with one of them, must abstain from commerce with the other, until commerce with the first has become forbidden him, *i.e.* until he has sold her, given her in marriage, or begun to enfranchise her by contract. The law does not, however, regard as having the same result a temporary cause preventing commerce with the slave in question, such as menstruation, *ihram*, †or having pledged her to a creditor. A master who marries a sister of one of his female slaves, or the husband who becomes the owner of his wife's sister, should cohabit with his wife, and abstain from commerce with his slave.

A slave cannot have more than two wives at a time, and a free man not more than four. A marriage concluded by a free man with five wives at once is null as regards all of them; but if he marries them one after the other, the fifth alone is void. Consequently the sister of the fifth wife can become the wife of the person in question, unless he must abstain from her on other grounds. Moreover, one has the right to take a fifth wife after repudiating irrevocably one of the four, even while the repudiated wife is still in her period of legal retreat; but this cannot be done if the repudiation is revocable.

A free man may repudiate his wife twice, and a slave his once, in a revocable way; but after this triple, or double, revocation, she cannot be taken back again until she has been the legitimate wife of another man, and this intermediate husband has had effective connection with her. Our school insists that this intermediate husband should be capable of performing conjugal functions; consequently an intermediate marriage of a woman with a young boy and her connection with him would be of no use. Neither can the intermediate marriage be on condition that the new husband shall repudiate his wife immediately after first having connection with her, and that she shall be *ipso facto* repudiated from that moment, or that the intermediate marriage shall *ipso facto* cease to exist from that moment. One authority, however, admits the first condition.

Section 2

One may not marry a woman of whom one is the proprietor, even in part only ; and the fact of becoming owner or part owner of a woman with whom one has already contracted marriage is of itself sufficient to annul it. Neither may a woman marry a slave of whom she is owner or part owner. A free man may not even marry the slave of another, except under the following conditions :—

1. That he has no free wife able to satisfy his passion ; or, according to some jurists, no free wife at all.

2. That he is unable to marry a free woman able to satisfy his passion ; or, according to some jurists, that he is unable to marry any free woman. On the other hand, most authorities permit a free man to marry the slave of another, in the case of the absence of the woman whom he could marry, when it is manifestly difficult for him to go to her, or when he is afraid that the excitement of desire will otherwise make him commit the crime of fornication. †A man who has not the means to pay the proportional dower a free woman could claim, and who finds some one willing to be content with a lower sum not in excess of his means, may not refuse this offer and marry a slave ; but when the free woman will not be content with a lower sum, but is disposed to give facilities as to payment, marriage with a slave is not prohibited.

3. That he is afraid of committing the crime of fornication if he does not marry ; †but the law admits this excuse only where he is unable to purchase a slave with whom cohabitation would be permitted him by right of ownership.

4. That the slave is a Moslem. A Moslem, whether free **or not, should never marry an infidel slave ; ††but an infidel, free or not, member of a religion founded upon a holy scripture, may marry an infidel slave.

A woman partly enfranchised is regarded for this purpose as entirely servile. A free man, who, after marrying a slave in conformity with the law, afterwards becomes enabled to marry a free woman, or who does in fact marry one though strictly speaking his means do not permit of it, keeps the slave all the same as a legitimate wife. But if, on the other hand, a free man, legally unable to marry a slave, nevertheless does marry both a slave and a free woman, *the contract is void so far as regards the slave, but remains valid as to the free woman.

SECTION 3

A Moslem may not marry a woman of a religion not founded upon some holy scripture. Thus, he may not marry an idolatress nor a fire-worshipper; but he may marry a Jewess or a Christian; though it is always blamable to marry a woman, whether Jewess or Christian, belonging to a nation not yet subjugated by our arms ††or even a woman belonging to infidel subjects of our Sovereign. By "infidels whose religion is founded upon a holy scripture," are understood those people who follow one of the actually existing divine revelations, though abrogated by the Koran, *i.e.* Jews and Christians; but not adherents of religious sects founded only on the psalms of David, and so on. Jewesses may become wives of Moslems, even when not strictly speaking of the race of Israel, *provided their nation was converted to Judaism before that revelation was abrogated by the Koran, and before the text of the law of Moses had been altered by theologians. Some jurists, however, consider only the first of these two conditions as strictly necessary. A Jewess or a Christian, the legitimate wife of a Moslem, has the same right to maintenance, sharing of marital favours, and with regard to repudiation, as Moslem wives, provided she observes the precepts of the law with regard to menstruation, lochia, *and grave impurities in general, and does not eat pork. A Moslem's wife, of whatever religion she may be, should at her husband's order wash herself, when any part of her body is affected by some impurity.

A Moslem may never marry an idolatress, even where the mother *or father of the woman in question is Jewish or Christian. And women belonging to Samaritan sects that have seceded from Judaism, or Sabaean sects seceded from Christianity, differing in each case as to some essential dogma, are deprived of the right to marry a Moslem. But women of Samaritan or Sabaean sects that differ from Judaism or Christianity only in secondary dogmas may marry a Moslem, just as Jewish or Christian women may. However, *since a Christian converted to Judaism, or a Jew converted to Christianity enjoy no longer the favour of our protection, neither may a woman in similar circumstances become the legitimate wife of a Moslem; and if a Moslem's wife is converted from Christianity to Judaism or *vice versâ*, she should be treated as a Moslem wife who has abjured the faith. A Jew or a Christian who wishes to change his religion should become a Moslem;

unless, according to one author, they are returning to their original religions after abandoning them. The same controversy exists as to whether a Jew or a Christian, who has become an idolater, can return to the religion they have left; but they can never enjoy our protection while remaining idolaters. An idolater who becomes a Jew or a Christian is equally incapable of enjoying our protection; nor can he return to his original religion. There is thus no course open to him but to embrace Islam, as if he were an apostate.

A woman that has abjured Islam can marry no one; and apostasy, whether of husband or wife, or both, before a marriage has been followed by cohabitation, involves *ipso facto* an immediate separation. Where, on the other hand, cohabitation has already taken place, the marriage remains in suspense, in the hope that the guilty party or parties will become convinced of their error before the end of the period of legal retirement. If this occurs, the marriage holds good as if nothing had happened; but otherwise separation is regarded as having taken effect from the moment of apostasy. In all cases, however, carnal enjoyment is forbidden to the parties while their marriage remains in suspense; though an infraction of this precept does not constitute the crime of fornication.

CHAPTER III.—THE MARRIAGE OF INFIDELS

SECTION 1

AN infidel of whatever religion who is converted to Islam while married to a woman whose religion is founded upon some holy scripture keeps her as his wife; but if she is an idolatress or a fire-worshipper, and is not converted with him, separation takes place immediately *ipso facto*, where the marriage has not yet been followed by cohabitation. Otherwise the continuation of the marriage depends upon whether the woman embraces the faith before the end of her period of legal retirement. If, before the expiry of this period the wife's conversion has not yet taken place, the marriage is considered to have been dissolved from the husband's conversion; and the same rule is observed if it is the wife who is converted, while the husband remains in a state of religious blindness. Where, on the other hand, both parties embrace the faith at the same time, the marriage remains valid. The conversion is regarded as simultaneous only where one of the parties begins his declaration before the other has finished.

Where the marriage remains valid, it is of no consequence whether it was originally contracted in contravention of our law, provided that the cause of illegality has ceased to exist at the time of conversion, and that the wife is then a woman who can lawfully be given to her husband. If, however, the cause of illegality still exists at the time of conversion, the marriage is regarded as having never been contracted. Moreover, it is not considered as an absolute illegality if the marriage was not concluded by a guardian, nor before witnesses. A continuation of the marriage must also be accepted in the following cases :—

1. When it has been contracted before the expiration of the period of legal retirement, provided that this period has expired at the moment of conversion.

2. In the case of a temporary marriage, where the parties have stipulated a term equivalent to perpetuity.

3. When, at the time of conversion, the woman is in retirement, owing to a cohabitation due to error, at least according to our school. On the other hand, a marriage with a person within the prohibited degrees cannot continue after conversion ; though our school admits the validity of the marriage, where the husband is first converted and places himself in a state of *ihram*, after which the wife is converted also, before her husband's *ihram* is over.

4. When an infidel who possesses a free wife and a slave wife is converted at the same time as they are, he keeps the free wife, according to our school, but should dismiss the slave. ††Marriages of infidels contracted in conformity with their own laws are recognised by ours as valid ; though some jurists maintain that our law never admits the validity of these marriages, while others consider their validity is recognised only where upon conversion it appears that the parties may lawfully remain together, but otherwise they must be regarded as null and void *ab initio*.

††An infidel who repudiates his wife three times and is converted to Islam can take her back again only after she has belonged to an intermediate husband.

An infidel who promised at his marriage a specified dower according to our law, is liable for it even after his conversion if the marriage is not thereby dissolved as we have explained above. But if the dower consists of prohibited things such as wine and so on, and the marriage remains valid after conversion, then the three following cases must be distinguished :—

1. Where at the moment of conversion the woman has already taken possession of the prohibited objects, she keeps them and can claim nothing further.

2. Where she has not yet taken possession, her husband owes her proportional dower.

3. Where she has only partly taken possession she can claim for the rest a reasonable part of the proportional dower.

A woman whose marriage has been dissolved, either by her conversion to Islam or by her husband's conversion, may claim the specified dower promised, provided it consists of permissible articles, and that the marriage, followed by cohabitation, is not otherwise attackable. If not, she can only claim proportional dower. If cohabitation has not yet taken place, a distinction is made between the case where the dissolution is a consequence of the wife's conversion, and that where it is caused by the husband's. In the first she can claim nothing, but in the second the husband owes her half of the specified dower promised, if consisting of permissible articles, and otherwise half of the proportional dower; all upon the condition already mentioned, that the marriage is dissolved solely by conversion and not from any other cause of nullity.

The court may not refuse to pronounce judgment if one of the parties is an infidel subject of our Sovereign, *or even where both are so; but should decide as if both were Moslems.

Section 2

An infidel who, at the time of his conversion to Islam, possesses more than four wives, should choose four to keep and dismiss the others; it being understood that all the four embrace the faith, either at the same time as their husband or before the termination of their period of retirement, or that they are followers of some religion founded upon a holy scripture. Where, on the other hand, only four wives embrace the faith, either with him or before the termination of their period of retirement, they remain his lawful wives to the exclusion of the others, even though he has not yet cohabited with them. An infidel who, at the time of his conversion is bound by marriage to a mother and to her daughter, and has had commerce with both, must subsequently abstain from both the one and the other. His cohabitation with them is in this case prohibited for ever, even though they may be followers of a religion founded upon a sacred book, or may have embraced the faith. But if he has cohabited with neither, the daughter remains his legitimate wife; though according to one author he may choose whichever he prefers. If he has cohabited with the daughter only, she remains his lawful wife; but if he has cohabited with the mother only, then cohabitation with both the one and the other is prohibited him for ever, though, according to one author, the mother may in this case remain his lawful wife.

An infidel who, at the time of his conversion, is married to a slave who follows his example either immediately or before the end of the period of retirement, may keep her as his lawful wife, unless coition with her is prohibited him on other grounds; but if the slave remains an infidel at the expiry of that term, separation takes place at once *ipso facto*. A convert married to several slave women who all follow his example either immediately or before the end of their period of retirement, should choose one to remain his wife; but this choice may not fall upon one with whom cohabitation was forbidden him at the time of conversion. Of these he may keep none. A convert married to a free woman and several slaves who are all converted with him, either immediately or before the end of the period of retirement, should keep the free woman as his sole wife and dismiss the others. He may choose one of his slave women only if his free wife perseveres in her errors at the end of her period of retirement. Where the convert has a free wife who embraces the faith at the same time as himself, and where also his slave wives obtain their liberty and are then converted before the end of their period of retirement, it is as if at the time of his conversion he had only free wives, and he may at his choice select the four wives whom he wishes to keep.

When signifying his wishes upon this subject, the convert may use the words: "I choose you," "I confirm our marriage," "I retain you," "I wish you to remain"; and he is considered to have implicitly chosen one of his wives if he repudiates her, †but not if he pronounces against her an injurious assimilation or an oath of continence. The convert may not make his decision subject to any condition; nor may he go back upon his choice. If he should choose five wives instead of four, he must afterwards indicate the one he wishes to dismiss. All the wives of a husband who has become a Moslem have an equal right to maintenance until he has decided which to retain. If he does not decide the court should force him to do so by imprisonment. Where a new convert dies before deciding, all his widows should observe the legal period of retirement; that is to say, a pregnant widow is in retirement until her churching; a widow having no fixed courses, or a widow who has had no commerce with her husband, for four months and ten days; a widow having regular courses, for three periods of purity, in all not less than four months and ten days. From the estate of a deceased convert must be reserved a sum sufficient to give his widows their due, when their respective rights have been ascertained.

SECTION 3

Where husband and wife embrace Islam together, the husband's obligation to maintain his wife is not interrupted. Where, on the contrary, she is not converted before the expiry of her period of retirement, he owes her nothing for the interval during which she has not been of the same religion as himself. This, at least, was Shafii's decision during his stay in Egypt. Where the woman's conversion precedes the man's, whether the latter takes place before the end of the period of legal retirement, or whether he continues in his errors, the woman may claim maintenance for the whole period of her retirement. A wife who abjures Islam loses at the same time all right to maintenance, even though she returns to the faith before the expiry of her period of retirement; but a wife whose husband becomes an apostate continues to be maintainable by him during the whole of the period of her retirement.

CHAPTER IV.—RIGHT OF OPTION, IFAF, AND MARRIAGE BETWEEN SLAVES

SECTION 1

ANY one who becomes aware that he has married a person afflicted with madness, elephantiasis or leprosy has a right to renounce the marriage. The law makes no distinction as to which party has been deceived in this way. A husband may also renounce a wife he has just married, on perceiving that she is *ratka* or *karna,* and consequently unsuited for coition; while a wife may renounce her husband on discovering him to be impotent or castrated. According to some authorities, however, a party possessing a defect discovered in the other has no right of option. Hermaphrodism alone does not give a right of option; at any rate if the hermaphrodite inclines manifestly towards the sex declared.

A wife's right to renounce her marriage by reason of her husband's defects is not limited to defects existing at the time of the contract, but extends to such as he may have acquired subsequently; with the exception of impotence, for a husband who becomes impotent after cohabiting with his wife can no longer be renounced by her. As to the husband, according to the opinion of Shafii in his second period, he as well as the wife has a right of option for redhibitory defects, even though these only become manifest during marriage; but in this case a right of option can never be exercised by the wife's guardian. Nor can he do this on account of castration or impotence existing at the time of the contract; but he can in the case of so-existing madness, †elephantiasis or leprosy of the husband. In all cases redhibition during marriage should be exercised soon after the discovery of the defect.

Renunciation of marriage on account of redhibitory defects previous to all carnal intercourse invalidates a woman's right to dower. If, on the contrary, the renunciation takes place after consummation a distinction must be made between proportional and fixed dower. †Proportional dower is due whether the defects existed at the time of the contract, or whether they became manifest between the time of the contract and the first coition; but in neither case must the party renouncing knowingly indulge in coition. †The fixed dower is due only where renunciation is based upon defects ascertained after the first coition. It is due also if after that event the apostasy of one of the parties entails renunciation. In no case can the husband proceed against the person who has deceived him, whether for dower due in consequence of cohabitation, or for cancellation on account of redhibitory defects; this is the opinion towards which Shafii inclined in his second period.

Impotence, †and the other redhibitory defects, have no legal effect until brought before the court. Impotence should be accepted as true, not only upon the admission of the party in court, but also upon proof that such admission has been made elsewhere. †It may also be proved by the claimant's oath, if the other party refuses to confirm his denial on oath. In whatever manner impotence has been proved, the court cannot immediately pronounce dissolution of marriage in consequence, but must grant the husband a year's delay in which to acquit himself of the physical obligations resulting from marriage. On its expiry the wife may summons her husband a second time. If the husband alleges cohabitation with his wife in the interval he must confirm this assertion upon oath, otherwise the woman is sworn. If she takes the oath tendered her, or if the husband admits impotence, she can of her own accord declare herself to be free from the bonds of matrimony, though some maintain she has not this right yet, unless the court authorises it or has itself pronounced dissolution of marriage in explicit terms. If during the year's probation the wife refuses to yield herself to coition, or if the husband cannot cohabit with her by reason of her sickness, or if she is imprisoned, the period during which the husband has been prevented from executing the order of the court is not taken account of. And the woman entirely loses her right to declare herself free on account of her husband's impotence, after the year's probation, if she is proved to have accepted him again ††or to have granted him further delay.

*Where there is a stipulation on the part of the husband that his wife must be a Moslem, or on the part of one of the parties that the other must be of an undisputed genealogy, free, etc., dissolution does not take place *ipso facto* because the party is not of the quality guaranteed. If the party in question is of better condition than that stipulated for, no right of option exists ; otherwise either wife †or husband may exercise this right. *Where the quality of Moslem or free woman has not been expressly guaranteed, but the husband merely had reason to believe the one or the other, he cannot renounce the marriage on perceiving subsequently that his wife is of another religion, provided that religion is founded upon some sacred book, or upon discovering that she is a slave ; provided always that cohabitation with her is not prohibited on other grounds. And similarly the wife, upon her side, after having consented to marry a man she believed was a suitable match for her, without making any express stipulation with regard to it, cannot exercise a right of option upon discovering that she has married a man of notorious misconduct, or that she has made an unsuitable match as regards her husband's genealogy or profession. [On the other hand, if the woman discovers too late that she has married a man with redhibitory defects or a slave she may exercise a right of option.]

Dissolution of marriage on the ground that a party does not answer to the conditions stipulated has the same result as regards dower and damages as dissolution on account of redhibitory defects, with this difference that in the case in question that the deceit must have existed at the time of the contract before it can become a ground for damages.

According to those authors who do not admit a dissolution of marriage follows immediately *ipso facto* where the husband having stipulated that his wife shall be a free woman discovers afterwards that she is a slave, a child born before discovery of the truth is free, and the father owes his wife's master the value of the child by way of damages. All this is without prejudice to his right of action against the person who has deceived him, if such action is permissible, and provided that it is not the master himself who has duped him by giving him his slave in marriage as if she were a free woman. Consequently, the value of the child is only due where the father has been deceived by the master's agent or by the slave herself ; it being understood that deception on the part of the slave also entails her having to compensate her husband as soon as she has the means of doing so, though she cannot be seized for this purpose. If through no one's fault the child is still-born, the husband owes nothing to his wife's master.

A woman who becomes enfranchised during her union with a slave, even a partially enfranchised slave, may claim a dissolution of marriage on this ground alone, *provided she takes proceedings at once. But the court may allow this last rule to be departed from where the woman declares upon oath her ignorance of the enfranchisement, and puts forward some probable ground for such ignorance, for example the absence of her master; *or where she declares that she was ignorant of her right of cancellation. Naturally an enfranchised woman whose marriage has been so dissolved, and who has not yet had commerce with her husband, can claim no dower; but she can claim the fixed dower promised where the dissolution has been demanded by her in consequence of an enfranchisement subsequent to the consummation of the marriage. Where, on the other hand, she does not make use of her right of cancellation until after commerce with her husband, and bases her claim upon a prior enfranchisement, she can only recover proportional dower; though some authorities allow her fixed dower in this case also. No right of option exists where the wife is only partially enfranchised, or is undergoing enfranchisement by contract. Nor does it exist in favour of an enfranchised husband united in the bonds of matrimony with a slave.

Section 2

Ifaf is an obligation recognised by law. It means that one must see to it that one's father, **father's father, or **mother's father, do not take to evil courses, by coming to their assistance, if they have not sufficient means to procure a female companion. One may acquit oneself of this duty—

1. By giving one's father or grandfather enough for a free woman's dower;
2. by saying to them, "Get married; I will pay the dower";
3. by contracting a marriage in their name, by virtue of an authorisation from them, but promising dower on one's own account; or
4. by giving them a female slave, or the money necessary to buy one.

The household expenses are also chargeable to the child or grandchild. The father or grandfather must be content with the way in which their child or grandchild wishes to discharge this duty. They cannot insist upon a legitimate wife if child or grandchild wishes to give a slave as concubine. Neither can they insist upon a particular person whose price or dower is very high; but if they are in agreement with child or grandchild as to the sum, then it is for them to obtain for that sum the person they prefer. One is even bound to supply a new companion to father or grandfather, not only where the first marriage or concubinage has been dissolved by death, apostasy or redhibitory defects in the woman, †but also where father or grandfather has repudiated his wife for some valid reason. *Ifaf* is obligatory only where a father or grandfather needs a companion but has not the means to procure one. The fact of need is legally established by the declaration of the interested party, which does not require to be confirmed on oath.

In no case may father or grandfather cohabit with a slave of child or grandchild; though, according to our school, an infraction of this rule entails only an obligation to pay dower, and not liability to punishment for fornication. A child born of such prohibited commerce is free, and his father's legitimate descendant; but if the contravention has been committed with regard to a slave of son or grandson already enfranchised by reason of maternity, the latter does not become the enfranchised slave of the father or grandfather because she has borne him a son. *But if she was not such an enfranchised slave to the son or grandson, she becomes so to the father or grandfather, who then owes the former her value plus dower, but not the value of the child. In consequence a father or grandfather cannot contract a lawful marriage with a slave of his son or grandson; †but where the son or grandson becomes the owner of his father's or grandfather's wife, the marriage remains valid. One cannot marry a slave of a male slave who is undergoing enfranchisement by contract; and where such male slave becomes owner of a female slave who is already his master's wife, this marriage is *ipso facto* dissolved.

Section 3

According to the opinion adopted by Shafii in his second period, a master who has authorised his slave to marry, is not obliged to undertake payment either of the dower or maintenance that the wife or children may claim. For these one may distrain upon what the slave gains by his ordinary work and also upon any accidental profits he may realise. In the case of a slave generally authorised, the profit he makes, †and even the capital furnished by his master, may be distrained upon for dower and maintenance. In the case of a slave who makes no profit and has not been generally authorised, both charges must be defrayed by him after his enfranchisement like a personal debt. Only one authority admits the master's responsibility in this case.

An authorisation to a slave to marry does not prejudice his master's right to acquire his company on a journey even though the slave may be in this way prevented from fulfilling his conjugal duties; but so long as the master does not take his slave on a journey, he should allow him to pass his nights with his wife. As to the master's right to the slave's services during the day, this exists only where the former has guaranteed payment of dower and maintenance, for otherwise he must dispense with the slave's services, until the latter, by his labour, has gained enough money for this purpose. If the master has guaranteed payment of dower and maintenance he may dispose of the slave's services and pay him a reasonable salary, or else himself entirely undertake to defray the cost of dower and maintenance, whichever he prefers as being most advantageous. Some authorities, however, allow him no choice in the matter, but consider him obliged to pay dower and maintenance, unless he prefers to forego the slave's services. A slave who, in contravention of the law, marries without his master's authorisation, is personally responsible for proportional dower, if the marriage has been followed by cohabitation. One authority even considers that payment of the dower in such case is a real charge involving if necessary the seizure of the slave after his enfranchisement. If it is not the case of a male but of a female slave whom the master has given in marriage, the latter retains a right to the fruit of her labour during the day, but must surrender her to her husband for the night. †In this case the husband is not liable for maintenance. †Neither is the husband obliged to accept an offer to remain with his wife in the master's house, even though the latter may be willing to allot a room specially for the use of the new *menage*. A master may take with him a married female slave on a journey, but in that case her husband has a right to accompany her.

Our school considers that there is no obligation on the part of the husband to pay dower to the master, if the latter has put the female slave to death, or if she has committed suicide, before the marriage has been really consummated. On the other hand, our school maintains the obligation of paying dower, if it is a free woman who has killed herself in similar circumstances; or if, instead of the master, it is another person who has killed the slave; or if the slave has died an accidental death. In all these cases dower is obligatory as in the case of an accidental death after a first cohabitation with a wife whether free or not. The master who sells a married slave may retain the dower obtained for her; and he may even keep half of it, if she is repudiated by her husband before cohabitation. Dower is not due if both parties belong to the same master.

BOOK 34.—DOWER

Section 1

The Sonna has introduced the practice of stipulating in the contract of marriage a fixed dower, though this stipulation is not rigorously necessary. Anything that may legally be sold may be made use of for dower. The husband who has promised a certain object as dower is liable for its loss before the bride has taken possession of it, as in other agreement, or according to one authority as if it were a deposit intrusted to him. If one admits, with the majority of jurists that a woman's title to a certain object stipulated as dower is not absolute, but merely contractual, before possession of it has been taken, one cannot allow her any right to dispose of it by way of sale, until it has been actually delivered to her.

From this principle it also follows :—

1. That in case of accidental loss, before taking possession, a husband owes proportional dower ; and the wife cannot demand the value of the thing originally promised.

2. That the woman is presumed to have taken possession, if she has herself caused the loss.

3. That in case of loss caused by the fault of another person, she may either claim from her husband the payment of proportional dower, transferring to him her claim against the other person, or transfer to that other person her claim against her husband, and recover damage from that person. That is the doctrine of our school.

Loss caused by the husband's fault has the same consequences as accidental loss ; or, according to others, as loss caused by another person ; and where one has promised as dower two specified slaves, one of whom dies before possession is taken, our school considers the agreement as cancelled so far as the deceased slave is concerned. The wife then has a right of option, *i.e.* she may either renounce the promised dower, or accept the surviving slave. In the first case the husband owes proportional dower ; in the second he must compensate her for the loss of the dead slave by giving her, in addition to the surviving one, a reasonable part of the proportional dower. Our school also grants a right of option to the wife, if the specified object that forms the dower has been damaged by redhibitory defects, before taking possession; but in these circumstances she may only choose between proportional dower and acceptance pure and simple of the defective objects. The husband, however, is never liable for accidental loss of produce from objects promised as dower, even where he may have been able to deliver them but have refused such delivery on the ground of his liability for the execution of the contract. Nor does our school consider him obliged to pay any indemnity for the use he may make of the promised object before delivery, *e.g.* by riding an animal included in the dower, or using it in any other way.

On the other hand, the woman is not obliged to place herself at her husband's disposition, until she has taken possession of the dower, at any rate when this consists of certain definite objects, and the parties have not stipulated any time of payment. †Where, on the other hand, dower is promised by a certain date, she cannot refuse cohabitation, on the ground that she has not yet taken possession, even though the time may have expired. In a case where the two parties have stipulated that neither shall be obliged to perform the duties resulting from the marriage contract, before the other has done so, it is the husband, according to one jurist, who should begin by delivering the dower; while, according to another, neither party can oblige the other to begin by fulfilling his or her engagements, but the one that begins can oblige the other to comply also. *But most authorities maintain that under these circumstances the parties should jointly fulfil their obligations; that is to say that the husband should begin by depositing the dower with some person of irreproachable conduct, the wife should then place herself at her husband's disposition, and after this the depositary should hand her the dower. A woman who, in spite of this stipulation of joint fulfilment, does not insist upon her husband's beginning by paying the dower, may claim it as soon as she has placed herself at his disposition; but if the husband does not accept her offer immediately upon her declaring her readiness, she may change her mind and refuse to surrender herself to him until he has discharged his pecuniary obligation. Where, on the contrary, the husband has immediately accepted cohabitation, his wife can no longer draw back. If the husband in spite of a stipulation of joint fulfilment, begins by paying, the woman must place herself at once at his disposition; and, according to the authority who considers the husband bound to pay in any case, he may even claim back the dower if she refuses without valid excuse. Finally, on insisting that his wife place herself at his disposition, the husband should at her request allow her a little time for her marriage toilet. The length of this delay may be fixed, if necessary, by the court, but must not exceed three days. A wife can never insist upon any delay on the ground that her menstrues are not yet finished; but a minor and a sick woman are not obliged to surrender themselves to their husband before being physically capable of fulfilling their conjugal duties.

A wife's right to dower becomes irrevocable by the fact of copulation, even where this is a prohibited act, *e.g.* during menstruation. The right becomes irrevocable also upon the death of one of the parties; but not, according to the opinion of Shafii in his Egyptian period, by the fact of the wife's having crossed the threshold of the bridal chamber without giving herself to the work of the flesh.

SECTION 2

A husband who has promised for dower things that cannot form the basis of a contract, *e.g.* wine, a free man, or something usurped, owes proportional dower, or, according to one jurist, the value the wine would have if it were vinegar, the man would have if he were a slave, or the usurped thing would have if it had remained in the possession of the rightful owner. *A promise to give something of which one is the rightful owner and also something usurped is null as regards the latter but valid as to the former, without prejudice to the wife's right—

1. To renounce the two promised objects, and claim proportional dower, or, according to one authority, the value of the two promised objects; or

2. To accept the object that may lawfully form the basis of a contract, plus a reasonable part of the proportional dower, in compensation for the loss of the other object.

Only one authority maintains that she must in all cases be content with the lawful object and nothing more, unless she prefers proportional dower.

By stipulating as follows: "I give you my daughter in marriage, and I also give you these clothes, if you will give me this slave here," one has legally combined a marriage, *a dower and an exchange, the slave constituting partly an equivalent for the clothes, and partly proportional dower. On the other hand, a stipulation "that the woman shall be given in marriage for a thousand pieces of money, which pieces belong or shall be given to her father," does not constitute, according to our rite, a legal promise of fixed dower; such a stipulation, though not affecting the validity of the marriage, obliges the husband to pay proportional dower.

A marriage cannot be concluded by granting one of the parties a conventional option of cancellation within a certain time; *but if such option has been stipulated, not with regard to the marriage itself but with regard to the dower, this clause only is null, while the marriage remains valid. As to the other conditions that may be added to a marriage contract, it is necessary to distinguish—

1. Conditions already implicit in the law relating to marriage, and such as are without any object. Both are considered as of no effect; but the marriage and the stipulation as to the dower remain valid.

2. Conditions inconsistent with the precepts of the law relating to marriage. Such are illicit, and have the effect of invalidating the stipulation as to dower; but they leave the marriage intact, so long as they are not incompatible with the fundamental object of that institution. Among such conditions are reckoned, for instance, a stipulation that the husband cannot take another wife so long as he is married to the first, or a stipulation that he is not liable for maintenance. Where, however, these conditions are incompatible with the fundamental object of marriage, *e.g.* a stipulation that would deprive a husband of his right of cohabitation with his wife, or a stipulation that he would repudiate her, the marriage itself is null and void.

*If, when marrying several wives at once, one promises a joint dower, the contract is illegal so far as concerns the dower, but the marriage remains intact, and each wife may claim proportional dower. *It is the same where a guardian concludes a marriage for his ward, while granting the bride a larger dower than she could claim as proportional dower; or where the father or grandfather, who may legally dispose of a girl's hand without asking her consent, stipulates for her a dower less than her proportional dower. When the parties agree in secret upon a certain dower, but declare publicly that they have agreed upon a larger dower, it is the dower which they really have in view that the husband should pay, at least according to our school. A marriage is null and void where a woman's guardian, after receiving from her a request to give her in marriage for a thousand pieces of money, gives her in marriage for a less sum. And similarly, where the woman has given her guardian no instructions as to dower, but he has stipulated for a sum inferior to her proportional dower. A single authority has maintained that in this case the marriage remains intact, but the stipulation is void and the woman can therefore insist upon proportional dower. [*In both of the two cases cited the marriage is valid; but the husband owes proportional dower.]

SECTION 3

When a woman whose intelligence is sufficiently developed for her to manage her property, asks her guardian to give her in marriage without dower, and he therefore refuses the dower offered by the husband, or does not stipulate one, this act is considered as a perfectly legal liberality. This is also the case where the master gives in marriage one of his female slaves, declaring at the same time that he wants no dower for her. But a free woman whose intelligence is not yet sufficiently developed for her to manage her property, cannot be legally married without stipulating some dower, even with her consent. *However, this remission of dower has this result only, that the husband owes his wife nothing in virtue of the marriage contract; but it does not prevent him from owing proportional dower if the marriage is consummated, †to be assessed according to the woman's condition at the time of the contract. A free woman thus given in marriage without dower, may also insist upon her husband assigning her a dower before cohabitation; and she need not place herself at her husband's disposition until it has been so assigned, †and delivered. It is also rigorously necessary that the wife should declare herself to be satisfied with the dower assigned her by her husband; *but the law does not require that the two parties should know exactly the amount that the woman would be able to claim as proportional dower. Under these circumstances the husband can validly assign a †dower within a certain time, or of an amount exceeding proportional dower. Only a few authorities have expressed the opinion that dower assigned in this way upon the wife's demand cannot exceed her proportional dower in the case where both dowers would consist in things of the same kind. If the husband refuses to assign his wife a dower under these circumstances, or if the two interested parties cannot come to an agreement upon the subject, the court must determine the amount in money current in the locality, and this amount can be claimed immediately. [The court can only give judgment for an amount that would appear to it to be reasonable as proportional dower; it should first therefore ascertain the amount of this latter.]

†A third party cannot lawfully assign a dower to a woman whose guardian has not stipulated for one, even though such person may be willing to pay it from his own property.

Dower assigned by the husband or determined by the court is subject to the same rules as ordinary fixed dower, that is to say that half is due upon repudiation before cohabitation, while nothing is due upon repudiation not only before cohabitation but even before assignment of the dower. *Death of one of the parties before cohabitation or assignment takes place does not make proportional dower obligatory. [*On the contrary, in this case proportional dower would really be due.]

Section 4

"Proportional dower" is the amount a woman may claim as dower in due proportion to the dowers stipulated or obtained by other women of the same condition. It is estimated—

1. According to the genealogy of the person in question, *i.e.* according to the dowers granted to the women who are the nearest agnates of the man from whom she derives her origin, such as her whole sister, her sister on the father's side, the daughters of her whole brother or brother on the father's side, her father's sisters, and so on. If there are no agnates who are women, or if they have not yet been given in marriage, or if their dowers are unknown, their relatives on the mother's side, such as mother's mother or sisters, are taken into consideration.

2. According to the wife's age, mental faculties, wealth, virginity, or otherwise, and in general all qualities usually appreciated in a spouse. If a wife has special qualities or defects, that give her greater or less value than her relations, she must also be granted a dower either greater or less as the case may be. The fact that one of her female relatives consented to receive an exceptionally small dower ought not to be taken into consideration; but the fact that they usually consent to receive a smaller dower when given in marriage to a member of the family ought to be so.

Proportional dower is always due after an illegal marriage followed by coition. In this case the amount is estimated according to the value of the woman upon the day the coition took place; or where cohabitation is prolonged, according to the highest value the woman had during the whole period she was in her husband's house.

[Prolonged cohabitation in consequence of an error as to the validity of the marriage obliges the husband to pay only a single dower; but if the error arose from several successive causes, *e.g.* if the husband cohabited with his wife at first under the belief that he had married her, and afterwards under the belief that she was his slave, he owes as many dowers as he has committed errors. Cohabitation with a usurped slave, or with a person forced to undergo forbidden carnal intercourse, has for effect that the woman may claim as many dowers as there have been acts of coition. Cohabitation, however, even prolonged, between a father and his son's slave, between the joint owner of a slave and that slave, or between a master and his slave undergoing enfranchisement by contract, necessitates payment of a single dower only; though there are some authorities who admit even in these circumstances a plurality of dowers, unless where there has been no separation between the acts of coition.]

SECTION 5

A separation of the parties before the consummation of the marriage, either at the wife's instance, or in consequence of some fact for which she is responsible, *e.g.* a dissolution of marriage by reason of redhibitory defects in the wife, puts an end to the husband's obligation to pay dower. Where separation before consummation has been caused, either by an act of the husband, such as repudiation, conversion, apostasy, anathema; or by reason of some third party, as relationship through fosterage, caused by an act of the mother of one of the parties; the husband is always liable for half the dower which the wife could have claimed had the marriage remained intact. The obligation to leave to the wife half the dower is explained by some authorities in this way that the husband has the right to renounce the marriage at the price of this sacrifice; ††but most jurists maintain that the half reverts to him *ipso facto* upon repudiation, etc.

Any increase derived from the dower after the separation belongs half to the husband, and if the wife separated from her husband has already taken possession of the dower, she must indemnify the husband if the dower has perished while in her possession. This compensation takes place by replacing the perished objects by other similar ones, if they are sold by measure or weight, or otherwise by paying their value. If the objects that form the dower have not perished but have merely become deteriorated while in the wife's possession, the husband can none the less recover the half if he is satisfied with that, or he can abandon the whole of the dower as it is to the wife, and claim half the value it had before deterioration. Deterioration before the wife has taken possession results under these circumstances in obliging the husband to be satisfied with half the dower as it is; but if this deterioration has been caused by a third party from whom the wife has recovered damages, she should give over half of this to her husband. As to increase derived from the dower before the separation of the parties, the wife profits by it where the increase has a separate existence from the principal object; but where this increase remains united to the principal object then half of it goes to the husband if the wife prefers to let him have his half in kind, but if she prefers to give him half of the original value she alone profits by the increase. The husband must in all cases respect the wife's decision as to this. Where an object that forms part of a dower has become both ameliorated and deteriorated before separation, *e.g.* if a palm tree has grown, or a slave become older or learnt a new trade, but has also become tainted with leprosy, the husband becomes part owner, *i.e.* owns half the object, if the interested parties agree to settle the account in that way, otherwise he receives only the original value of the half that reverts to him. The sowing of a field is considered a deterioration, its mere ploughing an amelioration. The pregnancy of a slave or of an animal counts as both profit and loss, though according to some jurists that of an animal is pure profit.

The production of a spathe on a palm-tree is considered as an increase that remains united to the principal object. Where a palm-tree forming a dower already at the moment of separation bears fertilised fruit, the wife is not obliged to pluck them, and if of her own accord she does so, she indicates by this her desire that the tree shall half belong to her. When, under these circumstances, the husband does not oppose the wife's request that only half the palm-tree shall be given him provided the fruit are not plucked before the season, †the wife cannot draw back from her proposal and must gather the fruits, while the tree becomes the joint and undivided property of the pair. When, on the other hand, it is the husband who makes the suggestion, the wife's consent does not prevent his changing his mind, and paying her half the value of the tree; provided always that the ownership of the half of the tree is never vested in the husband, so long as the party that has a right of option has not yet decided.

By "original value of dower" is understood the minimum value of the object between the day when dower was promised and the day the wife took possession.

Where a husband has promised his wife, in place of dower, to teach her the Koran, and where, by a repudiation before the instruction is complete, the fulfilment of this promise is impossible, then he owes her proportional dower; or, if the marriage has not been followed by cohabitation, only half.

A woman repudiated before consummation of marriage, who has already transferred the ownership of the dower of which she had taken possession, owes her husband half the value of what she received; †but if she has lost the dower and then regained it, it is on the original object itself that the husband may make good his claim.

*A woman who gives her husband her dower after receiving it, and is afterwards repudiated before consummation, still none the less owes him half of what she received; and by virtue of the same principle a wife who has given her husband only half of what she received, owes him the half of what is left, plus a quarter of the whole dower. Another jurist, however, allows the husband in these circumstances only the half of the remainder, while according to a third he may choose between half the whole amount of the dower, and half of the remainder plus a quarter of the whole. Where, on the other hand, the dower does not consist in a particular object but in an obligation on the husband's part, our school allows him nothing if, in the above circumstances, his wife has rendered it to him. According to the opinion adopted by Shafii in his second period, the wife's guardian can never give up the rights set out in this section.

Section 6

A woman repudiated before *or after consummation of marriage, to whom the law does not allow half dower, may demand a pecuniary indemnity called *motah*. This is so also in the case of separation, at any rate when this separation is not the result of anything for which the woman is responsible. It is recommended that the *motah* should never be less than thirty drahms, and where the parties cannot agree as to the amount of the *motah*, the decision rests with the court, which should take into account the condition of both the litigants. Some authorities, however, maintain that the court should have regard to the husband's condition only ; some only to that of the wife ; others admit no legal minimum, provided that the *motah* consists of something that can form the basis of a legal obligation.

Section 7

In case of proceedings as to the amount or the quality of the dower, the court should, in default of proof, administer an oath to the parties, and, if necessary, to their respective heirs. Where both sides take an oath, the law presumes that no fixed dower has been legally promised, and consequently the husband owes proportional dower. †The same rule applies to the case where the wife maintains in court that her husband promised her a specified dower, and he denies it. †If the wife alleges in court the existence of the marriage and the promise of a proportional dower ; while the husband admits the marriage, but denies the promise of dower, or says nothing upon this head ; the court should ask him to repeat his defence more precisely. If he then mentions an amount inferior to the proportional dower demanded by his wife, the general rule must be followed and an oath administered to both parties. But if the husband still denies the promise, or says nothing, the oath is administered to the woman only, and judgment entered according to her demand. †In the case where proceedings are taken about the amount of dower, not between the husband and wife, but between the husband

and the guardian of a minor or the curator of a lunatic, the rule mentioned above as to the mutual oaths of the parties is observed all the same. Where a wife alleges that her husband married her on such and such a day for a thousand pieces of money, and again on another following day for the same amount, he owes two thousand if the two contracts are established, either by an admission on his part, or by other proof. When the husband, in these circumstances, admits the two contracts, but denies his liability, either on the ground that he has not cohabited with his wife at all, or on the ground that he did not do so after one of the two marriages, and confirms this statement on oath, the presumption is in his favour, but he loses his right to recover half the dower he has paid. But if he asserts that on the second occasion he was merely repeating the words of the former contract, without intending to conclude a second marriage, this means of defence is not admissible.

Section 8

The marriage feast is an institution of the Sonna. According to one authority its observance is strictly necessary; and some even raise this idea to the rank of a dogma. An invitation to a marriage feast should be accepted as if it were an individual obligation, or, according to others, as one for which the Moslem community is collectively responsible. Some jurists, however, consider such acceptance merely as an obligation introduced by the Sonna, *i.e.* of the same nature as the marriage feast itself. Whatever may be its nature the obligation exists only under the following conditions:—

1. That the invitation is not only sent to rich persons from whom a present may be expected.

2. That the invitation is for one day only; for if the invitation mentions three consecutive days, the guests may excuse themselves from attending on the second day; while it will be even blamable in them to accept the invitation for the third day also.

3. That the invitation is not accepted from fear, or as a thing to be proud of.

4. That one is not afraid of meeting among the guests some one from whom one has received an injury, or with whom it is not fitting for one to appear in the same gathering.

5. That the feast is not accompanied by illicit amusements; unless one feels assured that one's presence will cause the shocking objects to be banished. By "shocking objects" are to be understood, *e.g.* silken carpets, representations of animals upon the ceiling, walls, cushions along the walls, curtains or garments; but such representations may

lawfully be depicted upon the floor, and upon carpets or cushions spread upon the floor. One may even depict upon the ceiling or the walls images of animals without heads, or representations of trees. For it is only forbidden to depict living things in their natural state.

Fasting is no reason for refusing an invitation to a wedding feast; and so far as regards a supererogatory fast, it is even preferable to break it if one's absence is likely to embarrass the host.

The guests should eat of the dishes offered them, without saying anything. They must not put their fingers in the dishes except to take out a piece of food offered to eat, unless it be from some motive that they know the host will approve. They may blamelessly throw pieces of sugar, etc., at the newly married pair. They may even pick up again what they have thrown; but it is better not to.

BOOK 35.—SHARING OF THE HUSBAND'S FAVOURS; AND DISOBEDIENCE OF WIVES

SECTION 1

THE husband should distribute his favours equally between his wives. If he falls into the habit of passing the night with one of them, he should do so with the others in rotation; but it is not considered a sin if he prefers to sleep by himself, whether he has many wives or only one. But this permission granted to the husband to sleep apart gives him no right to neglect his wives; in that case it would be blamable. A wife who is sick or *ratka* or *karna*, or who has menstrues or lochia that prevent coition, does not on that account lose her right to receive her husband in her turn; but a disobedient wife cannot claim this right.

A husband who has no room reserved for himself alone must visit his wives in their own rooms; and this is the preferable course even where he has a particular room to himself, though strictly speaking he may then make his wives come to him in rotation. But he is forbidden—

1. †To go and see one of his wives in her room, and make another come to his room, unless for some adequate reason, *e.g.* where the former is lodged nearer to him than the latter, or where he is afraid to make the former cross a garden or a road, or on account of her youth, etc.

2. To instal himself in the apartment of one of his wives, and there receive the visits of the others in rotation.

3. To lodge two wives in the same room, unless with their consent.

The husband may arrange as he pleases the way in which he visits his wives in turn, whether he goes in the morning and stays till next morning, or goes in the evening and stays till next evening; in any case it is the night that constitutes the essential part of the visit, and the day is merely an accessory. The only exception is for a husband whose occupation is at night, for instance, a watchman, in which case the rule is inverted. Where the night constitutes the basis of the visit, the husband should not leave the wife whose turn it is during the night to visit another wife, except in case of necessity, *e.g.* if the latter becomes dangerously ill. Even then, if the absence is prolonged, the wife whose turn it was should be afterwards compensated. During the day, however, the husband may go to his other wives, not only in case of necessity, but for any purpose, to arrange his things, etc., provided his absence is not excessively prolonged. †If during the day one leaves the wife whose turn it is, to make a necessary visit into the room of another, one need not compensate the former, provided always one does not have connection with the latter, though there is no objection to caressing her. ††But where, on the other hand, one leaves the wife whose turn it is to go and see another without adequate motive one must always compensate the former; though in general one is not obliged to pass an equal portion of the day with one's wives when visiting them in rotation.

The husband may regulate the duration of each periodic visit as he pleases, provided that the visits are not for less than one night and one accessory day, and provided, according to our school, that they are not for more than three nights and three days. It is to be recommended not to exceed the minimum. ††On the other hand, the husband may not himself choose which wife shall have the first turn, for this must be decided by lot. This rule, however, has been brought into question by some jurists who maintain that the husband may himself lawfully indicate in what order he shall periodically visit his wives. He may not grant to one of his wives a longer visit than he pays the others; except that a free wife may demand that her husband shall remain twice as long during each visit to her than with a slave wife; and with the further exception that if he takes a new wife he must be with her for seven consecutive nights if she is a virgin, or if otherwise, for three; and in both these cases he owes no compensation to his other wives. Finally, the Sonna has introduced the practice of allowing a new wife who is not a virgin the choice between three nights without subsequent compensation to the other wives, or seven nights with such compensation.

A wife who starts alone upon a journey, without being authorised to do so by her husband, should be considered as a disobedient wife who consequently cannot demand upon her return that her husband shall make up for the visits she has lost by her absence. When, on the contrary, she has undertaken the voyage with her husband's authorisation, one must distinguish, so far as concerns compensation, between a journey undertaken in the husband's interest or in the wife's. In the former case she should be subsequently compensated; in the latter, Shafii, during his Egyptian period, rejected compensation. A husband may not select some of his wives to accompany him upon a change of domicile; but in all other cases of change of abode, †whether for a long or a short journey, he may be accompanied by some of his wives, chosen by lot. He need not afterwards compensate those that remain behind unless at the end of his journey he makes a prolonged stay, in which case he must do so for the length of that stay, †but not for the time occupied in the return journey.

A husband may decline to allow one of his wives to transfer to another her right to his favours, but when he has consented, and one wife has renounced her rights in favour of another specially designated, he must pass with the latter all the nights which he would have passed with both. In these circumstances some authorities allow the husband to let the ordinary visit follow immediately upon that which is the result of this renunciation, even where these visits do not come next to one another in the usual order of rotation. Where a wife renounces her rights generally in favour of all the other wives, the husband should share his nights equally with the others; where she renounces in favour of the husband the latter may dispose of these free nights as he pleases; though, according to some jurists, he must even in this case observe an equal distribution.

Section 2

At the first indication of disobedience to marital authority a wife should be exhorted by her husband without his immediately breaking off relations with her. When she manifests her disobedience by an act which, though isolated, leaves no doubt as to her intentions, he should repeat his exhortations, and confine her to her chamber, but without striking her. [*He may have recourse to blows, even where disobedience is manifested by an isolated act.] Only where there are repeated acts of disobedience may a husband inflict corporal chastisement.

A husband who keeps from his wife what she may legally claim, *e.g.* refuses her her proper turn in his visits, or does not give her sufficient for her necessary maintenance, should be ordered by the court to fulfil his obligations. A husband of a worrying temperament, or one who treats his wife harshly without her giving him any cause for it, should first receive an exhortation from the court, and if this is without result must undergo what correction the court may think fit. Where husband and wife accuse each other, the court should appoint some reliable man to ascertain the facts of the case. The latter, after hearing what both parties have to say, should take whatever measures are rendered necessary by the circumstances in order that the party in the wrong may for the future perform his or her duty towards the injured party. In a case of very grave discord the court should appoint two arbitrators, one from the husband's family and one from the wife's, who should then arrange the matter as if they were the agents of the parties ; or, according to one jurist, by virtue of their nomination by the court. If they are considered as agents, the interested parties must approve their nomination, and the arbitrator for the husband must be authorised by him to pronounce repudiation, or to accept compensation for a divorce ; while the arbitrator for the wife should be authorised by her to offer compensation for a divorce, or to accept repudiation, also for a compensation.

BOOK 36.—DIVORCE

Section 1

Divorce is the separation of husband and wife for a compensation paid by the wife, whether the husband uses the word "repudiation" or the word "divorce." Divorce is permitted only to a husband who can lawfully repudiate his wife. Thus a slave or a man legally incapable by reason of lunacy can divorce only on condition that the master or curator receive the compensation paid. A female slave may claim a divorce even without her master's authorisation, whether the compensation consists in some obligation on her part or in some particular object. If it consists of some particular object the divorced slave is personally responsible to her former husband for proportional dower; or, according to one authority, for the value of the object she has promised. Where her master has authorised the slave to obtain a divorce he may either designate a particular object as compensation or fix the amount of the obligation she may contract towards her husband with this object. In the former case the husband may claim the object as his property, in the latter he may recover the amount from the slave's subsequent earnings, if she has not exceeded the limits of the authorisation. Where the authorisation has been given without any restriction as to the amount, compensation will still be paid from the slave's future earnings, and will consist of the proportional dower of the slave in question. When a husband proposes a divorce or a repudiation for a thousand pieces of money to his imbecile wife, her acceptance merely operates as a revocable repudiation; if she refuses the offer, she is not repudiated. On the other hand, a woman may lawfully obtain a divorce upon her death-bed, in which case the compensation is a debt due from the estate, unless it exceeds the proportional dower, when the excess becomes a charge upon the third of which she may dispose. *A revocable repudiation does not prevent a woman claiming a divorce, but an irrevocable one does.

Compensation has neither a maximum nor a minimum. It may consist of an obligation on the part of the wife, or of some particular thing, or even of the use of such thing. But a woman who has promised, *e.g.* an unknown thing, or a quantity of wine, owes proportional dower, instead of the compensation agreed upon. However, according to one jurist, the promise of a quantity of wine obliges the woman to pay its value instead.

Divorce may be effected by means of an agent, both on the one side and on the other; but the husband's agent may not consent to a divorce for a less sum than that fixed by his principal, nor for a sum less than the proportional dower where his principal has given him no instructions upon the matter. Where the agent has not observed this rule there is no divorce, nor repudiation; though one authority maintains that in these circumstances the divorce holds good and proportional dower is due *ipso facto*. Where the wife's agent has been authorised by her to offer a thousand pieces of money as compensation, and he has done so, the divorce is of course valid. And this is so also where the agent has promised two thousand pieces instead of one thousand, saying that he was acting in accordance with his instructions; but in that case the compensation is *ipso facto* reduced to the amount of the proportional dower; or, according to one authority, either to the sum fixed by the wife, or to the proportional dower, whichever is most advantageous for the husband. If the wife's agent effects the divorce upon his own responsibility, the act is considered as done by a third party, that is to say that the agent is personally responsible for the compensation promised. *If the agent omits to declare his capacity as agent, or the fact that he is acting upon his own responsibility, the wife owes the amount of compensation she had authorised her agent to offer, and the balance offered is owed by the agent. An infidel subject of a Moslem prince, a slave, and a person legally incapable through imbecility, may act as agents for offering or accepting a divorce; but legal incapacity prevents an agent from taking possession of the compensation. †A husband may lawfully appoint a woman to be his agent for divorce or repudiation. But husband and wife may not appoint the same individual to represent them in a divorce; though some jurists allow this.

Section 2

Separation in terms of a divorce is really a repudiation, and this must be taken into consideration where it is a question of the necessity of an intermediate husband, if one desires to remarry the woman in question. One jurist, however, maintains that a divorce has the same consequences as a dissolution of marriage for redhibitory defects, which means that in his opinion a divorce does not count as a repudiation, as regards the necessity for an intermediate husband.

According to those authorities who consider divorce as really repudiation, the word "dissolve" should be considered as an implicit term for describing divorce, †but the word "ransom" is, according to them, the equivalent of divorce; while the jurist who likens it to a dissolution of marriage for redhibitory defects is of a contrary opinion. According to the former theory, that divorce is repudiation, †the wife owes the husband as compensation the amount of the proportional dower, unless there is some special stipulation as to the amount. This theory considers also that the divorce is valid even though pronounced in terms that imply repudiation, provided that such is the intention; and even though use is made of some other language than Arabic. It is considered that a divorce is implied where the husband says, "I sell you yourself for so much," and the woman answers, "I buy myself."

Where the husband begins by making the offer, and adds the amount of compensation, *e.g.* by saying, "I want to repudiate you," or "I want to divorce you for so much," it is in any case a conditional offer to effect a bilateral agreement, even according to the theory that considers divorce equivalent to repudiation. Consequently the husband can always withdraw his words, so long as the wife has not declared her acceptance of the offer made her. Moreover, the law requires that in these circumstances acceptance must be declared before any considerable interval has elapsed from the time of the offer. The acceptance must relate to the offer. Thus there is no divorce where the husband says, "I want to repudiate you for one thousand pieces of money," and the wife accepts, replying, "It is agreed, but for two thousand," or *vice versâ*. Nor is there any divorce where the husband says, "I wish to repudiate you three times for one thousand pieces of money," and the wife answers, "I only accept one for a third of that amount." But where, on the other hand, there is no essential difference the divorce is valid. Thus if the husband says, "I wish to repudiate you three times for a thousand pieces of money," and the wife answers, "I accept one repudiation for that sum," he has legally repudiated her thrice for the amount declared. When it is not a conditional offer of divorce that the husband makes, but a conditional divorce that he pronounces, saying for example, "when you give me," or "when you have given me," the law allows no retractation on his part. In this case verbal acceptance is not required nor even immediate payment. The words "if you give me," or "whe you have given me," bring about identical legal consequences, except that they require payment to be made as soon as possible. If, instead of the husband, it is the wife who has taken the initiative in asking to be repudiated, and the husband has consented; this is a bilateral contract of the same nature as a piece of job work. In this case the wife may withdraw her request at any time before her husband has granted it; and he must make up his mind as soon as possible, otherwise the offer is considered as *ipso facto* withdrawn. A request on the wife's part "to be repudiated three times for one thousand pieces of money," granted by the husband for one repudiation only, and for a third of the amount, results in the woman being only once repudiated.

A divorce, or a repudiation for compensation, is never revocable, unless the parties have reserved this right; but such a reservation *ipso facto* annuls the stipulation as to the compensation. Only one authority considers, even where there has been this reserve, that the divorce has the effect of an irrevocable repudiation, and maintains that the wife owes proportional dower in addition. When a wife, after requesting to be repudiated for a certain amount, abjures Islam, and does not retract her error before the end of her period of legal retirement, she is considered to have lost her status as wife by the fact of apostasy, and owes nothing as compensation, whether her husband has or has not granted her request, and whether the marriage has or has not been consummated. But where the wife has returned to the faith before the expiry of her period of retirement; she is considered as repudiated for the sum offered; at least if the husband has in the meanwhile granted her request. A divorce is not rendered invalid because offer and acceptance are separated by some unimportant words.

SECTION 3

The following words on the part of a husband: "You are repudiated and you owe," or "you owe me so much," constitute merely a revocable repudiation, unless the wife has herself previously asked to be repudiated and offered the same amount as compensation. It does not even matter whether the wife accepts the offer made to her by the husband, for in any case the phrase does not imply that the money is due by her as compensation. †Only where the husband afterwards declares that he meant definitely to repudiate his wife for the amount mentioned, and she accepts this subsequent explanation, must she be considered as divorced. Where the wife has begun by asking for repudiation for a compensation, the above phrase is considered as a favourable reply to her request, and she is consequently divorced. According to our school the phrase, "You are repudiated on condition that you owe me so much," is equivalent to the phrase, "You are repudiated for so much;" that is to say that the wife, if she consents, is divorced, and owes the promised amount. It is the same where the husband says, "You will be repudiated if you will guarantee me a thousand pieces of money," provided that the wife gives an affirmative reply as soon as possible. The phrase, "When you guarantee me one thousand pieces of money you are repudiated," does not involve repudiation if the wife only guarantees some smaller sum, but it does if she guarantees the amount mentioned or double that amount. Similarly the following words pronounced by a husband against his wife, "If you guarantee me one thousand pieces of money you may yourself pronounce your repudiation," have the effect of divorcing her for one thousand pieces of money if she definitely accepts the entire proposal; but not if she merely guarantees the amount without divorcing herself, or repudiates herself without guaranteeing the amount. A repudiation pronounced on condition that the woman transfers some amount of money has effect as soon as the stipulated amount has been delivered to the husband, †who becomes its owner from that moment. A stipulation to deliver is equivalent, according to some, to a stipulation to transfer; but according to the greater number of authorities it is merely an ordinary suspensive condition. It is understood that in this case possession need not be taken immediately.

[By adding a condition to "deliver" instead of one to "transfer" the compensation, a mere revocable repudiation is pronounced; and the condition is fulfilled by the fact of the husband taking possession of the object, even as the result of some violence.]

A condition that a wife shall give a slave possessing certain specified qualities, as in a contract of *salam*, is not fulfilled if the slave given has not all the qualities stipulated, and the woman is consequently not considered to be repudiated; but if the slave, though possessed of the stipulated qualities, is tainted with redhibitory defects, the condition is fulfilled and the repudiation consummated; but without prejudice to the husband's right to return the slave on account of his defects, and to claim as compensation the amount of the proportional dower. According to one authority, however, he can claim in these circumstances only the value of the slave, had he had no defects. A condition to give "a slave," without further description, is fulfilled by the transfer of any slave, whatever his qualities may be; provided it is not a usurped slave, for in that case the husband can claim as compensation the amount of the proportional dower.

Where a woman asks her husband to repudiate her three times, for a thousand pieces of money, while the husband has only one repudiation left to pronounce, he has a right to demand the entire sum when pronouncing this repudiation. Others, however, maintain that only a third of the amount is due to him under these circumstances; while still others are of opinion that he can demand the thousand pieces if the woman acted knowingly, but only a third if she made a mistake as to the number of repudiations her husband could still pronounce. If the wife asks for a repudiation for a thousand pieces of money, and the husband replies by repudiating her for a hundred, she owes him only the amount declared by him. Others maintain that in this case she owes him a thousand; while still others do not admit any obligation, as there has been no consent. A request to be repudiated "to-morrow for a thousand pieces of money," results in the woman being obliged to pay proportional dower, if the husband repudiates her either on the next day or earlier without adding that she shall be free from the next day. According to one authority, however, there are jurists that do not allow this subtle interpretation, but consider the wife liable for the amount mentioned if the repudiation takes place, even though it may be before the day indicated by her. In any case this repudiation is irrevocable.

††Where a husband says to his wife, "When you enter the house you are repudiated for a thousand pieces of money," she is really repudiated if she accepts the proposal and enters the house, and she owes her husband the amount mentioned. A single authority maintains that in this case she owes proportional dower, and others raise this opinion to the rank of a dogma.

A third party may lawfully ask for the divorce of another's wife, even against her will. To this proposal must be applied all we have said about the expressions used in ordinary divorce and their consequences when used by or to the wife herself. A person appointed by the wife as her agent to ask for a divorce may do so either as her agent or upon his own responsibility. A third party may even appoint the wife herself an agent to ask for a divorce in the interests of that third party; but the wife may of course refuse to act as such agent. If a third party asks for a woman's divorce and falsely states that the wife has appointed such third party her agent, the husband's consent has no legal effect. A father may ask for his daughter's divorce like any other person; that is to say that when acting in his own name he is personally responsible for the compensation; but when acting on his daughter's account, either in his quality as guardian, or falsely alleging an appointment by her, there is no divorce. A father who of his own accord promises compensation from his daughter's property is as little justified as if he had promised his son-in-law a usurped object.

Section 4

Where the husband denies the fact of a divorce asserted by his wife, there is a presumption in his favour on his taking an oath. Where, on the other hand, the husband maintains that he has repudiated his wife for so much, while she asserts that she has been simply repudiated without compensation, the law presumes an irrevocable repudiation without compensation. In proceedings as to the nature or amount of the compensation the court should, in default of proof, administer an oath to the litigants ; when, if both take it, the wife owes proportional dower.

If a divorce has been obtained for a compensation of "a thousand" without specifying what, but the parties are in agreement as to the nature of the things of which this quantity has been stipulated, the wife owes her husband a thousand things of this kind. Some authorities, however, maintain that a stipulation of "a thousand" without adding what, is inadmissible in a court of law, and that the woman always owes in such a case proportional dower. The same controversy exists as to the case where one of the parties maintains that the stipulation of "a thousand" implies "dinars," and the other that it means "drahms" or copper money. According to the first theory the court should administer an oath to both parties ; but according to those authorities who do not admit the validity of such a vague stipulation, the wife owes proportional dower when she does not deny the husband's claim altogether, without its being necessary to administer an oath to the parties.

BOOK 37.—REPUDIATION

Section 1

In order that a repudiation should be valid the law requires that the husband should be a sane adult Moslem. A repudiation may be pronounced in a state of drunkenness. A repudiation is valid, even where pronounced unintentionally, if the husband uses explicit terms; but if he uses implicit terms, he must really intend to repudiate his wife.

By explicit terms are meant, "repudiation," "separation," "dismissal," "I repudiate you," "You are repudiated," "You are discharged," "O repudiated woman!"; †but where the mere words "you" and "repudiation," with or without the article, are pronounced without indicating the relation between them, such a meaningless exclamation has no legal effect. Our school admits that repudiation may be explicitly pronounced in any other language as well as in Arabic, provided the expressions employed correspond to the terms just mentioned. The following expressions are considered to be implicit terms: "I render you your liberty," or "You are free." †Local expressions specially used to denote repudiation, even though not actually mentioning repudiation itself, are considered by law as explicit. Thus some persons say, "the woman I was permitted to enjoy," or "the woman God permitted me to enjoy will henceforth be to me a person with whom connection is forbidden."

[†On the contrary these words should be considered as implicit.] As implicit terms are also considered the following: "You are henceforth isolated," "free," "separated," "cut off," "irrevocably repudiated," "You must observe on my account a period of legal retirement," or "period of purification," "Go back to your family," "Your rope is on your withers," "I have no further need of you," "Leave me," "Go away," "Leave me alone," "Bid me good-bye," etc. Enfranchisement is an implicit manner of announcing repudiation; and *vice versâ*, repudiation implies enfranchisement; but repudiation does not imply injurious comparison, nor *vice versâ*. Such phrases as: "Connection with you is henceforth forbidden me," or "I declare connection with you to be forbidden me," indicate either a repudiation or an injurious comparison, according to the husband's intention ; and if he had both in view he may afterwards declare which of the two he intends to effect. According to come authorities, however, these phrases always imply a repudiation, while according to others they always imply an injurious comparison. The phrase, "Your eye," or any other part of the body, "is forbidden me," does not render cohabitation with the woman positively prohibited to her husband, but the latter owes the expiation prescribed for perjury, *even though he may have had no intention of forbidding himself cohabitation with her. However, according to another doctrine, such phrases should be considered as not said. Such phrases as we have mentioned, if pronounced against a slave, have the effect of enfranchising her, if such is the master's intention ; but if he intended thus to forbid himself the right of cohabiting with her as regards the part of the body referred to, or if he had no particular intention when using these phrases, they have the same effect as regards the slave as in the case of the wife. If, in repudiation, one uses implicit terms, the intention must accompany the whole sentence ; or, according to some authorities, the first word.

A person who has the use of his tongue may not indicate repudiation by signs ; though some authorities admit signs in these circumstances as equivalent to implicit terms. As to a mute it is agreed that he may legally form and dissolve all kinds of obligations by means of signs ; and, where every one understands what he means, signs constitute on his part an explicit method of repudiation. Where, on the other hand, persons of highly developed intelligence can alone understand the signs, they are considered as an implicit manner of communicating the mute's ideas. A husband who, though having the use of his tongue, writes to his wife that she is repudiated, obtains the desired effect. But if he has so written without serious intention the marriage remains valid. If a husband writes to his wife : "You are repudiated from the time this letter reaches you," the repudiation is effected by the receipt of the letter ; but if he uses the phrase, "from the time you have read my letter," the result depends upon whether the woman can read. If she can, she is repudiated only from the moment she has read it herself, †not if another person reads it to her ; if she cannot and if the letter is read to her, this has the same effect as if she had read it herself.

Section 2

A husband may lawfully grant his wife the right to pronounce her own repudiation, a proceeding which Shafii in his second period likened to a transfer of property. The law requires that a wife so authorised should exercise the right soon afterwards. Thus one may say to one's wife: "You may yourself pronounce your repudiation for one thousand pieces of money," and after this she is irrevocably repudiated upon pronouncing the repudiation, and also owes the sum mentioned. One jurist, however, compares this proceeding to an appointment as agent by the husband, †and consequently does not insist on the wife's pronouncing the repudiation soon afterwards. Admitting this principle the difficulty arises whether the husband's offer must be formally accepted by the woman to enable her to use her right of pronouncing her own repudiation, a controversy we have discussed when speaking of the agent. However, whatever may be the nature of the proceeding, all are agreed that the husband may retract his words, so long as the wife is not really repudiated. When, on the other hand, the proceeding is admitted to be merely a transfer of property, the phrase, "When we are in the month of Ramadan you may pronounce your repudiation," though used by some, is devoid of meaning and consequently void.

Repudiation takes place also in the following cases:—

1. If the husband says to the wife, "Do the act that obliges me henceforth to abstain from you;" to which she replies, "I do it;" at any rate where the intention on both sides was to imply a repudiation, but not otherwise.

2. If the husband uses an explicit phrase, and the wife replies implicitly, intending to indicate repudiation.

3. If the husband uses an implicit phrase, intending to indicate repudiation, and the woman replies explicitly.

In virtue of these principles three repudiations are admitted, if such is the intention on both sides, even where neither the husband on granting his wife the right to repudiate herself, nor the wife on accepting the offer, may have actually spoken of "three." On the other hand, there is only one repudiation—

1. †Where neither of the parties speaks of "three," and only one intends to accomplish a triple-repudiation; and

2. Where one of the parties uses the number "three," but the other speaks of only one repudiation.

Section 3

Repudiation pronounced in a dream is void; and it is the same with regard to a repudiation pronounced by a husband by mistake, with no definite intention. The words used should always be interpreted in accordance with the succession of ideas they represent. Thus a woman whose name is Taliḳ is not repudiated by the mere words *O*

Talik, if the intention is to call her, †or where there is no special intention to call her. Even in the case of a woman of the name Tarik or Talib the law admits a presumption in favour of her husband who says to her *O Talik*, if he declares afterwards that he only meant to call her, but made a mistake in the letter. This, however, is without prejudice to the fact that a repudiation pronounced by way of banter or jest carries all the legal consequences of a real repudiation ; as does also a repudiation pronounced against a woman erroneously supposed not to be one's wife, either because her features cannot be distinguished in the obscurity, or because the husband does not yet know her, the marriage having been concluded by his tutor or agent. A stranger who pronounces a repudiation in Arabic without understanding the meaning of his words is not considered to have repudiated his wife ; though, according to some authorities, this repudiation is valid, if the husband's intention is to repudiate, even though he may not understand every word he uses.

A repudiation extorted by violence has no legal effect, unless it duly appears that the husband already had the intention of repudiating his wife, *e.g.* if after being constrained to pronounce a triple repudiation, he reduces it to a single one ; or if after being constrained to pronounce it explicitly or conditionally, he pronounces it implicitly or unconditionally ; or lastly if after having been forced to say, "I repudiate you," he says, "I dismiss you," or *vice versâ*. By "violence" in a legal sense is meant the power to cause a person the ill with which one has threatened him, whether such power consists in authority or legal force, provided the person in question cannot escape and really believes the threat will be carried out if he does not do what is demanded. Thus it is considered "violence" to threaten any one with serious blows, imprisonment, loss of property, etc. ; though, according to some authorities, a menace, to be a cause of nullity, must relate to a person's life, or to the loss of a limb, or to blows that would endanger life. Violence is a cause of absolute nullity, even if the person against whom it is exercised has made no mental reservation upon obeying. Only a few authorities assert that a person neglecting without valid excuse to make a mental reservation, when obeying violence, cannot claim nullity. By "mental reservation" is meant, *e.g.* the act of thinking of another person when repudiating one's own wife under pressure of a menace.

When one has temporarily lost one's reason through liquor or medicine, one is none the less capable of pronouncing repudiation or disposing of one's property in general ; and, according to our school, one is none the less responsible for one's words and actions. Only one of our jurists denies all consequence to the words or actions of a drunken man; while several admit his responsibility, but maintain that he can never derive any advantage from such a condition.

Repudiation is valid where reference is made to "A quarter of you," "A part of you," "One of your limbs," "Your liver," "One of your hairs," or "One of your nails," as being repudiated. According to our school it is the same where one says, "Your blood is repudiated;" but not if one speaks of that which comes from the human body, as saliva, sweat, sperm, or milk.

Our school does not accept a repudiation where the husband says to his wife whose right hand has been amputated, "Your right hand is repudiated." The phrase, "I am repudiated by you," spoken by the husband, implies a repudiation of his wife if such was his intention; but if by this obscure phrase he did not mean to indicate repudiation, †or even if his intention to repudiate did not specially refer to his wife, a repudiation does not take place. Intention to repudiate is also rigorously necessary where one says to one's wife, "I am irrevocably repudiated by you;" but authorities are not agreed as to whether these words must refer to some particular woman. Finally the phrase, "I am about to observe a period of purification," spoken by the husband is senseless and consequently void; though a few authorities consider it sufficient to repudiate one's wife if such was one's intention.

Section 4

A repudiation pronounced against a woman to whom one is not married is void, even where intended to apply to an eventual marriage. †On the other hand, a slave, though he can only pronounce a repudiation twice, may all the same pronounce a third to take effect upon his eventual enfranchisement, or upon the woman entering such and such a house after that event. In the first case the effect depends upon the enfranchisement, and in the second upon both the enfranchisement and an entry into the house mentioned. The reader, however, should be reminded that this conditional repudiation affects only a wife who has been revocably repudiated, and not one who has been divorced in the meanwhile. Similarly a condition upon which a free man has based a third repudiation, *e.g.* that the woman enters such and such a house, is not fulfilled where she is irrevocably separated for some other reason after the second repudiation, and taken back again by her former husband, and then enters the house mentioned. Under these circumstances it matters little whether she has *or has not previously entered the house when free. Another theory, however, admits these precepts only in case of irrevocable separation by divorce or of dissolution in consequence of redhibitory defects, but not in case of irrevocable separation caused by a new repudiation thrice repeated, occurring after the second repudiation.

A husband who repudiates his wife once or twice, but takes her back during her period of legal retirement, or marries her again after its expiry, and even after an intervening marriage with another husband, must, if he repudiates her again, take count of the former repudiations when determining whether this last one is or is not revocable. If, on the other hand, the new marriage has been effected after the woman has been previously repudiated thrice, she may again be three times repudiated before the new marriage is irrevocably dissolved.

A repudiation may lawfully be pronounced upon a death-bed. During a period of legal retirement rendered necessary by a revocable repudiation, the parties mutually retain their right of succession. This is not so in the case of an irrevocable repudiation; though Shafii in his first period admitted the wife's right, even in these circumstances.

Section 5

The phrase, "I repudiate you," or "You are repudiated," implies as many repudiations as the husband intends; and similarly with phrases indicating repudiation in an implicit manner. On the other hand, no account is taken of the number intended by the husband if he expressly says only once; though some authorities prefer, even in such a case, to keep to the intention and not to the letter. [On the contrary the majority maintain that in this case also the intention must be regarded; those authorities that would keep to the letter are in the minority.]

Where a husband is upon the point of saying, "You are repudiated thrice," and the phrase is interrupted by the sudden death of the woman, there is no repudiation if death occurs before the termination of the word "repudiated." If she dies between the words "repudiated" and "thrice" three repudiations must be admitted. Some authorities, however, admit in such a case only one repudiation, others none. If a husband says, "You are repudiated," "You are repudiated," "You are repudiated," these phrases equal three repudiations if separated by an interval. If, on the contrary, they follow immediately upon each other they constitute :—

1. A single repudiation, if the second and third phrases were merely intended by the husband to be reaffirmations of the first;
2. Three repudiations, if he intended to reiterate his will, *or had no definite intention in the matter;

3. Two repudiations, if he intended the second to reaffirm the first, and the third to be a reiteration of his will, or *vice versâ*; or

4. †Three repudiations, if the third phrase was a reaffirmation of the first, and the second a reiteration of his will.

When saying, "You are repudiated, and repudiated, and repudiated," the third "repudiated" may lawfully be used to reaffirm the second, but not so the second to reaffirm the first. All this as to reaffirmation and reiteration relates only to a woman whose marriage has been consummated; for where these phrases are pronounced against a wife before cohabitation there is only one repudiation. However, if one says to one's wife before cohabitation, "You are repudiated and repudiated, if you enter into such a place," the fact of entering is enough to cause her to be twice repudiated; and this is also the consequence of the phrase, "You will undergo one repudiation then another," or "accompanied by another," it making no difference in this case whether the marriage has been consummated †or not. The words "a repudiation followed by another," or "preceded by another" constitute two repudiations if the marriage has been consummated, and otherwise one; and the same with the words "a repudiation which follows another," or "which precedes another." If one says, "a repudiation upon a repudiation," it is necessary to distinguish between the cases where the preposition "upon" has been employed (1) in a conjunctive sense, (2) to indicate time or place, (3) in an arithmetical sense, or (4) without any specially indicated function. In the first case the phrase is admitted to imply two repudiations, and in the three others one. It must also be observed that the words, "The half of a repudiation upon the half of a repudiation," imply in all cases a single repudiation. The phrase, "A repudiation upon two repudiations" admits of the following explanations:—

1. It signifies three repudiations, when "upon" is used in a conjunctive sense.

2. It signifies one, when "upon" is used to indicate time and place.

3. It signifies two, when "upon" is taken in an arithmetical sense, *i.e* knowingly so taken; but only one when "upon" is taken in an arithmetical sense by a husband who does not know how to count, even if he intends to attribute to the phrase its ordinary meaning. Some authorities admit two repudiations in this last case.

4. It signifies one only where the husband does not intend to attribute to the word "upon" any special function; though one authority admits two in these circumstances, at any rate if the husband knows how to count.

"A partial repudiation" is equivalent to a whole one; and the same is true of the phrase, "Two halves of a repudiation," unless the husband adds that the two halves are distinct repudiations, for in that case there are two complete repudiations, by virtue of the explanation of "a partial repudiation." †"The half of two repudiations" means one; "three halves," and "the half of one repudiation plus the third of another," imply two; but "the half plus the third of a repudiation" constitutes one only. If one says to one's four wives, "I inflict upon you," or "You can share amongst you—a repudiation," or "two repudiations," or "three," or "four," all are repudiated once. However, where one intends each of the repudiations to be shared amongst the women, all are twice repudiated by two repudiations, and thrice by three repudiations or four repudiations. †It must, of course, be understood that one cannot afterwards declare that one intended the women to share amongst them the fractions of repudiations pronounced against them, as such a complication would be obviously inconsistent with the words themselves. Finally, if a husband repudiates one of his wives and then says to another, "I want you to share the repudiation with her," or "You are as she," they are both repudiated, otherwise not. The same rule applies also to a case where one husband repudiates his wife, and another says to his, "You are as she."

Section 6

A repudiation may be pronounced under some reservation, provided this reservation immediately follows the repudiation, except where one may stop to take breath, or because one is a stammerer. [†It is also rigorously necessary that there should be an intention to make a reservation before the oath is finished, where the repudiation is accompanied by an oath.] The law requires that a reservation should not be of a kind to render the whole act illusory. Hence the phrase, "You are repudiated thrice, less twice plus once," indicates at least one repudiation; and according to some authorities it indicates three. By virtue of the same principle the expression, "Two repudiations, plus one less one," indicates three repudiations, or, according to some authorities, two. A reservation may consist either in the negation of a positive fact, or in the affirmation of a negative. Consequently the words, "Three, less two less one," indicate two; "Three, less three less two," also two, or according to some three, and according to others one. "Five less three," mean two, or according to some jurists three; ††"Three less the half of another," mean three. A repudiation pronounced under the reservation, "If it please God," or "With God's permission, is of no effect where a suspensive condition is intended and similarly a repudiation may not be made dependent upon any suspensive condition consisting in some future fact announced under the same reservation of " If it please God," or " By God's permission." This rule applies not only to repudiation, but also to enfranchisement, to an oath or a vow, and in general to all ways of disposing of one's property. †On the other hand, the words, " O repudiated woman ! If it please God," must be considered effective ; for in this case the repudiation does not depend upon the will of God by way of condition ; but the words, " You are repudiated, with God's permission," constitute an illegal reservation.

Section 7

Any ambiguity in the phrasing of a repudiation should be interpreted in a sense favourable to the marriage, whether that ambiguity concerns the fact of the repudiation itself or the number of times it is pronounced. The husband cannot allege natural shyness as an excuse for ambiguity of expression.

When one husband says to his wife, " You are repudiated if this bird is a crow," and another husband adds, " If it is not a crow my wife is repudiated," the double repudiation does not take place where neither husband knows if it be a crow or not. But if the same person pronounces the two sentences against two of his wives, he wishes to divorce one of them ; and he must not only ascertain the nature of the bird, but must inform the wife concerned. Where a husband has repudiated one of his wives and forgets which, the affair remains in suspense until he remembers ; and under these circumstances he cannot be obliged by the wives concerned to put an end to the uncertainty. †A man who says to his wife and to another woman, " One of you is repudiated," and adds, " It is the other woman I meant," has a presumption in favour of the truth of his words, and the wife is not repudiated. ††Where, however, the wife is called Zainab, and he says, " Zainab is repudiated," he cannot afterwards assert that the words refer to another woman of the same name. The phrase, " One of you is repudiated," pronounced against two wives involves the repudiation of that one who is specially meant, and she must be informed ; but if neither be specially intended, it must be decided afterwards to which of the two it is to apply. In either case both wives are free until the husband has informed them of his previous intention or of his subsequent decision. He should do this as soon as possible, and he owes them ordinary maintenance until the matter has been decided one way or the other. The repudiation dates from the time of pronouncement. Only a small number of authorities make it date from the moment the husband communicates his decision, where he did not intend to indicate one particular wife at the time of pronouncement. It should also be pointed out to the reader that subsequent cohabitation with one of the wives is not enough to indicate which was intended, nor to decide which should be repudiated. Only a few jurists admit cohabitation to be a sufficient indication of a husband's subsequent decision. Where, on the other hand, in these circumstances the husband points to one of the wives and says, "This is the one I have repudiated," it is generally agreed that this is sufficient to indicate which of the two women he had specially in view when pronouncing the repudiation in the alternative; and where he says, "This one and that one," or "This one not more than that one," he has repudiated both. The obligation, either to say which wife was meant, or to decide to whom it shall apply, remains, though one or both should previously decease; for it affects not only the marriage but the right of succession. Consequently, in case of the husband's decease, before accomplishing this duty, *it is necessary to accept the declaration of his heir, as to the wife whom the deceased intended to repudiate; though the heir can never decide which shall be repudiated, if the deceased had not yet definitely decided. The words, "If this bird is a crow my wife is repudiated, and if it is not my slave is free," have as their consequence that the person who had spoken them, while ignorant of the nature of the bird, is deprived of his rights both over the wife and over the slave, until he has ascertained it. In this case, however, our school does not admit the declaration of the heir, in the case of the decease of the speaker; but the matter must be decided by casting lots. If the slave is thus selected he is *ipso facto* enfranchised. If the wife wins, the repudiation is inadmissible. †In this latter case the slave is not reduced to servitude, from which he has been in some sort liberated, but his situation remains in suspense.

Section 8

A repudiation is either in conformity with the Sonna, or contrary to it and consequently forbidden. Repudiations contrary to the Sonna are of two kinds:—

1. A repudiation during the menstruation of a woman with whom one has already cohabited. Some authorities admit repudiation in these circumstances when at the request of the woman herself; and all are agreed that menstruation is no obstacle to divorce, †except when the request is made by a third person. A repudiation in the words, "You are repudiated at the end of your present menstrues," †is in conformity with the Sonna; but our school considers as contrary

to the Sonna the expression, "At the end of your present period of purity," at least if the husband has not cohabited with his wife during that period.

2. A repudiation during a period of purity, when the husband has had connection with his wife in that period, and probably rendered her pregnant, though the existence of the fœtus may not have been ascertained. Neither may one lawfully repudiate a woman during a period of purity, †if one has cohabited with her during the menstruation that preceded that period; though there is no objection to a divorce in these circumstances, nor even to a repudiation where the existence of a fœtus has already been ascertained.

Where a woman has been repudiated in a manner contrary to the Sonna, the practice has been introduced by it of revoking the repudiation, after which the woman may be again repudiated, in the first following period of purity. If a man says to his wife during her menstrues, "You are repudiated contrary to the Sonna," the repudiation is immediately effected, though it has to be revoked as we have just said. But where, in these circumstances the husband says, "You are repudiated in accordance with the Sonna," it begins from the first following period of purity.

Where the repudiation is pronounced against the woman not during her menstrues, but during her period of purity, the law admits the two following distinctions :—

1. The expression, "You are repudiated in accordance with the Sonna," implies an immediate repudiation, if the wife has not had connection with her husband during her present period of purity; otherwise the repudiation takes effect from the end of her next menstruation.

2. The expression, "You are repudiated contrary to the Sonna," implies an immediate repudiation, if the wife has had connection with her husband during her present period of purity; otherwise the repudiation takes effect from the beginning of her next menstruation. In both cases, however, the repudiation may be revoked later.

The words, "A regular repudiation," "The most regular," or "The most perfect," are equivalent to "according to the Sonna," while the words "faulty," "the most faulty," or "the most abominable," are equivalent to "contrary to the Sonna." The expressions, "as much in accordance with as contrary to the Sonna," or "as regular as faulty," always designate an immediate repudiation.

Several repudiations may lawfully be pronounced at one and the same time; but the law does not permit the husband, after saying, "You are repudiated thrice," or "Thrice in accordance with the Sonna," to spread out these three repudiations over three of his wife's periods of purity; unless he belongs to a school which, like that of Malik, forbids pronouncing more than one repudiation at a time. †In this matter the court should respect the prescriptions of the school to which the husband belongs, even where his ideas are not in conformity with the precepts of our school, for it is a matter of personal status. This principle should be observed also in a case where the husband has used such expressions as, "You are repudiated, that is if you enter the house," or "If Zaid approves of it." †Where, on the other hand, the husband says, "All my wives are repudiated," or "Every wife I have is repudiated," adding, "I only meant some of them," no account can be taken of his individual opinions, as they are obviously opposed to common sense and public order. Such a reservation would only be admissible if it formed as it were a single locution with the principal phrase; where, *e.g.* one of his wives reproached a husband with having married other wives instead of confining himself to her, and he were to reply, "I repudiate all my wives," adding, "except you alone."

SECTION 9

The words, "You will be repudiated in such and such a month," "At the new moon of such and such a month," or "on the first of such and such a month," imply a term expiring at the commencement of the first night of the month. The term "the day" or "the first day" of the month expires upon the appearance of dawn on the first day; while the term "the end of the month" expires at the end of the last day of the month, or according to some at the beginning of the latter half. If one says during the night, "when a day shall have elapsed," one indicates the following sunset; but if one says it during the day one indicates the corresponding hour of the succeeding day. The expression "this day" pronounced during the day indicates a term expiring upon the next sunset; pronounced at night time it becomes a meaningless expression, and in consequence null and void. The terms "month" and "year" must be interpreted upon the same principles.

A repudiation commencing from some past time, *e.g.* "You are repudiated from yesterday," though referring to the past, counts only from the moment it was pronounced, if such was the husband's intention; though some maintain that such an intention is incompatible with the expression mentioned, and that the act is null and void. Where, on the other hand, the husband's intention really is that the repudiation should take effect from the previous day, the woman is already in her period of legal retirement, at the time when the repudiation is pronounced; and in these circumstances a declaration of the husband as to his intention is presumed to be true if substantiated on oath. And similarly where he declares he was referring to a previous marriage with the same wife; at any rate if his remarriage with her is a fact of public notoriety.

Conditional words or expressions, that is the words "whom," "if," "where," "when," "from the time that," "every time that," "whatever," do not necessarily imply that the act takes effect immediately where they refer to a definite future event, provided always that a divorce be not intended. The single exception to this rule is when the husband says, "You are repudiated if you like," for such a condition can refer only to the wishes of the woman concerned. The phrase "every time that" requires a repetition of the event upon which the repudiation depends; but this is not the case with the other expressions mentioned above. The words, "When I repudiate you, you are already repudiated," followed in fact by a repudiation, simple or conditional, constitute two repudiations, provided in the latter case the condition is fulfilled. The expression, "You are repudiated as many times as I can repudiate you," followed by a repudiation, constitutes three repudiations if the marriage has been consummated but otherwise only one. The words, "If I repudiate one of my wives, one of my slaves is freed; on the repudiation of two wives, two slaves; of three, three; of four, four," pronounced by a husband who has four wives, and followed by the repudiation of all four, either at once or in succession, implies the enfranchisement of ten slaves; ††and even of fifteen, if the condition is expressed by the phrase, "every time that." A condition that a certain event shall not take place, expressed by the word "if," *e.g.* "if you do not enter such and such a house," is fulfilled, according to our school, when it can no longer be reasonably supposed that the event will take place. But when such a negative condition is expressed in some other way, it is fulfilled only by the expiration of the time within which it is possible for the event to happen. Where, on the other hand, the husband has used the following words: "You are repudiated since you have entered the house," or "Because you have not entered it," it is known at once in a positive manner if the woman is repudiated or not. [Unless the husband is not strong in grammar, and consequently does not always observe the difference between the conjunctions "in" and "an"; for in this case the expression is considered as an ordinary condition.]

Section 10

A condition "that the wife is pregnant" is fulfilled as soon as the existence of the fœtus is ascertained. If it is not ascertained, an accouchement before six months is enough to indicate that the condition was fulfilled at the moment of repudiation; but if an accouchement does not take place until between six months and four years after the conditional repudiation, and if the woman in question has in the meantime cohabited again in such a way as may have rendered her pregnant, the condition is not fulfilled. †In the absence of subsequent cohabitation, the condition is fulfilled by an accouchement up to the extreme limit of four years after the repudiation. The phrase, "If you are pregnant of a son you are once repudiated, but if you are pregnant of a daughter you are twice repudiated," involves three repudiations if the wife gives birth to a son and a daughter; but the phrase, "If the child with which you are pregnant is a son you are repudiated once, and if it is a daughter twice" involves no repudiation in these circumstances. "If you have an accouchement you are repudiated," signifies that a woman giving birth to two children in succession one after the other, by the same husband, is repudiated for the first accouchement, and her period of legal retirement is regarded as terminated by the second; while the words, "Every time you have an accouchement you will be repudiated," implies the consequence that the giving birth to three children, not only by the same husband, but during the same accouchement, one after the other, involves two repudiations for the two first children, and the expiry of the period of legal retirement at the birth of the third. ††Now in this case the third repudiation has not yet taken place. If a husband pronounces against his four wives the words, "Every time one of you has an accouchement the others will be repudiated," and all four have an accouchement at one and the same time, each is repudiated thrice. Where, on the other hand, the accouchements are successive, the fourth wife is repudiated thrice, and also the first, provided that the latter's period of legal retirement has not expired at the time of the former's accouchement. As to the second wife, she is only repudiated once, upon the accouchement of the first; while the third is twice repudiated, *i.e.* upon the accouchements of the first and of the second; and further the periods of legal retirement of the second and third expire upon their respective accouchement. Some authorities, however, arrive at a different result, admitting that in such a case the first wife is not repudiated, and that each of her companions is repudiated once only. A special case exists where the wives in question have their accouchements two by two; then each of the two first is repudiated thrice, or according to some authorities once, and each of the two last twice.

A woman repudiated on condition she has her menstrues has a presumption in her favour on declaring upon oath that menstruation has begun ; †but no such presumption exists in the case of an accouchement, for that is a fact that can easily be otherwise established. Nor does any presumption exist where one wife's repudiation depends upon the menstruation of another. Consequently where a husband pronounces against two of his wives the words, "I repudiate you both if you are actually both in a period of menstruation," and subsequently denies the simultaneous menstruation alleged by the two women, he has a presumption in favour of his denial upon oath, and the double repudiation he has pronounced does not take effect. If he merely denies the menstruation of one of them, that one is repudiated as a consequence of the menstruation of the other, admitted by the husband.

The words "if," or "When I repudiate you, you are already previously repudiated thrice," followed really by a repudiation, involve only one ; though according to some authorities they constitute three, and according to others have no legal effect at all. This divergence of opinion exists also with regard to the words, "If I pronounce against you an injurious comparison," or "anathema," or "an oath of continence," or "If our marriage is dissolved on my demand on account of redhibitory defects, consider yourself as previously thrice repudiated," at least where these conditions are accomplished. However, a repudiation pronounced as follows, "If I have with you lawful carnal intercourse, you are previously repudiated," is null and void, even though carnal intercourse should take place.

Where a repudiation depends on the will of the wife, it should be declared within a short time, at least when the repudiation has been pronounced while speaking to her ; †but this is not rigorously necessary where the repudiation has been pronounced in the third person, nor where this act depends upon the will of a third party. If the person upon whose will the repudiation depends has really declared his decision, the repudiation has its full legal effect, even though that decision may be contrary to his own wishes ; though according to some jurists it is not in these circumstances mentally accomplished. A repudiation may not depend upon the will of a minor of either sex ; though some jurists admit such a suspensive condition in the case of a minor who has attained the age of discernment. In all cases where a repudiation has been pronounced on condition that either the wife or some third party wishes it, it cannot be retracted before the one or the other has decided. The phrase, "You are repudiated thrice, unless Zaid prefers that it should be only once," is no repudiation if Zaid says he wishes it to be once only ; some, however, admit in these circumstances a single repudiation. *When one has made a repudiation depend upon some act one is about to perform oneself, the fact of having accomplished this act, either without thinking of the consequences, or as the result of some violence, is not sufficient to fulfil the condition. The same principle must be followed where the repudiation depends upon the act of a third party, in all cases where the latter has an interest in the act, and knows what the consequences will be. For if it is an act indifferent to the third party, or if he is ignorant that the repudiation depends upon it, the fact of his accomplishing it without thinking, or as the result of some violence, is enough for the fulfilment of the condition.

Section 11

The words, "You are repudiated," followed by the act of lifting up two or three fingers, do not constitute two or three repudiations respectively, unless such was the intention of the husband who pronounced it; but where, under these circumstances, the husband adds, "so many times," then there are really either two or three repudiations. But where, even in this case, he declares upon oath that he raised the third finger only with the intention of indicating the two others united, the presumption is in his favour, and there are only two repudiations.

When a slave says to his wife, "At my master's death you will be repudiated twice," after which the master declares that the slave in question will be enfranchised at his death, †the master's decease causes the woman to be twice repudiated. These two repudiations, though originally pronounced by a slave, are considered to emanate from a free man, and are consequently revocable. It follows that the couple can remarry without an intermediate husband.

If a husband calls one of his wives and another answers and he says to her, "You are repudiated," believing himself to be speaking to the wife he called, †it is the wife that answers who is repudiated.

The words, "You are repudiated if you eat a pomegranate, and if you eat the half of a pomegranate," result in a wife being twice repudiated if she eats a whole pomegranate.

The law admits an oath as a way of rendering a repudiation conditional, whether the oath consists in an incitement to perform some act, or in its prohibition, or in the confirmation of some piece of news. Thus, upon saying, "You are repudiated if I confirm my words on oath," or "You are repudiated if you have not come out of such and such a house," or "If you have come out of it," or "If the matter is not as I have told you," a repudiation takes effect, by the fact of taking the oath, or by the fulfilment of the other conditions mentioned. When, on the other hand, the second condition consists in a fact about to happen, such as sunrise or the return of the pilgrimage, one cannot lawfully complete the repudiation by an oath, since in that case the first condition is replaced by the second.

If any one inquires from a husband whether he has repudiated his wife and he answers, "yes," it is an admission on his part; though he may afterwards declare that he was speaking of a former repudiation he had since revoked; and if he confirms this subsequent declaration upon oath, he has a presumption in favour of the truth of his words. But where the inquiry is not purely interrogative, but made with the intention of requesting the husband to proceed to a repudiation, the affirmative reply is an explicit manner of repudiation; or, according to some authorities, an implicit one.

Section 12

A condition of eating a piece of bread or a pomegranate is not fulfilled so long as there remains a crumb or a pip. Where a husband and wife eat together some dates and mix the seeds, and the husband says to the wife, "If you don't separate your seeds from mine you are repudiated," and the wife puts each seed aside, the condition of repudiation is not fulfilled and the marriage remains intact, unless the husband wishes her to indicate which seeds were hers. When a woman has a date in her mouth and her husband repudiates her on condition she swallows it, and then changes his mind and makes it depend on her spitting it out, and then changes his mind again and makes the repudiation depend upon her taking the date in the hollow of her hand, and the woman on hearing these words quickly swallows half the date and spits out the other half, the condition is not considered to be fulfilled. When a husband accuses his wife of theft, and says to her, "If you do not admit that my words are true you are repudiated," and she replies, "I did steal," adding, "I did not steal," no repudiation takes place. Where a husband says, "If you do not name the number of pips contained in this pomegranate you are repudiated," the fulfilment of the condition may be avoided by the wife first mentioning a number known to be a minimum, and then continuing by naming all numbers from that one up to what is known to be a maximum. It must be understood of course that it was not the husband's intention to ascertain the number of the pips, for in that case the wife could not escape the dilemma by such an evasive reply. This principle applies also to the evasive answer already cited with reference to a wife accused of theft. Where one says to three of one's wives, "I repudiate her who cannot tell me the number of *rakas* that are obligatory in twenty-four hours," and one of them answers "seventeen," and another "fifteen, that is to say, Friday," and the third "eleven, that is for a traveller," none are repudiated. When one says, "You are repudiated until such and such a time," or "from such a time," the time is due the moment that a single instant of that term is passed. The condition, "If you see so-and-so," or "If you touch him," or "If you accuse him unjustly of the crime of fornication," is fulfilled by the acts mentioned, whether the individual in question is dead or alive. This, however, is not the case with a condition referring, *e.g.* to the act "of giving him a blow," for this condition clearly implies that the individual in question is alive.

Where a wife pronounces against her husband words considered blamable, *e.g.* "O imbecile," or "O ignoble husband," and he replies, "If I am so you are repudiated," the repudiation really has effect if the husband's intention is to punish his wife for her insulting language, even though he may not be imbecile. Where, on the other hand, the husband, by so replying, wishes to make the repudiation really depend on the condition that he is imbecile, the marriage remains intact if he is not. †And the same is the case where the husband has no special intention in saying this. A charge of imbecility implies that the individual in question has not the free disposition of his property; and that of being ignoble means, according to some, that he sets more store by the things of the world than by religion, which is practically the same as saying that with him cupidity has the better of morality and seemliness.

BOOK 38.—RETURN TO CONJUGAL UNION

A **HUSBAND** who has repudiated his wife in a revocable manner has a right to take her back so long as she is still in her period of legal retirement; that is to say, he may retract his words and take his wife back again, without for this purpose effecting a new marriage, provided only that in the mean time the marriage has not become illicit for any other reason. ††When a husband, after pronouncing a revocable repudiation, goes mad, it is for his curator to exercise the right of revocation, whenever he would have been permitted to contract a new marriage for the person legally incapable confided to his care.

A return to conjugal union is accomplished by the words, "I take you back," "I return to you," "I bring you back," †and even the words "render" and "retain" are admitted as explicit in this sense. †On the other hand, the expressions "give in marriage" and "marry" are implicit terms. However, in using the word "render" one should add "to me" or "to marriage with me," otherwise this verb is not sufficient. Moreover, in his second period Shafii rejected the doctrine that a return to conjugal union must be effected in the presence of witnesses; and though the revocation may be enunciated in implicit terms, the law does not permit it to be made dependent upon any condition. A return to conjugal union cannot be effected tacitly, *e.g.* by coition; but one must declare that one takes one's wife back.

A right to return of conjugal union exists only—

1. If a woman has really cohabited with her husband.
2. If the repudiation was not pronounced for a compensation.
3. If the repudiation is not the third.
4. If the period of legal retirement is not yet expired.
5. If cohabitation between the parties has not become prohibited for some other reason.
6. If the wife has not in the mean time abjured Islam.

Where the woman pleads that her period of legal retirement is already expired, the following cases must be distinguished:—

1. Where the period is calculated by months, and the husband

denies that the period is expired, the presumption is in his favour, if he takes an oath.

2. †Where she claims that the period has expired by reason of an accouchement, and it is proved that she has menstrues and has not yet passed the age of child bearing, the presumption is in her favour, if she takes an oath, provided the accouchement has taken place within an admissible time. The shortest duration of a normal pregnancy is six months and two instants from the marriage; but if the pregnancy terminates by an abortion, it is one hundred and twenty days and two instants in a case where the fœtus already has a human form, and eighty days and two instants if the fœtus consists merely of a piece of shapeless flesh.

3. Where she pleads expiry of her period of legal retirement, on the ground that the three periods of purity required are passed, she has a presumption in her favour provided she takes an oath, and provided also that :—

(*a*) A free woman, repudiated during one of her periods of purity does not allege for the three periods together a shorter time than thirty-two days and two instants; nor, if repudiated during her menstrues, a shorter time than forty-seven days and one instant.

(*b*) A slave, repudiated in these circumstances, does not allege shorter times than sixteen days and two instants, or thirty-one days and one instant, respectively.

These rules must be observed both in a case where the alleged expiration is in conformity with a person's ordinary periods, and also where that person usually has shorter or longer periods.

Coition between a husband and wife revocably repudiated does not operate in prolonging the period of return to conjugal union; though the woman must begin a new period of legal retirement from the date of that illicit act. For carnal intercourse with the wife is prohibited during her period of legal retirement; though if the husband has intercourse with her in contravention of this rule, neither the punishment for the crime of fornication, nor any arbitrary punishment, is incurred; unless the misdeed is committed with full knowledge of this. In all cases, however, such cohabitation involves payment of proportional dower, if a return to conjugal union does not ensue; or even, according to our school, if it does.

A repudiation that admits of a return to conjugal union does not prevent a husband pronouncing an oath of continence, an injurious comparison, a new repudiation or an anathema, so long as the time of reconciliation has not expired. The right of succession of either party remains intact during this period.

The law also recognises the following presumptions, provided that the party in whose favour they are established confirms on oath the truth of his words :—

1. In favour of the wife ; if the husband alleges having insisted upon a return to conjugal union before the expiry of the term, though admitting that the period of legal retirement had expired before the time of the proceedings, while the woman denies that the husband exercised his right in time. The parties it is supposed are in agreement as to the date of expiry ; for example, if they agree that the period expired on Friday, but the husband alleges that there was a return to conjugal union on Thursday, while the wife says it was not till Saturday.

2. In favour of the husband ; if, in these circumstances, the parties agree as to the day upon which a return to conjugal union was demanded, but not as to the day of expiry of the period of legal retirement ; for example, if they agree that the husband demanded a return to conjugal union on Friday, alleging that the period expired on Saturday, while the wife says it expired on Thursday.

3. †In favour of the party whose assertion is impugned by an exception ; in a case where the husband maintains the priority of his demand, and the wife that of the expiry of her period of legal retirement, without either giving the exact date. There is a presumption in favour of the wife if she maintains that the time is expired, and the husband pleads in bar that he had already demanded a return to conjugal union ; and a presumption in favour of the husband if he maintains that he demanded a return to conjugal union before expiry of the period of legal retirement, and the wife pleads the illegality of the return, as it was only afterwards that the husband demanded it.

[If the parties are simultaneously cited to the court, so that it is not known which is the defendant, it is the wife who has the presumption in her favour upon taking oath.]

4. In favour of the husband, if he claims to have demanded a return to conjugal union, and the period of legal retirement is not yet expired at time of the hearing. Moreover, in all cases where the law admits a presumption in favour of the wife, she may retract it.

5. In favour of the wife, if the husband, after repudiating her once or twice claims to have had commerce with her during the marriage, and to be able in consequence to use his right of return to conjugal union, while the wife denies the coition, and consequently the right of return. Under these circumstances the husband has implicitly admitted that dower is due in virtue of coition, and if the wife has already taken possession of this dower, he cannot reclaim any part of it on the ground of the woman's denial of coition. On the other hand, if she has not taken possession, the wife can claim only half the dower.

BOOK 39.—OATH OF CONTINENCY

SECTION 1

AN oath of continency is an oath uttered by a husband who can legally repudiate his wife not to have carnal commerce with her, either for an indefinite period, or for some period exceeding three months. In his second period Shafii established the doctrine that this oath need not necessarily be expressed by invoking the name of God or one of his qualities but that it is sufficient to make a declaration, under penalty of repudiating a wife or enfranchising a slave in case of non-fulfilment; or even that it is enough to say, for example, " If I henceforth have any carnal commerce with you, I engage before God to accomplish a prayer, or a fast, or a supererogatory pilgrimage," or " to enfranchise such and such a slave." An oath not to have carnal commerce with a woman with whom one is not bound in the bonds of matrimony is an ordinary oath and not an oath of continency, even where one may subsequently marry the woman.

An oath of continence is not permitted by our school: (1) where the wife is *ratka* or *karna*; or (2) where the husband is emasculated.

The following words, " I shall not have commerce with you for four months, and at the end of that period, by God, I shall not for another four months, and so on," †do not constitute an oath of continence, because the original term does not exceed four months. By virtue of the same principle there can be no doubt that two perfectly distinct oaths of continence are implied in the words, " By God, I shall have no commerce with you for five months, and upon the expiry of that time I shall have none for a year." A man who declares he will abstain from his wife until after some event that will certainly not happen in four months, for instance the descent of Jesus Christ upon earth, utters a perfectly regular oath of continence; but this is not so where there is reason to believe that the event will take place within four months, or where it is not certain that the event will occur at a more distant date. An oath of continence may be equally well enunciated in explicit or in implicit terms. By explicit terms are understood those that imply carnal commerce without any doubt, *e.g.* "introduction of the penis," "coition," "copulation," and in the case of a virgin "deflowering." On the other hand, Shafii, in his second period, considered the following to be implicit terms: "touching," "contact," "cohabitation," "going to see," "covering," "approaching," etc.

Where one says, "If I afterwards cohabit with you, my slave shall be enfranchised," the oath of continence is broken *ipso facto* at the moment of losing in any way the ownership of the slave. The husband who, after pronouncing an injurious comparison against his wife, says to her, "If I cohabit again with you my slave shall be enfranchised in consequence of my injurious comparison," thereby utters a legal oath of continence; and even if he has not really pronounced previously an injurious comparison the court should none the less hold that he has uttered both an injurious comparison and an oath of continence, though perhaps mentally the man had no intention of pronouncing the one or the other. For the court is not concerned with what one thinks, but with what one says. If, however, the husband pronounces the words cited without a previous injurious comparison, and adds, "If I did pronounce an injurious comparison," he does not undergo the consequences of his oath unless such comparison was really uttered. An oath of continence has its full legal effect where one uses the words, "If I still cohabit with you, my other wife so-and-so will be repudiated," and in that case the latter's repudiation is effected *ipso facto* by an ulterior cohabitation with the wife against whom the words were pronounced; while the consequences of the oath cease to exist upon this repudiation.

He who says to his four wives, "By God, I will not cohabit with you any more," has uttered an oath of continence that renders illicit his cohabitation with all four of them, but not his cohabitation in general. Thus if he subsequently cohabits with three of them, he must abstain from the fourth; while the death of one or more of the wives, previous to any subsequent cohabitation, annuls the oath *ipso fdcto*. Where, on the other hand, he uses the words, "I will not cohabit with any of you," this is an oath of continence that at once renders illicit cohabitation with any one of them. *The words, "I will cohabit with you only once until the end of the year," constitute an oath of continence only on condition that more than four months of the year remain after the one cohabitation of which the husband speaks.

Section 2

Where a husband utters an oath of continence, the wife cannot complain of it to the court until the expiry of the term of four months, the period of indulgence beginning from the time the oath was pronounced; and, in the case of a woman revocably repudiated, from the moment the husband demands the return to conjugal union. If the marriage has been consummated the oath of continence is interrupted *ipso facto* by the apostasy of one of the parties during the period of indulgence; and the fact of her returning from her errors before the end of her period of legal retirement, causes another such period to be incurred. On the other hand, temporary causes on the husband's part that prevent coition during marriage, without affecting its validity, do not affect either the length or the period of indulgence. Among these causes are cited fasting, *ihram*, sickness, and madness. Where, on the other hand, these temporary causes of prevention are on the part of the woman, they interrupt the course of the period of indulgence if they are physical, *e.g.* minority or sickness, and a new period begins as soon as the causes in question cease to exist. A few authorities require that the time elapsed before the existence of the cause of prevention should be taken into account; consequently they consider the course of the period of indulgence not as interrupted, but as merely suspended. The legal causes of prevention on the woman's part have no influence upon the duration of the period of indulgence, causes among which should be mentioned menstrues, and supererogatory fasting; †while, by way of exception, the obligatory fasting of the woman has the same effect as a purely physical cause.

An oath of continence is broken by coition during the period of indulgence; and in default of coition during this period, the wife may summons her husband, in order that he may decide either to take her back or repudiate her. Her neglect to do this immediately does not prevent her subsequently exercising this right, so long as the term of the oath has not expired. Taking back the woman at her request is consummated only by a real penetration, not by voluptuous actions of any other kind. Consequently this right to summons her husband does not exist where the woman is unfit for coition from any cause, *e.g.* menstrues or sickness. In case of prevention on the husband's part, the woman must observe the two following distinctions:—

1. If the cause of prevention is purely physical, *e.g.* sickness, all she can insist upon is that her husband should declare himself to be ready to fulfil his conjugal duties as soon as he is capable of doing so.

2. If the cause of prevention arises from some legal provision, *e.g.* *ihram*, the wife, according to our school, can only ask for repudiation.

The wife has no right to summons her husband, if there has been any carnal commerce between them, even where such commerce does not amount to a regular coition. *Where the husband refuses to choose between the two alternative courses open to him, the court should pronounce a repudiation for him, *i.e.* one revocable repudiation, without allowing him a three days' respite. *Coition by order of the court does not excuse the husband from legal expiation for a broken oath.

BOOK 40.—INJURIOUS COMPARISON

SECTION 1

AN injurious comparison may legally be pronounced by any adult sane husband, even by the infidel subject of a Moslem prince, or by an emasculated person. A husband's drunkenness is no obstacle to the validity of an injurious comparison, nor to that of a repudiation.

The formulas by which the comparison may be explicitly announced are as follows:—

1. "You will be for me," or "in regard to me," or "with me," "as the back of my mother."

2. ††"You will be as the back of my mother," and nothing else.

3. "Your body," "your breast," or "your person will be as the breast," or "the body of my mother," or "like all the parts of the body of my mother."

4. *"You will be to me like the hand," "the bosom," or "the chest of my mother;" and even a comparison to the eye of one's mother must be considered to be valid, if the intention is to abuse one's wife; but not if the intention is to say something agreeable to her, or if there be no particular intention.

5. *"Your head," "your back," or "your hand will be to me as the back of my mother."

6. A comparison to one's grandmother by these formulas is also injurious, and our school extends this principle to all relatives within the prohibited degrees, with whom relationship is not accidental, *i.e.* with whom the husband could not be bound in the bonds of matrimony at any period of his life. Thus a nurse or a daughter-in-law are not included among relatives within the prohibited degrees, so far as concerns an injurious comparison. A comparison made either to a strange woman, or to a repudiated wife, or to a sister-in-law, or to one's father, or to a woman against whom one has pronounced an anathema, is null and void.

An injurious comparison may be made conditionally. Consequently the words, "If I pronounce an injurious comparison against my other wife, you also will be to me as the back of my mother," result in the comparison pronounced against the other wife affecting both. Where, on the other hand, instead of speaking of one's wife, one says, "If I pronounce a comparison against so-and-so," *i.e.* a woman with whom one is not bound in the bonds of matrimony, "you," that is one's wife, "will be," etc., the comparison has no consequence as regards either, unless the husband's intention was to make a comparison of his wife depend upon his pronouncing the words of comparison against any other person. It is possible, however, that this conditional comparison may be accomplished later; *i.e.* by marrying the person in question and pronouncing a comparison against her. This rule applies not only to the case where one has spoken of a woman with whom one is not bound in the bonds of matrimony, but also to the case where one says expressly, "So-and-so who is not my wife." However, there are authorities who deny that the rule is applicable to this case; and the following expression, "If I pronounce an injurious comparison against so-and-so, though she is not my wife," is null and void, whatever the circumstances may be.

The words, "You are repudiated like the back of my mother," involve the following consequences, according to the husband's intention:—

1. They constitute merely a repudiation,
   (*a*) if the husband had no definite intention in pronouncing them;
   (*b*) if he intended to repudiate his wife;
   (*c*) if he intended to pronounce merely an injurious comparison;
   (*d*) if he intended as much the one as the other; or
   (*e*) if he intended to pronounce an injurious comparison by the words, "You are repudiated," and a repudiation by the words, "Like the back of my mother."
2. They constitute a repudiation, and, when this is revocable, also an injurious comparison in addition, if the husband intended to repudiate his wife by the words, "You are repudiated," and to pronounce against her an injurious comparison by the words, "Like the back of my mother."

Section 2

After pronouncing an injurious comparison the husband owes an expiation, if he goes back upon his word and takes his wife again before being otherwise separated from her. For such renewal of cohabitation becomes impossible, and the comparison is *ipso facto* annulled, as soon as it is followed by any other sort of separation, *e.g.* death, dissolution of marriage on account of apostasy, or redhibitory defects, repudiation either irrevocable or revocable but not followed by a return to conjugal union, madness, †for the fact of becoming proprietor of one's wife, or of having pronounced an imprecation against her, at least where the accusation of the crime of fornication that led to the imprecation precedes the comparison. If the repudiation is followed by a return to conjugal union, our school considers this act as implying *ipso facto* a renewal of cohabitation, interrupted on account of the injurious comparison; but where the marriage has been dissolved on account of the husband's apostasy, his return to the faith has not the same result according to our school. This return would merely permit the husband to resume the interrupted cohabitation. Expiation, once prescribed, remains obligatory, even where a renewal of cohabitation has been followed by another separation. And the husband must first acquit himself of the expiation as a debt towards God before resuming cohabitation, and even before permitting himself any voluptuous act. [*Such acts are lawful even before expiation.]

An injurious comparison may be pronounced to take effect by a particular time, and in that case the term must be duly observed; though according to one jurist a comparison so limited has the effect of an unlimited comparison; and according to another it is null and void.

†According to the doctrine of most authorities, resumption of cohabitation can only be effected by carnal commerce while the consequences of the comparison are still in force; the mere fact of the woman living with her husband is not enough.

A husband who says to his four wives, "You are all to me as the back of my mother," thereby pronounces an injurious comparison against all four; and if he takes them back as wives, he owes four times the prescribed expiation; though, in his first period, Shafii maintained the opinion that in these circumstances the husband owes only a single expiation. But where the husband, without stopping, pronounces four times against his four wives the words, "You shall be to me as the back of my mother," there are four different comparisons, the first three of which are retracted. Where, on the other hand, he repeats the same words against one of his wives, it is necessary to distinguish :—

1. If the object of the repetition was to confirm his first words, in which case there is but one comparison; and—

2. *If the object was to reiterate them, in which case each repetition involves a new comparison, though each implies the retractation of that immediately preceding it.

BOOK 41.—EXPIATION WITH REGARD TO INJURIOUS COMPARISON

Expiation is possible only where the husband intends to reconcile himself with God ; but it is not rigorously necessary that this intention should specially refer to the injurious comparison.

Expiation, in a case of injurious comparison, consists in the enfranchisement of a slave of either sex, a Moslem, with no physical infirmities that would prevent his working for a master or gaining a living. It is enough then to enfranchise a slave who is a minor, or bald, or lame so long as he is not wholly unable to walk, or blind of one eye, or deaf, or deprived of the sense of smell, or one that has lost his nose, his ears, or his toes ; but it is an insufficient expiation to enfranchise a slave affected with some chronic malady, or one that has lost a foot or a ring-finger, or a little finger, or two other fingers [or a thumb].

For the same reason it is insufficient to enfranchise a decrepit old man, a madman even with some rare intervals of lucidity, or a sick person whose recovery cannot be hoped for. †It would be considered sufficient, however, if the sick slave unexpectedly recovered. A person who owes expiation cannot purchase a slave whose degree of relationship would render enfranchisement obligatory with the object of freeing him by way of expiation ; neither can he by way of expiation bestow full liberty upon a woman enfranchised by reason of maternity, or upon a slave undergoing enfranchisement by contract, at least if the contract is valid. On the other hand, one may lawfully, by way of expiation, bestow full liberty upon a slave enfranchised by a will or conditionally ; though it must be understood that after pronouncing a conditional enfranchisement in favour of one's slave, one may not recur to this idea and enfranchise him under the same condition by way of expiation. There is, however, no objection to making an enfranchisement by way of expiation depend upon some condition. One may also legally enfranchise two slaves for two different expiations, in such a way that each of the expiations consists in the enfranchisement of half of the one slave and half of the other. It is even lawful to enfranchise the halves of two slaves for a single expiation ; †on condition, if the expiator is an insolvent debtor, that the other halves have already been enfranchised.

Expiation cannot consist in an enfranchisement for an indemnity, for this would be a bilateral contract, as much as a repudiation for compensation, or a divorce. However, as a general rule, enfranchisement is perfectly legal where a third party says to the master, "Bestow full freedom, for a thousand pieces of money, upon your slave already enfranchised by reason of maternity," and the master agrees to it. The person in question then owes the sum mentioned; †and this rule is applicable not only to the case of a slave enfranchised by reason of maternity, but also to any other enfranchisement. If the third party uses the words, "Enfranchise the slave for me for so much," the enfranchisement, though effected by the master, would be none the less considered by the law as coming from the speaker who consequently owes the sum mentioned. †This means that the latter is supposed to become the owner of the slave, as soon as the enfranchisement is pronounced by the master, after which the enfranchisement is at his charge.

Where the person owing expiation possesses in full property either a slave who can be enfranchised in this way or money necessary to buy one, and where he is not in actual need of one or the other for himself or his family, for maintenance, clothing, lodging, or furniture, he should enfranchise the slave he possesses or can purchase. But it is never necessary to sell one's immovable property or valuable securities for the purpose of obtaining money to buy a slave for an expiatory enfranchisement, when such sale would bring in no more than is necessary for living. †Nor is it necessary to sell for this purpose the house one lives in, or the slave who is an old servant of many years' service, even though their value may be greater than what may be called strictly necessary. The person owing expiation is not obliged to buy a slave in order to acquit himself of the expiation, if this can be done without a sacrifice on his part. *The solvency of the debtor is ascertained at the moment he should perform the expiation.

A person who is not able to enfranchise a slave by way of expiation should in place of this fast for two consecutive months of the lunar year to expiate his fault; †but the law does not require the intention not to interrupt the fast. If the fast is begun in the middle of a month, the remaining days are taken into account, and also a number of days in the third month equal to the number of days in the first month before the fast began. The continuity of the fast is interrupted if a day is allowed to pass without fasting, unless it has been physically impossible to perform this duty, or one has been ill; this is the doctrine maintained by Shafii in his second period. On the other hand, continuity is not interrupted by ceasing to fast on account of menstruation; or even, according to our school, by an attack of madness.

A person owing expiation being unable to fast, either from decrepitude or sickness, may instead of fasting nourish sixty indigent or poor people. Most authorities, however, do not admit sickness as a cause of exemption, except in the three following cases :—

1. Where one cannot reasonably expect to recover.

2. Where fasting would be particularly painful for the sick person.

3. Where the sick person is afraid of aggravating his malady by fasting, even though the actual malady in itself may not be of a nature to justify a deviation from the law.

The indigent and poor persons may not be infidels, nor Banu Hashim nor Banu el Mottalib ; and the amount of nourishment due to each is a modd of provisions payable at the end of the annual fast. One may not give to the same indigent person a modd a day for sixty days instead of giving on one occasion sixty modds to sixty indigent persons, although the total quantity of modds is the same in the one case and the other. Nor may one give as provisions flour, or *sawik*, or bread, or provisions specially used at breakfast or supper.

BOOK 42.—IMPRECATION

Section 1

An imprecation may be pronounced only where there has previously been an accusation of the crime of fornication, and where this crime cannot be proved in the manner prescribed by law.

This accusation can be made explicitly or implicitly. It is made explicitly by the expressions, "You have rendered yourself guilty of the crime of fornication," "O man," or "O woman, guilty of fornication," or by an accusation of having knowingly introduced the penis into the vagina of a woman with whom commerce is prohibited, or into the podex of a man or of a hermaphrodite. The words, "You withdrew to the mountain," and even "You withdrew," are implicit; †but the expression, "You rendered yourself guilty of the crime of fornication in the mountain," is explicit. The following incriminatory expressions, "O libertine," and "O man of notorious misconduct," pronounced against a man, or "O wicked woman," and "You like deserted spots" uttered against a woman, or to say to one's wife, "You were no longer a virgin at the time of our marriage," imply an accusation of the crime of fornication, unless the person using them declares he had no such intention. In this latter case the law presumes that he is speaking the truth, provided he takes an oath to that effect. The words, "O son of a public woman," or "As for me I never rendered myself guilty of the crime of fornication," constitute insinuations against the person with regard to whom they are pronounced, but not a formal accusation, even if pronounced with that intention. The words, "I have had prohibited carnal commerce with you," constitute both a confession and an accusation of the crime of fornication. Where a husband says to his wife, "O woman, guilty of the crime of fornication," and she replies, "I never committed fornication except with you," or "You are more guilty than I," there is on the part of the husband an explicit, and on the part of the wife an implicit accusation. Where, on the other hand, the reply is, "It is true I committed the crime of fornication, but you were more guilty in the matter than I," there is a confession on the wife's part combined with an explicit accusation on the husband's.

The expressions, "Your vagina," or "Your penis has committed the crime of fornication," constitute an accusation of this crime; and it is the same where the speaker, instead of naming the genital parts, says, "your hand," or "your eye;" except that our school considers these latter expressions as implicit. Our school also considers as implicit the phrases, "You are not mine," or "You are not my son," spoken against one's child; but the accusation, "You are not the son of so-and-so," pronounced against the child of another is explicit, unless it relates to a child whose father has already disavowed it by a previous imprecation.

An accusation of the crime of fornication constitutes, when its truth cannot be proved in the manner prescribed by law, the crime of defamation. The defamer must suffer definitely prescribed corporal punishment, if the accusation is made against any one who is *mohsan;* otherwise he incurs only an arbitrary correction. By *mohsan* is understood any adult sane free Moslem man or woman abstaining from any carnal commerce that would render him liable to the prescribed penalty for fornication. Our rite regards as incompatible with such abstinence an act of cohabitation with a slave to whom one is related within the prohibited degrees; †but this incompatibility must not be extended to commerce with one's wife during her period of legal retirement, that results from a cohabitation due to error, nor to that with a slave belonging to one's son, nor to that with a woman one has married without the assistance of a guardian. If a person unlawfully accused of the crime of fornication commits this crime later, there is no ground for accusing and punishing as a defamer the person who accused him; but no such impunity results from the former losing his quality of *mohsan* in some other way, *e.g.* by apostasy. When one has once indulged in forbidden carnal commerce, one may never again in all one's life become *mohsan.* The right to demand the punishment of a person guilty of defamation passes to the heirs of an injured party; but this right lapses upon forgiveness. †Each inheritor may exercise this right without the concurrence of the others; and forgiveness by one transfers his right to the others.

Section 2

A husband may with impunity accuse his wife of the crime of fornication, even though he may be unable to furnish legal proof, when he knows for certain she has been guilty of it, or when he has grave and well-founded suspicions upon the subject. Among these may be included the fact of its being of public notoriety that the woman is guilty of the crime, and that so-and-so is her accomplice, and that the guilty pair were surprised together in a desert place.

If a woman gives birth to a child of whom her husband knows for certain he is not the father, he should disavow it, if he does not want it to be considered his. The law admits such disavowal only where—

1. The husband has had no carnal intercourse with his wife during the whole period of the marriage.

2. The accouchement takes place less than six months after their first coition, or more than four years after the last.

A child born between the limits of six months and four years after the first coition may only be disavowed upon the double condition that not only a menstruation subsequent to the last coition must prove that the woman cannot have been rendered pregnant by her husband, †but also that the child is born more than six months after this purificatory menstruation. ††A husband may never base his disavowal upon an assertion that during copulation he withdrew soon enough not to fecundate his wife. If the crime of fornication, though proved, took place at a moment that admits of the child being either that of the husband or of the woman's accomplice, the law declares illegal, not only the disavowal, ††but also the accusation of the crime of fornication, and the imprecation.

Section 3

An imprecation consists in the solemn declaration four times repeated, "God is my witness that I am sincere in accusing this my wife of the crime of fornication." If this accusation is not pronounced in presence of the accused, the name and descent must be indicated so as to leave no uncertainty as to the person intended. The husband must also invoke upon himself "the malediction of God," if he has brought the accusation in bad faith. If the imprecation is to be accompanied by the disavowal of a child the husband should mention it at once, adding to each enunciation of the formula, "And in asserting that the child to which she has just given birth," or "this child," "is an illegitimate child, of whom I am not the father." The woman on her side may rebut the accusation by repeating four times, "God is my witness that my husband brings this accusation in bad faith," and after that invoking "the wrath of God" upon herself, if her husband is sincere in his accusation. †It is rigorously necessary to use these particular words; an oath may not be lawfully substituted for the phrase, "God is my witness," nor may the words "malediction" and "wrath" be interchanged, †or inserted before the phrase, "God is my witness." It is also rigorously necessary that the imprecation should take place only upon an order of the court, which must contain the formula to be pronounced, with the legal consequences that result from its pronouncement. The woman may not pronounce her formula before the husband has finished his. A mute may choose between signs clearly indicating the meaning, and its reduction to writing. The formula may also be pronounced in a language other than Arabic; except in the case of persons who can speak Arabic even though it may not be their mother tongue.

An imprecation should be rendered more solemn—

1. By the choice of the time when it is pronounced, *i.e.* Friday, at the close of afternoon prayer.

2. By the choice of the place where it is pronounced, *i.e.* the most noteworthy spot in the town. Thus at Mecca an imprecation is uttered between the corner of the Kaba containing the "black stone," and the *Makam Ibrahim;* at Medina close to the pulpit in the sacred Mosque; at Jerusalem near the *Sakhra;* and in other cities near the pulpit in the great mosque. It is understood of course that a woman who is impure by reason of menstruation must pronounce her formula at the door of the building. Infidel subjects of a Moslem prince pronounce the imprecation in their churches or synagogues, and a fire-worshipper may even pronounce it in his temple; but an idolator may not lawfully pronounce it in a temple of idols.

3. By the number of persons present; that is to say that an imprecation must be pronounced in the presence of at least four persons.

These three rules, however, are considered by our school as being merely precepts of the Sonna, and consequently not of rigorous observance. The Sonna also prescribes that the court should give the interested parties such advice as may seem expedient, especially when they are about to pronounce the decisive fifth phrase. The Sonna also requires that an imprecation should be uttered standing.

Though in general a husband cannot pronounce an imprecation unless he is legally capable of repudiating his wife, the act is still valid :—

1. If the husband, apostatised after cohabitation with his wife, accuses her of the crime of fornication, but returns to the faith after the end of her period of legal retirement, and then pronounces an imprecation.

2. If the husband, in the same circumstances, pronounces an imprecation immediately after the accusation, and subsequently returns to the faith, provided always that it is before the expiration of the period of legal retirement.

Where, on the other hand, the husband does not repent from his errors until after the expiration of the period of legal retirement, the fact that the marriage is *ipso facto* dissolved is an obstacle to the imprecation.

An imprecation pronounced by a husband has the following consequences :—

1. The parties are separated, and marriage between them is for ever forbidden, even though the husband subsequently retracts his accusations.

2. The husband is not punishable as a defamer, though unable to furnish the testimony legally required to prove his wife's crime.

3. The wife is punishable for the crime of fornication, unless she in her turn pronounces the imprecation in the terms already mentioned.

4. The child whose paternity is disavowed by the husband's imprecation is not recognised as his by law.

The disavowal is unnecessary, and the child *ipso facto* illegitimate if not only is the husband certain he is not its father, but this is manifest to every one by the nature of things ; for instance, if the mother gives birth to it within six months from the marriage contract, or if the mother was repudiated immediately after the contract, in both cases before the marriage was consummated, or if the marriage was effected when one of the parties was in the East and the other in the West. On the other hand, the child's death does not extinguish the right of disavowal Shafii maintained, in his second period, that a disavowal should take place after no long interval, without prejudice, however, to its being effected at any time, on alleging some valid excuse for the delay. A husband may at his choice disavow a child of which his wife is pregnant either before or after her lying-in ; and if he excuses his delay in pronouncing his disavowal on the ground that the birth was concealed from him, the presumption is in his favour upon his taking an oath. This presumption, however, only exists where the husband was absent, or if present where the length of the delay is not incompatible with his ignorance. A husband to whom is spoken the following compliment, " May you have much pleasure from your child," or " God grant your son become a good man," and who replies, " Amen," or " Yes," may not subsequently disavow it ; but if, instead of making use of an expression implying avowal, the husband replies, " May God reward you," or " May God bless you," he is free afterwards to pronounce a disavowal. The possibility of furnishing legal proof of the crime of fornication is no obstacle to a husband's pronouncing an imprecation. And the woman's reply to her husband's imprecation according to the above-mentioned formula results in her not being liable to the definitely prescribed penalty for the crime of fornication, unless the husband produces the proof required by law.

Section 4

A husband may pronounce an imprecation not only in order to enjoy all the legal advantages which result from it; but also with one of the following special intentions:—

1. In order to disavow a child, even though his wife may have already pardoned his defamation, and the marriage been dissolved in some other manner.

2. In order to escape the definitely prescribed penalty for defamation, even though the marriage may have been already dissolved in some other manner, and there is no child to disavow.

3. In order to escape a discretional punishment for defamation, where particular circumstances rendered him not liable to the definitely prescribed penalty.

In any case an imprecation is never an excuse where it is a matter of defamation contrary to common-sense and manifestly false; and in a case of this sort the court is justified in inflicting upon the defamer a discretional punishment for his moral amelioration. Among such groundless defamations may be mentioned that of a girl still a minor and incapable of coition.

An imprecation cannot take place:—

1. If the woman is not pregnant as a result of the crime of which her husband accuses her, and also—

(*a*) She pardons the defamation pronounced.

(*b*) The husband can furnish the proof required by law that she has been guilty of the crime of fornication.

(*c*) The wife's crime is proved by her own avowal.

2. If the woman renounces her right to proceed against her husband before the court.

3. If the woman goes mad in consequence of the defamation pronounced against her.

On the other hand, an imprecation is admissible, even where the wife has been irrevocably repudiated, or where the marriage has been dissolved by her death, in a case where her husband accuses her of the crime of fornication, without being able to furnish legal proof of it, and the defamation is pronounced in general or with reference to a fact subsequent to the dissolution of the marriage, always on condition that there is a child which the husband is obliged to disavow if he does not wish to be considered its father. But an imprecation can never be pronounced after the irrevocable dissolution of a marriage, on account of a fact that took place before the marriage, †whether there is or is not a child to disavow. In all cases the husband must begin by accusing his wife of the crime of fornication before having recourse to an imprecation; and the law does not permit the husband to disavow one of two twin children and not the other; he must either disavow both or accept their joint paternity without any reservation.

BOOK 43.—PERIOD OF LEGAL RETIREMENT

Section 1

A woman's legal retirement after the dissolution of her marriage is of two categories, the first being that prescribed in consequence of a separation *inter vivos*, whether by repudiation or by any other method of dissolution of marriage. This kind of legal retirement need not be observed except when there has been carnal commerce between the parties; for where it is proved that the womb is intact retirement is not necessary. This, at any rate, was the doctrine maintained by Shafii during his Egyptian period.

The legal retirement of a free woman who has menstrues and regular periods of purity, is composed of three periods of purity; but it is understood that a woman separated in one of her periods of purity concludes her retirement at the beginning of the third menstruation, while one separated during one of her menstruations becomes free only upon the commencement of the fourth, including that during which she was repudiated. One authority insists that twenty-four hours should elapse before it can be said that menstruation has definitely commenced; and there is disagreement on the point whether a woman, who, upon the dissolution of her marriage, has not yet had menstrues but begins to experience them shortly afterwards, should or should not be considered as separated during a period of purity. This controversy derives from the other one as to whether the expression, "period of purity," signifies merely a transition from purity to menstruation or whether it implies an interval of purity between two menstruations. *In this latter controversy the second of these two views is to be preferred. The legal retirement of a woman whose hæmorrhages are prolonged beyond the term of her menstrues is fixed so as to take into consideration her habitual periods of purity and menstruation; but a woman who has irregular fluxes should in all cases observe a legal retirement of three months, or, according to some authorities, a retirement lasting for three months after menstruation has ceased to be manifested. A woman enfranchised by reason of maternity, a woman undergoing enfranchisement by contract, and in general all slave women, should observe a retirement of two periods of purity. *If they become completely enfranchised during their retirement, they should terminate it, in the case of a revocable repudiation, as if they had been free since the separation; but they should continue their retirement as if they were still slaves in the case of an irrevocable repudiation or any other kind of separation which, like divorce, has the same consequences as an irrevocable repudiation.

A free woman who has no menstrues, or has passed the age for them, should observe a retirement of three months, and, if the repudiation took place in the middle of a month, her retirement is not completed until after the appearance of two new moons plus the number of days wanting to complete thirty in the first month; all without prejudice to her obligation to observe the prescribed periods of purity, should she before the end of this time become subject to menstruation. A slave woman, including a woman enfranchised by reason of maternity, and one undergoing enfranchisement by contract, should, under these circumstances, observe a retirement for one month and a half, when they have no menstrues or have them no longer; though one authority prescribes them a retirement of two months, and another one of three. A woman whose menstrues are interrupted by some cause, such as suckling or sickness, should defer her retirement for three months until menstruation returns, or it appears evident that it will not do so; in his second period Shafii even declared this rule to be applicable to cases where the interruption is not due to any known cause. In his first period our Imam maintained that a woman in such a case, where the cause is not known, should begin by waiting nine months to see whether menstruation is going to return, and after that accomplish the ordinary three months' retirement.

In his second period Shafii also expressed the opinion that if the woman has reasons to think menstruation will not return, and consequently observes a retirement of three months, and the menstruation does return before the expiry of the three months, she should complete her retirement counting by periods of purity. *This is also what she should do, even though menstruation does not reappear until after the expiry of the three months, if she has not meanwhile become engaged in the bonds of another marriage; otherwise she is not obliged to observe a new period of retirement. As to whether a woman has good reason to think her menstruation will not return, this is a question which should be decided according to information obtained in each particular case from previous instances of near relatives both on the father's and mother's side; though, according to one authority, recourse may be had to observations with regard to women in general. [*I recommend this latter doctrine.]

Section 2

The legal retirement of a woman who is pregnant at the moment of separation terminates upon her accouchement, on the double condition that—

1. The child's father is the woman's lawful husband ; whether the paternity is established by law, or whether it can merely be considered possible, *e.g.* in case of disavowal.

2. The accouchement is terminated. This rule applies equally to "twins," though in this case the retirement expires only upon the birth of the last born. By "twins" are understood children born at a less interval than six months. The birth of a still-born child counts as an ordinary accouchement ; but not an abortion, at least where the fœtus consists merely in a lump of flesh without human form. On the other hand, if the fœtus already has a human form, though distinguishable only by a mid-wife, the abortion counts as an ordinary accouchement. Our school goes even further and allows that a retirement is terminated by an abortion, where the fœtus is merely a lump of flesh, but the midwives say it contains a principle of vitality.

A woman who begins by counting her retirement by periods of purity or by months, and perceives after its termination that she is pregnant, should still observe her period of retirement as if she had known of her pregnancy at the moment of the separation ; and even if she merely suspect her pregnancy without being sure of it, she cannot remarry before her suspicions are either dissipated or realised. Where, on the contrary, her suspicions arise only after the end of periods of purity or of months that constituted her period of legal retirement, the two following cases must be distinguished :—

1. If she has remarried, the second marriage remains intact, and the child has for father the new husband, unless born within six months after the contract.

2. If she has not remarried she should wait until her suspicions are dissipated or realised ; though a new marriage effected in contravention of this rule is not considered null by our school, unless the new husband has acted knowingly.

A child born four years after the irrevocable separation of the parties has the husband for father, unless the woman has remarried under the circumstances we have described ; but a child born later than this period is always illegitimate. In the case of a revocable repudiation, this period is counted from the moment of repudiation ; though, according to one authority, it should be calculated from the moment the period of legal retirement has expired. When a separated woman remarries after the end of her period of legal retirement, without suspecting her pregnancy, the fact that she has an accouchement within six months from the dissolution of the first marriage is enough to nullify the second ; but a child born later than this has for father the second husband.

A new marriage effected before the end of the period of legal retirement is illegal, and a child born during this marriage has for father the former husband, at least where the accouchement takes place within a period that renders this paternity alone admissible. The woman in question has then, by the fact of the accouchement, terminated the period of legal retirement necessary upon her separation from her former husband ; but after this must still observe an ordinary period of legal retirement for having cohabited with the second. On the other hand, if the time of the accouchement demonstrates the paternity of the second father the latter is regarded as the child's father, in spite of the illegality of the second marriage ; while, if the time of the accouchement admits equally well of the paternity of the one husband and of the other, the matter should be submitted to a physiognomist who should pronounce after examining the child, and whose decision carries with it the same consequences as if the paternity had been indicated by the time of the accouchement.

Section 3

Where a woman has to observe two periods of legal retirement of the same nature, resulting from her cohabitation with the same individual, one of the periods is included in the other. This is what takes place, for instance where a husband, after repudiating his wife revocably, indulges in coition with her before the expiration of her period. In this case it makes no difference—

1. Whether the retirement is calculated by periods of purity, or by months.
2. Whether coition has taken place knowingly or not.

In any case the final period of legal retirement begins from the last act of coition and involves *ipso facto* what remained to be accomplished of the retirement rendered necessary by the previous repudiation. And it is the same where the two periods of legal retirement are of a different kind ; for example, if one is calculated by periods of purity and the other is terminated by an accouchement. Then the accouchement determines the end of the final period of retirement, and the husband may exercise his right of return to conjugal union, until the accouchement has taken place. A small number of authorities do not admit this extension of the right of return to conjugal union where the pregnancy is the consequence of coition subsequent to the repudiation.

Where it is not the same individual whose successive cohabitation has rendered the two periods of legal retirement obligatory, the one is not included in the other. This happens, for instance—

1. Where a woman, repudiated by her husband, or who has committed cohabitation by error, indulges, before the expiration of her period of legal retirement, in coition with another whom she supposes to be her new husband, or who really is so but by virtue of an illegal marriage.

2. Where a woman who perceives that she has cohabited by error and who observes a legal period of retirement in consequence, is repudiated by her real husband before the expiration of that period.

When, in any of these cases, the woman is pregnant, she should always begin by observing the period of retirement rendered necessary by her pregnancy; and after her accouchement, she should observe that rendered necessary by the other cohabitation. If she is not pregnant, two cases must be distinguished.

1. The case mentioned above where the repudiation has priority over the coition committed by error. The woman should then first observe the legal period of retirement for repudiation, and afterwards begin the other period, all without prejudice to the right of return to conjugal union. If the husband exercises this right, the retirement for the repudiation ceases at the same time; but the woman should still accomplish the retirement on account of her coition with her supposed husband, before cohabiting with her true husband.

2. The case where the coition by error has the priority. In this case the retirement on account of the repudiation is first accomplished; though some authorities accord priority to the retirement on account of the coition by error.

Section 4

†Where a husband, after repudiating his wife irrevocably, continues to live with her during her period of legal retirement, counted either by periods of purity or by months, without, however, there being any carnal commerce between the parties, the retirement is carried out all the same, as if the separation had been complete. †Where, on the other hand, in these circumstances the repudiation is revocable, the retirement is not carried out until the parties cease to live together, though the right to return to conjugal union exists only during the prescribed periods of purity or months.

[The repudiation remains revocable as long as the period of legal retirement has not expired; and the fact of a woman living with any other than her husband causes a retirement rendered necessary by repudiation to terminate *ipso facto*.]

Where a woman who has been repudiated revocably remarries during her period of legal retirement, believing she may lawfully do so, the retirement is interrupted from the consummation of the new marriage; or, according to one authority, from the contract—an opinion which some elevate to the rank of a doctrine. So that, if the former husband exercises his right of return to conjugal union, and afterwards repudiates his wife a second time, she must begin her retirement again on account of the former repudiation. According, however, to the opinion of Shafii in his first period, the retirement is only suspended by the new marriage, so that the woman in these circumstances need only finish what is left over, provided that the return to the former union is not followed by coition. Where in these same circumstances the woman is rendered pregnant by her second husband and afterwards taken back by the first, the period of legal retirement does not terminate before the accouchement; and if she is again repudiated by her first husband, she must begin a new period of retirement. According to a small number of authorities there is no need to recommence a new period of legal retirement after the accouchement, unless there has been subsequent cohabitation with the first husband. Finally, where the first husband has successively married again and repudiated the woman from whom he was previously divorced, her final period of legal retirement commences from the repudiation; and this retirement includes that rendered necessary by the divorce.

Section 5

The second kind of legal retirement is that prescribed for a woman whose marriage is dissolved by the death of her husband. It admits of the following distinctions:—

1. Where the widow is not pregnant. In this case the period of legal retirement lasts for four months and ten days and nights for a free woman, and half of this time for a slave; it matters little whether the marriage has been consummated or not. A widow who at the moment of her husband's decease was already repudiated revocably should accomplish her retirement as if her husband had died while the marriage was still intact; but the widow who has been repudiated irrevocably should continue the retirement begun in consequence of the repudiation.

2. Where the widow is pregnant. She should then observe the legal period of retirement until after her accouchement, subject to the reservations already mentioned with regard to a pregnant woman whose marriage has been dissolved *inter vivos*. Consequently, a pregnant widow whose husband was a minor should observe a retirement as if she were not pregnant.

When a husband leaves two widows, of which one has been repudiated but it is not indicated which, they should both accomplish the legal period of retirement for widows that are not pregnant, supposing that there has been no consummation of their marriages. Where there has been consummation but the widows are not pregnant they need only observe the ordinary retirement of widows that are not pregnant, if the repudiation was revocable ; but if in these circumstances the revocation was irrevocable, then both must observe either the ordinary retirement of widows that are not pregnant or that of three periods of purity, whichever be the longer. It must be remembered that the legal retirement of widows commences from the husband's death, but periods of purity are calculated from the repudiation.

A wife whose husband is absent and who has heard no news of him may not contract another union unless certain that he is dead or that he has repudiated her. In his first period Shafii considered such a woman as able to remarry after her husband has been absent for four years and she has then observed a widow's retirement ; but during his stay in Egypt our Imam adopted the doctrine that even a judicial authorisation after four years' absence and a period of retirement are insufficient to render a remarriage unattackable. †But he conceded, during his second period, that a marriage effected in contravention of this rule is quite legal if it subsequently appears that the former husband was dead before its celebration.

A widow should be in mourning for her deceased husband during her period of legal retirement, but a woman revocably repudiated need not do so upon the dissolution of the marriage. On the other hand, this mourning is commendable in the case of a woman irrevocably separated *inter vivos;* one authority even maintains that it is *de rigueur*. A woman's mourning consists firstly in her abstaining from personal adornment in bright-coloured clothing even of a coarse material ; although some jurists permit her to wear material of which the threads are dyed first and woven afterwards, whatever the colour may be. A woman in mourning may legally wear all kinds of cloth, black or white, cotton, wool, linen, or silk. Bright coloured stuff is not forbidden if not worn for adornment. Secondly, a woman in mourning must wear no ornaments of gold or silver †or pearl. She must abstain from perfumes on the body, on the clothes, in food or in eye-wash, she must not paint her eyes with antimony, except in case of necessity, *e.g.* if she is blear-eyed; nor must she use white-lead nor unguents nor henna, etc. On the other hand, there is no objection to her making use of an ornamented bed or other objects, or to taking care of her person by washing her head, cutting her nails, or removing the dirt from her skin or her clothes.

[She is also permitted to do her hair and go to the bath, provided this is not a pretext for some unlawful outgoing. A woman who does not observe mourning regarded as an obligatory act commits a sin, and should terminate her period of legal retirement in the way to be explained in the next section when speaking of a woman who quits her husband's house during her period of legal retirement. A woman who hears of her husband's death or her repudiation after her period of retirement is terminated, need not observe any further mourning. A woman may wear mourning not only for her husband but also for other near male relatives or for her master; but this mourning may not exceed three days.]

Section 6

A woman who has been repudiated, even irrevocably, may insist upon her husband's giving her a suitable home during her period of legal retirement, unless she is rebellious to marital authority. *This right is accorded also to the widow, and, according to our school, to the wife whose marriage has been dissolved by reason of redhibitory defects, etc. The woman must spend her period of legal retirement in the house or in the apartment in which she was living at the moment of separation, and no one has a right to oblige her to remove elsewhere. Neither has she on her side the right to leave the house of her own accord.

[She may go out in the day-time, if the retirement is due to her husband's decease or to an irrevocable repudiation, provided these outgoings are for some lawful object, *e.g.* to buy provisions, thread, etc. She may even go out of an evening to visit one of her neighbours in order to spin together, or have a talk, etc.; but she must return home to sleep. She has the right to remove only if she is afraid the house is going to fall down, or, in case of a flood, or if her life is in danger, or her neighbours are troublesome, or even if her presence is very disagreeable to them.]

A removal, authorised by the husband, results in the woman being obliged to accomplish her period of retirement in the house he assigns her, at least where the cause of the retirement already existed at the time of the removal. This is Shafii's personal opinion. On the other hand, she should return to the house originally occupied to accomplish

.er retirement there if she has removed without authorisation, or if the .uthorisation was given before the cause of the retirement existed, or fter the removal took place. An authorisation given to a wife to take ıp her residence in another town has the same legal consequences as one given her to remove; but if the authorisation to remove elsewhere referred only to a journey undertaken either to perform the pilgrimage or for commerce, and the cause of retirement occurred on the way, the woman may either return to her domicile and accomplish her retirement there, or continue her journey while observing the retirement. In the atter case, however, she must, after attaining the object of her journey and finishing her business, return home and remain in retirement for the number of days still to be observed. When a woman goes to a house other than her domicile, and her husband repudiates her on the ground that the removal was unauthorised, there is a legal presumption in favour of the husband's assertion, provided he takes an oath. Our school admits a similar presumption in the husband's favour where the woman maintains that he authorised her to remove, while he alleges that he merely allowed her to go out on some business. The dwellings of nomads, and even their tents, are subject to the same law as fixed abodes.

When the husband owns a house in which his wife can suitably accomplish her period of legal retirement, he should assign it to her for that purpose, and cannot sell it, even by a fixed date, unless his wife calculates her period of retirement by months, and consequently he knows the exact date by which the house will be again at his disposal. In this latter case a sale by a certain date is permitted, in the same way as the sale of a house rented to a third party; only a few authorities consider such a sale as absolutely null under any circumstances. If a husband allots for the legal retirement of his wife a house lent him by another person, the woman should accept it; but if the lender asks for it back before the end of the period of legal retirement, and will not lend it any longer, even for a rent, the husband should allot his wife another house. The question of a house rented by the husband, where the lease expires before the end of the retirement, must be decided in accordance with the same principles. If the wife consents to accomplish her retirement in a house belonging to her, she may insist upon the husband paying her a rent for the time she is in it with that object. If the conjugal domicile is of great value, the husband may assign another for his wife's retirement, provided it is a suitable one. On her side the woman may refuse to spend her retirement in any house, even if it be the conjugal domicile, if it is not a suitable house for her to live in.

A husband has no right to remain in the house where his wife is in retirement, nor even to enter it, unless with her consent, or if it is a house inhabited by her in common with—

1. One of her own relatives within the prohibited degrees, who has attained the age of discernment ; or

2. One of his female relatives within the prohibited degrees, who has attained the age of discernment ; or

3. Another wife of her husband, or his female slave.

A husband may even lodge his wife against her will in an apartment separated from the other parts of the house where he lodges another wife, at least, if the wife in retirement has with her some relative within the prohibited degrees, or if it is an apartment with separate kitchen and latrines. But in this case it is commendable that the doors between these apartments should be locked, and that there should be no other means of communication. An upper storey assigned for a wife's legal retirement is to be regarded in the same way, with reference to the lower storey, as an apartment separated from the rest of a house.

BOOK 44.—PERIOD OF WAITING OF A SLAVE

A WAITING for purification is obligatory in the two following cases :—

1. A man who becomes the owner of a female slave by purchase, succession, donation, right of booty, redhibition, judicial oath, cancellation by agreement, may not lawfully cohabit with her by virtue of right of ownership until she has accomplished her days of waiting, whether she be a virgin or not. This period of waiting must be observed even though the seller abstained from cohabiting with her for a sufficient period, or she was obtained from a minor, or a woman, or any other person incapable of coition. This period of waiting is also *de rigueur* where a female slave undergoing emancipation by contract is unable to fulfil the engagement entered into by her with her master, and is consequently reduced to slavery ; †and also where a female slave after abjuring Islam repents of her errors and so becomes again her master's property. On the other hand, the period of waiting is not observed if the right of cohabitation has been suspended by some accidental circumstance, *e.g.* fasting, religious retirement, or *ihram ;* though as to this last circumstance authorities are not agreed. Waiting is commendable where one purchases a slave with whom one is already engaged in the bonds of matrimony ; some jurists even declare it to be obligatory in this case ; but it is not necessary in a case where one purchases a slave already married or observing her period of legal retirement, as then cohabitation with her by virtue of ownership would be quite illicit. *But an obligation to observe a period of waiting revives at the dissolution of the marriage or the end of the period of retirement.

2. A female slave who has cohabited with her master, or a woman enfranchised by reason of maternity, may not marry until after observing a period of waiting from the moment when they cease to be obliged to share their master's bed, whether he has enfranchised them unrestrictedly or they have obtained their liberty upon his decease. †A woman enfranchised by reason of maternity should observe a period of waiting even where her master, freeing her unrestrictedly or dying, has not cohabited with her for a sufficient time.

[A female slave who after sharing her master's bed is freed by him and left untouched during her period of waiting, need not observe any further period of waiting, but may be at once given in marriage, as her condition offers no resemblance to that of a married slave.]

One may not give in marriage either a female slave with whom one has cohabited, nor one enfranchised by reason of maternity, until they have observed the prescribed period of waiting; †but if the master himself wishes to marry his female slave enfranchised by reason of maternity, he may do so at once. Nor is there any need for waiting where a slave enfranchised by reason of maternity, after having been given in marriage to another, obtains her full liberty, either by simple enfranchisement by her master, or by his death, for cohabitation with a slave so emancipated was already forbidden him.

The period of waiting for a female slave having ordinary menstruation is composed of a single period of purity, *i.e.* it terminates after a single regular menstruation. This at least was maintained by Shafii in his second period. As to a slave whose period of legal retirement is calculated by months the period of waiting consists of a single month; or, according to one authority, of three months; while a pregnant woman, reduced to slavery in war, and a pregnant slave with whom her master has ceased to cohabit, should observe a period of waiting until the accouchement. As to a purchased slave, pregnant by marriage, we have already found that she need not observe the ordinary period of waiting until after the dissolution of the marriage.

[†An accouchement resulting from the crime of fornication has the same consequence as one resulting from lawful cohabitation.]

If one becomes owner of a female slave whose period of waiting has expired between the date of the conveyance and the taking of possession, it may be taken into consideration where the ownership is acquired by inheritance †or purchase, but not in the case of a gift. Where one purchases a slave with whom cohabitation is forbidden on some personal account, *e.g.* if she be a fire-worshipper, it is not enough that she has her menstrues after her acquisition, nor that the cause of prevention ceases, *e.g.* by her conversion; she must observe her period of waiting before one may cohabit with her.

The period of waiting results in rendering unlawful any corporal enjoyment of the master with the slave in question; but a woman reduced to slavery in war, though she must abstain from coition with her new master, may permit herself other voluptuous acts, though some authorities maintain that her condition is identical with that of other slaves. Moreover, a simple declaration by a female slave that she has had her menstrues is sufficient to establish a presumption in favour of the truth of her words; a similar presumption exists in the master's favour if, after the slave refuses to give herself to him, he asserts that she has already told him her menstruation is over, and her period of waiting therefore terminated.

A female slave is not considered to have cohabited with her master in a legal sense unless coition has really taken place; and the child born of this cohabitation has the master for his father, provided the accouchement takes place at a time admitting of such paternity. Our school, however, allows the master a right to disavow the child, while admitting the coition, if he can allege in favour of his statement the fact that after coition the slave observed her period of waiting; but if in this case the slave denies the period of waiting the master must assert upon oath that the child is not his. Some jurists even insist that the master must also allege the facts from which it can be concluded that the period of waiting really took place. ††There is no need for the master's oath where he denies cohabiting with his slave who maintains her enfranchisement by reason of maternity, for she then has no presumption in her favour, even if the fact of the accouchement is proved.

BOOK 45.—RELATIONSHIP BY FOSTERAGE

SECTION 1

RELATIONSHIP by fosterage exists where a child has taken the breast of a living woman who has at least completed her ninth year, or even if it has received as nourishment †either milk extracted from the breasts of a woman afterwards deceased, or a woman's milk curdled or skimmed, or mixed with some other liquid *in whatever proportion and whether it is all or only partly drunk—this, at least, is the opinion of some authorities. According to our school relationship by fosterage is established not only by the fact of suckling, but also by the introduction of milk into a child's body by the mouth or by the nose ; *but there is no such relationship where the introduction is effected by means of a washing. The law requires, moreover, as conditions essential to the establishment of relationship by fosterage that the nursling is alive at the moment of taking the milk, that it is not yet two years old, and that it has taken or sucked the milk at least five times. Custom must determine what is meant by "times" in this respect, but in any case a nursling takes milk as many times as it ceases to suck, except where it leaves the breast out of caprice to begin again immediately afterwards, or leaves one breast to take the other. When one has five times given a nursling milk at one night from its nurse's breast, or *vice versâ*, it is considered to have sucked only once ; though according to one authority, it has then sucked the five required times. In cases where it is doubtful whether the child has or has not sucked five times, and in cases where it is doubtful whether it has done so before it is two years old, there is no relationship by fosterage. A single jurist is of the contrary opinion where there is a doubt as to the age ; and this opinion is even considered by others as an admitted doctrine.

A nurse is her nursling's foster-mother ; the man who has rendered her pregnant and is consequently the cause of the milk is regarded as its foster-father ; and the prohibition extends not only to the nursling but also to its progeny. †One is even considered a foster-father where one possesses either five slaves enfranchised by reason of maternity or four wives and one such slave, and the nursling has taken the breast of each but once. Marriage with any of these five persons is for ever forbidden to the nursling as they have all cohabited with his foster-father. *This is why no relationship by fosterage would exist in the case supposed if it were a question not of slaves enfranchised by reason of maternity but daughters or married sisters of the man in question. The ancestors of the nurse on either side become the nursling's ancestors by fosterage, and the nurse's children its foster brothers and sisters, without distinction between natural ancestors and children and those that are so by fosterage Similarly the nurse's brothers and sisters are the nursling's maternal uncles and aunts by fosterage, and the father of the man who is the cause of the milk its foster grandfather, his brother its paternal uncle by fosterage, and so on.

A woman's milk is held *ipso facto* to be caused by the father of the child to which she gives birth, whether she is rendered pregnant by marriage or by error under the belief that cohabitation is lawful; but not if the pregnancy is the consequence of an act of criminal fornication. The disavowal of a child implies a disavowal of the mother's milk. In the case where a married woman has by error had carnal commerce with another than her husband, and even in the case where a woman has cohabited by error with two different husbands, the milk is considered to be caused by the man whom the law declares to be the father of the child, even where the paternity has been declared, in default of other proof, by a physiognomist. Moreover, relationship by fosterage with the man who is the cause of the milk exists in spite of the previous dissolution of the nurse's marriage by the death of her husband or by her repudiation, however long ago the separation took place, and even if the milk has disappeared from her breast and then returned to it. It is only when a separated woman accepts a new husband and has a child by him that the swelling of her breasts must be attributed to him. Consequently, where a woman who has married again sees her breasts swell before her accouchement of a child of the second marriage it is to the previous husband that this state of the breasts must be attributed, even where a new pregnancy is manifested. One jurist, however, in these last circumstances attributes the appearance of the milk to the second husband, and another to both of them together.

Section 2

If a man's mother, sister, or wife gives her breast to a very young girl who has been promised him in marriage, his marriage with the young girl is *ipso facto* dissolved, and he owes her half dower. He can, however, recover from the woman who without his knowledge has given her breast to the child half the proportional dower, or, according to one jurist, the whole proportional dower. If the breast has been given unconsciously, *e.g.* during sleep, the woman who has done so is not responsible, nor can the young girl claim anything. When one has two wives, one adult and one still a child, and the former's mother gives her breast to the latter, the marriage is *ipso facto* dissolved both with the one and with the other; but there is no objection to taking one of them back as wife. Under these circumstances the above principles must be observed as to the young girl's dower and the responsibility of the mother-in-law; and also to the adult wife's dower, provided she has not yet had commerce with her husband. Where, on the other hand, the husband has already cohabited with his adult wife and consequently owes her the whole dower, *he can recover from her mother what she would have been able to claim as proportional dower. Finally in the case where it is the daughter of one of his wives by a former marriage who has given her breast to the child-wife, commerce with the adult wife who is the nurse's mother is for ever forbidden the husband; while commerce with the child-wife is prohibited only where there has been cohabitation between him and the mother of the nurse in question.

Where a man, after accepting a minor as his wife, repudiates her, and some woman gives her breast to the child, that woman becomes none the less the husband's mother-in-law by fosterage, and cohabitation with her is consequently forbidden him. Where a repudiated wife remarries with a child she afterwards nourishes with the milk of her previous marriage, commerce with her becomes for ever forbidden both to her former husband and to the child she has accepted as her future husband; and, by virtue of the same principle, a slave emancipated by reason of maternity and given by her master as future wife to one of his young slaves, may no longer cohabit with the master nor with the slave if she gives the latter her breast, at least, if the master was the cause of the milk. Moreover, when a slave with whom her master has cohabited gives her breast to a young girl promised to the master as his future wife, he can have carnal commerce with neither, whether he or some other is the cause of the milk.

When a man has two wives, one an adult and the other still a minor, and the former gives her breast to the latter, not only is his marriage with the child-wife dissolved, as we have already seen, but even the nurse ceases to be his wife, and commerce with her is for ever forbidden him. Where a man has one adult wife and three child-wives, and the adult gives her breast to the others, coition with the adult wife is for ever forbidden the husband, but that with the child-wives is prohibited him only if he was the cause of the milk, or if he has at least cohabited with the wife who has become their nurse. Where, on the contrary, he has not yet cohabited with the adult wife the following distinctions should be made :—

1. If she nourishes the children at one and the same time, giving them suck the five required times. In this case the marriage with the young girls is dissolved, but the husband may subsequently marry each one separately.

2. If she nourishes them in a similar manner one after the other. In this case commerce with them is not forbidden for ever, but the marriage with the first and the third is dissolved because they have received the breast of their husband's wife, and the marriage with the second is dissolved as a consequence of the suckling of the third. One authority, however, considers the marriage of the second as remaining intact ; and the same divergence of opinion exists where there are two child-wives instead of three, suckled successively by a strange woman.

Section 3

Where one makes an admission that a certain person is one's daughter, sister, or brother by fosterage, one's marriage with such person is forbidden. Where husband and wife declare that their marriage was effected in contravention of the prescriptions relating to fosterage, this declaration suffices to bring about their separation, and causes the woman to lose her right to fixed dower. In these circumstances she can only claim proportional dower, at any rate if the marriage has been consummated, for otherwise she can claim nothing. Even if the husband alone maintains that there exists between him and his wife some prohibited relationship by fosterage, the marriage is dissolved even though the wife denies this relationship ; but in this case she can insist upon payment of the full definite dower, if there has been cohabitation, and otherwise half. Where, on the other hand, the wife alleges relationship by fosterage and the husband denies it, the law presumes that he is speaking the truth, provided he takes an oath, and provided that the wife consented to the marriage ; †for if she was given in marriage without her consent, the presumption is in her favour. She can in this latter case claim proportional dower, if there has been cohabitation ; otherwise she can claim nothing.

Where an oath is tendered to the party that denies the relationship by fosterage it is enough for him to affirm that he knows nothing of it ; but when it is tendered to the party that asserts that relationship, he must positively affirm its existence. Relationship by fosterage is proved—

1. By the deposition of two male witnesses, or of one man and two women, or of four women.

2. By admission; but it must be understood that an admission not made at the hearing must be proved by the deposition of two male witnesses.

The nurse herself is admissible as a witness to relationship by fosterage —at any rate where she has not taken a salary for her services. She may confine herself to affirming simply that a relationship by fosterage exists, †or she may prove a fact personal to herself from which that relationship follows, *e.g.* her giving the breast to the child in question. †As to other witnesses, relationship by fosterage is not sufficiently established by a deposition to the effect that "there exists between the husband and wife a prohibited relationship by fosterage," but the date must be mentioned, the number of times the nursling was given suck, and the fact that the milk penetrated into the body. This fact is the direct consequence of the circumstances that one has seen the child sucking, that the milk was introduced into the mouth and that the child swallowed it. It may also be established by indirect indications, *e.g.* that the child took the teat in its mouth, that the lips made a movement as if sucking, or that the throat moved either as if drinking the milk in gulps or as if swallowing it with a continuous movement, supposing it to be proved that the woman's breasts were not dry.

BOOK 46.—MAINTENANCE

SECTION 1

A MAN who is quite solvent owes two *modd* of provisions a day to each of his wives, but a man who is insolvent owes only one, and a man of moderate means one and a half. A *modd* is equivalent to one hundred and seventy-three drahms and a third. [†It is equivalent to one hundred and seventy-one drahms and three-sevenths of a drahm.]

By "insolvent" is understood in this connection a man who has been admitted amongst those having right to the charity tax through poverty or indigence. A husband who has no such right is regarded as being of moderate means if he cannot give his wives two *modd* a day without ruining himself or without thus coming to have a claim to the charity tax. Where, on the contrary, his means permit him to give two *modd* without ruining himself, he is called quite solvent.

Provisions due as maintenance are such as form the principal nourishment of the majority of the inhabitants of the locality. [If there is no principal nourishment in general use one must give one's wives some suitable nourishment. Solvency, insolvency, or a condition of moderate means must be determined for each day at dawn.] One may give one's wives provisions either in grain †or in the state of flour or bread; it being understood, however, that neither husband nor wife can be forced to give or to receive them except as grain, unless with their full consent. †The parties may also agree to substitute other objects for the provisions, provided only, according to our school, that the grains once given are not replaced by flour or bread of the same kind. †Moreover, a husband has no need to give provisions to a wife who comes and has her usual meals with him. [Where a wife is of limited intelligence the fact of her taking her meals with him does not free him from the obligation of giving her provisions, unless her curator consents to this.] Besides provisions properly so called, one must give one's wives the condiments in use in the locality, *e.g.* olive oil, butter, cheese, and dates, according to the season; but the court when determining the quantity and quality of the condiments should observe a difference between a solvent and insolvent husband. As to meat, it is local custom that determines whether it need only be given by a husband who is quite solvent, or whether this obligation exists also for the insolvent husband; condiments, on the other hand, are due by every husband, even though his wife receive no nourishment but bread.

A husband must not only supply his wife with necessary nourishment, but he must also give her—

1. Necessary clothing, that is to say, a chemise, a pair of drawers, a veil and a pair of sandals; and to this must in winter be added a cotton *jobba* †or, if local custom requires it, a *jobba* of some other material, *e.g.* linen or silk.

2. Something to sit on, *e.g.* a carpet, a piece of felt or a mat; †and a bed to lie on with a pillow, and in winter a blanket.

3. What is necessary for her toilet, *e.g.* a comb and pomade; what she requires for washing her head; litharge, etc., for removing the fetid odour of the body; but not eye ointments, nor ingredients for dyeing, nor what only serves for beautifying the person.

4. Medicines, when she is sick, and doctor's and surgeon's fees. She may insist on having her ordinary nourishment during her illness, both the principal nourishment and the condiments.

5. †Money enough for the usual bath, as often as is customary, and also for the special bath prescribed after coition and accouchement; but the husband is not bound to pay for the bath specially prescribed for menstruation and lascivious dreams, as these are impurities of which he is not the cause.

6. Utensils for eating, drinking, and preparing food, such as a pot, a basin, a vase, a jar, etc.

7. A suitable lodging; of which the law does not require the husband to be the owner.

8. Necessary servants, at least where the wife is of a social position which does not permit her to dispense with this. The servant may be either a free woman, or a female slave of the husband, or one he has hired, or a free or slave woman brought for the purpose by the wife from her father's house, whom the husband undertakes to support. As to the duty of procuring a servant for one's wife, the law makes no distinction between a solvent and an insolvent husband, nor even between a free man and a slave. If the servant is a free woman or a slave woman whose services the husband has hired, he is liable merely for the wages agreed upon; but if it is one of his own female slaves whom he has given his wife as servant, he owes her ordinary maintenance by virtue of his right of ownership. A servant brought by the wife from her father's house can claim from the husband the same nourishment as the wife, with the exception that she receives only one *modd* of

provisions from an insolvent husband †or one of moderate means, and one *modd* and a third from one quite solvent. Such a servant can also insist on the husband providing her with clothes †and suitable condiments, but not what is required for her toilet. On the other hand, it is only in case of repulsive dirtiness, *e.g.* the presence of vermin, that the husband may take notice of the servant's toilet and insist upon her taking better care of her person, at his expense. A wife who in conformity with custom may dispense with a servant, may claim one all the same if necessary, *e.g.* in case of sickness either acute or chronic. A slave wife can never claim a servant in ordinary circumstances; but in the case of a female slave of remarkable beauty jurists are not in agreement.

A wife must have the enjoyment of the premises she occupies; but her husband need not transfer the ownership to her. On the other hand, what she receives for her maintenance becomes her own, in the case of things that are consumed by use, like provisions. She may also dispose of them as she pleases; only if she imposes upon herself privations that affect her health, in order to make a profit out of what her husband gives her, has he the right to object. As to things that deteriorate but are not consumed by usage, such as clothes, household utensils, or a comb, these things also become the wife's property; though some authorities maintain that the husband is merely bound to procure her the enjoyment of them. A wife may insist upon her husband's giving her new clothes twice a year, *i.e.* at the beginning of winter and the beginning of summer; and where it is admitted that she becomes the owner of the things the husband is not bound to replace them in case of accidental loss. Where this doctrine is held, clothing given to a wife is not returned to the husband if she dies during the season for which such clothing was intended; but she can claim the clothes or their value even later, if she does not receive them at the prescribed period.

Section 2

During his stay in Egypt Shafii adopted the doctrine that a wife's maintenance is obligatory only if she puts herself at her husband's disposition, and not in virtue of the contract of marriage. The husband has a presumption in favour of his assertions in any proceedings as to the putting of the wife at his disposition. Consequently, a husband owes his wife no maintenance so long as she refuses to come to him; but owes it from the moment he hears she is willing to put herself at his disposition. If the husband is absent the court should send word to him that his wife wishes to come to him, through the court at the place where the husband is; and the husband should then either return to receive her, or appoint an agent to do so and supply her with the prescribed maintenance. If he does neither within a reasonable time, the court may apply his property to the maintenance of his wife. As to a wife affected by madness, or one not yet adult, the curator or guardian should place her at her husband's disposition; and this has the same consequence as when an adult or sane wife places herself at her husband's disposition.

A right to maintenance ceases if the wife is rebellious to marital authority; even if it be merely her husband's touch which she refuses to permit without valid excuse. The law considers, among others, as valid excuses, giving a wife a right to refuse herself to her husband, an excessive development of the genital organ in the husband, or a malady of the wife that would be aggravated by coition. Leaving the conjugal domicile without first asking permission also constitutes a fact incompatible with a wife's submission to marital authority, unless the house is threatening to fall down. A journey undertaken with the husband's consent, either to accompany him, or in his interest, does not in any way interrupt his obligation to maintain his wife. Only when the journey is undertaken in the particular and exclusive interest of the wife is she unable to claim maintenance during her absence. †If a disobedient wife returns to her duty during her husband's absence on a journey, she cannot immediately re-enter into the enjoyment of her rights. She must plead her cause before the court, in order that it may communicate the fact to the husband in the manner already explained. A woman who, in the absence of her husband, quits the conjugal domicile, even without leave, to go and see her family, etc., does not lose her right to maintenance. An adult who marries a young girl in her minority is not bound to supply her with the prescribed maintenance; but an adult woman married to a minor may claim this, since it is not her fault that the consummation of the marriage is deferred.

The entering into a state of *ihram* for the pilgrimage or the visit constitutes an act of disobedience on the part of the wife, if the husband has not authorised her to do so, and if he has not the right to break the *ihram*. Where he has this right the woman's conduct is not an act of disobedience, unless she quits the conjugal domicile. †In the latter case she is regarded as having undertaken a journey in her own interest, and must suffer all the consequences. †As to the wife whose husband has permitted her to undertake the *ihram*, she cannot claim ordinary maintenance from the moment of departure. The husband may object to his wife accomplishing a supererogatory fast, *and if she insists upon doing so in spite of his forbidding her, she is disobedient. †As to a fast which she is obliged to undertake late because the legal time is elapsed, the husband may object to his wife's keeping this as in the case of a supererogatory fast, provided that there is plenty of time; but in no case can he forbid his wife accomplishing her obligatory daily prayers as soon as the legal hour has come. †And the same is the case as to those acts of devotion introduced by the Sonna, that are accomplished at fixed hours.

A woman revocably repudiated may claim during her period of legal retirement everything that was previously her due, excepting the expenses of her toilet. Where in these circumstances a woman is reputed to be pregnant and her husband consequently maintains her beyond the period of ordinary retirement, he may recover what she has unduly received, if the pregnancy appears never to have existed. On the other hand, a woman irrevocably separated, either by divorce, or by three repudiations, cannot claim maintenance, including clothing, during her period of legal retirement, unless she is pregnant, for in this latter case she can claim both on her own account; or, according to one authority, by reason of the child she bears in her womb. Though we admit with the majority that she has this right on her own account, we cannot admit a right to maintenance of a woman who has become pregnant by the error of the husband who thought she was his wife, or who had really married her but in an illegal manner. [A woman whose marriage has been dissolved by her husband's decease can never claim maintenance during the period of her legal retirement out of the estate, even if she is pregnant.]

Maintenance during the period of legal retirement differs in no respect from maintenance during marriage; though, according to some authorities, the former consists only of what is strictly necessary. A woman, however, cannot claim maintenance on account of pregnancy before the existence of the fœtus has been ascertained; but in the latter case it must be accorded her day by day, or, according to others at the time of her accouchement. According to our school a woman's right to claim maintenance is not subject to limitation, *i.e.* her claim is receivable even after the expiration of the period of retirement.

Section 3

When a husband during his marriage becomes so insolvent that he can no longer give the minimum maintenance prescribed, but his wife in spite of this continues to live with him, the maintenance becomes a debt due to her from him and exigible at any moment. *If she no longer can bear such an insolvent husband, she can at once demand the dissolution of the marriage, since her husband no longer fulfils his obligations; †but no such claim is admissible against a solvent husband refusing his wife the prescribed maintenance. In this latter case it matters little if the husband be present or absent. On the other hand, a claim for dissolution is admissible if the husband is present and solvent but his property is elsewhere, at a distance so great as to admit of prayer being abridged. If this is not the case the woman cannot obtain the dissolution of the marriage; but the court should then order the husband to send for the necessary money. A woman is not obliged to accept from another as a gift the maintenance owed her by her husband.

If a husband gains enough money by his work to maintain his wife, it may be admitted that he has sufficient substance to allow him to discharge his pecuniary obligations towards her. And a claim for dissolution of marriage on account of complete insolvency is not admissible unless the husband is incapable of supplying his wife even with the maintenance due from an insolvent husband in ordinary circumstances. A degree of complete insolvency is manifested where a husband is unable to give not only the provisions that constitute the principal nourishment, but also the clothing, the †condiments, or the habitation that the law requires. [†A claim for dissolution should be rejected if it is founded merely upon the fact that the husband is unable to supply condiments.]

*Where a husband is unable to pay dower, dissolution of marriage is admissible, if the claim is brought by the woman before cohabitation; but not where the marriage has been consummated; and, moreover, the court can pronounce dissolution only where insolvency has been duly established. Where this insolvency is proved the court must either pronounce dissolution of the marriage or authorise the wife to pronounce it herself. *Three days' respite must, however, first be allowed. Only one jurist admits that dissolution may be pronounced without allowing any respite to the husband. Where, with the majority, a respite of three days is insisted upon, the wife is free to leave on the morning of the fourth day, unless the husband then gives her maintenance for this day. Where for two whole days the wife has not received her maintenance and the husband gives it her only on the third day, and then omits to do so on the fourth, the days of omission are added together and the woman is free on the fifth. Only a few authors maintain that three consecutive days' omission is necessary before the respite expires. All agree that during the respite enjoyed by the husband the wife may quit the conjugal domicile to get necessary provisions, provided she returns at night.

A husband cannot oppose a demand for dissolution of marriage by alleging that his wife has consented to share his pecuniary embarrassments, or that the marriage was entered into by her with full knowledge of the circumstances, for she is not obliged to do without maintenance longer than she likes. Where, on the other hand, it is not the prescribed maintenance but the dower that the husband cannot pay, he may oppose a demand for dissolution of marriage by a plea in bar. A demand for dissolution of marriage cannot be brought by the guardian of a minor wife, nor by the curator of a mad woman, unless a distinction be made between incapacity to furnish maintenance and that to pay dower. A demand for dissolution may be made by a free wife or by a slave wife, but not by a master where the woman wishes to share her husband's lot. A master may only persuade his female slave to demand a dissolution of marriage indirectly, *e.g.* by informing her that he will not maintain her so long as she remains the wife of an insolvent husband, and that she must therefore choose between dissolution of marriage and starvation.

Section 4

Ancestors and descendants should maintain each other mutually without distinction of sex or religion, on the sole condition that the individual against whom the claim is brought, himself possesses more than is necessary for the maintenance of himself and his household. One should even if necessary sell one's property to acquit oneself of this obligation, as if to pay an ordinary debt ; †and in default of property that can be realised, one should, if able to do so, work for this purpose. Only the man who has or gains just what he requires in order to live is not bound to maintain his ancestors or descendants ; though he should even then admit them to his house and his table, in the case of—

1. A person who has nothing and through illness cannot work.
2. A minor or a madman.

In all other cases the duty of maintaining one's ancestors or descendants is rigorously obligatory ; though some authorities do not admit this principle, and others admit it only as to sustenance due to ascendants. [*These last-mentioned authorities are evidently right.]

Maintenance due to ancestors or descendants consists only in what is strictly necessary, and a claim for it is limited to the term for which it is due ; unless there is a judgment ordering the performance of this duty, or permitting the claimant to borrow in the case of the absence or the refusal of the opposite party.

A mother should nourish her child with the milk which is manifested immediately after parturition; she should even continue to suckle it afterwards when no other nurse can be found but a foreign woman. Where, on the other hand, one can procure a nurse in the family, the mother is not obliged to give the child her breast, †and the child's father even has the right to oppose her performing this maternal duty. [†The husband's opposition is inadmissible; this at least is the opinion of most authorities.] Where husband and wife agree that the suckling shall be done by the mother herself, she may require from him a reasonable but not exorbitant remuneration. *But he is not obliged to agree to this demand for reasonable remuneration on the part of his wife, if a foreign woman offers to nourish the child for nothing, or for some inferior remuneration.

Maintenance is due from all the descendants together, if there is no difference between them; but if they are not equal under all respects †the obligation is incumbent on the nearest; and in case of equality of degree of relationship, it exists only for that person who will be called to the succession. Another doctrine, however, tends to consider that a right to the succession constitutes *primâ facie* the basis of the obligation to maintain one's ancestors, while the degree of relationship is of secondary importance; and besides this jurists are not agreed as to whether the heirs are jointly responsible for the nourishment, or only in proportion to their respective shares.

In the ascendant line a father is the first who should maintain his child; and it is only in a secondary degree that the child can require maintenance from its mother; only a few authors maintain that father and mother are equally responsible, at least towards an adult child. In default of father and mother, it is from one's nearest ancestors that one may claim nourishment, either those in the same line, or ancestors on the father's and on the mother's side. Some jurists, however, consider maintenance of descendants as a charge attached to the succession, while others consider it as a charge inhering to the right of guardianship or curatorship.

†A person who has both ancestors and descendants alive should first claim maintenance from the latter, without respect to the distance of degree of relationship. Where, on the other hand, one has several persons dependent upon one, one should first discharge one's duty towards one's wife, and then that towards one's nearest relative; or, according to some authorities, towards the one who will be called to the succession; or, according to others, to the one who would be called to duty of guardian or curator towards oneself.

Section 5

By the education of a child is understood—

1. Its supervision for all those matters in which it could not act for itself.

2. The care given to it, and the cultivation of its mind.

The first of these occupations is more particularly a woman's duty. It is confided first of all to the mother and her female ancestors through women, in order of proximity. During his Egyptian period Shafii embraced the doctrine that, in default of a mother and her female ancestors, through women, the education goes to the father's mother and her female ancestors through women, and after that to the grandfather's mother and her female ancestors through women. In his first period, however, the Imam allowed priority to sisters, and even to maternal aunts, over all female ancestors on the father's side. In any case a sister has priority over a maternal aunt, and the latter over a niece. A niece has priority over a paternal aunt, a full sister over a half sister on either side, †a half sister on the father's side over a half sister on the mother's side, and an aunt who is half sister on the father's side of the father or mother over one who is half sister on the mother's side of the father or mother. †An incapacity to inherit, due to a male degree of relationship between two women, suffices also to exclude female ancestors from the function of education; but incapacity to inherit is not a reason for the exclusion of other women whose degree of relationship would be no obstacle to marriage, *e.g.* a daughter of a maternal aunt. In default of women the education falls to the charge of all male inheritors within a prohibited degree, in the order in which they would be called to the succession, ††and secondarily it is confided to every male inheritor of a still more distant degree of relationship, such as the son of a paternal uncle. However, a young girl must never be confided to an inheritor with whom marriage is not prohibited and who shows a liking for her; but if her education falls to his charge, he must confide her to the care of some reliable woman chosen by him. Male relatives, of whatever degree, who are not called to the succession, †are not called to the duty of education; and in case of claims by male and female relatives, priority is accorded to the mother, then to the female ancestors through women, and lastly to the father; while according to some authorities even a maternal aunt and a half sister on the mother's side have priority over him. In general the ascendant line has priority always over a collateral one; where two persons are equally competent in this respect, priority belongs to the nearer; †if they are of the same degree the woman has the priority ; and if there is no legal difference the matter should be decided by lot.

The education of a child can never be entrusted to—

1. A slave, a mad man or woman, or a person of notorious misconduct.
2. An infidel, if the child is a Moslem.
3. Its mother, if she has married again ; unless with its paternal uncle, cousin on the father's side, or son of half brother on the father's side.

††The education of a child implies also the duty of suckling it or having it suckled, if it is not yet weaned. Personal incapacity to undertake the duty of education ceases with its cause ; and so does incapacity due to a marriage or repudiation. In case of the mother's absence or incapacity, her mother is invested with all her rights.

The rules mentioned in the present section relate only to a child who has not yet reached the age of discernment. If the child has attained this age it may choose with which of its parents it prefers to stay after their separation, provided neither the father nor the mother are mad, infidel, a slave or of notorious misconduct, and provided the mother has not married again. In any of these cases the child must remain with the other parent. It has the right to choose, not only between its father and mother, but also between its mother and father's father in case of the predecease of its father, and also, if there is occasion for this, between its brother, father's brother and father on the one side, and its sister, half sister, or mother's sister on the other. Even if it has once chosen, there is no objection to its afterwards choosing the other parent ; and if a son chooses his father, this does not prejudice his right to go and visit his mother when he likes. But a daughter loses this right, when she has declared that she prefers to remain with her father instead of with her mother as she would naturally do. But the father may never prevent the mother coming to see her children of either sex, provided there is no more than one visit on one day. In case of sickness a mother has by preference the right of tending her child of either sex, and, if necessary, of having it taken to her house for that purpose, if the father refuses to allow her to go and stay at his house. A son who chooses his mother only remains with her for the night, but must pass the day with his father, in order that the latter may form his character, send him to school, and make him learn a trade. On the other hand, a daughter must in these circumstances remain with her mother, day and night, without prejudice to the father's right to come and see her as often as may be customary. When a child wants to live with its father and with its mother, the matter should be decided by lot ; and if it refuses to choose the mother has the preference as the person to whom the law entrusts the education in the first place. Only a few authors require that in this case the matter should be decided by lot. If one of the parents has to leave on a necessary journey, a child of either sex must remain with the other, until the return of the former; but if the journey amounts to a change of domicile a father has a right to take his children with him, provided the place he is going to and the way there are safe. Some authorities also require that the new domicile must be at a distance permitting the abridgment of prayer.

In default of the father his agnates within the prohibited degrees are invested with his rights; and so is the cousin on the father's side, in the case of a boy, though not in that of a girl. In the latter case the child must be intrusted to the cousin's daughter, if she lives with him.

Section 6

A master must give his slaves the nourishment and clothing of which they have need, even if the slave be blind or sickly, or one enfranchised by the terms of a will, or on account of maternity. Nourishment includes ordinary provisions given to slaves in that locality; and the same with condiments. As to clothing, it is enough to give slaves merely what is sufficient to cover the shameful parts, but they must be clothed as local custom requires. The Sonna has also introduced the practice of giving them sound nourishment both in the principal food and in the condiments, and of supplying them with clothing suitable for the climate. A slave cannot afterwards claim damages for the maintenance his master has neglected to give him, but he should make a complaint at once to the court, which can proceed immediately to the sale of the master's property and apply the proceeds to the maintenance of the slave; or, in default of any such property, may order the sale or even the enfranchisement of the slave.

A master may oblige his female slave to suckle a child to which she has given birth; and even another's child, if she has more milk than is required to suckle her own. He may also oblige her, either to wean her child before the regular period of two years provided the weaning is not injurious to the nursling's health, or to continue suckling it after that term, provided this is not injurious to the health of the mother. It is only a free woman that has rights as to suckling and education which she can insist upon as against her husband. Thus, in case of marriage between free persons neither of the parties can cause the child to be weaned before the expiry of the prescribed period of two years, except with the other's consent; and this can only be given on condition that the child's health does not suffer by it. On the other hand, either party may insist upon the child's being weaned at the time prescribed by the law; while they may jointly agree to postpone this until after that term.

One may not exact from a slave any labour incompatible with his strength or aptitudes; nor can he on his part oblige his master to excuse him from performing any suitable task. The law admits the validity of the *mokharaja*, *i.e.* an agreement between a master and his slave by which the latter may dispose of his labour for a daily or weekly wage to be paid to the former.

One is obliged to maintain one's domestic animals, by giving them necessary fodder and water, and if this duty is neglected the court may oblige the master either to sell the animal or suitably maintain it; or kill it, at least if it is an animal that can be used as human food, otherwise the master has no choice between sale or maintenance. An animal must not be milked in such a way as to injure the young to which she has given birth; but as to inanimate objects, such as an aqueduct or a house, the master may use or abuse them as he pleases, and no one can oblige him to see to their upkeep.

BOOK 47.—CRIMES AGAINST THE PERSON

CHAPTER I.—GENERAL PROVISIONS

Section 1

HOMICIDE is of three categories; it may be premeditated, involuntary, or voluntary; only premeditated homicide involves a penalty under the law of talion. Premeditation in homicide consists in the intention of attacking the person of a particular individual with a cutting, piercing, or blunt instrument, capable in ordinary circumstances of causing death. Where, on the other hand, there is no intention of committing a crime, or a crime against a particular individual, there is involuntary homicide, *e.g.* if one falls upon a person one knows to be underneath and kills that person, or if one wants to shoot at a tree and the projectile strikes some one. Voluntary homicide is intentionally attacking a particular individual with an instrument that under ordinary circumstances does not cause death, *e.g.* striking him with a whip or a stick. Thus premeditated homicide will include the act of introducing a needle into any part of the body if there ensues so painful a wound as to cause the death of the victim; but it is only voluntary homicide where the prick is in some part of body where a wound is not mortal, and has left no visible trace, though death is caused. Other authorities, however, admit premeditation in these circumstances; still others consider that such an act incurs no penalty at all, and all jurists agree in this where death has been caused by thrusting a needle, *e.g.*, into the callosity of the heel, *i.e.* a place where there is no sensation.

The fact of having confined a person, and not only withheld necessary food and drink, but also prevented their being obtained by that person, so that death results, is premeditated homicide. It is understood that this confinement must have lasted long enough to be able in ordinary circumstances to cause death from inanition. It is only voluntary homicide if death occurs earlier than this, unless the victim had been deprived of food and drink before being confined, and the criminal was aware of this circumstance. In this case there is premeditated homicide all the same; *but not where the criminal did not know that the person confined had already previously been deprived of food and drink.

The law of talion is applied not only to the immediate authors of a premeditated homicide, but also to the moral and distant authors. Thus, for example, if two witnesses by their testimony cause an innocent person to be condemned to death, and afterwards declare that they intentionally gave false evidence, they also should be put to death; unless the representative of the person put to death declares that he knew the testimony was false, before the penalty had been pronounced.

A person who receives into his house a minor, or a madman, and offers him poisoned food, so that death results, incurs a penalty under the law of talion; but where a sane adult tastes of a dish whose contents are unknown to him, the guilty person is simply liable for the price of blood, in consequence of his neglect to remove this dangerous dish. In this case there is only voluntary homicide; though, according to one authority there is also premeditation and consequently the law of talion applies. On the other hand, another jurist has maintained that in this case there is no punishable crime, as the stranger takes the dish of his own accord. A similar controversy exists as to the nature of the act of poisoning dishes belonging to another, of which he is in the habit of partaking, and which he does in fact unsuspectingly eat, so that death ensues. One is still punishable under the law of talion though the injured person neglects to have a mortal wound one has given him attended to, at least if he dies in consequence.

Death caused by drowning admits of the following distinctions:—

1. Where the water into which the victim is thrown is so shallow that it cannot be considered likely to drown a man. If the victim rests lying on his side until he is drowned, this is not punishable, as it is the victim himself who has killed himself.

2. Where the water is so deep that escape is only possible by swimming, the following cases must be distinguished:—

(a) it is premeditated homicide, if the victim cannot swim, or is prevented from doing so by being pinioned or by some chronic malady such as paralysis.

(b) it is voluntary homicide if the victim is prevented from saving himself by swimming owing to some accidental circumstance, such as wind or waves;

(c) *the act is not a crime at all, and the guilty person is not even liable to the price of blood, if the victim could have saved himself, but voluntarily abstained from doing so.

Authorities are not agreed as to whether the act of throwing some one into the fire, admits of similar distinctions; or whether this act should not always be regarded as premeditated homicide, where death has ensued.

When one kills a person whom another has seized, or throws him into a well which another has dug; or when one throws him down from a height, and another waits underneath to cut him in two, there is no complicity; and each individual is separately liable, under the law of talion, for killing, throwing down, or cutting in two the victim. *Where, on the other hand, one throws some one into the water in a place where under ordinary circumstances he could be drowned, but he is instead devoured by a fish, one is liable to the law of talion, though not the immediate cause of his death. If the water was not deep enough to drown the victim under ordinary circumstances, but he has nevertheless been devoured by a fish, the guilty person is not liable to punishment.

Premeditated homicide, committed under coercion by violence renders liable under the law of talion not only the person who exercised the coercion *but also the person who allowed himself to be intimidated; for the law regards them as accomplices. In case of homicide that is not premeditated they should jointly pay the price of blood, if this is required; and if one of them is not liable to the law of talion by reason of social superiority to the victim, the other must undergo it none the less. Only where the violence is irresistible, *e.g.* used by an adult to a minor, the former alone is amenable to the law of talion; and this is admitted even by those authorities who in general allow that premeditation may exist in the case of a minor. Moreover, where one forces some one to shoot at a distant object one knows to be a man but the other thinks is game one incurs a penalty under the law of talion as the immediate cause; but that other who has done the material act cannot be considered as an author of the homicide. The law of talion cannot be applied to any one where a hunter, obliged to shoot at game, by misfortune hits a man; nor where some one, obliged to climb a tree, falls, causing death. In the latter case, however, there is voluntary homicide, and according to some jurists, it is premeditated. A person who forces some one to commit suicide is *not punishable under the law of talion; nor, according to our school, if he kills some one who said to him, "Kill me, or I will kill you." In this latter case there is no ground either for a claim for the price of blood. On the other hand, where one person says to another, "Kill either Zaid or Amr, or I will kill you," there is no violence in the legal sense, and the person is punishable if he commits the homicide.

SECTION 2

Where two persons together attack and kill another, they are accomplices in premeditated homicide, and are both punishable under the law of talion. This rule applies first of all to the case where both crimina deal the victim an immediately mortal blow, *e.g.* if one cuts off his head, and the other cuts him in two ; but it is just the same if each deals him a blow that causes a grave but not immediately mortal wound, *e.g.* if each cuts off a limb. If one of two persons attacks another and leaves him for dead, *i.e.* unable to see or speak or communicate by signs, and the other gives him a wound that finishes him, the former alone is punishable under the law of talion, the other incurring only a correction at the discretion of the court. When, on the other hand, it is the former who merely deals the wound, and the second attacks the victim and leaves him for dead, the latter is considered guilty of premeditated homicide if the wound dealt by him is one immediately mortal, *i.e.* if he has cut off a wounded person's head. Under these circumstances the person who deals the first blow is punishable for that wound only, *i.e.* he is liable either under the law of talion or to a pecuniary penalty.

The premeditated homicide of a sick person at the point of death is punishable under the law of talion, although he has already lost consciousness.

Section 3

When one kills a Moslem in an enemy's country, under the belief that he is an infidel not subject to Moslem authority, one is liable neither to a penalty under the law of talion *nor to payment of the price of blood ; but when this act occurs in the territory of a believing ruler, the one or the other is applicable according to circumstances ; though one authority calls in question the applicability of the law of talion. On the other hand, our school admits a recourse to the law of talion in a case of premeditated homicide committed against some one designated as an apostate by public notoriety, or an infidel subject of a Moslem ruler, or a slave, or a reputed parricide, if it appears later that the person killed had not the legal character rendering inadmissible an application of the law of talion. It is in accordance with the same principles that a person is liable to the law of talion who strikes a sick person of whose dangerous state he was not aware, but who dies immediately, though in ordinary circumstances the blow would not have been mortal. This, however, is denied by some authorities.

To render applicable the law of talion it is legally necessary—

1. That the deceased was a Moslem, or an infidel enjoying our protection, on some ground or other. An infidel not subject to a Moslem ruler, and an apostate, are proscribed, and may be killed with impunity ; but the premeditated murder of a condemned criminal by any one other than the representative of the murdered man, the magistrate or the executioner is punishable like any other murder. As to a person guilty

of the crime of fornication, if he is *mohsan* and consequently punishable with lapidation, his premeditated murder by an infidel subject of a Moslem prince involves an application of the law of talion; †but this is not so if he is killed by a Moslem.

2. That the criminal is a sane adult. Drunkenness is not considered an excuse by our school. If the guilty person alleges as an excuse his minority or madness on the day of the crime, this assertion is presumed by law to be true, upon the double condition that the criminal takes an oath to that effect, and that his real age is not incompatible with his statement, or that his madness is of public notoriety. In a case where the guilty person declares in court that he has not yet attained his majority, his assertion is sufficient even though not on oath, provided a presumption is admitted in favour of the truth of his statement. An infidel not subject to Moslem authority is not liable to a penalty under the law of talion, as he is already proscribed by virtue of his belief; but religion is not a cause of impunity for an apostate, nor for an infidel in any way under our protection.

3. That the criminal is not of a social position superior to that of the victim. Thus a Moslem cannot be put to death for killing an infidel, even though the latter may be the subject of a Moslem prince; but an infidel who kills a Moslem or an infidel is liable to the law of talion, even though the two infidels are not of the same religion, or the criminal embraces the faith after committing the crime. This rule must also be observed in a case where the infidel in question, having merely wounded another, is immediately converted, and the victim dies of his wounds. But in both these cases the conversion of the criminal has this consequence that neither the Sovereign nor his delegate the judge can of their own initiative pronounce a penalty under the law of talion, but must wait until the representative of the victim claims its application. *An apostate is to be put to death for killing an infidel subject of a Moslem prince or another apostate; but not an infidel subject of a Moslem prince for killing an apostate, nor a free man for killing a slave, even though the latter be partially enfranchised. A slave, a slave enfranchised by testament, a slave undergoing enfranchisement by contract, and a female slave enfranchised by reason of maternity, are all equal in this respect. But a slave enfranchised after killing another, or in the interval between the wounding and death of the victim, follows the rule as to the conversion of an infidel criminal; while the death penalty is never applicable to a slave partially enfranchised who kills another, provided, according to some authorities, that he is free to a greater degree than his victim. By virtue of the same principles the law of talion is inapplicable to a premeditated homicide committed

against a Moslem slave by a free infidel subject of a Moslem prince, or *vice versâ;* and also to an infanticide, *i.e.* a premeditated homicide against one's child or other descendant; but it is applicable to parricide, *i.e.* the premeditated murder of one's ancestor. The premeditated murder by one of two parties of the person whose paternity they dispute is punishable under the law of talion if the paternity is adjudged to the other party, even if this is done upon the expert testimony of a physiognomist, but not if the paternity is adjudged to the party who has committed the crime.

Where one of two brothers commits the premeditated murder of his father and the other of his mother, the following cases must be distinguished:—

1. If the two homicides are committed at the same time, each of the two criminals may claim in court the punishment of the other for killing an ancestor whom he represents; and which of the two is to bring the first accusation must be chosen by lot. When one of the guilty brothers has thus been put to death on the demand of the other, whether the latter has been so designated by lot, or whether he presented himself first of his own accord, it is the representative of the brother that has been executed who should demand an application of the death penalty against the other; at least where one admits that the faculty of representing the victim by virtue of the right of succession is lost as well by the fact of rightful as of unjust killing.

2. If the two homicides are committed one after the other, a case which again admits of two distinctions—

(*a*) If the marriage between father and mother was dissolved before the first homicide, the first criminal must begin by demanding the execution of the other, after which the representative of the latter must demand the execution of the former, without any drawing of lots.

(*b*) If the marriage between the father and the mother still existed intact at the time of the first homicide, it is only the brother who has just committed the second homicide who is put to death upon the demand of the other.

Where several individuals have concurred in the homicide of another they are all punishable under the law of talion, if it is applicable; but the representative of the victim may remit the capital punishment for some of the criminals, and content himself with the price of blood from them, in proportion to the number of criminals whose execution he has claimed. An accomplice in a case of homicide cannot be punished with death, if the principal acted without premeditation and committed only a voluntary or involuntary homicide; but the accomplice of a father the premeditated murder of one of his children should be put to death in spite of the principal's impunity. Similarly, a slave who is the accomplice of a free man in the premeditated homicide of a slave, or an infidel subject of a Moslem prince who is the accomplice of a Moslem in the premeditated homicide of an infidel like himself, must none the less undergo the death penalty, though the free man and the Moslem are not liable to it, by reason of their respective personal qualities. *The same principle requires an application of the law of talion in the following cases of complicity :—

1. With an infidel not subject to Moslem authority, who has committed premeditated homicide, though we have just seen that a demand for an application of the law of talion cannot be brought against such infidel.

2. With an executioner or other person who carries out a sentence under the law of talion, or some definitely prescribed penalty, when this consists only in the loss of a bodily member or in a wound ; *e.g.* if a person gives the criminal another wound after he has suffered the penalty, which together with the first causes his death.

3. With a suicide, *e.g.* by giving a wound to some one who has already wounded himself intentionally, but who dies only because of receiving the second as well.

4. With a person on whose part the act constitutes only legitimate self-defence.

On the contrary, the law of talion is not applicable in the following cases :—

1. Where one gives the victim two wounds of which one is premeditated and the other involuntary, death resulting from the two combined.

2. Where one wounds an infidel not subject to Moslem authority or an apostate, who then becomes converted ; and after this one gives him another wound which in conjunction with the first is fatal.

3. Where one gives a wound that is not mortal to a person who applies to it an immediately fatal poison. Where the person in question has, in these circumstances, applied to the wound a substance that does not usually cause death, but appears to be fatal in this instance, the causer of the wound is guilty only of voluntary homicide. Where, however, the substance, though not in the category of immediately fatal poisons, ordinarily causes death in similar circumstances, and the victim knowingly applies it to the wound, the latter commits a suicide of which the causer of the wound is an accomplice. Other authorities, however, maintain that in this case there is only involuntary suicide.

†Where several persons give another cuts with the lash so that death

is the consequence, though each stroke by itself is not mortal, the law of talion is applicable only if the attack is made by a joint agreement. This rule, however, is the subject of controversy. Where, on the other hand, a single person has successively killed several others, he should suffer the penalty of death for the first victim, and his estate is liable for the price of blood as regards the others. In the case of the premeditated homicide of several persons at once, it must first be decided by lot for which of the victims the criminal is to suffer death, after which his estate is liable for the price of blood of the others. [Where in these circumstances the criminal is put to death by the representative of one of the victims other than that one for whose homicide he ought to suffer death, it is a crime rendering that representative himself liable to the law of talion; and the representative of the victim to whose homicide the law of talion applied, can claim the price of blood.]

SECTION 4

No responsibility is incurred by mortally wounding an infidel not subject to a Moslem prince, or an apostate, even though he should repent of his errors before death. This principle extends also to a master who mortally wounds his slave, and then frees him before his death. Others, however, do not admit impunity in these circumstances, but maintain that one is then liable for the price of blood. Where, on the other hand, one shoots at such infidel, or an apostate or one's own slave, after which the infidel or the apostate is converted, or one frees the slave, before the projectile hits him, our school exacts the price of blood on the lighter scale, for the killing of a free Moslem. This price of blood is exigible either from the criminal or from his *aakila*. Where one wounds an individual who abjures Islam before dying of the wound one is considered to have killed a proscribed person; *but one is nevertheless liable for the wound inflicted, under the law of talion, and the nearest relative of the apostate should claim the application of the penalty. Only a few authorities consider that this is the duty of the Sovereign; while if the nature of the wound does not admit of an application of the law of talion, but requires a pecuniary penalty, the criminal owes either an indemnity or the price of blood, whichever is the more advantageous. Some authorities insist in these circumstances upon the payment of an indemnity always; others maintain that there is no punishable offence. Where one wounds a Moslem who thereupon abjures his faith but afterwards repents before dying of the wound, one is not punishable with death, unless, according to some authorities, the apostasy of the victim has lasted only a very short time. But one is always liable in these circumstances for the price of blood, or, according to one authority, to half the price of blood. When a Moslem wounds an infidel subject of one of our princes, and he embraces the faith after receiving the wound, or when a free man wounds another's slave who is enfranchised after being wounded, the victim's death in consequence of the wound does not render the criminal liable to the law of talion, but he owes the price of blood prescribed for the homicide of a free Moslem. In the case of an enfranchised slave this price of blood is payable to his former master in proportion to his value as a slave, and to his heirs for the remainder. If the slave's wound consists in the loss of a hand, and his master grants him his freedom before he dies in consequence of the wound, his master can claim either the price of blood due for the mutilation, or half the value of the slave, at the criminal's choice. One authority alone gives the criminal a choice between the price of blood and the full value of the slave. Where one man cuts off the hand of a slave whom his master thereupon frees, and two others then each give the slave a new wound, which combined with the loss of the hand cause the death of the victim, it is these two latter persons who should suffer the penalty under the law of talion, and not the one who cut off the hand.

Section 5

Punishment under the law of talion for the loss of one of the members of the body or for some other wound is regulated by the same principles as we have just explained relating to the application of the law of talion for homicide. Thus, for example, where several persons have concurred in the act of cutting off the victim's hand by placing a sabre upon his wrist and each giving it a blow so as to sever the hand from the arm, each must have his hand cut off under the law of talion.

Wounds on the head and face are of ten different kinds--

1. *Harisa, i.e.* if only the skin has been cut or scraped.
2. *Damia,* if blood has flowed.
3. *Badia,* if the flesh has been injured.
4. *Mutalahima,* if the flesh has been penetrated.
5. *Simhak,* if the membrane enters the flesh and the bone is injured.
6. *Mudiha,* if the bone has been uncovered.
7. *Hashima,* if the bone itself has been injured.
8. *Munakkila,* if the bone is broken, so that the fragments are separated.
9. *Mamuma,* if the membrane of the brain has been injured.
10. *Damigha,* if the brain is injured.

The law of talion is applicable only to wounds of the sixth category or, according to some authorities, to categories 2–6. As to other bodily wounds they involve an application of the law of talion where the bone is exposed, or where there has been mutilation of a part of the nose or of the ears without exposure of the bone. This penalty is also incurred by any one who cuts a member at a joint, even if this is at the beginning of a thigh or of an arm, at any rate where such an amputation can take place without wounding the interior of the body of the criminal. ††If this is impossible a mutilation under the law of talion cannot take place, for fear lest the punishment should exceed the crime. The law of talion applies also to a person who tears out an eye, or cuts off an ear, an eyelid, the nose, a lip, the tongue, the penis, the testicles, †the buttocks, †or the edges of the vagina. On the other hand, the law of talion does not apply to the breaking of a bone ; in this case it is enough to amputate the bone of the criminal at the nearest lower joint, and make him pay the fine, if the amputation is less serious than the hurt to the injured party. In the case of a wound under the category *mudiha* and also under the category *hashima*, the law of talion should be applied for the former, and a price of blood of five camels exacted for the latter. In the case of a wound under the category *mudiha* and also under *munak kila*, an application of the law of talion may be claimed for the former, and a price of blood of ten camels for the latter.

A person who may demand that the criminal's wrist be severed under the law of talion may not aggravate the penalty by exacting a separate amputation of each finger ; and if he has in this way exceeded his just due the court should inflict upon him a discretionary punishment, without, however, condemning him to pay any price of blood. †This punishment for an amputation of the fingers does not prevent an amputation of the criminal's hand.

Where the criminal breaks some one's bone in the upper part of the arm, and afterwards cuts the lower part, an amputation under the law of talion is effected only at the elbow, and a fine is also due for rendering useless the upper part of the arm. †The injured party may also content himself with the amputation of the criminal's wrist, together with the price of blood for the part of the arm comprised between the wrist and the place where the bone was broken.

A criminal who has caused some one a wound on the head under the category *mudiha*, in consequence of which the injured party loses his sight, should suffer a *mudiha* of the same kind under the law of talion ; and if the criminal then loses his sight the matter may be considered at an end. Otherwise he must suffer the loss of his sight in the most expeditious manner possible, *e.g.* by having a red-hot iron held close to his eyeballs. And the same procedure must be followed in a case where one of the parties has given the other a blow likely in ordinary circumstances to cause loss of sight, a blow which in fact does cause blindness. Hearing is subject to exactly the same principles as sight; and the loss of either of these faculties involves an application of the law of talion, even though it may be an indirect and not an immediate consequence of the wound. †The same principles regulate a case of loss of bodily strength, of taste, or of the sense of smell. On the other hand, where one has cut some one's finger, and the victim loses another in consequence of the wound, one is liable under the law of talion only for the finger one has cut, and not for the other lost as an indirect consequence of the wound.

CHAPTER II.—METHOD OF PUNISHMENT UNDER THE LAW OF TALION, AND THE PERSONS WHO CAN DEMAND ITS APPLICATION.

Section 1

The left hand may not be amputated, by way of talion, in exchange for the right hand; nor the lower lip instead of the upper; nor *vice versâ*. Nor may the end of one finger be substituted for that of another; nor a member at one part of the body for a member at another. On the other hand, it is of no consequence if the member of the criminal to be amputated is thicker, longer, or stronger than that of the victim, whether such member be †or be not an organic member.

As to wounds of the category of the *mudiha*, *i.e.* the only ones that admit of an application of the law of talion, the length and width—but not the thickness—of the flesh and of the skin must be taken into consideration. If the *mudiha* extends to the entire surface of the skull, and the criminal's skull is smaller than that of the victim, it is enough to give him a similar wound extending to the entire surface of the skull, but not affecting the face or the neck. The criminal then owes in addition a pecuniary indemnity proportional to the greater gravity of the victim's wound. Where, on the other hand, the criminal's skull is the greater it is enough to give him a wound of the same extent as that of the victim, even though this does not affect the entire skull; ††and in this case the criminal may even indicate the part of the skull upon which he prefers to receive the wound. In the case of a *mudiha* that removes the scalp, this is applied to the criminal to the same extent, even though that part of the skull should be smaller than in the injured person, and that in consequence the wound inflicted by way of talion extends beyond the scalp. A person who may demand an application of the law of talion for a *mudiha*, and who exceeds the measure of the *mudiha* received, is liable himself under the law of talion for the excess. In a case where the injured party has involuntarily exceeded this measure, and also where the criminal is contented with a pecuniary penalty for the injury wrongly suffered by him, the injured party owes him the indemnity prescribed for the wound as a whole; though some authorities consider that the injured party is liable merely for an indemnity proportional to the gravity of the excessive punishment he has inflicted. Where several persons jointly inflict a *mudiha* upon another, they are each individually liable to a *mudiha*; or, according to some authorities, to a single *mudiha* in common, so that the total does not exceed the injury suffered by the victim.

A sound hand or a foot is not to be cut off for a mutilated hand or foot, even with the criminal's consent; but if one commits a contravention of this rule, one is not liable under the law of talion, but only for the price of blood. Should, however, the criminal die in consequence of such an abuse, the injured party is liable under the law of talion to the punishment for premeditated homicide. On the other hand, a mutilated hand or foot may be amputated for a sound hand or foot, unless experts declare that it will be impossible to stop the flow of blood. And the injured party must in any case be content with the amputation of the mutilated member, and cannot claim any fine in addition. A sound hand or foot may be amputated for a crooked or lame hand or foot; and no attention need be paid to the colour of the nails of the member to be amputated. ††A place where a nail has disappeared is amputated for an entire nail; but not *vice versâ*. The penis is subject to the same principles as the hand or the foot, so far as regards normal or mutilated state; but it must be understood that the term "mutilated" applies to a penis that has lost its natural elasticity, but not to one that has merely lost its power of erection. Consequently the penis of a man in full enjoyment of his virile faculties may be amputated for that of a castrated or impotent person. Similarly, a sound nose is amputated for a nose that has lost the sense of smell, a sound ear for a deaf one; but not a good eye for a blind eye, nor a sound tongue for a mute tongue.

The law of talion applies to the extraction but not to the breaking of a tooth. Nothing is due for the moment from a person who tears out a tooth from a child that still has its milk teeth, but if it subsequently appears when the child changes its teeth that the tooth in question is not replaced, and experts declare it to be due to a defect in the jaw occasioned by the wound, the criminal is liable to the law of talion, but never before the child comes of age. *In the case of a tooth torn out from a person who has already lost his milk teeth, an application of the law of talion does not depend upon the ascertainment of a new tooth in the alveole.

If one cuts off a person's sound hand, having oneself a hand with only four fingers, one must suffer the amputation of this incomplete hand, and pay in addition an indemnity for the injured party's other finger. Where, on the other hand, it is the injured party who lacked a finger, he cannot claim the amputation of the criminal's hand, but must limit his demand either to the price of blood of his four fingers and nothing else, or to the amputation of four fingers of the criminal, †plus a fine for the part of the hand where the fingers were joined to it, †all without prejudice to a fine of one-fifth of the price of blood for the hand, due in the one case and in the other. Where, on the other hand, one cuts some one's hand that has no fingers at all, one is not liable under the law of talion unless one has oneself a similar hand. Where one cuts a sound hand, but lacks five fingers oneself, one suffers amputation of the mutilated hand, and pays in addition the price of blood of the victim's five fingers. Where a criminal who has only two mutilated fingers cuts the victim's sound hand, the latter may choose between the amputation of the criminal's three remaining fingers, plus the price of blood for the two others he has lost, and the amputation of the criminal's hand and nothing more.

Section 2

*When one cuts in two a person enveloped in some piece of cloth, and then maintains it was a corpse, the legal presumption is in favour of the representative of the victim, provided he takes an oath, and asserts the victim was alive at the moment of the crime. According to our school this presumption exists in favour of the criminal, though not on oath, when, summoned to court for cutting a member of the body, he alleges that the member had a natural defect, at least in the case of a member usually visible. In any other case the presumption is inadmissible. †Where one cuts some one's two hands and then his two feet, and the victim dies, and one maintains that death was the consequence of the wounds, while the victim's representative alleges the contrary, either on the ground that there was a sufficient interval for the victim to be healed, or because death was due to some other cause, the representative enjoys the benefit of the legal presumption, and the criminal owes the price of blood, not for killing the victim, but for cutting the two hands and the two feet, that is to say, the double. The representative also enjoys this presumption if the criminal has cut only one of the victim's hands, and maintains that death is due to some other cause, while the representative maintains that it is due to the wound, and that consequently he may claim the price of blood for homicide and not for the wound. When one gives some one two wounds of the category *mudiha*, and then removes a portion of the skin between the two, in order to make them appear to be only one, and so to be liable for only one indemnity, one has a presumption in one's favour if one alleges that the new wound was made before the two others were healed, at least if this is possible. In this case the injured party may confirm on oath his statement that the new wound was caused after the healing of the others, and the criminal must pay two indemnities, or even three, according to some authorities.

Section 3

††The victim's heirs have a joint right to demand the punishment of a criminal guilty of homicide, and if there are among them absentees, minors, or lunatics, the prosecution must be adjourned until the first return, the second come of age, and the last recover their reason. The criminal must remain in prison until then; and he cannot claim to be released on bail. The heirs, however, should designate one of their number to conduct the prosecution in their name as representative of the victim; and if they cannot agree it must be decided by lot who is to discharge this duty. Where, under these circumstances, there is chosen by lot a person who is in some respect unsuitable to perform the task satisfactorily, he should be replaced by a substitute. According to some authorities unsuitable persons should not be among those among whom the lots are cast. *Moreover, where, in contravention of this principle, one of the heirs presents himself of his own accord and proceeds to the application of the death penalty after obtaining the necessary authorisation, he does not himself become liable under the law of talion, and his coinheritors may still claim their share of the price of blood in the criminal's estate. Only one jurist maintains that it is the inheritor who has thus overstepped the limits of his authority who owes them this indemnity. If the heirs had already pardoned the criminal the inheritor who on his own initiative has carried on a prosecution and applied the capital punishment, is himself punishable with death under the law of talion. This rule, however, is limited by some authorities to the case where the inheritor in question, though knowing the others had pardoned the criminal, still proceeded to the application of the penalty in spite of the prohibition of the court.

Punishment under the law of talion may be carried out only after the authorisation of the Sovereign or of his deputy. An injured party or his representative who acts on his own initiative is liable to punishment at the discretion of the court. In any case the claimant is authorised personally to apply the penalty only when that penalty is death. In the case of all other punishments under the law of talion, such as the amputation of a bodily member, etc., it is the official executioner who must be charged with the duty of carrying them out. The penalty of death must be carried out in the manner ordered by the judgment. Thus a person who has been authorised to cut off the criminal's head, and who intentionally strikes him in another part of the body not indicated in the judgment, is liable to punishment at the discretion of the court, though his right to execute the judgment remains in its entirety. Where, on the other hand, this person declares that he erroneously struck the criminal in a place not indicated by the judgment, and the circumstances admit of the truth of this assertion, the court should transfer the execution of the judgment to some one else, without pronouncing any punishment. ††The hire of the executioner is defrayed by the condemned person.

A penalty under the law of talion must be executed no long time after the condemnation, without paying any attention to whether one is in the sacred territory of Mecca, or whether it is hot or cold, or whether the condemned person is sick. A death penalty or amputation cannot be carried out immediately in the case of a pregnant woman. She must remain in prison not only until she has suckled her child with the first milk occurring after her accouchement, but also until another nurse has been found, and if necessary until the child is weaned, that is, until it is two years old. ††The simple declaration of a condemned woman that she is pregnant is sufficient, even in the absence of visible signs.

Where the victim has been killed by means of an instrument for cutting, or by strangulation, burning, drowning, or starving, etc., the criminal must be put to death in the same way; but if the homicide has been committed by means of magic, he must perish by the sword. †This is also the case where the criminal killed his victim by making him swallow wine, or by pederasty. If in case of homicide by starvation the criminal remains without food for the same number of days as his victim without death resulting, the execution must continue until death ensues. According to one authority, however, the criminal should then perish by the sword. A criminal who has killed his victim by the sword may demand to be executed in the same way. If the victim did not immediately succumb from the wound received, but did so later the representative may at his choice either at once cut off the condemned person's head, or first give him the wound he gave his victim and then either cut his head off or leave him to die of the first wound. If the victim succumbed to an internal wound, or to the breaking of his upper arm, the criminal should have his head cut off. Only one author maintains that the criminal should then receive the same wound as the victim, *and that if he does not die he cannot be given another wound to finish him. For instance, if the victim's wound consists in the loss of a hand, and he succumbs to the consequences of this wound after amputation of the criminal's hand under the law of talion, the victim's representative may either cut off the criminal's head, or pardon him for half the price of blood for homicide. When, in these circumstances the victim's wound consists in the loss of both hands, the representative may none the less cut off the criminal's head after he has suffered under the law of talion for the two hands; but if he pardons him he can claim nothing more.

No responsibility is incurred where the criminal dies from wounds given him under the law of talion. Thus, where there is the loss of a hand, nothing is due from either side, when both the injured party and the criminal die simultaneously of their wounds. And it is the same where the injured party dies before the criminal. †But if in these circumstances the criminal dies first, the injured party may still claim the half of the price of blood.

Where the criminal, told to present his right hand to be amputated under the law of talion, presents his left, in order to have it also cut off, nothing is due by the person who has obtained the judgment if he in fact cuts off that left hand; and he may then proceed to the amputation of the right hand. †But when, in these same circumstances, the criminal declares that he presented the left hand in order to suffer with it the penalty under the law of talion, and the injured party is not content with this, the amputation of the criminal's right hand may be proceeded with, but the price of blood must be paid for the left hand amputated by mistake. One is not liable under the law of talion in this respect. The same rule is applicable where the criminal declares that he presented the left hand in the confusion of the moment, believing it to be the right, and the injured party says he also made the same mistake.

SECTION 4

All premeditated crimes are punishable under the law of talion and subsidiarily by the price of blood; or, according to one jurist, either by the one or the other. In any case, however, the representative of the victim has the right to pardon the criminal, *i.e.* to grant him a remission of the penalty under the law of talion and content himself with the price of blood, even though this may be against the criminal's wish. However.

if it be admitted that the price of blood is only a subsidiary penalty in place of that under the law of talion, an unreserved remission of the latter has, according to our school, the effect of implying a remission of the price of blood; while the remission of the price of blood alone is invalid and forms no obstacle to a subsequent remission of the penalty under the law of talion for this same price of blood. A remission of the penalty under the law of talion may take place for an indemnity of some other nature than the price of blood prescribed by law; but in that case the criminal's consent is necessary, and in default of this the remission is considered to be *ipso facto* retracted, so that the law of talion may be applied. Where it is admitted that the law of talion and the price of blood are equally applicable in the first instance, and that consequently a remission of the price of blood alone is possible, a bankrupt may not grant this remission. On the other hand, in the system maintained by the majority of jurists a remission of the penalty under the law of talion by a bankrupt for the price of blood, has the effect of rendering this price of blood claimable, and the unreserved remission of the penalty under the law of talion implies the remission of the price of blood as we have just shown. Even the remission of the penalty under the law of talion on the part of a bankrupt, on the special condition that no pecuniary penalty should be incurred at all, is lawful, at least according to our school. A person legally incapable by reason of prodigality is, so far as regards the subject with which we are now occupied, in the same position as the bankrupt; or, according to other authorities, as the minor. The remission of the penalty under the law of talion for an indemnity of a similar nature to but greater than the price of blood, *e.g.* of two hundred camels, is void, in the second system referred to, even though the criminal consents; †but, according to the authorities who consider the price of blood as a subsidiary penalty, such a compromise would be lawful.

An adult whose intelligence is sufficiently developed to allow of his managing his property may legally ask some one to give him a wound. In such a case there is no crime on the part of the person who gives the wound; nor even where the individual in question asks to be killed at once. One jurist, however, considers such person to be liable for the price of blood.

Remission either of the penalty under the law of talion or of the indemnity has for its consequence that the criminal owes nothing, either in case of homicide or in case of a wound. Even where death is the indirect consequence of a wound for which remission of the penalty has been granted, the remission prevents any application of the law of talion; but as to the indemnity due for the wound it is only considered to be remitted as well, under these circumstances, where the remission is made—

1. By the terms of a legacy, *e.g.* if one says, "I leave to the criminal the indemnity he owes me"; or

2. Where one uses the explicit terms "remission," "abolition," or "pardon." According to some authorities this also would be a legacy.

All these provisions relate only to the amount of the original indemnity, that prescribed for the wound; consequently, in case of subsequent death from the wound, the criminal owes the difference between this indemnity and the price of blood for homicide. Only one jurist considers a remission granted to the person who inflicts a wound as implying also the price of blood prescribed for loss of life, in all cases where one specially stipulates that this remission relates not only to the crime itself but also to its consequences. †Where a wound inflicted upon a member of the body does not cause death, but only the loss of another member, the criminal still owes, in case of a remission of the penalty under the law of talion for the original wound, the price of blood for the second member of the body lost by the victim as an indirect consequence of the crime. When one has the right to claim a criminal's execution because the wound he has inflicted upon the injured party has indirectly caused death, one cannot exact a penalty under the law of talion for that wound, after granting pardon for the loss of life. †But, on the other hand, a pardon granted for the wound does not imply a remission of the capital penalty; *but the criminal in these circumstances may claim to be executed in the most merciful way, by having his head cut off. Where the penalty for the wound under the law of talion has been already suffered, and the injured party then grants the criminal a remission of what he might claim in case his life was lost in consequence of the wound, this remission is *ipso facto* null and void, if the wound does in reality cause death, unless it has been granted for a consideration.

If the principal, after telling an agent to see to the application of the law of talion, pardons the criminal; but the agent in ignorance of this carries out his instructions, he is not liable under the law of talion for the blood that has been unnecessarily shed. *But he is personally liable for the price of blood, to the exclusion of his *aakila*, without proceeding against the principal.

Where a woman incurs a penalty under the law of talion for a wound, she is freed from liability by marrying the injured party; but if the parties are separated before the consummation of the marriage the woman in question owes the half of the indemnity, or, according to one authority, the half of her proportional dower.

BOOK 48.—THE PRICE OF BLOOD

CHAPTER I.—GENERAL PROVISIONS

SECTION 1

THE price of blood for the homicide of a free Moslem is one hundred camels; that is to say—

1. In a case of premeditated homicide—thirty *hikka*. thirty *jazaa*, and forty *khalifa*, or pregnant camels.

2. In a case of involuntary homicide—twenty *bent-makhad*, twenty *bent-labun*, twenty *ibu-labun*, twenty *hikka*, and twenty *jazaa*, or four-year-old camels.

Involuntary homicide committed—

1. Within the sacred territory of Mecca, or

2. In one of the sacred months, *Zulkaida*, *Zul-Hejja*, *Muharram*, or *Rejab*, or

3. Upon a relative within the prohibited degrees, is punishable with the price of blood on the heavier scale, prescribed for cases of premeditation.

The price of blood for involuntary homicide, even when aggravated by one of the three circumstances just mentioned, is a debt for which the *aakila* of the criminal are responsible; but the price of blood for premeditated homicide can only be recovered from the criminal himself, and is due at any moment. As to voluntary homicide, this involves payment of the price of blood under the heavier scale by a certain time, and may be recovered from the *aakila*.

Camels that are sick or that have redhibitory defects cannot be given except with the consent of the injured party; and the state of the *khalifa* should be ascertained by experts. †On the other hand, it is of no consequence whether the *khalifa* have attained their fifth year, before which period camels do not usually become pregnant. One may give camels of one's own herd, without regard to the particular species, provided they have the required qualities; though some jurists maintain that one can only give camels of that locality. Where one is not a camel owner it is agreed that one may only give camels of the locality.

A nomad must give camels of his tribe. If there are no camels of the locality then camels of the nearest locality must be given. But it is forbidden to give camels without the required qualities or not of the necessary age; or even to pay the value of the camels due, except by mutual consent. If there are absolutely no camels one can oblige the injured party to accept, instead of camels, a thousand *dinar* or twelve thousand drahms. Such was Shafii's original doctrine; but during his stay in Egypt he changed his opinion, and maintained that in such a case one should substitute for the camels their equivalent in the money current in the locality. Finally in a case where the camels can be procured only in part, it is enough to give as many camels as one can, and the money value of those that are wanting.

A woman, or a hermaphrodite, is worth half a man, whether in a case of homicide or in a case of wounding. A Jew or a Christian is worth the third of a Moslem. A fire-worshipper, or even an idolater who has a safe conduct, is worth a fifth. According to our school individuals belonging to foreign nations who have not yet been invited to embrace the faith, and whose religion has not been expressly abolished by the Prophet, keep their personal status so far as concerns crimes committed against their person. Consequently, if one kills or wounds them, one must pay the price of blood prescribed by their respective religions. Where, however, the invitation to be converted to Islam has been made to them, or where their religion has been expressly abolished, crimes committed against their person incur payment of the price of blood of a fire-worshipper.

SECTION 2 (1)

As regards wounds on the head or face, the indemnities due for causing such wounds to a free Moslem are as follows:—

1. For a *mudiha*, five camels.

2. For a *hashima*, which is also a *mudiha*, ten camels; otherwise five. According to some authorities a *hashima* which is not a *mudiha*, is punishable with a fine.

3. For a *munakkila*, fifteen camels.

4. For a *mamuma*, a third of the price of blood prescribed for homicide.

Where, of four individuals, one gives the victim a *mudiha*, another a *hashima*, a third a *munakkila*, and the fourth a *mamuma*, the three first each owe five camels, and the fourth must make up what is wanting to amount to a third of the price of blood for homicide. Wounds on the head and face, classified as less serious than a *mudiha*, necessitate an indemnity fixed according to their gravity in due proportion to a *mudiha*. Where this proportion cannot be ascertained such wounds involve a fine, just in the same way as all other " external " wounds that do not come under the law of talion. As to " internal " wounds, these are punishable with a third of the price of blood for homicide. By " internal wound " is understood any wound that penetrates into the cavities of the body, such as the stomach, the chest, the hollow at the top of the sternum, the sides and the hips. The indemnity due for a *mudiha* is always the same, whatever the extent may be; but two *mudihas* are counted as two distinct wounds if separated from each other by pieces of flesh and skin; or, according to some jurists, if separated either by pieces of flesh or by pieces of skin. And each *mudiha* constitutes a distinct wound if one has been intentionally and the other involuntarily given; or even if a *mudiha* extends both to the head and to the face. This rule, however, is rejected by some authorities. If one enlarges a *mudiha* one has given to the injured party ††this *mudiha* is still none the less a single wound; but there are two where one enlarges a *mudiha* given by a third party. Internal wounds also follow this rule †except that there are considered to be two wounds if the weapon enters the body on one side and comes out of it on the other. And the same is the case with a wound made by a two-pointed lance. The indemnity is due, even though the wound should close up, without distinction between a *mudiha* and an internal wound.

According to our school the price of blood prescribed for homicide is due to the full amount by a criminal who cuts off some one's two ears; but if they withered away, the offence is punishable by fine only.

The loss of an eye involves payment of half the price of blood prescribed for homicide, even in the case of a squint-eyed, short-sighted, or one-eyed person, or in the case of an eye covered with a white pellicle not affecting the sight. But if the sight is affected only a proportional indemnity is owing, unless the proportion cannot be ascertained, in which case the fine is due.

For the loss of each eyelid the criminal owes a quarter of the price of blood prescribed for homicide, even where the injured party is blind.

For a loss of the nose the full price of blood prescribed for homicide is due. For each side of the nose, or for the diaphragm, the price of blood is one-third, though according to others the loss of the diaphragm involves the fine, and that of the two sides of the nose the full price of blood.

Each lip is paid for by half the price of blood prescribed for homicide. †By " lip " is understood that part of the face comprised from right to left between the two corners of the mouth, and from above to below in what covers the gums.

A loss of the tongue involves payment of the price of blood for homicide, even if the injured party spoke with difficulty, or if he was a stammerer, or if he had the defect of pronunciation called *tothgha,* or if he stuttered because still a child. However, as to little children, some authorities consider them to be mutes, as long as they give no signs of having the tongue sufficiently developed, such as making a movement of the tongue when crying or sucking. Now in the case of a mute person a loss of the tongue does not involve payment of the price of blood but a fine.

The loss of each tooth of a free Moslem is indemnified by five camels, whether in the case of a broken tooth of which no remains are visible in the mouth, but of which the root remains intact, or in the case of a tooth completely torn out. A tooth in excess of the ordinary number is paid for by a fine; while a tooth which is a little shaky is considered as a tooth that is quite intact. Only where the tooth is so shaky that it is of no use is the fine prescribed instead of the price of blood; but it is of no consequence whether a shaky tooth causes trouble in manducation. A person who tears out a milk tooth from a child, owes merely the prescribed indemnity, if it appears at the time of the second teething that the child has no other in the empty alveole owing to a lesion of the jaw. *Consequently nothing is due if the child dies before the time of the second teething; but a person who tears out a permanent tooth is liable for payment of the indemnity even though another tooth has appeared in the injured place. Moreover, the tearing out of several teeth involves payment of the indemnity as many times as there are teeth torn out; only one jurist admits the restriction that the indemnity for the whole set can never exceed the amount of the price of blood prescribed for homicide, except where there is more than one offence, and more than one criminal. Half the price of blood is due for each half of the jaw, without prejudice to the indemnity due for the teeth.

The loss of each hand involves half the price of blood prescribed for homicide, provided the wound is not inflicted above the wrist, for in that case one is also liable to a fine. Each finger is paid for by ten camels; each finger joint by a third of this amount, and each joint of the thumb by the half. The feet follow the same rule.

The two teats of a woman involve the price of blood for homicide; but if this wound has been suffered by a man, the offender is punishable with fine. One authority, however, does not admit this distinction, and insists upon the price of blood whatever may be the sex of the person wounded.

The price of blood for homicide is also due in a case of the removal of the two testicles or of the penis; even though the wounded person should be incapable of coition through youth, age, or impotence. The price of blood for homicide is due for the loss of the two buttocks, or for that of the two sides of the vagina, as also for flaying the victim. Where it is ascertained that the victim's life was not imperilled by the flaying, the criminal is not punishable with death, even though the victim may have lost his life later, *e.g.* by decapitation at the hands of a third party.

Section 2 (2)

One owes the price of blood for homicide if one causes some one to lose his reason, and if madness is the consequence of a wound itself involving an indemnity or a fine, the criminal should pay one or other in addition. One jurist, however, maintains that in such a case the greater sum includes the less. If the affair took place in some isolated spot, and the injured party declares he lost his reason in consequence of the wound so received, the price of blood is adjudged to him without its being necessary for him to take an oath, even though his declaration may be somewhat incoherent.

The price of blood for homicide is due in case of loss of hearing; and half is due if this loss is limited to one ear. Other authorities, however, admit in the latter case only a price of blood proportional to the damage sustained. The loss of both ears and of the sense of hearing involves payment of twice the price of blood for homicide. Loss of hearing is proved by the oath of the injured party, unless circumstances indicate that his assertion is false, *e.g.* if he jumps up at some cry uttered while he was asleep or not thinking of the part he was playing. In a case of incomplete deafness the criminal owes a proportional price of blood if the degree of deafness can be ascertained, but otherwise a fine of which the court should fix the amount after examination. According to some jurists the degree of deafness can always be ascertained by comparison with the strength of hearing of a normal individual of the same age as the injured person. Thus the proportional degree of deafness even of a single ear may be ascertained by first closing the wounded ear and ascertaining the strength of hearing of that still uninjured, and then closing that one and testing the strength of hearing of the other.

For loss of sight in each eye the criminal owes the half of the price of blood for homicide; and if the eye is torn out nothing more is due. Blindness is ascertained by experts; or, if necessary, by suddenly putting close to the alleged insensible eye a scorpion or a red-hot iron, when, if the injured party remains motionless the truth of his words may be believed. Partial loss of sight follows the same rule as that already established for cases of partial deafness.

††Loss of smell involves payment of the price of blood for homicide.

Loss of the faculty of speaking also involves payment of the price of blood for homicide; but a loss of the faculty of pronouncing certain letters is estimated proportionally, taking the Arabic alphabet as a basis, *i.e.* twenty-eight letters, though some authorities do not count labials and gutturals. In the case of a person who cannot pronounce certain letters of the alphabet, the calculation differs according to whether this defect is an original one, or the consequence of some malady sent from heaven or resulting from a lesion. Now, if the defect was original or the consequence of a malady the price of blood is due as if the defect did not exist; though some authorities in such case admit only a proportional price of blood; whereas, if the defect was the consequence of a lesion, our school insists upon a proportional price of blood. A loss of half the tongue as well as a loss of the faculty of pronouncing a quarter of the letters renders the criminal liable to a payment of half the price of blood. For a total loss of voice the law exacts payment of the full price of blood for homicide. If the tongue has at the same time lost its mobility, so as no longer to be able to articulate or vibrate, the criminal is liable for twice the price of blood; but some authorities have called this last rule in question.

The sense of taste is equally rated upon the price of blood for homicide. By taste is understood normally the human faculty of distinguishing if a thing be sweet, sour, bitter, salt, or agreeable; and a partial loss of the faculty of distinguishing one or several of these five qualities involves payment of a proportional price of blood. If this partial loss means that one can still imperfectly distinguish all five, the criminal owes a fine.

Payment of the price of blood for homicide is, however, incurred for causing the loss of:—

1. The power to masticate.
2. The power to emit sperm, on account of some lesion of the spine.
3. A woman's power to become pregnant.
4. Pleasurable feeling in the act of coition.

The price of blood is claimable also in a case where a husband or another tears the perineum in the act of copulation. Some authorities deduce the same consequence from a tearing by coition of the separation between the vagina and the urethra; and coition is forbidden, even to the husband, if this act cannot be effected without causing the woman such a wound.

As to loss of virginity, the following cases must be distinguished :—

1. Where it is caused by an individual who has no right to do so. Here again the following distinctions must be made :—

(*a*) If it is caused in some other manner than by the introduction of the penis into the vagina an indemnity is necessary.

(*b*) If it is caused by an introduction of the penis, either by mutual error, or by violation, there is necessary a payment of the proportional dower which the girl could claim after being deflowered, as well as an indemnity for the offence. According to other authorities the girl can claim only the proportional dower that she was worth before her deflowerment.

2. Where it is caused by some one who has the right to do so. In this case there is nothing punishable, though according to some authorities an indemnity is due even in this case, whenever copulation has taken place otherwise than by the introduction of the penis into the vagina.

Loss of muscular force or power of walking involves payment of the price of blood for homicide ; and a fine is due for partial loss of one or the other. Lesion of the spine, involving not only loss of power to walk, but also of pleasurable feeling in the act of coition or of power to emit sperm, is compensated by twice the price of blood for homicide, a rule, however, that is not accepted by some jurists who think that the price of blood is due only once.

Section 2 (3)

The price of blood for the members of the body and for the bodily organs is cumulative ; but if the victim dies from his wounds the price of blood for homicide is due and nothing more. †This is so even if the criminal cuts off his victim's head before the wounds that he has made are healed, provided only that the wounds and the mortal blow are of the same nature, *i.e.* that one of the crimes has not been perpetrated with premeditation and the other involuntarily. There is also plurality in the price of blood, where the wounds and the mortal blow were not caused by the same person.

Section 3

A fine is due for wounds that are not rated by law. The amount is determined by the court in accordance with the seriousness of the case, and in due proportion to the price of blood due for homicide ; or, according to some jurists, with the price of blood due for the wounded member. The proportion to be observed in the application of the fine is the same as the diminution in the value of a slave of the same qualities as the victim due to a similar mutilation. But a fine for the wounding or partial loss of a bodily member should always be less than the legal indemnity prescribed for the total loss of that member; and where an application of the above rule would lead to another result, the court should reduce the fine to an amount that appears to it to be reasonable. In the case of a member such as the thigh, for which no indemnity has been prescribed, the fine should always be less than the price of blood for homicide. The penalty for a wound should be estimated after healing, and where it appears that the victim has not suffered any appreciable permanent lesion, the gravity of the lesion must be taken into consideration immediately before complete recovery. Other authorities, however, maintain that in such a case the court should fix a reasonable amount as the fine, while yet others think that in these circumstances there is no occasion for a fine. Wounds rated by the law, such as the *mudiha*, may be taken as a basis for fixing the amount of fines due for disfigurement: †but fines for wounds not so rated may never be taken as a basis for fixing the amount of others.

The price of blood for the homicide of a slave is the value of the slave. As to lesions suffered by a slave, the price of blood varies in proportion to his value, at any rate in the case of wounds not rated for a free man. In the case of wounds that are rated by law, the same proportion must be observed between the price of blood and the value of the slave as between the price of blood for a similar wound to a free man, and the price of blood for the homicide of a similar individual. A single authority in these circumstances allows the amount to be estimated according to the diminution in the specific value of the slave. *Cutting off a slave's penis and testicles is punishable with a fine amounting to twice the value of the slave. It is true that another doctrine tends to maintain that even in this case the criminal should indemnify the master for the diminution in the slave's value. Finally the offender owes nothing for wounds that do not appreciably diminish the value of the slave.

CHAPTER II.—OBLIGATION TO PAY THE PRICE OF BLOOD; THE *AAKILA*: AND EXPIATION

SECTION 1

WHEN a minor who has not yet attained the age of discernment is upon the edge of a terrace, and is frightened at the cry of a passer-by, and falls down and is killed, the passer by owes the price of blood on the higher scale, and the obligation to pay it falls also on the *aakila*. According to one authority the law of talion may even be applied in these circumstances. †Where, on the other hand, the minor is on the ground, or where it is an adult who is on the edge of the terrace, an unexpected cry causing a fatal fall does not involve a payment of the price of blood. Under the above circumstance, drawing a sword is the same as uttering a cry; while a minor who is almost an adult is the same as an adult in this respect, provided he has a lively intelligence. Where a person utters a cry as a warning of the presence of a wild beast, and thereby so frightens a minor on the edge of a terrace that he falls down and is killed, the price of blood on the lower scale is due by the *aakila*.

If the Sultan, or a judge, etc., sends for a pregnant woman accused of some offence, and frightens her so that she has an untimely birth, he is responsible for the abortion.

There is no punishable offence where a minor placed in a cave of wild beasts is devoured by them; provided, according to some authorities, that he could have saved himself. Nor is there any punishable offence where one pursues with a drawn sword a person who from fear throws himself into the water or into the fire or from the top of a terrace and so kills himself; but if the person so pursued does not throw himself down, but falls accidentally, either through blindness or in the dark, †or if the terrace gives way under him, the pursuer is responsible for the accident. Where a minor, sent to a swimming master to learn how to swim, is drowned, the master is responsible for the price of blood.

One is responsible for digging a well into which some one has fallen, if the digging was in itself illicit. Consequently a man who digs a well on his own ground or on uncultivated ground, is not responsible for the accidents which may result from it; but if he does so in the courtyard of his house, he is responsible for the fall of a person he may invite to such a spot which he knows to be dangerous. And besides this, a responsibility for accidents exists where a well has been dug—

1. On another's land without his knowledge.
2. On a piece of land of which one is only the co-proprietor.
3. On a narrow public way, so as to obstruct it. But where the road is not obstructed there is no responsibility for a person who has dug a well on the public roadway in the following cases:—

(*a*) If the Sovereign has approved it.

(*b*) *If the well is dug for the benefit of the public; for where the profit is merely personal the responsibility does exist.

In this matter a mosque is subject to the same rules as a public road.

One is responsible for accidents caused by the construction of a balcony opening upon a public road; and even, according to the opinion of Shafii in his second period, for having given too much prominence to the pipes collecting the rainwater from the roofs, although this is an act permitted to each proprietor. If the balcony or the water-pipe partly rests upon a wall, and the protruding portion of the balcony or the pipe falls, the proprietor is entirely responsible for the accident; †while he is only responsible for half of it, where the part which rests upon the wall and the protruding portion both fall. A wall that leans upon the side of a public road follows the same rule as a balcony; but no responsibility is incurred for accidents caused by the fall of a wall constructed in vertical equilibrium that afterwards leans over. Other authorities, however, admit this principle only where the proprietor could not have prevented the accident by a demolition or reparation of the wall that threatened to fall down. †The responsibility never extends to accidents that are the remote consequences of the fall of the wall on the public road, *e.g.* if some passer-by stumbles against the *débris* and falls, or where this *débris* affects another's property. ††On the other hand, one is responsible for throwing into the road ordures, melon skins, or other slippery objects that cause a passer-by to fall.

In a case where two causes of accident coincide, it is the more immediate which determines the responsibility. Consequently where one of two persons digs a well and the other places a stone at the edge of it, the latter alone is responsible if another person stumbles against the stone and falls into the well, where both of the two have acted illegally. Where, on the other hand the person who places the stone thereby commits no illegal act, traditional doctrine admits the responsibility of the person who dug the well. Where one person places a stone somewhere and two others follow his example and together place another stone, and a passer-by stumbles against them and falls, all three are responsible for the accident; though some authorities maintain that the first individual is responsible for the half, and the two others jointly for the other half. He who stumbles against a stone deposited by another person and so pushes it before him, and another then stumbles against it, is responsible for this latter accident; but where he stumbles on a big wide road against some one sitting or sleeping upon it, or merely stopping upon it, no responsibility is incurred by either party even if the accident causes the death of either or both. Where, on the other hand, the accident occurs upon a narrow road, our school allows that the death of the person sitting or asleep involves no responsibility in the person who has stumbled against him; but considers that the former would be responsible for the death of the latter. In similar circumstances a moving person is responsible for an accident to a person stopping upon the road, but not *vice versâ.*

SECTION 2

Where two persons inadvertently stumble against each other, the *aakila* of both are mutually liable for half the price of blood on the lighter scale, if the accident has caused the death of both. If the affair is intentional on both sides the *aakila* are responsible for half the price of blood on the heavier scale; if intentional upon one side only, each should be condemned to pay the price of blood prescribed for its particular case. ††In such a collision both estates are charged with double expiation. Where the death of the two individuals is caused by the collision of their respective mounts the consequences are the same except that each estate is charged also with half the value of the other's mount, if the accident involved the death or mutilation of the animals. And similarly where there is a collision, not between two sane adults, but between two minors or two lunatics; though according to some jurists the guardian or the curator must personally guarantee the minor or lunatic committed to their charge from the consequences of the suit if he advised him to ride. Where a third party has caused a minor or a lunatic to ride, jurists unanimously consider him to be responsible for the prices of blood and injuries and damage due on both sides. A collision between two pregnant women resulting in a double abortion is punishable with the price of blood in the way we have explained, ††and four times the expiation in each case; while the *aakila* of the two parties owe each other half the *ghorra* prescribed for abortions. A collision between two slaves that results in the death of both constitutes no offence.

A collision between two ships is regulated by the principles set out with reference to riders, so far as concerns their captains, at any rate where ships and cargoes belong to them. If the ships are loaded with goods belonging to other persons, each captain owes the charterers half the damage sustained by each of them. Finally, in a case where neither the goods nor the ships belong to the captains, these latter are liable for half the value both of the ships and of the goods committed to their charge.

When a vessel is in danger of shipwreck everything in it may be cast into the sea, and this course is even obligatory if it appears that the lives of the crew or of the passengers depend upon it. An indemnity is due for goods so cast that belong to a third party, unless he consented. The words, "Throw out your goods on my account," or "Throw out your goods, I will be responsible," involve an obligation to indemnify the owner; but our school does not recognise this obligation where one merely says, even in the midst of a storm, "Throw out your goods," and nothing more. The responsibility we are speaking of exists only where the request to throw away the goods is made through fear of sinking, and not if made when there is no danger; and it is of no legal consequence whether the casting is or is not profitable to the person making it.

When the projectile from an engine of war rebounds and returns and kills one of the soldiers serving it, the price of blood is divided into as many portions as the original number of soldiers, and each of the dead man's comrades owes his share to the estate. If the victim did not belong to the working of the engine of war the fact constitutes an involuntary homicide, if it is proved that the projectile was not aimed at the victim; but it becomes a premeditated homicide if the thing is knowingly pointed at the victim, and the projectile can strike at that distance in ordinary circumstances.

Section 3

The price of blood for voluntary or involuntary homicide constitutes a debt recoverable in the first instance from the offender, and subsidiarily from his *aakila*, *i.e.* his agnates in collateral line. Some authorities also consider a son to be amongst the *aakila*, provided he is at the same time grandson of his father's brother, as may occur where a homicide is committed by a woman who has married her cousin on the father's side. Responsibility falls first upon the nearest *aakila*, and, if all the sum due cannot be recovered from him, then from his nearest full agnate, or, according to Shafii's first doctrine, from his nearest agnates whether full or only on the father's side. After this it is the offender's patron who is responsible as *aakila*, then his agnates, then the patron's patron and his agnates. After this again the responsibility falls upon the patron of the offender's father, then upon his agnates, his patron and his agnates, and so on. The *aakila* of a woman are responsible for that woman's freed slave, and if there is more than one owner, they are jointly responsible for the total amount due; whereas each agnate of a patron is responsible only for the obligation of his principal. *An enfranchised slave is never considered as being amongst the *aakila* of his patron.

In default of *aakila*, or if their contributions are insufficient, the State is responsible for a Moslem offender; *and if for some reason or other the amount cannot be recovered from the State, the responsibility relapses entirely upon the offender himself.

The *aakila* should acquit themselves of their obligation within the space of three years, if the price of blood is for the homicide of a free Moslem, *i.e.* a third each year. The price of blood for the homicide of an infidel subject of a Moslem prince must be paid in one year; and that for the homicide of a woman in two years, *i.e.* a third of the full price of blood the first year and a sixth the second. However, according to some jurists, the price of blood for such infidel and that for a woman must be paid for in three years. The *aakila* are responsible just the same *if the victim is a slave; but whatever may have been the slave's value, the *aakila* are never obliged to pay each year more than a third of the ordinary price of blood. According to some other authorities, however, they must see that the total price of the slave is paid up within the three years. In case of a homicide committed upon two victims the two prices of blood must be paid within the three years like a single one; but according to some authorities the debt need only be paid within six years. As for the price of blood for a wound or for the loss of a bodily member, one need not pay more each year than a third of the price of blood prescribed for homicide. Other authorities, however, maintain that this is a debt payable in entirety at the end of the first year. All the limits of time we have mentioned are calculated in case of homicide from the moment of the victim's death, and in case of other offences from the moment the crime is committed.

The decease of one of the *aakila* in the course of the year has for its consequence that his debt falls upon the others; but no such responsibility ever attaches to a poor man, a slave, a minor, or a madman. A Moslem *aakila* is not responsible for an infidel offender, nor an infidel *aakila* for a Moslem offender; *but a Jew may be responsible for a Christian offender, and *vice versâ*. The responsibility of a rich *aakila* never exceeds half a *dinar*, nor that of a man of moderate means a quarter per annum; or, according to others, for the three years. The state of the fortune of the debtor is ascertained at the end of each year; while he who becomes insolvent in the course of the year owes nothing.

Section 4

The person of a slave may be seized in satisfaction of a debt due for an offence committed by him, but his master may, instead of abandoning the culpable slave to be put up to auction, ransom him either with his value or with the indemnity prescribed for a lesion, whichever is the more advantageous for him. In his first period Shafii did not accept this doctrine, maintaining that the prescribed indemnity is due in any case, if the master wishes to avoid the seizure of the slave. *The money due for the offending slave is a material debt, and not an obligation for which he is personally responsible after being enfranchised. If the slave, after being ransomed by his master, is guilty of another offence, the master has again the choice between seizure and ransom; but if the second offence is committed before the payment of the first ransom the slave may be seized for the total of the two debts, unless his master ransoms him either with his value, or with the indemnities prescribed for the two crimes, whichever is the more advantageous for him. In these circumstances Shafii's first doctrine allowed only the ransom with the two indemnities. In the case of the enfranchisement or sale of the slave after the offence, and supposing that the validity of these acts depends upon the master's solvency, the latter can no longer abandon his slave, but is obliged to ransom him, in the manner already explained. And it is the same if the master kills the slave after the offence. According, however, to other authorities Shafii's first doctrine insisted even in these circumstances upon the prescribed indemnity; but the master owes nothing where the slave, after committing the offence, takes to flight or dies a natural or accidental death, unless the master previously opposes his seizure. If he opposes the seizure he implies an intention to ransom the slave, †and though in ordinary circumstances he may withdraw from a promise to ransom his slave and declare that he prefers to abandon him, such retractation is no longer permissible as soon as the slave's death has rendered his seizure impossible. A master may ransom his female slave enfranchised by reason of maternity in the same way as his other slaves; though according to some jurists Shafii originally insisted for her also upon payment of the indemnity as the only possible ransom. *A plurality of offences committed by such female slave does not in any way affect her master's right of ransom.

Section 5

Abortion involves the *ghorra* as price of blood for the fœtus if brought forth dead in consequence of the crime, without prejudice to the price of blood for the mother, where the abortion causes her death also. †It is the same if the fœtus appears to be dead in the mother's womb in consequence of the crime, and cannot be extracted because of her death. If it is a question not of a fœtus but of a child brought forth by abortive means, and remaining some time alive without showing signs of pain, its death is presumed to be natural and nothing is due for the abortion; but if the child dies immediately after birth, or some time afterwards, but with constant signs of pain, the person causing the abortion owes the ordinary price of blood due in case of homicide.

If there are two fœtuses there are also two *ghorras*. The *ghorra* is due in full even where there issues from the womb merely a hand or a piece of flesh virtually containing a human form, according to the midwives; or even, according to some jurists, where there remains in the womb a piece of flesh which, according to the midwives, could take a human form.

The *ghorra* consists in a male or female slave of the age of discernment without redhibitory defects. †Thus one may give as *ghorra* a slave of a certain age, provided that age does not approach decrepitude The value of the slave must not be less than one-twentieth of the price of blood due for homicide; and in default of a slave answering all these conditions one owes five camels. Some authorities, however, do not insist upon the slave having the value mentioned. In default of camels their value must be substituted for them. The *ghorra* is payable to the heirs of the fœtus, and is a debt for which the *aakila* of the offender are responsible; though according to some jurists the offender alone is responsible if the abortion has been caused with premeditation. According to some authorities the *ghorra* is the same for a fœtus which at its birth would have been Moslem as for one that would have been Jewish or Christian. According to others nothing is due for the abortion of a fœtus which would have been infidel by birth; †but the majority allow for this fœtus a *ghorra* of the amount of one-third of that for a fœtus which would have been Moslem. The abortion of a female slave is punished with one-tenth of her value upon the day of the offence; or, according to others, on the day of the abortion; and the amount goes to the profit of the master. †If the mother is deprived of a bodily member or organ, but the fœtus is without bodily defects, the value of which one-tenth is due is the mother's original value. *And the tenth due for the abortion of a female slave is also a debt for which the *aakila* are responsible.

Section 6

A homicide requires an expiation, even where the offender is a minor, a lunatic, a slave, or an infidel subject of a Moslem prince; and it makes no difference whether the homicide is premeditated, voluntary, or involuntary. Expiation is even necessary:—

1. In case of excusable homicide, at least where the victim is a Moslem.

2. In case of homicide committed upon the territory of infidels not subject to Moslem authority, at least where the victim is a Moslem.

3. Where the victim is an infidel subject of a Moslem prince.

4. Where the victim is still in his mother's womb.

5. Where the victim is the offender's slave.

6. In case of suicide. This, however, has been called in question.

Expiation is not due—

1. For homicide committed upon an infidel woman or minor not subject to our authority.

2. For homicide committed upon a rebel.

3. In case of legitimate defence.

4. Where homicide is committed under the law of talion.

†An expiation is due for each accomplice. This expiation is equal to that prescribed for injurious comparison; *with the exception of the option of maintaining sixty indigent persons.

BOOK 49.—PROCEDURE IN CASE OF CRIMES AGAINST THE PERSON

Section 1

The accuser must give a precise account of the offence, mentioning whether it was premeditated or involuntary, whether the criminal had accomplices or not, and so on; and if he does not do this the court shall require him to give details of his complaint; or, according to some authorities, it should dismiss him on the ground of there being no case. According to others the accuser should also name in his complaint the particular person alleged to have committed the crime. †Thus where the accuser confines himself to asserting that only one of several accused persons committed a homicide, the court has no right to compel them to take an oath, if they deny it. †This principle applies not only to the procedure we are here concerned with, but also in cases of usurpation, theft, and destruction. Moreover, an accusation can only be received from a sane adult, whether a Moslem or an infidel subject of our Sovereign or enjoying our protection, provided in the two last cases that the accused is of the same quality.

One may not accuse a person of homicide after having previously accused another person of the same offence, at any rate where one asserted there were no accomplices; *but there is no objection to first bringing an accusation of premeditated homicide, and afterwards limiting it to that of voluntary homicide.

An oath fifty times repeated is admissible as legal proof only in case of grave suspicion, *e.g.* if the victim is found in the camp or village of his enemies, if a band of men run away leaving a corpse lying on the ground, or if two bands fight together furiously and a victim remains on the spot. In this last case suspicion falls upon the band to which the victim did not belong; but if the bands did not fight, the fact of the victim remaining dead at that place constitutes a grave suspicion that he was killed by the band to which he belonged. The deposition of a single witness of irreproachable character or that of several slaves or women also constitutes a grave suspicion; on condition, according to some authorities, that the latter are separately examined. †A similar suspicion results from the deposition of persons of notorious misconduct, of minors, or of infidels. On the other hand, grave suspicion never exists where the matter is open to doubt, *e.g.* where one of two sons of the victim declares that so-and-so is guilty, and the other asserts the contrary. A single jurist admits suspicion, even in these circumstances; while others do not admit as a ground of doubt the denial of a person of notorious misconduct. Where, however, in the circumstances above mentioned, one of the sons declares that the homicide was committed by Zaid in complicity with a person he does not know, and the other declares it was committed by Amr in complicity with a person he does not know, each son may confirm upon oath, fifty times repeated, the truth of his deposition, and then afterwards claim from the person he has indicated one-quarter of the price of blood. As to grave suspicion falling upon a band of men, an accused person who denies having formed part of it has a presumption in his favour if he confirms his statement upon oath. †The oath fifty times repeated is not to be taken by an accuser, if the grave suspicion relates only to the material fact of homicide, and does not indicate whether it is premeditated or not; and it can only be taken in case of homicide, not in cases of wounding or destruction of property, unless the object destroyed is a slave.

This oath consists in the accuser swearing fifty times that his complaint is true; but our school does not insist upon the ceremony taking place without interruption. Consequently an accuser struck with an attack of madness or fainting may continue his oath upon coming to himself. ††But if the accuser dies before finishing the fifty oaths required, no right of continuation devolves upon his heir, who may, however, on his part, pronounce a new series of fifty oaths. Where the victim leaves several heirs who may jointly demand the punishment of the guilty person, the fifty oaths are divided among them in proportion to their respective shares in the estate; except that any one who would in this way take merely part of an oath, must take it in its entirety. One authority even maintains that the oath should be taken fifty times by each heir. The refusal of an heir to take this oath makes his right pass to his coinheritor; and if one of two coinheritors cannot perform his oaths through absence the other may either take by himself the fifty oaths prescribed and receive at once his portion of the price of blood, or await the return of the absent coinheritor. Finally, in cases of crimes against the person, our school insists all the same upon the repetition of the oath fifty times—

1. When it is taken by the accused, in default of grave suspicion.

2. When it is taken by the accuser, or by the accused, in case of grave suspicion.

3. When it is taken to supplement the deposition of a single witness.

The result of the repeating of the oath fifty times is that the price of blood becomes obligatory both for the criminal and for his *aakila*, in case of voluntary or involuntary homicide, and that it is due from the criminal alone in case of premeditated homicide. In his first period Shafii considered that even in this last case the repetition of the oath fifty times was sufficient proof for the law of talion.

Where there is grave suspicion of premeditated homicide against three persons of whom one only has been arrested, the accuser begins by taking an oath fifty times to give his complaint greater force against the one arrested; and after this the latter owes one-third of the price of blood. If afterwards another of the accused persons is arrested, the accuser again repeats the oath fifty times with respect to him; but doubt has been cast on this rule by a jurist who maintains that only twenty-five oaths can be insisted on against the second accused, if the accused does not mention him upon the first occasion. This jurist, however, admits, as do the majority, that on the contrary supposition the new oaths are of no value; †in that case suffice the first fifty oaths legally pronounced in the absence of the second accused.

The oath fifty times repeated is administered also to an individual who can claim only a pecuniary penalty in place of talion, for instance, to the master of a slave, even where the master in question is a slave undergoing enfranchisement by contract. As to an accuser who becomes an apostate it is preferable not to administer to him the oath with which we are concerned, until he returns from his errors; though according to our school the validity of the oath is unquestionable if taken at once. And finally, the oath repeated fifty times is not administered if the victim leaves no heir.

Section 2

No one can be condemned to a penalty under the law of talion unless the fact has been proved, either by a confession, or by two male witnesses of irreproachable conduct. But a criminal's condemnation to a pecuniary penalty may be based as well upon the deposition of a single male witness, corroborated by that of two women or by an oath; †with the single exception that where an accuser demands an application of the law of talion and afterwards finds that he can produce as witnesses only one man and two women, he may not change his mind and remit any proceeding under the law of talion and content himself with asking for a pecuniary penalty; although these witnesses would have sufficed had he in the first instance applied for the imposition of a fine. And, in accordance with the same principle, where a *hashima*, constituting in the first instance a *mudiha*, is established by a man and two women, the penalty prescribed for a *hashima* cannot be exacted, at least according to our school, as the *mudiha* involves the law of talion, and consequently cannot be proved in that manner. The depositions should indicate precisely the fact with which the accused is charged. Thus a deposition to the effect that "the accused struck the victim with his sword and wounded him and he is dead," is not enough until completed by a deposition to the effect that "death was the consequence of the blow," or that "it was the accused who killed him." A *damia* is proved by a deposition that "the accused struck the victim on the head in such a way as to cause it to bleed," or "to make the blood spurt forth;" a *mudiha* by a deposition that the accused struck him in such a way as to uncover the bone; though according to some authorities it is enough to prove that the accused dealt the victim a *mudiha* upon the head. In the case of a *mudiha* the deposition should also indicate precisely the place and gravity of the wound, as otherwise it would be impossible to apply the law of talion. A homicide committed by means of magic is proved only by the criminal's confession, and not by the testimony of witnesses.

A deposition to the effect that a certain person, of whom one is the heir, has been wounded by another, is admissible only when the wound has been completely healed. Nor may one depose, in a civil action, in favour of any one of whom one is the heir, during that person's last malady; as the principle is admitted that no one may depose in his own favour. Consequently the *aakila* cannot give evidence to the effect that the witnesses for the accuser are of notorious misconduct, at any rate where these same *aakila* would contribute to the price of blood in case of condemnation. If two witnesses assert that two persons have killed some one, but these two accused persons in their turn accuse the two witnesses of being themselves the only guilty parties, the latter are none the less condemned, if the representative of the victim sides with the witnesses. On the other hand, the accusation on both sides should be rejected, if the representative sides with the accused, or if he declares that both the accused and the witnesses are guilty, or if he declares that they are all lying. A penalty may not be pronounced under the law of talion, where some of the heirs of the victim admit that their coheritors have already remitted this penalty; and the depositions of two witnesses who contradict one another as to the time, the place, the instrument or the circumstances of the crime, are void and of no effect. Some authorities admit depositions of this nature merely as establishing grave suspicions.

BOOK 50.—REBELS

SECTION 1

By rebels are understood those who revolt against the Sovereign, either by attacking him, or by disobeying his orders, or by refusing services or taxes legally due to him. In case of armed rebellion in which the guilty parties are organised under chiefs, they must be marched against and reduced to obedience; provided, according to some authorities, that there exists a Sovereign, recognised as their head by all Moslems. As to persons whose rebellion consists only in their deviation from recognised orthodox doctrine, those, for instance, who no longer observe public prayer, or commit grave sins in secret, these must be left alone, unless they trouble the internal security of the state with armed force, for then they must be fought and punished like brigands.

Rebels remain capable of deposing as witnesses, and the judgments rendered by their courts may be executed, except judgments that would be illegal even if delivered by our courts, or such as approve of hostile acts committed against true believers. †Our courts may reply to letters of requisition addressed to them by rebel courts, and may accept as evidence informations drawn up by them. Definite penalties pronounced and carried into effect by them are recognised as legal; as are also their charity tax, poll-tax, and land-tax, and even the application of the proceeds of the charity-tax to the support of their soldiers. This last rule, however, is doubtful.

Rebels are civilly responsible for all damage caused by them to the property of loyal subjects; and the latter are similarly responsible for all damage caused by them to the property of the rebels otherwise than in the war. One jurist, however, does not admit the responsibility of loyal subjects in any case. Individuals forming part of an organisation, though not united in armed bands, are civilly responsible for any destructive act, just like any other person; but those who, though not organised, are united in armed bands, should be considered in this respect as rebels, even where there are no chiefs among them, and they offer no opposition to lawful authority.

Rebels may not be fought with, until there has been previously sent them some trustworthy and intelligent person, capable of advising them to lay down their arms. He should begin by inquiring as to their grievances, and if they complain of vexatious treatment or error on the part of the lawful authorities, he should put a stop to this at once, and give the advice that may be necessary for the submission of the rebels. If the rebels refuse to take this advice, the Sovereign should threaten to reduce them to obedience by force of arms; and if they ask for a delay he may accord or refuse it as seems to him best.

It is forbidden to kill rebels when they take to flight, or when disabled or when made prisoners. Prisoners, including minors and women, must be retained until the end of the war and the complete dispersion of the rebel bands, unless they declare their submission to lawful authority. After the pacification captured arms and horses are to be returned to their owners, provided that nothing further is to be feared from them. In warfare against rebels it is forbidden to make use of the arms and horses taken from them, except in case of absolute necessity, or to use methods of great destructiveness, such as fire or warlike machines, unless such a course is rendered necessary by the rebels themselves using these things in their defence, or by there being no other means for our escape when surrounded by them.

It is equally forbidden to reduce rebels to obedience by means of troops recruited from amongst the infidels, or even from amongst Moslems who, like followers of the school of Abu Hanifa, maintain that rebels who have taken to flight may be killed. Infidels not subject to Moslem authority, enrolled by rebels in a war against us, and thus enjoying their protection, have no title to be so considered by us; †the rebels themselves, however, are bound to observe the engagements they have contracted with the infidels in question. Infidel subjects of our Sovereign who take part with the rebels against us, knowingly, and of their own free will, lose all right to our protection; but if they are forced to join in the war, our engagements towards them remain intact. It is the same where the infidels in question declare that they believed in good faith that it was lawful for them to take part in the war, and that the rebels were in the right. At least this is the theory of our school. In all these circumstances infidel subjects of our Sovereign should be treated in warfare like the rebels themselves.

Section 2

Essential requisites for a Sovereign are to be a free, sane, adult, male Moslem of the tribe of the Koraish; of sufficient courage, discretion and knowledge of the law; of sound sight, hearing, and speech.

Sovereignty is conferred—

1. By election; †to be carried out by the best scholars, chiefs, and other persons occupying a high social position, or so many of them as can be united in one place.

2. By designation; the Sovereign having the right to designate his successor, and even to grant to several persons the right of designating one of them to be his successor.

3. By the right of the stronger; and this title to the supreme authority is to be recognised not only where the Sovereign who is thus imposed upon the faithful unites in his person all the requisite qualities, †but also if he possesses none of them, and is even of notorious misconduct, or an ignorant person.

[A tax-payer who alleges that he has paid the rebels the tax due from him, has a presumption in his favour; but this presumption does not exist with regard to the poll-tax †or the land-tax. The same presumption exists in favour of a person who asserts that he has suffered a definite penalty, unless the crime was proved by witnesses; or unless no trace of punishment can be found on the criminal's body.]

BOOK 51.—APOSTASY

Apostasy consists in the abjuration of Islam, either mentally, or by words, or by acts incompatible with faith. As to oral abjuration it matters little whether the words are said in joke, or through a spirit of contradiction, or in good faith. But before such words can be considered as a sign of apostasy, they must contain a precise declaration—

1. That one does not believe in the existence of the Creator, or of His apostles; or

2. That Muhammad, or one of the other apostles, is an impostor; or

3. That one considers lawful what is strictly forbidden by the *ijmaa*, *e.g.* the crime of fornication; or

4. That one considers to be forbidden what is lawful according to the *ijmaa*.

5. That one is not obliged to follow the precepts of the *ijmaa*, as well positive as negative; or

6. That one intends shortly to change one's religion; or that one has doubts upon the subject of the truth of Islam, etc.

As to acts, these are not considered to be incompatible with faith, unless they show a clear indication of a mockery or denial of religion, as, *e.g.* throwing the Koran upon a muck heap, or prostrating oneself before an idol, or worshipping the sun. No account is taken of the apostasy of a minor or a lunatic, nor of acts committed under violent compulsion. Even where the guilty person, after pronouncing the words or committing the acts, becomes mad, he may not be put to death until he has recovered his sanity. This favour, however, does not, according to our school, extend to the case of drunkenness. Apostasy, and a declaration of having returned from one's errors, pronounced by a drunken person, have the ordinary legal consequences.

Witnesses need not recount in all their details the facts that constitute apostasy; they may confine themselves to affirming that the guilty person is an apostate. Other authorities are of the contrary opinion; but the majority go so far as to make no account of the mere denial of the accused, even where the assertions of the witnesses are made in general terms. But where, on the other hand, the accused declares that he acted under compulsion, and the circumstances render this assertion plausible, *e.g.* if he has been kept a prisoner by infidels, he has a presumption in his favour, provided he takes an oath ; but this presumption does not arise in the absence of such circumstances. Only where the two witnesses required by law do not declare that "the accused is apostate," but that "the words pronounced by him are words implying apostasy," and the accused then maintains that he only pronounced them under compulsion, the presumption is in his favour, and it is not necessary for him to give more detailed explanations. Where, after the death of an individual whose faith has never been suspected, one of his sons who are both Moslems declares that his father abjured Islam and died impenitent, and adds the cause of the apostasy, this son alone is excluded from the succession, and his portion escheats to the state as a tax ; but his deposition has no effect upon the rights of his coinheritors. *The same rule applies also where the cause of the crime is not mentioned, and the son limits himself to saying that his father died apostate.

An attempt should be made to induce the apostate to return from his or her errors ; though, according to one authority, this is only a commendable proceeding. The exhortation should take place immediately, or, according to one jurist, in the first three days ; and if it is of no effect, the guilty man or woman should be put to death. Where, on the contrary, the guilty party returns from his or her errors, this conversion must be accepted as sincere, and the converted person left alone ; unless, according to some authorities, he has embraced an occult religion such as the Zend, whose adherents, while professing Islam, are none the less infidels in their heart, or some doctrine admitting of a mystic or allegorical interpretation of the Koran.

The child of an apostate remains a Moslem, without regard to the time of its conception, or to one of its parents remaining a Moslem or not. One authority, however, considers the child whose father and mother have abjured the faith to be an apostate ; while another considers such a child to be by origin an infidel. [*The child should be considered as an apostate. This is what the jurists of Irak have handed down to us as the universally accepted theory.]

*As to the ownership of the property of an apostate dead in impenitence, it remains in suspense, *i.e.* the law considers it as lost from the moment of abjuration of the faith, but in case of repentance it is considered to have been never lost. However, there are several other theories upon the subject ; though all authorities agree that debts contracted before apostasy, as well as the personal maintenance of the apostate during the period of exhortation, are charges upon the estate. †It is the same with any damages due in consequence of pecuniary prejudice caused to other persons, the maintenance of his wives, whose marriage remains in suspense, and the maintenance of his ascendants or descendants. Where it is admitted that ownership remains in suspense, the same principle must be applied to dispositions subsequent to apostasy, in so far as they are capable of being suspended, such as enfranchisement by will, and legacies, which all remain intact where the exhortation is successful, though not otherwise. On the other hand, dispositions which, by their very nature, do not admit of such suspension, such as sale, pledging, gift, and enfranchisement by contract, are null and void *ab initio ;* though Shafii, in his first period, wished to leave them in suspense. All authorities, moreover, are agreed that an apostate's property may in no case be left at his disposition from the moment that a state of apostasy has been ascertained, but must be deposited in charge of some person of irreproachable character. But a female slave may not be so entrusted to a man ; she must be confided to some trustworthy woman. An apostate's property must be leased out ; and it is to the court that his slave undergoing enfranchisment by contract should make his periodical payments.

BOOK 52.—FORNICATION

The crime of fornication consists in the introduction of the penis into the vagina of a woman with whom one has no right of coition, without one being able to allege any cause of error. The crime is punishable with a definite penalty; and this punishment is also applicable, according to our school, to whoever introduces his penis into the podex of a man or of a woman. On the other hand, the penalty does not apply to a person who merely indulges in voluptuous touching of the thighs, nor to coition—

1. With one's own wife or female slave during their menstrues, during a fast, or while in a state of *ihram*.

2. *With one's own female slave married to another man.

3. *With one's wife, during her period of legal retirement.

4. *With a female slave of whom one is the owner, in case of relationship or affinity within the prohibited degrees.

5. *Under violent compulsion.

6. ††In cases where authorities are not in agreement as to the illegality of coition, *e.g.* in case of a marriage concluded without witnesses, of which the Malekites do not admit the absolute nullity.

7. †With a corpse, *or with an animal.

Thus the law only punishes coition with a free woman, or with the slave of another person, in the case of an individual—

1. With whom one is not engaged in the bonds of matrimony, and who has surrendered herself for nothing or for a remuneration.

2. With whom one is related by family or marriage within the prohibited degrees, even though one may have married her in fact, but in contravention of the law.

One is not punishable for the crime of fornication unless one is an adult sane Moslem, and unless one knew the act was forbidden. Drunkenness cannot be pleaded as an excuse.

The penalty is as follows.

1. For a guilty person whom the law considers as *mohsan*, by which word is understood in this respect an adult sane free Moslem man or woman who has already experienced coition in a legitimate marriage, the penalty is lapidation. *If this marriage is attackable in any respect,

the penalty of lapidation cannot be pronounced. †It is necessary that coition under the marriage must have consisted in the introduction of the penis into the vagina, and that the man should have been an adult sane free Moslem at the moment. Infidel subjects of our Sovereign are considered as Moslems so far as regards this matter. †The fact that one of the accomplices in the crime of fornication does not satisfy all the conditions required for lapidation, constitutes no excuse for the other.

2. For a free person who is not *mohsan*, the punishment for fornication is one hundred stripes, followed by banishment for one year to a distance at least permitting prayer to be abridged; †and if the Sovereign designates a particular spot as the criminal's residence, he must submit to this aggravation of his punishment. In any case, during the period of his banishment, the criminal may not remain in the place where the crime was committed, nor in the place of his domicile; †and if he makes his appearance in one or other of these places, the authorities should drive him away. †A banished woman need not set out on her journey alone; she has a right to be accompanied either by her husband, or by some one within the prohibited degrees, at the expense of the state when she has not sufficient means of her own. †But no one can be obliged to accompany the guilty woman, even for hire.

3. For a slave, the punishment for fornication is fifty stripes, followed by banishment for half a year, or according to one authority a whole year. One jurist, however, does not admit banishment as a punishment where the criminal is a slave.

The crime of fornication is proved only by the evidence of witnesses and by confession. A confession need only be uttered once, and has no effect when retracted; †but a retraction is null and void where the guilty party asks for pardon or takes to flight. As to the evidence of witness the reader must note that the law requires four male witnesses; but the definite penalty is not pronounced, even on the deposition of these four witnesses, if four women ascertain that the woman accused is still a virgin. But the deposition of these four women is not enough to convict the accuser of defamation. If one of the witnesses indicates a certain part of the house where the crime was committed, and the three others a different place, the legal proof is not attained.

It is the Sovereign or his delegate who should have the definite penalty executed, where the criminal is free or partially enfranchised; and it is preferable that the execution of the sentence should take place in presence of the person who ordered it, and of the witnesses. In the case of a slave the execution of the sentence should be ordered either by his master or, by the Sovereign, †the latter having priority in case of a dispute. †As to banishment it is always the master who should see to the execution of the sentence in the case of a slave; but in this matter a slave undergoing enfranchisement by contract is considered as a free man. †The right of the master to see to the execution of a sentence of definite punishment pronounced against his slave exists none the less should the master be a man of notorious misconduct, or an infidel, or himself a slave undergoing enfranchisement by contract; and in the case of a penalty at the discretion of the court, the right of execution of the sentence belongs exclusively to the master. †The master may also examine the witnesses in a penal matter.

Lapidation takes place by means of pieces of dry earth or of stones of convenient form and size. If the criminal is a man, he is not half buried in the ground; †but this procedure is commendable in the case of a woman, at least where the crime has been established by the evidence of witnesses. The sickness of the criminal, excessive heat or cold, are no grounds for postponing the execution; unless, according to some authorities, where the proof of the crime is a confession. On the other hand, sickness is a good ground for postponing the execution of a sentence of flogging, unless no hope can be entertained of a cure. In these circumstances, however, flogging is effected by means of one stroke with a rod with a hundred bands, instead of by means of one hundred strokes with a whip with a thong; if it is impossible to procure a rod with more than fifty bands, then the flogging consists of two strokes. Even in this case, however, the flogging must be done in such a way that the criminal experiences some pain; *i.e.* that the bands must all touch him or at least contribute by their weight to make the instrument fall more heavily; for if the patient unexpectedly recover, that is no reason for repeating the flogging. Flogging should not take place at a moment when it is excessively hot or cold; though, according to Shafii's personal opinion, the Sovereign, if he proceeds to carry out the execution of the sentence, in spite of the criminal's sickness, is not responsible for the consequences that may ensue. According to that view it is merely commendable to adjourn the punishment in that case, but it is not a rule of rigorous observance.

BOOK 53.—DEFAMATION

DEFAMATION is punishable only when committed by a sane adult Moslem. Drunkenness is no excuse. The law requires that the crime should have been committed spontaneously. As to a minor who has attained the age of discernment, he is punishable at the discretion of the court. Ascendants are not punishable for defamation against their descendants.

The penalty for a free person is eighty stripes, and for a slave forty, provided that the injured party possesses the character of *mohsan, i.e.* would be punishable with lapidation if the accusation were well founded. As to the legal meaning of the word *mohsan,* we explained this when treating of imprecation.

There are punishable as defamers : *witnesses who prove in court the crime of fornication, but are not of the prescribed number of four ; and even witnesses, of whatever number, who are not male, free, and, according to our school, Moslem. On the other hand, a witness cannot be punished as a defamer who proves that the accused confessed the crime of fornication, even though he be the only witness.

Where two persons mutually defame each other there is no ground for compensation ; and where the injured party has himself of his own accord applied the definite prescribed penalty, the flogging has not been legally executed, and must be repeated.

BOOK 54.—CRIMES PUNISHABLE WITH AMPUTATION

CHAPTER I.—THEFT

Section 1

Amputation for theft is applicable only under the following circumstances :—

1. That at least the quarter of an entire *dinar* has been stolen, or an object of that value. †Thus if one steals a piece of unminted gold of the volume of a quarter of a *dinar*, that would not have this volume after being placed under the die, one is not liable to the definite prescribed penalty. This penalty should be pronounced against a thief who takes several *dinars*, believing them to be pieces of copper of less than the required value ; †and also against a person who steals an old coat of less than the required value ; but in the pocket of which, accidentally and without his knowledge, there is something of which the value, added to that of the coat, does amount to the value required. Where one commits two thefts at the same place, each less than the quarter of a *dinar*, but more when taken together, one has committed two non-punishable thefts, if the owner perceived the first before the second took place, and repaired the fastening in the meanwhile. †Otherwise there is considered to be only one theft, of the required amount, and consequently the thief is punishable with amputation. †The penalty is applicable also to the case of a person who makes an opening in a sack of corn, etc., so that its contents are abstracted, to the minimum value required. Two persons committing this abstraction together are punishable with amputation only when they take twice the minimum, as otherwise each would be considered to have taken an inferior amount. Amputation is never applicable to a person who steals things impure in themselves, and consequently without legal value, such as wine, pork, a dog, or the untanned skin of an animal that has died a natural death or been killed in any other manner than by slaughtering or in hunting in accordance with the precepts of the law. ††But where the vessel in which some prohibited liquid is

contained is stolen at the same time, and the value of this vessel reaches the required minimum, amputation should be pronounced, without regard to the contents. And in accordance with this same principle amputation does not take place for the theft of a guitar or other instrument of music, though some authorities exact it where the different fragments of the guitar have the required value. [†These authorities are right.]

2. That the stolen property belongs to another. Consequently amputation does not take place where the stolen object has already become the property of the thief before its abstraction; even though this may be unknown to him, as by succession. Nor does it take place where the original value of the things stolen has already diminished, before their abstraction, below the minimum, as where the owner eats some of his provisions, etc. According to Shafii's personal opinion it is not absolutely necessary that one should be the owner of the object to render amputation inapplicable; it is enough if one has claimed it in a court of justice. †Where only one of two accomplices makes some claim to an object either for himself or for both of them, while the other opposes this claim, the former alone is exempt from amputation; his claim does not save his accomplice from amputation. *And it follows also from this principle that amputation is not rigorously required in the case of theft of an object of which one is co-proprietor, when this object is in a jointly owned shop, however small may be the thief's share.

3. That the abstraction cannot have been committed by error. Consequently amputation does not take place for abstractions to the prejudice of one's ascendants or descendants, nor for those committed by a slave to the prejudice of his master; *though amputation is rigorously necessary for abstractions committed by one of two married persons to the prejudice of the other. As to thefts to the prejudice of the public treasury, they do not involve amputation in the following cases:—

(*a*) Where the stolen object is intended specially for a corporation of which the thief is a member.

(*b*) †Where the thief has a claim to the stolen object under some respect, *e.g.* where a Moslem steals money intended for the public good, or where a poor person steals money forming part of the charity tax.

Our school insists upon amputation for taking a door or a beam from a mosque, but not for taking a mat or a lighted lamp. †On the other hand, amputation is rigorously necessary for any one who steals any fixed object, or carries off a female slave enfranchised on account of maternity, asleep or mad.

4. That the stolen object is kept sufficiently safe, either in sight, or in a sure place. When one deposits an object on a desert plain or in a mosque one ought not to lose sight of it; but when one deposits it somewhere inside an enclosed place, it is sufficient to take the usual amount of care to see to the fastenings. A stable is a sure place for animals, but not for household goods or wearing apparel; the courtyard of a house and the *soffa* are sure places for utensils and daily clothes, but not for finery, nor for gold and silver coin. If one lies down upon a coat in a desert plain or in a mosque, or uses something as a pillow, these objects are kept sufficiently safe, provided the sleeper does not turn over in his sleep and does not lie down to the side. A coat or other object placed upon a desert plain close to the owner are considered to be kept safely so long as he does not lose sight of them, and is able to defend them from attack, either by his own strength or by calling for assistance. A solitary house is a safe place if a strong man is in charge of it, it matters little if the door is open or closed. A house surrounded by other houses is a safe place if the door is closed, and there is a guardian, even though he should be in the habit of going to sleep; but if the guardian goes to bed leaving the door open the house is not a safe place by night, †or by day. †It is the same where a guardian is a person to be easily duped by thieves. An uninhabited house, surrounded by other houses, constitutes a safe place, according to our school, only during the day; provided it is during a time of peace, and the door is closed. A tent in a desert plain, if the ropes are not stretched tight and the lower extremities not firmly attached to the soil, is regarded, with everything it contains, in the same way as objects placed upon the plain. If the ropes are stretched tight, and the extremities attached to the soil, the tent is a safe place, if it has a strong guardian, even though he is in the habit of going to sleep. Cattle in a stable or an enclosed place belonging to a house is sufficiently safe even without a guardian; but such a place in a desert requires a guardian, who need not, however, always be awake. As to camels on a desert plain they are sufficiently guarded if in charge of a herdsman; and the same is the case with camels or elephants attached to one another, so as to walk in file, provided that their conductor ascertains every hour that they are all there, and provided there are no more than nine head. †Animals not attached to one another on the march are not considered to be sufficiently guarded. A shroud is sufficiently guarded in a tomb situated in some closed construction, †or in a cemetery on the outskirts of habitations, but not in a tomb situated in some desert place.

SECTION 2

The lessor †or the lender of a shop is punishable with amputation for abstracting an object deposited in the shop by the lessee or borrower; but if the shop is occupied by a person who has usurped it, neither the owner †nor any one else is punishable for committing such abstraction.

Nor is amputation applicable :—

1. If a person who has usurped an object places it in a shop which belongs to him, and the owner of the object so usurped comes and takes another object belonging to the usurper and deposited in the same shop.

2. †If any other person takes the usurped object from the shop.

3. In case of open theft, or robbery, or denial of a deposit.

†Amputation is applicable to a person who penetrates a wall and by this means steals something the next night. [Unless before the theft the owner is informed of the fact that a hole has been made in his wall, or the hole is visible to passers by, for under these circumstances the place is insufficiently safe and consequently there is no ground for amputation.]

In a case where one criminal makes a hole in the wall, and another makes use of it for theft, neither are liable to amputation; and where both together make the hole but only one commits the abstraction, the latter alone suffers amputation. Even if one of the two places the stolen object close to the hole and the other takes it, the latter alone is punishable with amputation; *and this principle is carried so far that amputation is not pronounced against the accomplice even though he places the object in the middle of the hole and the value exceeds twice the legal minimum.

Amputation is rigorously necessary where the object is taken from the owner under the following circumstances :—

1. If the thief throws the thing to some one who is about to go away.

2. If he throws it into running water.

3. If he places it on the back of a moving animal.

4. If he exposes it in the open when a violent wind is blowing.

†On the other hand, this penalty is not applicable where the thief merely places the object upon the back of an animal that happens to stop at that place, and goes on with it as a load. A free person, not being an object of commerce, cannot be stolen; consequently one is not punishable with amputation for carrying off a free person; †even though it may be a small child wearing a collar the value of which reaches the legal minimum. It follows from this principle that one

who finds a slave sleeping on a camel and leads the beast far from the caravan without waking the sleeper, should be amputated; †but if the sleeper is a free man he is still in possession of his mount, and consequently amputation is not applicable. On the other hand, amputation is prescribed for transporting an object belonging to another from a closed room into the courtyard of the house if the main door is open, but not if the room is open and the house door shut. According to some authorities amputation is rigorously necessary even where the doors of both room and house are shut; †while the same rules are applicable in the case of a room at an inn from which one has abstracted another's baggage and deposited it in the courtyard.

Section 3

Theft committed by a minor or a lunatic, or under violent compulsion does not involve amputation; but it is of small consequence whether the injured party or the criminal are Moslems or infidel subjects of our Sovereign. As to an infidel living among us by virtue of a safe conduct or an armistice jurists are not in agreement, though the better doctrine tends to regard as liable to amputation those who are expressly subject to our laws in this respect. [The generally accepted doctrine forbids the amputation of such infidel.]

Theft is proved †by the accuser's oath, if the accused challenges him to it; and also by the accused's confession, which may, however be retracted, according to our school. ††Where the accused confesses some crime incurring a penalty of reparation towards God and consequently not remissible, the court should have it explained to him that retractation is permissible, without however, imposing it upon him as an order. Moreover, if any one of his own accord presents himself before the court and admits having stolen the property of another person who is absent, †the penalty of amputation may not be pronounced before the return of the injured party, and his confirmation of the fact; †but execution should take place at once where the accused admits forcing the slave of another to commit the crime of fornication. Theft is also proved by the deposition of two male witnesses; the deposition of one man and two women is not sufficient for pronouncing the definite prescribed penalty, though enough for the civil action resulting from the crime. The witnesses should make a detailed account of the fact, and if the details do not agree, if, for example one of the witnesses declares that it happened at dawn, and the other at the beginning of the night, their depositions cancel each other.

Without prejudice to the penalty incurred the thief should be condemned to a restitution of the object stolen, or if it be lost to a payment of its value.

Amputation of the right hand takes place for the first offence; that of the left foot for the second; that of the left hand for the third, and that of the right foot for the fourth. Subsequent offences are punishable at the discretion of the court. The joint where the amputation is to be effected should first be anointed with boiled fat and oil. This act is considered by some jurists as a necessary accompaniment of the penalty. †The majority, however, regard it as the sufferer's right, so that he has to bear the expense, and the Sovereign need not order it *ex officio*. The hand is amputated at the wrist, and the foot at the joint below the ankle. A person who commits several thefts for the first time suffers only the amputation of the right hand, even though there were missing from it four fingers [†or even five]. The hand is amputated without regard to the fact that it may have an extra finger. If the criminal has already lost the right hand in consequence of some malady, amputation does not take place for the first theft. But, according to our school, it is not a reason for dispensing with the amputation of the right hand that the sufferer has already lost the left, although on that account the penalty is in his case much more serious than it otherwise would be.

CHAPTER II.—BRIGANDS

SECTION 1

BY "brigand" is understood an adult sane Moslem who troubles the security of the roads by armed force; but not a person who furtively joins the rear of a caravan, intending to escape after a few thefts. Those who confine themselves to attacking and robbing travellers who are alone or in small groups should be considered as brigands in respect to the persons they can get the better of, but not in respect of a large caravan. Besides, in the term brigandage is not included an attack at a moment, when, or in a place where, one can call for help; but the term does cover an attack when this is not the case, either on account of distance, or on account of the weakness of persons living near by, even though it may be in a town.

Brigands who trouble the security of the roads by menace only, and do not rob or murder travellers should be punished by the Sovereign with imprisonment, etc., by way of punishment at discretion; but a brigand guilty of theft, to an amount usually involving amputation, should lose the right hand and the left foot; or, for a second offence, the left hand and the right foot. Homicide committed by a brigand renders rigorously necessary an application of the death penalty; and homicide accompanied by theft is punished with death; and the corpse is exposed for three days upon a cross. After this period it should be taken down. According, however, to some authorities it should remain until a clear liquid begins to flow from it. One jurist even maintains that the guilty person should first be crucified for some time and then taken down to be put to death.

A person who takes part in the misdeeds of brigands, and joins their band, but is not employed in it, and is not guilty of any criminal act, should be punished with imprisonment, banishment, etc., by way of punishment at discretion. As to banishment, some jurists maintain that the Sovereign should indicate the place where the guilty party should reside.

The death penalty, to which a brigand is liable for homicide, is equivalent to a penalty under the law of talion; though, according to one authority, it is even then a definite prescribed penalty. According to the theory adopted by the majority a brigand cannot be put to death for killing his descendant or an infidel subject of our Sovereign; and if he dies before execution the price of blood due for his victims constitutes a debt payable from his estate. If a brigand has committed several homicides this theory requires that he should be put to death for one of these homicides, while his estate remains burdened with the price of blood due for the others; but even when one adopts that theory the brigand should none the less be put to death as subject to a definite prescribed penalty when the representative of the victim pardons him for a fine, though the talion does not exist in these circumstances. A brigand who kills his victim either by means of a blunt instrument, or by cutting off a limb, should suffer death in the same way; but if his victim recovers from the effects of his wound, the brigand is not punishable under the law of talion. Nor is he liable to the special penalties formulated against him, if he changes his conduct before falling into the hands of the authorities; all without prejudice to the penalties to be pronounced for the special offences of which he is guilty. As to a brigand whose repentance is only manifested after his arrest, our school grants him no such favour; *and in general the other definite prescribed penalties should be undergone in spite of the criminal's repentance.

Section 2

In a case where the offender has to undergo several penalties for offences against men, and consequently capable of being remitted, such as the death penalty, amputation of a limb, and the penalty for defamation, he is first flogged, then suffers amputation, and is finally put to death. The death penalty should be executed immediately after the amputation. Consequently the latter penalty should be put off in the absence of the person who has the right to demand the penalty of death, †and even if he is present and insists upon proceeding at once to amputation. On the other hand, where the person who has the right to demand the death penalty, wishes the execution to be put off, there is no objection to proceeding at once to the flogging; and this penalty should be followed immediately by amputation, if the person who has the right to exact the death penalty pardons the criminal. In a case where the person who can exact the penalty of amputation, wishes its execution to be put off, the person who can exact the penalty of flogging need not wait; but the penalty of death may not on any consideration be executed before amputation; and the person who proceeds in spite of this to the execution of the criminal owes to the injured party who had the right to exact amputation the price of blood for the limb that should have been amputated. The person who has the right to exact flogging may oblige the two others to wait as long as he pleases; this at least is what strict logic requires. Where the offender has to suffer not penalties capable of remission, but penalties for offences committed against God, the lightest is executed first, and so on in order. If he has to undergo a penalty for an offence against God and also a penalty that may be remitted, a penalty pronounced for defamation has priority over one pronounced for fornication, †or over one pronounced for wine-drinking. †And similarly a penalty under the law of talion, whether of death or of amputation, has priority over a penalty incurred for the crime of fornication.

BOOK 55.—OF FORBIDDEN BEVERAGES, AND OF PUNISHMENT AT THE DISCRETION OF THE COURT

SECTION 1

EVERY beverage that induces intoxication when taken in great quantity is forbidden, even when only a small quantity is taken. The fact of taking it involves an application of the definite prescribed penalty. This penalty, however, is applicable neither to a minor, nor to a lunatic, nor to an infidel, whether he be or be not the subject of a Moslem prince, nor to any one into whose mouth the drink has been introduced by force, nor, according to our school, to any one who has been otherwise forced to drink it. He who drinks wine without knowing what it is is not punishable; and it is the same with a new convert to Islam who drinks it without knowing that it is forbidden; the punishment, however, is incurred by a new convert who merely alleges as his excuse that he knew the drink was forbidden but was not aware of the punishment. It is also incurred for taking the lees of wine, but not for eating bread that has been kneaded with wine, or preserves prepared with wine, †nor for introducing forbidden liquid into one's body by means of injection or sniffing. Besides this, one may take wine in case of immediate necessity, *e.g.* if there is in the throat a piece of food which it is difficult to get down, and there is no other liquid handy at the moment; †but one is liable to punishment if one takes wine as medicine or to quench one's thirst.

The definite prescribed penalty for the crime we are here concerned with is forty stripes, if the guilty person is free, and twenty if a slave. In case of attenuating circumstances the strokes may be given not only with a lash, but also with the hand, with a sandal, or with the end of a coat rolled round like a cord. Few authorities require in all cases stripes with a lash. The Sovereign, or his deputy the judge, has a right to increase the number of blows †up to the double if it seems good to him, but in that case these extra blows constitute a punishment at the discretion of the court. According to others they should be considered also as the definite prescribed penalty.

The crime is proved either by the culprit's confession or by the testimony of two male witnesses; the odour of the breath, drunkenness or vomiting are insufficient by themselves to establish it. It is enough that the accused states that he drank wine, etc., or that the witnesses state they saw him drink wine, etc., without its being necessary to enter into more precise details; provided that it is also established, according to some authorities, that the act was done knowingly and willingly.

Whipping cannot be administered during the state of drunkenness resulting from the crime. It is effected, as in all cases of definite prescribed punishment, by means of a whip with a handle of a thickness between a stalk and a stick, neither green nor quite dry. The stripes should be administered upon all the limbs of the body, except places where the wound would be mortal. One should avoid hitting the face, and, according to some, the head. The hands of the sufferer are not tied, nor is he made to put down his clothes; but the blows should be repeated rapidly in such a way as to make him cry out and inflict upon him an exemplary chastisement.

Section 2

Contraventions that are not punishable with some definite prescribed penalty, and involve no sort of expiation, should be punished at the discretion of the court either by imprisonment, whipping, a slap, or a reprimand. The nature and gravity of the punishment are at the discretion of the Sovereign or his deputy the judge; except that, according to some authorities a simple reprimand is not sufficient if the offence is committed against men, but only where it is committed against God. Whipping should always be under twenty strokes in the case of a slave, and forty in the case of a free man; though some think that twenty is the limit for any person. †Moreover, the principle that a punishment at discretion should always be below the minimum pronounced as a definite prescribed penalty extends to all contraventions.

†Where the injured party grants a remission to the criminal, *e.g.* of the definite prescribed penalty for defamation, the Sovereign may not substitute for it a punishment at his discretion; but the remission of a punishment at discretion, by the injured party, leaves intact the right of the Sovereign to inflict upon the guilty person the punishment he deserves.

BOOK 56.—EXCUSABLE HOMICIDE, WOUNDING AND RESPONSIBILITY FOR DAMAGE

Section 1

One has a right to resist any attack upon one's life, property, bodily members, or modesty; and if the person so assailed kills the aggressor, the law admits no responsibility in the matter. Defence against attacks upon one's property, though recognised as legitimate, is not obligatory; but one ought to defend one's life or one's modesty, *at least when one's life is attacked by an infidel or an animal, but not when attacked by a Moslem. Defence of another is regulated by the same principles as defence of one's own person, though according to some authorities it is always obligatory. †When a jar falls accidentally upon some one who cannot protect himself against it without breaking the jar, he is civilly responsible for damages. An aggressor should be repulsed with the least possible roughness; thus one should not have recourse to blows if the object can be attained by words or by calling for assistance; strokes with a whip are forbidden where a slap would be enough; a stick is forbidden where a whip would be sufficient; and one must not kill the aggressor, if one could render him incapable of any hurt by cutting a limb. Where one can save oneself by flight our school requires that this should be done, instead of defending oneself; and where the aggressor has taken one's hand between his teeth, one should withdraw it in such a way as to cause him the least possible pain, *i.e.* by opening the jaws and striking the corners of the mouth; but if one is obliged to withdraw one's hand by force, one is not responsible for making the aggressor lose some of his teeth.

A person who perceives a man intentionally looking through a sky-light or a hole at the women of the house, may throw at the indiscreet man some light object, such as a pebble, and if by accident the missile causes the man to lose his sight, or causes a wound near the eye, the person is not responsible, even should death be the consequence. Only in the case where the woman observed is a relative of the man within the prohibited degrees, or his wife, it is not permissible to use missiles to drive him away. Some authorities also add a reservation that the woman in question is not veiled ; others require a previous admonition before adopting the extreme course of throwing a missile.

A guardian, chief, husband, or schoolmaster, inflicting punishment upon the persons submitted to their authority are responsible for the consequences, except in the following cases :—

1. In the case of a definite prescribed penalty, applied to the guilty person within the limits allowed by law.

2. ††Where a drinker of forbidden beverages is beaten with a sandal or a piece of clothing.

3. **Where one inflicts upon a drunkard the prescribed forty stripes with a lash ; but where the number of blows exceeds forty, the person ordering them is responsible for the consequences in proportion to the excess, or, according to one jurist, up to half the price of blood. This controversy exists also with regard to the crime of defamation ; where, for example, eighty-one strokes are inflicted upon the guilty party.

Any free, adult, sane person may cut a tumour appearing upon his body, unless the operation would be dangerous, and there is no danger in leaving the tumour, or at any rate the danger of the operation is the greater. In the case of a minor or of a lunatic, it is for the father or grandfather to order the operation, even if there is some danger, provided that in this case the danger incurred by not proceeding with the operation is yet greater. The Sultan may not order an operation in these circumstances as subsidiary guardian, nor may his deputy the judge. It is only where the operation is not dangerous that the Sultan, as well as the father or grandfather, may give his authorisation for the operation to be performed.

†A surgeon who bleeds a patient or applies leeches to him does not incur any responsibility, even though the sick man succumbs, provided that the operator does not overstep the limits imposed by science in operations of that nature. The Sultan, or his deputy the judge, as subsidiary guardian, who goes beyond his competence and orders a minor to undergo an operation, is personally responsible for the price of blood on the higher scale ; while the price of blood due for an error on his part, either in the application of a definite prescribed penalty or in his decisions, is a debt recoverable from his *aakila*, or, according to one authority, from the public treasury. All jurists admit the responsibility of the magistrate who pronounces a definite prescribed penalty upon the deposition of two witnesses who subsequently turn out to be slaves, infidel subjects of a Moslem prince, or minors near their majority, at least if he accepted them as witnesses without preliminary inquiry ; but jurists are not in agreement as to the magistrate's responsibility where he has done all he could in the matter. But where

it is admitted that the *aakila* or the public treasury can be held responsible for the price of blood, due to an error of judgment, †one cannot admit any right to proceed against the witnesses who turn out not to have the requisite qualities. A surgeon who, on proper authorisation, bleeds any one or applies leeches to him, is in no way responsible for the consequences; and an executioner who carries out a sentence of death or of flogging upon the authorisation of the Sovereign is merely the latter's instrument, unless he knows that the order is from a tyrant, or given in error. In these two cases he would himself be liable under the law of talion, unless acting under violent compulsion.

The circumcision of a woman is effected by the removal of a little of her flesh, in the upper part of the vagina, and that of a man by the removal of the foreskin. It is not obligatory before majority, though it is recommended to proceed to this operation on the seventh day after birth, and not to put it off unless the child has not yet sufficient strength to support it. Any one who performs circumcision at an age when the child is not yet strong enough to support it is liable under the law of talion if the operation causes death. This rule, however, does not apply to the child's ascendants. †On the other hand a guardian is not responsible for the consequences of circumcision effected at an epoch when the child has a constitution sufficiently developed to be able to undergo the operation. The hire of the person who performs the circumcision is at the charge of the patient.

Section 2

One is responsible for the damage caused by animals in one's charge, both as regards the person and the property of others, and both by day and by night. However, the person in charge is not responsible for accidents that may happen to people or property by reason of the animal passing water upon the public road or making it filthy with their excrement. But care must be taken that the animals do not do anything extraordinary as, for example, even excessive trampling in the mire. The person in charge is responsible for acts not natural to the animals in question. Any one who carries wood upon his back, or loads an animal with it, is responsible for the consequences of the fall of the wood, if it is caused by a collision with some building. When a person carrying wood, or some one in charge of an animal with a load of wood, enters a market and causes damage to person or property, he is responsible if there is a crowd, but not otherwise. A blind man, or a person with his back turned at the moment the animal passes, may only make a claim against the individual we are speaking of, if he has torn their clothes without warning them to get out of the way. This responsibility, however, only exists where the owner of the things damaged has committed no imprudence; for if he has, for example, deposited things on the public road, or placed them before the animal, his claim is unfounded. The owner of a domestic animal that has broken its leash and damaged a sown field is not responsible for the accident if the damage is caused by day. On the other hand, he is responsible if it happens by night, unless:—

1. The animal escapes after being properly tied up.

2. The owner of the field was present at the spot, but neglected to protect his crop from the trespassing animal.

3. †The field was surrounded by a wall or other inclosure in which there was a gate that the owner had left open.

†The owner of a cat that has eaten a bird or some food belonging to another person is responsible only if he knew that the animal was particularly voracious. It is of no consequence whether the fact occurred by night or by day. †Where, on the contrary, the owner was ignorant of the cat's voracity he is not responsible for the damage it has caused.

BOOK 57.—MILITARY EXPEDITIONS

SECTION 1

WAR against infidels was already during the lifetime of the Prophet an obligation for which the Moslem community was jointly responsible; though some authorities maintain that at that period it was an obligation incumbent upon each individual Moslem. As to the nature of this obligation in modern times the following distinctions must be made:—

1. War against infidels living in their own country is a common obligation; that is to say that if a sufficient number of Moslems acquit themselves of it, the others may lawfully remain at home. Among obligations for which the Moslem community is responsible in common, and not individually, are also included that of defending the faith and refuting infidel errors; that of solving difficulties as to religious practices; that of the study of the sciences relating to the law, such as the interpretation of the Koran and the criticism of traditions; that of the study of the solution of subordinate questions of jurisprudence, so that justice may be done; that of exhorting people to do good and abstain from evil; that of taking care that the sacred temple of Mecca should be visited each year by a large number of the faithful; that of relieving the sufferings of Moslems by giving clothing and nourishment to those that are in need, at any rate if the charity tax and the public treasury do not suffice; that of appearing as witness and making a deposition; and that of making a study of trades, arts, and all that serves to ameliorate the lot of man. For an assembly it is a common obligation to return a salutation. As to this last obligation, the reader should be informed that the Sonna has introduced the practice that a person who is performing a duty of nature, or is at table or in a bath, need not either give or acknowledge a salutation; even individually. To return to the subject, the obligation to take part in the war against infidels does not apply to a minor, a lunatic a woman, a sick person, a man obviously lame, a man wanting a hand or a foot, or one of whose limbs is mutilated, a slave, nor to a man who has not the arms and equipment necessary for the war. Moreover, any excuse that is valid for not accomplishing the pilgrimage, is also valid for not taking part in the war

for the propagation of the faith, except fear of being assaulted on the way by the infidels, ††or by highway robbers even though Moslems. Debts due instanter are an obstacle to the departure of the debtor, whether for the war against the infidels or for any other journey, unless it is undertaken with his creditor's consent; but debts due upon a certain date to come are no obstacle to one's quitting one's domicile; unless, according to some authorities, the journey is one of exceptional danger. Nor can one lawfully depart for a war against infidels until authorised to do so by one's ascendants, if Moslems; such authorisation, however, is not necessary for a traveller who goes for the purpose of inquiry as to his religious duties, whether individual †or collective. An authorisation by a creditor or by ascendants is revocable so long as one is not actually enrolled; but if the revocation does not occur until one is about to fight, it is rigorously forbidden to pay any attention to it.

2. Infidels who invade our territory should be driven out by armed force by all possible means, and by all the inhabitants of the territory invaded, poor, children, debtors, and slaves, without previous authorisation. According to a few authorities a slave should obtain his master's authorisation where there are enough free men If it is impossible to offer the enemy an organised resistance, each Moslem attacked by infidels should defend his life by all possible means, if he has to deal with miscreants who do not allow quarter; otherwise he may allow himself to be taken prisoner. Under these circumstances to enroll oneself is a duty not only for persons domiciled in the threatened locality, but also for all who live at a distance not permitting of the abridgment of prayer. Travellers from a greater distance than this, who happen to be temporarily at the spot, are obliged to take arms if the inhabitants of the town and suburbs need assistance; and even this condition is disallowed by some authorities. †When the infidels have made a Moslem prisoner of war, they should be attacked immediately in order to deliver him, if there is any chance of success.

Section 2

It is blamable to invade the territory of infidels without the authorisation of the Sovereign or of his deputy. The Sonna also requires that the Sovereign should give precise and detailed instructions to the commander he has appointed for each detachment ordered upon an expedition, and should have an oath administered to each warrior to remain faithful to the flag.

The Sovereign has a right to enroll as auxiliary troops—

1. Infidels whose treachery he does not fear; provided that the

number of Moslems is always high enough to oppose twice the number of infidels.

2. Slaves, with their master's consent.

3. Minors near their majority, and of sufficient strength to stand a campaign.

All these irregular troops receive their ammunition, equipment, arms, etc., either from the public treasury, or from particular funds of the Sovereign. Moreover, it is not lawful to enroll Moslems, for the war against the infidels, as mercenaries, for the propagation of the faith is a religious duty for each believer; but the Sovereign may legally enroll in that manner his infidel subjects; and indeed, according to some authorities, any person may do so.

It is blamable for a Moslem forming part of an army in campaign to kill his near relatives who are infidels, and all the more his relatives within the prohibited degrees. [Unless he hears them blaspheme God and the Prophet.]

In a war against infidels it is forbidden to kill minors, lunatics, women, and hermaphrodites that do not incline towards the masculine sex; *but one may lawfully kill monks, mercenaries in the service of the infidels, old men, persons that are weak, blind, or sickly, even though they have taken no part in the fighting, nor given information to the enemy. If they are not killed, they must at any rate be reduced to slavery. The wives of infidels should also be reduced to slavery, and infidels' property should be confiscated. It is lawful to besiege infidels in their towns and fortresses, and employ against them inundation, fire, and warlike machines; and to attack them unawares at night, without having regard to the presence among them of a Moslem prisoner or merchant, for whom these general methods of destruction may be equally dangerous. This is the doctrine of our school. By virtue of this same principle one may even shoot women and children, if the infidels continue the combat while hiding behind them; *but this must not be done if the infidels conceal themselves thus with the sole object of saving their own lives, and the nature of the military operations does not make it absolutely necessary to have recourse to extreme measures. †The same principles must be followed where infidels conceal themselves behind Moslems. Our combatants have no right to retire before the infidels, unless the number of the latter exceeds twice that of our troops, except in the case where one retires in order to return to the charge on another side, or where one falls back upon the reserve in order to recruit strength. In such a case one may retire, †even if the reserve is at some distance; but in that case one cannot claim one's share in the booty captured in one's absence; †as one may do if the reserve is close by. On the other hand, one may legally retire before the enemy, where their number exceeds twice the number of our troops; †with the single exception that if, *e.g.* one hundred able-bodied Moslems are attacked by one hundred and one infidels, the Moslems must hold out against them if the infidels are wholly or partly weak men.

Each Moslem soldier may engage in single combat with an infidel soldier. It is even commendable to accept a challenge; but the Moslem who sends a challenge is praiseworthy only if he is certain of his aptitude in handling his arms, and the Sovereign gives his consent.

It is lawful to destroy the houses and plantations of infidels, where this is necessary from a military point of view, or if it renders the victory easier; it is even a good thing to have recourse to this measure in all cases where it is unlikely that the houses and plantations will one day become our property. Where this is probable it is better not to proceed to destroy them. It is rigorously forbidden to kill infidels' domestic animals, except cattle for our food, and their cavalry horses which can always be killed either in the defence or in the attack. Where it is feared that the cattle taken from the enemy may fall again into their hands, or that this cattle may cause us some annoyance, it may be killed.

Section 3

Women and minors of the infidels made prisoners of war should be reduced to slavery; and slaves taken in their country become ours. As to free adults, males, the Sovereign may choose between the five following courses, as seems to him most advantageous for the Moslems; that is to say he may either:—

1. Put them to death.
2. Give them their liberty.
3. Exchange them for Moslem prisoners of war.
4. Release them for a ransom.
5. Reduce them to slavery.

Where circumstances do not indicate which of these measures is to be preferred, the prisoners should be retained until the best method becomes clear. Some authorities do not allow an idolater to be made a slave, and one jurist considers this to be unlawful for a pagan Arab. An infidel prisoner of war who embraces the faith saves his life in all cases by so doing; and the Sovereign has with regard to him a choice between methods Nos. 2 to 5. According, however, to other authorities, such a prisoner must always be reduced to slavery. The conversion of an infidel before his defeat assures him not only of life but of possession of his property and of his children who are under age; but our school does not extend this favour to his wife.

A woman who is reduced to slavery ceases immediately to belong to her husband; though, according to some authorities, the marriage, if it has been consummated, remains good until the end of the period of legal retirement, as the woman may be enfranchised before its termination. The wife of an infidel subject of our Sovereign made a prisoner of war, †or a prisoner of war previously enfranchised by such infidel, may be reduced to slavery; but not, according to our school, the infidel wife or infidel enfranchised slave of a Moslem. The captivity of both husband and wife, or of one of them, involves the dissolution of the marriage, in the case of free persons; and even, according to some authorities, in the case of persons already slaves. But captivity does not affect the debts contracted by the prisoner of war during his freedom in favour of a Moslem or of an infidel subject of our Sovereign. These debts are recoverable from the prisoner's property seized after his reduction to slavery. Where two infidels not our subjects have contracted a debt towards each other, or one has bought something from the other, the agreement holds good if both embrace the faith, or become the subjects of our Sovereign liable to a poll-tax. †But damages due for some material loss cannot be recovered if both embrace Islam.

By the term " booty of war " is understood—

1. Property taken by force from the enemy.

2. Property abstracted from the territory of the enemy, either by oneself or in the company of others, in a furtive manner.

3. †Property found upon the enemy's territory that cannot be supposed to belong to a Moslem; for otherwise the regular announcements must be made, and the appropriation take place, in conformity with the requirements of the law relating to things found.

Soldiers may freely take from the booty all necessary food, and also what is required for preparing it, including meat, fat, and other ordinary provisions. They may also take the necessary forage for their animals, straw, barley, and so on; they may kill the infidels' cattle for their personal needs, ††and they may take not only food properly so-called, but also fruit. ††They are not liable for the value of the cattle thus killed, and need not limit themselves to what is strictly necessary; but these requisitions are forbidden to marauders who only join the army after the end of the war, and after the booty has been collected. ††And the portion that has been levied by way of requisition and not yet employed upon return to Moslem territory must go into the total booty to be divided. It is only upon the territory of the enemy that these requisitions may be levied, †and also upon the space between the utmost Moslem habitations and the boundaries of our Empire.

A lawful claimant may renounce his share in the booty, provided he is capable of administrating his property himself; even if he happens to have been declared bankrupt. The only condition required is that he must declare his intention before the partition, †or rather before the reservation of the fifth to be shared amongst those who have taken the booty. Such renunciation need not be expressed by each individual, but may be the intention of a whole troop. In no case may a member of the Prophet's family renounce his claim to the share reserved to him; nor may one renounce one's right to the equipment of a slain foe. A person renouncing his share in the booty is in the same position as one not present at the battle. The claim of a soldier who dies before receiving his share falls to his heirs.

The booty becomes the property of those entitled to it only by the fact of distribution; though before this they may take possession of it provisionally. Some jurists consider that right of property in the booty is acquired at the moment the booty is taken; and others attribute to the distribution a retroactive force, which means that if the booty taken by a soldier is assigned him as his share, he is considered to have had full ownership of it from the moment he took it, whereas on the contrary supposition his right of ownership has never existed. The immovable property forming part of the booty is, so far as regards appropriation, regulated by the same law as movable property; even objects forbidden to Moslems, such as dogs, may be attributed to the person having a claim to them, and who wishes to accept them, provided he can make some profit out of them. If claims are made to forbidden things by several persons entitled to them, they must be equally divided between them; and where this is impossible, the matter must be decided by casting lots.

††The country of Sawad in Irak was conquered from the infidels and divided amongst the soldiers of the army, who afterwards made a gift of it to the state. It was then made *wakaf* in favour of the Moslem community; and the annual land tax paid by the cultivators has become the rent. The revenue has been employed in the public interest. The country of Sawad extends in length from Abbadan to Haditha in the neighbourhood of Mosul, and in breadth from Kadisia to Holwan [††The town and suburb of Basra, though included in the country of Sawad, is regulated by this law only so far as concerns one spot situated to the west of the Tigris and another situated to the east of that river.]

The city of Mecca surrendered to the Prophet by virtue of

capitulation, and was not taken by assault; consequently its houses and cultivated fields remained in the full possession of their inhabitants.

SECTION 4

An adult, sane Moslem may grant a safe-conduct or quarter to one or more enemies; provided it is for a fixed number, and the act is done of his own free will, and not under any constraint. †Thus a Moslem who is a prisoner of war amongst infidels, cannot grant a safe-conduct. But the law does not insist, for the validity of either safe-conduct or quarter, that any special words shall be used, provided the terms employed clearly express the intention. A document may be drawn up, or the grant may be made by letter, provided only that the infidel whom one wishes to benefit is informed of it. A safe-conduct or a grant of quarter is null and void if the infidel declares that he declines it; †or even if he does not formally accept it; but the acceptance may, however, if necessary, be expressed by signs.

A safe-conduct or a grant of quarter cannot be given for a period exceeding four months; only one authority admits a validity for any period less than a year. Moreover, the law requires that the grant should not prejudice the interest of the Moslems; it is forbidden, for example, to grant a safe-conduct to a spy. On the other hand, the Sovereign should respect a safe-conduct or a grant of quarter duly obtained, so long as he has no reason to fear fraud or intrigue on the part of the infidel. A safe-conduct or a grant of quarter are purely personal, and cannot be transferred to the family or property of the infidel, whether these are still in the enemy's territory, †or the infidel has taken them with him; all without prejudice to any special stipulations that may be made upon the subject.

The law recommends a Moslem inhabiting an infidel country to emigrate, even though he may enjoy there the free exercise of his religion; and this emigration becomes obligatory if he is deprived of the exercise of his religion, and he possesses the means enabling him to emigrate. A Moslem made prisoner of war by infidels should endeavour to escape upon the first opportunity. If released unreservedly he may do the enemy all the harm he can even by means of an ambush. On the other hand, this is forbidden where he has accepted liberty in exchange for granting infidels a safe-conduct, or granting them quarter. Infidels endeavouring to accompany the prisoner must be repulsed, and if necessary, killed; and it is forbidden to keep a promise to remain in the territory of the enemy, after being released on parole.

The Sovereign may take one of the infidels into his service as a guide to point out the way to some fortress, and promise him by way of recompense some gift such as one of the young women to be made prisoners. Under these circumstances the woman must be given him if the fortress is taken in consequence of the information supplied, †but not if it is taken in some other manner. If the fortress is not taken the guide receives nothing. Some authorities allow him even then a reasonable remuneration in proportion to the service he has rendered; unless there was an express stipulation that nothing would be due to him in case of failure. Moreover, the contract with the guide admits of the following distinctions:—

1. Nothing is due to him if there is no young woman in the fortress; or if she was already dead at the time the contract was made; or even if she died after this, but before the fortress was taken.

2. The guide should be remunerated in some other manner:—

(*a*) If the young woman dies after the taking of the fortress, but before being handed over to the guide.

(*b*) If she embraces the faith, at any rate according to our school.

The remuneration consists in a reasonable sum; or, according to some authorities, in the value of the young woman.

BOOK 58.—THE POLL-TAX

CHAPTER I.—GENERAL PROVISIONS

SECTION 1

WHEN it is desired to impose a poll-tax upon infidels the following terms are employed :—" I establish you upon Moslem territory," or " I grant you permission to live there on condition of paying a poll-tax, and submitting to our laws." †It is necessary to stipulate the amount of the tax ; but it is not necessary to add a clause to the effect that the infidels must abstain from uttering insults against God, Mohammed, or Islam. Our school forbids stipulating for a poll-tax for a specified term ; and moreover an agreement to pay the tax is not complete unless it is formally accepted by the infidels. An infidel found upon Moslem territory, without any such agreement, who declares that he has come there either to hear the word of God, or as ambassador, or under a safe-conduct granted by a Moslem, has a presumption in his favour. This presumption is only rebuttable as to the safe-conduct.

An agreement for the payment of poll-tax can be concluded only by the Sovereign or his deputy. The proposals of the infidels with regard to this must be taken into consideration, unless the person charged by them with the negotiation is a suspected person. Such an agreement may be come to only with Jews, Christians, and Fire-worshippers, provided the peoples concerned already practised their religion before the mission of Mohammed, or at any rate at some uncertain date. This benefit extends also to those who think themselves in possession of books revealed to Abraham or of the Psalter of David ; it even extends, according to our rite, to individuals one of whose parents is an adherent of a religion founded upon some holy book, and the other an idolater.

A woman, a hermaphrodite, a slave even when partially enfranchised, a minor and a lunatic are exempt from poll-tax. A lunatic, however, owes the tax, if he has only rare attacks of madness, *e.g.* once a month or once a year ; †as to a lunatic whose attacks are in rapid succession, *e.g.* every day, he owes payment of the tax only when his lucid intervals added together amount to a year. The son of an infidel subject of our Sovereign owes, upon his majority the same poll-tax as the other inhabitants of his country ; and as soon as he has paid it, the law assumes that a new agreement has been come to with him to this effect ; though, according to some authorities, the agreement effected with his father should be considered as *ipso facto* extending to him. Our school insists upon the payment of poll-tax by sickly persons, old men, even if decrepit, blind men, monks, workmen, and poor persons incapable of exercising a trade. As to persons who are found to be insolvent at the end of the year, the amount of the tax remains due from them until they become solvent again.

No infidel may establish his domicile in the Hejaz, *i.e.* at Mecca, Medina, Yamama, or the villages situated in the suburbs of these sacred cities. Some jurists, it is true, allow that they may have their domicile on the side of the great roads uniting these towns. An infidel may not even enter the Hejaz without the permission of the Sovereign, even to cross the country, under penalty of being taken to the frontier, and also of having to undergo punishment at the discretion of the court, if he acts knowingly. An infidel, however, who asks for permission to cross the Hejaz should obtain it if his journey is in the interest of Moslems, *e.g.* if he comes as ambassador or to import necessities for the inhabitants. But if he wishes to import other things the Sovereign may not permit it without levying a tax upon his goods and requiring him to leave within three days. Entry into the sacred territory of Mecca is absolutely forbidden to infidels, even as ambassadors. If a duly qualified ambassador should approach, the Sovereign or his delegate should go out to meet him and give him audience upon the limit of the territory. An infidel who, in spite of the prohibition, enters the sacred territory and falls sick there, should be carried out to the boundary, even though this is likely to cause death ; and if he dies upon the sacred territory not only must he not be buried in it, but if the burial has already taken place the corpse must be disinterred. Where, on the other hand, it is not upon the sacred territory of Mecca, but in some other part of the Hejaz, there the infidel falls sick, and the carrying out of the body would involve great difficulty, it may be left at the spot where it is ; otherwise it must be immediately taken away. By virtue of the same principle the corpse of an infidel who has died in any other part of the Hejaz than the sacred territory of Mecca requires merely to be carried out beyond the limits of that province, where this can be done without too great inconvenience, but otherwise it may be buried in the place where it is.

SECTION 2

The minimum amount of the poll-tax is one dinar per person per annum; but it is commendable to raise the amount, if it be possible to two dinars, for those possessed of moderate means, and to four for rich persons. Infidels who promise payment of the tax at a higher rate are none the less liable for this higher amount, although they may subsequently discover that, strictly speaking, they need not have promised more than the minimum of one dinar; †and if they refuse to pay the amount agreed upon, they should be treated as people who fail to carry out their engagements towards us. An infidel who embraces Islam in the third year after the conquest owes poll-tax only for the two previous years, and not for the third; and the same rule applies to the infidel who dies during the third year. In the latter case the amount due by him is a debt owing by his estate in preference to the legacies, but ranking equal with other civil debts according to our school. In case of conversion or decease during the course of any year a proportional amount of poll-tax is due for that year; according to one jurist nothing at all is due in these circumstances.

An infidel who has to pay his poll-tax should be treated by the tax-collector with disdain; the collector remaining seated and the infidel standing before him, the head bent and the body bowed. The infidel should personally place the money in the balance, while the collector holds him by the beard and strikes him upon both cheeks. These practices, however, according to most jurists, are merely commendable, but not obligatory, as some think. The latter forbid an infidel to commission a Moslem to pay the poll-tax for him, or to pay it by means of the transfer of a debt due to him by a Moslem, or to get a Moslem to be answerable for it. Most jurists, however, permit these usages. [For a collector to act in the manner here described is absolutely forbidden, and it is a grave error to declare it to be commendable.]

The law recommends that the Sovereign should also stipulate that the infidels should as much as possible practice hospitality in regard to Moslem travellers passing through their country, all without prejudice to the legal minimum of the poll-tax. It is true that some jurists maintain that this charge may be taken into account when it is desired to ascertain whether the infidels do pay the minimum. †In any case, however, the duty of hospitality must not be imposed upon the poor, but only upon the rich and those in the enjoyment of moderate means. When stipulating for the practice of hospitality the Sovereign should mention the number of guests each individual must receive, the men and their horses; the nature and the quantity of the food, as well principal as accessory, due to each individual; and the forage for the animals. The guests should be lodged either in the church or in the synagogue or in the best uninhabited house in the place. The length of stay should be stipulated up to a maximum of three days.

The Sovereign may accept the offer of the infidels to pay the charity-tax, instead of the poll-tax, provided that the interest of the Moslems is not opposed to that course; and provided that the charity-tax paid by the infidels is double that of the ordinary charity-tax; that is to say that they pay two *shahs* for five camels, two " bent *makhad* " for twenty-five camels, one *dinar* for twenty *dinars*, ten *drahms* for two hundred *drahms*, and a fifth instead of a tenth. †Moreover, the excess that the tax-payer may recover by giving two " bent *makhad* " is not doubled in the case of an infidel; *but where the taxable property does not reach the minimum taxable a proportional charity-tax is not exacted. The charity tax levied in this way is legally considered as a poll-tax, and is so distributed. In consequence it follows that nothing is levied from persons who are for some reason exempt from poll-tax, *e.g.* women, even where their property reaches the minimum taxable.

Section 3

The obligations which we undertake, when stipulating for a poll-tax, are as follows:—

1. To abstain from any hostile act against the infidels concerned; that is to say that we are responsible for any damage illegally caused by us to their person or property.

2. To protect them against attacks on the part of infidels not subject to our laws; and also against other enemies, external and internal. This obligation, however, does not exist, according to some jurists, where the tax-payers do not fix their domicile amongst us, but occupy a separate territory.

Infidels who by virtue of the poll-tax are subjects of our Sovereign must be forbidden to build churches or synagogues in a town founded by us and whose inhabitants embraced Islam of their own free will. As to places taken by assault the infidels must abstain, not from building new churches or synagogues there, †but even from using for that purpose any such edifices as may be already there. Where, on the other hand, the country submitted by virtue of a capitulation, the following cases must be distinguished:—

1. If the capitulation is to the effect that the land shall be ours, but the infidels are to remain there by title of hereditary possession, they may continue to make use of it; †but if nothing is decided upon the subject of these edifices, they may not put them to that use.

2. If the capitulation is to the effect that the infidels continue to be owners of the land, they may not only continue to make use of their churches or synagogues, †but may even build new ones.

Some jurists merely recommend, but the majority declare it obligatory, that the infidels should be forbidden to have houses higher than those of their Moslem neighbours, †or even to have them as high; a rule, however, that does not apply to the infidels who inhabit a separate quarter. An infidel subject of our Sovereign may not ride a horse; but a donkey or a mule is permitted him, whatever may be its value. He must use an *ikaf*, and wooden spurs, those of iron being forbidden him, as well as a saddle. He must go to the side of the road to let a Moslem pass. He must not be treated as a person of importance, nor given the first place at a gathering. He should be distinguished by a suit of coloured cloth and a girdle outside his clothes. If he enters a bathing-house where there are Moslems, or if he undresses anywhere else in their presence, the infidel should wear round his neck an iron or leaden necklace, or some other mark of servitude. He is forbidden to offend Moslems, either by making them hear his false doctrines, or by speaking aloud of Esdras or of the Messiah, or by ostentatiously drinking wine or eating pork. And infidels are forbidden to sound the bells of their churches or of their synagogues, or celebrate ostentatiously their sacrilegious rites.

When the infidels do not observe the conditions imposed on them, the agreement made with them remains none the less intact, but they must be forced from that time to fulfil their engagements more strictly. It is only when they make war upon us, or refuse to pay the poll-tax or to submit to our laws, that the agreement is *ipso facto* broken, and we are freed from our obligations in that respect. When an infidel commits the crime of fornication with a Moslem woman, or makes her his wife; or shows our enemies the places where our frontiers are exposed; or seeks to turn a Moslem from the faith, or speaks insultingly of Islam or of the Koran, or defames the Prophet—†the agreement, so far as it concerns him is *ipso facto* broken, provided that this penal clause has been expressly stipulated. *An infidel who breaks the agreement by armed force should be at once resisted and killed. An infidel who breaks the agreement in any other way cannot claim to be deported to his own country; but the Sovereign may have him killed or reduced to slavery, or may pardon him or release him for a ransom, as may seem to him most advantageous. He cannot, however, be made a slave if he embraces Islam before the Sovereign decides upon his fate. †The loss of a safe conduct, or of a grant of quarter, does not affect an infidel's wife or children. An infidel who renounces the agreement made with us, and asks to be henceforth considered as an enemy, has a right to be conveyed in safety beyond our frontiers.

CHAPTER II.—ARMISTICES

THE Sovereign or his deputy has the right to grant an armistice to the infidels, in the case of the inhabitants of a country; in the case of the inhabitants of a town, the governor of the frontier province may also grant it. An armistice is permitted only when there is some advantage for the Moslems; if, for example, we are weak in number; or if money and munitions of war fail us; or if there is reason to hope that the infidels will be converted, or will offer to submit and pay poll-tax. An armistice which, though advantageous, is not caused by our weakness, may be agreed upon for four months; *or more, provided it is for less than one year; but if we are the weaker, a maximum period of ten years may be stipulated for. Where this maximum has been exceeded all jurists regard the armistice as valid for the legal period, and only the excess period to be illegal; but an armistice is invalid where no precise period has been stipulated for; ††or where some illegal clause is included in it. It is considered, for instance, an illegal clause to stipulate that persons made prisoners of war by the infidel shall not be released; or that infidels shall retain property they have captured; or that they shall pay a poll-tax of less than one *dinar* per person; or that we shall pay them tribute, etc. On the other hand, it is quite lawful that the Sovereign, when granting an armistice should reserve the right of recommencing hostilities when he pleases. In any case the Sovereign should abstain from committing any act of hostility so long as the armistice lasts; he should not begin again to wage war until after the legal expiration of the armistice, unless the infidels themselves terminate it by an explicit and formal declaration, or by again taking up arms, or by giving information to our enemies as to the places where our frontiers are exposed, or by killing a Moslem. At the end of the armistice one may attack the enemy immediately, either by day or by night. The armistice is broken as to all the infidels if some of them take up arms again, unless the others oppose it by words or actions. If these latter prove that they do not wish to break the armistice, and separate from those who are recommencing hostilities, and inform our Sovereign that they intend to keep their engagements, the armistice remains intact so far as they are concerned. All this, however, does not prevent the Sovereign from revoking the armistice at any moment, if he has reason to fear that the infidels have only consented to it in order to weave some intrigue; in this case those who have established themselves in our country upon the faith of the treaty must be conveyed to the frontier. But the Sovereign must never revoke an armistice upon ill-founded suspicions.

In an armistice one may not promise to the infidels the extradition of a Moslem woman who has taken refuge with us; an infraction of this rule renders illegal not only the clause but the whole treaty. *Even in a case where one has stipulated the extradition "of all the refugees," or said nothing about extradition, it is not necessary to restore to her husband the dower of a woman who has taken refuge with us. Extradition is also illegal in the case of a minor, a lunatic, and, according to our school, a slave or a free man who has no near relatives on the father's side. If a refugee has such relatives, the extradition may take place only upon their demand; but if the refugee has some power over the person who demands the extradition, and can consequently return to us when he pleases, extradition is lawful even upon the demand of some person not a near relative on the father's side. Extradition consists in our ceasing to retain or to protect the individual claimed; but the Sovereign should never force him to return to his country. The individual is free to remain amongst us; and he may, if necessary, in the exercise of his right of legitimate defence, kill with impunity any one who seeks to take him. We may exhort him to resist, but may not formally counsel him to kill the person who seeks to take him. A stipulation that the infidels should surrender apostates from us is lawful and should be faithfully executed by them, under penalty of the armistice being considered *ipso facto* broken; *though it may also be stipulated that apostates shall not be extradited.

BOOK 59.—HUNTING AND SLAUGHTER OF ANIMALS

SECTION 1

IN order that one may lawfully eat of the flesh of animals suitable for the nourishment of the body, the neck should be cut if possible either in the upper or the lower part ; where this is impossible, as in hunting, it is enough to cause some mortal wound. Flesh of animals otherwise slaughtered is forbidden to Moslems ; moreover the butcher and the hunter should be Moslems, or at any rate belong to those religious persuasions among whom Moslems may choose their wives. One may also eat of the flesh of an animal killed by a female infidel slave, professing a religion founded upon some holy book, although she cannot become the wife of a Moslem. The law forbids to eat of the flesh of an animal slaughtered or killed in hunting by a Moslem with the assistance of a fire-worshipper ; but where the Moslem and the fire-worshipper have both set their dogs or fired upon a piece of game, and it is the Moslem's dog or arrow that has killed it, before the other's dog or arrow reached it, this game may lawfully be eaten. It is the same where the game was not killed immediately, but left for dead upon the spot. Where, on the contrary, it is the fire-worshipper who has out-distanced the Moslem under these circumstances, or where they have both wounded the animal without causing immediate death, the flesh is forbidden. It does not matter then whether they wounded it at the same moment, or one after the other, or if they do not know which wound was the first. An animal is lawfully killed by a minor, *even though he may not have attained the age of discernment ; *by a lunatic ; *or by a drunkard ; but it is blamable for a blind man to undertake doing so ; †and hunting both by shooting and by coursing, is rigorously forbidden him.

Fish and locusts may be eaten, even if they have died a natural death, or been killed by a fire-worshipper ; †and the rules about slaughtering do not apply either to worms in food, such as vinegar and certain fruit, provided that these worms are swallowed with the food in which they occur. †And one may, strictly speaking, kill a fish by cutting it in pieces, or swallowing it alive ; though these cruelties are always blamable.

When one fires at a piece of game, or a fugitive camel or sheep, or when one lets loose upon these animals a hunting beast or a bird of prey, and when in this way they are wounded and die in a few moments, the flesh may be eaten although the neck has not been cut. A domestic animal that has fallen into a well where its neck cannot be cut is subject to the same law as the fugitive camel. [†One should not kill a domestic animal fallen into a well by letting loose upon it a hunting dog, at any rate it has been so established by Er Royani and Esh Shashi.]

An animal may not be killed in any other than the ordinary way if it is easy to run after it and catch it, or to do so by the help of another person. In any case the law requires that a fugitive domestic animal, or one fallen into a well, should receive a mortal wound; and some jurists even maintain that the wound should cause immediate death.

One may lawfully eat of a piece of game killed by means of an arrow, or of a hunting dog, or of a bird of prey, if one only reached it at the moment it ceased to live, or even after its death, and so could not give it the *coup de grace*, and it died of the wound it had received. This is, however, on condition that it is not the hunter's fault that he was unable to deal the animal the decisive blow, *e.g.* if it was dead before he could draw his knife, or before he could get hold of it so as to kill it. Consequently, an animal killed while hunting in the manner we have just described is forbidden, if the hunter by his fault has let it die of the wound it received, although this wound was not immediately mortal, *e.g.* if he went out hunting without his knife, or if he let another hunter take it, or if the knife was firmly fixed in the sheath. When one fires upon a piece of game so as to cut it in two, the flesh of each half may lawfully be eaten; and even when a member of the animal's body has been cut in this way, both this member and the rest of the body may be eaten, provided the wound was immediately fatal. But if the wound did not immediately cause death, so that the animal has had to be killed either in the normal way, or by giving it a second and decisive blow, the rest of the body may be eaten, but not the member cut by the original wound. Only where it is impossible to give the animal a decisive wound or to kill it in the ordinary way may all the body be eaten. Some authorities, however, consider that the cut member is prohibited even in these circumstances.

The slaughtering of any animal that has been in one's power is effected by cutting the larynx and the œsophagus; it is commendable to cut also at the same time the two jugular veins. To slaughter an animal by cutting the nape of the neck is forbidden; and the flesh of an animal so killed may be eaten only if the butcher perceives his error and cuts at once the larynx and the œsophagus, before the animal ceases to live.

Nor may one eat the flesh of a fox that has been killed by introducing a knife into the ears, as some hunters do in order not to spoil the skin.

The Sonna has introduced the following practices relative to the slaughtering of animals :—

1. Camels are killed by cutting the throat near the chest ; in the case of bullocks and small cattle the throat is cut higher up ; though, strictly speaking, one may do the opposite of this.

2. Camels are killed standing upon their four legs ; as to bullocks and small cattle, they are made to lie upon the left side, the right foreleg being free and the three others strongly bound.

3. The slaughtering knife is sharpened.

4. The animal's head is turned in the direction of the holy temple of Mecca.

5. One should pronounce the formula, " In the name of God," and invoke His blessing upon the Prophet ; but one should never say, " In the name of God and of Mahommed," as do some of the faithful.

Section 2

For the regular slaughtering of animals that one has had in one's power, and for the hunting of animals that one has not had in one's power, one may lawfully use any instrument for cutting, suitable for causing a wound, without caring whether it is an instrument of iron, copper, gold, wood, reed, stone, or glass ; provided it is not of horn, ivory, or bone. The law forbids the eating of the flesh of animals killed by an instrument for bruising, or for both bruising and cutting, such as a ball, a lash, an arrow without a point, and not sharpened, an arrow and a ball together, or an arrow whose point and shaft have both dealt a mortal wound while the game was in motion. The same principle prevents one eating the flesh of animals strangled in a hunter's net, or of an animal wounded by an arrow and fallen from some height and killed by the fall.

Hunting by coursing is lawful, either with hunting beasts or by birds of prey ; as *e.g.* with a dog, a cheetah, or a white or ordinary falcon, provided that these animals are trained to remain quiet upon their master's order, to attack the game the moment they are let loose, and to seize it with their claws or their teeth without eating it. *This last condition, however, concerns only birds of prey and not dogs, etc. Its training must have accustomed the beast to hunting so that one may be sure that it will not eat the game. Where the hunting beast devours the game in spite of this, the flesh is prohibited, and the beast must be trained again. It matters little if the beast licks the blood of its prey. As to the part of the body rendered impure by the dog's bite, it need merely be washed with water and sand, in order to become lawfully edible. It is not necessary to take out and throw away this part of the body. *It is also lawful to eat a piece of game attacked by a hunting beast or a bird of prey and killed by the beast's weight or the force of the fall.

The law forbids eating—

1. A piece of game wounded by a knife dropped from the hand by accident.

2. A sheep that has rubbed or knocked against a knife held in the hand, so that the throat is cut, even though both larynx and œsophagus may be cut through.

3. A piece of game pursued and killed by a dog of its own accord; even though the master, seeing the dog started, may have urged it on.

On the other hand, the game is lawfully killed where an arrow reaches it driven accidentally by the wind; †though its flesh is forbidden if the arrow has been drawn at random, to test it, or upon some object, and then driven by the wind upon the game so as to kill it. A person who fires upon a piece of game that he took for a stone, or upon a troop of gazelles of which he hit only one, may eat of the flesh of the slain animal. †And similarly, if he fires upon a particular piece of game and kills another. When a dog let loose upon a piece of game flies away out of sight of the hunter, and the game is afterwards found dead, the law forbids that it should be eaten. *The same principle requires one to abstain from eating the flesh of a piece of game that has escaped from the hunter's sight after he has wounded it, and the body of which has only been found later.

Section 3

A hunter becomes owner of the game he has seized in his hand, or upon which he has inflicted an immediately mortal wound, or which he has rendered incapable of defending itself or of escaping, or whose wings he has broken, or which he has taken in a net placed for that object, or which he has driven into a place from which it cannot escape. †The owner of a piece of land has not yet acquired the ownership of a piece of game that comes upon his land and remains in the mud, etc., until he actually takes possession of it. The ownership of the game, once acquired, remains until the animal escapes, by its own effort or by the act of the owner. Thus a pigeon perched upon another person's dove-cot should be restored to the owner, and where the pigeon is so mixed up among the other pigeons of the dove-cot that it can no longer be distinguished, then neither the owner of the dove-cot where it is, nor the owner of the pigeon, can by sale or gift transfer the ownership of any of the pigeons of the dove-cot ; †though such a transfer, made by the owner of the pigeon to the owner of the dove-cot is perfectly valid. The owner of the pigeon and that of the dove-cot can, moreover, jointly transfer the whole of the dove-cot and pigeons to any one else, provided that the number of the pigeons is known, and that they are all of the same value.

Where two persons fire, one after the other, upon the same piece of game, and both wound it, the following cases must be distinguished :—

1. If the second hunter causes the game a wound immediately mortal or so serious as to render the animal incapable of defending itself or of escaping, it belongs to him. In this case the wound given by the first hunter is of no consequence.

2. If the wound caused by the first hunter is immediately mortal or so serious as to render the animal incapable of defending itself or of escaping, the game belongs to him unless the wound caused by the second hunter cuts the larynx and the œsophagus. In these latter circumstances the game belongs to the second hunter, and may be lawfully eaten provided he pays the first hunter damage for having killed the game which the first hunter had already secured. If the second hunter kills the game, already incapable of defending itself or of escaping, not by cutting the larynx and œsophagus but in some other manner, or if he gives it a wound not immediately mortal in itself, but fatal in combination with the previous wound, the flesh of that game is forbidden. But the second hunter must pay the first its value.

Where the two hunters fire at the same time and wound the game, either in some way immediately fatal, or so seriously as to render it incapable of defending itself or of escaping, the game belongs to them both in common. If only one of the two caused the wound in question, the game belongs to him. But our school forbids that the game should be eaten if one of the hunters causes a wound immediately fatal, and the other a wound rendering it incapable of defending itself or of escaping, and it is not known which of the two wounds was given first.

BOOK 60.—SACRIFICES

SECTION 1

THE Sonna has introduced the custom of sacrifices that are obligatory only for the person who has imposed them upon himself as a duty. The Sonna prescribes moreover to him who would immolate a victim upon the tenth day of the month Zul Hejja not to cut his hair or his nails before completing this act of devotion, and to discharge the duty in person, or at least be present. One cannot immolate by way of sacrifice any other animals but camels, bullocks, and small cattle ; and the camels must have attained their sixteenth year, the bullocks and goats their third, and the sheep their second. It matters little if the animal be male or female or castrated. Though a camel or a bullock suffices for seven persons, and one head of small cattle for one person only, it is preferable to immolate a camel on one's own account, a bullock taking the second rank, a sheep the third, and a goat the last. Seven head of small cattle are preferable to a camel. It is commendable to immolate a single head of small cattle on one's own account, rather than to join with others in immolating a camel. The animal sacrificed should be exempt from defects that prejudice the quantity or quality of the flesh ; one cannot take a thin animal, or one attacked by rabies ; or an animal wanting an ear or an eye ; or a lame, sickly or manifestly mangy beast. But there is no objection to immolating an animal that is but slightly affected by one of these physical defects, or one that has lost its horns, or one that has its ears split, torn, or pierced.

[†As to mange, it is enough that the animal should be affected by it, to however slight an extent, to render it unsuitable for sacrifice. This is Shafii's personal opinion.]

The hour of sacrifice on the occasion of the pilgrimage, on the prescribed day called *yaum en nahr*, is that when the sun has reached the height of a lance, after which one must still pray two *rakas* and listen to two short sermons before proceeding to the ceremony. It must be finished by the last of the three following days, called *ayyam at tashrik*, at sunset. [It is merely preferable, but not obligatory, that the sun should have risen to such and such a height ; for, strictly speaking, one may proceed to the ceremony as soon as the sun has risen and the time necessary for the *rakas* and the sermons has elapsed.]

The believer who has made a vow to immolate a particular animal by saying, " By God, I undertake to immolate such-and-such an animal," must keep his engagement at the hour prescribed ; but if the animal dies before this he owes nothing unless he killed it himself. In the latter case he must buy another animal of equal value and sacrifice it. On the other hand, the believer who vows to sacrifice an animal, and afterwards specifies a particular beast, must keep his engagement at the hour prescribed ; †but if the animal dies the original vow still remains obligatory.

The act of immolation should be accompanied by an intention ; except in case of a particular victim, †for where one has already uttered the words, " This animal will serve for my sacrifice." A person who does not perform the sacrifice himself may express his intention either at the moment he gives the animal to his agent or when the latter proceeds to the immolation.

The sacrificer may himself eat the flesh of a supererogatory victim, or give it to his guests, even though the latter may be rich enough to pay for their own meal ; in this latter case, however, they may not be permitted to take away any of the flesh. For one's private table one may only dispose of a third, or, according to one authority, of a half; of the flesh. The rest, or, better still, the whole, should be given to the poor ; with the exception, however, of one or two mouthfuls which must always be eaten as a sacrament. As to the skin one may either give it away or make use of it oneself, as one chooses. In the case of an obligatory sacrifice a believer has a right to eat the whole of the victim, as well as the young of the animal immolated, which, though it has a separate existence, follows the same rule as its mother. Milk left in the udder of the animal may be drunk.

A slave may not sacrifice. If his master authorises him to perform such act of devotion, it is in his master's favour. Even a slave undergoing enfranchisement by contract may not sacrifice without his master's consent. Nor may one immolate a victim for a third party without his consent ; nor for a deceased person who has not so directed in his will.

Section 2

The Sonna has also introduced the practice of a sacrifice upon the occasion of the first shaving of a child's head. This sacrifice consists of two *shahs* for a boy, and one *shah* for a girl ; it being of course understood that the victim is subject to the already mentioned prescriptions as regards age, absence of physical defects, and also as to the permission of eating the flesh or giving it to other persons to eat.

The Sonna requires for this sacrifice in particular—

1. That the victim should be cooked without breaking the bones.

2. That it should be immolated upon the seventh day after the birth of the child.

3. That on the same day the child should be given a name.

4. That the child's head should be shaved after the sacrifice ; and the weight of the hair in gold or silver given to the poor.

5. That the first call to prayer should be uttered into the child's ear immediately after birth.

6. That its palate should be rubbed with dates.

BOOK 61.—EATABLES

ALL manner of fish may serve as lawful nourishment, however they have been killed or if they have died a natural death; †and it is the same with aquatic animals that are not fish properly so called. Some authorities, however, maintain that aquatic animals not comprised under the denomination of fish cannot be eaten; others consider that this depends upon whether their terrestrial namesakes are eatable or not. Consequently neither the dog-fish nor the sea-hog can be eaten any more than a dog or a pig. Amphibians such as frogs, crayfish, and serpents are all forbidden food.

Amongst animals living only upon the land, the flesh of which may lawfully be eaten, may be mentioned cattle belonging to the camel, bovine, caprine, or ovine race; one may also eat the flesh of the horse, the antelope, the onager, the gazelle, the hyæna, the African lizard, the hare, the fox, the jerboa, the fennec and the sable. On the other hand, the law forbids eating the mule and the domestic ass; all quadrupeds and birds that have means of defence such as claws and talons, *e.g.* the lion, leopard, wolf, bear, elephant, monkey, falcon of any kind, vulture, and eagle; †as well as the jackal and wild cat. †Forbidden also is any animal which it is recommended to slay, such as a serpent, scorpion, Egyptian crow, kite, rat, and in general any carnivorous animal, and even the *rakhama* and the *baghath*. †The harvest crow may lawfully be eaten; but not the parrot, nor the peacock. One may eat the ostrich, crane, duck, goose, fowl, pigeon—by which term is legally understood any bird that drinks by sucking in the water and that coos—sparrow of any colour and species, *e.g.* nightingale, bull-finch, starling; but one may not eat swallows, ants, bees, flies, nor any kind of vermin, such as beetles or worms. All animals born of an animal that can be eaten and of one that cannot are forbidden.

As to those animals about which the law makes no express provision, they can be eaten if well-to-do and respectable Arabs eat them under ordinary circumstances; but one must abstain from food that such persons regard with abhorrence and eat only in time of famine. Where there is a doubt as to the proper name by which an animal should be described these same persons should be consulted. If even they do not know the proper name of it, it may be called by the name of the animal that is like it.

An animal of any kind is forbidden as food if it eats ordure, and its skin shows traces of this habit. According to others, however, the use of such an animal's skin is merely blameworthy. [†This latter doctrine seems to me to be preferred.] The flesh of such an animal may, however, be eaten when the skin has lost its repulsive quality, through the animal being fed for some time on pure and wholesome food.

It is also forbidden to make use of provisions that have become impure, at least where it is impossible to purify them, or to cut away the contaminated portion, as in the case of liquids, such as vinegar or liquefied date syrup. This principle is carried so far that it is considered blamable to eat food obtained as the wages of some impure labour such as applying leeches or sweeping a house. Such eatables are given, in conformity with the Sonna, to slaves and beasts of burden, not to free men. A fœtus found dead in the body of an animal killed in accordance with the precepts of the law may serve as lawful nourishment.

Any one who fears that he will die of inanition, or at least fall dangerously ill, should make use of any sort of eatable, even those most rigorously forbidden, if there is a hope of saving his life by so doing. According, however, to other authorities an individual who fears death from inanition is never obliged to eat forbidden food, he is merely permitted to do so; and if he has near by him eatables that are forbidden, he may in no case partake of more forbidden food than is absolutely necessary to keep him alive. Where there are no eatables not forbidden within reach, he can, according to one authority, eat forbidden food until he is replete; *but most jurists insist that no more may be taken than is absolutely necessary to keep one alive, unless one fears death if the appetite is not completely satisfied. In case of urgency one may even eat a human corpse, or kill an apostate or an infidel not subject to Moslem authority in order to eat him; but one may never kill for this purpose an infidel subject of a Moslem prince, or an infidel minor not so subject, nor an infidel who has obtained a safe-conduct. [†In case of urgency one may kill and eat even a minor or a woman among infidels not subject to Moslem authority.]

A person suffering from hunger who can only find eatables belonging to an absent person, has a right to take them on condition of restoring their equivalent in kind or money; but the owner of eatables who has immediate want of them himself, is not obliged to share them with another suffering from hunger who asks him to do so. Such a sacrifice is even forbidden unless it is a Moslem who makes the request. But the person who is not in immediate want of his own provisions should give to another who asks for food, saying he is suffering from hunger, provided that other is either a Moslem or an infidel subject of one of our princes; and in case of a refusal the owner may even be forced to comply, under menace of death. Those who use their right to take another's provisions should restore the value immediately, if they have money with them; but otherwise they should be allowed time for payment. †A person who gives nourishment to a really famished person, without stipulating for any recompense, is considered to have acted from generosity, and can claim nothing for it. A person suffering from hunger who finds a corpse, and at the same time eatables not forbidden but belonging to another, should, according to our school, eat the corpse, rather then take the eatables that do not belong to him. Our school extends this rule even to a person in a state of *ihram* who finds upon the sacred territory a corpse and a piece of game that he could kill if hunting were not forbidden him. †The law forbids a Moslem to cut off a limb of his body and eat it. [†This act is lawful if one is upon the point of dying of inanition and cannot find even a corpse to eat, and has a better chance of remaining alive by cutting off a bodily member than by braving hunger. But one may in no case cut off a limb of one's own body in order to nourish another person, nor cut off the limb of another person under one's protection in order to nourish oneself.

BOOK 62.—RACING AND SHOOTING COMPETITIONS

THE Sonna permits challenges to racing matches or shooting competitions even for a prize. The shooting may lawfully be effected not only with arrows, but according to our school also with javelins, lances, stones, balisters, or other weapon of war. On the other hand, the law forbids challenges to a game of mall on horseback, throwing the ball, swimming, chess, or the game of rings; it forbids also challenges to certain bodily exercises, such as standing upon one foot, and challenges to certain games of chance, as, for instance, guessing the number of the objects held closed in the hand. The law allows challenges as to horse races, *and even as to races of elephants, mules or donkeys; †challenges are forbidden only in case of a flight of birds, or of a fight.

*Challenges to racing matches or shooting competitions become obligatory on both sides once they have been accepted; neither of the parties can then cancel the agreement of his own accord without the other's consent. A person who accepts a challenge cannot withdraw from it, either before acting in prosecution of it or after. And neither the conditions of the challenge, nor the prize, can be altered in any way after it has been accepted.

Essential conditions for a challenge to a racing match are—

1. That both parties are acquainted with the place of departure and the goal of the course.

2. That each has an equal chance with regard to the line travelled and the distance.

3. That it is a matter of certain specified horses, belonging to certain specified persons.

4. That it is possible for either party to reach the goal first.

5. That both know the amount of the prize.

The prize may be offered by one of the parties or by a third person, *e.q.* the Sovereign. In this last case it is offered in the following words:—" To whichever of you two whose courser arrives first I will give a draft upon the Treasury for so much," or " I will pay so much." A prize offered by one of the competitors is in these terms: " If you win this race I will pay you so much," and one may if one likes add, " and if I win you need not give me anything." The parties are forbidden to offer each other an equal prize, unless a third competitor takes part in the race, without any wager, and his courser is strong enough to rival the coursers of the two parties who have challenged each other. In this last case, however, the law admits the following distinctions :—

1. If the third courser, whose master has offered no prize, reaches the goal first, his master takes the wagers of both the other competitors.

2. If the coursers of the parties who gave the challenge beat the third courser, or if the three arrive together at the goal, no one pays anything.

3. If the third courser reaches the goal at the same time as one of the others, the master of the latter keeps his wager and divides that of the one who has lost with the master of the third courser.

4. If the courser of one of the parties who gave the challenge wins and the courser of the third party comes in second, †the owner of the winning horse takes the wager of the other challenging party.

Where three or more persons challenge one another, the agreement becomes illegal if the second party stipulates for a prize equal to that of the first; †but if the price stipulated by the second person remains lower than that which the first reserves to himself in case of success, the validity of the contract is admitted.

In a camel race the animal whose shoulder first reaches the goal wins the prize; in a horse race the result depends on whether the neck reaches the goal; according to some authorities victory is always decided by the forefeet reaching the goal.

In a shooting competition it is necessary to stipulate in advance—

1. Whether it is of the kind called *mobadara*, where the prize is gained by whoever first hits the mark a certain number of times; or of the kind called *mohatta*, where the winner is the man who first hits the mark a certain number of times in excess of his rival.

2. The number of times each person may fire, as a maximum; and the number of times he must hit the mark.

3. The distance, the length and the breadth of the target, except in case of a habitual known shooting range.

4. What is meant by "hitting the target." Thus it may be agreed that it is enough to hit the target without leaving a mark, or that the projectile must pierce the target without necessarily remaining fixed in it, or that it must remain so fixed, or that it must traverse it. Where not otherwise specified the first of these arrangements is assumed to have been come to.

The prize at a shooting competition is subject to the same rules as in the case of a racing match, both as regards the cases in which it is permitted to be offered, and as regards the conditions that must be satisfied. But it is not necessary to use certain particular bows and arrows, and a clause to that effect would even be null and void. Thus, at any moment a bow or an arrow may be changed for another of the same sort; and any stipulation interfering with this liberty to change would cause the agreement to become illegal. *It is necessary to stipulate in advance which of the competitors is to shoot first.

Where a great number of competitors wish to take part in the shooting match, it is lawful for two of them to be chosen as chiefs, and for these in their turn to choose the shooters who will form their troop; but the law does not permit this to be decided by casting lots. When one of the chiefs has placed in the number of the shooters some one he supposed had come to take part in the shooting, but who appears later to have been present at the contest merely by chance, the choice is null and void as regards that individual, and one of the competitors in the rival group must abstain from taking part in the shooting. As to the other individuals chosen to make up the two groups, there is the same divergence of opinion as upon the subject of the combination of an illegal with a valid contract; but if it is admitted that the choice of the others remains intact, each competitor should be given a right of option, as to whether he desires to adhere to the agreement or to withdraw from it. Even where all declare that they wish to continue the shooting, the agreement is *ipso facto* dissolved, if no agreement can be come to as to which person shall be eliminated for the individual wrongly chosen by the chief of the opposite troop. In this sort of shooting the prize is shared among the winners in proportion to the number of times they have each hit the mark; or, according to other authorities, in equal parts.

When special stipulations are made as to what is to be understood by "hitting the mark," arrows that do not hit it in the manner agreed upon do not count; but it is of no consequence if the shooter when discharging the arrow breaks the bow-string or the bow, or if the arrow hits the mark only by glancing off from some object, unexpectedly presenting itself between the shooter and the target. Even where the wind carries the target away after the arrow has sped, it must be considered to have hit the mark, if it touches the place where the target was at the moment it left the bow. Arrows that miss the mark, either because they glance off from something, or because the target is carried away by the wind, are not counted in favour of the opponent. But if it is agreed that an arrow must remain fixed in the target, an arrow that pierces it and remains fixed there may be counted, even though it afterwards falls out. And it is the same with an arrow that does not pierce the target, because it hits it at some spot of exceptional hardness.

BOOK 63.—OATHS

Section 1

An oath creates an obligation for the person uttering it only when there is invoked one of the attributes or qualities of God, *e.g.* in the phrases "by God," "by the Master of all created things," "by Him that lives and never dies," "by Him in whose hand is my life," and in general for all expressions employed to designate the supreme being. When one makes use of one of these expressions one may not add a reservation to the effect that one did not intend to take an oath; but if one makes use of an expression which, though it may be used to designate God, may also be used of a human being, such a reservation may be added. Such expressions are "the merciful," "the creator," "the nourisher," "the lord," etc. Expressions that are strictly applicable both to God and man, such as "being," "he who exists," "the wise," or "he who is in life," constitute an oath only where such is the intention of the person using them. The use of one of the qualities of God as a substantive, *e.g.* "by the greatness of God," "by His glory," "by His word," "by His majesty," "by His knowledge," "by His power," or "by His will," constitute an oath if one had not the intention of designating the knowledge, power, etc., that emanate from him upon men. Thus the expression "by the *hakk* of God" implies an oath where the word *hakk* is used in the sense of "justice"; but not where it is used in the sense of "law," for then it means the religious ceremonies of which God may exact the accomplishment as His right. Arabic prefixes, denoting an oath are *bi, wa, ta;* it being understood that the prefix *ta* is only employed with the noun *Allah;* in default of these prefixes the noun *Allah,* without distinction between the nominative, the accusative, and the genitive, implies an oath only where such is the intention of the person using it. The words, "I swear" or "I will swear," "I take oath" or "I will take oath by God that I will do such and such a thing," constitute an oath whether such is the intention or whether they are pronounced without any special intention. Only when one formally declares that one did not intend to make an oath, but merely to state a present or future fact one has a presumption in one's favour that one merely intended to state that fact, and nothing more, and to state it in explicit terms, according to our school. He who says to some one, "By God, I implore you," or "By God, I ask you to do such-and-such a thing," has taken an oath if such was his intention; but it is no oath if he says, "If I did that I am a Jew," or "I abjure Islam," whatever his intention may be. And it is the same where, without thinking of their meaning, one utters words which necessarily imply an oath. But it is of small consequence whether one uses the past tense or the aorist.

It is blamable to take an oath that has not for its special object a work pleasing to God. A person commits a grave sin who takes an oath to neglect an obligatory act of devotion, or to accomplish some forbidden act. In such case he must perjure himself and have recourse to expiation. And the Sonna prescribes expiation to any one who swears to abstain from some commendable act, or to accomplish a blamable action; but in the case of some indifferent act one may have sworn to refrain from or to accomplish, it is always better to keep one's oath. Some authorities, however, prefer even then that a person should perjure himself and have recourse to expiation, on the principle that any oath is blamable when its object is not some work certainly pleasing to God. Where the expiation does not consist in a fast, one may acquit oneself of it in anticipation, before perjuring oneself, in all cases where such perjury is lawful; and even, according to some authorities, where it is forbidden. [†I adopt the doctrine of the latter.]

By virtue of this principle one may acquit oneself of an expiation due for injurious comparison, before resuming cohabitation; or of one due for homicide before the death of the victim; and one may perform the expiation prescribed for the non-fulfilment of a vow before that non-fulfilment has occurred, provided that the vow consists merely in a money obligation.

Section 2

A person who owes expiation for perjury may at his choice either enfranchise a slave, of the same quality as one enfranchised to expiate an injurious comparison, or give to each of ten indigent persons a *modd* of vegetables, forming the principal nourishment of that locality, or clothe them by giving them, *e.g.* a shirt, a turban, or a cloak, but not boots, a pair of gloves, or a belt. The law does not require that the person receiving the clothes must be able to wear them; and one may give a short pair of trousers to a tall individual, and garments of cotton, linen, or silk indifferently to a man or to a woman, and such old clothes as have not quite lost their utility. A person who cannot perform his expiation in one of these three ways must fast for three days, *not necessarily consecutive; but where this incapacity of performance is only temporary, as when he has property elsewhere, he should wait until the means of performing his expiation reach him, rather than have recourse immediately to a fast. It is understood that a slave cannot impose upon himself a pecuniary expiation, unless his master supplies him with the provisions and clothing necessary for acquitting himself of his obligation, and unless it is admitted that he may become owner. In default of such liberality on the master's part, or when it is not admitted that the slave can ever become owner, and consequently donator, the slave must in all cases have recourse to a fast, provided that this act does not prejudice his work or his health. And in this case the fast can take place without the master's special authorisation only when he has authorised the slave to take the oath and then avoid its fulfilment. But where, on the other hand, these two acts have taken place without previous authorisation the master may object to a fast prejudicial to the slave's work or health. †Where the master has authorised his slave to swear but not to forswear, or *vice versâ*, it is the authorisation or want of authorisation that decides, according to the principles we have mentioned, whether he can or cannot oppose a prejudicial fast. A partially enfranchised slave, who possesses savings, should acquit himself of his expiation by giving food and clothing, but not by freeing a slave.

Section 3

An oath taken *e.g.* by a tenant "to stop no longer," or "to live no longer" in a house obliges him to quit it immediately, under penalty of becoming perjured if he personally remains in it without lawful excuse. The time required to remove his effects or his family or to dress himself does not constitute a case of perjury. An oath "not to remain as the neighbour of so-and-so in such and such a house" is accomplished by the swearer or his neighbour quitting the house immediately, †or even by the house being divided into two by a wall, each part with a separate entrance. An oath "not to enter a certain house," or "not to leave it," uttered when respectively inside or outside, implies no obligation to change one's position; for he who remains where he is neither leaves nor enters. Where, however, the act from which one must abstain does not consist in a simple isolated fact, like entering or leaving a house, but in some continuous course of action, as, for example, when one swears not to marry, or wash, or dress, or ride, or stand up, or sit down while being already married, etc., one becomes perjured by the fact of remaining married, etc. [This rule is a mistake as to marriage or ablution; †and similarly one cannot regard as "perfuming oneself" the mere fact of not having removed the perfumes with which one had previously scented oneself. The rule is also applicable to an oath not to indulge in coition, not to fast, or not to pray.]

A person who swears not to enter such-and-such a house becomes perjured if he enters the vestibule; and it does not matter whether the vestibule is situated between the door and the rooms, or between the front door and the back door; but there is no breaking of the oath if he enters the arcade in front of the door, or mounts upon the terrace surrounded or not by a wall. Nor is there any breaking of the oath by putting into the house one's hand, head, or foot; but the introduction of both feet supporting the body constitutes a perjury. The prohibition to enter remains intact in the case of a fall of the house, as long as the foundations of the walls are still visible, and then applies to the site. It ceases only when the land has been completely levelled, or when the house has become a place open to the public, such as a mosque or a bath-house, or where the site has become a garden with the outer walls partly left standing as an inclosure.

A person who swears "not to enter Zaid's house" cannot enter a house occupied by Zaid as owner, but may enter one occupied by Zaid as borrower, lodger, or usurper; unless one intended to refer in general to any house inhabited by Zaid, for in that case the prohibition applies to any house which Zaid borrows, rents or usurps. The phrase cited includes also any house of which Zaid is the owner, though not living in it; unless one intended to refer specially to his habitation and not to his ownership. In accordance with the same principles an oath "not to enter Zaid's house" or "not to speak to Zaid's slave" or "wife," ceases to be of effect as regards a house or slave which Zaid has sold, or a wife whom he has repudiated; but where one refers to such-and-such a house, or such-and-such a wife, or such-and-such a slave of Zaid, one is understood to refer to that particular building or person. In that case words indicating that they belong to Zaid merely make the definition more exact. These last quoted expressions would only admit that the validity of the oath should cease with the actual right of property or status of marriage if such was manifestly the intention of the person taking the oath. †An oath "not to enter the house by such-and-such a door" does not prevent one's entering by that door when it has been removed to another place. An oath "not to enter any room" applies to every room, large or small, or any shed made of clay, stone, brick, or wood, and even to a tent; but not to a mosque, a bath-house, a church, or a mountain cave. Similarly, an oath "not to go to Zaid's" is violated by entering the chamber occupied by Zaid in common with another person, at least according to one jurist, unless the person taking the oath intended to visit this person and not Zaid. As to the consequences of a visit to a place where the presence of Zaid was not known there is the same controversy as to whether the violation of an oath by inadvertence constitutes perjury. [*An oath "not to salute Zaid" is violated by saluting a group of men including Zaid, unless he is specially excepted.]

Section 4

An oath "not to eat animals' heads," without specifying any particular animals, implies an obligation not to eat the head of any animal whose head is sold separately. This oath does not apply to birds, fish, or game that are ordinarily prepared for food without cutting off the head, unless local custom has introduced the practice of selling separately the heads of these animals. The word "eggs" includes all eggs that are eaten without killing the animal that lays them, such as hen's eggs, ostrich eggs, and pigeon's eggs; but not the eggs of fish, that are only eaten as roe after the fish has been killed; nor locust's eggs, that are not eaten at all unless in the body of the animal that bears them. The word "meat" is used of cattle, horses, game, and birds, but not of fish, nor of fat in the interior of the body, †nor of the intestines, the liver, the spleen, nor the heart. †The word "meat" includes the flesh of the head or the tongue, and the fat of the back and sides. The word "fat" in general does not include the fat upon the back nor on the thighs nor on the hump, parts of the animal's body to which the word "meat" does not apply either. The "fat upon the thighs" may not be confounded with "the fat upon the hump," and where one wishes to indicate both one must use the Arabic word *dasam*, which signifies all the fat parts of the body and consequently implies not only the fat properly so called, but also the fat upon the back or in the interior of the body. Any expression signifying beef applies also to buffalo meat.

When one indicates wheat and swears "not to eat any," one must abstain from wheat in grains, as well as from wheat in the state of flour or loaf; but when one swears, "I will not eat of this wheat," and utters the word wheat, one need abstain from it only when the grains have been cooked, mixed with fat, or fried; not when flour, a decoction, a paste, or bread, has been made of it. An oath as to "dates freshly gathered" includes neither dry dates nor dates that are not yet ripe, though they may be large enough, and *vice versâ*. The word "grape" does not include raisins, and *vice versâ*. †And a person who swears not to eat "these freshly plucked dates" is not obliged to abstain from them when they are dry. Similarly, if he swears "not to speak to such-and-such a young man," he can speak to him all the same when he has become an old one. The word "bread" includes as well wheaten bread as barley bread, or bread made of rice, beans, millet, chick peas, etc., and an oath to abstain from it applies also to bread cut in pieces and dipped in soup. An oath "not to eat of a certain decoction" includes an obligation not to introduce it into the mouth with the tongue or the fingers; but the decoction may freely be drunk when diluted with water. Where, on the other hand, one has used the expression "not to drink the decoction," one may introduce it into the mouth with the tongue or the fingers, but not dilute nor drink it. An oath "not to eat milk" or any other liquid requires abstention from eating bread prepared with milk, but not from drinking milk; an oath "not to drink" the liquid in question requires one to abstain from this act but not from eating bread prepared with the liquid. An oath "not to eat butter" is violated by eating it upon one's bread either in a solid or a liquid state, but not by drinking it in a liquid state, nor by eating it in the preparation called *asida*, unless the butter is manifestly apparent. The word "fruit" (*fakiha*) includes dates, grapes, pomegranates, and citrons, either immediately after plucking, or dried. [It is the same with lemons and lotus-fruit, melons and pistachio nuts or filberts. On the other hand, the word "*fakiha*" does not include cucumbers, nor egg-plants, nor parsnip; while the word "*thamar*," though a synonym of *fakiha*, does not include dried fruits.

A person who speaks of melons, dates, or nuts, and nothing more, is not understood to refer to those called "Indian," *i.e.* water-melons, tamarinds, and coco-nuts. In "foodstuffs" are included both the principal nourishment and also fruit, seasoning, and cakes. An oath "not to eat of a certain cow" only applies to the flesh, but not to the calf nor to the milk; a similar oath with regard to a "tree" includes only the fruit, and not the leaves nor the ends of the branches.

Section 5

An oath "not to eat such-and-such a date" is not violated when that date is mixed with other dates, and one eats all but one date, without knowing exactly whether it is the date in question. On the other hand, an oath "to eat such-and-such a date" can only be accomplished by eating all the dates with which it is mixed; and an oath "to eat such-and-such a pomegranate" by eating all the pips. If one swears "not to wear these two coats" one becomes perjured by doing so either at once or one after the other, but one need have no fear in wearing one. To render such an act unlawful it would be necessary to have said "neither this coat nor that coat."

An oath "to eat certain food to-morrow" has no consequence if the person who takes it dies before the time comes; but if he dies, or if the food is destroyed, upon the day on which he should have kept his oath, it is necessary to make the following distinction:—

1. In a case where the person's death or the loss of the food takes place at an hour by which he could already have eaten it, he becomes perjured, even though the day be not entirely passed by.

2. In a case where the person's death or the loss of the food takes place at an hour by which the person in question has not been able to eat the food there exists the same controversy as about a person who becomes perjured in consequence of some violence used towards him.

Where the person taking the oath is himself the cause of the loss of the food before the time indicated, either by eating it or in any other manner he has *ipso facto* failed to fulfil his obligation. Here one must again decide in accordance with the principles relating to violence when the food is lost accidentally or by the fault of a third party before the expiry of the time. An oath in the following terms: "I will pay you your debt at the beginning of next month" obliges the debtor to pay at sunset on the last day of the current month; but the oath is violated by an anticipated payment, or if the debtor allows to pass by, after the sunset, an interval in which he might have acquitted his engagement. However, one is not perjured if in these circumstances one has begun to measure out the articles promised, even though the quantity does not admit of the operation being finished in a short time.

An oath "not to speak" does not prevent one exclaiming, "Praise to God," nor does it prevent a recitation of the Koran; but a person who swears "not to speak to so-and-so," violates his oath by merely saluting him. Shafii, however, in his second period, did not consider as a violation the fact of writing him a letter, or sending him a message, or pointing him out with the hand. This oath does not permit one to intimate to such person what one wants by reciting a verse of the Koran, unless this act is accomplished with the single intention of making a recitation.

An oath to the effect "that so-and-so has no property" means that the individual in question possesses nothing at all of any value, not even the coat he wears, nor a slave to be enfranchised by will, nor a slave whose enfranchisement depends upon a condition, nor an object he has bequeathed to another person, nor a debt due †or to become due. †On the other hand, this oath is not violated by the circumstance that the individual in question has a slave undergoing enfranchisement by contract, *i.e.* one who has ceased to be marketable.

An oath to "beat so-and-so" is accomplished by any act constituting a blow," without its being necessary that the patient should experience any pain, unless one added the adverb "soundly." The mere fact, however, of touching the patient's body with a whip cannot be considered as a blow, nor merely biting him, nor partly strangling him, nor tearing out his hair, nor even, according to some authorities, giving him a buffet or pushing him away. An oath "to inflict upon some one one hundred lashes with a whip" is fulfilled by inflicting a single blow with one hundred whips or batons bound together, or with a bough with a hundred branches, provided only that one is certain that each whip and branch has touched, or at least that all together, one upon another, have contributed to the sufferer's pain. [In case of doubt it should be admitted that all the whips, batons, or branches have had their effect; this is Shafii's personal opinion.] Where, on the other hand, the oath was to the effect that one would go and beat the patient one hundred times one may not limit oneself to a single blow in this way.

If one swears to the effect that "I will not leave you until the payment of my debt," one is not perjured if the debtor runs away and one is not able to pursue him. [††Even if one can pursue the debtor one is not obliged to do so, and one does not become perjured by allowing him to escape.] For an oath in these terms only obliges one not to separate from the debtor; not to stop when he walks on; not to remit the debt if one is walking with him; not to quit him, even after transferring the debt to a third party, or after the debtor is declared bankrupt, and even though in this latter case it should be in order to allow him to put his affairs in order. On the other hand, one can always leave the debtor after the debt has been paid. It matters little then if one discovers afterwards that one has not received all that one might claim, *e.g.* if the debtor has given things of inferior quality, though of the stipulated kind. Where the creditor accepts articles of another kind, but not knowingly, there is the same controversy as to becoming perjured by inadvertence.

An oath to bring to the knowledge of the judge any blamable act to which one may be a witness is violated if the person bound by it, on seeing a bad action committed, omits to bring a complaint before the court, though he is able to do so; and if he dies before repairing his neglect. By the word "judge" is understood the judge of the locality, for one cannot bring the matter before another court; but one may bring it before the successor of the man who was the judge at the time, in case of the death or dismissal of the latter. Where, on the other hand, one does not say "before the judge," but "before a judge," one may bring the case in any court. The expression "before such-and-such a judge" admits of a distinction—

1. It may mean "before so-and-so, as long as he is a judge." In

this case one becomes perjured, if, upon seeing some blamable action, one does not bring it to the knowledge of the judge indicated, though one is able to do so, even though the judge may be subsequently dismissed. If it is impossible to bring the matter before the judge while he remains in office, one is then in the same position as a person perjured in consequence of some violence

2. It may mean the judge personally and not officially. In this case the matter should be brought before him even after his dismissal.

Section 6

A person who swears " not to sell " or " not to buy " should abstain from selling or buying, whether upon his own account or for another; but he may sell or buy through an agent. Similarly an oath not to " give in marriage " or " repudiate " or " enfranchise " or " beat " is no obstacle to doing these things through an agent, unless one intended to say that one would not do these things either personally or through a third party. On the other hand, an oath " not to marry " prevents marriage by proxy, but does not prevent one accepting a woman in marriage as agent for a third party. An oath not to sell Zaid's things refers only to a sale with Zaid's consent. An oath " not to make a donation to Zaid " is not violated by offering him something he does not accept, †or something he accepts but does not take possession of; but such an oath prevents giving him a life interest, or a donation revocable at the donor's death, or a charitable gift. On the other hand, one may lend or bequeath him something, or even immobilise property in his favour. †A man who swears " not to give some one an alms," is not perjured by making him a donation properly so called. A person swearing " not to eat the provisions Zaid has just bought," may eat those purchased by Zaid jointly with another person. †And it is the same if the expression is " provisions " instead of " the provisions." Such an oath refers not only to a sale properly so called but also to a sale by advance. Where food bought by Zaid is mixed with food bought by another, eating the mixture does not involve perjury unless one is certain to have really taken food bought by Zaid. And an oath " not to enter the house Zaid has just bought " does not include a house acquired by Zaid in virtue of his right of redemption.

BOOK 64.—VOWS

Section 1

Vows are of two kinds—

1. A vow with a penalty, consisting, *e.g.*, in the following words :—"If I speak to him I engage before God to fast," or "to enfranchise a slave." If not kept this vow obliges the person formulating it to accomplish the expiation prescribed for perjury, or, according to one authority, to accomplish the expiatory action promised. A single authority gives the person who owes expiation a choice between the expiation for perjury and the expiatory act promised. [†It is to this latter doctrine I give the preference, as do the jurists of Irak.] On the other hand, a person who says, "If I enter such-and-such a house I engage to perform the expiation prescribed for perjury, need only undergo the expiation for perjury.

2. A vow of gratitude, consisting in an engagement towards God to acquit oneself of some good work in the hope of obtaining from Him some favour or of avoiding some calamity. This vow may be formulated, for example, in the following terms :—"If God heals my sickness I engage to accomplish before Him such-and-such an act," or "I engage to perform such-and-such an action." A promise such as this should be accomplished if the event hoped for takes place, *i.e.* if the condition is fulfilled. *The accomplishment of the promise is obligatory even where it is not made dependent upon a condition, for example, if one says, "I engage before God to fast."

A vow may not have for its object an action that is unjust or that is already obligatory. A person who vows to perform some indifferent action, or to abstain from it, need not keep his engagement, provided he acquits himself of the expiation for perjury, at least according to the theory which is to be preferred.

Where one vows to fast for several days it is commendable to do this as soon as possible. One may even fast for the promised number of days separately as well as together, unless a special restriction was made as to this. A vow to fast for a specified year renders a fast obligatory during the whole of this year, with the exception of the days of the great annual festivals, and of the days called *ayyam at tashrik;* and it is understood of course that the fast of the month of Ramadan must be accomplished as it is by everybody, without its being afterwards necessary to repeat it by way of reparation for the month thus deducted from the vow. *When a woman makes such a vow, but is obliged to break her fast in consequence of menstruation or lochia, she must make up subsequently for the days thus lost. [*This precept is not obligatory, in the opinion of most authorities.] The vow in question involves, however, the obligation to accomplish afterwards every other day of fasting lost without this being caused by *force majeure.* And the reader should also be informed that the believer need not begin a new fast of a whole year when he accomplishes afterwards in this way the days of fasting that have been lost, †unless he has expressly announced that the days of fasting are to be uninterrupted.

A vow to fast for a year, without specifying what year, admits of the following distinctions:—

1. Even in the case where one promises to observe the days of the fast without interruption, it does not lose its validity by the intercalation of the obligatory fast of Ramadan, nor by the forced interruption of the days of the two great annual festivals, and of the days called *ayyam at tashrik,* during which fasting is not permitted. But all the fasting days not kept should be made up for during the next year by an equal number of consecutive days. Nor is this fast invalidated by an interruption consequent upon menstruation; though it is true that there is upon this subject the same divergence of opinion we have mentioned already with regard to a similar interruption of a vow to fast during a specified year.

2. Where the vow does not make any mention of an uninterrupted succession of days the difficulties mentioned under No. 1 do not exist, and the fast lasts only for a lunar year, *i.e.* for 360 days chosen at those periods which are most convenient with regard to one's other duties to God.

A vow "to fast every Monday" does not oblige one to fast over again for the Mondays in Ramadan, nor for the Mondays upon which the fasting is suspended in consequence of the two festivals or the days called *ayyam-at-tashrik.* But where, on the other hand, it is a question of the Mondays belonging to the period during which one has to fast for two consecutive months by way of expiation, one must then make up for the Mondays not observed. A single authority does not admit this theory in a case where the obligatory expiation was antecedent to the vow. [*It is the doctrine maintained by this latter jurist that I prefer.] *In the case of a vow of this kind a woman should make up later for the Mondays upon which the fast is interrupted by menstruation or lochia.

A vow "to fast upon a certain day" cannot be regarded as properly observed if the fast is anticipated. A person who makes a vow to fast upon a certain day of a certain week, and then forgets the day of observance, should fast upon the last possible day of that week, *i.e.* the Friday. This fast can then be taken into account as an act of devotion accomplished too late, if it should transpire that the specified day was not a Friday. ††And a supererogatory fast becomes obligatory for whoever makes a vow to complete, while he is accomplishing it. A vow "to fast for a part of a day" has no legal consequences, though, according to some authorities one should fast then for a whole day. *A vow to fast "the day of Zaid's arrival" should be accomplished, unless Zaid arrives during the night or the day of one of the two annual festivals, or in the month of Ramadan, for in these cases the vow is considered as void. The arrival of Zaid upon a day upon which one has already broken one's fast, or begun another fast one had vowed to perform, obliges one to fast another day. And it is the same if Zaid arrives upon a day when one is already engaged in performing some supererogatory fast. Some authorities, however, maintain that in this latter case one need only terminate the fast already begun, which then counts for the fast one vowed to observe. When one utters the following vow:—"If Zaid arrives I will fast the day after his arrival, and if Amr arrives I will fast the first Thursday after his arrival," and both Zaid and Amr arrive on the same Wednesday, the fast is put off for a day, that is to say, one fasts on Thursday for the arrival of Zaid, and afterwards on another day for that of Amr.

SECTION 2

A vow "to walk to the holy temple of Mecca" or "to go there" renders it obligatory, according to our rite, to accomplish the pilgrimage or the visit; with this one difference that a vow "to go there" does not necessarily imply going on foot. *Walking is obligatory only if one has formulated a vow to "walk to the holy temple," or "to accomplish either the pilgrimage or the visit on foot." Where this last-mentioned expression is made use of, it is enough to begin walking on placing oneself in a state of *ihram*; †but if one says, "I will walk to the holy temple," the journey must be made on foot from the place where one has left one's family. This journey on foot does not prevent the believer taking a ride, *if he cannot otherwise continue his journey, **or even if he allow himself this convenience without valid excuse. *But in either case he must make up for his fault by an expiatory sacrifice. This pilgrimage or this visit that one has vowed to accomplish should be made in person unless the pilgrim is physically incapable of going to Mecca, in which case he may be replaced by an agent. In any case it is commendable to acquit oneself of the journey as soon as possible. If a person puts the journey off and is surprised by death before he has accomplished it, though he was capable of doing so, the law prescribes that the cost of sending an agent to perform the pilgrimage or the visit must be borne by the estate. A vow " to accomplish the pilgrimage in a particular year " obliges the person taking the oath to accomplish it during the year specified, if this is possible ; and if he is prevented from doing this by sickness, he must acquit himself of it subsequently. *But the law requires nothing of this sort where the preventing cause is wholly objective, *e.g.* a state of war. As to a prayer or a fast one has vowed to accomplish on a particular day or at a particular hour, one must always acquit oneself of it afterwards if prevented, whether the cause be sickness or a state of war.

A vow " to sacrifice a victim," without anything else, implies that one must conduct the victim to Mecca and give it to the proper persons there ; but where one has specially mentioned that the victim must be given to the proper persons in a particular locality, the victim must be sacrificed there. On the other hand, a vow " to fast " does not imply that the fast must be accomplished in the place where the vow is taken. And the same is the case with a vow to accomplish a prayer, unless it is uttered in the great mosque at Mecca, or, according to one authority, in that of Medina or that of Jerusalem. [*These two mosques are, so far as regards this subject, to be regarded exactly in the same way as that of Mecca.]

A vow " to fast," and nothing else, obliges one to fast for a single day only ; while that " to fast for a few days " implies a fast of at least three days.

A vow of " an alms " is accomplished by a gift of anything. A vow to accomplish " a prayer " implies two *rakas*, or, according to one jurist, a single one, even without adding the *kiyam*. This act is, on the other hand, obligatory in each *raka*, according to the authorities who insist upon two, unless the believer is unable to accomplish it.

A vow to " enfranchise a slave " means a slave capable of being enfranchised by way of expiation, or, according to one authority, any slave. [*It is the latter who is right.]

Where one has vowed to enfranchise " an infidel slave with redhibitory-defects one may acquit oneself of one's vow by the enfranchisement of an infidel slave exempt from such defects, unless the particular defects have been specially mentioned. By virtue of this same principle one

cannot remain seated when making a prayer, if one has vowed to accomplish it standing ; but the contrary is quite lawful. One must adhere rigorously to the terms of one's vow with regard to a recitation of the Koran for a certain lapse of time, or of a certain chapter of the Koran, or with regard to a public prayer. ††One may promise, by way of a vow, to perform any work, provided it be one agreeable to God, and not an obligatory act, such as looking after a sick person, making a salutation, or accompanying a funeral to the grave.

BOOK 65.—ADMINISTRATION OF JUSTICE

CHAPTER I.—GENERAL PROVISIONS

SECTION 1

THE Moslem community is collectively responsible for the administration of justice. A Moslem who feels himself specially capable of exercising the functions of a judge, should solicit those functions; but any individual may accept these duties if the Sovereign entrusts them to him, even though some other individual may be more capable than he. Some jurists, however, have thrown doubt upon this rule. But in such a case it is undoubtedly blamable to solicit the function of judge; and some authorities even go further and wholly forbid any such solicitation. Where one considers oneself not inferior to another in juridical capacity, one may, it is universally agreed, accept the position of judge; it is even commendable to solicit it where, being learned but obscure, one hopes in this way to be able to make one's light shine for the good of humanity, or create for oneself a respectable social position. [††Solicitation is always blamable, except in case of eminent capacity.] To know whether one has special aptitudes for the magistracy, it is only necessary to compare oneself with the other inhabitants of the district.

A judge must be Moslem, adult, sane, free, male, of irreproachable character; sound of hearing, sight, and speech; educated, and enjoying a certain degree of authority in matters of law. Such an authority can be attributed only to one who understands the Koran and the Sonna, and all the texts relating to jurisprudence; and who knows, moreover, whether these texts have a general or special significance; whether they are or are not still in need of explanation; whether they abrogate other texts, or are themselves abrogated by later ones; whether a certain tradition is or is not based upon an uninterrupted line of reporters; whether the origin of a tradition goes back to the companions of the Prophet, or only to the first generation after him; and whether the authority of the reporters is strong or weak. A person wishing to obtain a certain amount of authority in matters of law should also know—

1. The Arabic language, both as to the employment of words and as to grammatical rules; and also the opinions of jurists, beginning with the companions of the Prophet.

2. Whether these opinions are in harmony with one another, or if there is some divergence between them.

3. The reasonings upon which these opinions are based.

Where, however, there is no one fulfilling these requirements, the Sultan may, if necessary, appoint as judge an individual of notorious misconduct or one absolutely incompetent, in order to decide a particular question. It is then admitted, so far as regards that case, that the decisions of the individual so appointed are regarded as final, provided only that he has been nominated by a prince really invested with supreme authority.

The Sovereign is recommended to authorise a person appointed judge to choose his own substitute. Where, however, this authorisation has been formally refused him, a judge has no right to choose his own substitute; and where nothing has been said about it he may only choose one for the cases he is unable to decide personally, not for the others. The substitute must possess the same qualifications as the ordinary judge, unless he has been designated for some special duty, *e.g.* the hearing of witnesses. In this latter case only the qualifications necessary for that particular duty can be insisted on. A substitute who enjoys a certain amount of authority in matters of law may decide cases himself; but otherwise he should in all cases refer to the authority of the jurist whose opinions he has embraced; and one has no right to give him any other instructions.

All proceedings may be compounded, except where penalties are incurred for offences against God, *i.e.* unremissible penalties, provided that the arbitrator is a man capable of exercising the functions of judge. A single authority does not admit arbitration; while others limit it to cases where there is no judge in the locality, and yet others to proceedings that only involve pecuniary consequences and so deny its legality in disputes as to the penalty of talion, marriage, etc. In no case, however, is an arbitration of effect as against third parties. Thus, even where a composition is admitted on the part of a person guilty of homicide, the arbitral decision cannot be enforced against his *aakila* for the price of blood. Either party may revoke his offer of composition so long as the arbitrator has not pronounced his decision; *but once this has been done no one's approval is necessary for the execution of the judgment.

The Sovereign may appoint two judges in the same district, either nominating each one to special judicial functions, or to a particular portion of the locality, or for a particular time or for a certain kind of proceedings; or nominating both of them to the same functions, except that it is not lawful to order them to give judgment together.

Section 2

Lunacy or unconsciousness on the part of the judge, or loss of sight or of any of the intellectual or moral qualifications required, or carelessness or forgetfulness, has the consequence of annulling his decrees; †and it is the same where he is of notorious misconduct. †A judge who becomes incompetent for one of these reasons cannot resume his duties of his own accord, even where the cause of his incompetence has ceased to exist.

The Sovereign may dismiss any judge who appears to him to be incapable of performing his duties; or even a judge who is in every respect capable, if he can find one still more capable. Where the Sovereign has found an individual neither more nor less capable than the actual judge, he may, nevertheless, effect the change if it be for the public interest, or if, for instance, he hopes thereby to appease a sedition. †And the dismissal of a judge has full legal validity in spite of its being in contravention of the principles we have mentioned. According to our school the dismissal of a judge has effect from the moment he is informed of it. Thus where the Sovereign writes to him, "Consider yourself dismissed from the moment you have read this letter," the judge is dismissed, not only when he reads the letter himself, †but also when another person reads it to him.

A person specially nominated by a judge for some particular judicial duty, *e.g.* the sale of the property of a deceased person, ceases *ipso facto* to be so authorised, either upon the death or upon the destitution of the judge who nominated him. And it is the same in the case of a substitute, if the Sovereign had not empowered the judge to choose one; or if the authorisation was given in the following terms, "You may choose a substitute of your own accord," or without mentioning if the substitute was to be appointed by the Sovereign or the judge. Where, on the other hand, the authorisation is to the effect that the judge may take a substitute, but the latter's authority is to be derived from the Sovereign alone, the substitute remains in the exercise of his duties in spite of the death or dismissal of the judge who nominated him. The death of the Sovereign does not *ipso facto* involve the dismissal of the judges appointed by him; nor does the death of the judge involve the dismissal of the persons he has charged with the administration of the property of orphans, or of *wakafs*.

A judge who has been dismissed no longer enjoys a legal presumption in favour of the truth of his words, where he wishes to establish by a simple declaration the contents of a judgment he delivered before his dismissal; ††and a declaration of this nature from him is no longer accepted in evidence, even though confirmed by the testimony of another witness. But a dismissed judge may depose as an ordinary witness to prove the existence of a legally delivered arbitration award. A judge who is not yet dismissed may establish by his mere declaration the contents of the judgments he has delivered; provided always, however, that these judgments were within his competence, for otherwise he should be considered in the matter as a judge already dismissed.

Where, after his dismissal, a judge is accused of pronouncing an unjust pecuniary award, either because he was bribed or because, for example, he has accepted as sufficient the evidence of two slaves, legal proceedings should be taken against him for damages. An accusation is even admissible, and a summons may be issued, upon the evidence accepted by the judge, *e.g.* the deposition of two slaves, without the plaintiff having to plead that he has suffered any pecuniary loss; though according to some authorities the dismissed judge can only be summoned where this is the case, unless the facts alleged have already been proved. †If, when he is accused, the judge appears in person and denies the charge, the presumption is in his favour without his taking an oath. [†He does not enjoy this presumption unless he takes an oath.]

The accusation of a magistrate in the exercise of his functions, implying deceit or fraud upon his part, is never admissible, unless the facts alleged have been already proved.

In every proceeding against a judge, even when not amounting to an accusation; his functions should be performed by his substitute, and the case should, if necessary, be transferred to the court of another district.

SECTION 3

An appointment of a judge by the Sovereign should not only be drawn up in writing, but must be before two witnesses, who should accompany the new judge to his district in order to prove the authenticity of his appointment. †Public notoriety, however, is sufficient as to this authenticity; but our school never admits in any case the nomination of a judge by means of an ordinary letter.

The new judge should begin by making inquiries as to the learned jurists and persons of irreproachable character in the principal town of his district; he should make his entry there upon a Monday; and he should alight in the centre of the town, and first of all inspect the prisons. He should order those prisoners who admit having been lawfully incarcerated to remain there; but if any of them maintain that they have been wrongfully imprisoned, and produce plausible arguments in support of their allegations, the judge should examine into the matter, and issue a summons to the adverse parties if they are not upon the spot. Secondly, after that the new judge should meet all testamentary executors and make inquiries under what circumstances the administration of the legacies was entrusted to them. He should also examine into their conduct and their administration, and if he perceives that either the one or the other leaves something to be desired, he should withdraw from their custody the funds entrusted to them. Where, on the contrary, he perceives that errors have been committed in the administration in good faith, and merely through want of capacity and firmness, he should limit his action to attaching to the testamentary executors a special adviser to assist them in their duties. In the third place the judge should choose a *mozakki*, *i.e.* an employé to give him information as to the witnesses, and an usher. This latter should be a Moslem of irreproachable character and of sufficient education to be able to draw up the record of proceedings and the judgments; and it is recommendable that he should have some knowledge of law, a quick intelligence, and a good hand-writing. *The judge should also appoint the interpreters, who must be free persons of irreproachable character; but it is not necessary that they shall be able to see. If the judge is hard of hearing several interpreters must be nominated. And, finally, the judge must prepare the instruments necessary for the execution of his sentences, *e.g.* a whip for flagellation, and a prison for bodily restraint and for punishment at the discretion of the court.

It is to be recommended that the judge should hold the sittings of the court in some large open court, where the audience may be sheltered from heat and cold, adapted to the season and to the object of the hearing. It is forbidden to hold sittings in a mosque. It is blamable in a judge to deliver a judgment when he is angry, or hungry, or in a state of excessive satiety, or in general when he is in any physical state likely to trouble his mind. The law recommends a judge to consult the jurists of the town before pronouncing a decision.

A judge is recommended not to go personally to make his purchases or sell his goods, and even not to have a recognised man of business. He is rigorously forbidden to receive a present from one of the litigants, unless such person was in the habit of making him similar presents before his appointment; but he need have no fear in continuing to receive presents as usual from those who already gave him such presents before his appointment, and who are not concerned in any proceedings before him. But even in this case it is preferable to return the presents received.

A judgment delivered by a judge in his own favour, or in that of his slave, or of his partner in the same firm, has no legal effect; ††and similarly with a judgment in favour of his ancestors or descendants. In all these cases the judge should decline to hear the case, and should refer the matter to the Sovereign, or to another judge, or to his substitute.

On the demand of a successful litigant the judge should have it established by witnesses that the defendant has made a judicial admission, or that the defendant has won his case upon taking an oath administered to him, etc. He cannot evade the obligation to pronounce sentence before witnesses, where the case is ripe for decision. It is to be recommended that the judge should cause to be delivered to the successful litigant upon his request a minute of all the proceedings in court together with a copy of the judgment delivered in his favour. According to some authorities this is even obligatory. It is also commendable that the proceedings and judgments should be made out in duplicate, one for the successful litigant and the other to be deposited in the archives of the court. A judgment that subsequently appears to be at variance with a text of the Koran, with the Sonna, or with the general opinion of jurists, or with common-sense, should be quashed, either by the judge who delivered it, or by his colleagues, substitutes, or successors, even where there is no doubt as to his competence. Where, on the other hand, the only flaw in the judgment is of a subtle nature, the decision holds good and cannot become the subject of new proceedings. And it must be observed in this connection that the meaning of a judgment depends upon what is formally decided in it, not upon what the magistrate meant to say. And there is general agreement that even where the matter is legally proved a judge should never pronounce a sentence against any one unless he is himself convinced that that party is in the wrong; *and he may even sentence a person upon his own conviction alone, except in the case of an irremissible penalty for which a special proof is required by law.

Where some one presents to the judge a document containing one of his judgments, or where two witnesses declare to him that he delivered a certain judgment, he may not accept the document or the testimony unless he remembers the judgment in question. This principle applies also to witnesses who, unless they can remember the matter, may not refer either to a document containing their deposition, or to the assertions of other persons affirming that they were witnesses of the event.

Authorities are not, however, agreed upon these principles in the case of a document carefully kept by the judge or by the interested witness. One may affirm upon oath that a person to whom one is heir had a claim or acquitted himself of an obligation, on no other ground than documents written by him, at least where one can recognise the deceased's hand-writing, and has faith in his sincerity. ††And, finally, one may depose upon the faith of a document, containing the affirmation of a fact, provided that it has always remained in the possession of the witness.

SECTION 4

A judge should treat the parties who appear before him in an impartial manner. If he gets up or remains seated upon the entry of the one he should do the same for the other; and he should listen to their respective pleadings without giving any sign of approbation or of blame. He should return the salutations of both and make them sit in the same row. †But where one of the adversaries is a Moslem, and the other an infidel subject of our Sovereign, he is permitted to show more respect to the former than to the latter. As soon as the parties have taken their places the judge should cause silence to be made in the court, then call upon the plaintiff to address him, and it is only after the plaintiff has finished what he has to say that the defendant is called upon. Where the defendant admits the claim the matter is simple, and the plaintiff wins his case; but if the defendant denies, the judge should call upon the plaintiff to produce proof of his allegations, and then be silent. If the plaintiff, though able to produce the required proof, declares that he prefers that an oath to determine the matter should be administered to the opposite party, this request should be complied with; †and the plaintiff still be permitted to produce his proof, even though at first he said he had none. Where several persons wish to be admitted to the hearing, the first applicant has the priority; where it is not known which applied first, or where all applied at the same time, recourse must be had to casting lots to decide which case should be heard first. Priority must-always be given to urgent cases of travellers, and to women's cases, even though of later application, unless their number is exorbitant. Priority accorded to some one either in consequence of prior application, or because the lot was drawn in his favour, applies only to a single case, and not to all the cases he may claim to bring before the court.

A judge is forbidden to designate certain persons to have the exclusive right of deposing before him as witnesses. If a judge knows that a certain witness who comes to make a deposition is of irreproachable character, or if he knows that another such witness is of notorious misconduct, he should accept or reject the testimony without further inquiry ; but if he has not this knowledge for certain, he cannot either accept or reject the deposition until he has made inquiry as to the moral character of the witness. This he may do by taking note of the name, etc., of the witness and of the two litigants, ††and the substance of the claim, and referring the matter to the *mozakki* or officer employed in obtaining further information upon the subject. The latter then makes a verbal report to the judge of the result of his inquiries ; though, according to some authorities, the report may, if necessary, be made in writing. A *mozakki* should not only possess all the qualifications required of a witness ; he should also have an intelligence sufficiently developed to decide whether a witness is or is not of irreproachable conduct. He cannot make this declaration unless he knows the witness intimately, either as his friend or his neighbour, or as having had business dealings with him. †The *mozakki* when making his report, should make use of the formal words of a deposition, " I bear witness that," but he need not enter into the reasons for considering a person to be irreproachable. Only a few authorities require that the *mozakki* should state it to be his personal opinion. On the other hand, when the *mozakki* declares that some one's testimony should be rejected in consequence of his notorious misconduct, he must give his reasons for that opinion, founded either upon what he has himself observed, or upon public notoriety. The proof that a witness is of notorious misconduct has the value of a positive fact, and has preponderance over the negative proof that he is irreproachable ; unless the person who maintains his character to be irreproachable cannot give any positive fact as the ground of his opinion, *e.g.* where he declares that the witness, though formerly of notorious misconduct, has since become an honourable citizen. †In order to establish an irreproachable character it is not sufficient that the defendant should admit this circumstance, while declaring that the witness is mistaken in his deposition.

CHAPTER II.—JUDGMENTS BY DEFAULT

SECTION 1

JUDGMENT may be given against some one by default, where the plaintiff alleges that his adversary denies the claim and produces sufficient proof of his case. †A plaintiff may also be allowed to prove the facts alleged by him, though he make no declaration as to the position taken up by the defaulting party, and in no case is it necessary for the judge to appoint some one to maintain before him the denial of the absent defendant. The plaintiff, after proving his case, is obliged to swear that his claim still exists and has not been satisfied, *e.g.* by payment on the part of the debtor. According, however, to other authorities, it is only commendable and not obligatory to administer this additional oath; and the same controversy exists as to this oath when administered in proceedings against a minor or a lunatic who has no legal representative at the hearing. Where the proceedings against the defaulter are not taken by the plaintiff in person, but by his agent, the oath we have spoken of is not administered to the latter; and should the defendant be present and reply to the agent, "Your principal has freed me from my obligation," this assertion, unless proved, is not enough even to cause the judgment to be postponed. A judgment against a defaulter may be executed upon the property which he possesses within the jurisdiction of the court; and if he has none, the plaintiff may demand that the case be transferred to the court in whose jurisdiction the defaulter is. This transfer may take place either by having sent to the latter court the depositions of the witnesses, in order that judgment may be entered there and executed without any further informations being necessary; or by sending the judgment of the first court to the second to be executed. For the transfer it is enough to establish by two witnesses of irreproachable character what has taken place at the first hearing; but the first court is recommended to have sent to the second a document sealed with its seal in which the defaulter is indicated in a way sufficient to establish his identity. The two witnesses should give evidence against the defaulter if he perseveres in his denial; where, on the other hand, he declares, without admitting or denying anything, that he does not bear the name indicated in the letter of requisition, he has a presumption in his favour, provided he confirms his declaration upon oath; and in this latter case the plaintiff must prove that the person in question is really the adverse party whose name and parentage are mentioned in the letter. When this proof is forthcoming, and the adverse party maintains that though bearing the same name he is not the person meant by the former court, such a defence cannot be admitted, unless there be in that locality a similar name answering to the same qualities. In this case the person of the same name is summoned, and if he admits he is the person described, the proceeding should be continued against him, and the former defendant dismissed. Where, on the other hand, the person of the same name denies that he is the person described, the matter should be sent back to the former court, in order to obtain by the evidence of witnesses fuller information as to the identity of the person to be summoned, and the minutes of these fresh proceedings should then be forwarded to the second court. If the judge in whose jurisdiction the defaulter is, arrives at the place where the proceedings were originally taken, he should consult his colleague as to the decision to be come to. As to the question whether the judge, on returning to his jurisdiction, may give judgment in accordance with the personal information he has thus obtained, there is the same divergence of opinion as to whether he should give judgment in accordance with his own certain knowledge without attending to the legal proof. But a judge may order the execution of the judgment whether the defaulter is upon the boundary of his jurisdiction or whether he has summoned him before him at the ordinary hearing.

Where, in a case of default, the court limits itself to a hearing of witnesses, it should have minutes drawn up of the depositions it has received, and add the name of the party against whom these depositions have been made. It should also add the names, etc., of the witnesses, in all cases where it has not itself acknowledged their character to be irreproachable, in order that the judge before whom the proceedings are continued may be able to make inquiries upon the subject. †But where the court before which the depositions were made certifies in the minutes of the proceedings that the witnesses are of irreproachable character, no further information is required upon the matter.

A case may be transferred, however short may be the distance between the courts; ††but requisitorial letters for the hearing of witnesses cannot be addressed to a court whose jurisdiction is not distant at least as far as would permit of having recourse to hear-say evidence to establish the depositions of the original witnesses.

Section 2

When a case is about a certain, definite object, not in the jurisdiction of the court, but not of a kind to be easily confused with any other object, such as a piece of immovable property, a slave, or a horse, all of which are known, the court may permit the parties to prove their rights, and then give judgment; and after this he should communicate in writing with the court in whose jurisdiction the subject of the suit is situated, in order that the latter may have it given into the possession of the successful litigant. In the case of immovable property it is sufficient in these circumstances to indicate its limits. *Where, on the other hand, the object in dispute is of a nature to be easily confused with other things the court cannot allow the parties to prove their claims until the plaintiff has first given as minute a description of it as possible, and stated its value. *Then the court should hear the parties, but not decide immediately in a case of this sort; he should communicate in writing with the court in whose jurisdiction the thing is, and inform him of its distinctive marks, in order that the latter may order it to be seized and sent to him. The witnesses that have been summoned should then declare whether they recognise the object; *and this cannot be handed over to the plaintiff in the meantime unless he furnishes a personal security for it. The security can only be released when the court that has given the plaintiff the object receives from the court before which the proceedings are being taken a letter informing it that the object has been recognised by the witnesses. And if the object is not recognised by the witnesses the plaintiff who has obtained temporary possession of it must pay the expense of restoring it to the original owner. In the case of something which is in the jurisdiction of the court but is not brought to the hearing, this must first of all be sent for, if it is possible, in order that the witnesses may establish its identity, for in such a case recourse may not be had, even provisionally, to a mere description.

Where the defendant declares that he possesses no object of the kind claimed from him, he has a presumption in his favour, provided he confirms his declaration upon oath; and unless the plaintiff is able to prove that it is false, he must confine himself to an action for damages. If the defendant refuses to take the oath, and the plaintiff is ready to swear that the defendant really has the thing in his possession, or if he can prove it, the defendant should be ordered to produce the object in dispute, and if necessary imprisoned until he complies with the order, or until he proves in court that the object no longer exists. In case of doubt on the part of the plaintiff as to the loss of the object, so that he does not know whether to claim its return or its value, he may formulate his claim as follows: "The adverse party has usurped such-and-such a thing which belongs to me, and I demand its restitution, or in case it has been destroyed, its value." Some authorities, however, do not allow of such an alternative claim; they insist first upon a claim for the return, and then an oath, according to the procedure we have mentioned; and only after this has been done do they allow of a claim being made for the value. This same controversy exists also in a case where one gives a coat to a broker to sell, and he denies the fact, so that one does not know whether he has sold, lost, or kept it; and as to whether one should bring against him a personal action for payment of the price obtained, or for the value, or for its return.

Where it is admitted that the object should be brought to the hearing, the expense of its transport must be borne by the defendant, in the case where the claim of the plaintiff upon the thing in dispute is recognised by the court; and if the claim is dismissed, the plaintiff must pay not only the expense of bringing the thing to the hearing, but also that of restoring it to the defendant.

Section 3

As to procedure in case of absence, the law insists that the defaulter must be at a "considerable" distance, that is to say that if one starts in the morning to look for him, one has not returned by the following night. Other authorities say that the distance should be such as enables to abbreviate prayer. On the other hand, where the defendant is in the neighbourhood, the court may not proceed in his absence to the hearing of the plaintiff's witnesses, nor give judgment; unless he keeps himself hidden, or occupies too high a social position to be summoned to attend the court.

*Judgment by default is permitted not only in civil matters, but also in cases of crimes against the person, and in cases of defamation; but a person guilty of any other crime may not be sentenced in his absence.

Evidence given in court against a defaulter who appears before judgment is pronounced does not need to be given a second time in his presence; it is enough to inform him of what has been done in his absence in order that he may have an opportunity of challenging the witnesses, etc. On the other hand, the whole proceedings must be begun afresh if, after the plaintiff's witnesses have been heard, the judge is dismissed and then reappointed.

The summonsing of an individual who is in the district in which the court is held is effected either by sending him the seal of the court upon a piece of clay, etc., or by means of an usher. If the defendant refuses to appear without valid excuse the court may have him brought before it by force, and may also inflict upon him a punishment at its discretion. On the other hand, in the case of an absent person the following cases must be distinguished :—

1. If the absent person is not within the jurisdiction of the court, he cannot be summonsed, nor made to appear by force.

2. If the absent person is within the jurisdiction of the court at a place where the judge has a substitute, the court should limit itself to hearing the witnesses for the plaintiff, and then send the proceedings to the substitute.

3. If the absent person is within the jurisdiction of the court at a place where the judge has no substitute, he may be summonsed and, if

necessary, brought by force, provided that the distance does not prevent this; *i.e.* provided that the bearer of the summons can leave in the morning and be back again by the next night.

†A young woman, even though she lives close to the court, may not be summonsed, when she is *mokhaddara*, *i.e.* when she is not in the habit of going out, except in case of absolute necessity.

CHAPTER III.—DISTRIBUTION OF ESTATES

The distribution of an inheritance or of a joint estate is effected either by the inheritors or the persons entitled themselves, or by an expert chosen by them, or by an expert appointed by the Sovereign. The official expert must be a free male of irreproachable character, versed in geometry and arithmetic. Where the distribution necessitates a valuation of some sort, this must be made by two experts; but in all other cases one is enough. One jurist maintains that two experts are always necessary. The expert appointed by the Sovereign to preside at distributions may also be authorised to decide difference in the matter of valuation; in which case the valuation itself is effected by two special experts having the qualifications of irreproachable witnesses; while a distribution properly so called is always effected by the official expert himself. The official expert receives a remuneration from the public treasury; and it is only in times of penury that his payment has to be borne by the inheritors or other persons entitled. In a case where the sharers themselves choose an expert, and agree with him upon the amount of his remuneration, and the proportion of it to be paid by each of them, each one owes him the amount stipulated. In default of any special agreement about it the stipulated remuneration is levied proportionately upon the shares; a single authority maintaining that the sharers are then separately responsible.

Where there are articles that it is not possible to divide up without a considerable diminution in their value, such as a valuable diamond, a costly dress, or a pair of boots, the court may not order their distribution, even upon the request of all the parties entitled. But it cannot oppose it, if the parties entitled carry out the division themselves, and the object does not thereby lose all its utility; as, *e.g.* in the case of a sabre which can still cut though broken into pieces. †Even in the case of something which by its division, without precisely losing much of its value, can no longer serve the purpose for which it was made, such as a bath or a small millstone, the court cannot accede to an application to order its distribution. Such a request could only be complied with where, for example, the bath is of a size that admits of its being made into two. †By virtue of the same principle if of two proprietors of a house one is entitled to nine-tenths, and the other to one-tenth, only the former may apply for its distribution if the tenth by itself is uninhabitable.

As to things whose nature admits of their being effectively divided without any considerable diminution in their value, the following cases must be distinguished :—

1. The distribution may be effected by a simple division into equal parts in the case, *e.g.* of things that can be estimated by measure, of a house that consists of several constructions of the same kind, or of a piece of land of the same quality or nature throughout. In this case any person entitled may oblige his co-proprietors to proceed to a division, which is carried out in the following way. As many equal lots are made as there are persons entitled, these lots being determined by measure or weight ; and after this there is written upon a piece of paper either the name of each sharer, or the description of each lot, mentioning, for example, its boundaries and situation. These pieces of paper are rolled round little balls of equal size, and finally these balls are drawn by some one who was not present on the spot at the moment when the pieces of paper were rolled round them. The first ball is drawn for the first lot which is in consequence given to the person whose name is upon the piece of paper, and so on with the others. Where, on the other hand, it is the lots that have been mentioned on the pieces of paper, the first ball is for that one of the sharers previously designated ; he is given the lot indicated on the first to come out, and so on with the others. Where all the coproprietors are not entitled to the same fraction, *e.g.* where three persons may claim respectively the half, the third and the sixth of a parcel of land, the land must be divided into as many lots as is indicated by the denominator of the smallest of the fractions, and after this has been done the distribution should proceed in the manner already explained. But in these circumstances care must be taken not to assign to one person lots that are separated from one another, and so do not form one continuous bit of land.

2. Equal distribution, *i.e.* a division into lots of different sizes, but of equal value, is called for in the case of land that is not of uniform value throughout, in consequence of one corner being more fertile or nearer water than another. *This circumstance does not prevent distribution taking place upon the application of each coproprietor. Equal distribution is impossible in the case of two houses or of two shops, even where of equal intrinsic value ; in this case neither of two persons entitled may insist upon one being assigned to him

and the other to his coproprietor. In the case of movable property, *i.e.* slaves or clothes of the same value and kind, one may ask for equal distribution; but where the slaves or the clothes, though having the same value, are of different kinds, such an application is inadmissible.

3. Adjustment is called for where, for example, a parcel of land is divided into several lots in one of which is a well or a tree which it is impossible to distribute. In this case the person so favoured owes to the other a proportional compensation; but no one can force his coproprietor to such a division, as it is in reality a sale, and this principle is extended by our school even to an equal distribution as explained under the preceding paragraph No. 2. On the other hand, distribution by a simple division, as in No. 1, is in truth merely the act of rendering to each the exclusive possession of what was already his property. A distribution by adjustment and compensation requires also the consent of the interested parties after their respective portions have been assigned them by lot. †And subsequent consent is always necessary where one of the coproprietors could not have forced the others to proceed to a distribution, being expressed as follows: "We accept the distribution that has been effected," or "We accept what has been assigned to us by lot."

Obligatory distribution should be rescinded upon the application of any person entitled who can prove that there has been error or fraudulent infraction of his rights. Even where such claimant cannot furnish any legal proof of this, he may still have an oath administered to his former coproprietors. Where, however, the distribution is really a sale, there is no ground for rescission on account of error, and an application for rescission could not be received. [In cases where the distribution is merely the act of rendering to each person the exclusive possession of what is already his property, there is ground for rescission in case of error legally proved or established by oath.] Legal seizure of a portion of the succession or joint estate has the effect of annulling the distribution as far as concerns the property seized. As to the question whether in spite of this the distribution remains good for the remainder there is the same difference of opinion as with regard to the partial dissolution of a bargain. Where the seizure concerns something certain and definite, the distribution remains good if each lot is subject to an equal or proportional diminution in value; but in all other cases the distribution is *ipso facto* annulled by the circumstances mentioned.

BOOK 66.—EVIDENCE OF WITNESSES

SECTION 1

No one can be a witness except a free, adult, sane Moslem of irreproachable and serious character, not liable to suspicion. It is necessary, to constitute irreproachable character, that the witness should have abstained entirely from committing capital sins, and should not be in the habit of committing sins of a less serious nature. Amongst illicit pleasures that offend respectability are counted the game of backgammon ††which is rigorously forbidden, and that of chess which is merely blamable where there is a stake, for in this case chess is considered as a true game of chance, and in consequence rigorously forbidden. It is lawful to sing and listen to the song to which the camel-drivers make their animals walk; but the law blames all other singing not accompanied by instruments of music; and it forbids the use and the sound of any musical instrument tending to excite to the use of forbidden drinks, such as the guitar, lute, cymbal, and Persian flute. †On the other hand, the flageolet is an instrument of music which the law permits. [The flageolet also is rigorously forbidden.] A tambourine may be used at a marriage or a circumcision †or any other festival, even when bells are attached to it; but one must never beat the *kuba*, *i.e.* a long drum narrow in the middle.

The law permits dancing, provided it is not of an enervating character like that of effeminate persons. The declamation and recitation of poetry is permitted, provided there are no satiric or obscene verses, nor any allusion to some particular woman.

By a man of "serious" character is meant one who models his conduct upon the respectable among his contemporaries and fellow-countrymen. Certain actions are essentially incompatible with a serious character. One should regard, for example, as wanting in seriousness a person who eats in public places and walks there bare-headed; who embraces his wife or his slave in the presence of other persons; who is always telling funny stories; who wears a gown and pointed cap as a professional jurist though this is not the custom of the place; who habitually plays chess or sings or listens to singing, or who dances for an excessively long time. It is well, however, so far as these acts are concerned, to take into consideration the individuals, circumstances and places. Besides this, there are occupations so base in themselves as to be incompatible with the character of a witness; for example, that of a person who applies leeches, or sweeps houses, or tans leather; persons following such occupations, even though they may be of as high social position, cannot depose as witnesses. †These occupations, however, when exercised as a trade by an individual whose father before him was a barber, a sweeper, or a tanner, form no obstacle to a deposition. By "liable to suspicion" is meant a person who allows himself to be influenced by the idea of procuring some advantage, or protecting himself against some damage.

Interested witnesses may always be challenged. Consequently one cannot depose in favour of one's slave or dependent undergoing enfranchisement by contract, nor can one give evidence with regard to an estate inherited by one's debtor, nor in favour of one's debtor who has been declared bankrupt. For the same reason may be challenged a witness with regard to a matter about which he has been appointed an agent, or with regard to the remittance of a debt for which he is security, or with regard to an assault against a person of whom he is the heir. On the other hand, there is objection to accepting in a question of real property or of money the deposition of a sick or wounded person in favour of another of whom he is the heir, even before his recovery. The *aakila* cannot testify to the notorious misconduct of the witnesses of a homicide, nor can the creditors of a bankrupt testify to the notorious misconduct of witnesses called by another person to establish another debt. †Where, however, two witnesses prove a testamentary disposition in favour of two other persons, and these latter subsequently declare that the witnesses themselves were mentioned in the same will, none of this evidence can be challenged as it really relates to different things. And finally, one cannot depose in favour of one's ancestors or descendants, though one may legally do so against them, *and the law even specially allows a son the privilege of deposing against his father as to a repudiation or a defamation uttered by the latter against a wife who is not the mother of that son. *Evidence given in favour both of one's own descendants and also of a third party, is valid only for the latter. [Husband and wife may give evidence in favour of each other, and one may even depose in favour of one's brother or of one's friend.]

The deposition of an enemy is not admissible, *i.e.* of an individual who hates the adverse party to such a degree as to wish to see him fall into misery, to envy his prosperity, and rejoice in his misfortune; but the favourable deposition of such an enemy is admissible. An enemy's testimony should be accepted in all cases where the ill-feeling is not personal, for example, if it is the result of a difference of religion. Consequently a Moslem may depose against an infidel or a heretic, and a heretic whom we do not regard as an infidel does not lose his right to give evidence. It is permitted to challenge the testimony of persons who are too eager to give evidence, or so indifferently careless that one can put no trust in their words ; but one must accept the evidence of police agents or of other persons as to the accomplishment of a person's obligations towards God, and the actions of private life that confer an irrevocable right to a third party, *e.g.* repudiation, enfranchisement, remission of a penalty under the law of talion, existence or expiration of a period of legal retirement, penalties of a non-remissible character, ††and even affiliation.

Judgments delivered upon the testimony of two witnesses who afterwards are found to be infidels, slaves, or minors, should be quashed either by the court that delivered them or by any other court ; *and the same is the case where it appears too late that the witnesses were of notorious misconduct. But the depositions of an infidel, a slave, or a minor should be accepted if they repeat them after the cause of their incapacity has ceased to exist ; though the law does not accord this favour to individuals of notorious misconduct who afterwards lead a changed life. It is only after a sufficient interval has elapsed to admit of the sincerity of the change that they can again be accepted as witnesses, and most authorities fix the duration of this interval at one whole year. Where the notorious misconduct is the consequence of a verbal insult to some one, it is enough to make a verbal retractation ; where, for example, a person proceeded against for defamation declares that he withdraws the insulting expressions used, and adds that he feels for them profound regret, and that he will in future abstain from such a crime, the court may accept his testimony. This rule applies also to false evidence. [Insults not expressed in words but by acts are made reparation for by ceasing to manifest them, by showing one's regret, and proposing to abstain from such things in future ; and also by compensating the insulted party, so far as this is within human power.]

Section 2

The testimony of a single individual is not enough to prove any fact, *except the appearance of the new moon in the month of Ramadan. In order to prove the crime of fornication four male witnesses must be produced, and two to prove the culprit's confession, though in this latter case also one jurist considers that four are necessary. Real property claims, and contracts having consequences that are merely pecuniary, such as sale, cancellation by consent, transfer of debts due to one, and security, as well as the rights resulting from these contracts, such as right of option, or a term for payment, may all be proved by the testimony of two male witnesses, or of one male witness and two women. Two male witnesses are rigorously required in all other contested cases, whether it be a matter of non-remissible penalties, except that for fornication, or of remissible ones, or of some dispute as to an act of private life ordinarily affected before men and in their sight, such as marriage, repudiation, return to conjugal union, conversion, apostasy, notorious misconduct, irreproachability, death, insolvency, appointment of an agent, testamentary dispositions, and the testimony which two witnesses have made a certain deposition. On the other hand, what is specially liable to come under the observation of women, and in general facts which do not usually take place in the presence and in the sight of men, such as the existence of virginity, accouchement, menstruation, suckling, redhibitory defects in women and in parts of the body usually covered, are proved as well by the evidence of two men as by that of four women.

Facts which cannot be proved by the evidence of one male witness and of two women, cannot be so either by the deposition of one male witness and by a supplementary oath; but this oath may replace the evidence of two women in all cases where their deposition together with that of a man is admissible, except only that of women's redhibitory defects. In no case can the deposition of two women, plus a supplementary oath, be accepted as sufficient proof of anything. A supplementary oath is administered to a plaintiff only after the hearing of his witness, and after the latter has been recognised to be of irreproachable character. This oath should contain an affirmation of the truth of the deposition. But the plaintiff has a right to waive his claim to take the oath, and to have it offered to his opponent, who in his turn has also a right to refuse to take it. *In this latter case the plaintiff may still take it. Where some one owns a slave and her child another person may prove enfranchisement by reason of maternity, producing in support of it a single male witness, and swearing that the slave is the child's mother; *but neither affiliation nor the freedom of the child can be established in this way. Our school admits that a slave ceases to be his master's property and becomes free when another person declares upon oath that the slave in question belonged to and was enfranchised by him, and these facts are corroborated by the evidence of a male witness. Where some one's heirs claim some property which they allege to have belonged to the deceased, though they can only produce a single male witness of the truth of this, while only a part of these heirs are ready to confirm their claim by a supplementary oath, the property in question must be adjudged to these latter only, in proportion to their respective shares in the succession. As to the other heirs who have not taken the oath, not only are they not admitted as persons entitled to the property adjudged to their coinheritors, but any claim on their part is rejected, at any rate if they have refused to take the oath while capable of doing so. But if they have been prevented from taking the oath, *e.g.* in case of absence, minority, or lunacy, our school, though rejecting their claim, allows them the right of taking the oath afterwards, so soon as the cause of their incapacity has been removed. The part they claim should then be adjudged them, without its being necessary for them to produce again the witness who has already deposed in their favour.

Witnesses called to prove a material fact, such as fornication, usurpation, destruction of property, or accouchement, should have actually seen the fact themselves; consequently a deaf man may lawfully give evidence in such cases. On the other hand, witnesses called to prove that the adverse party has spoken certain words; for example, that he has made a bargain, or made an admission, or repudiated a wife, should not only have seen the individual in question, but also heard the words in dispute. Thus a blind man cannot give evidence, ††unless it be in the case, *e.g.* of an admission uttered in his ear by a person who has not since left him, until the moment of the deposition. And it is understood, of course, that a blind person can give evidence of a fact which he saw before he was struck with blindness, provided that he knows the name and origin of the two litigants. A witness who has heard the words and seen the act of a person he knows, and whose name and origin he knows, should point out that person if present at the hearing; but he need merely mention the name and origin, if the person be absent or deceased. A witness who has forgotten the name and origin of the person in question cannot depose. In the case of a veiled woman a witness cannot rely upon her voice to prove her identity, unless he could recognise her figure, and knows her name and origin. Even in these circumstances the witness should limit himself to declaring, as to her identity, what he knows for certain, without adding his conclusions. Strictly speaking, he cannot either identify the woman by referring to one or two persons, even though these may be of irreproachable character; but the practice does not accord with the precept. Where the plaintiff, after proving his claim against some one present at the hearing, demands a sentence in writing, the judge should describe that person by his appearance, and add his name and origin only where these have been proved before him.

A witness may prove in court some one's name and origin, according to what he has heard as to the names of the father, the tribe, †or the mother. Our school also permits to be established in the same way upon the ground of public notoriety, the deçease of any person, without its being necessary for the witness to have seen the dead body himself. †Such hearsay evidence, however, is inadmissible in case of enfranchisement, patronage, conversion of property into real estate, marriage, or ownership. [†According to the majority of authorities of repute evidence grounded upon public notoriety is accepted in all these cases. Public notoriety consists in the fact of hearing an occurrence related in the same manner by several individuals whose words can be trusted ; though, according to some authorities it is enough to have heard it told by two persons of irreproachable conduct. A witness cannot declare that a certain individual is owner on the mere ground that the latter possesses the object in dispute, nor even because he has had possession of it and disposed of it for a short time. †Where, on the other hand, the period during which the individual has had possession of and has disposed of the object is long, this fact must be accepted as affording a presumption of ownership, on the sole condition that the ways in which it has been disposed of are of such a nature that such a conclusion may be deduced from them, *e.g.* if they consist in the fact of having inhabited, demolished, built, sold, or pledged a house. Insolvency may be proved by alleging indications and arguments showing that the individual in question has been struck by a series of misfortunes and has lost his fortune.

Section 3

The Moslem community is collectively responsible for the presence of witnesses at marriages, †confessions, pecuniary, or real property dispositions, and the drawing up of documents, in order to give these different acts the necessary authority. If an affair of this sort happens in presence of two persons only they cannot refuse to be witnesses. This principle is carried so far that one cannot shirk this obligation if the other declares he is ready to undertake it, even where the party claiming their services only needs a single witness, to be supplemented by an oath in case of proceedings. When the affair happens in the presence of several persons, the joint obligation requires that if the interested party claims the services of two of them they should consent, †and have no right to refer the interested party to other witnesses. When the affair happens in the presence of a single individual he must give his services, unless it is a fact that cannot be proved by a single witness and a supplementary oath, for in this case the testimony of a single witness would be of no use. According, however, to some jurists the obligation to serve as a witness is incumbent only upon those who are intentionally present at the act, not upon the persons who happen accidentally to be there.

The law requires also for a person's appearance as a witness :—

1. That the distance from the home of the witness does not exceed that within which the court may order a personal summons ; or, according to some authorities, that the distance should be less than that permitting of the abridgment of prayer.

2. That the witness should be of irreproachable character ; for notorious misconduct may be a reason for refusing his services as useless. However, a refusal to be a witness, founded upon notorious misconduct, is admissible only in the case of conduct that every one disapproves. Only a few authorities maintain that such refusal may also be founded upon misconduct of which some doubt the perversity.

3. That the witness should not be prevented from appearing through sickness, etc. And in this case the evidence of the witness who does not appear may be proved at the hearing by two other witnesses, or the court may send some one to take the deposition of the said witness at his domicile.

SECTION 4

Hearsay or secondary evidence is a deposition to the effect that a certain witness has proved this or that fact. This evidence is admissible in civil cases, and according to our school in criminal cases also, except in those in which the penalties are not remissible. Such evidence, however, is only to be admitted in the following cases :—

1. Where the original says to the secondary witness, "I was a witness of such-and-such fact, and I call you to be a witness of my statement," or "Be a witness to this statement."

2. Where the secondary witness has heard the original witness give evidence in court.

3. Where the secondary witness has heard from the original witness a detailed account, for example as follows : "I bear witness that so-and-so owes so-and-so a thousand pieces of money as the price of such-and-such a thing bought," or on some other ground ; and it is necessary in this case that the original witness should have specially asked the second to bear witness to his words.

The validity, however, of hearsay evidence in the circumstances set out under sub-section 3 is not to be relied upon ; and it is never enough for the secondary witness simply to say—

1. That he has "heard say" by so-and-so that one of the

litigants owes such-and-such a sum; that is, without adding that the person whose words he is repeating uttered them as a piece of evidence.

2. That he has heard say by so-and-so, ".I am a witness of that debt," or " I can be called as a witness to that;" that is, without adding the cause of the obligation.

A deposition by hearsay should contain the cause of its validity; though, strictly speaking, the court can also accept a hearsay piece of evidence where the cause is not expressed, if the judge is morally certain of the truth of the deposition. Hearsay evidence may never rest upon the words of a witness who is to be rejected; nor can one produce women as secondary witnesses, even where it is a matter of facts that may be proved by women as original witnesses. But the validity of hearsay evidence is not invalidated where the original witness is prevented from deposing by some physical cause such as death, absence, or sickness; though where the right of deposition has been lost owing to apostasy, notorious misconduct, or enmity, one cannot have recourse to hearsay evidence in order to bring in a deposition that has become inadmissible. ††Lunacy has the same effect as death. It matters little whether the witness giving hearsay evidence is of notorious misconduct or a slave at the moment of hearing the original statement, provided he is capable of deposing at the moment of the hearing.

The deposition of the original witnesses is proved legally by two hearsay witnesses; though, according to one jurist the deposition of each original witness should be proved separately, without distinction of sex, by at least two male witnesses.

In any case secondary evidence is only permissible :—

1. Where the original witness has been prevented from coming, or can only come personally with difficulty, *e.g.* in consequence of disease, blindness, serious illness or absence, at least if the distance is such that the court could not order a personal summons, or, according to some authorities, if the distance is such as to permit of the abridgment of prayer.

2. Where the names of the original witnesses are given at the hearing by the witnesses who give the hearsay evidence, though the latter need not guarantee their irreproachability. There is, however, no objection to their affirming at the same time the irreproachability of the original witnesses. Hearsay evidence in which the names of the original witnesses are not given is valueless, even where the persons making the original statements are really irreproachable, and more than sufficient in number.

Section 5

The retractation of a piece of evidence before judgment has been delivered has as its consequence that the court cannot take this evidence into consideration as a ground for its decision. Where the retractation takes place after sentence has been delivered, but before it has been executed, the order holds good in a civil, but not in a criminal matter. A retractation after execution of sentence has no effect upon the validity of the judgment, either in a civil or in a criminal case.

Where, after execution of a death penalty, either under the law of talion, or for apostasy, or even by stoning or whipping, the witnesses declare that they have made a false declaration, intentionally, against the executed person, they are punishable either with death under the law of talion, or with payment of the price of blood on the higher scale, according to circumstances. If the judge himself, in such a case, declares that he has intentionally delivered an unjust sentence, he should be punished with death by way of talion, whether the victim has undergone capital punishment, or suffered death in consequence of the application of some other penalty. Where judge and witnesses both declare they have intentionally contributed to the condemnation, and consequently to the death, of the victim, they are all punishable under the law of talion; but where they merely declare that they have committed injustice by error, half the price of blood should be borne by the judge, and the other half by the witnesses jointly. A *mozakki* who subsequently declares that he has given false information with regard to the irreproachability of witnesses, should be punished himself as a false witness; while the representative of the victim who confesses that he has wrongly slain an innocent person under the law of talion, after that person had been sentenced for premeditated homicide, incurs a penalty under the law of talion, or liability to payment of the price of blood, according to circumstances, whether his retractation is or is not accompanied by those of the witnesses. In this latter case, however, some authorities consider the representative and the witnesses as accomplices, each owing only a portion of the price of blood, where this is due.

Where two witnesses prove an irrevocable repudiation, relationship by fosterage, or imprecation, and the court decrees in consequence a separation, this separation is not annulled by a subsequent retractation of the depositions; but the false witnesses owe the woman proportional dower; or, according to one authority, they owe the half of this dower if the marriage has not yet been consummated. On the other hand, where the separation is decreed, *e.g.* for a cause of repudiation, upon the testimony of two persons who subsequently declare that their evidence is false, but it is proved that the marriage was nevertheless illegal in consequence of relationship by fosterage, the false witnesses owe no reparation.

*False witnesses in monetary matters or matters of real property are only liable, upon retractation of their depositions, for damages where these have really been sustained. This means that, if all retract, they must make joint reparation for the wrong that they have done; but the retractation of one or some of them has no consequence, provided that the number of witnesses who maintain the truth of their depositions is sufficient to make the judgment valid. However, according to some authorities, the witnesses who have in this way retracted their statements, are liable in any case for damages, in proportion to their number, or having regard to the number of witnesses maintaining their statements. Where, on the other hand, after retractation by some of the witnesses, there are not enough left to furnish legal proof, the following cases must be distinguished:—

1. Where the total number of witnesses heard does not exceed the number required by law, the witnesses who retract are liable for damages in proportion to the number of witnesses required.

2. Where the total number of witnesses heard exceeds the number required by law, the witnesses who retract are liable for damages, in proportion to the number of witnesses required; or, according to some authorities, in proportion to the total number of witnesses heard.

In accordance with the same principles it is necessary to determine whether the witnesses were not of the same sex. Where, for example, a fact has been proved by the deposition of a man and two women, and all retract their statements, the man is liable for half the damages, and the two women jointly for the other half. Where it is a matter of some fact, such as relationship by fosterage, to prove which the law requires either the evidence of one man and two women, or that of four women, while the fact has actually been proved by one man and four women, the consequence of a retractation by all of them is that the man owes merely one-third of the damages, and the four women jointly two-thirds. †Where, on the contrary, in the instance just mentioned either the man, or two of the four women, retract their deposition, there is no liability, for the fact remains legally proved. †Finally, in the case of a real or pecuniary obligation, where the law requires the evidence of two men, or that of one man and two women, but in which one man and four women actually testify, a retractation by two of the women is of no consequence; while that of all four women renders them liable for half the damage. The other half has then to be borne by the man in case of a retractation on his part. According, however, to some authorities, one must decide in this case as in a matter of relationship by fosterage, which can, strictly speaking, be proved by four women. †In proceedings for the crime of fornication, a retractation of witnesses who have merely established the status of *mohsan* has no consequence so far as they are concerned ; and the same is the case with witnesses who retract their statements in a matter of repudiation of enfranchisement, in which they have merely proved the modality or suspensive condition.

BOOK 67.—PROCEDURE

SECTION 1

IN a criminal matter, even a case under the law of talion, or the case of a penalty for defamation, no one may exercise his right to carry out the law against the guilty party until he has obtained against him a judgment delivered by the court. But when it is the case of a real right, such as the ownership of some particular object, one may of one's own accord seize the object in question, without having recourse to the court, unless one fears thereby to commit some injustice. Where it is the matter of a debt due from some one who does not refuse to pay, one must confine oneself to asking for payment, and never seize the debtor's goods of one's own accord; but one may seize objects of the same kind as those that are due, if the debtor denies his obligation, and one is unable to prove its existence. This seizure may, if necessary, according to our school, be extended to things of a different nature from those due, where the debtor has no things of a similar kind. One may act in the same way towards a debtor who admits his obligation but refuses to pay, and against one who denies the debt which the creditor is able to prove. But in this case some authors require a previous recourse to the decision of the court.

A person who may legally seize something of his own accord has the right, if necessary, to break a door, or pierce through the walls of a shop or house where it is. If the objects thus seized are of the same kind as those due, the creditor becomes their owner by the fact of the seizure; otherwise he must put them up to auction, and repay himself out of the amount so realised. Some jurists maintain that this sale can only take place after a new authorisation by the court. †Things seized are at the risk and peril of the person seizing them; that is to say that he is responsible for their loss, even if accidental, before he becomes their owner, or before the sale, as the case may be. The person seizing them should not seize more than is necessary for recovering his debt, except where the nature of the things seized does not permit this to be limited exactly to the amount due. Finally the law recognises the legality of a seizure of things in the possession of the debtor's debtor.

*By "plaintiff" is understood that party who maintains that the ordinary appearance of things is not the truth; and by "defendant" is understood the party that maintains the contrary. Thus where husband and wife embrace Islam before cohabitation, and the husband maintains that the two conversions took place together, and that therefore the marriage remains valid, while the woman maintains that the one conversion preceded the other, it is the husband who is the plaintiff, and the burden of proof is upon him. The claim should be precise; thus, in the matter of a sum of money, the nature and coinage of the pieces should be mentioned, their amount and whether they were intact or not, where these details have any bearing upon the value. In the case of some particular object that may be sufficiently well described by its qualities, *e.g.* an animal, a description of it must be given, as in a contract of *salam;* and according to some jurists the price must also be mentioned. And this is without doubt rigorously necessary where the claim is for damages for the loss of something not capable of measurement. Where the plaintiff maintains the existence of a marriage, †it is not enough to mention this engagement and nothing more, but he should say, "I married such-and-such a woman; she was given me by a guardian capable of so doing, before two witnesses of irreproachable character." It is even necessary to add that it was with the full consent of the woman in question, if the law requires her consent for the validity of the marriage. †Where the wife is a slave the husband should add that he took the woman because he had not the means of paying the dower of a free woman, and that he was afraid of his misconduct if he remained celibate. †It is only when one maintains the existence of a contract having merely pecuniary consequences, such as a sale, a lease, or a gift, that it is enough to mention it, without entering into fuller details as to the formalities or the cause.

A party against whom a fact has been proved has no right to have the supplementary oath administered again to the plaintiff; unless he opposes to it a rebuttal such as payment, return, purchase, gift followed by a taking of possession, etc., for then the defendant may demand from the plaintiff his oath that the rebutting circumstance is unfounded. †And it is the same where the defendant alleges that the plaintiff knew of the notorious misconduct or the want of veracity of his own witnesses. Where the defendant asks for a postponement to produce proof of the contrary, he must be allowed three days.

When the plaintiff maintains in court that a certain adult individual is a slave, and the latter alleges that he is free, this latter assertion is presumed to be true; but a claim of this nature brought against a minor not in one's power is inadmissible, even with the consent of the minor in question. In this case the plaintiff must always prove his allegation. But in the case of a minor already in one's power a simple declaration that this possession is due to a right of ownership is enough for the child to be adjudged to one, unless the court is certainly aware that the possession of the child is due to having found it. In all these cases a contrary affirmation upon the part of the minor is of no effect, even though he may have already attained the age of discernment; some authorities, however, consider a minor who has attained the age of discernment as subject to the same rules as an adult.

†The payment of a debt not yet due can never be claimed in a court of law.

Section 2

A defendant who refuses to say anything at the hearing should be treated as being contumacious; but his silence cannot be considered as an admission. Where the claim, for example, is for ten pieces of money, the defendant cannot even limit himself to declaring that he does not owe this amount; he must also add that he does not owe any portion of it before it is possible, in default of proof, to have an oath administered to him in order to confirm the presumption that exists in favour of every one who denies owing anything. Where, then, the defendant is only willing to swear that he does not owe the amount claimed, instead of swearing that he owes nothing at all, he must be treated as contumacious, and the plaintiff may swear that the defendant owes him any sum not exceeding the ten pieces originally claimed, and proceed to the seizure of the amount definitely adjudged. Where the claim of a sum of money is accompanied by the reason, for example, where the plaintiff alleges that such-and-such a sum was lent to the defendant, it is enough for the latter to reply that "the plaintiff has no claim against me," without its being necessary for him to deny the loan in so many words. Thus one may oppose to a claim of pre-emption the simple statement that "the plaintiff has no claim against me," or "the plaintiff cannot insist upon delivery of the share in the immovable property in question." In this case the defendant need only swear to the truth of his statement; but if he has also formally denied the claim, he should also, upon the order of the court, confirm his denial of it by an oath. According to some authorities, however, it is enough, even in this case, to confirm upon oath a general denial.

The person who has actual possession of something that has been engaged or hired by him, may reply to the owner, "that he is not obliged to return it to him," and nothing more; ††but if he admits the ownership alleged by his adversary, and bases his refusal to surrender the object upon the terms of the contract of pledge or lease, this defence throws upon him, in case it is denied, the burden of proving the existence cf this contract. Where, in these circumstances, the defendant is unable to prove the contract, and is afraid that if he admits the ownership at the beginning, the plaintiff will not admit on his part the pledging or the hiring, he may oppose to the claim the following reply.—" If you claim the thing simply because you are its owner, I have no need to return it to you; but if you claim it as a pledge or a thing hired, then say so, in order that I may make my reply to that." †Where the plaintiff claims some particular object, and the defendant replies that he cannot return it, " because he is not the owner," or " because the thing belongs to a third party whom he does not know," or " because the object belongs to his son who is a minor," or " because it is a capital invested for the profit " either " of the poor," or " of such-and-such a mosque," the defendant is not thereby dismissed. But the plaintiff cannot proceed immediately to seize the object in dispute, until he has proved his case, or, in default of proof, had an oath administered to the defendant, to the effect " that he is not obliged to return him the thing in dispute." Where, on the other hand, the defendant declares that the object belongs to such-and-such a third party, and this person can be summoned to appear in court, so that the proceedings may be begun again against him, and an oath if necessary administered to him, that person should be summoned. Where he admits the truth of the assertion of the original defendant, he alone should be proceeded against; but if he denies it, the proceedings should be continued against the original defendant. And until the court delivers judgment, the original defendant should remain in possession of the object claimed, in spite of his admission that in any case the thing is not his. According to some jurists, however, the thing should in this case be given provisionally to the plaintiff, while others require the court to order its sequestration until the rightful owner be known. †Where the defendant admits that the object belongs to a third party who cannot be summoned by reason of absence, the proceedings must be adjourned until the return of that person, unless the plaintiff can prove the truth of his case and take the oath required by the law in cases of default. According to some authorities there is no default in the case mentioned, and consequently the supplementary oath is not to be administered.

In a criminal matter the confession of a slave is admissible. The case should be brought against the guilty slave personally, and it is he who should plead; but in a claim for damages, *i.e.* a case in which the admission of a slave is not binding, proceedings should be taken against his master, even though arising out of an act of the slave.

Section 3

A judicial oath, whether of a plaintiff or of a defendant, should be rendered more solemn by repetition in all cases where the proceedings do not relate exclusively to some real property claim, or to some pecuniary obligation. This aggravation is even obligatory in proceedings about some merely pecuniary claim, where the amount in dispute reaches the minimum subject to the charity tax. We have already explained, when speaking of imprecation, what an aggravation of the oath implies.

The oath should contain a pertinent declaration as to the fact attested, where this is to the personal knowledge of the party, and even when the act has been done by some one else, if one affirms its existence; but where one denies a fact alleged to have been done by another, it is enough to declare that one knows nothing of it. Thus, where one has summoned the debtor of a person of whom one is the heir, and the debtor pleads a remission of the debt by the deceased, it is enough to declare upon oath that one knows nothing of this remission. †On the other hand, where, for example, one maintains that the slave of the adverse party has committed a crime by which damage has been caused one, the master should, if the fact is denied, swear positively that the slave did not commit the alleged crime, if it is to his personal knowledge. [Even where the damage is alleged to have been caused by an animal, the responsible owner should, if he can, affirm upon oath that the animal has not caused the damage of which the plaintiff complains.]

One may take an affirmative oath, not only where one has personally examined or observed the thing in dispute, but also where one believes firmly in the authenticity of some fact upon the faith of one's own writing or that of one's father.

The full bearing of a judicial oath depends upon the intention of the judge, and not upon that of the individual who takes it. Consequently, neither a mental reservation, nor an interpretation contrary to the meaning of the words, nor a reservation made in an undertone which the judge cannot hear, can free the witness from having committed the sin of perjury.

A person who admits the claim against him should be ordered to fulfil the resulting obligation; but one who denies should confirm his denial upon oath, if the plaintiff is unable to prove his case. A judge, however, who has been called to account, can never be called upon to swear "that he has not delivered judgment in bad faith"; nor can a witness be made to swear "that his deposition is in conformity with the truth;" as the refusal to take such an oath would be the self-accusation of the person in question. Where the defendant alleges "that he has not yet attained his majority, this assertion is presumed to be true, without his being obliged to confirm it upon oath; and this simple declaration is enough to adjourn the proceedings until he has come of age. Moreover, an oath taken by the defendant, in default of proof on the part of the plaintiff, results only in a lapse of the proceedings, not in destroying the plaintiff's right. Consequently the latter, after losing his case in this way, can begin it again, if he can prove in court the truth of the facts upon which his claim is founded. †Where, however, the plaintiff begins his case again, without being able to prove his facts otherwise than by having an oath administered to the defendant, the latter may plead the previous judgment, and the fact that the oath has been already administered to him. If the plaintiff denies this previous decision, the defendant may insist upon his confirming this denial by an oath, before taking new proceedings. Where in these circumstances the defendant, instead of refusing, proposes that the oath offered him in default of plaintiff's proof, should be administered to the plaintiff instead, the latter may still affirm upon oath that his case is well founded, and win it, without, however, the defendant being thereby considered to be contumacious. For one is only contumacious where one declares formally, "I refuse to obey the order of the court to take an oath," or where one replies to the order of the court by saying, "I will not swear." Then one is contumacious by the mere fact of uttering these words; but if the defendant, when ordered by the court to swear, merely keeps an obstinate silence, he is not *ipso facto* contumacious. But the court may declare him to be contumacious; even implicitly, by administering an oath to the plaintiff.

An oath, whether administered to the plaintiff at the instance of the defendant, or by the judge in case of the plaintiff's contumacy, has the same effect, according to one jurist, as if the claim were proved; *but according to most authorities this oath is equivalent to the admission of the defendant. It results from this latter doctrine that the defendant is estopped from subsequently proving a previous extinction of the debt by payment or remission. A plaintiff who declines to take the oath so offered to him loses his right to take it afterwards, and cannot in any case begin the proceedings again, even though he may be able to furnish the necessary proof. Where, on the contrary, he declines the oath because he prefers to prove his claim, or because he wishes first to verify his accounts, he must be given a respite of three days; and, according to some authorities, the hearing should even be suspended until he desires that it should be resumed. If it is the plaintiff who, before deciding as to the oath offered him, asks for a respite in which to verify his accounts, his application should be rejected ; though, according to some jurists, the court should allow him also a delay of three days. The application for adjournment can only be made by the plaintiff before he has entered into the merits of the case, and he cannot be allowed for this purpose a longer delay than to the end of the hearing.

†A person asked to pay in his share of the charity tax cannot limit his defence to stating that he has paid it to another collector, or that the expert has made a mistake ; he must also take an oath ; and if he refuses to do this he must be sentenced to perform his duty again, even where it is impossible for him to have an oath administered to the plaintiff. All this is, however, upon condition that the oath of the tax-payer is required by law when he acquits himself of his obligation in ordinary circumstances. A guardian who, on the account of his pupil, claims in court the payment of a debt, cannot be obliged to take an oath, in case of a denial of the claim and a refusal to be sworn on the part of the defendant ; unless, according to some authorities, the cause of the debt is a fact within the personal knowledge of the guardian.

Section 4

Where two persons claim a certain particular object in the possession of a third party, and both are in a position to prove their statements, the two claims mutually annul one another. However, according to one jurist, the usufruct of the thing in dispute should in this case be adjudged to the two claimants jointly ; according to another, the object should be divided between them ; according to a third, recourse should be had to casting lots ; while a fourth is of opinion that the thing should be sequestrated, until the truth of the matter is manifested, or the interested parties have come to a settlement. In a case where two persons have undivided possession of something of which both can prove exclusive ownership, nothing is changed in the mutual relation of the parties with regard to the object in question. Where, however, a third party claims an object and proves his right of ownership, while the actual possessor does the same, the latter has a presumption in his favour. A possessor's claim to prove his right of ownership is inadmissible, unless a case is brought against him.

Where one has been obliged to give up a thing in one's possession in consequence of a legally proved claim, to which one was able to oppose a mere denial, in consequence, *e.g.*, of the absence of witnesses, one may still take proceedings to prove that one is the rightful owner, and, in consequence, the legitimate possessor. And in these circumstances, the fact of the possession one has lost constitutes a presumption in one's favour. This rule, however, has been denied by some authorities.

Where the plaintiff claims a thing, and alleges that he has become the owner of it because the defendant has sold it to him, and the latter merely opposes to this claim his right of ownership, without denying the transfer asserted by the plaintiff, the fact that the defendant is actually in possession of the thing in dispute gives rise to no presumption in his favour, where both parties produce evidence in support of their case. A person who admits that a certain thing belongs to so-and-so cannot afterwards claim that thing except by virtue of a subsequent transfer; †but such a transfer need not be alleged by a person who, after surrendering his property in consequence of a claim brought and legally proved against him, subsequently obtains the required proof to show that he is the rightful owner. Should he then come and claim the object, his claim is still admissible, as we have just seen. Where two parties both produce evidence in support of their assertions, our school allows no preponderance to the party that happens to have the greater number of witnesses; nor to one who has two male witnesses, while the other has one male and two female. *But where one of the parties can produce two male witnesses, and the other only one whose deposition is confirmed by a supplementary oath, the preponderance is, by an exception, accorded to the former, though strictly speaking, one witness and the oath would be enough to prove the fact. *In a case where one of the parties can prove he has been owner for a longer period, he wins his case; and he may claim from the third party actually in possession the rent and profits since that time. According to our school, however, such a preponderance cannot be accorded to a party who proves that he has been owner from a definite date, over one that proves he has been owner, without mentioning any date. But our school maintains a presumption in favour of the possessor in all cases where he can prove a right of more recent date than the right of the adverse party. Our school does not admit as sufficient proof of actual ownership a deposition that "yesterday so-and-so was still owner," without adding who the present owner is, unless the witnesses declare that the person in question has not lost the ownership since the date mentioned, or, at least, that they are not aware of anything likely to cause such loss. The witnesses may even in this way prove that so-and-so is the actual owner, where they know that the ownership has been acquired by him by way of succession, purchase, etc., and are not aware of any subsequent transfer. An admission that the plaintiff is owner, made just before by the defendant, and duly established at the hearing, is presumed to apply still to the actual ownership.

From the fact that one is the rightful owner of an animal or of a tree it does not follow that one is also the owner of the frui. actually upon the tree, or of the young of the animal; †but the fœtus belongs in all cases to the owner of the mother by right of accession.

The purchaser of an object seized in consequence of a claim, even though the latter be indefinite as regards the date of the claimant's ownership, has a remedy against the vendor for the amount of the price he has paid; though, according to some authorities, such recovery is admissible only where the claimant's title is prior to the purchase. The testimony is not invalidated because the plaintiff alleges his right of ownership without mentioning the transfer of title, while the witnesses add by what title he obtained the object; but where the claimant alleges some particular title, and the witnesses another, their deposition is of no value.

SECTION 5

Where one ligitant maintains that he has rented a room to another for ten pieces of money, and the other says that the whole house was rented to him for that sum, and both can bring evidence in support of their case, the two claims mutually annul one another. According to one jurist, however, the tenant has a presumption in his favour.

Where two persons claim something in the possession of a third, each alleging that he has bought and paid for the object in question, and each bringing evidence in support of their claim, the object should be adjudged to that purchaser whose contract has the priority. Where it is not clear which is the earlier, the two claims mutually annul each other. Where two persons prove in court that they have sold an object to a third, for such-and-such an amount, the two claims mutually annul each other, if the alleged sales are of the same date. On the other hand, the purchaser should pay twice the amount agreed upon, where the two claimants prove that the sales took place at different times; †or if neither of the sales is of a certain date; or if one of the sales is proved to have been effected at a certain date, but not the other.

Where a deceased person leaves two sons, one a Moslem and the other a Christian, who each maintain that their father died in the religion he professes, the following cases must be distinguished:—

1. Where it is a matter of public notoriety that the father was a Christian, then—

(*a*) In default of proof, the assertion of the Christian son is presumed to be true.

(*b*) The same presumption exists in favour of the Moslem son, if both sons have furnished general legal proof of the truth of their statements.

(*c*) If the proofs furnished do not concern generally the religion professed by the father, but special circumstances from which his religion may be inferred, *e.g.* his last words, the two claims are mutually annulled.

2. Where the religion of the deceased is not a matter of public notoriety, and each son produces proof of the truth of his statements, in this case also the two claims are mutually annulled.

A Christian leaves a Moslem son and a Christian son. The former declares that he only embraced the faith after his father's death, so that he ought not to be excluded from the succession in consequence of difference of religion, while the son who has remained a Christian alleges that his brother was already converted. In this case the Moslem, in default of legal proof, has a presumption in his favour, provided he takes an oath to that effect. On the other hand, if in these circumstances, both sons prove the truth of their assertions, the presumption is in favour of the Christian. And the latter also has the presumption in his favour, in default of proof, where both brothers agree that the conversion took place, *e.g.* in the month of Ramadan, but the Moslem maintains that their father died in the preceding month of Shaban, while according to the Christian the decease did not take place until the following month of Shawal. Where, however, both sons can call evidence in support of their assertions, the presumption is in favour of the Moslem. Where the deceased has left an infidel father and mother, and two Moslem sons, who all maintain that the deceased died in their religion, the parents enjoy a presumption in their favour, provided they take an oath; though according to one jurist, the matter should then remain in suspense until the truth is known or the litigants come to a compromise.

In a case where one litigant proves that the deceased enfranchised upon his death-bed a slave called Salim, while the adverse party brings proof to show that it was Ghanim who was thus freed, and the enfranchisement of either would just exhaust the third capable of being disposed of, the law considers to be preponderant the proof of the earlier enfranchisement. If it is proved that the enfranchisements took place simultaneously, whether Salim or Ghanim shall be freed must be decided by casting lots. According to some authorities this method of decision should also be had recourse to where neither of the enfranchisements are of certain date; according to others one jurist maintained the opinion that the two slaves are both half-freed. [This latter theory is that of our school.] Finally, in a case where two persons unconnected with the deceased declare that he bequeathed his liberty to his slave Salim, while two residuary inheritors declare that the deceased retracted this disposition and left his liberty to another of his slaves called Ghanim, and the enfranchisement of either would exhaust the third capable of being disposed of, it is Ghanim that the law considers to be enfranchised. Where, however, the two inheritors may be challenged as witnesses on account of notorious misconduct, the retractation cannot be proved by their deposition, and Salim is freed altogether. In order to punish the inheritors, Ghanim also is enfranchised, up to the amount of the third of the succession that remains, after deducting the value of Salim.

SECTION 6

A physiognomist cannot be summoned as a witness unless he is a Moslem of irreproachable character and of long experience. †The law also requires that he should be free, and a man; but it does not insist upon recourse being always had to more than one physiognomist, nor that he must belong to the Arab tribe of the Beni Modlij. The report of a physiognomist is indispensable in the case of proceedings relative to filiation; or with regard to a person whose parentage is not known, for example, a foundling; or a person of whom two others may consider themselves to be the father, for example, a child born of a woman who has had commerce with two men within a short interval. This can happen, even in good faith, in the following cases:—

1. Where each has exercised coition with her, believing her to be his own wife.

2. Where the woman was their joint slave.

3. Where one repudiates his wife immediately after coition; and the other then has her in his bed by error, or by virtue of an illegal marriage.

4. Where a master sells his female slave after coition, and the purchaser cohabits with her without observing her period of purification.

5. †Where a master cohabits with his married slave.

In all these cases the matter must be submitted to a physiognomist, where a child is born within a period between six months after the later and four months after the earlier act of coition, and each man claims the child as his. But where there has been a menstruation between two cohabitations the law considers the later as the sole cause of the pregnancy. To this rule there is but one exception, that is to say, where the earlier act of coition has been accomplished by the legal husband, and the later by error or by fornication; but it is of little consequence whether the persons who consider themselves to be the father are or are not free Moslems.

BOOK 68.—SIMPLE MANUMISSION

SECTION 1

THE manumission of a slave is legal only on the part of a master who has the free disposition of his property. Enfranchisement may be made to depend upon a condition, and may be limited either to a member of the body or to a fraction of the slave; but in these two last cases the slave is none the less wholly freed in accordance with the distinctions which we shall afterwards set out.

Enfranchisement may be expressed in explicit terms, such as, "I make you free," "I enfranchise you," †or "You are no longer liable to the law of property." It is then of no consequence whether one has or has not the intention to manumit. On the other hand, such intention is rigorously necessary when one makes use of implicit terms, such as, "I have no longer upon you the right of property," "I have no longer any power over you," "There is no longer any bond between you and me," "I have no longer the right to make use of your services," "You can go where you please," "You will be henceforward under my patronage." Moreover, the law considers as implicit terms for expressing manumission all phrases that declare repudiation, explicitly or implicitly. The words, "You are free," said to a slave of either sex constitute an explicit manumission; and the validity of the act is in no way affected if the master in saying them commits a fault against grammatical gender. Where a master says to his slave, "Your enfranchisement is given you," or "I permit you to choose between slavery and liberty," intending to grant him his freedom, the slave is free as soon as he declares that he wishes to make use of this permission. And the same is the case where—

1. The master says, "I enfranchise you for one thousand pieces of money," or "You are free for one thousand pieces of money," and the slave accepts.

2. The slave asks his master to free him for one thousand pieces of money, and the master consents to do so.

In both cases the sum mentioned is immediately due by the slave. When the master offers to allow the slave to redeem himself for one thousand pieces of money, and the slave accepts, this sale is, according to our school, not only perfectly valid, but the slave is immediately free, though liable to his master for the amount mentioned, and remaining under his patronage.

The manumission of a pregnant female slave at the same time includes *ipso facto* the freedom of the fœtus in her womb; and any special reservation of this at the time of the mother's enfranchisement is null and void. Granting freedom to the fœtus alone, and nothing more, does not imply that of the mother, and where mother and fœtus belong to different persons the manumission of the one never implies that of the other.

A slave belonging in common to two masters, of whom one manumits him, either entirely or partially, obtains his liberty in this way only as regards the share of that master; and if the latter is insolvent, the part share of the other is unaffected by this act. Where, however, the master who enfranchises a slave of whom he is coproprietor is solvent, the share of the slave that has not been freed returns to him all the same by virtue of the right of redemption, but he must indemnify his coproprietor in proportion to the latter's rights, and according to the value of the slave upon the day of manumission. Then, where the master who enfranchises can only pay a portion of the value of the slave, he must indemnify the coproprietor according to his means, and the slave remains, so far as the latter is concerned, in his original condition, due proportion being kept between the manumitted share and the indemnity received. Enfranchisement by virtue of right of redemption is an immediate consequence of the original manumission; or, according to one jurist, a consequence of the payment of the indemnity. Another authority maintains, however, that the payment of the indemnity has retrospective force, in the sense that this fact indicates the existence of the manumission by virtue of the right of redemption from the moment of the original enfranchisement. Manumission by reason of maternity on the part of one of two coproprietors has the same consequence as regards right of redemption as simple manumission, with the exception that the part owner who enfranchises in this way, though solvent, should not only indemnify the other part-owner for the slave but also for the proportional dower. As to the question from what moment a manumission by virtue of right of redemption in these circumstances counts, opinions are divided as we have explained when speaking of simple manumission; but it must be understood that the theories set out upon this subject, both firstly and lastly, do not imply that the part-owner who enfranchises must indemnify the other for the value of the child born to the slave. Enfranchisement by will on the part of one of the coproprietors does not imply a right of redemption; *but the fact that a part-owner who enfranchises, though solvent, has contracted debts that exhaust his fortune, is no obstacle to this right. When one says to one's coproprietor, "You have enfranchised your share in the slave, and so you should indemnify me for mine," he has a presumption in his favour, provided he takes an oath, if the manumission is denied. However, those jurists who consider enfranchisement by virtue of a right of redemption as an immediate consequence of the original manumission maintain that in this case, the share of the speaker is *ipso facto* enfranchised, by reason of his implied admission; but without admitting a right of redemption in consequence of this secondary manumission. According to these same jurists there is even ground for a right of redemption and indemnity when one's coproprietor says to one, "If you enfranchise your share in our slave, my share will also be free after your manumission," but on condition that the person to whom this phrase is addressed is solvent. Where, however, in this phrase, one uses the words, "My share will be free before yours," an enfranchisement by the coproprietor thus addressed, has for its effect that the share of the other owner becomes free, even if he is insolvent, by the accomplishment of the condition, and not by reason of the right of redemption. The patronage falls in these circumstances to the two masters by their own right. Where, on the other hand, the co-proprietor who spoke the words in question is solvent, the same effect is caused only where the validity of such a retrospective condition is not admitted. Where it is admitted, and the speaker is solvent, there is no manumission by virtue of right of redemption. In the case where a slave belongs for a half, a third, and a sixth to three different masters, of whom the two last enfranchise their respective shares, our school considers that each owes the first half the indemnity. Moreover, an essential condition for right of redemption is that manumission takes place willingly. Consequently, there is no right of redemption where, by right of succession, for instance, a father becomes coproprietor of his son. And, finally, a person who is dangerously ill should be considered insolvent, so far as regards this point, as to any amount exceeding the third of which he can dispose; and a deceased person should even be considered as absolutely insolvent. Consequently, right of redemption cannot be exercised where a testamentary executor is charged with manumitting a slave of whom a share belonged to the deceased.

Section 2

Where a person, capable of alienating his property for nothing becomes owner of one of his ascendants or descendants who are slaves, that ascendant or descendant is *ipso facto* freed, without distinction of sex or degree. In the case of a person who is incapable of alienating his property for nothing, his guardian or curator may not purchase for him one of his ascendants or descendants. If a minor obtains the ownership of one of his ascendants by way of gift or legacy, his guardian should accept the liberality only where the slave in question is capable of exercising a trade. In this case the slave is *ipso facto* enfranchised; but he need not be maintained by the donee, because of the relationship. Where, on the other hand, the slave in question is not in a state to maintain himself, the guardian should accept only in the case of the insolvency of his pupil, because then the relative has to be maintained out of the public treasury; but he is rigorously forbidden to accept the gift or legacy of an ascendant or descendant incapable of exercising a trade, if his pupil is solvent and maintenance will consequently have to be paid for by him.

Where some one upon his death-bed becomes gratuitously the owner of his ascendant or descendant, that relative is *ipso facto* freed, and his value is levied upon the third of which the testator can dispose; or, according to some authorities upon the estate; but where the acquisition is effected for a consideration, the two following cases must be distinguished.

1. If the acquisition for a consideration is effected without the seller, when stipulating the price, making any sacrifice upon his part, the enfranchisement must be paid for out of the third of which the deceased can dispose, and the slave has no share out of the succession. If the sick man, when making the acquisition was insolvent, some authorities do not admit the validity of such a purchase; but the majority consider that the acquisition holds good, though in that case enfranchisement does not result. In these circumstances the slave should be sold again to satisfy the creditors.

2. If, on the other hand, the acquisition for a consideration is affected for a very low price, with which the vendor is content out of consideration for the purchaser, the difference between the price stipulated and the real value of the slave constitutes a gift upon the part of the vendor, so that the manumission is a charge upon the third of which the testator can dispose only for the amount of the stipulated price.

Where a third party makes a gift to a slave of a share in another slave, who is the ascendant or descendant of the donee, and the slave accepts this donation, the share of the ascendant or descendant thus given is *ipso facto* enfranchised; at least where it is admitted that the slave can accept a gift of his own accord. And besides, the master must indemnify the coproprietors of the relative by reason of the right of redemption.

SECTION 3

Where some one upon his death-bed voluntarily manumits a slave, the sole property he possesses, the enfranchisement is valid only for one-third ; and, in case of the master's insolvency, the act has no effect at all. By virtue of the same principle, the manumission upon a death-bed of three slaves, all of equal value, effected by an individual having no other property, should be limited in its effect to one of them ; and which of the three is to be freed must in this case be determined by casting lots. And recourse must also be had to casting lots when the deceased in these circumstances says to his three slaves all of equal value, " I enfranchise a third of you three," " A third of you three is free," or " I enfranchise a third of all my slaves." In this last case, however, according to some jurists, all the three are free for one-third.

A recourse to casting lots takes place as follows :—Three pieces of paper are taken of equal size ; on two of them is written the word " slavery," and upon the third the word " enfranchisement," and they are rolled round three balls, as we mentioned before. A ball is then drawn for one of the slaves, and if it is that upon which is the paper with " enfranchisement " written upon it, that slave is free, and the others remain slaves. Where, on the other hand, the one drawn contains the word " slavery," that slave remains a slave ; and a second ball is drawn for one of the two others. The names of the three slaves may also be written upon papers, and the slave whose name is first drawn be freed, while the others remain slaves. When the decision has to be made between three slaves of different value, for example, when one is worth one hundred pieces of money, the second two hundred, and the third three hundred, and the deceased has left no other property, two balls are placed in the urn with the word " slavery " on them, and a single one with the word " enfranchisement." If the one with the word " enfranchisement " is drawn for the slave worth two hundred, he alone is free and entirely free ; but if this word is drawn for the one worth three hundred, he is freed only for two-thirds. Finally, if the word has been drawn for the slave worth one hundred pieces, not only is this slave entirely free, but there must be another drawing with two balls labelled " slavery " and " enfranchisement." That one of the two slaves for whom this latter ball is drawn becomes enfranchised up to the limit of what remains of the third of which the testator could dispose, deducting the former manumission. Where, in these circumstances, there are more than three slaves, of whom the number and value permit of a threefold partition, for example, six slaves all of the same value, the same procedure is adopted in casting lots, except that each of the three lots refer to two persons instead of one. Where, on the other hand, it is only the total value and not the number that can be divided into three portions, where, for example, of six slaves one is worth one hundred pieces of money, two others one hundred together, and also the three others together one hundred, one lot must be made for the first slave, one for the next two, and one for the three others. But where neither the number nor the value permit of being divided into three lots, for example, where there are four slaves all of an equal value not divisible by three, one authority recommends to proceed as follows:—The number of the slaves is divided into three lots, two of which are composed of a single slave and the third of two slaves, and when the ball bearing the word "enfranchisement" is drawn for one of the two first lots, the slave included in this lot is freed. After this it is decided by casting lots which of the three other slaves is to be freed, up to the amount that remains of the third that can be disposed of, deducting the cost of the first manumission. Where it is the third lot that wins, the two slaves that compose the first and second lots remain slaves, and lots must be drawn to decide between the two slaves forming the third lot, to know which of the two is to be completely enfranchised, and which is to be enfranchised only up to what remains of the third of which one can dispose, deducting the cost of the first enfranchisement. Another jurist, however, recommends writing the names of the slaves upon four different pieces of paper, and afterwards proceeding to the drawing; the one whose name first comes out of the urn is enfranchised up to the amount that remains of the third that can be disposed of, after deducting the cost of the first manumission. [*The former procedure is preferable.] But the entire controversy as to procedure in drawing lots refers only to precepts of the Sonna. Some authorities, however, regard these precepts as obligatory.

Where the manumission can only be partially effected, because a complete enfranchisement would exceed the third that can be disposed of, but other property belonging to the estate is found afterwards, the manumission must be continued up to the third of the total net assets. Slaves manumitted afterwards in this way may keep for themselves what they have gained by their labour from the day of their enfranchisement by the deceased; and the heir may not even claim the restitution of what he has already spent for their maintenance. Where it transpires later that the deceased, besides the slaves manumitted, had another slave whom he had just enfranchised, the latter has a right to be admitted to the drawing of lots for manumission. A slave, enfranchised by drawing lots, is considered as free from the day when the deceased declared his manumission; and the value of this slave to be allowed for in the partition is his value at that moment. In consequence what the slave gains is really his, and cannot be included when determining the amount of the third that can be disposed of. On the other hand, those that remain slaves because the drawing of the lots was unfavourable to them should be assessed according to their value upon the day of the decease; they form a portion of the two-thirds due to the heirs, including what they have gained from that moment, provided that this gain is composed of things still existing in kind. Gain earned after the decease goes always, not to the estate, but to the heir to whom the slave is assigned at the distribution. Thus, where the deceased only had three slaves whom he enfranchised upon his death-bed, each of whom is worth one hundred pieces of money, but one of whom has made, between the manumission and the decease, a gain of one hundred pieces, lots are first of all drawn, and if this slave wins, not only is he enfranchised, but he keeps as well the hundred pieces which he has gained. Where, on the other hand, the result of the drawing is to manumit one of the two slaves who have gained nothing by their labour, lots must be drawn again, and if the other slave that has gained nothing wins he is freed for one-third. But where upon this second drawing the slave that has made some gain wins, he is only free for one quarter. Over and above this he must be given as earnings one-quarter of what he has gained, and the other three-quarters of this gain go to the heir whose property he becomes for three-quarters on distribution.

SECTION 4

A person who frees a slave retains over him a right of patronage, without any distinction between simple manumission, or liberation under the terms of a will, or enfranchisement by contract, or on account of maternity or relationship or right of redemption. In case of the master's decease the right passes to his agnates. A woman is never called to the succession by right of patronage, unless it be to that of some one she herself has manumitted, or of his children or enfranchised slaves. For example, where a daughter becomes the owner of her father who is a slave the latter is *ipso facto* liberated; and where the father in his turn manumits one of his slaves, and then dies, and later this slave also dies, and neither leaves heirs, the daughter is called to the succession as the slave's patroness, and not as his patron's daughter. In case of the patron's decease the patronage can be exercised only by the nearest agnate as a personal right, and in general a manumitted slave can have no other patron but his master or his master's agnates. If a slave marries an enfranchised woman, the child born of this union is free and under the patronage of its mother's patron; but if the father is afterwards enfranchised, the patronage of the child passes to the father's patron. If the father dies a slave, and afterwards the father's father is manumitted, the patronage of the child passes to the patron of this relative; and it is the same where the liberation of the father's father takes place during the lifetime and slavery of the father, except that in this case the patronage is transferred to the father's patron, if the father is afterwards enfranchised. According to other authorities, however, the patronage remains with the mother's patron, so long as the father is a slave, and is only transferred to the patron of the father's father by the father's death. Where, finally, the child in question becomes the property of his slave father, he is *ipso facto* liberated; but, if there is occasion for it, the patronage of the father's other children, *i.e.* his brothers and sisters, and half brothers and half sisters on the father's side, †and of himself, is acquired by that child. [†According to Shafii's personal opinion this patronage of a person over himself cannot exist.]

BOOK 69.—TESTAMENTARY MANUMISSION

SECTION 1

ENFRANCHISEMENT by will may be expressed explicitly by the phrase "You will be free after my death," "when I am dead," or "as soon as I am dead," or by the phrase, "I manumit you after my death." According to our school the expressions "I make you," or "You will be my testamentary enfranchised slave," are also explicit. This manumission may also be legally expressed by all terms that imply a simple manumission, such as, "My death will dissolve the bond between you and me," but in such a case the master must have really had the intention to accomplish that act. One may pronounce a testamentary manumission subject to a restriction, *e.g.* "If I die this month," or "in this sickness," "you are free;" or make it depend upon a condition, as for example, "If you enter the house you will be free after my death." In these cases the enfranchisement depends upon the operation of the restriction or the accomplishment of the condition. In the example last given the slave must enter the house before his master's death; but the entry should, on the contrary, be after that event if the master says, "You will be free if you enter the house after my death." In this latter case, however, the slave need not make his entry immediately after his master's death, and the heir cannot sell him in the mean time. Where the master says, "You will be free as soon as one month has passed after my death," the heir cannot sell the slave during this period, but there is no objection to his employing him in his service in the meantime, both in this case and in the preceding one. Manumission in the words, "If you like you can be my testamentary enfranchised slave," or "If you like you can be my enfranchised slave after my death," requires that the slave should say at once what he decides to do, but if the master says, "As soon as you have expressed your wishes in the matter," the slave need not do so immediately. Where two part-owners of a slave declare that he will be free "after their death," he is not completely enfranchised until after the death of both of them; though after the death of one, his heir cannot sell the share of the slave forming part of the inheritance.

Testamentary manumission is forbidden to the lunatic or the minor, *even where the latter has attained the age of discernment. On the other hand, it is permitted to imbeciles and infidels. As to an apostate there is the same divergence of opinion as about his right of ownership. Our school, however, maintains in all cases a testamentary manumission spoken before apostasy; and the apostasy of a slave, enfranchised by will while he was still a believer, does not cause him to lose his liberty. An infidel who is not a subject has a right to take his testamentary enfranchised slave who is an infidel into his own country; but when an infidel of any kind grants his liberty to a Moslem slave by his will, the act is null and void, because the law prescribes that such a slave should be seized and sold on his account. In the case of an infidel slave, enfranchised by his master's will, his master also an infidel, who after his manumission embraces the faith, without his master revoking his former disposition, this conversion is enough to withdraw him from his master's control, and he can then work for his master's account and repay him the gain resulting from this labour. According to one jurist, however, even in this case the enfranchised slave should be sold, and the price given to his master.

The master of a testamentary enfranchised slave may sell him, and this sale *ipso facto* annuls the manumission. For a testamentary enfranchisement is nothing more than a simple manumission, depending upon a condition, or according to one authority a legacy. According to our school the enfranchisement remains none the less annulled where one again becomes the owner of the testamentary enfranchised slave that one had sold. As to the revocation of the sort of manumission with which we are here occupied, excepting the case where it is a necessary consequence of the sale, it is not lawful unless it be admitted that the act constitutes a legacy. One may then express the revocation by the words—"I annul," "I declare dissolved," "I break," or "I revoke the testamentary manumission." If, on the other hand, one admits, with most authorities, that the act constitutes a simple manumission depending on a condition, one cannot revoke it.

There is no objection to manumitting in the ordinary way a slave one has already enfranchised by will, and making this later manumission depend upon a condition, or naming a specified time for its operation. In the latter case the slave becomes free as soon as one of the following things happens—the master's death, or the accomplishment of the condition, or the expiry of the term. The testamentary manumission of a slave does not prevent her master, during his lifetime, having the right to cohabit with her, and this act leaves the previous enfranchisement intact, unless the slave becomes a mother, in which case the testamentary manumission is annulled and becomes a liberation on account of maternity. On the other hand, enfranchisement on account of maternity cannot become a testamentary manumission. The liberation under the terms of a will of a slave undergoing enfranchisement by contract, and the manumission by contract of a testamentary enfranchised slave are both permitted by law.

Section 2

*When a testamentary enfranchised slave gives birth to a child during her master's lifetime either in consequence of her marriage, or of the crime of fornication, it remains a slave until the master's death. Where, on the other hand, testamentary enfranchisement is granted to a pregnant slave our school permits not only that the child should be included in its mother's manumission, but also that it should be considered a testamentary enfranchised slave, where the manumission of the mother does not actually take place, either in consequence of her previous death, or of a revocation. Some authorities, however, maintain that the child, before its birth, follows its mother's condition in case of revocation. Moreover, a fœtus in the mother's womb is capable of testamentary enfranchisement before birth, and this manumission does not involve that of the mother, though her sale before accouchement implies *ipso facto* the revocation of the enfranchisement of the fœtus. Where a slave, manumitted in the ordinary way, under some condition gives birth to a child, it is not *ipso facto* enfranchised with its mother when that condition is fulfilled. According to a single authority the child is *ipso facto* manumitted when the condition is accomplished during the mother's lifetime, but remains a slave when the condition is only fulfilled after the mother's death. A testamentary manumission in favour of a male slave never extends to his children.

In the matter of crimes against the person a testamentary enfranchised slave of either sex remains during the master's lifetime subject to the ordinary law applicable to slaves. At his master's death the testamentary enfranchised slave obtains his entire freedom, and his value is debited to the third of the estate of which the master could dispose, after deducting the debts. If this third is not sufficient, the slave becomes only partially free. For the same reason is debited to the third of the estate a simple manumission depending upon a condition relative to the last illness; for example, where the deceased declares, " You will be free if you enter the house during my last sickness;" *but where the condition may be fulfilled while the testator is in good health, the fact that it is accidentally accomplished during his last malady does not prevent the manumission being debited to the entire estate.

Where a slave maintains in a court of law that he was enfranchised by will, and the master denies this, the latter must take an oath and declare that this contradiction is equivalent to a revocation, and that in consequence the claim is inadmissible. This rule is admitted even by the authority who assimilates testamentary manumission to a legacy, and who consequently admits its revocability.

Where a testamentary enfranchised slave, on becoming free, finds himself in the possession of a sum of money, and declares that he gained it after his master's death, while the heir maintains that it is his earnings amassed during the master's lifetime, and that in consequence it should be paid in to the assets of the estate, the enfranchised slave has a presumption in his favour, provided he takes an oath. Even where, in these circumstances, the two parties can bring evidence in support of their assertions, the enfranchised slave still has the presumption in his favour.

BOOK 70.—ENFRANCHISEMENT BY CONTRACT

SECTION 1

ENFRANCHISEMENT by contract is a meritorious act upon the master's part, when asked for by a slave worthy of confidence and capable of exercising a trade. According to some authorities even this last condition is not necessary to render the act meritorious, and in any case enfranchisement by contract is never blamable. The words by which the master may legally manifest his wish to enfranchise in this way are, "I make you my enfranchised slave by contract for such and such a sum which you will pay by periodical instalments; and when the whole has been paid you will be free." The number of instalments must be mentioned, and the amount of the debt to be paid upon each occasion; but the contract remains valid even where one may have omitted to add the condition upon which the liberation depends, *i.e.* the concluding phrase, "and when," etc.; provided always that the intention to enfranchise is not wanting, for in that case our school does not admit the validity of the act. And, moreover, the law insists that the slave should formally declare that he accepts the offer made by his master, and that the contracting parties, that is to say both the slave and his master, are adult sane Moslems capable of the free disposition of their property. It follows from this latter condition that enfranchisement by contract effected by a master in his last illness is debited to the third of the estate of which he can dispose. Where in these circumstances a master leaves three slaves all of equal value, the enfranchisement by contract of one of them is perfectly legal. And it is the same where the slave thus enfranchised, though the only property of the deceased, has already paid during his master's lifetime two hundred pieces of money, while he was only rated at one hundred. If the slave had only paid one hundred his enfranchisement would have counted only for two-thirds. The validity of an enfranchisement by contract effected by an apostate depends upon the question whether his right of ownership ceases to exist or not. Where it is admitted that his right of ownership remains in suspense, there must be admitted also the nullity of the enfranchisement by contract, according to the opinion adopted by Shafii during his stay in Egypt. A slave pledged or hired can no longer be enfranchised by contract by his master during the continuance of the engagement.

The equivalent that is due by the slave for his liberty is upon his part a debt for a term, even where this debt only consists in the use of something, or of his services. The debt should be paid in at least two instalments; although, according to some jurists, one may also stipulate that the whole debt shall be due immediately where the slave is only partially owned by the master, and is otherwise free. If one has stipulated, as an equivalent, that the slave should continue to give his services for a month, and pay at the end of it one *dinar*, a regular enfranchisement has been contracted for; but it would be irregular if the master stipulated as an equivalent that the slave should sell him such and such an object. Where the master stipulates as follows: "I contract to make you my enfranchised slave, if you buy from me this coat for one thousand pieces of money, payable by instalments, your liberation not to take place until the debt has been paid," our school admits only the validity of the enfranchisement, but not that of the debt. Where one manumits several slaves at once for a single sum of money to be paid by instalments, on condition that no one of them is to be free before the whole of the debt is paid, this enfranchisement is valid, according to Shafii's personal opinion. Then, however, the sum mentioned is *ipso facto* divided in proportion to the respective value of each of the slaves upon the day of the contract, so that the one who pays his becomes free, and the one who does not remains a slave.

Enfranchisement by contract may also be effected with regard to a slave who has already been previously and partially enfranchised, *and a contract to enfranchise such a slave entirely is limited *ipso facto* to the portion still capable of being enfranchised. Enfranchisement by contract cannot be effected by one of two coproprietors even if the other subsequently consents to it, at least according to our school; and a contract to partially enfranchise a slave of whom one is the sole owner is also forbidden by our school. Enfranchisement by contract of a slave belonging to two masters may lawfully take place when both at the same time give their consent either personally or by agent, and both stipulate the same terms of payment. The sum stipulated is then divided in proportion to their reciprocal rights. Where the slave is not in a condition to fulfil his engagement, and one of the coproprietors considers that for this reason the contract should be cancelled—but the other thinks it should remain good, it is as if the contract for enfranchisement had been effected only by one of the coproprietors, and the act is then illegal. According to other authorities, however, these circumstances do not invalidate the contract. Where, finally, one of the co-proprietors remits what the slave owes, or manumits him later in the ordinary way, then only this owner's portion becomes free, subject to indemnity and right of redemption, if the coproprietor is solvent.

Section 2

The master is obliged either to remit the slave a portion of his debt, or to return him a part of the sum received. Remission, however, is preferable, especially in the case of the last instalment. †The law does not prescribe either a maximum or a minimum for remission or restitution, but either must be something capable of being the subject of obligation. †Remission or restitution should take place immediately before complete enfranchisement, and it is commendable to make it consist of a quarter or a seventh of the sum stipulated

The law forbids a master to cohabit with his female slave undergoing enfranchisement by contract, in the exercise of his right of ownership ; but a contravention of this rule does not incur the definite penalty for fornication. The master, however, in these circumstances is liable for dower, and a child born of this illicit union is free. On the other hand, the master is not obliged as well to pay the mother the value of the child, at least according to our school. As to the slave herself, she becomes enfranchised on account of maternity ; without prejudice to the contract of enfranchisement, that is to say that in case of non-execution of her obligations under it, she none the less becomes free upon her master's death. *A child born of a slave under a contract of enfranchisement, either in consequence of a marriage or of the crime of fornication, is also under the contract and follows the condition of his mother, whether slave or free. The child, however, owes nothing for his own liberty, though he remains the property of the master, or, according to one authority, the property of his mother, until his complete liberation. In case of homicide the value of the child goes to the owner, but the pecuniary consequences of a crime committed by the child must be borne by itself. The profits which it gains, either by its work or in any other way, *e.g.* as dower, should be employed in the first place for its necessary maintenance, and the remainder should be sequestrated in order to be returned to it on its freedom, or to the master if it is not freed.

A slave under a contract of enfranchisement does not obtain his liberty, even partially, until he has paid the whole of the amount he owes. Where such slave wishes his master to accept in payment something which the latter is of opinion cannot be given, in default of legal proof it is the slave who has a presumption in his favour, and should swear that it is a thing the use of which is permitted him. The master is then obliged to accept it, or to give a receipt for the amount offered by the slave; or if necessary the latter may deposit the thing in court. Should the slave under the contract refuse to take an oath, it should be administered to the master. Where the thing is seized by legal process the master may insist upon the slave giving him another thing of the same kind and value, and where a dispute of this sort arises as to the last of the periodic payments, complete enfranchisement is suspended until the legal claim has been dismissed, or the slave has given something else. This rule must be observed, even where the master on receiving the object says, "Now you are free." Restitution on account of redhibitory defects has the same consequences as legal seizure.

A slave under contract of enfranchisement cannot be married without the master's consent, until he has paid up the whole of the debt. Our school even forbids him to cohabit with one of his slaves by virtue of his right of ownership, even though the master authorises him to do so. This prohibition to cohabit with one of his slaves does not, however, prevent his purchasing slaves, *e.g.* for trading in them. Besides, a contravention in this respect does not involve a penalty for the crime of fornication, and a child born of such illicit union is none the less its father's legitimate child. Such child follows the condition of his father as regards freedom or slavery, when he is born either before his father's complete enfranchisement, or within six months after that event; *but in these circumstances the mother never becomes enfranchised on account of maternity. But a child born of such a union six months or more after the father's complete manumission is free, and then the mother also becomes free by reason of maternity.

A master is not obliged to accept payment in anticipation, where he can give a valid reason for his refusal, *e.g.* that thus the expense of keeping the money or other things received will fall upon him, or that he is afraid of losing them. On the other hand, where there is no valid reason the master cannot object to a slave under contract of enfranchisement paying him before the due date, and the latter may then, if necessary, be liberated by a judicial order. But an anticipation of the instalments can never be a ground for any diminution in the debt, even with the consent of the interested parties. These instalments cannot be transferred by sale, or exchange, before the master takes possession; *and when the slave under contract of enfranchisement pays a purchaser of the debt, he does not obtain his liberty. For the master may none the less insist upon full payment; though in this case the slave has a remedy against the purchaser for the amount he has erroneously paid him.

According to the opinion of Shafii in his second period a slave under contract of enfranchisement cannot any longer be sold by his master, and if sold in spite of this does not become free upon making the stipulated payments to his new master. Gift is equivalent to sale in this respect. Nor can the master dispose of the earnings of a slave under contract of enfranchisement, nor liberate nor give in marriage a slave of such slave.

Finally, where a third party asks a master " to liberate immediately his slave under contract of enfranchisement for such and such an amount," and the master agrees, it is this third party and not the slave who is liable for the sum promised.

Section 3

An enfranchisement by contract, legally executed, does not admit of a revocation by the master, except where its terms are not carried out by the slave; but the latter may renounce it when he pleases, simply by ceasing to make the periodic payments, though he may be quite capable of continuing them. Where a slave under a contract of service declares himself to be incapable of paying, the master may either give him time or dissolve the agreement. This dissolution for non-execution has no need to be pronounced by the court; it can not only be enounced by the master, but even by the slave himself, where the master is not willing to cancel the contract in spite of the slave's wishes. When at the end of one of the periods the slave under contract of enfranchisement asks for some delay, it is recommendable to grant it him; but this indulgence on the part of the master leaves intact his right to insist later, whenever he pleases, upon a dissolution of the contract for non-execution. Where the slave cannot pay but still possesses some property, the delay allowed should be long enough to allow of its realisation; but where the goods are unsaleable the master is not obliged to grant for this purpose a longer delay than three days. As to the property of the slave under contract of enfranchisement, property that is in another place, the master must grant him merely the delay necessary to send for them if the distance is less than two days' march. If upon the expiry of a period the slave is absent, the master may cancel the contract for non-execution, even although the slave has in the place property in sufficient quantity. For no one, not even the court, may use these things to pay the debt, without the previous authorisation of the slave in question. Enfranchisement by contract is not vitiated by the slave's lunacy, for then the court can proceed to the payment of the instalments, but in this case the slave should pay his curator, and cannot obtain his liberty by payments to the master in person.

Premeditated homicide of a master by his slave under contract of enfranchisement gives the master's heir the right to demand an application of the law of talion; and in the case of pardon or of voluntary or involuntary homicide all the slave's property may be seized to satisfy the price of blood. †In default of property the heir may dissolve the contract for non-execution, so that the slave resumes his previous state of slavery. If it is not a case of homicide, but of a wound, it is the master himself who can demand either an application of the law of talion, or the price of blood, as we have explained in reference to the heir in the case of homicide. Premeditated homicide or wounding, committed by a slave under contract of enfranchisement with respect to any other person than his master, also involves an application of the law of talion, unless the injured party or his representative grants pardon. In this latter case, as also in case of voluntary or involuntary homicide, not only all that the slave possesses, but also all that he subsequently gains, can be seized, up to the value of the slave himself or of the indemnity, whichever is the more advantageous for him. In default of goods to seize the injured party or his representative may ask the court to declare the slave incapable of fulfilling his obligation; and after this the slave returns to ordinary servitude, and is put up to auction, up to the amount of the indemnity. If his value exceeds this amount the contract of enfranchisement remains intact, and even in the contrary hypothesis the master always has the right to ransom him for this amount and thus keep him as his slave under contract of enfranchisement. Simple manumission, or a remission of instalments upon the part of the master, after the slave has committed the crime, cannot be attacked by the injured party; but the master must then pay ransom, because the slave's sale has become impossible. A contract of enfranchisement is annulled by the premeditated homicide of the slave, for in these circumstances he is considered to have died in a state of slavery. Consequently the master may demand an application of the law of talion if the criminal is not of a social position superior to that of his victim; otherwise he may exact payment of the value of the slave killed.

A slave under contract of enfranchisement may of his own accord freely dispose of his property, provided that it is not for nothing, or part of a hazardous speculation, *unless the master has authorised acts of this nature. He may even buy a slave whose enfranchisement would be obligatory for his master; and such a slave becomes in fact free *ipso facto*, if he falls into the master's possession by a dissolution of the contract in consequence of non-execution. Where, on the contrary, it is a case of the purchase of a slave whose enfranchisement would be obligatory for the slave himself who is under contract, the act is illegal if without the master's authorisation, but not where this has been obtained. Where the validity of the act in question is admitted the slave whose enfranchisement should *ipso facto* take place, becomes the master's slave under contract of enfranchisement. But our school forbids a slave under a contract of enfranchisement to manumit another slave in his turn, either simply or by contract, even though authorised so to do.

SECTION 4

A contract of enfranchisement into which there has been introduced an illicit condition, equivalent, or term, is illegal, but not absolutely null. Such an enfranchisement has the same consequences as a regular contract of enfranchisement for all that concerns the slave's capacity to gain money on his own account, the obligation to pay an indemnity for a crime, the right to claim dower, even for erroneous cohabitation, complete enfranchisement upon payment of the entire sum stipulated, and the right to keep for himself any gain that may have been made in the mean time. The illegal contract of enfranchisement of which we are here speaking is assimilated to a regular contract of enfranchisement depending upon a condition in respect that the slave does not become free when the master remits his debt; that the master's death annuls the agreement; that the master may dispose by will of the slave; and that the latter does not participate in the portion of the charity tax appropriated to the use of slaves under contract of enfranchisement. And this illegal contract has another peculiarity in that the master may revoke it when he pleases, and that the master does not become the owner of the property acquired by the slave; these revert in kind to the latter at the moment of complete enfranchisement if they are of any value. The slave, however, should then pay the master his own value upon the day of his liberation. Where master and slave each owe the other something in these respects, a balance is struck between them, and the excess alone can be claimed. [†The striking of the balance extinguishes the smaller sum due, *ipso facto*, and whether the parties are aware of it or not. According to another opinion, however, this can only take place with their consent. According to a third opinion it takes place upon the desire of one of the parties; while according to a fourth it is not a cause of extinction at all.]

The illegal contract of enfranchisement with which we are concerned can be revoked by the master. This revocation should take place before witnesses; for in default of legal proof the slave who denies this revocation has a presumption in his favour, provided he takes an oath. Thus a master cannot refuse an offered payment upon the ground of such revocation. †Lunacy, unconsciousness, or legal incapacity, on the part of the master, annul *ipso facto* this illegal contract of enfranchisement; but the slave's lunacy does not do so. A master or his heir who denies the contract alleged by his slave, has a presumption in favour of the truth of his statement. The heir should also swear that he is ignorant of the fact. Where the proceedings relate only to the quantity or the nature of the periodic payments, the parties should, in default of legal proof, swear to the truth of what they maintain; after which the following cases must be distinguished:—

1. ††If the master has not yet taken possession of what he alleges he stipulated, the enfranchisement by contract, not yet being *ipso facto* broken, should be declared to be dissolved by the court where the parties cannot agree.

2. If the master has already taken possession of what he alleges to have been stipulated, while the slave maintains that the master has received a portion of that sum, not as periodic payments, but as a deposit; the slave obtains immediately his complete freedom; and the master must return him all he has received. On the other hand, the slave owes the master, as an equivalent, his own value; but these debts may be balanced against each other, if there is occasion for this.

A master who declares that he effected a contract of enfranchisement while in a state of lunacy or legal incapacity in other respects, has a presumption in his favour if the slave denies it, provided that it is a matter of public notoriety that he was in the condition alleged; otherwise there is a presumption in favour of the slave who maintains that he was legally enfranchised. The master still enjoys a presumption in his favour, where he alleges that he remitted the first instalment, or a portion of the periodic payments; while the slave maintains that it was the last or all of the instalments that were remitted.

Where a master leaves two sons and a slave who maintains that the master enfranchised him by contract, the two sons have a presumption in their favour if they both deny it. If both admit it the slave becomes under contract of enfranchisement. †Where, in this latter case, one of the sons manumits his portion later in the ordinary way, this portion does not become free immediately but remains in suspense until the slave has acquitted himself of his obligation towards the other son. Then the patronage falls to the sons, not on their own account, but as their father's heirs. Where in these circumstances it appears that the slave is unable to complete his engagement, there is a right of redemption and the value of the slave should be paid by the son who has just manumitted nim, if he is solvent. If not, only the enfranchised portion of the slave becomes free immediately, without prejudice to the other son's right cf ownership over the portion remaining in slavery. [*On the contrary, a simple manumission of his portion by one of the sons does not remain in suspense, but takes effect immediately.] Where, in these circumstances, one of the two sons admits the contract of enfranchisement, his portion becomes enfranchised, while the other portion remains as before. Where, however, the son who admits the contract afterwards, manumits the slave for his portion in the ordinary way, there is still a right of redemption, at least according to our school; and the son who thus manumits should indemnify his brother, if he is solvent.

BOOK 71.—FREEDOM ON ACCOUNT OF MATERNITY

When a master has cohabited with one of his female slaves, and rendered her pregnant, she becomes free upon her master's death, whether the child to which she gives birth is living or dead. But if it is still-born the law insists that it must have attained a development sufficient to be an occasion for *ghorra* in case of abortion. A child born of a slave belonging to another, to whom one is married, is not free but remains the property of that slave's master. Such a slave does not become free on account of maternity where her husband afterwards becomes her master. Where, on the other hand, a child is born of the slave of a third party, with whom one has cohabited through error, the child is free, and is regarded as its father's legitimate son; but the mother does not become free on account of maternity should the man who rendered her pregnant subsequently become her master.

Freedom on account of maternity leaves intact the master's right to cohabit with the slave during his lifetime by reason of his ownership; he may even employ her in his service, or hire out her services to another; she may be seized for the indemnity if she commits a crime; †and the master may even give her in marriage without her consent. Her sale, pledging, or gift are the only things forbidden him. The master also remains the owner of any child born of the slave, either in consequence of marriage with another person, or of the crime of fornication, but the child is always free upon the master's death. On the other hand, children that the woman in question gave birth to before her enfranchisement on account of maternity remain slaves and do not become free upon the master's death; whether they were conceived in marriage or by the crime of fornication. Consequently the master may sell these children as he pleases. Finally, upon the master's death, the consequences of enfranchisement on account of maternity must be defrayed out of the whole estate, and not out of the third of which he can dispose.

Glory to God, the lord of all created things. God grant His grace to our master Muhammad. God grant him His grace and His blessing; to him and his family and his companions. May He grant them all His grace and His blessing. God sufficeth for us. He is the supreme mediator. There is no force nor power but in God Most High.

GLOSSARY

OF ARABIC WORDS AND NAMES

Aakila, male relatives of a criminal or other person, who are liable to pay penalty due for injury, 424.

Aariya, loan, 195.

Aashura, tenth, *i.e.* tenth day of the month of Muhurram, 103.

Aatakaf, religious retirement, 104.

Aatidal, a posture of the body at prayer, 27.

Abu Hanifa, 434. Abn Hanifa ibn Thabit, an eminent Muhammadan scholar, was born A.D. 699 at Kufa, where he lectured on law, and died at Baghdad in 767. He made considerable use of analogy and equity, like other jurists; but more especially of a doctrine of preference for such rules as suit local conditions. Some eighty or ninety million Moslems now belong to his school, being the bulk of the Muhammadan population of the Indian, Ottoman, Russian, and Chinese empires.

Adhhar, literally, clearer; indicates a doctrine preferred by Nawawi, though the contrary opinion is widely accepted, xii., xiv.

Adhiya, sacrifices, 477.

Ahia-el-muat, vivification of the dead, so, occupation of waste land, 226.

Akdariya, a particular case of succession, 253.

Alas, a species of wheat, 84.

Arafa, Mount, 115. A small hill on a plain a few hours to the east of Mecca, where the pilgrims assemble in the afternoon of the 9th of Dulhejja and utter pious ejaculations, and loud shouts of **labbaika.**

Araya, a permissible bartering of certain fruits, 144.

Asahh, literally, surer; indicates a doctrine preferred by Nawawi, though the contrary opinion is maintained by authorities of repute, xii., xiv.

Ashriba, beverages that are forbidden, 451.

Atama, eatables, 480.

Awl, proportional reduction in share of estate, 252.

Ayyam-at-tashrik, the three days after the great festival, *i.e.* the 11th, 12th, and 13th of the pilgrim month, 477.

Azan, the first call to prayer, 21.

Badana, an expiatory sacrifice, 120.

Badia, a wound, when the flesh has been injured, 403.

Baghawi, el, 280. Abu Muhammad of Bagh in Khorasan was a jurist of the school of Shafii, in the eleventh century of our era. He compiled the *Masabih es Sunna* or book of traditions arranged in each chapter according to their worth, *i.e.* sound traditions from the collections of Bokhari and Muslim, others merely good, and others unsound.

Banu Hashim, Hashim was the great-grandfather of the prophet Muhammad, 274.

Banu Muttalib, Abdul Muttalib was the grandfather of the prophet, 274.

Banu Shaiba, 112. The family to whose custody were entrusted the keys of the Kaba. The gate was apparently that now represented by the circular archway to the north-east of the sanctuary in the court of the Musjid-el-haram.

Bent-labun, 80, two-year-old she-camel.

Bent-makhad, 80, yearling she-camel.

Bia, sale or barter, 123.

Bokhari, el. 40, 67. Muhammad ibn Ismail, of Bokhara. He was born in A.D. 810 and died in 870; and was the author of the principal canonical collection of 7275 sound traditions of the teaching and practice of the prophet Muhammad. It was known, like that of Muslim, as the *Sahih*. He was apparently of the school of Shafii.

Bowaiti, 67. A contemporary and friend of Shafii.

Bughat, rebels, 433.

Damia, a wound, where blood has flowed, 403.

Damigha, a wound, where the brain is injured, 403.

Dawa, prosecution, 428, 526.

Debah, slaughtering, 472.

Deman, responsibility, for damage, 455.

Dhihar, injurious comparison, 352.

Dhohr, midday prayer, 19.

Dinar, denarius aureus; a gold coin, of 66 grains, worth about ten shillings, 124.

Diya, price of blood, 412.

Doha, a late morning prayer, 41.

Drahm, drachme; a silver coin, worth about sixpence, 124.

Fatiha, "opening" chapter of the Koran, 26.

Feraid, distribution of estates, succession, 246.

Ghasb, usurpation, 198.

Ghorra, price of blood in case of crime or njury causing abortion. 426.

Hadd el Kazf, defamation, 442. *Literally*,, limit of censure.

Hajj, pilgrimage to Mecca, 107.

Harim, 226, land that may not be occupied, owing to its proximity to other land.

Harisa, a wound where only the skin has been cut or scraped, 403.

Hashima, a wound where a bone has been injured, 403.

Hiba, gifts, 234.

Hikk, or **hikka**, 80, three-year-old camel, or she-camel.

Ibu-labun, 80, two-year-old camel.

Idda, period of retirement of a widow or divorced woman, 364.

Ifaf, an obligation to assist a father or grandfather in certain circumstances, 302.

Ifrad, performing the hajj and then the omra, 118.

Iftirash, a manner of sitting, in prayer, 25.

Ihram, state of a person accomplishing the pilgrimage, 109, 386.

Ijara, contract of hiring, 218.

Ijmaa, general agreement of the Moslem community, 436. It is defined by Professor Goldziher as "the general usage of the community which has been established by agreement in the larger circles of believers independent of the written traditional or inferred law."

Ikama, the second call to prayer, 21.

Ikrar, admission, 188.

Ila, oath of continency, 348.

Imam, leader, at public prayer, 44. Of a school of law, *E.g.* esh-Shafii, 234, 366. Also means the Sovereign, the Caliph.

Irak, 437, 495. Babylonia and Persia. The expression "jurists of Irak" is practically synonymous with that of the school of Hanifa. Its most distinguished other representatives were his teacher Hammad b. Abi Suleiman, his two pupils Abu Yusuf and Muhammad, and el Khassaf, author of *Adab-el-Kadi*.

Isha, the prayer of the night, 19.

Istibra, period of waiting of a slave, 375.

Itk, simple manumission, 537.
Izar, a garment worn at the pilgrimage, 111.

Jaala, job-work, 244.
Jama masjid, 104. *Lit.* "assembly place of prostration," *i.e.* mosque for public prayer on Fridays.
Jamrat-al-akaba, heap of stones at Mina, 116.
Jazaa, 81, four-year-old she-camel.
Jaziya, poll-tax, 465.
Jelus, a sitting posture, at prayer, 28.
Jenaza, funeral ceremonies, 70.
Jerah, wounds; and so, crimes against the person, 395.
Jesus Christ, 348. Like the Christians of the first century, the early Moslems would seem to have believed in the imminence of the last judgment. The glorious appearing of the Nabi Isa was, however, to be preceded by the seven years' reign of the Mahdi, and this is presumably the meaning of the passage referred to.
Jobba, a cloak, 384.

Kada, administration of justice, 500.
Kafara, expiation, with regard to injurious comparison, 355.
Kafiz, a measure, 223.
Kanut, a formula of prayer, 27.
Karna, a defect in a woman giving rise to right of option upon marriage, 299.
Kataba, writing; contract of enfranchisement, 549.
Kati et trik, brigands, 448.
Kaud, a sitting posture, at prayer, 29.
Kesm, partition, thus sharing of husband's favours, 316.
Kesm el fi wa el ghanima, distribution of the profits of war and of booty, 273.
Kesm es Sadakat, distribution of the proceeds of the charity tax, 277.
Keta-es-sarika, body-cutting; *i.e.* crimes punishable with amputation, 440.
Khalifa, pregnant camel, 413.
Khula, divorce, 320.
Kibla, direction of prayer, 23.
Kiraa, recitation, of the Koran, at prayer, 26.
Kirad, a joint-stock company, 210.
Kiran, joint accomplishment of hajj and omra, 111.
Kisas, law of talion, 405.
Kiyam, standing up, in prayer, 25.
Kolla, 1, 2, a jar or pitcher, a measure.
Kuba, a forbidden kind of drum, 515.

Lekit, foundlings, 240.
Lian, imprecation, 358.
Lokta, things found, 236.

Maghrib, evening prayer, 19.
Mahr, dower, equivalent of sadak, 305.
Majlis, *lit.* sitting; right to cancel a contract before separation of the parties, 129.
Makam Ibrahim, a small building to the eastward of the Kaba, in the Masjid-et haram, at Mecca, where the imam of the School of Shafii takes his station, and leads the prayers of the congregation, 361.
Malik, 337, 338, 439. Malik ibn Anas was born in A.D. 718 and died in 795. He was a judge and jurist, and lived and died at Medina, where he lectured on law. In his teaching he emphasized the principles of public advantage and general agreement. His book the *Muwat'a* is one of the earliest collections of traditions, and contains about 1700. To his school belong nearly all the Muhammadans of Africa, with the single important exception of those of Lower Egypt, a total of some thirty millions.

Mamuma, a wound, where the membrane of the brain has been injured, 403.

Marwa, a spot in Mecca, a little to the north-west of the Masjid-el-haram, 115.

Mashhur, *literally*, well-known ; indicates a doctrine preferred by Nawawi, and that the contrary opinion is not widely accepted, xii., xiv.

Masjid-el-haram, the great court and colonnades round the Kaba at Mecca, 119.

Mihrab, a niche or other sign in a mosque wall denoting the kibla or direction of prayer towards Mecca, 59.

Mina, a valley to the east of Mecca, where the pilgrims perform their sacrifices on the tenth of Dulhejja, 116.

Minhaj, a guide or manual, (title-page). *Minhaj-et-Talibin* may therefore mean the students' guide.

Mithkal, a weight, equal to one drahm and a half, 85.

Mobadara, a kind of shooting competition, 484.

Modaraba, a joint-stock company, 210.

Modd, a measure of capacity of about four gallons, 383.

Mohakala, a forbidden bartering of corn in the ear for husked corn, 143.

Moharrar, *literally*, the freed ; title of a law book upon which the *Minhaj-et-Talibin* is based, xi., xii.

Mohatta, a kind of shooting competition, 484.

Mohsan, a respectable man, 359, 439, 442.

Mokhabara, a kind of lease, 215.

Mokhaddara, a young woman not in the habit of going out, 512.

Mokharaja, hire of a slave for his master's profit, 394.

Mosaka, a farming lease, 215.

Mosharaka, a particular case of succession, 250.

Mosinna, a two-year-old calf, 81.

Motah, a pecuniary indemnity in certain cases of repudiation, 313.

Mozabana, a forbidden bartering of dates on the tree for dry dates, 143.

Mozakki, an *employé* for informing a court as to the character of witnesses, 504, 507.

Mozaraa, a kind of lease, 215.

Mozdalifa, a village between Mount Arafa and Mina, where the pilgrims to Mecca pass the night between the ninth and tenth of Dulhejja, 116.

Muballigh, 47, a repeater of the imam's words and movements at public prayer.

Mudiha, a wound, where the bone has been uncovered, 403.

Muezzin, the man who utters the call to prayer, 22.

Munadala, shooting competitions, 483.

Munakkila, a wound, where a bone is broken so that the fragments are separated, 403.

Musabaka, racing, 483.

Muslim, 29, 67, 280. Muslim ibn el Hajjaj, jurist of Nishapur, was born in A.D. 815 and died in 875. He compiled a canonical collection of sound traditions, known, like that of his friend el-Bokhari, by the name of *Sahih*, and of yet greater accuracy. His introduction treats fully of the science of tradition in general.

Mutalahima, a wound, where the flesh has been penetrated, 403.

Nafakah, maintenance, 383.

Nawawi, (title-page). Abu Zakariya ibn Sharaf en Nawawi was born in A.D. 1233, at the town of Nawa, between Galilee and the Hauran. He became professor of tradition at the Ashrafiya school in Damascus, in 1267, and was the author of a number of works, including the present book, the *Minhaj-et-Talibin*. He died in 1278.

Nazr, vows, 495.

Neshuz, disobedience of wives, 318.

Nikah, marriage, 281.

Nisab, taxable minimum, 83.

Niya, intention, 24.

Omra, visit to Mecca, 107.

Radaa, relationship by fosterage, 378.
Rafii, er, Abu Kasim er Rafii, author of the Moharrar, upon which the *Minhaj-et-Talibin* is based. He lived about half a century before Nawawi, xi., xii.
Rahn, pledge or security, 152.
Raka, the recital of a prayer; thus "two rakas" means a prayer said twice, 216.
Ramal, a way of making the circuit of the Kaba, 113.
Ratka, a defect in a woman giving rise to a right of option upon marriage, 299.
Rda, a garment worn at the pilgrimage, 111.
Rejaa, return to conjugal union, 345.
Retel, about 1 lb. av. dry measure; about 17¼ lbs. av. weight, 83, 84.
Ridda, apostasy, 436.
Rokna, bending of the body at prayer, 27.
Royani, er, 473. A medieval writer, author of the *Bahr-el-Madhab*.

Saa, a measure, equal to about eight handfuls of corn, 124.
Sabæans, 294. These Sabæan sects should more properly be called Sabians, and are not to be confused with the ancient people of Yemen. They were a semi-Christian sect of Babylonia, also known as Elkesaites, and were regarded by the early Moslems as possessing a written scripture, and so entitled to toleration. A little later the surviving pagans of Harran also came to be regarded as Sabæans.
Sadak, dower, 305.
Safa, a small mound in Mecca to the south-east of the Masjid-el-haram, and corresponding gate, 114.
Sahih, *literally* authentic; indicates a doctrine preferred by Nawawi, and that the contrary opinion is not maintained by authorities of repute, xii., xiv.
Sakhra, the "rock," possibly part of the great altar of sacrifice in front of the Jewish temple, now within the building known as the Kubbet-es-Sakhra, in the Haram-esh-Sherif at Jerusalem, 361.
Sala, prayer, 19.
Salam, salutation; at prayer, 30.
Salam, contract of; a sale by advance, 147.
Salat el jemaa, public prayer, 43.
Sawad, 462, a district in Irak.
Sawik, a kind of infusion or decoction, 357.
Sayd, hunting, 472.
Sejud, prostration at prayer, 28.
Shafii, xii. Muhammad ibn Idris esh-Shafii was born in A.D. 767 at Gaza or Ascalon. After studying law under Malik at Medina he went to Baghdad and was taught there by jurists of the school of Hanifa. He himself lectured at Baghdad between 811 and 814, but afterwards went to Egypt, where he lived at Fostat or Old Cairo, and taught with great authority until 820, when he died. Professor Goldziher says that "he systematized the method for the deduction of laws from the sources of law and laid down the exact limits within which each might be used. In his *Risala* he created the science of the use which could be made of speculative deduction without lessening the undisputed prerogatives of scripture and tradition; he regulated their application and limited their arbitrary use by strict rules." The adherents of the school of Shafii number some sixty or seventy million persons, of whom about a half are in the Netherlands Indies, and the rest in Egypt and Syria, the Hadramaut, Southern India and Malaya.
Shah, 80, a young lamb or kid.
Shahada, testimony, 515.
Shashi, esh, 473. A medieval writer, author of the *Hilyat-el-Ulema*.
Shefaa, pre-emption, 205.
Sherka, partnership, 179.
Sherkat-al-abdan (with Sh^t-al-mofawada and sh^t-al-wujuh). Forbidden kinds of partnership, 179.

Sherkat-al-inan, the only permissible kind of partnership, 179.
Siaf, excusable homicide, 453.
Siam, fasting, 95.
Siar, military expeditions, 457.
Simhak, a wound, if the membrane enters the flesh and the bone is injured, 403.
Sobh, the morning prayer, 19.
Soffa, bench, porch or vestibule of a Moslem house in Egypt, 445.
Solt, a species of grain, 84.
Sonna, 336, 361, 542. The word Sonna or Sunna is used in more senses than one. In its commoner signification it means the way or usage of the prophet Muhammad as handed down by oral tradition. This Sonna is an integral portion of the law and of the same binding force as a precept of the Koran. But in the *Minhaj-et-Talibin* the word generally signifies later practices which, though observed by the majority of the faithful, have not acquired the binding force of the *ijmaa*, but are merely regarded by most persons as commendable.
Tabia, a yearling calf, 81.
Tadbir, testamentary manumission, 545.
Taflis, bankruptcy, 161.
Tahajud, an early morning prayer, 41.
Tahallol, normal condition, in contrast to a state of ihram, 117.
Tahara, purity, 1.
Takbir, 25, the exclamation "Allah akbar," "God is most great."
Talak, repudiation, 327.
Talibin, students, (title-page).
Tamatto, performing the omra and then the hajj, 119.
Tashahud, the confession of faith, 29.
Tasua, ninth, *i.e.* ninth day of the month of Muharram, 103.
Tawarok, a sitting posture, at prayer, 29.
Tertib, regular ordering; at prayer, 30.
Thaniya, 81, five-year-old she-camel.

Umhat-el-awlad, *literally*, motherhood of children; and so, freedom on account of maternity, 558.

Wadiya, deposits, 269.
Wakaf, 230, a religious or charitable foundation.
Wakala, agency, *i.e.* relations between principal and agent, 181.
Wars, 83, a plant, *memecylon tinctorium.*
Wasaya, wills, 259.
Wask, 83, a measure; *lit.* a cargo.
Witr, a prayer consisting of an odd number of rakas, 40.

Yeman, oaths, 486.
Yum-en-nahr, day of immolation of victims at Mina on the tenth of the pilgrim month, 477.

Zakat, alms contribution or charity tax, 80.
Zam-zam, a spring to the east of the Kaba, in court of the Masjid-el-Haram at Mecca, the water of which is drunk by the pilgrims, 118.
Zina, fornication, 430.

SUBJECT INDEX